STRATEGIC HUMAN RESOURCE DEVELOPMENT

STRATEGIC HUMAN RESOURCE DEVELOPMENT

William J. Rothwell, Ph.D.
Management Development Director
The Franklin Life Insurance Company
Springfield, Illinois

H. C. Kazanas, Ph.D.
Professor
University of Illinois
Champaign, Illinois

Prentice Hall
Englewood Cliffs, New Jersey 07632

Library of Congress Cataloging-in-Publication Data

Kazanas, H. C.
  Strategic human resource development.

  Bibliography: p.
  Includes index.
  1. Manpower planning. 2. Personnel management.
I. Rothwell, William J. II. Title.
HF5549.5.M3K39 1989 658.3′01 88-25301
ISBN 0-13-851742-8

Editorial/production supervision: Jacqueline A. Jeglinski
Manufacturing buyer: Mary Ann Gloriande

© 1989 by Prentice-Hall, Inc.
A division of Simon & Schuster
Englewood Cliffs, New Jersey 07632

The publisher offers discounts on this book when ordered
in bulk quantities. For more information, write:

    Special Sales/College Marketing
    Prentice-Hall, Inc.
    College Technical and Reference Division
    Englewood Cliffs, NJ 07632

All rights reserved. No part of this book may be
reproduced, in any form or by any means,
without permission in writing from the publisher.

Printed in the United States of America
10 9 8 7 6 5 4 3 2 1

ISBN 0-13-851742-8

Prentice-Hall International (UK) Limited, *London*
Prentice-Hall of Australia Pty. Limited, *Sydney*
Prentice-Hall Canada Inc., *Toronto*
Prentice-Hall Hispanoamericana, S.A., *Mexico*
Prentice-Hall of India Private Limited, *New Delhi*
Prentice-Hall of Japan, Inc., *Tokyo*
Simon & Schuster Asia Pte. Ltd., *Singapore*
Editora Prentice-Hall do Brasil, Ltda., *Rio de Janeiro*

CONTENTS

PREFACE ix

PART 1 THE BACKGROUND AND PURPOSE OF HRD

CHAPTER 1 BACKGROUND ISSUES 1
Strategic Business Planning **2**
Human Resources Planning **11**
Strategic Human Resource Development **16**
The Scope of HRD **21**
Activities of HRD Practitioners **24**
The Traditional Focus of HRD **36**

CHAPTER 2 THE PURPOSE OF THE HRD EFFORT 45
What Is Purpose? **45**
How Important Is Purpose? **47**
What Are Possible Relationships Between Strategic Business Plans,
   HR Plans, and HRD? **48**
How Is the Purpose of an HRD Effort Clarified? **61**
What Are the Effects of Organizational Philosophy and Culture
   on the Purpose of the HRD Effort? **63**

PART 2 ASSESSING NEEDS AND SCANNING THE ENVIRONMENT

CHAPTER 3 COMPREHENSIVE NEEDS ASSESSMENT 79
Comprehensive Needs Assessment: Definition and Description 80
Needs Assessment: Background Issues 80
Steps in Comprehensive Needs Assessment 87
Identifying Learners 88
Classifying Learners by Market Segment 89
Comparing Actual to Desired Knowledge and Skills 97
Identifying Present Learning Needs by Market
 or Market Segment 105

CHAPTER 4 ENVIRONMENTAL SCANNING 112
Environmental Scanning: Definition and Description 113
The State of the Environmental Scanning Art
 in Business Planning 114
Environmental Scanning for HRD 117
Environmental Scanning and Curriculum Needs Assessment 117
Steps in Environmental Scanning for HRD 118

PART 3 CHOOSING AND IMPLEMENTING ORGANIZATIONAL STRATEGY FOR HRD

CHAPTER 5 CHOOSING ORGANIZATIONAL STRATEGY FOR HRD 152
Choosing Organizational Strategy for HRD:
 Definition and Importance 152
Prescriptions About Choosing Organizational Strategy
 for HRD 153
Choosing Organizational Strategy for HRD: The Process 155
Special Issues to Consider in Choosing Organizational
 Strategy for HRD 165
Planning for Contingencies 172
Choosing Organizational Strategy for HRD: The Product 173
Results of Curriculum Planning and Choice of Organizational
 Strategy for HRD 193

CHAPTER 6 IMPLEMENTING ORGANIZATIONAL STRATEGY FOR HRD 201
Steps in Implementing Organizational Strategy for HRD 202
Establishing Operational Objectives for the HRD Effort 202
Creating, Reviewing, and Revising HRD Policies 208
Examining Leadership 209
Reviewing Structure 211
Reviewing Reward Systems 214
Budgeting for Necessary Resources 216
Communicating About Strategy 218
Developing Functional Strategies for HRD 223

PART 4 FUNCTIONAL STRATEGIES FOR HRD

CHAPTER 7 ORGANIZATION DEVELOPMENT 236
- Definition of Organization Development 236
- How Is Organization Development Distinguishable from Other Change Methods? 237
- What Is the Relationship Between Organization Development and Organizational Learning? 237
- Problems Associated with Traditional Organization Development Interventions 250
- Strategic Organization Development 250

CHAPTER 8 NONEMPLOYEE DEVELOPMENT 259
- Steps in Nonemployee Development 260
- Creating Classification Schemes 260
- Analyzing Relationships Between the Corporation, Its Public, and Its Stakeholders 263
- Analyzing Present and Future Criteria 266
- Pinpointing Discrepancies 268
- Separating Instructional from Noninstructional Needs 268
- Deciding What Changes Should Occur 269
- Designing Instruction Consistent with Desired Changes 271
- Selecting Content and Delivery Methods 272
- Following Up on Instructional Needs 274
- The Relationship Between Organizational Strategy for HRD and the HRD Effort Planned for Groups Outside the Organization 275

CHAPTER 9 EMPLOYEE DEVELOPMENT 302
- Definition of Employee Development 302
- Identifying ED Needs 303
- Specialized Methods for Employee Development 306
- Problems with Traditional Employee Development Programs 319
- Strategic Employee Development 320
- Specialized Employee Development Methods for Meeting Long-Term Organizational Needs 321

CHAPTER 10 EMPLOYEE EDUCATION 340
- What Is Employee Education? 340
- Career Planning: Some Considerations 342
- Career Planning in Organizations 343
- Career Planning: Individual Issues 354
- Employee Education 357
- Tying Employee Education to Organizational Strategy for HRD 380

CHAPTER 11 EMPLOYEE TRAINING 397
- What Is Employee Training? 397
- What Is Job Performance? 399

*What Is the Relationship Between Training
and Job Performance?* **399**
How Is Training Related to Planning? **399**
A Model for Designing and Delivering Training **400**
Problems with the Traditional Model of Training **423**
Strategic Training **425**
How Is Strategic Training Related to Planning? **425**
*When Should Strategic Training Be Used Instead of Traditional
Training?* **426**
A Model of Strategic Training **426**

PART 5   EVALUATING HRD

CHAPTER 12   EVALUATING HRD   **464**
   What Is Evaluation? **464**
   Why Is Evaluation Worthwhile? **465**
   What Are Some Ways of Thinking About Evaluation? **467**
   Evaluating Training **476**
   Evaluating Development **492**
   Evaluating the HRD Effort **494**
REFERENCES   **507**
NAME INDEX   **547**
SUBJECT INDEX   **554**

PREFACE

This text applies Strategic Business Planning principles to Human Resource Development.

    This subject has captured the attention of HRD practitioners in recent years, for good reasons. First, we live in a time when nothing is constant except change. People unwilling to change cannot survive for long. Learning is a form of changing, and planned learning in organizations is important for realizing Strategic Business Plans. HRD is synonymous with planned learning in organizations.

    Second, managers in U.S. businesses are frequently accused of shortsightedness. Among others, Hayes and Abernathy (1980) complain that managers are rewarded for short-term results only. Nearly 76 percent of 1,000 executives responding to one survey agree that businesses do not gain from a short-term focus (Heidrick & Struggles, Inc., 1981). Shortsightedness has been cited as the culprit in the declining global competitive position of U.S. business generally—and to the derailing of executives who never quite make it to the top (Johnston, 1986; McCall & Lombardo, 1983).

    Farsightedness is learned. Managers, and indeed all employees, must learn to anticipate rapid changes in their jobs, careers, work groups, and organizations. Human Resource Development can contribute to this learning by basing organized training, education, and development on expected future needs when appropriate to do so. HRD should be guided by a comprehensive, unified plan for learning in the organization. We call this plan *the Organizational Strategy for HRD*.

Three tasks are undertaken in this text.

The first task is to present a model of Strategic Human Resource Development that differs from the traditional and past-oriented model of HRD. SHRD is neither past-oriented nor reactive; rather, it is future-oriented and proactive.

The second task is to show HRD practitioners how to unify planned learning activities intended to

1. change organizational culture and work group norms;
2. improve relations between an organization and its general public and key external stakeholders;
3. match up collective skills of a work unit with its present or expected future responsibilities;
4. help individuals achieve their career objectives; and
5. match skills of job incumbents with job responsibilities.

The first activity is associated with Organization Development; the second is associated with Nonemployee (Stakeholders) Development; the third is associated with Employee Development; the fourth is associated with Education; and the fifth is associated with Training.

The third task is to provide HRD practitioners with activities and case studies to help guide their thinking. By completing them, practitioners should be better equipped to formulate and implement a unified Organizational Strategy for HRD.

This text is structured in five parts and twelve chapters. Part One provides important background information about Strategic Business Planning, HR Planning, and HRD. It also treats how to formulate a purpose or mission for an organization's HRD Effort. Strategic Human Resource Development (SHRD) is the process of changing an organization, stakeholders outside it, groups inside it, and people employed by it through planned learning so that they possess knowledge and skills needed in the future. To understand SHRD, HRD practitioners should understand Strategic Business Planning, Human Resource Planning, and the status of HRD activities in the U.S. Chapter 1 deals with these issues.

A unified Strategy for HRD stems from a sense of purpose that deals with the means by which HRD contributes to meeting organizational and individual needs. Chapter 2 establishes this framework. It dramatizes the range of possible purposes for a comprehensive HRD Effort.

Part Two covers analysis of present strengths/weaknesses and future threats/opportunities affecting groups, individuals, and jobs.

To formulate an integrated Organizational Strategy for HRD, HRD practitioners, line managers, and learners require information about present learning needs and future environmental conditions confronting

- groups outside the business,
- groups inside the business,
- individuals, and
- jobs.

Chapter 3 focuses on comprehensive needs assessment. It identifies broad learning needs and thus underscores significant, strategic weaknesses. Further, it identifies unique talents (strengths). As used in formulating Organizational Strategy for HRD, comprehensive needs assessment is geared to the present.

Chapter 4 focuses on environmental scanning. It explains how to pinpoint possible future needs, and thus underscores threats or opportunities for performance. As used in formulating Organizational Strategy for HRD, environmental scanning can be applied broadly to all instructional programs or more restrictedly to only one or two instructional programs.

Part Three focuses on choosing and implementing Organizational Strategy for HRD. *Choosing HRD Strategy* means selecting a comprehensive, general plan for learning in an organization. It results from comparing strengths (present talents/skills), weaknesses (present learning needs), threats (possible future learning needs), and opportunities (possible future talents/skills). The culmination of this choice is an integrated direction for planned learning in an organization.

Implementing HRD Strategy means turning plans into actions. It activates learning plans and sets the stage for unifying such HRD functions as Organization Development, Nonemployee Development, Employee Development, Education, and Training.

Part Four treats each functional strategy for HRD that can be used in implementing a comprehensive Organizational Strategy for HRD. These functional strategies serve different purposes:

- *Organization Development* is intended to change the culture of an organization or work group.
- *Nonemployee Development* is intended to improve relations between an organization and groups outside it with which it deals.
- *Employee Development* is intended to match up collective skills of a work unit and the responsibilities assigned to the unit by the organization.
- *Education* is intended to help individuals achieve their career objectives.
- *Training* is intended to furnish people with knowledge and skills needed to perform their jobs.

Each component of Organizational Strategy for HRD can be viewed separately or together. In addition, Development, Education, or Training can be treated from a past-oriented or future-oriented perspective.

Part Five closes the circle, describing evaluation methods for each component of the HRD Effort and the overall HRD Effort itself. Evaluation means placing worth on something. Evaluating HRD closes the circle on strategic decision making and action taking, providing feedback of use in subsequently

- defining the purpose of the HRD Effort,
- assessing comprehensive learning needs,
- scanning the environment,
- choosing Organizational Strategy for HRD,

- implementing Organizational Strategy for HRD, and
- implementing functional strategies such as Organization Development, Nonemployee Development, Employee Development, Education, and Training.

William J. Rothwell			H. C. Kazanas
Springfield, IL			Champaign, IL

PART 1
THE BACKGROUND AND PURPOSE OF HRD

1

BACKGROUND ISSUES

Many articles have appeared in academic and practitioner journals about strategic planning for HRD departments and about the role of HRD practitioners as strategists. The American Society for Training and Development's study of what HRD practitioners do, *Models for Excellence* (1983), identifies "strategist" as one of fifteen roles of HRD practitioners. Acting in this role, practitioners "develop long-range plans for what the training and development structure, organization, direction, policies, programs, services, and practices will be in order to accomplish the training and development mission" (*Models for Excellence,* 1983, p. 91).

This definition is rare. Most writings on this subject imply that the practitioner's chief responsibility is *to manage the HRD department strategically* rather than *to lead efforts to formulate and implement a unified plan to guide the direction of learning in an organization.* Departmental planning is important, but not as important as organizational planning for learning. What the HRD department should do (its strategy) is related to what the organization should do to encourage planned learning that supports business and staffing plans.

Some confusion on this topic is understandable. HRD practitioners are rarely included in top-level discussions about business plans (Rothwell, 1985b; Rothwell & Kazanas, 1986). Though HRD is the one area of human resource practice most amenable to supporting business plans (Zemke, 1981), it is also the one area of HR practice least often used for this purpose by top managers ("Human resources," 1982).

HRD practitioners are too often cut off from strategic decision-making and are left to set their own direction. It is scarcely surprising, then, that HRD practitioners are frequently admonished to formulate their own plans when Strategic Business Plans are unclear, are not followed by top managers, or are not expressed in ways that imply action in the HR area.

Strategic Human Resource Development (SHRD) is the process of changing an organization, stakeholders outside it, groups inside it, and people employed by it through planned learning so that they possess the knowledge and skills needed in the future. SHRD focuses on the *HRD Effort,* defined as the coordinated learning activities undertaken by HRD practitioners, operating managers, and employees to support business and HR plans. The result of SHRD is an *Organizational Strategy for HRD.* This is a comprehensive, coordinated plan for major learning initiatives by which a firm's managers intend to meet business and staffing objectives through organized learning.

To understand SHRD, practitioners should first learn about Strategic Business Planning and HR planning. The reason is that SHRD is only a tool for helping implement these plans. This chapter provides this necessary background information. It describes Strategic Business Planning, HR planning, and SHRD. Further, it clarifies how they may support each other. Finally, it summarizes the scope of HRD activities in the U.S., describes the roles of HRD practitioners, and provides other background information about the HRD field.

STRATEGIC BUSINESS PLANNING*

In the most fundamental sense, Strategic Business Planning (SBP) involves choosing how an organization will compete (Hosmer, 1982). A plan of this kind is usually considered a chief concern of top-level corporate executives and should command the highest priority of corporate top managers. It requires consideration of an organization's present internal strengths and weaknesses and future external threats or opportunities.

Until the 1950s, managers tended to worry more about coordinating their businesses than about dealing with changes outside their businesses. The world was less turbulent than it is today. Businesses operated in defined geographical areas, marketed products or services to distinct groups of customers, and restricted their range of products and services (Chandler, 1962). In such settings, managers separated the world outside the business (the external environment) from the world inside (the internal environment). Long-range or *first generation planning* was used to examine the external environment. Managers assumed the future would be like the past. Planning concentrated on building from past successes and on developing existing markets for the firm's product or service. Handled by staff specialists who prepared reports for top managers, planning did not command much real attention (Holloway, 1986). The main focus was on the internal environment, because coordination within the organi-

---

*This section and the one following it relies on material from Hofer and Schendel (1978) and from Sredl and Rothwell (1987).

zation was needed. Without coordination, such classic *functions* as production/operations, marketing, finance, and personnel worked at cross-purposes. Top managers used *policies,* which are guidelines for action, to coordinate functions within their organizations (Hofer & Schendel, 1978). During the annual budgeting process, differences between long-range plans and internal policies were ironed out. This process was not systematic.

In the 1960s, managers found themselves facing conditions unlike the past. The external environment was growing increasingly unpredictable. The government passed laws, created regulations, and handed down court rulings that affected hiring, employee appraisal, training, financial matters, health and safety, and much more. The first shortages in raw materials since wartime were experienced. Technological innovation became more important as the gap narrowed between basic and applied research.

At the same time, organizations became larger and more complex. Businesses expanded into overseas markets, new industries, and multiple product or service lines. Consumer preferences began to change faster. It became harder to manage the businesses themselves.

Amid more dynamic external and more complex internal environments, managers found it inappropriate to

1. separate examinations of external and internal environments without making greater efforts to integrate them,
2. extend assumptions about a certain past into an uncertain future, and
3. use identical policies to coordinate operations across autonomous businesses in different industries operating under one corporate banner.

First generation planning proved inadequate for dealing with this complexity (Hofer & Schendel, 1978). *Second generation (strategic) planning* emerged at this time as a tool for use by top corporate executives in managing amidst growing complexity and environmental turbulence. Initially, plans of this kind were rather inflexible. *Third generation (strategic) planning* added consideration of alternative plans in the event of possible changes in the environment as a plan was implemented.

A Model of Strategic Business Planning

Strategic Business Planning is a process in which decision-makers (Glueck & Jauch, 1984; Holloway, 1986; Sredl & Rothwell, 1987):

1. *Clarify purpose.* What is the purpose of the firm? What should it be?
2. *Select goals and objectives.* What is the firm trying to achieve? How can achievement be measured?
3. *Identify present strengths and weaknesses.* What is the firm doing well? not so well?
4. *Analyze future threats and opportunities.* What opportunities or threats will the external environment pose to the organization in the future?

5. *Compare strengths/weaknesses to threats/opportunites.* How can the firm take advantage of future opportunities and avert future threats posed by the environment, considering its present internal strengths and weaknesses?
6. *Decide on long-term strategy.* What should be the long-term direction (strategy) pursued by an organization so that it can take advantage of opportunities and avert threats posed by the environment?
7. *Implement strategy.* What changes need to be made inside the organization so its chosen strategy can be pursued with the greatest likelihood of success?
8. *Evaluate strategy.* How well do decision-makers think the strategy will work? How well is it working? How well has it worked?

The first step in SBP is clarifying the organization's purpose. A purpose statement clarifies beliefs and assumptions. When written down and communicated, it is a rallying point and a stimulant for action. At the same time, it also helps create a vision of what the organization should be like in the future. This vision should be concrete and understandable by others. Ideally, it should also excite their enthusiasm, motivating everyone in the firm to make this ideal view a future reality.

A purpose statement can also be the economic rationale for a firm's existence. To address this issue, decision-makers should ask such questions as these (Gilmore & Brandenburg, 1962):

1. In what areas of business activity should the firm operate?
2. How much opportunity does a business activity offer the company in terms of growth? Flexibility? Stability? Return on investment?
3. What does it take to succeed in the business?
4. What are the firm's capabilities?
5. How well do the firm's capabilities match up to what is needed to succeed in the business?
6. What is the firm's likelihood of success in the business activity?
7. What methods of doing business can be considered?
8. How do these choices compare on the basis of feasibility?
9. How do these choices compare on the basis of potential profitability?
10. What business activities should the firm enter in the future? What should be its purpose?

More than just an exercise in paperwork, the process of clarifying purpose is an essential starting point in formulating Strategic Business Plans.

The second step in SBP is selecting objectives and goals. Objectives and goals operationalize purpose. Goals identify broad areas in which action is to be taken. Objectives state what measurable results are desired over a specific time period. (Some writers reverse the terms, using objectives to mean broad activity statements and goals to mean measurable counterparts. See Ryans & Shanklin, 1985). Goals are usually timeless. Objectives are not. In fact, it is possible to think of *levels of objectives*—some long-term, some intermediate-term, and some short-term.

The third step in SBP is identifying organizational strengths and weaknesses. Strategists ponder what the firm is doing especially well at present and what it is not doing so well. Strengths and weaknesses are often viewed in competitive terms. In other words, top managers think of their firm's strengths and weaknesses relative to competitors. To this end, they should first identify key factors leading to success in a business or industry and then assess how well their firm compares on those factors to key competitors.

The fourth step in SBP is analyzing future threats and opportunities posed by the external environment. Strategists consider what events or trends, outside the immediate control of the organization, are likely to affect it in the future and what resulting threats or opportunities these events/trends will pose to the organization. An *event* is a one-time occurrence; a *trend* is a gradual tendency toward change in the world. The Arab Oil Embargo of 1973 was a major event which threatened the operations of many U.S. firms. Trends are identifiable in the industry, laws and regulations, economic conditions, social mores, technology, and consumer preferences. Any change in the world may pose threats to an organization's survival or opportunities worth taking advantage of.

The fifth step in SBP is comparing organizational strengths and weaknesses to environmental threats and opportunities. Strategists ponder how well-prepared the firm is to cope with expected future environmental changes, and what managers have to do to turn expected future opportunities to advantage or avoid expected threats created by environmental conditions.

The sixth step in SBP is deciding on long-term strategy. Decision-makers ponder what actions should be taken to achieve organizational goals and objectives, given present internal conditions and expected future external conditions. They may then select a long-term plan to ensure that these actions will be taken over time. Strategists then decide on a long-term direction for the organization, and "accommodate [the organization] to changes in its environment which are often beyond its control or influence" (Utterback, 1979, p. 135). The Chief Executive bears primary responsibility for strategy selection (Saunders, 1980).

The seventh step in SBP is implementation. This has frequently been the weakest link in SBP (Keichel, 1982), because top managers too often change strategy without making adjustments to support the change within the organization. Common problems in implementation usually stem from failures to align duties, reporting relationships, leadership talent, employee talent, incentives, and policies with desired strategy.

The eighth and final step in SBP is evaluation. Strategists ponder:

1. What is the likelihood that a given SBP will produce desired results? (This question is addressed prior to implementation.)
2. What has been the progress to date? (This question is addressed during annual strategic review meetings.)
3. What were the overall results? (This question is addressed at the time a new SBP is first contemplated.)

Many approaches to evaluation have been proposed. Perhaps the simplest is to compare results to the intentions expressed through goals and objectives.

A model is helpful in conceptualizing the SBP process. However, it is only a model—literally, a simplified depiction of a more complicated process. In the real world, strategists may skip steps in the model, reorder them, call them by different names, drop some steps, or perform several steps concurrently.

Key Assumptions of Strategic Business Planning

Authors writing about SBP traditionally make assumptions about it. These assumptions are worth reviewing in order to clarify what SBP can and cannot do.

The first assumption: *Strategy-making begins with clarification of organizational purpose.* Strategists should agree on organizational purpose as a starting point for planning. Since many people have a stake in what the organization is or should be, strategic managers function as arbiters of organizational purpose against a backdrop of differing interests. Sharplin (1985) emphasizes this by defining purpose as "the organization's continuing [reasons for existence] with regard to certain categories of persons—in short, what is to be accomplished for whom?" (p. 49).

Important stakeholders include owners or shareholders, consumers, employees, managers, and members of the general public. Each group has its own expectations about what the organization is and what it should be.

The second assumption: *Strategy-making is based, in part, on identification of organizational strengths and weaknesses.* Traditionally, writers on SBP assume that managers are capable of identifying the present status of the organization. However, managers have a hard time examining their organizations critically. After all, managers made the decisions initially. Rarely can they step back and attack their own logic and results. In any case, there are enough examples of organizations in which top management strategists are less, not more, aware of operational problems than frontline employees. One reason is that top managers receive distorted information because people reporting to them are interested in looking good to them so as to reap desired rewards.

The third assumption: *Strategy-making is based on examination of the future and the external environment.* SBP assumes that managers can identify important trends or events likely to affect the organization in the future and draw accurate inferences about the effects of trends or events. These assumptions are not always valid, because strategists seldom possess all relevant information about trends or events, cannot predict all ramifications of trends or events even if they are identified, and rarely enjoy complete freedom to change an organization to anticipate future external trends or events. About the best that can be hoped for is that *major* trends or events will be identified, their *major* ramifications will be anticipated, and *some* changes will be made in the firm.

The fourth assumption: *Strategy-making is about future implications of present decisions, not future decisions.* Strategists should first identify future conditions and then, stepping back to the present, establish plans to take those conditions into account.

The fifth assumption: *Strategy-making is a mental activity which requires holistic thinking* (Holloway, 1986). Hence, creativity and problem-solving skills are essential to the process.

Value of Strategic Business Planning

How much, if any, does SBP improve organizational performance? Numerous academic studies have sought answers to this question. While research methods have varied, results have not conclusively shown whether any correlation exists between planning and corporate success (Leontiades & Tezel, 1980). As Byars (1984) observes, "some organizations either through luck or intuitive genius of their leadership have been successful without formal strategic management systems" (p. 24). Yet it would seem reasonable to assume that any effort to anticipate the future would be superior to dependence on mere luck, chance, or good fortune. An old saying states the case succinctly: "The organization with a plan beats those without plans every time."

Levels of Planning

There are several levels of Strategic Business Planning in most large corporations. There are also types of planning distinct from SBP.

Consider Figure 1-1, which illustrates the simplified structure of a large, diversified corporation. *Grand Strategy* is established at the highest corporate level. However, each business possesses its own *enterprise or business unit strategy.* In each en-

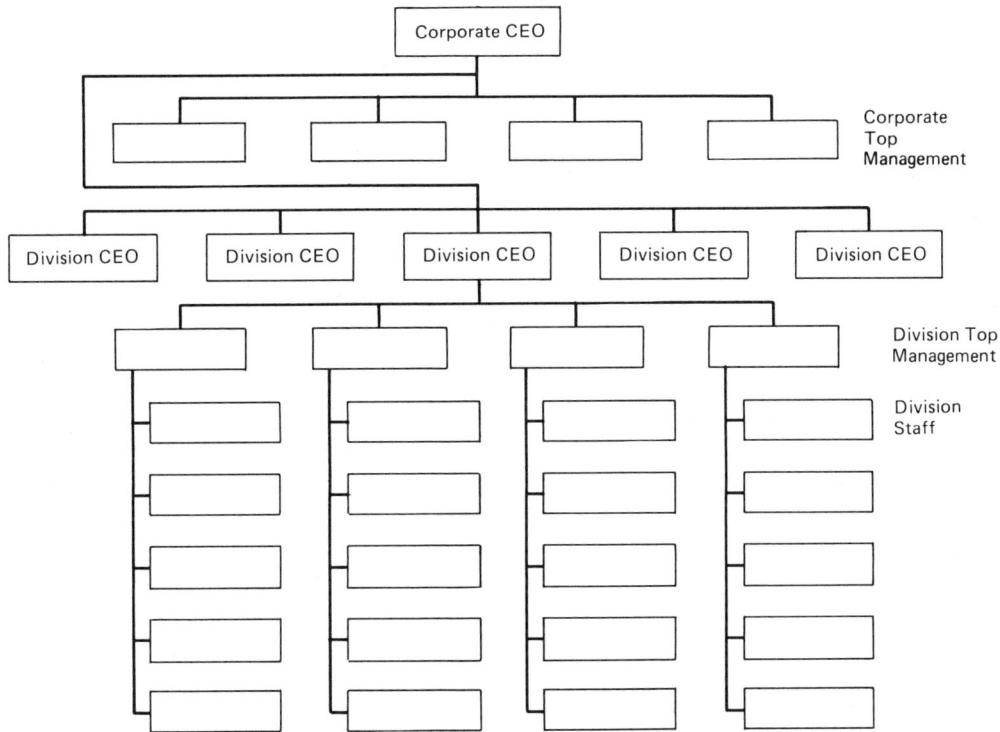

Figure 1-1: A Simplified Representation of the Structure of a Large, Diversified Corporation

terprise, functions such as operations/production, finance, marketing, and personnel have their own functional strategies, each related to business strategy and supportive of it.

Grand Strategy is the responsibility of the corporate Chief Executive and the corporate Board of Directors. It defines the overall character of the corporation, the ways it competes, and the means by which corporate goals and objectives are to be achieved. Grand Strategy ties together all other plans so that they do not work at cross-purposes.

Enterprise strategy is the plan for a single business within the corporation. An enterprise is often called a *strategic business unit* (SBU) to emphasize its relative autonomy. A diversified corporation, by definition, is engaged in various businesses. At the level of SBU, decision-makers focus on a single organization in one industry. They consider such questions as (Sharplin, 1985): (1) "What specific products or services does the SBU produce?" (2) "Who are the SBU's customers or clients?" and (3) "How can the SBU best compete in its particular product/service segments?" (p. 7). These questions are quite different from those considered at the corporate level, where Grand Strategy necessarily focuses on overall corporate mission and on methods of tying together distinct SBUs into a corporate portfolio of businesses.

Functional strategy is the plan for one activity area within an enterprise. *Functions* include finance, marketing, production/operations, and personnel/human resources. Any major department is also a function. To cite one example outside business: A large university will have a Grand Strategy that defines its overall purpose and desired relationships with such key external stakeholders as government, community, alumni, business, and other segments of society; each school or college within the university has an enterprise strategy that defines its purpose, its services, and groups whose needs it is intended to serve; and each department within a college or school has its own functional strategy that defines a segment of the enterprise, its purpose, its services, its programs, its service users, and its relationship to the college, school, and university. Hence, functional strategy means the planned direction for key activity areas within an enterprise.

Enterprise and functional plans are also part of a planning hierarchy that reflects differing concerns and time periods. There are three levels (Huse, 1982): (1) strategic; (2) coordinative or tactical; and (3) operational. They are illustrated and briefly summarized in Table 1-1.

Strategic planning is chiefly the concern of top-level managers. It is directed toward achieving long-term goals and objectives over several years. Strategic plans are uncertain and involve high degrees of risk. They help decision-makers anticipate changes in a largely uncontrollable external environment and play a high-stakes game of organizational success or failure.

Coordinative planning is intermediate-term. It is primarily the concern of middle-level managers. Less risky than strategy-making, coordinative plans "determine how certain areas of a business will deploy resources to reach objectives by following the policies and strategies that have been established in the strategic planning process" (Huse, 1982, p. 144).

Operational planning is short-term. It is the primary concern of first-line supervisors. Annual budgets are expressions of operational plans. Less risky than strategic

TABLE 1-1 LEVELS OF PLANNING

	Strategic plans	• The concern of top management • Long-term time horizon • Encompasses the entire organization • Primary focus: external
	Coordinative (tactical) plans	• The concern of middle managers • Intermediate-term time horizon • Encompasses only part of the organization • Primary focus: internal
	Operational plans	• The concern of supervisors • Short-term time horizon • Encompasses only a small segment of an organization's full range of activities • Primary focus: internal

or coordinative plans, operational plans involve scheduling and moving needed resources. These plans are tied to their longer-term strategic and coordinative counterparts.

Methods of Planning

Some firms have relatively formal planning processes; others, less formal ones. Large diversified corporations obviously face conditions somewhat different from those confronting medium-sized or small, single-product firms. Methods match conditions. In large corporations, planning is complicated and often resembles the process depicted in Figure 1-2. A full-time, professionally-trained corporate planning staff conducts studies for top managers. Top corporate executives concentrate on evaluations of overall corporate mission, goals, objectives, environmental conditions, internal strengths, and weaknesses across the corporation's portfolio of SBUs, and they also concentrate on resource acquisition and allocation. Middle-level managers operate within broad corporate objectives, but devise their own specific objectives and allocate resources by priority area. Lower-level department heads in each division establish objectives in line with middle-managers, and devise corresponding action plans (Huse, 1982).

Medium-sized companies with a single line of products or services can copy the structured planning approach of larger organizations, the less structured approach of smaller organizations, or devise some combination (Huse, 1982). External consultants can be used instead of a full-time planning staff. Top executives may solicit ideas from managers of such functional departments as finance, marketing, production/operations, and personnel/human resources about appropriate initiatives for the firm, information about competitors, and legal issues. This information provides the basis for planning.

In small companies, a team approach to strategic planning may suffice (Huse, 1982). A formal committee, headed up by the Chief Executive, develops plans. Meetings are vehicles for the process. Results of a 1986 survey of corporate planners and

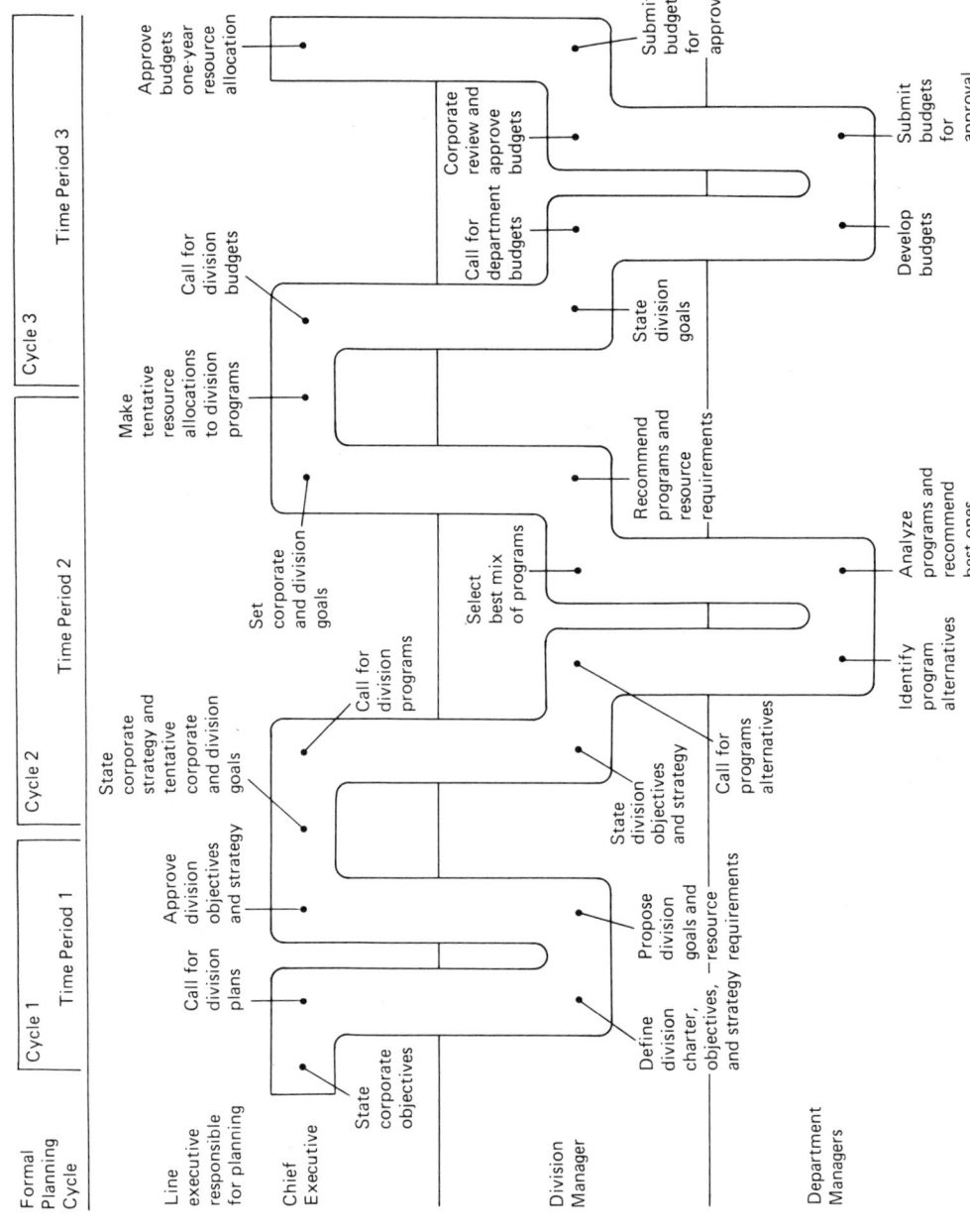

Figure 1-2: The Cycles of Planning. *Source:* Vancil and Lorange, 1975, p. 84. Reprinted with permission of *Harvard Business Review*.

training directors revealed that meetings are common vehicles for planning even in *Fortune* 500 firms (see Table 1-2).

Much has been written about the planning process (for example, O'Connor, 1980a & 1980b; Paine & Naumes, 1974; Roach & Allen, 1983; Ryans & Shanklin, 1985). Several points about it are clear. First, the planning process should be highly innovative, creative, and experiential. Second, formal planning encompasses only a tiny fraction of strategic decision-making. As much as 75 to 90 percent is informal, falling outside formal processes and meetings (Dyer, 1984). Third, planning has to do with organizational culture, because any SBP activity involves cultural change. Fourth and finally, people are essential for formulating and implementing strategy. Strategic plans stem from *human* values, beliefs, decisions, and problem-solving. Likewise, successful implementation of Strategic Business Plans depends on the availability and application of *human* skills and knowledge.

HUMAN RESOURCES PLANNING

Human resources planning means ensuring that the right numbers and types of people are available to apply the right skills needed to realize Strategic Business Plans. The outgrowth of HRP is a Grand Strategy "for ensuring that the organization's human

TABLE 1-2   METHODS OF CONDUCTING STRATEGIC PLANNING

Question
How does your organization conduct long-term (strategic) planning?

Method	Respondents			
	Planners		Trainers	
	Frequency	Percentage	Frequency	Percentage
No Formal Method	6	8.8%	8	11.6%
Budgeting	2	2.9%	6	6.5%
Management Meetings/Retreats	22	32.4%	15	27.6%
Management by Objectives (MBO)	9	13.2%	13	15.8%
Budgeting and Management Meetings	7	10.3%	11	12.9%
Budgeting and MBO	2	2.9%	1	2.2%
Management Meetings and MBO	8	11.8%	2	7.2%
All Formal Methods	11	16.2%	7	13.9%
Other	1	1.5%	6	5.0%

Source: Rothwell & Kazanas (1986–1988).

resources will be capable of fulfilling the stated business mission" (Roberts & Wolf, 1983, p. 15-2). Prior to the middle of this century, managers rarely worried about HRP. Most work involved physical, not mental, labor. It was easy enough to find warm bodies on short notice.

The earliest efforts to plan for labor were tied to financial forecasting and budgeting (Alpander, 1982). It was readily apparent to managers, even early in this century, that labor was a major production expense. It is not surprising, then, that the first fitful attempts to plan for labor stemmed from the need to estimate product demand and production levels. In this pioneering period, budgeters—not personnel practitioners—handled estimates of labor needs (Alpander, 1982).

During the 1960s, *manpower planning* first appeared (Alpander, 1982). It focused on forecasting supplies of personnel by examining movements into organizations and through various jobs. Forecasting demand for labor was another matter. Distinct from supply forecasting, its focus is directed to numbers and kinds of people needed to produce goods at a desired level of output. It was handled by corporate planners and budgeters, if by anyone (Alpander, 1982).

During the 1970s, managers began to devote more attention to the human side of their enterprises. Manpower planning was gradually supplanted by *human resources planning* (HRP) to denote a comprehensive approach to forecasting personnel supplies and demands, and planning personnel initiatives to help meet organizational needs (Alpander, 1982).

A Model of HRP

Think of HRP as a process in which decision-makers (Rothwell & Kazanas, 1988; Sredl & Rothwell, 1987):

1. link the purpose, goals, and objectives of the HR department and/or HR plan to the purpose, goals, and objectives of the organization,
2. assess the present status of HR in the organization by analyzing the work performed, the people who perform it, and the HR department,
3. scan the environment to assess how work will probably change over time, how people will probably have to change over time to keep up with work changes, and how the HR department will probably be affected over time by changes inside and outside the organization,
4. compare present work being done to expected future work and compare present people doing the work and those needed in the future,
5. consider unified, long-term HR strategies that will help close planning gaps in the work and work force (the one selected becomes an HR Grand Strategy),
6. implement HR Grand Strategy through coordination of such HR practice areas as career management programs, HRD, recruitment, job design, organization development, labor relations, employee assistance programs, and compensation/benefits,
7. manage HR activities so that they are effective for helping implement HR Grand Strategy by changing people and jobs, and

8. Evaluate HR Grand Strategy before, during, and after implementation.

Those who are curious about this model are advised to see our book-length treatment (Rothwell & Kazanas, 1988). For now it is sufficient to note that HRP is a long-term, functional planning activity intended to change jobs, people, and the department so that they support implementation of Strategic Business Plans.

Key Assumptions of HRP

Authors writing on HRP traditionally make several assumptions about it. First, they assume it should be *handled from the top down.* There is a distinct tendency in the literature to suggest that the HR needs for an entire corporation should be forecast and programs established from the top down. Yet much evidence suggests that comprehensive HR plans are rare (Nkomo, 1986; Rothwell & Kazanas, 1986; Rowland & Summers, 1981). More often than not, incremental changes—individual promotion, training, and pay decisions—are more common (Roberts & Wolf, 1983; Schein, 1978).

Second, they assume it should *integrate the many different programs and activities of the HR department.* Few authorities in HRP dispute the importance of integrating HR programs so that they are mutually supportive. Yet there is little evidence that such integration has been occurring (Craft, 1980; Nkomo, 1986).

Third, authorities assume HRP should be *supportive of, yet distinctive from, Strategic Business Plans.* HR plans should not merely be driven by Strategic Business Plans; rather, HRP should be interactive, at once influencing Strategic Business Plans and being influenced by them. The people presently available have an important influence on what strategies an organization can or should undertake—and even on what strategies are chosen. If a new venture is contemplated, one question to ask is this: Does the organization now employ people with appropriate skills and abilities? If not, the venture is handicapped from the start. HR Strategy must support business strategy ("Strategy and HR Policy," 1988).

Value of HRP

How much does HRP contribute to successful organizational performance? This question is difficult to answer. Definitions of HRP vary. Not all organizations even attempt it. However, at least one study on this subject has been undertaken.

Misa and Stein (1983) prepared a list of companies known for productivity improvement. They then compared this group to a matching sample of twenty-four companies from the *Fortune* 500. Their overall conclusion: "We found that the [productivity] leaders manage their human resources function strategically" (p. 27). Productivity leaders consistently outperformed comparison firms on the basis of return on total capital, return on equity, and net profit margin.

What characteristics distinguish the HR practices of productivity leaders from less productive counterparts? According to Misa and Stein (1983):

   1. "Leaders define the human resource role in terms of the function's participation in business decisions and the implementation of business strategies."

2. "Leaders focus the current resources devoted to the human resource function on important problems before they add new programs or seek additional resources."
3. "Leader human resource staffs initiate programs and communication with line management."
4. "Leaders' line management share in the responsibility for human resource programs."
5. "Leaders' corporate staffs share responsibility for human resource policy formation and program administration across organizational levels" (p. 28).

In a different study, Stella Nkomo (1986) found that few *Fortune* 500 companies—only 14.8 percent of 264 firms responding to her survey—make *any* attempt to plan comprehensively for HR. In most firms responding to Nkomo's survey (57 percent), no attempt is made to integrate HR plans and Strategic Business Plans.

Levels of HRP

Traditionally, writers have not discussed different levels of HRP. The usual assumption is that there is only one. However, there are obviously different HR needs for corporate, enterprise, and functional levels. Perhaps it helps, then, to speak in terms of different levels of HR Planning. Of course, this idea is based on analogy with corporate planning.

Consider Figure 1-3, which illustrates a simplified relationship between organi-

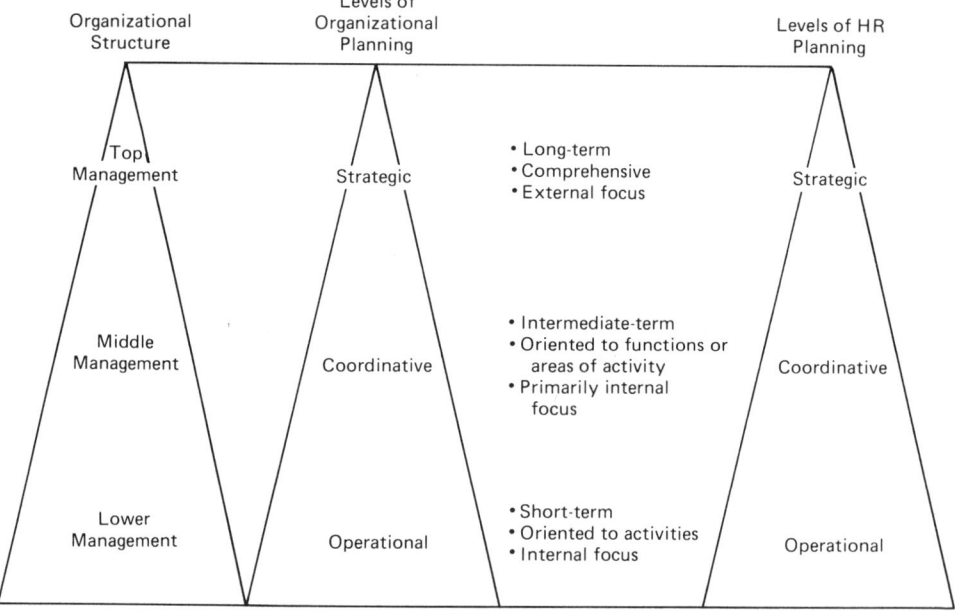

Figure 1-3: A Simplified Representation of the Relationships Between Organizational Structure, Organizational Plans, and Human Resource Plans

14   Background Issues   Chap. 1

zational structure, plans, and HR initiatives. Note that comprehensive, corporate-wide HR Grand Strategy is established at the highest levels. Each autonomous business (SBU), however, devises its own HR plans in keeping with broad corporate guidelines. Within each enterprise, functional HR plans guide and integrate HR practice areas such as career management, recruitment, HRD, organization development, job redesign, employee assistance, labor relations, and compensation/benefits.

HR Grand Strategy, like its corporate planning counterpart, is ultimately the responsibility of the top HR Executive, the Chief Executive (CEO), and key line executives. It establishes the relationship between the corporate HR function and corporate Grand Strategy.

HR Enterprise Strategy is more detailed, encompassing the HR plan for only one business in the corporation. At this level, the highest-ranking HR Executive works with CEO and key line managers to address such questions as:

1. What are the chief products/services of HR? What should they be?
2. What are the major responsibilities of HR practitioners, line managers, and employees in working toward realization of HR Plans? What should they be?
3. What HR initiatives are desirable in light of enterprise strategy? What resources are available to pursue those initiatives?
4. Who is the *chief* client or customer of HR activities: line managers? top managers? employees? Who should be the chief client or customer?
5. Given the major responsibilities of the HR department, how can it *best* serve its *chief* client? Other clients?

Seeking answers to there questions should help link the purpose, goals, and objectives of HR to those of the enterprise.

HR Functional Strategy is more specific than enterprise or corporate HR strategy. Its focus is providing guidelines for HR practice areas within the HR department at the enterprise level. These HR practice areas include recruitment/selection, HRD, organization development, and compensation/benefits. Any division or subcomponent of the HR department is a function. (Another way to look at it is that any HR activity, with or without someone assigned responsibility for it, is a function.) Each function has its own purpose, goals, objectives; each function operates in its own environment; each function possesses its own strengths and weaknesses; and each function can establish its own strategies.

The notion of HR functional strategy is important because any HRD department's strategic plans are, by this logic, functional plans. In other words, HRD practitioners are relatively free to establish their own departmental strategies, though these strategies should be consistent with broad enterprise HR strategy, corporate HR strategy, and functional strategies of other HR practice areas.

Methods of HRP

Some firms use sophisticated computer simulations and models to forecast HR demands, movements between job categories, and available HR supplies inside and outside the organization. Much of what is known about HRP comes from published case studies about methods (for a detailed bibliography of these studies, see Frantzreb, 1984).

Large, diversified corporations often employ HRP specialists. Most are placed within the HR department, have background in HR, and devote only part of their time to HRP (Strauss & Burack, 1983). In most *Fortune* 500 firms, HRP is handled by the HR department alone (Nkomo, 1986), with limited participation by line departments (Rothwell & Kazanas, 1988).

Forecasting HR demands and supplies has often been called the heart of HRP (Walker, 1980). Most firms—52 percent—forecast HR demand, but only 6 percent forecast supplies (Neihaus & Sheridan, 1984). Various advanced quantitative techniques are used in forecasting. Firms employing around 33,000 people are more likely than their larger or smaller counterparts to attempt linkage between SBP and HRP (Nkomo, 1986).

Despite academic interest in HRP for many years—long enough for academic research efforts to direct practitioner attention to this area—actual practices lag far behind theory. Several reasons may account for this gap. As Stella Nkomo (1986) points out, more lip service than real support is paid to HR generally. Second, managers often assume that the right people for the right jobs are always available. Third, HR practitioners lack credibility and skills. Fourth and finally, managers rely more on informal than formal HRP methods.

STRATEGIC HUMAN RESOURCE DEVELOPMENT

As defined earlier in the chapter, Strategic Human Resource Development (SHRD) means the process of changing an organization, stakeholders outside it, groups inside it, and people employed by it through planned learning so they possess the knowledge and skills needed in the future. SHRD helps implement Strategic Business Plans and HR plans by cultivating the skills of people inside the firm or changing the knowledge and skills of stakeholders outside it. One possible relationship between Strategic Business Plans, HR plans, and SHRD is illustrated in Figure 1-4.

SHRD is more holistic than traditional HRD. The outgrowth of SHRD is an Organizational Strategy for the HRD Effort which guides, unifies, and provides direction to planned learning sponsored by an organization. In SHRD, the focus of planning centers around roles and responsibilities of everyone—HRD practitioners, line managers, and participants. This focus on an HRD Effort—a broad undertaking in which many people have roles to play—differs from mere HRD department planning.

A second distinction between traditional and strategic HRD has to do with the role of experience. Experience denotes awareness based on participation in past problem-solving. It occupies a central place in most human endeavors. Everyone has heard the old saying, "Experience is the best teacher." Many people believe that 95 percent of all learning occurs through experience (Watson, 1979).

Traditional HRD activities provide individuals, otherwise lacking knowledge or skill, with structured opportunities to receive the fruits of distilled organizational experience. Those who advocate this view think of HRD in much the same way that John Dewey's (1938) critics thought of education: "the subject-matter of education

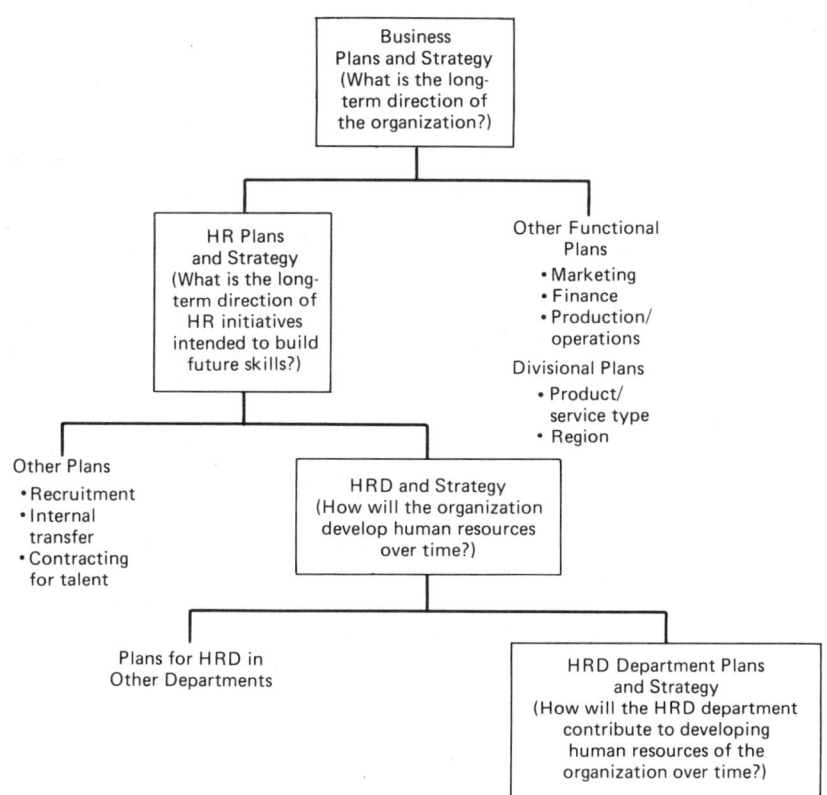

Figure 1-4: One Possible Relationship Between Business Plans, HR Plans, and HRD

consists of bodies of information and skills that have been worked out in the past; therefore, the chief business of the school is to transmit them to the new generation" (p. 17).

When viewed in this traditional way, HRD is a *maintenance subsystem*, intended to improve organizational efficiency by increasing routinization and predictability of human behavior (Katz & Kahn, 1978). It facilitates socialization of newcomers into the corporate culture, work group, and job. In a sense, traditional HRD is a rite of passage furnishing newcomers with ideas, techniques, and approaches worked out in the past. As Berger (1986) explains, *"teaching the correct way* has direct implications for HRD professionals. Culture fosters continuity and transmits to organization members the solutions that have worked well in the past and will work well in the future. Successful practices, basic assumptions, and theories about cause and effect are communicated (explicitly and subtly) to future generations. This transmission process . . . is the primary mission of HRD professionals" (p. 51).

It is appropriate to rely on experience if future events and situations will be similar to, and call for knowledge and skills derived from, the past. If future problems will be much like problems faced in the past, then few can question the wisdom of relying on what has been learned in the past as the basis for planned learning.

The trouble is, experience is not always appropriate in preparing for the future. There are many reasons why this is so. New knowledge is created faster today than it was in the past. Computers increase the speed with which information can be processed—but not the speed at which human beings can absorb it or use it. Organizations face more competition and must anticipate competitive challenges if they are to survive. The same principle applies to individuals who are competing with others for career success.

A new approach to HRD is needed to cope with a future that is not always like the past. This approach should help individuals anticipate knowledge and skills needed in the future rather than react after problems become apparent. SHRD does this. It can aid in planning one-time learning experiences as much as long-term learning encompassing multiple experiences. In SHRD, the practitioner's role is not solely to distill *past* experience or help solve *past* performance problems stemming from lack of individual knowledge or skill; rather, practitioners guide organizational members in a continuing, creative process of discovery so that they can prepare for knowledge and skills needed in the future.

This is not to say that SHRD always differs from its traditional counterpart. Traditional HRD and SHRD coincide when the external environment of the organization, individual, or job is relatively stable. If the future will be like the past, then traditional and strategic HRD intersect. But if the future will be utterly unlike the past due to external environmental change, then SHRD is appropriate for equipping people with new knowledge and skills.

A Model of SHRD

SHRD resembles Strategic Business Planning and long-term HR planning. HRD practitioners work with operating managers to (Sredl & Rothwell, 1987):*

1. Clarify the purpose of the HRD Effort.
2. Assess present conditions. What are the strengths and weaknesses of the organization viewed in terms of human skills?
3. Scan the external environment. What threats and opportunities affecting human performance are likely to result from changes outside the organization? Department? Work group? Occupation? Job?
4. Compare present strengths and weaknesses to future threats and opportunities.
5. Choose a long-term Organizational Strategy for HRD which is likely to help prepare individuals and the organization for the future.
6. Implement Organizational Strategy for HRD through
    a. organization development,
    b. nonemployee development,
    c. employee development,
    d. employee education, and

*A similar model is described in Sredl and Rothwell, 1987.

e. employee training.
7. Evaluate HRD.

These steps, illustrated in Figure 1-5, are the basis for the structure of this text.

With slight modifications, this model can also guide an HRD department or an operating department in planning its role in the HRD Effort. After all, both an HRD department and operating departments should support a unified Organization Strategy for HRD (see Figure 1-6).

Key Assumptions of SHRD

Generally speaking, an organization's HRD Effort can be effectively managed in line with Strategic Business Plans and human resource plans when each of the following conditions is true.

First, *there should be an overall purpose statement for the corporation, and the HRD Effort should be related to it* (Nininger, 1982). It is important to link business mission to that of planned learning sponsored by the business. In this way, few hard-

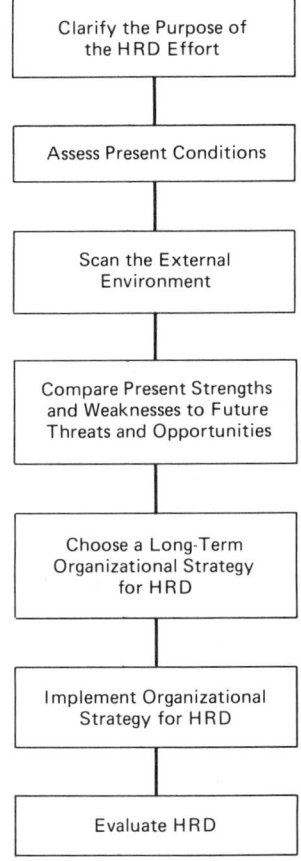

Figure 1-5: A Simplified Model of the SHRD Process

Strategic Human Resource Development

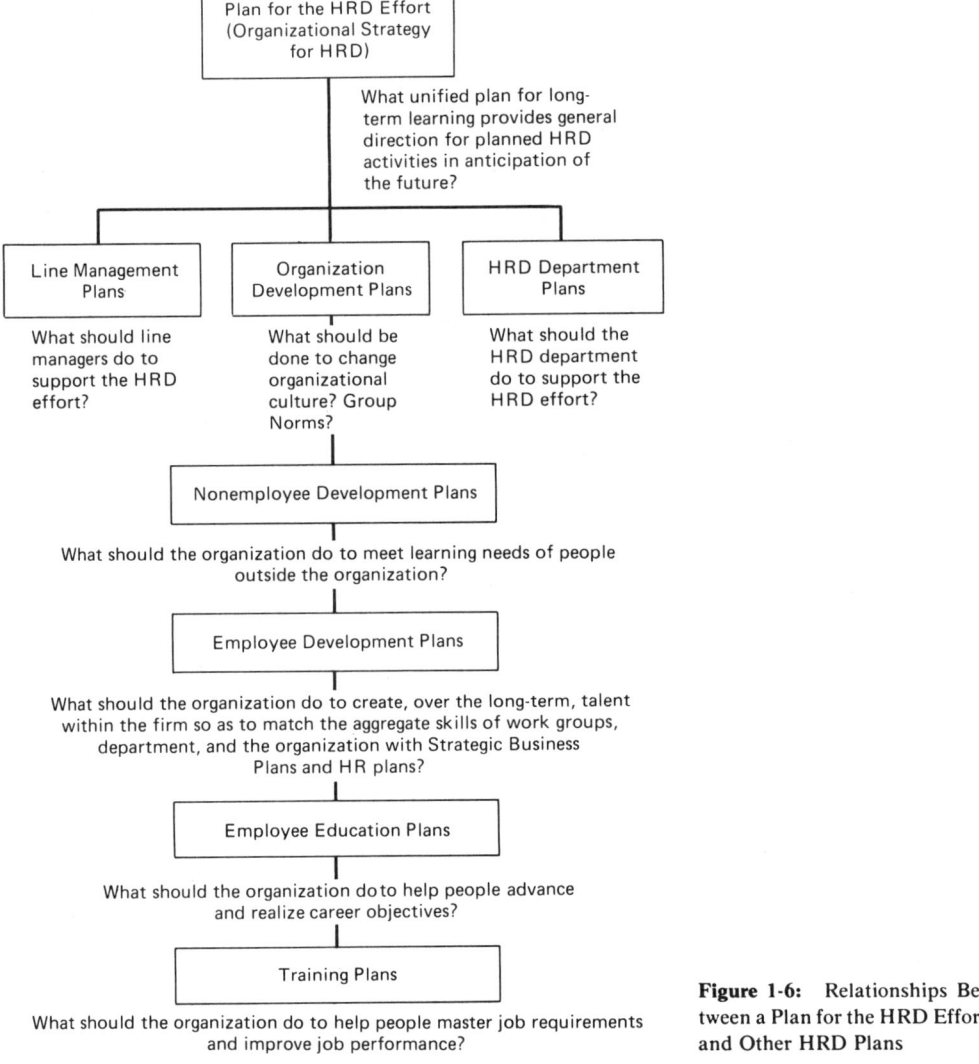

Figure 1-6: Relationships Between a Plan for the HRD Effort and Other HRD Plans

eyed critics can question the value of HRD unless they also question the value of the corporation.

Second, *every major plan of the corporation should be weighed in terms of human skills available to implement it and alternative ways of obtaining those skills.* HRD is not the *only* way to obtain needed skills. Alternatives include external recruitment or contracting for talent, internal transfer on a short-term or long-term basis, worksharing, redesign of jobs, or reliance on part-time employees. Nevertheless, any plan implies that human skills will be needed. Where and how to obtain these skills should be explicitly considered.

Third, *people at all levels in the organization's chain of command should share responsibility and accountability for HRD.* Planned learning is an important part of every supervisor's and employee's job. It is not enough to give lip service to training, education, and development. Supervisors and employees should be evaluated, in part, on how well they develop themselves and contribute to the development of others. Pay decisions, promotions, and transfers should depend in part on how well people are contributing to the HRD Effort for themselves and others.

Fourth, *there should be a formal, systematic, and holistic planning process for the corporation, personnel department, and HRD.* It is difficult for HRD to support Strategic Business Planning and long-term HR planning if nothing is articulated clearly. Formal planning is desirable. It furnishes opportunities for linkages and information-sharing. Unlike informal planning, formal planning calls for a deliberate and systematic approach to specifying what should be done, when it should be done, and who should be accountable for results.

Value of SHRD

SHRD is worthwhile for several reasons. First, it makes HRD activities proactive rather than reactive. Necessary knowledge and skills are furnished *before* or *as* they are needed rather than *after* performance problems are evident. *In this way, problems are headed off before they occur.* Second, SHRD ties learning to a comprehensive instructional planning process that supports and relates to Strategic Business Plans and Human Resources plans. Top managers apparently want this integration (Foltz, Rosenberg, & Foehrenbach, 1982). Third, businesses known for their excellence in productivity improvement handle their human resources strategically (Misa & Stein, 1983). HRD can help improve employee productivity and can lend itself, perhaps better than any other HR activity, to the support of Strategic Business Plans (Zemke, 1981). Finally, HRD practitioners will increasingly have to think strategically if they are to enjoy long-term career success (Baird & Meshoulam, 1984). For all these reasons, SHRD is important.

However, SHRD is not a panacea. It can serve to anticipate and furnish knowledge and skills needed in the future. In this respect, it may support Strategic Business Plans, long-term plans, and individual career plans. But it cannot anticipate future problems stemming from lack of individual ability, poor motivation, inappropriate reward systems, lack of supervision or leadership, or inadequate feedback on performance. These issues should properly be considered as part of a total *strategic performance system,* which is a topic too broad for discussion in this text.

THE SCOPE OF HRD

The scope of HRD efforts in the U.S. is staggering. Employers spend between $30 and $50 billion per year on formal employee training and education (Calvert, 1985; Carnevale & Goldstein, 1983; "Employee training in America," 1986). Approximately $180 billion per year is spent on informal, on-the-job training (Calvert, 1985). One in eight Americans receives formal, employer-sponsored job training each year (Carnevale & Goldstein, 1983). In-house HRD departments offer more instruction per employee than such alternative sources as external vendors, educational institutions, or trade and professional associations (Calvert, 1985; Gordon, 1986). White-collar employees, as a group, receive the most training and education (Carnevale, 1986; Gordon, 1986). Employees under age forty-five receive substantially more employer-sponsored in-house training than employees in other age groups (Carnevale, 1986).

A decade ago, HRD was largely unknown to government policymakers and academicians. They concentrated their attention almost exclusively on educational programs geared to improving employment prospects of the economically disadvantaged. But with productivity declines in the 1970s, policymakers began to realize "that people *are* productivity—and how efficiently people are trained is an important factor in the productivity equation" (Charles, 1986). Many pieces of legislation in recent years have been introduced to deal with training-related issues. One recent presidential candidate even inserted an item about HRD in his campaign platform (Charles, 1986).

At present, there are more than 250,000 full-time HRD practitioners in the U.S. and about 700,000 part-time practitioners ("How many trainers," 1983; "Trainer tally varies," 1982). Full-time practitioners usually possess college degrees in education and business (see Tables 1-3 and 1-4), come from backgrounds as personnel specialists (see Tables 1-5 and 1-6), and aspire to future positions in HRD or top management (see Table 1-7).

The HRD field is becoming more professional. HRD departments were once dumping grounds for line managers who could not perform and for people killing time until retirement. Rarely is that the case at present. Few organizations can afford the luxury of supporting hangers-on. Managers are increasingly sensitive to the crucial importance of training employees to be more productive in how they work—and to *think smarter* rather than just *work harder*.

The professionalism of the HRD field has been partly a result of a growing number of formal college degree programs in the field at both undergraduate and graduate levels. More than 200 of these programs exist at present (*Directory of Academic Programs,* 1983–1984). Many high-quality, non-degree-related workshops exist as well—

TABLE 1-3	EDUCATION—BACHELOR'S DEGREES OF HRD PRACTITIONERS
Specialty	% of sample
Education	17.6
Business/Management	16.0
Social Sciences	14.7
Psychology	10.8
Engineering	5.5
Letters	5.4
Communications	4.4
Health Services	3.2
Physical Sciences	2.9
Biological Sciences	2.6
Industrial Relations	2.1
HRD/Training and Development	1.9
Other	13.1

Source: Lee, 1985b, p. 75. Reprinted with permission from *Training.*

TABLE 1-4 EDUCATION—POST-GRADUATE DEGREES OF HRD PRACTITIONERS

Specialty	% of sample
Education	31.6
Business/Management	18.6
Psychology	10.4
Social Sciences	6.7
HRD/Training and Development	6.1
Communications	2.4
Industrial Relations	2.2
Health Services	2.2
Letters	2.0
Engineering	1.7
Other	16.0

Source: Lee, 1985b, p. 76. Reprinted with permission from *Training*.

and are often more up-to-date than offerings in educational institutions. The best workshops and seminars are offered by the many professional societies in the HRD field.

However, entry to the HRD field is not easy for those peering in from the outside. Some firms promote HRD practitioners only from within, and will not hire outsiders, no matter how well-qualified (*Careers in Training*, 1983). Some firms do hire entry-level employees with college training in HRD, but prefer graduates of academic HRD programs offered by colleges of business or psychology to graduates of similar and

TABLE 1-5 TRAINERS' BACKGROUND: WHERE HRD PRACTITIONERS COME FROM

Former Position	% of sample
Personnel Specialist	11.7
College/University Instructor	7.8
Schoolteacher	
(primary)	
(secondary)	9.5
Line Manager	10.4
Staff Manager	7.2
Sales	7.2
First-line Supervisor (line function)	6.3
First-line Supervisor (staff function)	3.5
Technical Specialist	11.2
Other Professional	10.5
Student	3.4
Other	11.3

Source: Lee, 1985b, p. 76. Reprinted with permission from *Training*.

TABLE 1-6 CURRENT POSITION OF HRD PRACTITIONERS BY FORMER POSITION

Former job	Training/HRD manager	Training/HRD specialist	Other (nontraining/HRD manager, consultant, personnel professional, etc.)
Personnel Specialist	9.9	2.8	22.9
College/University Professor	8.2	7.2	7.5
Schoolteacher	11.3	9.7	5.2
Line Manager	10.2	11.2	11.8
Staff Manager	7.2	6.0	9.2
Sales	8.0	5.2	5.6
1st Line Supervisor—line	6.2	9.2	3.3
1st Line Supervisor—staff	3.1	3.6	3.3
Technical Specialist	12.3	14.0	7.5
Other Professional	9.7	16.5	8.8
Student	2.5	5.6	4.2
Other	11.9	8.8	10.9

Source: Lee, 1985b, p. 77. Reprinted with permission from *Training*.

equally good programs offered by colleges of education or communication. Still others favor specializations—such as degrees in "Instructional Technology"—to generalized HRD preparation. Readers interested in entering the field should purchase Stump's (1985) simple but useful guide to careers in the HRD field and review it carefully. It is available from the American Society for Training and Development (1630 Duke Street, P.O. Box 1443, Alexandria, VA 22313).

ACTIVITIES OF HRD PRACTITIONERS

Many research studies have attempted to describe what HRD practitioners do (for example, *Competency analysis,* 1979; Pinto & Walker, 1978; Varney, 1980). These efforts have been confounded, at least in part, by unclear definitions of HRD and by the sheer variety of philosophies and approaches to the HRD field. Yet there is clearly a need to know what practitioners do in order to: (1) provide guidance and plan instruction for those who would like to enter, or sharpen their skills in, the field; (2) explain and justify HRD to others in organizational settings; (3) provide guidance for HRD managers in selecting, developing, and evaluating HRD staff; and (4) chart career paths in the field.

Two recent studies have shed light on the nature of professional HRD practice. The first, *Models for Excellence* (1983), was sponsored by the largest single professional association in the HRD field, the American Society for Training and Development. The second, *Instructional Design Competencies: The Standards* (1986), was carried out by a joint task force organized by the Association for Educational Communications and Technology (AECT) and the National Society for Performance and In-

TABLE 1-7 LONG-TERM CAREER ASPIRATIONS OF HRD PRACTITIONERS	
Career	% of sample
Training and Development Specialist or Manager	24.6
Chief Executive/Operating Officer	15.7
Other Personnel Responsibilities (personnel manager, labor relations, etc.)	15.0
Consultant	14.7
Other Organizational Functions (marketing, production, etc.)	12.9
Educator/Teacher/Academician	6.5
Owner of Business Other Than Consulting	5.7
Other	5.0

Source: Lee, 1985b, p. 78. Reprinted with permission from *Training*.

struction (NSPI). Though these studies were conducted in different ways, focused on different facets of the HRD field, and produced different outcomes, each is worth a brief overview, because they tell more about what HRD practitioners do than any other existing sources.

Models for Excellence (1983) began with an extensive review of prior research about the HRD practitioner's job. It culminated in an impressive description of HRD "roles," "competencies," and "work outputs." In this context, a "role" means a cluster of behaviors, an activity area; a "competency" means an underlying skill required to enact the role; and a "work output" means a tangible result of role behavior or application of a competency. Presently under revision (at this writing), the 1983 study pinpointed 15 possible roles, 31 competencies, and 102 work outputs of HRD practitioners. They are listed in Tables 1-8, 1-9, and 1-10.

Instructional Design Competencies: The Standards (1986) does not describe all practitioner "roles"; rather, it is limited to competencies "which enable a skilled instructional designer to enter an organization, diagnose a performance problem caused by knowledge or skill deficit, plan a training or non-training intervention, execute the plan, and evaluate the results" (p. 1). Each competency is described in terms of purpose, performance, and assumptions. Each "performance" is further explained in terms of (a) conditions necessary to exhibit it, (b) behavior associated with it, and (c) yardsticks for assessing it. The "core competencies" are illustrated in Table 1-11. Of course, the role of instructional designer is only one of many parts played by HRD practitioners.

How important are the competencies identified in these research studies? The answers to this question must be based on information about present and expected future activities of HRD practitioners.

Each year since 1982, *Training Magazine* has commissioned a survey study of HRD activities in the U.S. Basing conclusions on a sample of over 2,000 organizations (a 16.8 percent response rate on a mailing to 15,000 firms), this survey is one of the best current sources of information about activities of HRD practitioners. According to the 1986 survey results, practitioners spend substantial time training and developing middle managers and executives (see Table 1-12). Management skills receive much attention (see Table 1-13); so too does new employee orientation (see Table 1-

TABLE 1-8 THE FIFTEEN KEY ROLES OF HRD PRACTITIONERS

- EVALUATOR . . . The role of identifying the extent of a program, service, or product's impact.
- GROUP FACILITATOR . . . The role of managing group discussions and group process so that individuals learn and group members feel the experience is positive.
- INDIVIDUAL DEVELOPMENT COUNSELOR . . . The role of helping an individual assess personal competencies, values, goals, and identify and plan development and career actions.
- INSTRUCTIONAL WRITER . . . The role of preparing written learning and instructional materials.
- INSTRUCTOR . . . The role of presenting information and directing structured learning experiences so that individuals learn.
- MANAGER OF TRAINING AND DEVELOPMENT . . . The role of planning, organizing, staffing, controlling training and development operations or training and development projects and of linking training and development operations with other organization units.
- MARKETER . . . The role of selling Training and Development viewpoints, learning packages, programs and services to target audiences outside one's own work unit.
- MEDIA SPECIALIST . . . The role of producing software for and using audio, visual, computer, and other hardware-based technologies for training and development.
- NEEDS ANALYST . . . The role of defining gaps between ideal and actual performance and specifying the cause of the gaps.
- PROGRAM ADMINISTRATOR . . . The role of ensuring that the facilities, equipment, materials, participants, and other components of a learning event are present and that program logistics run smoothly.
- PROGRAM DESIGNER . . . The role of preparing objectives, defining content, selecting and sequencing activities for a specific program.
- STRATEGIST . . . The role of developing long-range plans for what the training and development structure, organization, direction, policies, programs, services, and practices will be in order to accomplish the training and development mission.
- TASK ANALYST . . . Identifying activities, tasks, subtasks, human resource, and support requirements necessary to accomplish specific results in a job or organization.
- THEORETICIAN . . . The role of developing and testing theories of learning, training, and development.
- TRANSFER AGENT . . . The role of helping individuals apply learning after the learning experience.

Source: Models for Excellence, 1983, p. 29. Reprinted with permission from the American Society for Training and Development.

14). Despite the computer revolution, lecture remains the most common instructional delivery method (Gordon, 1986). Hence, effective small-group presentation skill remains a key competency for HRD practitioners, especially for those new to the field. It becomes less important as the practitioner progresses beyond entry level, accepting increasing responsibility for preparing instructional materials and ultimately for supervising other practitioners (Sredl & Rothwell, 1987).

Most practitioners report to personnel department chiefs, suggesting that long-term career paths are often in personnel management rather than in HRD. This reporting relationship is less preferable for professionally-prepared, career-oriented practitioners than the second most common reporting relationship—to the HRD department chief. The reason is that personnel practitioners have historically been inter-

TABLE 1-9 TRAINING AND DEVELOPMENT COMPETENCIES

1. *Adult Learning Understanding* . . . Knowing how adults acquire and use knowledge, skills, attitudes. Understanding individual differences in learning.
2. *A/V Skill* . . . Selecting and using audio/visual hardware and software.
3. *Career Development Knowledge* . . . Understanding the personal and organizational issues and practices relevant to individual careers.
4. *Competency Identification Skill* . . . Identifying the knowledge and skill requirements of jobs, tasks, roles.
5. *Computer Competence* . . . Understanding and being able to use computers.
6. *Cost-Benefit Analysis Skill* . . . Assessing alternatives in terms of their financial, psychological, and strategic advantages and disadvantages.
7. *Counseling Skill* . . . Helping individuals recognize and understand personal needs, values, problems, alternatives, and goals.
8. *Data Reduction Skill* . . . Scanning, synthesizing, and drawing conclusions from data.
9. *Delegation Skill* . . . Assigning task responsibility and authority to others.
10. *Facilities Skill* . . . Planning and coordinating logistics in an efficient and cost-effective manner.
11. *Feedback Skill* . . . Communicating opinions, observations, and conclusions such that they are understood.
12. *Futuring Skill* . . . Projecting trends and visualizing possible and probable futures and their implications.
13. *Group Process Skill* . . . Influencing groups to both accomplish tasks and fulfill the needs of their members.
14. *Industry Understanding* . . . Knowing the key concepts and variables that define an industry or sector (e.g., critical issues, economic vulnerabilities, measurements, distribution channels, inputs, outputs, information sources).
15. *Intellectual Versatility* . . . Recognizing, exploring, and using a broad range of ideas and practices. Thinking logically and creatively without undue influence from personal biases.
16. *Library Skills* . . . Gathering information from printed and other recorded sources. Identifying and using information specialists and reference services and aids.
17. *Model Building Skill* . . . Developing theoretical and practical frameworks which describe complex ideas in understandable, usable ways.
18. *Negotiation Skill* . . . Securing win-win agreements while successfully representing a special interest in a decision situation.
19. *Objectives Preparation Skill* . . . Preparing clear statements which describe desired outputs.
20. *Organization Behavior Understanding* . . . Seeing organizations as dynamic, political, economic, and social systems which have multiple goals; using this larger perspective as a framework for understanding and influencing events and change.
21. *Organization Understanding* . . . Knowing the strategy, structure, power networks, financial position, systems of a SPECIFIC organization.
22. *Performance Observation Skills* . . . Tracking and describing behaviors and their effects.
23. *Personnel/HR Field Understanding* . . . Understanding issues and practices in other HR areas (Organization Development, Organization Job Design, Human Resource Planning, Selection and Staffing, Personnel Research and Information Systems, Compensation and Benefits, Employee Assistance, Union/Labor Relations).
24. *Presentation Skills* . . . Verbally presenting information such that the intended purpose is achieved.
25. *Questioning Skill* . . . Gathering information from and stimulating insight in individuals and groups through the use of interviews, questionnaires, and other probing methods.
26. *Records Management Skill* . . . Storing data in easily retrievable form.

TABLE 1-9 Continued.

27. *Relationship Versatility* . . . Adjusting behavior in order to establish relationships across a broad range of people and groups.
28. *Research Skills* . . . Selecting, developing, and using methodologies, statistical, and data collection techniques for a formal inquiry.
29. *Training and Development Field Understanding* . . . Knowing the technological, social, economic, professional, and regulatory issues in the field; understanding the role T&D plays in helping individuals learn for current and future jobs.
30. *Training and Development Techniques Understanding* . . . Knowing the techniques and methods used in training; understanding their appropriate uses.
31. *Writing Skills* . . . Preparing written material which follows generally accepted rules of style and form, is appropriate for the audience, creative, and accomplishes its intended purposes.

Source: Models for Excellence. 1983, p. 36. Reprinted with permission from the American Society for Training and Development.

TABLE 1-10 THE CRITICAL OUTPUTS FOR THE TRAINING AND DEVELOPMENT FIELD

Evaluator:

1. Instruments to assess individual change in knowledge, skill, attitude, behavior, results
2. Instruments to assess program and instructional quality
3. Reports (written and oral) of program impact on individuals
4. Reports (written and oral) of program impact on an organization
5. Evaluation and validation designs and plans (written and oral)
6. Written instruments to collect and interpret data

Group Facilitator:

7. Group discussions in which issues and needs are constructively assessed
8. Group decisions where individuals all feel committed to action
9. Cohesive teams
10. Enhanced awareness of group process, self, and others

Individual Development Counselor:

11. Individual career development plans
12. Enhanced skills on the part of an individual to identify and carry out his/her own department needs/goals
13. Referrals to professional counseling
14. Increased knowledge by the individual about where to get development support
15. Tools, resources needed in career development
16. Tools for managers to facilitate employees' career development
17. An individual who initiates feedback, monitors, and manages career plans

Instructional Writer:

18. Exercises, workbooks, worksheets
19. Teaching guides
20. Scripts (for video, film, audio)
21. Manuals and job aids
22. Computer software
23. Tests and evaluation forms
24. Written role plays, simulations, games
25. Written case studies

TABLE 1-10 Continued.

Instructor:

26. Video tapes, films, audio tapes, computer-aided instruction, and other AV materials facilitated
27. Case studies, role plays, games, tests, and other structured learning events directed
28. Lectures, presentations, stories delivered
29. Examinations administered and feedback given
30. Students' needs addressed
31. An individual with new knowledge, skills, attitudes, or behavior in his/her repertoire

Manager of Training and Development:

32. T&D department or project operating objectives
33. T&D budgets developed and monitored
34. Positive work climate in the T&D function or project group
35. Department/project staffed
36. T&D standards, policies, and procedures
37. Outside suppliers/consultants selected
38. Solutions to department/project problems
39. T&D actions congruent with other HR and organization actions
40. Relevant information exchanged with clients/departments (internal and external)
41. Staff evaluated
42. Staff developed

Marketer:

43. Promotional materials for T&D programs and curricula
44. Sales presentations
45. Program overviews
46. Leads
47. Contracts with T&D clients (internal and external) negotiated
48. Marketing plan (developed and implemented)
49. T&D program/services visible to target markets

Media Specialist:

50. T&D computer software
51. Lists (written and oral) of recommended instructional hardware
52. Graphics
53. Video-based material
54. Audio tapes
55. Computer hardware in working order
56. AV equipment in working order
57. Media users advised/counseled
58. Production plans
59. Purchasing specifications/recommendations for instructional/training software
60. Purchasing specifications/recommendations for instructional/training hardware

Needs Analyst:

61. Performance problems and discrepancies identified and reported (written/oral)
62. Knowledge, skill, attitude problems and discrepancies identified and reported (written/oral)
63. Tools to assess the knowledge, skill attitude, and performance level of individuals and organizations
64. Needs analysis strategies
65. Causes of discrepancies inferred

TABLE 1-10 Continued.

Program Administrator:
66. Facilities and equipment selected and scheduled
67. Participant attendance secured, recorded
68. Hotel/conference center staff managed
69. Faculty scheduled
70. Course material distributed (on-site, pre-course, post-course)
71. Contingency plans for back-ups, emergencies
72. Physical environment maintained
73. Program follow-up accomplished

Program Designer:
74. Lists of learning objectives
75. Written program plans/designs
76. Specifications and priorities of training content, activities, materials, and methods
77. Sequencing plans for training content, activities, materials, and methods
78. Instructional contingency plans and implementations strategies

Strategist:
79. T&D long-range plans included in the broad human resource strategy of the client organization
80. Identification (written/oral) of long-range T&D strengths, weaknesses, opportunities, threats
81. Descriptions of the T&D function and its outputs in the future
82. Identification of forces/trends (technical, social, economic, etc.) impacting T&D
83. Guidelines/plans for implementing long-range goals
84. Alternative directions for T&D
85. Cost/benefit analyses of the impact of T&D on the organization

Task Analyst:
86. Lists of key job/unit outputs
87. Lists of key job/unit tasks
88. Lists of knowledge/skill/attitude requirements of a job/unit
89. Descriptions of the performance levels required in a job/unit
90. Job design, enlargement, enrichment implications/alternatives identified
91. Subtasks, tasks, and job clustered
92. Conditions described under which jobs/tasks are performed

Theoretician:
93. New concepts and theories of learning and behavior change
94. Articles on T&D issues/theories for scientific journals and trade publications
95. Research designs
96. Research reports
97. Training models and applications of theory
98. Existing learning/training theories and concepts evaluated

Transfer Agent:
99. Individual action plans for on-the-job/real world application
100. Plans (written/oral) for the support of transfer of learning in and around the application environment
101. Job aids to support performance and learning
102. On-the-job environment modified to support learning

Source: Models for Excellence, 1983, pp. 31–33. Reprinted with permission from the American Society for Training and Development.

TABLE 1-11 SUMMARY OF CORE COMPETENCIES OF THE INSTRUCTIONAL DESIGNER (HRD PRACTITIONER)

1. Determine projects that are appropriate for instructional design.
2. Conduct a needs assessment.
3. Assess the relevant characteristics of learners/trainees.
4. Analyze the characteristics of a setting.
5. Perform job, task, and/or content analysis.
6. Write statements of performance objectives.
7. Develop the performance measurements.
8. Sequence the performance objectives.
9. Specify the instructional strategies.
10. Design the instructional materials.
11. Evaluate the instruction/training.
12. Design the instructional management system.
13. Plan and monitor instructional design projects.
14. Communicate effectively in visual, oral, and written form.
15. Interact effectively with other people.
16. Promote the use of instructional design.

Source: Instructional Design Competencies, 1986, p. 3. Reprinted with permission from the International Board of Standards of Training, Performance, and Instruction.

ested in putting people in "boxes" on organization charts; in contrast, HRD practitioners are—or should be—more interested in developing people for new "boxes" or getting away from the restrictiveness of boxes completely (Laird, 1985, Nadler, 1979).

What does the future hold in store for HRD? As HRD practitioners emerge from formal college degree programs, the state of the art will become increasingly sophisticated. Newcomers to the field will simply be better prepared than their predecessors. They may place greater reliance on computer-based training (CBT), an area in which college students receive more instruction than their predecessors. The process of identifying what training is needed will be increasingly recognized as important, and data collection methods will become more sophisticated as recent college graduates in HRD bring their newly-learned skills in questionnaire design and interviewing to analyzing training needs.

Two other trends are worth special note. First, there is a trend for practitioners to make greater use of public seminars, so named because they are open to the general public. Between 1983 and 1986, public seminars increased as a percentage of HRD development and delivery options (see Table 1-15). Second, there is another trend for HRD departments to use one-on-one instruction rather than group classroom instruction (see Figure 1-7). One reason is that one-on-one instruction can be paced to meet immediate needs and fit individual time schedules in ways that classroom instruction cannot.

What do these trends mean? Practitioners will devote more time to the "individual development counselor" role described in *Models for Excellence.* More than that, they will need to train supervisors to act in this role. Increasingly, employees are yearning for individualized counseling about personal and career growth. What they want is

TABLE 1-12 WHO GETS THE TRAINING

Job category	Organizations providing training (%)[1]	Mean number of individuals trained[2]	Projected number of individuals trained[3] (in millions)	Mean number of hours delivered[4]	Projected total hours of training delivered[5] (in millions)
Middle Managers	68.9	20.4	3.22	44.2	142.5
Professionals	46.1	50.7	5.36	42.3	226.8
Executives	69.5	5.2	0.83	40.9	33.9
Salespeople	29.7	38.3	2.61	39.9	104.1
First-line Supervisors	61.2	28.4	3.99	39.6	157.9
Senior Managers	60.6	9.1	1.26	38.9	49.2
Production Workers	25.3	153.7	8.92	34.6	308.6
Customer Service People	34.2	60.4	4.74	33.3	157.8
Administrative Employees	48.8	19.6	2.19	22.0	48.3
Office/Clerical	50.8	29.1	3.39	18.3	62.0
Total			36.52		1,291.0

[1] Percent of all U.S. organizations with 50 or more employees that provide training to people in these categories.
[2] Average number of individuals trained, based only on those organizations that do provide some training.
[3] Total number of people trained in all organizations (in millions).
[4] Average hours of training per individual, based only on organizations that do provide some training.
[5] Total man-hours of training delivered by all organizations to all employees in these categories (in millions).

Source: Gordon, 1986, p. 49. Reprinted with permission from *Training*.

TABLE 1-13 GENERAL TYPES OF TRAINING BY SIZE OF ORGANIZATION*

Types of training	Number of employees					
	50–99	100–499	500–999	1,000–2,499	2,500–9,999	10,000 or more
Management Skills/Development	69.0	82.4	88.9	91.7	89.7	92.4
Technical Skills/Knowledge	65.5	73.1	75.2	80.8	82.0	86.1
Supervisory Skills	58.4	78.2	82.9	86.1	89.7	88.4
Communication Skills	60.7	69.5	76.1	83.1	87.2	85.7
New Methods/Procedures	56.0	59.9	66.7	64.7	66.4	67.1
Clerical/Secretarial Skills	56.0	59.4	60.7	67.6	71.8	67.5
Executive Development	54.8	58.4	60.7	72.9	74.4	79.1
Computer Literacy/Basic Computer Skills	51.2	51.6	58.1	66.6	71.8	78.3
Customer Relations/Services	44.1	58.2	56.4	60.4	64.1	66.7
Personal Growth	47.6	52.1	58.1	61.3	64.1	63.3
Sales Skills	41.7	44.8	43.6	43.3	48.7	60.0
Employee/Labor Relations	36.9	41.6	49.6	56.2	64.1	64.9
Disease Prevention/Health Promotion	35.8	43.0	47.0	53.1	48.7	48.0
Customer Education	33.4	27.0	29.1	33.0	35.9	40.2
Remedial Basic Education	11.9	16.7	19.7	20.7	25.6	28.3

*Percent of organizations providing these types of training to employees.
Source: Gordon, 1986, p. 62. Reprinted with permission from *Training*.

TABLE 1-14 SPECIFIC TYPES OF TRAINING

Types of training	Percent providing	In-house only (%)	Outside only (%)	Both (%)
New Employee Orientation	80.8	74.4	.0	4.5
Performance Appraisals	66.2	44.8	7.2	4.2
New Equipment Orientation	57.4	31.7	0.2	5.5
Leadership	54.2	15.9	4.2	14.0
Time Management	52.8	14.4	21.0	7.3
Train-the-Trainer	47.1	20.8	11.4	4.9
Word Processing	46.0	22.1	9.8	4.0
Hiring/Selection Process	45.8	23.9	7.3	4.6
Goal-Setting	45.6	28.2	7.5	9.9
Interpersonal Skills	45.3	18.0	9.2	18.1
Product Knowledge	42.9	30.6	10.9	11.4
Public Speaking/Presentation	41.6	16.3	10.0	15.3
Team-Building	39.4	17.1	11.6	10.7
Problem-Solving	38.5	14.9	9.5	4.1
Stress Management	38.5	11.3	12.2	5.0
Computer Programming	38.3	10.4	10.9	7.0
Motivation	38.1	16.9	7.9	3.3
Planning	37.3	19.2	5.3	2.8
Safety	36.8	16.7	2.9	7.2
Personal Computer Use	35.4	11.3	10.3	3.8
Data Processing	33.1	8.5	8.2	16.4
Listening Skills	33.0	12.4	13.5	.7
Writing Skills	32.1	10.0	2.7	3.6
Conducting Meetings	31.7	18.0	9.8	11.0
Delegation Skills	31.4	12.6	6.9	9.0
Decision-Making	30.3	14.0	8.1	9.4
Strategic Planning	28.6	11.2	8.1	9.3
Management Information Systems	26.1	7.8	8.0	10.2
Negotiating Skills	20.9	7.6	5.3	5.3
Manufacturing (e.g., production planning, cost estimating)	17.2	4.4	5.3	7.5
Outplacement/Retirement Planning	16.9	7.2	5.6	4.1
Creativity/Creative Thinking	16.3	8.1	1.7	6.5
Purchasing	14.8	5.7	3.3	5.8
Finance	14.5	3.5	3.6	7.4
Other (subjects not listed)	13.2	1.4	5.3	6.5
Nutrition	12.4	4.9	1.9	5.6
Reading Skills	9.5	2.1	5.3	2.1
Foreign Language	5.5	1.6	3.5	3.4

Source: Gordon, 1986, p. 62. Reprinted with permission from *Training*.

TABLE 1-15   DEVELOPMENT AND DELIVERY OF TRAINING

			Percentage of organization's total training effort (mean)	
Type of training	Developed by	Delivered by	1983	1986
Seminars/Workshops (In-House)	In-House Training Staff	In-House Training Staff	42.5	30.4
Seminars/Workshops (Off-Shelf)	Vendor	In-House Training Staff	16.0	14.8
Seminars/Workshops (Public)	Various External Sources	Various External Sources	15.8	21.5
Seminars/Workshops (Closed—i.e., for organization's employees only)	Vendor/Consultant	Vendor/Consultant	9.8	10.2
Self-Instruction	In-House Training Staff	N/A	6.5	12.0
Self-Instruction	Off-Shelf	N/A	6.6	8.6
Self-Instruction	Custom-Built by Vendor	N/A	2.8	2.5

Source: Zemke, 1986, p. 58. Reprinted with permission from *Training.*

not traditional employee performance appraisal; rather, they are searching for the kind of meeting described by Blessing (1986):

> What if . . . each support employee had the opportunity to take charge of a special meeting with the supervisor, devoted solely to that employee's on-the-job growth? The meeting wouldn't cover promotion or salary issues, but would put the manager and employee in the role of associates who are exploring avenues within the current job to develop the assets of the individual employee (p. 92).

The learning plan growing out of such meetings will be unique to one person, positioning HRD practitioners as enabling agents who help others find means to meet their own learning needs. This role requires an entirely different set of skills and assumptions about people than have typified HRD practice to date.

The future looks bright for skilled HRD practitioners. As professionally-trained managers with advanced degrees assume more responsibility, the demand for HRD services is likely to grow. The reason is that highly-educated managers tend to appreciate HRD activities more than their less-educated counterparts and are more likely to support and even require those activities.

Activities of HRD Practitioners

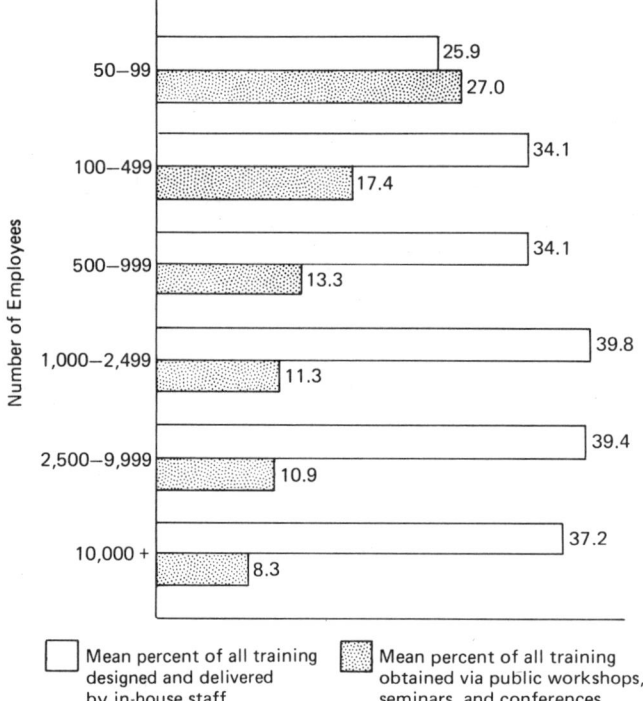

Figure 1-7: Development and Delivery of Training as a Function of Organizational Size. *Source:* Zemke, 1986, p. 59. Reprinted with permission of *Training*.

THE TRADITIONAL FOCUS OF HRD

HRD focuses on change through learning. Though this idea is simple, its implications are powerful and far-reaching. After all, there are different kinds of change and different kinds of learning.

Nadler (1979) distinguishes between three types of HRD activities: (1) *training*, geared to immediate change in *job* performance; (2) *education*, geared to intermediate change in *individual* capabilities; and (3) *development*, geared to *general and long-term improvement in the individual*. He also distinguishes between three categories of human resource activities: (1) *HRD*, intended to improve the individual in the future, (2) *HRU*, intended to make use of an individual's present skills, and (3) *HRE*, intended to change the context in which an individual is presently working.

Consider the placement of individuals in organizational settings. Individuals are at once

- *unique human beings* with their own talents, skills, abilities, capabilities, and career aspirations,
- *job incumbents*, hired to carry out particular tasks and presumably achieve certain results or outcomes,
- *members of work groups*, typically reporting to one supervisor, who share concerns with others in their group,

- *members of friendship groups,* consisting of people who like each other (these may or may not overlap with work groups),
- *members of one organization* facing its own problems, competitors, and placement within the society and community, and
- *members of a national culture or a country,* facing its own problems and its own rivals.

Individuals are also family members and members of certain occupations.

These "placements" are obvious. What is not so obvious is that each can imply learning needs. In addition, each placement may imply different needs over time.

Think about a newly-hired worker. From the supervisor's standpoint, the first order of business is to train the newcomer about job tasks, work procedures, and organizational expectations. This training *must* take place, even if the newcomer has extensive prior education about the work or even experience doing it. Educational preparation in school settings is generalized and is *not* adequate, as HRD activities are, to prepare *one* person to do *one* job in *one* organization. In any case, organizations vary by culture; jobs within and between organizations vary somewhat by duties; and supervisors vary in what work and how much of it they expect. As a result, any newcomer needs training to reach a minimally acceptable level of performance. Training is thus an important part of every supervisor's job. The change effort is short-term, furnishing an individual with skills and knowledge that can be immediately applied.

Training can also serve another, related purpose. From the newcomer's standpoint, the first order of business is often to learn not only about the job but also about other people—supervisors, coworkers, and perhaps even subordinates. Learning how to get along with others is often as important for newcomers as learning job tasks, work procedures, and organizational expectations. In this sense, training facilitates socialization, defined as "activities by which an individual comes to appreciate the values, abilities, expected behaviors, and social knowledge that are essential for assuming an organizational role and for participating as an organizational member" (Gibson, Ivancevich, & Donnelly, 1985, p. G15). It is a gradual process in which newcomers become committed to values and beliefs of organizational members (Wanous, 1978).

As individuals gain experience and reach at least an acceptable level of performance in their jobs, other learning needs emerge. For instance, it may become important to

- Expand the range of skills applied to the individual's present job.
- Keep the individual up-to-date on changes affecting the job.
- Prepare the individual for new job responsibilities.
- Help the individual realize career goals.

HRD practitioners call this *employee education.* As Nadler (1984) points out, it focuses on individuals rather than jobs. It is an intermediate-term change effort extending over several years as an individual is gradually groomed for new job duties, updated on new techniques in an occupational specialty, or furnished with a broader range of skills than is typical for newcomers.

There are other types of HRD activities beyond employee training and education. They are: (1) organization development; (2) nonemployee development; and (3) employee development.

Organization development is a long-term effort designed to change the culture of an organization or group. It emphasizes interpersonal relations (how people interact) and assumptions about appropriate group behavior (what people should do).

Nonemployee development is another long-term change effort. It is focused on planned learning activities geared to groups *outside* the organization. Such groups include members of the general public, citizens of communities in which the firm is based or is doing business, employees of other firms with which the organization does business, and customers who purchase the organization's products or use its services.

Different groups have different learning needs. Members of the general public may well be interested in social issues. For example, they may be concerned about the firm's handling of such matters as Affirmative Action, pollution, and safety. Citizens of communities in which a firm is doing business are interested in economic issues, such as the firm's capability to produce new jobs and maintain or increase the number of people it employs. Employees of other firms may have unique needs: (1) those working for suppliers may require specialized training or information so as to serve their customer's needs better; and (2) those working for organizations which market a firm's products or services may have to know about those products or services to do a credible job in selling them. Customers may need training to use the firm's products properly. The purpose of nonemployee development is to change a firm's external environment by providing the knowledge and skills people need to deal with the firm or its products and/or services.

Employee development focuses on the long-term cultivation of skills necessary to implement organizational plans. It is directed to changing aggregate abilities of a group, not one person. In a sense, then, it aims to change what a work group, department, or organization is able to do by changing the collective skills and knowledge of people staffing those groups.

HRD activities are thus carried out to address the learning needs of individuals inside and outside organizational settings. Training is intended to improve job performance. It is a short-term change effort. Employee education is intended to update individual skills and prepare people for new jobs or duties. It is an intermediate-term change effort. Organization development (OD), long-term in nature, emphasizes interpersonal relations and cultural adaptation to changing conditions. Nonemployee development meets learning needs of people outside the firm. Employee development prepares groups of people so that they collectively possess the knowledge and skills necessary to meet responsibilities of their work units.

These activities should not be carried out separately, each divorced from others. Instead, they should be viewed holistically and planned so that each supports others in an integrated Organizational Strategy for HRD.

ACTIVITY 1-1 A Checklist on Strategic HRD

This checklist is intended to serve two purposes.

First, it introduces the complete model of Strategic HRD described in this text. In this sense, it is an overview of SHRD.

Second, this checklist can aid HRD practitioners and operating managers who are brave enough to fight the tendency toward short-term, crisis-oriented planning for HRD which prevails in many organizations. It is useful as a list of activities—a "to do list"—for creating and implementing an Organizational Strategy for HRD.

For each activity listed in the left column, check (✓) an appropriate response in the middle column. The choice of responses is limited to "yes," "no," and "not applicable." If you wish, write any remarks to yourself in the right column.

Since organizations vary by culture, you may need to add—or subtract—steps and activities in the SHRD process so that the steps apply to your firm.

In formulating and implementing a comprehensive Organizational Strategy for HRD, have HRD practitioners and operating managers worked together to:	YES (✓)	NO (✓)	N/A (✓)	REMARKS
CLARIFYING PURPOSE OF HRD				
1. Clarify the purpose of the HRD Effort in the organization?	( )	( )	( )	
2. Create a purpose statement for the HRD Effort that is a. articulated in writing? b. communicated widely?	 ( ) ( )	 ( ) ( )	 ( ) ( )	
3. Prepare a purpose statement for the HRD Effort that describes a. the role of HRD in the organization? b. the part to be played by HRD in each area of the organization? c. how HRD helps meet needs of people inside and outside the organization? d. how HRD is related to the organization's philosophy of doing business?	 ( ) ( ) ( ) ( )	 ( ) ( ) ( ) ( )	 ( ) ( ) ( ) ( )	

The Traditional Focus of HRD

	YES (✓)	NO (✓)	N/A (✓)	REMARKS
ASSESSING PRESENT NEEDS				
4. Assess present strengths and weaknesses of human resources in the organization?	( )	( )	( )	
5. Identify learners to be served by the HRD Effort over time? More specifically, is it clear a. who are the learners? b. where they are located? c. how many are there? d. how they can be reached for carrying out planned instruction? e. how intense their motivation is to learn? f. when they are most interested in learning?	( ) ( ) ( ) ( ) ( ) ( )	( ) ( ) ( ) ( ) ( ) ( )	( ) ( ) ( ) ( ) ( ) ( )	
6. Classify learners into broad "market segments" to be served by the HRD Effort?	( )	( )	( )	
7. Compare actual to desired knowledge and skills at present in each market segment of learners?	( )	( )	( )	
8. Identify present a. *strengths* (competencies) in each market? b. *weaknesses* (learning needs) in each market segment of learners?	 ( ) ( )	 ( ) ( )	 ( ) ( )	
SCANNING THE ENVIRONMENT				
9. Classify the external environment into discrete sectors or components for analysis?	( )	( )	( )	

	YES (✓)	NO (✓)	N/A (✓)	REMARKS
10. Decide on a time horizon appropriate for scanning for HRD?	( )	( )	( )	
11. Examine environmental sectors for expected changes over the time horizon that has been chosen?	( )	( )	( )	
12. Infer effects of environmental changes on a. the public? b. key external stakeholders? c. departments/work groups inside the organization? d. individuals (and career prospects)? e. job requirements?	( ) ( ) ( ) ( ) ( )	( ) ( ) ( ) ( ) ( )	( ) ( ) ( ) ( ) ( )	
13. Identify future a. *threats* affecting each market segment of learners? b. *opportunities* affecting each market segment of learners?	( ) ( )	( ) ( )	( ) ( )	
COMPARING PRESENT STRENGTHS/WEAKNESSES TO FUTURE THREATS/ OPPORTUNITIES				
14. Compare present strengths/weaknesses to future threats/opportunities relative to a. corporate interactions with external groups? b. interactions between groups in the corporation? c. knowledge and skills needed by departments and work groups in the organization? d. knowledge and skills needed by individuals in order to achieve future career goals?	( ) ( ) ( ) ( )	( ) ( ) ( ) ( )	( ) ( ) ( ) ( )	

	YES (✔)	NO (✔)	N/A (✔)	REMARKS
e. knowledge and skills needed by individuals to improve present performance on the job?	( )	( )	( )	

CHOOSING ORGANIZATIONAL STRATEGY FOR HRD

	YES	NO	N/A	REMARKS
15. Choose an organizational strategy for HRD such as				
a. *growing*—that is, by increasing HRD activities?	( )	( )	( )	
b. *retrenching*—that is, by decreasing HRD activities?	( )	( )	( )	
c. *diversifying*—that is, by changing learners served, needs addressed, emphasis placed on potential markets of learners, etc.?	( )	( )	( )	
d. *integrating*—that is, by establishing closer ties to other functions inside the firm or to groups outside it?	( )	( )	( )	
e. *turning around*—that is, by retrenching and then pursuing another Organizational Strategy for HRD?	( )	( )	( )	
f. *combining*—that is, by pursuing 2 or more strategies at the same time?	( )	( )	( )	

IMPLEMENTING ORGANIZATIONAL STRATEGY FOR HRD

	YES	NO	N/A	REMARKS
16. Implement Organizational Strategy for HRD through coordinating development, education, and training?	( )	( )	( )	
17. Establish operational objectives for the HRD Effort so as to unify development, education, and training?	( )	( )	( )	

	YES (✓)	NO (✓)	N/A (✓)	REMARKS
18. Review and revise HRD policies in light of a new Organizational Strategy for HRD?	( )	( )	( )	
19. Examine leadership in the organization relative to the new Organizational Strategy for HRD?	( )	( )	( )	
20. Review structure relative to Organizational Strategy for HRD in a. the organization? b. the HRD department?	( ) ( )	( ) ( )	( ) ( )	
21. Review reward systems relative to Organizational Strategy for HRD?	( )	( )	( )	
22. Budget for resources necessary to implement Organizational Strategy for HRD?	( )	( )	( )	
23. Establish means to communicate about Organizational Strategy for HRD?	( )	( )	( )	
24. Develop functional strategies for HRD in line with Organizational Strategy for HRD? (These functional strategies direct Organization Development, Nonemployee Development, Employee Development, Employee Education, and Employee Training.)	( )	( )	( )	

	YES (✔)	NO (✔)	N/A (✔)	REMARKS
EVALUATING HRD				

25. Clarify
    a. who wants information from evaluation of HRD?
    b. who will do the evaluating?
    c. what is the primary focus of interest?
    d. when should evaluation be carried out?
    e. why is evaluation necessary?
    f. how will evaluation be conducted?
    g. how will each of the following be evaluated:
      • Organization Development?
      • Nonemployee Development?
      • Employee Development?
      • Employee Education?
      • Employee Training?
      • The HRD Effort as a whole?
	( )
	( )
	( )
	( )
	( )
	( )
	
	( )
	( )
	( )
	( )
	( )
	( )
		( )
		( )
		( )
		( )
		( )
		( )
		
		( )
		( )
		( )
		( )
		( )
		( )
			( )
			( )
			( )
			( )
			( )
			( )
			
			( )
			( )
			( )
			( )
			( )
			( )	

26. Clarify when there is a need to *change* Organizational Strategy for HRD?	( )	( )	( )	

REMARKS

2

THE PURPOSE OF THE HRD EFFORT

An organization's purpose statement is a starting point for Strategic Business Planning. Policymakers should first identify what business they are operating in before they formulate a strategy to succeed in that business. A statement of purpose is equally important for an HRD Effort. It is a starting point for SHRD.

WHAT IS PURPOSE?

Purpose—sometimes called *mission*—is the fundamental reason for an organization's existence. It "defines activities the organization performs or intends to perform and the kind of organization it is or intends to be" (Byars, 1984, p. 20). In HRD, purpose is sometimes synonymous with "intention." While the value of specifying instructional intentions has sparked substantial debate, it is advantageous because it (1) helps guide design and development efforts, (2) helps learners understand what they are supposed to learn, (3) provides means to evaluate the relative success of subsequent instructional efforts, and (4) provides information worth communicating to employees and operating managers about what instruction is intended to do. A sense of purpose, whether for an organization or instruction, instills confidence. It gives people the feeling that they know "where they are going" and helps them understand "why they are doing what they are doing."

Perhaps the best description of a formal purpose statement is Morrisey's (1976):

> For the total organization, the statement [of purpose] should include the broad identification of the type of operation for which it is responsible, its major areas of service, clientele or user groups, organizational approach, plus the philosophical basis for its operation (p. 25).

A purpose statement thus answers such questions as : (1) What is our business? What should it be? (2) What are the major parts of the business? What should they be? (3) Who are the customers? Who should the organization be serving? (4) How is the business presently meeting needs of each customer group? How should it be meeting those needs? and (5) What do managers believe about the business, customers, and methods of operation? What should they believe?

Strategic Business Planning theorists prefer to direct their primary attention to "customers" during the process of formulating purpose. Rothschild (1976), for instance, suggests pondering these questions:

Who?
>Who are your customers?
>How can they be classified?
>Which classification is most important to you and your competitors?
>Will this classification still be most important in the future?

Why?
>Why do customers buy when and as much as they do?
>What are their objectives?
>Which objectives are most important?
>Are the reasons for purchasing and their ranking in importance likely to change?

What if . . . ?
>What could cause a change in customers' objectives?
>What information will help anticipate these changes?

So what?
>What are the implications of change in customer behavior and objectives?
>Will the impact be positive or negative on you, relative to the impact on your competition?

What then?
>How will this customer classification add to your understanding of the total market, size, mix, growth rate, and time? (pp. 29–30; reprinted with permission)

Customer analysis of this kind provides valuable clues about the purpose of the business—and profitable strategies for the future.

It does not require much imagination to see that these questions are applicable to HRD. Indeed, a good starting point for long-term planning of an HRD Effort is to pose the same kind of questions that Rothschild suggests. Consider:

- What purposes does the HRD Effort seek to attain inside the organization? Outside it?
- What part of this purpose is the responsibility of the HRD department? Operating managers? Learners?
- What is known about the learners? How can they be classified? How can this classification scheme be used in planning instruction?
- How are HRD activities presently benefiting the organization? How should they benefit the organization?
- How are HRD activities presently meeting learner needs? How should they meet learner needs in the future?
- What is the organization's present philosophy about HRD? What should that philosophy be in the future?

By posing these questions, HRD practitioners stimulate a meaningful dialogue about the HRD Effort in their organization. This information, in turn, helps set priorities. Use Activity 2-1 (at the end of this chapter) to consider the purpose of the HRD Effort in an organization.

HOW IMPORTANT IS PURPOSE?

Without a sense of purpose, HRD practitioners may successfully complete many projects or activities but may never know how they are contributing to the organization or to improvements in job performance. Nor will they be able to demonstrate their value in a convincing way if asked to do so. As Robert Mager (1975) notes, "if you don't know where you're going, it is difficult to select a suitable means for getting there" (p. 5). Similarly, if HRD practitioners or line managers lack purpose for the HRD Effort, they will scarcely be able to establish a strategy for realizing that purpose.

If common sense is not a compelling reason for clarifying purpose, consider the results of a survey study conducted by Rothwell and Kazanas (1986–1988), who mailed questionnaires to 250 corporate planners and 250 HRD practitioners to investigate relationships between Strategic Business Planning and HRD. One-hundred forty-two completed surveys were returned (a 28.4 percent response rate). Both corporate planners and HRD practitioners agreed that three conditions are essential if HRD is to support Strategic Business Plans: (1) a written statement of the organization's purpose must exist; (2) a formal Strategic Business Planning process must exist in the organization; and (3) top management support for HRD must be demonstrated by ample resources devoted to such activities. To these, HRD practitioners added a fourth: (4) a written statement must clarify HRD's purpose in the organization.

These findings reinforce results of another study. Beginning in 1979, thirteen senior human resource executives in ten large Canadian corporations met to share insights about desirable linkages between Strategic Business Plans and human resources management activities. Carried out under the sponsorship of the Canadian Conference Board, the study produced seven principles characteristic of effective relationships between Strategic Business Plans and personnel management. Three conditions are similar to those identified by Rothwell and Kazanas. The Canadian executives agreed that, "in the context of overall business planning, effective HR management is facilitated to the extent that (1) there is an overall corporate purpose and the human resource dimensions of that purpose are evident; (2) a process of developing strategy within the organization exists, and there is explicit consideration of human resource dimensions; and (3) the office of chief executive provides the climate for integrating human resource considerations to needs of the business" (Nininger, 1982, p. x).

In both studies, a clearly-defined organizational purpose is thus an important precondition for linking Strategic Business Plans and HR activities. Rothwell and Kazanas (1986-1988) also found that corporate HRD practitioners believe clarifying the purpose of HRD is an important activity in its own right.

WHAT ARE POSSIBLE RELATIONSHIPS BETWEEN STRATEGIC BUSINESS PLANS, HR PLANS, AND HRD?

There are many possible relationships between HRD, Strategic Business Plans, and HR plans. These can be summarized a follows:

1. HRD can be driven by organizational and HR plans. This is the *top-down approach*.
2. HRD can be driven by perceived future learning needs of managers and employees. This is the *market-driven approach*.
3. HRD can be driven by comparisons between individual career plans/objectives and organizational plans/objectives. This is the *career planning approach*.
4. HRD serves as a tool for helping top management strategists formulate business and HR plans. This is the *futuring approach*.
5. HRD furnishes learners with artificial experience tied to organizational and HR plans. This is the *artificial experience approach*.
6. HRD provides feedback about implementation of plans for use by top managers in subsequent planning. This is the *pulse-taking approach*.
7. HRD provides information to strategists about organizational strengths and weaknesses. This is the *performance diagnosis approach*.
8. HRD teaches people how to think strategically. This is the *educational approach*.
9. HRD serves the inarticulated needs and interests of strategists. This is the *interpersonal approach*.
10. HRD focuses on specific issues, problems, or projects of major strategic significance to the organization. This is the *"rifle" approach*.

Table 2-1 summarizes all ten approaches. Note that they are not mutually exclusive. In fact, they may overlap conceptually. Each approach is worth describing in more detail. Remember: each approach implies a purpose for an HRD Effort.

TABLE 2-1 A SUMMARY OF RELATIONSHIPS BETWEEN STRATEGIC BUSINESS PLANS, HR PLANS, AND HRD

Approach	Brief description
Top-Down	The HRD Effort is used to support implementation of organizational and HR plans and is driven by those plans.
Market-driven	The HRD Effort is used to identify future learning needs and to convince people to meet those needs.
Career Planning	The HRD Effort is a tool for helping individuals realize their own career plans.
Futuring	HRD is used to provide assistance to top management strategists in formulating strategic plans.
Artificial Experience	HRD is used to simulate future conditions, helping individuals identify their own learning needs.
Pulse-Taking	In the course of offering instruction, HRD practitioners collect information about how well strategic plans are being implemented and later feed it back to strategists.
Performance Diagnosis	In the course of assessing needs, HRD practitioners identify problems of larger scope and provide that information to strategists for their use in strategic business planning.
Educational	HRD practitioners teach people how to think strategically.
Interpersonal	HRD practitioners interact with strategists, identifying their beliefs and communicating them to others.
Rifle	HRD practitioners concentrate their attention on issues, problems, or projects of strategic importance.

The top-down approach. Perhaps the most common way to think of the relationship between Strategic Business Plans, HR plans, and HRD is from this perspective. As Roberts and Wolf (1983) explain:

> Human resources . . . must be approached within the context of what needs to occur in order to facilitate achievement of the enterprise's strategy. Thus, human resources strategy takes its cue from the key plans, performance measures, and climate requirements of the enterprise. . . . Human resources strategy is driven by a top-down awareness of what does and does not constitute support for the achievement of the enterprise's strategic vision and plan (p. 15-3).

To express this idea another way, top managers envision the organization as it exists in the future and as it is positioned relative to the external environment. This vision is embodied in a formal strategic plan (a product); however, planning is synonymous with visioning (a process).

To make this vision a reality, human knowledge and skills are necessary. Indeed, any plan implies that knowledge and skills will be needed for proper implementation. Of course, plans also require adequate resources—money and time. But without human qualities to mobilize and apply resources, no plan can ever be implemented.

Theorists have long argued that, to implement a Strategic Plan successfully, top managers should devote attention to matching appropriate leaders to the strategy. Each part of the organization should be led by someone who wants the strategy to succeed and possesses the skills necessary for success. Unfortunately, it is difficult to find the right person for the right leadership job at the right time if nobody worries about the issue until the need arises. This problem is a major one confronting all U.S. corporations (Gerstein & Reisman, 1983; *Wanted: A Manager*, 1980; *What's Wrong with Management?*, 1982).

Despite evidence that HR practitioners are aware of this problem (Rowland & Summers, 1981; Walker, 1980), top managers consistently cite a need for better long-term planning for management talent (*Basic HRD*, 1981; Foltz, Rosenberg, & Foehrenbach, 1982). By virtue of position, top managers are acutely aware of how important leadership can be in implementing a business plan. Generally, top managers direct less attention to comprehensive HR planning than to leadership planning. The aim of comprehensive HRP is to match available numbers and skills of employees in different job categories to requirements implicit in Strategic Business Plans. Unfortunately, forecasting future *skill* requirements has been a traditional weakness of HR planning. The reason is that the common practice is to compare *numbers* of people needed to fill job categories to *numbers* of people available (Director, 1985). Nor do top managers establish overall direction for all personnel programs to match them to corporate strategy (for more on this subject, see Craft, 1980; Roberts & Wolf, 1983; Rothwell & Kazanas, 1988; Walker, 1980).

In the top-down approach, a comprehensive HR plan is necessary before strategy can be formulated to guide the HRD Effort, because knowledge and skills to implement Strategic Business Plans are available from more than one source. It is thus necessary to consider alternative ways of obtaining them. Suppose managers need an individual who possesses unique skills. They can: (1) recruit from outside the organization; (2) transfer somebody possessing the skills from a different part of the firm on a temporary or permanent basis; (3) contract for talent externally on a short-term or long-term basis; (4) use innovative techniques like worksharing to get more than one person's talents mobilized to deal with the job's tasks; (5) simplify or change job duties; or (6) train, educate, or develop individuals within the firm. HRD activities are appropriate only for the last of these choices. For this reason, other methods of obtaining necessary skills have to be considered before HRD plans are formulated. A comprehensive HR planning process affords the means to make these choices.

To use a top-down approach, HRD practitioners have to link up HRD plans to plans of the personnel department and the organization. Figure 2-1 illustrates the process. As the figure shows, organizational and HR plans must be decided on *first* before HRD plans are formulated. The HRD Effort is forced into a role in which it can only support these plans (see Figure 2-2). It is driven by them and has little or no effect on how they are formulated.

The market-driven approach. A second way to think of the relationship between Strategic Business Plans, HR plans, and HRD is from a market-oriented per-

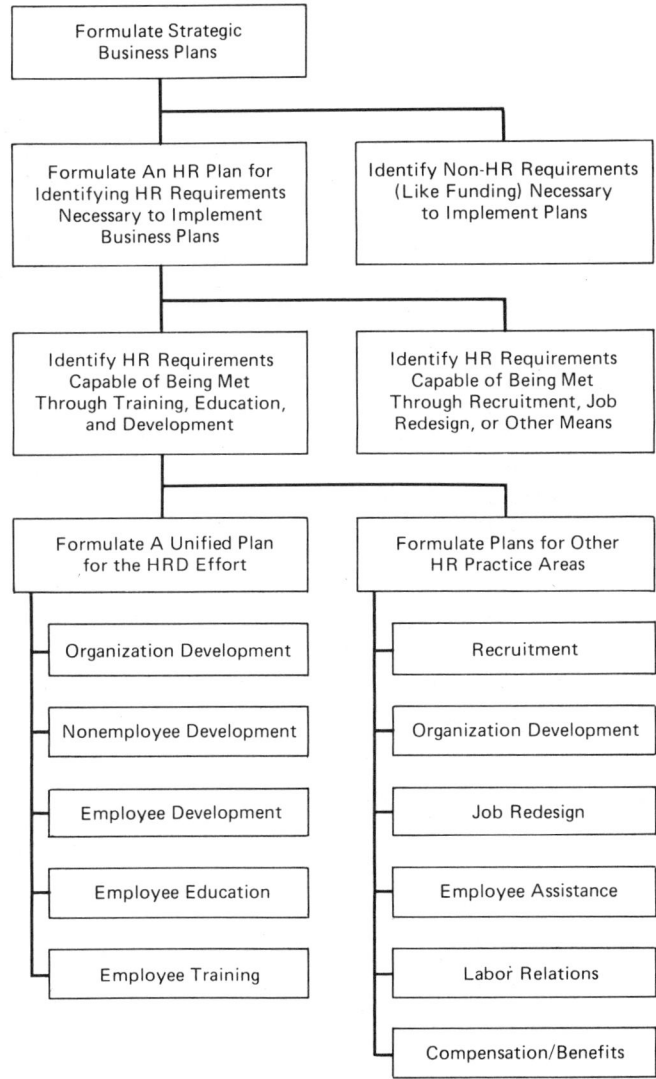

Figure 2-1: A Simplified Model of Steps in the Top-Down Approach

spective. HRD practitioners must "convince the organization that their products and services should be utilized; they [HRD practitioners] must see themselves as selling a specific set of products and services to the organization" (Zemke, 1981, p. 26).

A major problem with the market-driven approach results from the tendency of managers and employees alike to identify learning needs on the basis of past problems.

Much effort must be exerted to get people to think about long-term needs that anticipate future requirements. HRD practitioners contribute to a past-oriented bias by using learning needs assessment techniques that "too often rely heavily on the examination of past deficiencies or past behaviors as a basis for planning instruction intended to equip learners for meeting future conditions" (Rothwell, 1984d, p. 19).

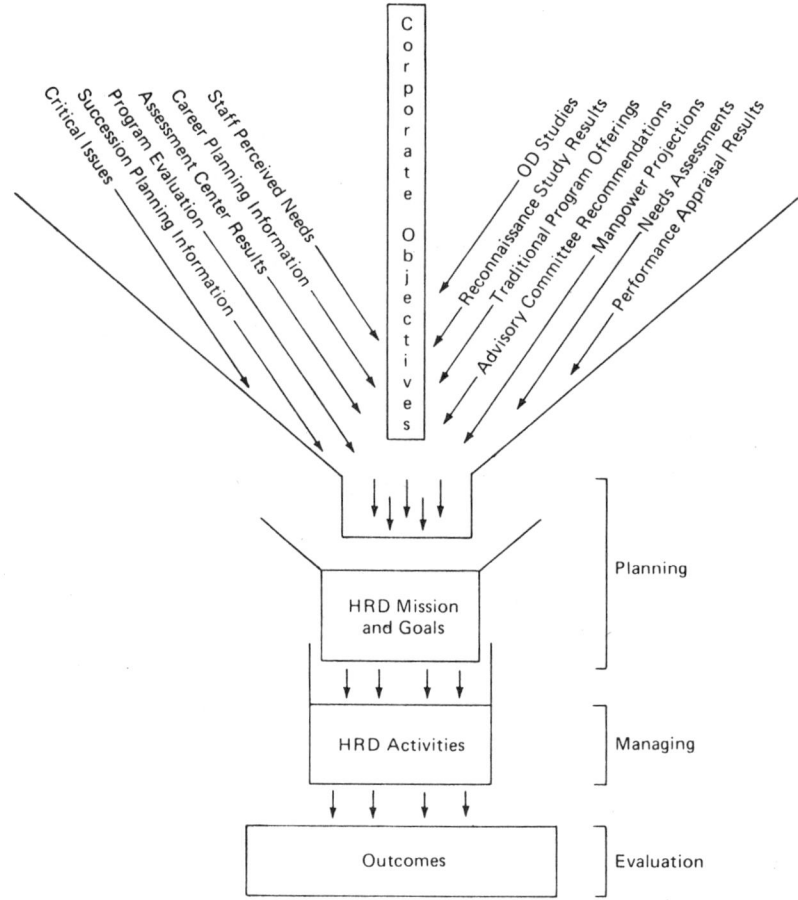

Figure 2-2: The Top-Down Approach: Inputs to the HRD Planning Process. *Source:* Harvey, 1983, p. 52. Reprinted with permission from *Personnel Administrator.*

Think of this problem from another perspective. Suppose Company X creates a new product with which consumers are not familiar. At one time, most products were in this category. Consumers experience a need which the new product can satisfy but are unaware of the need, the product, or both. Products of this kind are called *unsought goods.*

To promote these goods, marketing specialists suggest starting with informational advertising. Consumers have to be informed about the product *and* convinced of their need for it before they will buy. This step is the beginning of a *product development life cycle.* The introduction of a new product begins the cycle. As consumers learn about the product and the needs it satisfies, they purchase it. The product thus gains popularity. More firms begin manufacturing the same, or a substitute, product. As competition grows stiffer, firms enjoying marketplace advantage due to size, name recognition, or other strengths drive out firms not enjoying such advantages. Eventually, the number of competing firms stabilizes. The product development life cycle is essentially a *learning curve.* A visionary entrepreneur begins the cycle by introducing a new product or service. Consumers and competitors learn about the product. Eventually, market factors reduce the number of firms making the product.

Consider HRD from this perspective. Acting like entrepreneurs, HRD practitioners can take the lead to identify learning needs *before* others are aware they exist. The Strategic Business Plan is a good source for identifying these needs, because it clarifies the firm's direction. HRD practitioners promote instruction designed to meet these unsought needs, showing learners and their superiors what the instruction is and why it will be useful to them in the future.

To use the market-oriented approach, HRD practitioners: (1) classify employees into distinct groups, perhaps by job category, (2) predict what knowledge or skills employees will probably need in the future to perform in ways consistent with business strategy; (3) assess knowledge/skills that are available in each employee group at present; (4) decide how to close gaps between present and future knowledge and skill requirements; (5) plan training, education, and development to close gaps over time in each group of employees; and, (6) mount a promotional campaign to inform managers and employees about Strategic Business Plans and HR plans, implications of those plans for them, and the value of HRD programs in preparing for the future.

The career planning approach. A third way to think of relationships between Strategic Business Plans, HR plans, and the HRD Effort is from the individual's perspective. As Schein (1978) explains:

> The dialogue between manager and career occupant is, in a sense, the critical juncture in the total HRPD [Human Resource Planning and Development] system. Here individual and organizational needs meet, and some kind of ultimate matching must take place. If the organization has done its homework in the form of adequate planning and inventorying and if the individual has done his or her homework in the sense of getting some self-insight into needs, goals, and aspirations, a real dialogue can occur (pp. 196-97).

Individual career plans must be taken into account if employees are to be committed to Strategic Business Plans. The organization's plans must be translated into terms that are directly applicable to present and possible future jobs. Individuals, to be motivated, must see "what's in it for them." They must see how they fit in at a future time and be convinced that they benefit if Strategic Business Plans are realized.

To use this approach, HRD practitioners: (1) establish individual development programs to provide structure for negotiations between individuals and their superiors; (2) identify learning experiences that will help individuals achieve their career objectives and will, at the same time, help the organization implement its business and HR plans; and (3) deliver these learning experiences. Schein (1978) and Lee (1981) propose alternative models of the same kind.

An individual development program (IDP) must be organized if this approach is to work. An IDP is designed to produce an individualized development plan or contract which "deals with mutually agreed on steps to be taken by an individual and/or company to prepare an individual for higher level responsibilities and a method of monitoring such progress to a point of mutual satisfaction" (Deegan, 1986, p. 41). It is similar to employee performance appraisal—except that the resulting plan is geared to achieving the individual's future career objectives in line with company staffing needs.

The futuring approach. A fourth way to tie together Strategic Business Plans, HR plans, and the HRD Effort is through the strategy formulation process itself. Formulation can occur formally or informally. If it is *formal,* then top executives come up with a written business plan. If it is *informal,* then executives make daily decisions consistent with a formal plan. As Dyer (1984) notes, between 75 and 80 percent of strategy-making is informal. The essence of strategy formulation is *futuring,* defined as the ability to "project future trends and visualize possible and probable futures and their implications" (Gentilman & Nelson, 1983, p. 32; *Models for Excellence,* 1983, p. 49).

HRD practitioners contribute to the strategy formulation process by facilitating effective interaction of strategists, whether in meetings common to formal planning or in daily relations between top managers. In either case, *group process*—how strategists get along with each other—is important in obtaining results. Skilled in group facilitation skills, HRD practitioners are well-suited to leading creative small-group experiences—precisely what strategic planning meetings should be. In addition, HRD practitioners are also well-suited to help strategists cooperate to implement plans through daily decisions.

HRD practitioners may also contribute to strategy formulation by designing structured exercises which aid decision-making. Examples of such exercises include brainstorming, the delphi procedure, nominal group technique, and scenario generation. Each elicits new ideas which can be important in strategy formulation (Paine & Naumes, 1974).

To use this approach, HRD practitioners: (1) describe elements of a creative group to strategists prior to formal planning meetings (see Table 2-2); (2) stimulate strategists to identify ways in which formal meetings could be improved so that group members work together more effectively; (3) encourage strategists to surface and deal with problems of group interaction; (4) use group facilitation skills during formal meetings to help participants interact; and (5) design experimental exercises to help group members structure their thinking on strategic issues.

The artificial experience approach. A fifth way to tie together Strategic Business Plans, HR plans, and HRD is through simulations of future conditions.

As noted earlier, one major problem confronts those who try to integrate planning and HRD activities: managers and learners alike tend to associate learning needs with historical problems they have experienced. The trouble is that, to bring a plan into reality, responding to past needs may not work. After all, future conditions may be quite different from the past.

The same problem confronts planners. Plans should not be based on the assumption that the future will be like the past. Nor should planning be a one-shot, one-time-a-year affair. It should instead be approached as a continuous learning process. Strategy formulation produces long-term objectives, but they should be considered tentative. Objectives should be revised as managers acquire experience or confront new environmental conditions. In fact, "organizations adjust their activities based on

TABLE 2-2 CHARACTERISTICS OF A CREATIVE GROUP

GROUP PROCESSES: The problem-solving process is characterized by:
a. spontaneous communication between members (not focused on the leader)
b. full participation from each member
c. separation of idea generation from idea evaluation
d. separation of problem definition from generation of solution strategies
e. shifting of roles, so that interaction which mediates problem solving (particularly search activities and clarification by means of constant questioning directed both to individual members and the whole group) is not the sole responsibility of the leader
f. suspension of judgment and avoidance of early concern with solutions, so that emphasis is on analysis and exploration, rather than on early solution commitment.

GROUP STYLE: The social-emotional tone of the group is characterized by:
a. a relaxed, nonstressful environment
b. ego-supportive interaction, where open give-and-take between members is at the same time courteous
c. behavior which is motivated by interest in the problem, rather than concern with short-run payoff
d. absence of penalties attached to any espoused idea or position.

GROUP NORMS:
a. are supportive of originality, and unusual ideas, and allow for eccentricity
b. seek behavior which separates source from content in evaluating information and ideas
c. stress a nonauthoritarian view, with a relativistic view of life and independence of judgment
d. support humor and undisciplined exploration of viewpoints
e. seek openness in communication, where mature, self-confident individuals offer "crude" ideas to the group for mutual exploration without threat to the individual for "exposing" himself
f. deliberately avoid credence to short-run results, or short-run decisiveness
g. seek consensus, but accept majority rule when consensus is unobtainable.

Source: Delbecq, 1967, pp. 334–35. Reprinted with permission from *Academy of Management Journal.*

past experiences. . . . " (Bedeian, 1984, p. 261). Unfortunately, mistakes have already been made by the time objectives are revised. The point is that problems have to be *experienced* before people feel the need to learn or before managers feel the need to change.

Is an organization's HRD Effort thus doomed to be reactive, geared to meeting needs only after learners recognize them? Not necessarily. One way to get around the problem is to *simulate* future conditions. This has been done before in planning by using scenarios, defined as brief narrative descriptions of a possible future. Decision-makers use scenarios to plan what to do and how to do it under future conditions (Zentner, 1985).

HRD practitioners can design learning to produce artificial experience. Such learning does not produce improved skills or more knowledge; rather, it results in the discovery of possible future learning needs. Trainees—and their supervisors—are jolted into firsthand awareness of skills and the knowledge that will be necessary to grapple with future problems confronting them. It is the reverse of the traditional training process: learners end up with, rather than begin with, heightened awareness of learning needs. They *create* rather than *receive* information. They are then motivated to seek people, resources, and activities that help them anticipate future problems they may encounter. Many so-called "experiential methods"—case studies, critical incidents, role plays, simulations, and games—can be directed to anticipating future learning needs in this way. They thrust learners into a simulated future world so they experience it firsthand.

To use this approach, HRD practitioners should (1) apply special approaches to job analysis in order to identify what the future may hold in store for job incumbents (see Rothwell & Kazanas, 1988); (2) prepare descriptions of future conditions; (3) design exercises set in the future to give learners vicarious, artificial experience; (4) lead learners through discoveries during the exercises; (5) discuss results of exercises with learners, prompting new insights; (6) guide learners to discover their future learning needs; and (7) help learners prepare action plans so they can anticipate and meet future learning needs.

There is one major drawback to this approach: the future is not as certain or well-defined as the past or present. Learners may thus have to assess relative probabilities of *several* alternative futures as they assess their needs. Their learning plans may have to include contingency plans in the event of unexpected changes.

The pulse-taking approach. There is a sixth way to tie together a Strategic Business Plan, an HR plan, and an HRD Effort. Training, education, and developmental activities can be used to collect information about how well Strategic Business Plans are being implemented. Small groups become vehicles for surfacing problems posed by implementation of plans and for brainstorming solutions to those problems. Group instructional efforts "take the pulse" of the organization.

To use this approach, HRD practitioners focus classroom-based instructional offerings on a few key issues pertinent to organizational plans and objectives. Practitioners concentrate on helping participants (Mason & Mitroff, 1981): (1) surface problems which impede progress on business plans; (2) define or clarify the problem(s); (3) consider solutions; (4) examine the value of solutions by using the classroom setting for "reality testing," and (5) devise action steps to implement solution(s).

The performance diagnosis approach. A seventh way to tie together a Strategic Business Plan, an HR plan, and an HRD Effort is to use instructional needs assessment for examining the organization's internal strengths and weaknesses. This information is valuable to managers contemplating changes to Strategic Business Plans.

Traditionally, strategists think of strengths and weaknesses from a marketplace perspective. As Sharplin (1985) explains, "strengths are special attributes or distinctive competencies an organization possesses in comparison with other organizations, especially competitors, which give it an advantage over them" (p. 191). A weakness is the reverse; it is anything giving an organization a competitive disadvantage. In this sense, strengths and weaknesses exist only in comparison to competitors.

There are, however, other ways to think of organizational strengths and weaknesses. They may have to do with differences between:

1. *the ideal and the actual:* How well does the organization measure up to what strategists would like it to be? Where it does measure up, it possesses strengths; where it does not measure up, it possesses weaknesses.

2. *the possible and the actual:* Are some divisions, work groups, or individuals performing better than others? What accounts for these differences? When differences do not exist, the organization possesses strength; where variations exist, there is weakness.

3. *desirable state-of-the-art methods and those that are less effective, efficient, or progressive:* How well is the organization taking advantage of new ideas and technology? When the organization is not taking advantage of new ideas or technology, weakness exists; where it is taking advantage of new ideas, strength exists.

Assessments of strengths and weaknesses provide clues about possible strategy. There are two basic approaches to strategy formulation. The first, called the *inside-outside approach* (Huse, 1982), examines strengths and weaknesses to determine what an organization is doing better than its competitors. Strategy is based on identifying organizational strengths and building on them. The second, called the *outside-inside approach* (Huse, 1982), examines the world outside the organization to identify trends that may pose future threats and/or opportunities to the firm. The key to strategy selection is averting threats or taking advantage of opportunities.

In analyzing performance problems, HRD practitioners frequently encounter information of value in strategy-making. Instructional efforts only solve performance problems caused by lack of knowledge or skill. Yet poor performance quite often stems from more than one cause. Examples of other causes include: inappropriate reward systems; poor feedback on performance; mismatches between duties and people doing them; and conflicts between individuals or work groups stemming from poor organization or job design.

Information about performance problems, collected during needs assessment or during instructional delivery, can be fed back to strategists for use in subsequent planning so that corrective action can be taken. This approach provides a descriptive element lacking in the stark figures of financial reporting. This information is needed because "decision-makers at all levels of organizations are hard-pressed to provide logical and supportable explanations for the effectiveness of their organization" (Van de Ven & Morgan, 1980, p. 217)—or, by the same token, for the ineffectiveness.

The educational approach. An eighth way to tie together a Strategic Business Plan, an HR plan, and an HRD Effort is to offer instruction on strategic thinking skills. Much has been written on this subject (for example, Ajimal, 1985; Easterly-Smith & Davies, 1983; Mason, 1986; Stone & Heany, 1984; Weber, 1984). Many problems are attributable to short-term thinking (Diebold, 1982). Instruction in strategic thinking may help correct these problems.

Rothwell (1985b) hypothesized that HRD departments which offer training on strategic planning are more likely to become involved in strategy formulation than those which do not. While this hypothesis is difficult to prove—HRD departments may, in fact, offer training on strategic thinking *after* involvement in formulating organizational plans—there is evidence that many firms do offer training on planning (see Table 2-3).

There are at least three forms of instruction on strategic thinking. The first is

TABLE 2-3 ORGANIZATIONS OFFERING TRAINING ON PLANNING

Question: Does your organization presently offer training on strategic planning?

Answer	Planners		HRD Practitioners	
	Frequency	Percent	Frequency	Percent
No	50	73.5%	51	75.0%
Yes	18	26.5%	17	25.0%

Source: Rothwell & Kazanas, 1986–1988.

education. Participants learn generally about the theory of strategic thinking. Applying on the job what they learn in training is left up to them. The second is *education tied to training*. Participants learn generally about the theory of strategic thinking; then about the strategic plan of *their* organization; and finally, they develop action plans to relate what they do in their jobs to what must happen if Strategic Business Plans are to be successfully implemented. The third is *training*. Participants are taught specific skills they need to achieve strategic objectives.

Off-the-shelf instructional programs can be purchased from commercial publishers for pure education. Education tied to training requires HRD practitioners to do much instructional design work themselves, so that training content is carefully tailored to the unique requirements of their employer. Pure training may also require much tailor-made instruction. Stonich (1982), however, describes one training intervention that is more general:

> Business school faculty are called in to give lectures and discuss business cases that relate directly to the issues that managers face. . . . Managers then break into teams for intensive workshop sessions, where they work on a "live issue". . . . External facilitators, or "coaches," with expertise in attacking such issues, guide each team toward the best practical approaches to dealing effectively with these issues (p. 81–82).

As a consequence, managers learn what they need to do to implement Strategic Business Plans. They can then return to their respective work groups and develop joint action plans with subordinates along similar lines.

To use the educational approach, HRD practitioners should first clarify their primary purpose. Is it to help individuals become better strategic thinkers? If so, pure education is appropriate. Is it to help individuals learn generally about strategic thinking *and* about the applications of it in their jobs? If so, education tied to training is appropriate. Is the purpose to help those at every level of the organization learn how to translate broad, general Strategic Business Plans into specific action plans to guide their work groups or jobs? If so, pure training is appropriate.

Once purpose has been clarified, it is then possible to select or design instructional materials consistent with it, deliver instruction, and follow up after instruction to see how well it is applied.

The interpersonal approach. There is a ninth way to link a Strategic Business Plan, an HR plan, and an HRD Effort: HRD practitioners can improve their access to top managers. A substantial percentage of corporate strategy is informal, existing only in the minds of top managers. As Linkow (1985) explains:

> Managed by top corporate and divisional general managers, the informal [planning] process often produces the essential corporate strategy. This process recognizes that people, not organizations, have values, so it focuses on the political and behavioral concerns that mediate economic results (p. 85).

For HRD practitioners to be aware of informal plans, they must increase interaction with—and serve the interests of—top managers. Both corporate planners and corporate HRD practitioners agree that greater access to top managers is desirable (see Table 2-4).

Increasing interaction with top managers is, of course, easier said than done. Too often, HRD managers are accorded junior rather than senior executive status. They are denied direct access to the Chief Executive and perhaps to other top officers as well. Perhaps the Vice President for Human Resources is the only top officer to whom they have access. As a consequence, information they receive is filtered through a third party—the Personnel Chief—as are messages they try to communicate (Rothwell, 1985b; Sredl & Rothwell, 1987).

What can be done about this problem? The answer depends on the situation. Recently hired or promoted HRD managers may be able to take advantage of the license accorded newcomers to "get a foot in the door," so to speak, with top managers (Sredl & Rothwell, 1987). They can request appointments with higher-ups and, in so doing, establish a foothold denied to their predecessors. Once the foothold is established, they can take full advantage of it.

For those who do not enjoy the license accorded newcomers but who wish to gain access to strategists, several approaches are possible:

1. Identify a problem which troubles people at the top. Take action on it in a highly visible way.

TABLE 2-4 WHAT HRD PRACTITIONERS SHOULD STRIVE FOR

Question: To improve the extent that HRD supports implementation of organizational plans, do you feel HRD practitioners should strive *the* most for...

	Planners		HRD Practitioners	
	Frequency	Percent	Frequency	Percent
...Greater Access to Organizational Plans	9	20.5	7	14.9
...Greater Access to Top Managers	16	36.4	11	23.4
...Greater Participation in the Planning Process	18	40.9	29	61.7
...Other	1	2.3	0	0.0

Source: Rothwell & Kazanas, 1986–1988.

2. Schedule a meeting and discuss the importance of access to top managers. Ask to form a management or training advisory committee consisting of Senior Executives. (The worst that can happen is that the request will be denied.) Ask the Chief Executive to help organize such a committee—and ask him or her to be a member.
3. Lobby for support from people who already have access to top managers. Use "grassroots pressure" in hopes that it may lead to success.

Do some brainstorming if none of these alternatives seems to fit the situation. What can *you* do to get a foot in the door with Senior Executives?

Those who succeed can ask strategists this question: What HRD activities can help solve their problems? If that question does not produce useful answers, ask them to describe the organization as they would like to see it at some point in the future—and what barriers seem to make that vision difficult to realize. Instruction can then be planned to remove the barriers.

The rifle approach. A tenth way to tie together a Strategic Business Plan, an HR plan, and an HRD Effort is to restrict the scope of training, education, and development so they focus on just a few strategic objectives of the organization. The term "rifle" is apt to describe this approach because it connotes a highly directed, concentrated effort. It differs from a "scattergun" approach that attempts to link HRD activities to all strategic objectives.

Some HRD practitioners think *all* their activities should be linked directly to corporate plans. That need not be the case. Instead, they can single out a few major problems impeding strategy implementation. One way is to start small and score a highly visible success. Early success is very important in any change effort (Beer & Driscoll, 1977; Greiner, 1967). One small success often leads to future encouragement and greater opportunities (Beer, 1980).

To use the rifle approach, HRD practitioners should identify one or two problems lending themselves to solutions through training, education, or development. These problems should also be related to the organization's strategic business objectives. Practitioners should then analyze the problems, consider and implement solutions, communicate results so that others will be interested in similar efforts in the future, and repeat this process. These steps may lead to incremental change in the organization through HRD initiatives.

Choosing an approach. Each approach described in the preceding sections is a way to link a Strategic Business Plan, an HR plan, and an HRD Effort. But when is one more appropriate to use than another?

Generally speaking, practitioners should strive for as many linkages between HRD activities and business plans as possible—provided that top managers devote more than mere lip service to formal planning (the process) and are committed to implementing plans (products of the planning process). But even when top managers are not committed to formal planning processes and products, HRD practitioners still bear responsibility to act in ways that help strategists realize their vision of the future, no matter how poorly that vision is conceptualized or communicated.

In each organizational setting, HRD practitioners and operating managers should decide for themselves what relationships should exist between Strategic Business Plans, HR plans, and planned learning activities. They will then need to establish—or strengthen—these relationships. Finally, they have to come up with their own vision of the HRD effort and the role of the HRD department in helping make the vision a reality. Armed with this information, HRD practitioners will find it easy to clarify the purpose of the HRD Effort and the HRD department.

Use Activity 2-2 (at the end of this chapter) to consider how to use each approach described in this part of the chapter in order to tie together a Strategic Business Plan, an HR Plan, and an HRD Effort in an organization.

HOW IS THE PURPOSE OF AN HRD EFFORT CLARIFIED?

The HRD Effort is only a tool for identifying and meeting the learning needs of an organization and the individuals employed in it. But how is the purpose of the HRD Effort clarified? Previous sections of this chapter have provided clues. At this point, it is appropriate to describe concrete ways to clarify the formal purpose of an HRD Effort.

Formulating the purpose of the HRD Effort. There are at least two ways to formulate a purpose statement for an HRD Effort.

The first is perhaps easiest. Beginning with the formal purpose statement of the organization, assuming that such a statement exists, the highest-level HRD executive should break down that statement into components pertaining to the organization's business, major areas of service, customers served, methods of competition, and philosophy (Morrisey, 1976). Working with top managers of the organization, the HRD executive should then construct a rough draft purpose statement for the HRD Effort based on that of the organization. This purpose statement specifies *how* the organization's planned learning activities will contribute to the organization's purpose. It should also answer the following questions:

1. What should be the role of the HRD Effort in the organization?
2. What should be the role played by the HRD Effort in each part of the organization?
3. How should the HRD Effort meet learning needs of each stakeholder group?
4. How should the HRD Effort help the organization compete against other firms?
5. How should the HRD Effort reflect what strategists believe about the way the business should be conducted?

This draft purpose statement should then be circulated for comment to key stakeholders of HRD activities. Using these comments, the HRD Executive can revise the purpose statement. Finally, he or she should communicate this statement to others through new employee orientation, budget documents, course descriptions, and training brochures.

A purpose statement of this kind clarifies what the HRD Effort is supposed to do, and why. In addition, it makes explicit how the HRD Effort contributes to the organization's purpose. It also helps guide operations, keeping HRD practitioners and operating managers on track by reminding them about appropriate areas for action. While it is possible to clarify the purpose of the HRD Effort without obtaining comment from others, the process of circulating the formal purpose statement is a way to communicate the role of the HRD Effort, build support from others, and clarify responsibilities. Generally, participation by others in this clarification process is highly desirable (Lundberg, 1984).

A second way to formulate a purpose statement for an HRD Effort is to begin with *possible* relationships between HRD, Strategic Business Plans, and HR plans. HRD practitioners first examine how well the Effort is presently:

- supporting Strategic Business Plans and HR plans,
- meeting future learning needs of managers and employees,
- helping individuals realize their career aspirations,
- contributing to the formulation of Strategic Business Plans and HR plans,
- providing artificial experiences of the future,
- furnishing top managers with information of use in planning,
- helping managers identify organizational strengths and weaknesses,
- educating managers about strategic thinking,
- serving strategists' needs, and
- contributing solutions to problems of long-term significance to the organization.

As a second step, HRD practitioners and operating managers clarify what they believe to be a desirable relationship between the HRD Effort and any number of issues listed previously. Practitioners and operating managers can then (1) pinpoint gaps between present and desirable relationships of the HRD Effort to any of these issues, and (2) clarify the role of HRD in closing the gaps. The resulting purpose statement links the HRD Effort directly to a specific issue or group of issues. However, no explicit linkage exists between the organization's purpose and that of the HRD Effort. Use Activity 2-3 (at the end of this chapter) to ponder the HRD Effort's purpose using this approach.

We have described two distinct ways to formulate a purpose statement for an HRD Effort. These are not mutually exclusive, however. They may be used separately or together, depending on the preferences of those using them. It is important, though, that time be taken to formulate some kind of formal purpose statement for the HRD Effort. Without it, HRD practitioners and operating managers will not be able to carry out subsequent steps in Strategic HRD.

Changing the purpose statement. How much attention should be devoted to formulating the purpose statement of the HRD Effort? When should this statement be reviewed or changed?

The proper amount of attention to devote to formulating a purpose statement depends on the benefits expected to result from the process. The time spent is worthwhile if it builds support among operating managers, motivates HRD staff, clarifies accountability, establishes a clearer sense of direction about the HRD Effort among operating managers and HRD staff, and excites enthusiasm for HRD. The process of discussing the purpose of the HRD Effort is probably more important than the product of these discussions. After all, the process is likely to increase the commitment of participants.

As long as the formal purpose statement guides and describes the HRD Effort, it need not be changed. However, the purpose statement—and its underlying assumptions—should be reviewed when:

1. Managers perceive that HRD activities are mediocre or do not meet the needs of those they are intended to serve.
2. People compare the HRD Effort unfavorably to typical practices in the industry or to practices in other firms, even those in other industries.
3. The organization changes its Strategic Business Plan or undergoes a merger, takeover, or buy-out.
4. Major new initiatives are about to be undertaken in the organization's HR practices—such as compensation/benefits or labor relations.
5. A new top management team or a new CEO enters the organization.
6. A new Director of HRD is appointed.
7. External environmental conditions place new and unexpected demands on people in the organization.

In each case, new conditions may render past assumptions out of date.

WHAT ARE THE EFFECTS OF ORGANIZATIONAL PHILOSOPHY AND CULTURE ON THE PURPOSE OF THE HRD EFFORT?

Organizational philosophy and culture are important to consider in articulating the purpose of an HRD Effort. *Philosophy* means "beliefs about what we do and why we do it"; *culture* means shared values, beliefs, and norms unique to one organizational setting (Smircich, 1983).

Philosophy of HRD. Practitioners in any field vary in what they believe about what they do. Though "philosophy" has a vaguely abstract sound, it rests at the heart of any purposeful activity. It is a system of beliefs and values. Philosophy is useful because it helps determine purpose, define roles of people working in HRD departments, change HRD activities and strategies, and set priorities among competing alternatives. Though not as specific as a formal purpose statement, philosophy is more important because it guides daily decision-making in pervasive yet elusive ways.

What is known about the personal philosophies of HRD practitioners? Ron Zemke (1985b) reports the results of one study in which practitioners were asked to rate four statements of philosophy and five HRD purpose statements. As Table 2-5 shows, most practitioners believe the most appropriate philosophy for HRD is "to

TABLE 2-5 TRAINING PHILOSOPHY/VALUES

Philosophy/Value statement	Appropriate	Inappropriate	Reflects my values
to prepare employees to develop specific skills necessary to perform effectively in their current job assignments	98.1	1.9	44.3
to help employees recognize and realize their full potential as human beings	84.0	16.0	23.5
to build skills and impart knowledge that will make employees more effective in a variety of possible job roles	92.3	7.7	17.5
to prepare employees to take on broader or more demanding job assignments in the future	94.1	5.9	14.7

Source: Zemke, 1985b, p. 93. Reprinted with permission from *Training*.

prepare employees to develop specific skills necessary to perform effectively in their current job assignments." Fewer than 40 percent, however, indicate that this statement reflects their own values. In short, practitioners *say* that training—a short-term, job-specific change effort—is the most appropriate focus of an HRD Effort. Statements associated more with employee education are ranked slightly less. Practitioners indicate the least appropriate philosophy, also the one associated with long-term employee development, is "to help employees recognize and realize their full potential as human beings." Yet it was rated second highest as reflecting their personal values. This discrepancy between what practitioners *value* and what they consider *appropriate* merely underscores the pressure they face to adopt a short-term orientation. (Zemke suggests that it is a result of the "bottom-line" emphasis purveyed in most organizations.)

A different survey on appropriate "objectives" of HRD yielded results similar to Zemke's (see Table 2-6).

Most respondents in Zemke's study perceive the purpose of the HRD Effort as providing "a basic curriculum of programs and courses that management can access to ensure employees can do their jobs" (see Table 2-7). This purpose is heavily past- or

TABLE 2-6 TRAINING OBJECTIVES

Objective	Percent very important
helping employees perform their present jobs well	81%
orienting new employees	78%
keeping employees informed of technical and procedural changes occurring within the organization	64%
providing an opportunity for employees to develop their personal skills and knowledge	37%
helping employees qualify for future jobs within the corporation	30%

Source: "Employee training in America," 1986, p. 36. Reprinted with permission from the American Society for Training and Development.

TABLE 2-7	TRAINING DEPARTMENT MISSION
Mission description	Represents my HRD department—percent
to establish a basic curriculum of programs and courses that management can access to ensure that employees can do their jobs	32.7
to anticipate changing conditions (internal and external) and provide programs to help employees cope with the changes	22.0
to provide expertise in analyzing performance problems and devise appropriate solutions	16.4
to provide programs that will improve productivity	14.6
to respond to requests from individual managers/supervisors for employee T&D	14.3
Source: Zemke, 1985b, p. 96. Reprinted with permission from *Training*.	

present-oriented because traditional training is designed that way (Rothwell, 1984b). The second largest number of respondents, however, favored a more strategic orientation. Responses having to do with productivity improvement and meeting "felt needs" of managers were least favored. Zemke concludes from these results that practitioners favor "a very traditional academy-like approach" (p. 96) to improving employee performance.

What is the starting point for articulating an HRD philosophy? Perhaps the best place to start is to do some soul-searching. What do *you* believe about HRD? How would *you* rank the importance of items in Table 2-5? How would you rank the objectives in Table 2-6? How would you describe the mission of the HRD department in Table 2-7? *Why* would you answer as you do?

Organizational culture. Practitioners are not completely free to behave in ways consistent with their own personal philosophies. After all, they function in organizational settings which have their own meanings. The meanings implicit in a setting are synonymous with *culture,* "the pattern of basic assumptions that a given group has invented, discovered, or developed in learning to cope with problems . . . and that have worked well enough to be considered valid, and therefore to be taught to new members as the correct way to perceive, think, and feel in relation to those problems" (Schein, 1984, p. 3). Culture and formal purpose are related when people in an organization share beliefs and act in ways generally consistent with values implicit in a purpose statement; organizational culture and HRD philosophy are related when HRD practitioners share beliefs of organizational members and act in accordance with formal and informal norms of conduct.

Culture is a topic that has received much attention in recent years (see Baker, 1980; Berger, 1986; Davis, 1985; Deal & Kennedy, 1982; Marshall, 1982; Martin, Feldman, Hatch, & Sitkin, 1983; Peters & Waterman, 1982; Pettigrew, 1979; Schein, 1985). Robbins (1986) identifies seven major characteristics of culture:

1. *individual autonomy:* To what degree do people feel they are responsible for results? Are they independent in their work? Do they have freedom to exercise initiative?

2. *structure:* To what degree do people feel their behavior is guided by organizational rules and regulations? Do they receive adequate supervision?
3. *support:* Do people feel they receive adequate assistance from their organizational superiors? Do they experience close interpersonal relations with their superiors?
4. *identity:* Do people identify with shared beliefs in the organization? What are those beliefs?
5. *linkages between performance and rewards:* To what extent do people feel that explicit linkages exist between their performance and the rewards they receive?
6. *conflict tolerance:* Do people feel the existence of destructive interpersonal conflicts which mar relations among peers and between groups? Do they feel there is a willingness to be open and honest about differences of opinions in the organization?
7. *risk tolerance:* Do people feel they have enough freedom to take risks?

Culture is essentially a descriptive term that has more to do with perceptions and feelings than with concrete, objective facts (Robbins, 1986).

Strategic Business Planning theorists have long debated whether culture poses more of a constraint or an opportunity for planning. Some believe that changing culture is too expensive and takes too long to be useful in implementing strategic plans (Uttal, 1983). Others disagree with this view (Byars, 1984; Cleland, 1981; Inzerilli & Rosen, 1983; Kanter, 1983; Schein, 1983). It is clear, however, that too often top managers are not well-versed enough about particular strengths and weaknesses of their organization. When a firm is doing poorly, top managers are quick to suggest change. Yet problems may have less to do with the wrong culture, strategy, or goals than with poor alignment between existing goals and the organization (Pastin, 1986). In some cases, strategy fails because it conflicts with corporate purpose or identity (Stone & Heany, 1984).

A formal purpose statement can be the highest expression of culture. It can encapsulate in one sentence or paragraph the official view of what the organization should be and how it should serve the needs of its consumers or stakeholders. However, the process of formulating this statement is an empty exercise when it is focused only on economic issues like return on investment (Toffler, 1980), is the product of only a few executives (Ackoff, 1981), and is merely descriptive of what the organization has been instead of what it should become in the future (Zemke, 1985).

A change in formal purpose implies a change in strategy *and* culture. This change should trigger a chain reaction, in which the purpose of each unit or structural component is reexamined as it relates to the whole organization. At the same time, members of each unit experience *role crisis,* in which they are temporarily unsure of how their jobs relate to the unit and how the unit relates to the organization. For strategic change to be implemented successfully, it is important to reduce the duration of this role crisis so that individuals carry out their work in ways consistent with a new Strategic Business Plan.

Any HRD Effort should reflect, at least to some extent, the organizational culture of the firm. Of course, some practitioners may be interested in changing that culture or in helping others to do so. Even in these cases, it is important to begin the change effort from the standpoint of a thorough understanding of *what the culture is* before taking action or drawing conclusions about *what the culture should be.*

Perhaps the best place to start is with a *culture audit,* a systematic examination of organizational beliefs (Wilkins, 1983). To conduct such an audit, HRD practitioners should begin with a survey of key stakeholders and others so as to collect stories and myths about the firm. Ethnographic interviewing techniques can be very helpful for this purpose (Spradley, 1979). These stories can then be used as the basis for case studies and other experiential exercises of value in training newcomers or problem performers—"how things are done here" (Albert, 1987). Some organizations have more pronounced cultures than others, making the execution of audits of this kind all the more challenging (Wilkins & Ouchi, 1983).

Information about culture can also furnish valuable input to the process of clarifying an HRD Effort's purpose. Use Activity 2-3 (at the end of this chapter) to think about this issue.

ACTIVITY 2-1 The Purpose of an HRD Effort

Directions: Use this activity to do some brainstorming about the purpose of an HRD Effort in an organization. For each question in the left column, provide an answer in the right column. (There are no right or wrong answers, though some answers may be better than others in some organizations.) Continue your answer on additional paper if needed. At the end, prepare a rough draft purpose statement applicable to the HRD Effort in the organization you are examining.

Questions	Answers
1. What *is* the responsibility of the HRD Effort in contributing to overall business objectives?	
2. What *should be* the responsibility of the HRD Effort in contributing to overall business objectives?	
3. What are the organization's major areas of service? What *is* the responsibility of HRD in each area?	
4. What *should be* the responsibility of HRD in each area of the organization's services?	
5. What are the major groups of stakeholders with which the organization must deal? What *is* the responsibility of the HRD Effort to meet the learning needs of each group?	
6. What *should be* the responsibility of the HRD Effort to meet the learning needs of each stakeholder group?	

7. What is the organization's philosophy of doing business? How *do* HRD activities contribute to the practice of that philosophy?

8. How *should* HRD activities contribute to the organization's philosophy of doing business?

9. What *is* the purpose of the HRD Effort in dealing with such cultural issues in the organization as
   - individual autonomy?
   - structure?
   - support?
   - identity?
   - linkages between performance and rewards?
   - conflict tolerance?
   - risk tolerance?

10. What *should be* the responsibility of the HRD Effort in dealing with such cultural issues in the organization as
    - individual autonomy?
    - structure?
    - support?
    - identity?
    - linkages between performance and rewards?
    - conflict tolerance?
    - risk tolerance?

ACTIVITY 2-1 Continued

Questions	Answers
11. What *is* the responsibility of the HRD Effort in the organization for • supporting implementation of Strategic Business Plans? HR plans? • meeting perceived future learning needs of managers and employees? • helping individuals realize their career aspirations? • formulating Strategic Business Plans and HR plans? • providing employees with artificial experiences of the future so that they can identify their own learning needs? • providing top managers with information for use in Strategic Business Planning? • identifying organizational strengths and weaknesses? • educating managers and employees to think strategically? • serving needs of strategists? • dealing with specific issues, problems, or projects of strategic importance to the organization?	
12. What *should be* the responsibility of the HRD Effort in • supporting implementation of Strategic Business Plans? HR plans?	

- meeting perceived future learning needs of managers and employees?
- helping individuals realize their career aspirations?
- formulating Strategic Business Plans and HR plans?
- providing employees with artificial experiences of the future so that they can identify their own learning needs?
- providing top managers with information for use in Strategic Business Planning?
- identifying organizational strengths and weaknesses?
- educating managers and employees to think strategically?
- serving needs of strategists?
- dealing with specific issues, problems, or projects of strategic importance to the organization?

The Purpose Statement

Using the answers to the preceding questions, prepare a rough draft purpose statement for the HRD Effort in the organization. Try to keep it as short and concise as possible, yet be sure to include the most important areas of responsibility. Remember: any purpose statement should answer the question "why are we doing this?"

ACTIVITY 2-2 Improving Relationships Between a Strategic Business Plan, an HR Plan, and an HRD Effort

Directions: Use this simple activity to organize your thinking. For each approach listed below in column 1 and briefly described in column 2, describe in column 3 what could be done in an organization to use this approach *or* improve the way that the approach is being used. Continue your answer on additional paper if needed. There are no right or wrong answers.

Column 1	Column 2	Column 3
Approach	Brief Description	What can be done in an organization to 1. use the approach? or 2. improve the way the approach is being used?
1. Top-down	Use HRD to support implementation of Strategic Business Plans and HR plans.	
2. Market-driven	Use HRD to meet the perceived future needs of managers and employees.	
3. Career planning	Help individuals realize their career aspirations as the organization changes in line with Strategic Business Plans.	

4. Futuring	Provide support/techniques for managers involved in formulating Strategic Business Plans.						
5. Artificial experience	Provide individuals with artificial experiences of the future so they can identify their own learning needs.						
6. Pulse-taking	Identify how well strategy is being implemented.						
7. Performance diagnosis	Identify organizational strengths and weaknesses, providing feedback to strategists.						
8. Educational	Teach people how to think strategically.						
9. Interpersonal	Serve needs of strategists.						
10. Rifle	Deal with HRD implications of specific issues, problems, and projects of strategic importance to the organization.						

ACTIVITY 2-3 A Culture Audit

Directions: Use this activity to structure your thinking about the status of the organization's culture and the role of the HRD Effort in dealing with it. While the activity may be used by members of the HRD department, it can be readily converted to a survey for use in collecting data from the organization's employees.

For each question in column 1 below, circle a code in column 2 representing the *present* status of the organization and a code in column 3 representing the *desired* status. (There are no right or wrong answers.) Finally, in column 4, briefly describe what should be the role of an HRD effort in narrowing gaps between organizational culture as it is and as it should be. There is space for remarks at the end of the activity. Use the following scale in marking your responses to columns 2 and 3:

0 represents no amount
1 represents a very small amount
2 represents a small amount
3 represents an adequate amount
4 represents a large amount
5 represents a very large amount

COLUMN 1	COLUMN 2	COLUMN 3	COLUMN 4
Questions about Culture How much do you feel that:	Actual Conditions No　　　　Very large amount　　　amount 0　1　2　3　4　5	Desired Conditions No　　　　Very large amount　　　amount 0　1　2　3　4　5	What should be the role of an HRD Effort in narrowing gaps between actual and desired cultural conditions in this organization?
1. Employees perceive they have responsibility for results?	0　1　2　3　4　5	0　1　2　3　4　5	
2. Employees perceive they have independence to carry out their work?	0　1　2　3　4　5	0　1　2　3　4　5	

3. Employees perceive that they are free to exercise individual initiative?	0 1 2 3 4 5	0 1 2 3 4 5	
4. Employees perceive that their work behavior is guided significantly by organizational rules and regulations?	0 1 2 3 4 5	0 1 2 3 4 5	
5. Employees perceive that they receive adequate supervision?	0 1 2 3 4 5	0 1 2 3 4 5	
6. Employees receive adequate assistance from their superiors?	0 1 2 3 4 5	0 1 2 3 4 5	
7. Employees enjoy close interpersonal relations with their superiors?	0 1 2 3 4 5	0 1 2 3 4 5	
8. Employees feel that their primary allegiance is to the organization as a whole?			
9. Employees perceive that there is a strong link between how they perform individually and the rewards they receive?			

ACTIVITY 2-3 Continued

Questions about Culture How much do you feel that:	Actual Conditions No Very large amount amount 0 1 2 3 4 5	Desired Conditions No Very large amount amount 0 1 2 3 4 5	What should be the role of an HRD Effort in narrowing gaps between actual and desired cultural conditions in this organization?
10. Employees perceive that significant, destructive conflict exists in relationships between their peers?			
11. Employees perceive that significant, destructive conflict exists in relationships between work groups in the organization?			
12. People in the organization confront conflict openly?			

13. Employees perceive there is freedom to take risks in the organization?		
14. There are other characteristics of the organization's culture which are important? Specify: _____ _____ _____ _____ _____		
Remarks		

ACTIVITY 2-4   A Case Study on the Purpose of the HRD Effort

Directions: Read over the case which follows and answer the questions at the end.

George P. Willis has just been hired to set up an HRD department in a large bank, the Larson Trust.*

Larson is over 100 years old and employs 10,000 people in a large metropolitan area in the Eastern United States. Larson's management has long been skeptical of planned learning activities of any kind. Though nationally known for its innovations in banking, its reputation for HRD is backward for the industry (to say the least). The bank's senior officers have undertaken this initiative in HRD because of widespread complaints by middle management.

George Willis has been hired from another large bank, where for ten years he ran a comprehensive HRD program. Willis is an HRD zealot. He earned an M.B.A. from the Wharton School and completed a Ph.D. in Education from Indiana University.

Willis has a free hand to start up the HRD Effort however he wants. His budget for the present year is negligible, but he has been told that "no reasonable request will be refused." Company management is watching Willis closely.

Questions

1. What should Willis do to clarify the role of the HRD Effort?
2. If you were in Willis's position, what would you do during the first month? The first year? Why? Explain your reasoning.

*This case is fictitious, but does bear similarities to several real situations.

PART 2
ASSESSING NEEDS AND SCANNING THE ENVIRONMENT

3

COMPREHENSIVE NEEDS ASSESSMENT

Ask experienced HRD practitioners "what is the starting point for planning an HRD program?" and most will give the same answer: needs assessment. (A few streetwise types may respond "management commitment," but let's focus on the most common answer.) If needs assessment is the starting point for planning *one* HRD experience, what should be the starting point for planning *all* organized learning events in an organization? The answer is *comprehensive needs assessment,* which is defined as a broad, systematic examination of conditions conducted for the purpose of identifying general differences between what people should know or do and what they actually know or do.

Comprehensive needs assessment is the second step in the model of SHRD presented in Chapter 1. It naturally follows the first step in the model—determining the purpose of the HRD effort. Managers and employees must be thoroughly familiar with present conditions before they can effectively plan for the future and consistently act in line with a predetermined purpose. "Strategy fails," Pastin (1986) explains, "because managers are not sufficiently concerned with the present. For a map to be useful, it must have an 'X' marking present location. The best map in the world will not keep you from getting lost if you don't know the location from which you are starting. In the same way, Strategic [Business] Planning must start with an assessment of where the organization is and whether it is aligned with its present goals" (p. 50). The same basic principle applies whether attention is focused on a Strategic *Business* Plan or on a Strategic *Learning* Plan.

COMPREHENSIVE NEEDS ASSESSMENT: DEFINITION AND DESCRIPTION

Comprehensive needs assessment is similar to *situation analysis* in Strategic Business Planning. Situation analysis is an "assessment of the company's performance" (Rowe, Mason, & Dickel, 1986, p. 56). Its focus is usually on present relationships between the organization and its competitors. Its purpose is to evaluate the status of the organization.

In educational settings, instructional planners sometimes undertake a similar kind of analysis. When assessing needs for a "course," they may focus on one discipline, issue, or problem. But when assessment is directed to a *curriculum* as *an instructional plan spanning all learning experiences sponsored by a school*, their focus is more general:

> For a school . . . embarking on a major consideration of its curriculum, it is preferable not to reduce the overall issue [of needs] in the first instance to questions of what to teach . . . but to consider the whole range of human needs and capabilities . . . the primary question in a general [curriculum] needs assessment is *what human needs should the school endeavor to meet?* (Pratt, 1980, p. 80).

This broad philosophical question must be addressed on many levels, not just one. First, what needs must be addressed due to public policy and legal mandate? Second, what needs must be addressed so that the school is responsive to the community and the society it serves? Third, what needs do learners and teachers feel should be addressed? Fourth, what needs result from economic and labor market conditions, technological change, or other matters?

Unfortunately, educators seldom address all these issues. Tradition, not analysis, drives most educational planning at primary and secondary school levels (Lodge, 1983). Nor do HRD practitioners handle the process much better in work settings: formal needs assessment is rarely carried out (Digman, 1980; Feuer, 1986a). When it is, no attempt is made to plan for meeting long-term learning needs (Rothwell & Kazanas, 1986–1988); rather, the focus is typically on specific problems and specific training intended to solve them. Yet clearly, Strategic Business Plans imply needs for human skills, and an HRD Effort is one means to meet those learning needs through the development of skills within the firm over time.

Viewed in this context, *comprehensive needs assessment is the process of specifying present but general gaps between what people should know or do and what they actually know or do*. It pinpoints not just needs (*weaknesses*) but also significant talents, skills, or competencies (*strengths*). It thus clarifies what people are doing well and not so well.

NEEDS ASSESSMENT: BACKGROUND ISSUES

Ralph Tyler (1949) expressed the classic definition of an instructional need:

> Studies of the learner suggest educational objectives only when the information about the learner is compared with some desirable standards, some conception of acceptable

norms, so that the difference between the present condition of the learner and the acceptable norm can be identified. The difference or gap is what is generally referred to as a need (p. 6).

An instructional need is thus traditionally considered to be a deficiency between *what is* and *what should be*, between present condition and criteria. An important point to stress is this: an instructional need implies that the deficiency is caused by lack of learner knowledge or skill. Needs *can* stem from other causes, such as poor motivation or lack of ability, but they are *not* appropriately met through instruction.

The history of needs assessment in HRD begins with the work of McGehee and Thayer (1961). They suggested that needs should be identified by synthesizing the results of three different examinations. First, HRD practitioners should analyze the organization and identify instructional needs stemming from production, legal, and other requirements. This is called *organization analysis*. Second, practitioners should direct attention to jobs and identify instructional needs stemming from work tasks. This is called *operation or work analysis*. Third, practitioners should focus on people working in the organization and identify instructional needs stemming from individual performance problems. This is called *individual analysis*. Each analysis should be separately performed and the results compared to yield instructional needs. Sources of information vary for each type of analysis (see Tables 3-1, 3-2, & 3-3).

Traditional needs assessment is thus based on problem-solving. When decision-makers perceive that a difference exists between their expectations and actual results, a problem warrants attention. If the problem is caused by a lack of knowledge or skill, it is properly classified as an *instructional need*. If the problem is caused by something other than a lack of knowledge or skill—like poor motivation or morale, poor job structure, poor work incentives, or another cause—it is a *noninstructional need* requiring action other than training, education, or development. Thomas Gilbert (1967) was among the first to draw this distinction between instructional and noninstructional needs. He contended that HRD practitioners should look beyond mere instructional solutions to any appropriate, cost-effective performance improvement strategy for dealing with problems. Building on this idea, Geary Rummler (1976) proposed comprehensive performance audits to identify improvement programs yielding high payoffs by making jobs more efficient and effective. Audits of this kind examine (1) job context, (2) incumbents, (3) desired actions or decisions, (4) results, and (5) feedback to incumbents on results (Rummler, 1976). There are three levels of analysis: (1) *policy*, focusing on identifying performance improvement programs yielding the highest payoff; (2) *strategy*, focusing on ways of defining and improving a job; and (3) *tactics*, focusing on specific ways to make people more efficient. (See Table 3-4.)

Dugan Laird (1985) distinguished between two types of instructional needs. The first type he called a *microtraining need*, arising from individuals. Whenever one person or a small group faces change of any kind requiring new knowledge or a new skill, a microtraining need exists. Whenever people are hired, promoted, transferred, or temporarily reassigned to a new job, they may require special instruction in order to perform effectively. Microtraining needs may also be identified through examinations of individual performance appraisals, career contracts, group production records, or quality control reports.

TABLE 3-1 ORGANIZATIONAL DATA SOURCES

Data source recommended	Training need implications
1. Organizational Goals and Objectives	Where training emphasis can and should be placed. These provide normative standards of both direction and expected impact which can highlight deviations from objectives and performance problems.
2. Manpower Inventory	Where training is needed to fill gaps caused by retirement, turnover, age, etc. This provides an important demographic data base regarding possible scope of training needs.
3. Skills Inventory	Number of employees in each skill group, knowledge and skill levels, training time per job; etc. This provides an estimate of the magnitude of specific training needs. Useful in cost benefit analysis of training projects.
4. Organizational Climate Indices	These "quality of working life" indicators at the organization level may help focus on problems that have training components.
a. Labor-Management data—strikes, lockouts, etc.	All of these items related to either work participation or productivity are useful both in discrepancy analysis and in helping management set a value on the behaviors it wishes improved through training once training has been established as a relevant solution.
b. Grievances	
c. Turnover	
d. Absenteeism	
e. Suggestions	
f. Productivity	
g. Accidents	
h. Short-term sickness	
i. Observation of employee behavior	
j. Attitude surveys	Good for locating discrepancies between organizational expectations and perceived results.
k. Customer complaints	Valuable feedback; look especially for patterns and repeat complaints.
5. Analysis of Efficiency Indices	Cost accounting concepts may represent ratio between actual performance and desired or standard performance.
a. Costs of labor	
b. Costs of materials	
c. Quality of product	
d. Equipment utilization	
e. Costs of distribution	
f. Waste	
g. Down time	
h. Late deliveries	
i. Repairs	
6. Changes in System or Subsystem	New or changed equipment may present training problem.
7. Management Requests or Management Interrogation	One of most common techniques of training needs determination.

TABLE 3-1 Continued.	
Data source recommended	Training need implications
8. Exit Interviews	Often information not otherwise available can be obtained in these. Problem areas and supervisory training needs especially.
9. MBO or Work Planning and Review Systems	Provides performance review, potential review, and long-term business objectives. Provides actual performance data on a recurring basis so that base-line measurements may be known and subsequent improvement or deterioration of performance can be identified and analyzed.

Source: Moore & Dutton, 1978, p. 537. Reprinted with permission from *Academy of Management Review*.

The second type is a *macrotraining need,* arising from change in the organization. Whenever groups of people face change requiring new knowledge or skills, a macrotraining need exists. For example, macrotraining needs stem from changes in Strategic Business Plans, personnel policies, organizational structure, production methods, sales policies, and government laws or regulations. Laird's diagnostic model for identifying macrotraining needs is shown in Figure 3-1.

Laird's distinction between micro and macro training needs is important for several reasons. First, it positions the HRD practitioner in a role somewhat like that of an air traffic controller. To speak figuratively, the practitioner monitors a radar screen sweeping the environment. Changes occurring inside or outside the organization appear as blips on the screen. Some blips require action—that is, planned learning activities intended to equip people to cope with change. Second, change differs by degree. Not all blips are the same size or are configured the same way. The scope of corrective action depends on the scope of the problem. Third and finally, Laird implies that some changes are predictable, even cyclical. They recur. No matter how stable the organization, some needs keep coming up. Newly hired, transferred, or promoted employees have to be oriented to new jobs, for instance. This need recurs every time an individual's duties change. On the other hand, some are neither predictable nor recurrent. An industry's deregulation may be apparent for years, but will probably not unfold in any predictable way. Yet this trend may require planned learning activities so that people learn new skills or master new knowledge pertinent to the change.

From long tradition, HRD practitioners have thus viewed instruction as a means of rectifying deficiencies or solving performance problems. Needs assessment is really a form of deficiency analysis. It uncovers areas in which present conditions are not as good as desired conditions.

There is another side to performance, of course. In some areas, people excel: the organization outperforms competitors; individuals do better than the minimum standards established for them; and job results turn out better than expected. In each case, condition is better than criteria. When the cause of this favorable discrepancy stems from human knowledge and skill, it is a special talent or competency.

TABLE 3-2 OPERATIONAL ANALYSIS SOURCES

Technique for obtaining job data	Training need implications
1. Job Descriptions	Outlines the job in terms of typical duties and responsibilities but is not meant to be all-inclusive. Helps define performance discrepancies.
2. Job Specifications or Task Analysis	List specified tasks required for each job. More specific than job descriptions. Specifications may extend to judgments of knowledge and skills required of job incumbents.
3. Performance Standards	Objectives of the tasks of job and standards by which they are judged. This may include baseline data as well.
4. Perform the Job	Most effective way of determining specific tasks but has serious limitations the higher the level of the job in that performance requirements typically have longer gaps between performance and resulting outcomes.
5. Observe Job—Work Sampling	

6. Review Literature Concerning the Job
  a. Research in other industries
  b. Professional journals
  c. Documents
  d. Government sources
  e. Ph.D. theses
	Possibly useful in comparison analyses of job structures but far removed from either unique aspects of the job structure within any *specific* organization or specific performance requirements.

7. Ask Questions about the Job
  a. Of the job holder
  b. Of the supervisor
  c. Of higher management	

8. Training Committees or Conferences	Inputs from several viewpoints can often reveal training needs or training desires.

9. Analysis of Operating Problems
  a. Down time reports
  b. Waste
  c. Repairs
  d. Late deliveries
  e. Quality control
	Indications of task interference, environmental factors, etc.

10. Card Sort	Utilized in training conferences. "How to" statements sorted by training importance.

Source: Moore & Dutton, 1978, p. 537. Reprinted with permission from *Academy of Management Review.*

TABLE 3-3 INDIVIDUAL ANALYSIS SOURCES

Technique or data obtained	Training need implications
1. Performance Data or Appraisals as Indicators of "Sickness"	Include weaknesses and area of improvement as well as strong points. Easy to analyze and quantify for purposes of determining subjects and kinds of training needed. These data can be used to *identify* performance discrepancies.

a. Productivity
   b. Absenteeism or Tardiness
   c. Accidents
   d. Short-term sickness
   e. Grievances
   f. Waste
   g. Late deliveries
   h. Product Quality
   i. Down time
   j. Repairs
   k. Equipment utilization
   l. Customer complaints	

2. Observation—Work Sampling	More subjective technique but provides both employee behavior and results of the behavior.
3. Interviews	Individual is only one who knows what he (she) believes he (she) needs to learn. Involvement in need analysis can also motivate employees to make an effort to learn.
4. Questionnaires	Same approach as the interview. Easily tailored to specific characteristics of the organization. May produce bias through the necessity of pre-structure categories.
5. Tests	Can be tailor-made or standardized. Care must be taken so that they measure job-related qualities.

a. Job knowledge
   b. Skills
   c. Achievement	

6. Attitude Surveys	On the individual basis, useful in determining morale, motivation or satisfaction of each employee.
7. Checklists or Training Progress Charts	Up-to-date listing of each employee's skills. Indicates future training requirements for each job.
8. Rating Scales	Care must be taken to insure relevant, reliable, and objective employee ratings.
9. Critical Incidents	Observed actions which are critical to the successful or unsuccessful performance of the job.
10. Diaries	Individual employee records details of his (her) job.

Needs Assessment: Background Issues

TABLE 3-3 Continued.	
Technique or data obtained	Training need implications

11. Devised Situations
   a. Role play
   b. Case study
   c. Conference leadership training sessions
   d. Business games
   e. In-baskets
	Certain knowledge, skills and attitudes are demonstrated in these techniques.

12. Diagnostic Rating	Check lists are factor analyzed to yield diagnostic ratings.
13. Assessment Centers	Combination of several of the above techniques into an intensive assessment program.
14. Coaching	Similar to interview—one-to-one.
15. MBO or Work Planning and Review Systems	Provides actual performance data on a recurring basis related to organizational (and individually or group-negotiated standards) so that base-line measurements may be known and subsequent improvement or deterioration of performance may be identified and analyzed. This performance review and potential review is keyed to larger organization goals and objectives.

Source: Moore & Dutton, 1978, pp. 539. Reprinted with permission from *Academy of Management Review.*

TABLE 3-4 LEVELS OF ANALYSIS IN PERFORMANCE AUDITS		
Level	Focus	HRD issue
I (Policy)	the structure and goals of the organization and the kind of environment it provides for the job	Which program will give the highest payoff for improving performance?
II (Strategy)	the theory and accomplishments of a job itself and how it helps fulfill the goals of the organization	What are the strategies of defining and improving a job?
III (Tactics)	the kind of changes that must be made in the behavior of individuals if they are to accomplish the job	What specific things must you do to make people more efficient in doing a job?

Source: Reprinted from Rummler, 1976, p. 14-10 with permission from McGraw-Hill Book Company.

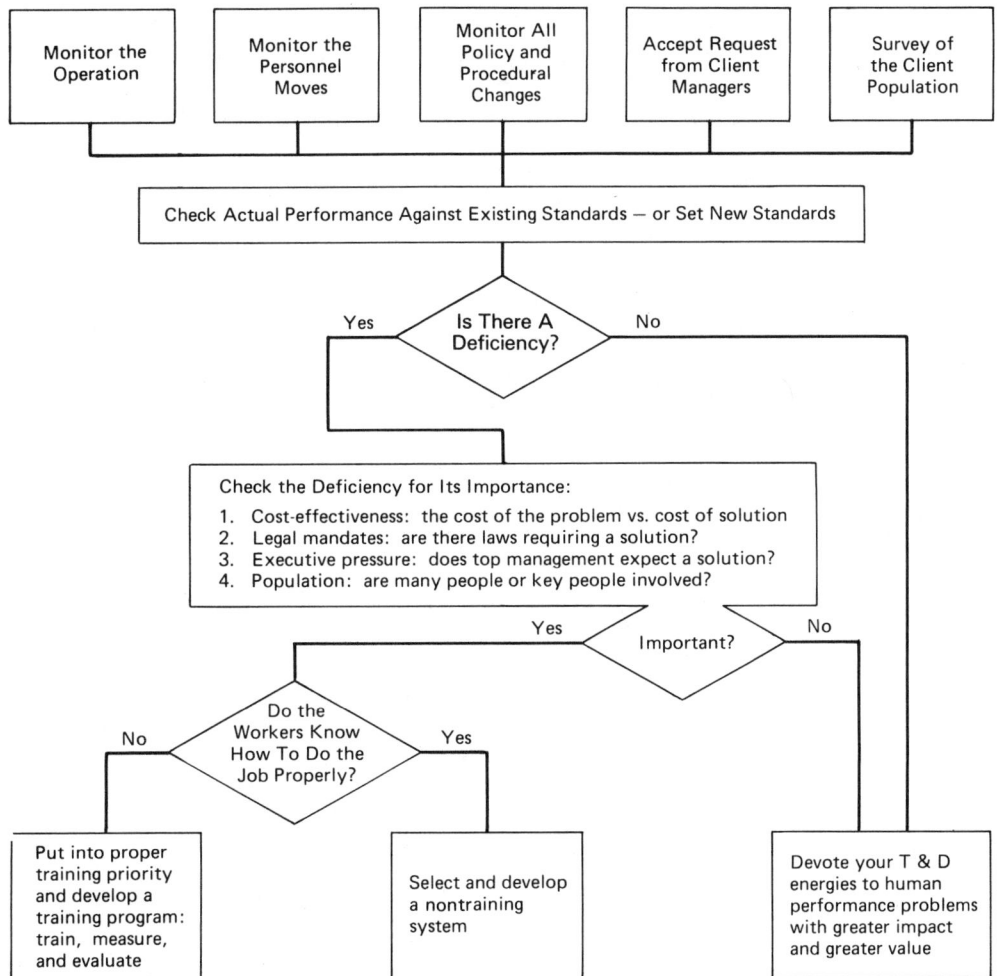

Figure 3-1: Identifying Macrotraining Needs. *Source:* Laird, 1985, p. 62. Reprinted with permission of Addison-Wesley.

STEPS IN COMPREHENSIVE NEEDS ASSESSMENT

There are several "right" ways to carry out a comprehensive needs assessment. However, at some point HRD practitioners and line managers should:

1. Identify learners to be served by the HRD Effort over time. More specifically, who are the learners and prospective learners? Where are they located? How many are there? How can the learners be reached? How intense is their motivation to learn? When are they most interested in learning?
2. Classify learners into broad "market segments."
3. Compare actual to desired knowledge and skills at present for each market segment of learners.

4. Identify present learning needs for each market and market segment of learners. When actual knowledge and skills (AKS) minus desired knowledge and skills (DKS) equals a *deficiency,* then it is classified as a *weakness.* On the other hand, if AKS minus DKS equals a *proficiency,* then it is classified as a *strength.*

These steps are worth considering in more detail.

IDENTIFYING LEARNERS

In order to assess instructional needs, HRD practitioners should collect as much information as possible about present and prospective learners and clients. *A learner is one receiving and participating in planned learning activities. A client is one who wants and benefits directly from those activities.* The distinction between learner and client is sometimes vague. There are several reasons why: (1) learners benefit directly from instruction and are sometimes the only clients; (2) employees' superiors at all levels are responsible for HRD activities and are properly considered clients; and (3) superiors may participate in design and delivery of planned learning—and may learn in the process—but are not considered learners when learning strategies are intended to meet needs of their subordinates.

HRD practitioners are always engaged in meeting the needs of at least two markets—learners and their organizational superiors. The strategic implications of this should not be ignored. HRD practitioners, like marketing specialists, have two basic options: (1) to satisfy perceived needs of both groups—learners and clients/supervisors—as much as possible; or (2) to concentrate on satisfying needs of one group more than the other's. Most practitioners try to satisfy needs of both groups while gearing their efforts to meeting needs which would be difficult for alternative sources of instruction (like external vendors, colleges, or universities) to supply. External providers of education or training are competitors to in-house HRD departments when instructional activities are not tailored to the learners' precise working conditions.

HRD practitioners are well-positioned to detect learning needs and gather detailed information. In this respect, they enjoy a competitive advantage over external providers of instruction. In short, in-house instruction is more easily tailored to the employing firm. Specific instruction "is of use only to the firm that provides it" (Marshall, Briggs, & King, 1984, p. 328); general instruction is readily transferable to other firms and improves the employability of learners. Managers have an incentive to offer specific instruction in-house because learners receiving it are far less likely to quit and thus take personal advantage of company-funded improvement of their skills. The learners also have an incentive to participate in such in-house learning experiences because "company-provided programs are most likely to increase earnings" (Geber, 1987, p. 80).

To identify instructional needs, HRD practitioners have to research their markets—that is, learners and clients. If the HRD Effort is geared solely to employees, then information has to be collected about them. If it is geared solely to the external consumers of company products or services, then information has to be collected about them. If the HRD Effort is comprehensive, then information has to be collected both about learners and clients.

The purpose of the HRD Effort provides direction to information-gathering by clarifying targeted learners, types of instructional activities to be offered, methods of offering those services, and follow-up activities to ensure that learning is subsequently applied.

CLASSIFYING LEARNERS BY MARKET SEGMENT

HRD practitioners have to assess learning needs and talents according to precise learner characteristics. Separate but comprehensive needs assessments can be focused on different learner markets and, within each market, on different segments. A *market* is an identifiable group of people. A *market segment* is a subgroup which has "special needs and preferences and which represents sufficient pockets of demand to justify separate marketing strategies" (Buell, 1984, p. 66).

There are at least four possible markets for an HRD Effort: (1) the job market; (2) the individual/career market; (3) the work group market; and (4) the external market. The first three are found inside an organization; the fourth is outside.

The job market. One way to classify learners is by their job tasks, results, and responsibilities. Employee training, a short-term change effort, traditionally focuses on jobs (Nadler, 1979). It is geared to producing immediate, observable results and to socializing individuals into an organization.

When examining the job market, HRD practitioners should be familiar with certain terminology. A *task* is "a discrete unit of work"; a *position* is a group of related tasks performed by one person in one organization; a *job* is a group of similar positions; a *job class* is a group of related and/or unrelated jobs occupying the same level of responsibility and bearing certain similarities as a result; a *job category* or *job family* is a group of related jobs but at different levels of responsibility; and an *occupation* is a group of similar jobs existing in different organizations. A brief example will help clarify the meanings of these terms.

Harry Smith is an Accountant I in Acme Chemical Company. Harry occupies a *position* similar to other Accountant I *jobs* at Acme. Accountants IIs, IIIs, and IVs at Acme are in the same job family. Finance experts, personnel experts, and marketing experts are in the same job class. Accountants at other companies share a common occupation with Harry.

All Accountants at Acme share certain common training needs as they are socialized into the organization. They are hired on the basis of qualifications. For instance, every new accountant has an accounting degree. But each newcomer has to learn "the Acme way" of performing the Accountant I's job and getting along with other people. The same principle holds true for all other job classes. Each job class has recurring needs arising from movement into, through, and out of the class (see Table 3-5).

Job families have similarities. For example, all supervisors share common responsibilities: they oversee daily operations and are responsible for front-line activi-

TABLE 3-5 RECURRING INSTRUCTIONAL NEEDS STEMMING FROM MOVEMENTS OF PERSONNEL

Stages	Key issues	Instructional implications/needs
Presocialization	What learning experiences can prepare an individual for entry to an occupation?	How well does formal schooling prepare individuals for entry to an occupation? Job? Job class?
Recruitment	How can an organization attract qualified talent in line with its needs?	What do applicants need to know about the organization and job that will help them select themselves?
Selection	How can an organization select effective performers?	What does the organization need to know about individuals applying for entry?
Job/Group Orientation	How can an individual be oriented to the position? Job? The work group?	What training focused on job tasks should be given to newcomers? When?
		How can individuals be helped to learn norms of their work groups? Culture of the organization?
Stable Performance	How can deficiencies in individual performance on the job be identified and corrected?	What training will help correct problems in job performance?

ties. Similarly, professional employees are hired for their expertise, which they put to special use.

To design a long-term learning plan to meet recurring instructional needs, HRD practitioners "need to look at all divisions and functions and superimpose a logical grouping." An example is illustrated in Table 3-6. "Even though titles differ, this group is based on common responsibilities" (Galosy, 1983, p. 49). Training courses and/or experiences can then be focused on these responsibilities.

One way to create logical groupings is to classify job titles into the following categories and then assess recurring training needs for each group: (1) executives; (2) senior managers; (3) middle managers; (4) first-line supervisors; (5) sales personnel; (6) professionals; (7) administrative employees; (8) clerical support; (9) skilled production or service workers; (10) unskilled production or service workers; (11) customer representatives; and (12) others.* Several job titles may be grouped into each category.

Each category represents a different market segment. Each requires a different long-term learning plan to meet recurring training needs. (See Activity 3-2 at the end of this chapter for help in identifying groupings applicable to a specific organization.)

Individual/career market. A second way to classify learners is by individual performance and career aspirations. Employee education, an intermediate-term change effort, focuses on this market. It prepares an individual for movement to another job. It also upgrades skills and elicits new insights.

*Based on categories found in Gordon, 1986.

TABLE 3-6	MANAGEMENT GROUPINGS		
Sales	Data processing	Operations	Finance
Exec. V.P.	Exec. V.P.	Exec. V.P.	Exec. V.P. Treasurer
Senior V.P.s Regional V.P.s V.P.s	Research V.P.s	Senior V.P.s Regional V.P.s	Vice Presidents
Directors Dist. Mgrs.	Directors Project Mgrs.	Directors Dist. Mgrs.	Comptroller Assistant Comptroller
Managers Supervisors	Supervisors	Managers Supervisors	Managers Supervisors

Source: Galosy, 1983, p. 49. Reprinted with permission from American Society for Training and Development.

To be successful, employee education has to be based on training, education, experience, and personal characteristics equated with successful performance at each level. In consultation with supervisors, individuals can plan for career movement by gradually acquiring the knowledge and skills they need to succeed in other jobs or job families.

For instance, Martina Short is an experienced welder who wants to be a first-line supervisor in the welding department. By comparing her present skills to those required for successful performance as a welding supervisor, Martina is able to devise a learning plan that will gradually bring her skills in line with those needed by a welding supervisor. To establish this plan, Martina negotiates a learning contract with her supervisor. In this process, Martina makes explicit her desire for promotion and her plans for obtaining the necessary skills needed for that promotion. The supervisor makes no promises and raises no unrealistic expectations, but does assure Martina that, without the skills she plans to acquire, she will never be eligible for promotion.

It is more difficult to assess employee educational needs than training needs and to devise categories for an employee education curriculum than a training curriculum. But it is not impossible. On the basis of employee performance appraisals and other information, individuals can be classified according to how much they are worth as educational investments. For instance, Odiorne (1984) suggests that employees can be classified as (1) *workhorses,* "people who have reached a high peak of performance but have definitely limited potential" (p. 66); (2) *stars,* "people of high potential who are performing at the highest level of that potential" (p. 67); (3) *problem employees,* "people who have great potential but who are working well below their capacity and with mixed results" (p. 67); and (4) *deadwood,* "people whose performance and potential are both low" (p. 66). "Stars" are ranked first for investment; deadwood is ranked last. If individuals are classified into these categories, supervisors can determine how much each individual is worthy of the cost of skill improvement—and what kind of skill improvement the individual should receive.

Another way to classify individuals is by life cycle stage. While it is important to avoid age discrimination, people in each age bracket have central life concerns which differ from those in other age brackets and affect their motivation to learn. (See Table 3-7 for a list of central life concerns of different age groups.) These central life concerns are worth considering when assessing individuals needs. They may imply what the individual is motivated to learn about.

See Activity 3-3 at the end of the chapter for help in classifying individuals in an organization by life cycle stage.

The work group or department market. A third way to classify learners is by their placement within the organization. Long-term change efforts like organization and employee development focus on this market. Organization Development is geared to changing culture. Employee development is geared to creating a collective mix of employee skills appropriate to the responsibilities of the work group or department. In this context, a *work group* means a supervisor and his or her immediate subordinates.

TABLE 3-7 LIFE CYCLE STAGES OF AMERICAN ADULTS		
Early adulthood (18–30)		
Vocation and career	Home and family living	Personal development
Exploring career options	Courting	Improving your reading ability
Choosing a career line	Selecting a mate	Improving your writing ability
Getting a job	Preparing for marriage	Improving your speaking ability
Being interviewed	Family planning	Improving your listening ability
Learning job skills	Preparing for children	
Getting along at work	Raising children	Continuing your general education
Getting ahead at work	Understanding children	
Getting job protection of military service	Preparing children for school	Developing your religious faith
	Helping children in school	Improving problem-solving skills
Getting vocational counseling	Solving marital problems	
Changing jobs	Using family counseling	Making better decisions
	Managing a home	Getting along with people
	Financial planning	Understanding yourself
	Managing money	Finding your self-identity
	Buying goods and services	Discovering your aptitudes
	Making home repairs	Clarifying your values
	Gardening	Understanding other people
		Learning to be self-directing
		Improving personal appearance
		Establishing intimate relations
		Dealing with conflict
		Making use of personal counseling

Source: Knowles, 1984, p. 153. Reprinted with permission from Gulf Publishing.

TABLE 3-7 Continued.

Enjoyment of leisure	Health	Community living
Choosing hobbies Finding new friends Joining organizations Planning your time Buying equipment Planning family recreation Leading recreational activities	Keeping fit Planning diets Finding and using health services Preventing accidents Using first aid Understanding children's diseases Understanding how the human body functions Buying and using drugs and medicines Developing a healthy life-style Recognizing the symptoms of physical and mental illness	Relating to school and teachers Learning about community resources Learning how to get help Learning how to exert influence Preparing to vote Developing leadership skills Keeping up with the world Taking action in the community Organizing community activities for children and youth

Middle adulthood
(30–65)

Vocation and career	Home and family living	Personal development
Learning advanced job skills Supervising others Changing careers Dealing with unemployment Planning for retirement Making second careers for mothers	Helping teenage children to become adults Letting your children go Relating to your spouse as a person Adjusting to aging parents Learning to cook for two Planning for retirement	Finding new interests Keeping out of a rut Compensating for physiological changes Dealing with change Developing emotional flexibility Learning to cope with crises Developing a realistic time perspective

Enjoyment of leisure	Health	Community living
Finding less active hobbies Broadening your cultural interests Learning new recreational skills Finding new friends Joining new organizations Planning recreation for two	Adjusting to physiological changes Changing diets Controlling weight Getting exercise Having annual medical exams Compensating for losses in strength	Taking more social responsibility Taking leadership roles in organizations Working for the welfare of others Engaging in politics Organizing community improvement activities

Source: Knowles, 1984, p. 155. Reprinted with permission from Gulf Publishing.

TABLE 3-7 Continued.

Later adulthood (65 and over)		
Vocation and career	Home and family living	Personal development
Adjusting to retirement Finding new ways to be useful Understanding social security, medicare, and welfare	Adjusting to reduced income Establishing new living arrangements Adjusting to death of spouse Learning to live alone Relating to grandchildren Establishing new intimate relationships Putting your estate in order	Developing compensatory abilities Understanding the aging process Reexamining your values Keeping future-oriented Keeping your morale up Keeping up to date Keeping in touch with young people Keeping curious Keeping up personal appearance Keeping an open mind Finding a new self-identity Developing a new time perspective Preparing for death
Enjoyment of leisure	Health	Community living
Establishing affiliations with the older age group Finding new hobbies Learning new recreational skills Planning a balanced recreational program	Adjusting to decreasing strength and health Keeping fit Changing your diet Having regular medical exams Getting appropriate exercise Using drugs and medicines wisely Learning to deal with stress Maintaining your reserves	Working for improved conditions for the elderly Giving volunteer services Maintaining organizational ties

Source: Knowles, 1984, p. 155. Reprinted with permission from Gulf Publishing.

Work groups are—or should be—readily identifiable with the aid of an organization chart. Simply begin at the top and circle supervisor and subordinates in each group (see Figure 3-2 for an example.) The first work group consists of the Chief Executive and his or her immediate subordinates. Each subordinate, in turn, serves as supervisor for a group of subordinates. Continue this process from top to bottom of the organization to identify all work groups.

No two organizations are structured in quite the same way. Differences exist both in what kinds of departments or work groups are created *and* in the kinds and numbers of people or jobs reporting to the same supervisor.

Regardless of structure, human skills are essential. To meet the responsibilities of each department or work group, managers need the right numbers and types of

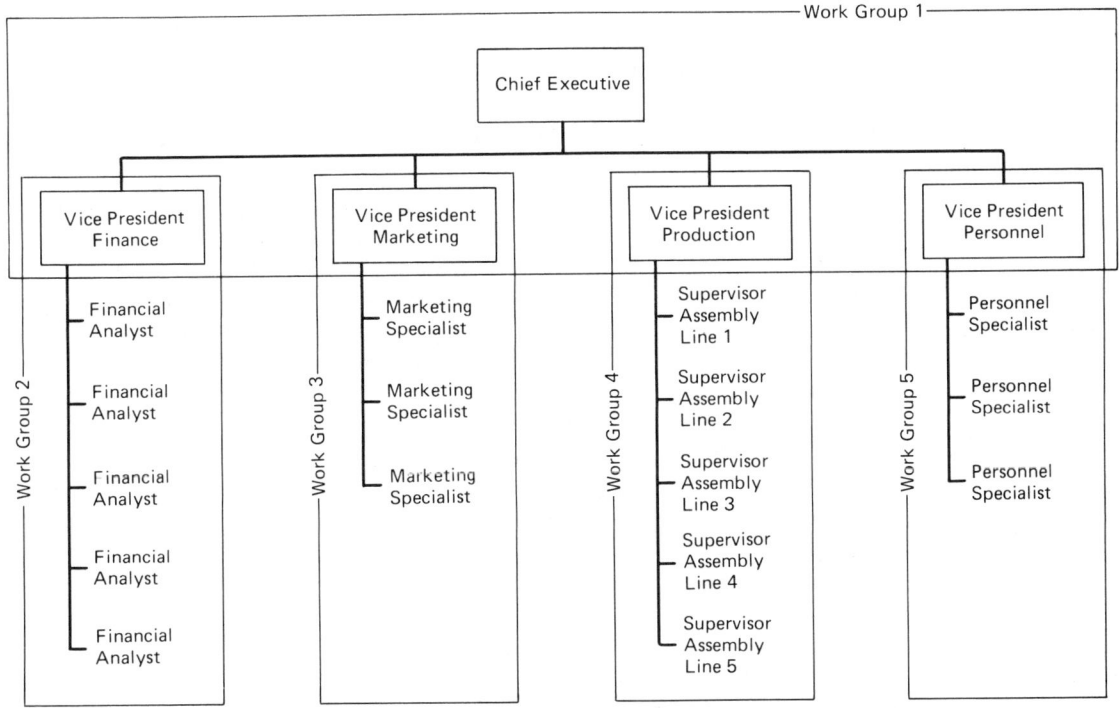

Figure 3-2: A Simplified Organization Chart with Work Groups Designated

people. While staffing requirements can be met in many ways, employee development is one way to ensure that the collective skills of a group match up to its responsibilities. A long-term learning plan for each group is thus necessary to clarify when and how these skills can be obtained.

To prepare a long-term plan for employee development, each supervisor should examine (1) the purpose of the work group, (2) the differences between how the group should be performing and how it is actually performing, (3) the human skills and knowledge which can narrow the gap between desired and actual group results over time, and (4) the methods of obtaining necessary skills and knowledge.

The external market. Employees are not the only ones who can be classified as learners. Nor are employees or supervisors the only potential clients of planned learning activities. People outside an organization may also have learning needs worth addressing. To state the case succinctly:

> Street-smart marketing types understand the value of training in selling a new product, especially a high-tech one. After all, what employer wants to invest megabucks in a piece of alien equipment that nobody understands how to use? The manufacturer better realize that somebody has to teach the buyer's employees how to use the machinery (*A marriage*, 1987, p. 12).

Classifying LEARNERS by Market Segment

Nonemployee development, ranging from short-term to long-term instructional efforts geared to meeting the learning needs of people outside an organization, focuses on this market. It creates consumers who know how to use company products and services, suppliers who are aware of unique needs of an organization with which they transact business, distributors who are familiar enough with company products or services to market them effectively to consumers, and members of the general public or community who understand the unique needs and problems of an employer.

To develop a long-term learning plan for the external market, HRD practitioners should consider such questions as: (1) What groups outside the organization are particularly critical to sales and/or long-term survival and success? (2) What strengths and weaknesses are evident in relations between the organization and each external group? (3) How much are these strengths and weaknesses attributable to lack of knowledge or skills? (4) How much is each weakness attributable to an external group's lack of knowledge about the organization? On the other hand, how much is each weakness attributable to lack of employee knowledge about the external group? and (5) What planned learning experiences over time can help correct weaknesses attributable to lack of knowledge, and build on the unique strengths of the group that stem from group competencies?

Perhaps two examples will clarify these issues.

First, consider the case of a computer company that introduces a wristwatch-size computer. At first, consumers are unaware of the product's existence and capabilities. This problem can be addressed through mass media advertising. While costly, advertising does create product demand and familiarizes consumers with general product capabilities. Subsequent instruction is necessary, however, to demonstrate to specific consumers how the product can help meet their unique needs. In fact, a whole series of seminars can be designed around different consumer applications of the product. This instruction becomes an important marketing tool and, potentially, a profit-making enterprise of its own.

Consider a different case. Managers of the Acer Corporation want to open a new plant, which will employ 720 people, on a tract of land in rural Mississippi. The plant will benefit from a very attractive incentives package, including tax breaks and free land, provided by the State. However, some local residents fear problems will accompany the plant's opening. For example, they are concerned about toxic wastes and environmental pollution, an influx of "big city types" who will bring with them a crime wave, and the possible drain on local utilities. To address these concerns, the company mounts a massive public education effort using various media: spot advertisements on local television and radio; full-page letters to residents published in local newspapers; speeches to community and school groups; and door-to-door interviews with residents. The result of this effort is that the learning needs of the community are met and strong community support for the new plant is secured.

Planned learning experiences can also be directed to satisfying the learning needs of critical suppliers, distributors, government regulatory agencies, and other key groups which can affect the business. In each case, HRD practitioners examine problems in relations between the organization and a specific external group, and design planned learning activities which satisfy learning needs and thus help improve relations with that group.

COMPARING ACTUAL TO DESIRED KNOWLEDGE AND SKILLS

Most books and articles on HRD devote considerable attention to data collection methods used in needs assessment. Few writers distinguish between short-term and long-term needs assessment. Most writers, like most practitioners, assume needs assessment is focused on the short-term *training* needs of an identifiable learner group. That does not have to be the case, however.

Levels of assessment and assessment strategy. Learning needs can be viewed on three levels, much like corporate plans.

Strategic needs are most general and comprehensive. They require the longest time to satisfy. By meeting strategic learning needs, HRD practitioners create cultural change. Organization development, employee development, and much nonemployee development are focused on this level.

Coordinative needs are not as general nor as comprehensive as strategic needs. They do not take as much time to deal with. Meeting them produces change in line with individual career plans. Employee education is focused on this level.

Operational needs are most specific and require the least time to deal with. Meeting them produces immediate changes in job performance. Employee training is focused on this level.

Comprehensive needs assessment requires an integrated approach so that needs can be assessed on all three levels at once. Integration is important so that short-term, intermediate-term, and long-term instructional efforts are coordinated and unified.

What is necessary, then, is a strategy for needs assessment that ensures this integration. Generally, there are three possible strategies: (1) *top-down;* (2) *bottom-up;* and (3) *negotiated*. If a top-down strategy is chosen, needs assessment is carried out by a handful of people at the top. Quite often they are the same decision-makers who formulate Strategic Business Plans. The participation of many people builds commitment for subsequent learning and helps tie the resulting learning plans to other kinds of plans (Nilsson, 1987). A bottom-up strategy results from a compilation of numerous separate assessments carried out by first-line supervisors or employees. A negotiated strategy is quite literally negotiated between top managers and other people in the firm.

There is no right or wrong strategy for needs assessment. However, there may be a right or wrong approach in one organizational culture. A good clue is how Strategic Business Plans are formulated. Are they formulated at the top and imposed downward? Are they compiled from separate plans formulated at the bottom and forwarded up the hierarchy? Is some form of negotiation used? Whatever the pattern used in formulating Strategic Business Plans, needs assessment should be carried out in a similar fashion—if not as part of the Strategic Business Planning process itself (Dyer, 1984).

Data collection methods. The essence of needs assessment is a comparison between *what is* and *what should be*. Condition is the same as *what is;* criterion is the same as *what should be*. Instruction is an appropriate way of narrowing the gap between condition and criterion when the deficiency is caused by lack of knowledge or skill, and taking action is consistent with the purpose of the HRD Effort. (See Figure

3-3). Instruction may also be used to build on proficiencies—that is, exceptional knowledge, skills, or talents. The same principle applies whether the focus is organization development, nonemployee development, employee development, education, or training.

Different data collection methods can be used to compare condition and criteria in needs assessment and thus uncover deficiencies (weaknesses) and proficiencies (strengths). These methods include: (1) interviews; (2) surveys; (3) observation; (4) task analysis; (5) performance/productivity measures; (6) employee performance appraisals; (7) assessment centers; (8) group discussions; (9) critical incident techniques; (10) delphi procedures; and (11) nominal group techniques. There are more (see Kaufman & English, 1978; Laird, 1985; Tracey, 1984; Ulschak, 1983). Not every method is appropriate for a comprehensive needs assessment. Some are appropriate only for identifying specific training, education, or development needs. However, interviews are widely applicable and are probably the most commonly used data collection method (see Table 3-8).

An *interview* is essentially a conversation. Interviews can be formal or informal. A formal interview relies on a highly structured series of questions prepared and tested in advance. HRD practitioners are not free to vary the wording or the sequencing of questions. They record responses directly on a form (called a *schedule*). Informal interviews rely on an outline of subjects, topics, or issues. HRD practitioners can vary the wording or sequencing of questions. They record notes directly on the form (called a *guide*). Formal interviews preserve consistency across respondents but sacrifice the potential for intensive probing; informal interviews sacrifice consistency across respondents for the potential to probe for additional information.

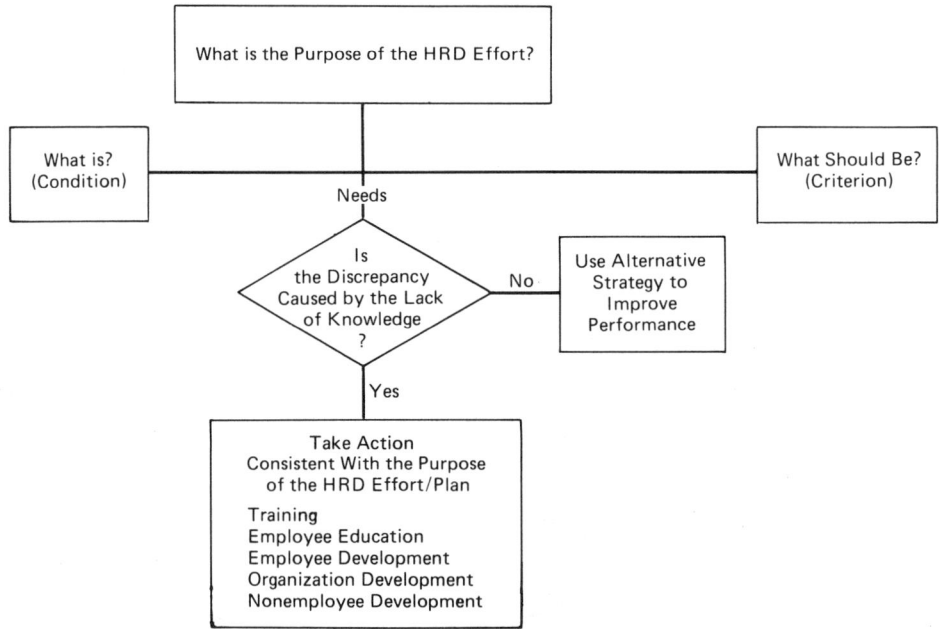

Figure 3-3: Instructional Needs Assessment: A Simple Model

TABLE 3-8	NEEDS ASSESSMENT TECHNIQUES COMMONLY USED
Type of technique	Percent who use technique
Interviews	83%
Direct observation of work	80%
Examination of performance or productivity measures	75%
Questionnaires	66%
Task analysis	64%

Source: "Employee Training in America," 1986, p. 35. Reprinted with permission from the American Society for Training and Development.

Interviews are flexible enough to be used in identifying training, education, and development needs. The difference between them depends on *who is interviewed* and *what they are asked about.* Experienced job incumbents and their supervisors are appropriately interviewed to plan training or education; supervisors are interviewed to plan employee development; many people are interviewed to plan organization development; and members of external groups are interviewed to plan nonemployee development. In each case, they can be questioned both about deficiencies (weaknesses) and proficiencies (strengths).

Surveys are also flexible, just as interviews are. Most people associate surveys with written questionnaires, but they can be conducted over the telephone. A survey is essentially an interview reduced to writing. Open-ended surveys call for essay responses; closed-ended surveys require respondents to mark a choice like yes or no, agree or disagree, or important or unimportant. Scaled surveys ask respondents to indicate how much they agree or disagree or how they feel about specific issues.

Surveys are cheaper than face-to-face interviews and are useful in collecting much information from scattered locations in a short time. But they do not allow for extensive probing or easy follow-up, as interviews often do. Open-ended surveys yield essay responses that are difficult to analyze; closed-ended surveys yield numerical responses that provide an illusion of certainty. For more on this subject, see Fink and Kosecoff (1985).

Surveys are sufficiently flexible to be used in identifying training, education, or development needs. Surveys on job requirements help identify training needs; surveys on education or experience in preparation for promotion help identify educational needs; surveys on work group skills help identify employee development needs; surveys on intragroup or group feelings help identify organization development needs; and surveys of consumers, stockholders, suppliers, distributors, and the general public help identify nonemployee development needs. Like interviews, surveys can focus on uncovering deficiencies (weaknesses) and proficiencies (strengths).

Observation is not as flexible as surveys or interviews. It is appropriately used in identifying the training and sometimes the educational needs of manual laborers. It is not appropriate for identifying employee or nonemployee development needs, nor for identifying the training/educational needs of white-collar workers.

Observation is simple enough to do. HRD practitioners watch experienced or exemplary performers while they work. Practitioners then record the frequency of work behaviors on specially-designed behavioral observation forms, which resemble interview schedules, except that HRD practitioners use them during observation.

Task analysis is the name for a whole range of methods using structured observation (Fleishman & Quaintance, 1984; Gibbons, 1977). It is appropriate for assessing the training and educational needs of manual workers. In some rare cases it is used to identify the instructional needs of consumers using products. To analyze tasks, HRD practitioners: (1) Identify what tasks are performed in a job; (2) Observe how tasks are performed in terms of work results, methods of carrying out work activities, who or what received the action, and why the task is performed (Goldstein, 1986); and, (3) Rate task importance for instructional purposes. For example, which tasks are most important for successful job performance? Which ones are most difficult to learn? Which ones are changing?

To design a training program, HRD practitioners reassemble and act out the tasks to ensure that the analysis represents a complete description of work activities.

Performances or productivity measures are unobtrusive. Employees are unaware that their work is being scrutinized. HRD practitioners compare actual work group outputs to (1) *work standards,* minimally acceptable levels of scrap, downtime, or product rejects, (2) *objectives,* preestablished targets for producing quantity or quality, or (3) *exemplars,* individuals or groups producing far more or making far fewer errors than other individuals or groups.

Performance or productivity measures help HRD practitioners identify proficient or deficient performance, but do not reveal the cause(s). While differences in group performance are attributable to causes other than the lack of an appropriate mix of skills within the group, this is *one* possible cause. HRD practitioners need only compare the prior training, education, and experience of high performing to low performing groups. Differences *may* reveal employee development needs in low performing groups and unique competencies in high performing groups.

Employee performance appraisals are especially appropriate for identifying individual training and educational needs. After all, an appraisal "is a systematic process designed to assess the extent to which employees are performing jobs effectively" (Milkovich & Glueck, 1985, p. 363). Information from appraisal is used to assess training needs in 8 percent of small organizations and 9.4 percent of large ones (Locker & Teel, 1977).

Appraisals serve a two-fold purpose. First, they furnish employees with feedback on past performance. Second, they provide a starting point for planning future performance improvement. These two purposes may not be balanced equally. Deficiencies stemming from the lack of individual knowledge or skill are appropriately used to identify traditional training needs; proficiencies are traditionally used to plan employee educational activities leading to promotion or other future career moves for individuals.

There are different kinds of employee performance appraisal. Perhaps least useful are so-called trait ratings, which evaluate individual performance on so-called traits like "ambition," "dependability," and "output." When paired up with a scale like "exceeds expectations," "meets expectations," and "falls below expectations," trait ratings are too vague to be very helpful for identifying specific deficiencies or proficiencies.

Behaviorally-anchored rating scales (BARS) are more concrete and are thus more effective in providing supervisory feedback on individual behavior. The approach is based on short narratives describing behaviors that are solicited from knowledgeable supervisors or experienced job incumbents. These incidents are clustered into five to ten performance dimensions, which are then ranked in order from most to least preferable by a second group of knowledgeable people. The resulting behavioral anchors become a foundation for employee appraisals, job descriptions, and training curricula. Research on BARS indicates that the approach does not work well in organizations facing turbulent external environments (Greenlaw & Kohl, 1986).

Management by Objectives (MBO) is also an employee appraisal method. Supervisors and employees meet at the beginning of an appraisal period to negotiate future goals, methods of measuring goal achievement, and times to review progress. This process of negotiating goals begins at the top of the organization when the CEO negotiates goals with subordinates, who in turn negotiate goals with their subordinates, and so on.

MBO is more than just an appraisal method. It is also useful in business planning and in changing a culture from authoritarian to participative (Migliore, 1983). It is forward-looking, because measurable employee performance objectives are established up front. While MBO has been criticized on numerous counts, it is one way to plan for employee training, education, and development.

Assessment centers are not strictly used in collecting information to identify instructional needs. In fact, an assessment center is "a standardized form of employee appraisal that relies on multiple types of evaluation and multiple raters" (Werther & Davis, 1985, p. 300). Individuals are interviewed, tested, and asked to participate in various individual or group exercises. The exercises are based on the activities of a job as identified through job analysis. Performance is assessed by trained evaluators, who are also seasoned managers. The independent assessments of these evaluators are then compiled and fed back to individuals who use them to plan training and education. Theoretically, an assessment center could be used to assess the skills of a work group and thus help identify employee development needs. In the same vein, an assessment center could be used to assess the skills of customers using the products, and thereby identify nonemployee development needs. In more practical terms, assessment centers are commonly used in selection, promotion, and transfer decisions. They have also been used in assessing individual training needs (Beck, 1983).

Group discussions are general enough to be used for almost any purpose. They range from *group interviews,* in which HRD practitioners question job incumbents about work tasks, to *open forums,* in which supervisors openly explore employee development needs with members of a work group. They can also be useful in developing a general training plan by job class and in identifying employee educational needs or nonemployee development needs.

The *critical incident technique* structures experience. A panel of knowledgeable people—supervisors, experienced job incumbents, or exemplary performers—is assembled. They are then asked to reflect on their experience and describe situations which exemplify extremely proficient or deficient performance. These situations are categorized to describe behaviors leading to job success or failure.

Critical incidents are highly flexible. They reveal: (1) *training needs,* if focused on job behaviors; (2) *educational needs,* if focused on career, promotion, or transfer matters; (3) *employee development needs,* if focused on important, recurring problem situations which emerge in work groups; and (4) *nonemployee development needs,* if focused on past company dealings with suppliers, customers, distributors, stockholders, or members of the general public.

However, critical incidents have drawbacks (Johnson, 1983). Their value is heavily dependent on who is chosen to research problems. Slight differences in the instructions given to participants may produce radically different results across panels of experts. Data collection is time-consuming and thus potentially expensive. Finally, critical incidents reveal more about exceptions from norms than about norms themselves.

The delphi procedure, named for the ancient Greek oracle of Apollo, was developed by the Rand Corporation and has been widely applied to research problems. Typically, delphi participants are chosen for their special expertise. Participants remain anonymous and never assemble as a group. Instead, information is solicited from them by written survey. The results are compiled by researchers, are fed back to participants with more questions, and this process continues until participants agree on key issues.

To apply this approach to instructional needs assessment, HRD practitioners begin by clarifying purpose. They decide (for example) to assess recurring training needs of job incumbents, career or educational interests of people facing different central life concerns, career routes through an organization, developmental needs of a work group, or nonemployee development needs. Whatever the purpose, HRD practitioners begin by developing a questionnaire. They can do so by themselves (without the help of others), or they can interview people and use the interview results as the basis for survey questions. The participants should be chosen with care and should be knowledgeable about the subject. HRD practitioners then contact participants, secure their cooperation, explain the delphi procedure to them, finalize questions on the delphi survey, send the survey to participants, receive completed surveys, compile the results, send the results back to participants for comment and critique, and continue this process until participants agree on key responses.

The delphi's chief advantage is that participants are not pressured, as they sometimes are in meetings, to conform to the ideas expressed by articulate or respected group members (Rath & Stoyanoff, 1983). Chief disadvantages include the cost and time needed to carry out a delphi. Moreover, separate delphi studies must be carried out to identify job training needs, career educational needs, and work group developmental needs.

The *nominal group technique* (NGT) takes its name from the way the process itself works. People are assembled in a small group. However, the group exists in name only—that is, *nominally.* In many ways similar to the delphi, NGT has been applied to Strategic Business Planning, HR planning, training needs assessment, and futures research.

NGT may help assess training, education, or development needs—depending on what issues are examined. HRD practitioners (Delbecq, Van de Ven, & Gustafson, 1975): (1) select one or more panels of knowledgeable people; (2) assemble group members in one place; (3) explain NGT to participants; (4) ask participants to generate ideas, identify performance problems, assess needs or prioritize instruction, and record their ideas on slips of paper, one idea to each slip; (5) have participants hand in their slips to the group facilitator (the HRD practitioner); (5) record each idea on a blackboard, flipchart, or overhead transparency so that all group members can see it; (7) encourage discussion following the generation of ideas; and (8) rank ideas by majority vote.

NGT is advantageous for two reasons. First, the silent generation of ideas prevents group pressures for conformity from affecting individuals. Second, ideas stem from participants rather than HRD practitioners or others. NGT is disadvantageous for three reasons. First, voting on ideas forces individuals to set priorities even when they see no need for action. Second, individuals may be subtly pressured to conform to group opinions during discussion or voting. Third, it is difficult to follow up on the many ideas that can be generated in NGT (Martinko & Gepson, 1983), with the result that good ideas are lost and participants are sometimes frustrated.

Other approaches to instructional needs assessment are briefly summarized in Table 3-9.

Selecting data collection methods. What specific data collection method should be used in an instructional needs assessment? Answering this question is not always easy.

TABLE 3-9 APPROACHES TO INSTRUCTIONAL NEEDS ASSESSMENT

Approach	Brief description
Advisory Committee	An advisory committee is a group of employees and/or line supervisors who provide advice to HRD practitioners about instructional needs, designs, and delivery methods.
Attitude Survey	An attitude survey is not conducted solely for the purpose of assessing instructional needs; rather, it is intended to identify problems in the organization, some of which may be corrected through planned instruction.
Exit Interviews	An exit interview is administered to terminating employees to explore reasons for their departure and methods for improving training, education, or development.
Management Requests	Any request for training from a supervisor or manager is a "management request." Quite often, these requests stem from interpretations or perceptions about problems.
Performance Documents	A performance document is a record of individual or group productivity. Daily production, downtime, or scrap rate records are performance documents.
Skill Tests	A skill test is administered to employees in the work setting to identify performance strengths/weaknesses of job incumbents for purposes of identifying training needs. The incumbent performs a job task and is observed by experienced people who assess needs based on the performance.

More than one writer in the HRD field has addressed this subject (for example, Newstrom & Lilyquist, 1979; Steadham, 1980; Ulschak, 1983). In choosing a data collection method, these writers suggest that HRD practitioners consider such issues as these:

1. *employee involvement:* Should the assessment process build learner commitment to meeting needs once they are identified? How important is learner commitment?
2. *time required:* How much time is available to carry out the assessment process? When are results needed?
3. *cost:* What are the expected costs of alternative data collection methods? What financial constraints exist?
4. *relevance:* Will a given data collection method produce useful results in a form capable of being used?
5. *practitioner skills:* How capable are HRD practitioners to use alternative data collection methods? For instance, do practitioners possess the necessary skills to prepare a survey, conduct interviews, or carry out task analyses?
6. *respondent skills:* Do intended respondents possess the necessary skills to provide useful information?
7. *relations between needs assessors and respondents:* How dependent is a data collection method on good relations between the needs assessor and respondents? For example, it may be difficult to schedule interviews or carry out surveys when respondents distrust the motives of the assessor or when trust is lacking in an organization. In these cases, people are reluctant to speak their minds, much less commit themselves to writing, for fear of repercussions.
8. *level of awareness:* How important do prospective learners or clients view a specific need area? When their awareness level is high, data collection efforts are easier, because people readily see benefits in responding.
9. *management preferences:* Do supervisors or managers prefer one data collection method over others? For instance, obtaining needs assessment information from attitude survey results may be difficult if supervisors fear that poor morale in their work groups will reflect on their competence. In any given situation, one data collection method may well be more appropriate than others. See Table 3-10 for an incomplete listing of various data collection methods and their relative strengths and weaknesses.

Involving others in data collection and analysis. HRD practitioners should give careful thought to *who* should be involved in collecting data and determining instructional needs. There are several key issues to consider. First is *the importance of the need area.* If widespread commitment is important, it is worthwhile to take more time to arrive at decisions. The second consideration is *other constraints.* What are the constraints on time, money, and staff? When constraints are tight, then the number of people to involve in data collection or analysis should be reduced to hold down costs.

TABLE 3-10 STRENGTHS AND WEAKNESSES OF SELECTED DATA COLLECTION METHODS

Methods	Incumbent involvement	Management involvement	Time requirement	Cost	Relevant quantifiable data
Advisory Committees	Low	Moderate	Moderate	Low	Low
Assessment Centers (external)	High	Low	High	High	High
Attitude Surveys	Moderate	Low	Moderate	Moderate	Low
Group Discussions	High	Moderate	Moderate	Moderate	Moderate
Employee Interviews (by trainer)	High	Low	High	High	Moderate
Exit Interviews (by personnel dept.)	Low	Low	Low	Low	Low
Management Requests	Low	High	Low	Low	Low
Observations of Behavior (by trainer)	Moderate	Low	High	High	Moderate
Performance Appraisals	Moderate	High	Moderate	Low	High
Performance Documents	Low	Moderate	Low	Low	High
Questionnaire Surveys and Inventories	High	High	Moderate	Moderate	High
Skills Tests	High	Low	High	High	High

Source: Newstrom & Lilyquist, 1979, p. 56. Reprinted with permission from the American Society for Training and Development.

As a general rule, practitioners should involve as many interested parties as possible in data collection and analysis. The reason is that greater involvement in the needs assessment process tends to produce greater commitment to subsequent learning activities carried out to satisfy learning needs. As Nilsson (1987) writes, "this does not mean involving everyone but enough individuals to comprise a meaningful sample. A key objective [should be] to get ownership by those whose support . . . is critical" (p. 135). Participation in identifying instruction needs may well be a key factor in integrating HRD and planning activities (Rothwell & Kazanas, 1987).

IDENTIFYING PRESENT LEARNING NEEDS BY MARKET OR MARKET SEGMENT

Strategic Business Planners have long noted the existence of strengths and weaknesses in organizational performance. Strengths lead to success against competitors. Weaknesses, if not handled carefully, lead to competitive failure. Generally, strategists can choose either to build on strengths or correct weaknesses. *Analysis of corporate strengths and weaknesses* furnishes valuable information about what businesses to enter or leave, what resources to allocate to what activities, and how to manage interactions between business units (Sharplin, 1985). *Analysis of business unit strengths and weaknesses* helps strategists decide what products or services to offer, what resources to concentrate on each product or service, and how to manage relations between functions (Sharplin, 1985). *Analysis of functional strengths and weaknesses* provides insight into what contributions each function should be making to the organization, what resources each should receive, and how to manage the activities of each function (Sharplin, 1985). Sweeping examinations of organizational strengths and weaknesses aid decision-making, and unify subsequent action.

The same principle applies to learning needs assessment. Broad analysis of strengths and weaknesses of job incumbents yields valuable information to plan job training and socialization efforts spanning many related learning experiences. Broad analysis of individual strengths and weaknesses yields valuable information to plan employee education. Analysis of the strengths and weaknesses of each work group yields information to plan employee and organization development. Finally, broad analysis of strengths and weaknesses in an organization's relations with its product or service users, suppliers, distributors, and the general public yields information to plan nonemployee development.

Instructional needs assessment traditionally focuses on specific problems facing identifiable learners at one time. Results of assessment are then used to plan one-shot training courses to correct these problems. That makes training a "fix-it" tool. However, assessment can also be used to focus on the general strengths and weaknesses of job incumbents, individuals, work groups, or external groups. *Sweeping examinations of strengths and weaknesses make the HRD effort a tool for long-term and continuous improvement with a unified direction.*

A *training curriculum* can thus be planned for each job class or job category (Sredl & Rothwell, 1987). Working with others in the organization, HRD practitioners analyze the strengths and weaknesses of each job class or category. From the result of this analysis, an organized but generalized sequence of learning experiences can be designed to orient and socialize newcomers to each job class or category.

An *educational curriculum* can also be planned to prepare individuals for promotion or other career moves, to upgrade skills, and to elicit creative solutions to problems. An educational curriculum stems from the analysis of present strengths/weaknesses of individuals compared to the requirements for success in possible future jobs. Employee education helps individuals achieve their career objectives.

A *developmental curriculum* results from comparison of present work group strengths and weaknesses. It consists of planned learning experiences designed to build a collective pool of group skills adequate for tasks facing a group. A *nonemployee development curriculum* consists of planned learning experiences intended to correct deficiencies or build on proficiencies in relations between an organization and external groups relevant to it.

However, the world changes. Jobs, individuals, work groups, and groups outside organizations do not remain static. Consequently, analysis of past or present strengths and weaknesses is not alone sufficient to plan for meeting future learning needs. Further analysis is necessary. The next chapter deals with this issue. Its focus is anticipating environmental changes which change training, education, and development needs.

ACTIVITY 3-1 Information for Instructional Needs Assessment	
Directions: Use this activity to structure your thinking about instructional needs assessment in an organization. For each question in the left column below, provide an answer in the right column. Continue your answer on additional paper if necessary.	
Questions	Answers
1. Who are the learners served by the HRD Effort? Are some of them particularly important? If so, which ones? Why are they important?	
2. Who are the clients served by the HRD Effort? Are some of them particularly important? If so, which ones? Why are they important?	
3. What is known about present learners served by the HRD Effort? (Describe common characteristics.)	
4. What is known about prospective future learners to be served by the HRD Effort?	
5. What is known about present clients served by the HRD Effort?	
6. What is known about prospective future clients to be served by the HRD Effort?	
7. Are some learners concentrated in some locations more than in others? If so, which locations and what learners?	
8. What are the major work activities of targeted learners?	

ACTIVITY 3-1 Continued	
Questions	Answers
9. What are the major work activities of the clients?	
10. What do other people say about the targeted learners?	
11. What do other people say about the clients?	
12. What problems have historically faced the learners?	
13. What problems have historically faced the clients?	
14. How motivated are learners to learn? What accounts for this level of motivation? Is it likely to change?	
15. How motivated are clients to encourage learners to learn? What accounts for this level of motivation? Is it likely to change?	

ACTIVITY 3-2 Job Groupings

Directions: Use this activity to create job groupings in your organization. For each group listed in the left column, list job titles which fall into the grouping in the organization and the major responsibilities of the jobs. If the organization is small, some groupings may not have corresponding jobs. If that is the case, write "not applicable" in the column. Continue your answer on additional paper if necessary.

Job Grouping*	Job Titles in the Grouping, in the Organization	Major Responsibilities Common to Jobs in this Grouping
Executives		
Senior Managers		
Middle Managers		
First-Line Supervisors		
Sales Personnel		
Professionals		
Administrative Employees		
Clerical Support		
Skilled Production or Service Workers		
Unskilled Production or Service Workers		
Customer Representatives		
Others		

*Based on categories found in Gordon, 1986.

Identifying Present Learning Needs

ACTIVITY 3-3   Classifying Individuals

Directions: Use this activity to classify individuals. List life cycle stages in the left column. List individuals in a work group in the center column. Finally, in the right column, describe the implications of the individuals' life cycle stages on likely learning interests of those individuals. Continue your answer on additional paper if necessary. (A separate analysis for each work group in an organization would be necessary for a comprehensive analysis.)

Life Cycle Stage	Individuals	Implications of Individuals' Life Cycle Stages on Likely Learning Interests of Those Individuals

ACTIVITY 3-4 A Case Study on the Strengths and Weaknesses of the HRD Effort

Directions: Read over the case which follows and answer the questions at the end.

Rhesus is a giant retail corporation, one of the largest in the retail industry.* Rhesus stores sell a wide selection of goods and are found in just about every medium- to large-sized city in the U.S.

However, Rhesus is not particularly an industry leader in its HRD activities. Several years ago, the corporate-level HRD department at Rhesus was completely eliminated in the midst of downsizing. Recently, it was revived. At its helm is Harold Anderson, a five-year company employee destined for higher-level responsibilities at Rhesus. His one-year-old HRD department is staffed with six long-time company employees. (The company will not hire professional HRD practitioners.) Anderson is to set up a department servicing the corporate office only. The corporate office employs several hundred people. Anderson has a free hand, more or less, to establish the purpose of the department and offer planned learning activities of value to Rhesus's corporate employees and managers.

The retail industry is hotly competitive. Like other retailers, Rhesus plans a major program to change its stores. This program will eventually change just about every fixture in most stores—including product display, advertising, inventory control, and even store layout and staffing. Within ten years the plans will be a reality. In the meantime, Rhesus will continue as it always has—a dominant force in the industry.

Questions

1. What should Anderson do to analyze the present strengths and weaknesses of the HRD Effort at Rhesus?
2. What problems will Anderson encounter in his start-up effort? What can he do to avert them? What can he do to minimize their effects?

*A fictitious company.

4

ENVIRONMENTAL SCANNING

Try an experiment. Select several managers at random. Ask them this: "What are the *future* training, education, and development needs of your employees?" If your organization is like most, this question should elicit some interesting responses. A few might sound like these:

- "First explain the difference between training, education, and development."
- "Our work is so diverse that anything will help."
- "I just don't know."
- "They have no needs at all."

After you get the answers, ask another question: "How do you know that your answer is correct?" Managers who feel that their employees do have needs will then recount anecdotes about past problems they have experienced.

The point of this exercise will not be lost on perceptive practitioners. All too often, managers perceive learning needs as stemming from major problems experienced in the past, anecdotal evidence, and specific people or events. Managers are thus like most people: they remember significant more than insignificant events; they color their memory with interpretations; their memories are anecdotal; and they find it easier to think in specific rather than global terms. You can also bet that, when confronting an immediate problem, managers are sure to grasp at any possible solution—including HRD. It is probably not unreasonable to assume that managers, like most adults, are highly motivated to learn about problems which they are presently confronting (Knowles, 1984). They probably identify employee instructional needs on the same short-term basis (Rothwell, 1985b). Since HRD practitioners rarely conduct any systematic needs assessment (Feuer, 1986a), they probably believe the managers.

It is easy to see what happens as a result. Instructional programs are designed on the basis of faulty memory, interpretations of special cases which took place in the past, or problems confronting people at present. Not surprisingly, the short-term focus of these instructional programs—not to mention their weak foundation—is at odds with the necessity to (1) deal with real performance issues, not perceived ones; (2) anticipate future requirements of the organization; and, (3) tap individual motivation to learn by dealing with matters concerning employees. In any case, past or present problems may not stay the same under changing conditions in the future.

Managers, learners, and HRD practitioners alike must therefore look beyond traditional approaches to instructional needs assessment which are too often focused on the past and limited to major problems. They should recognize "a growing need to become more future-oriented in decisionmaking. The only way we can cope with today's rate of change is to try to extend ourselves further into the future. We need to develop a 'blueprint' for the future, rather than to let the future arrive by chance" (Tregoe & Zimmerman, 1985, p. 95). It is thus necessary to (1) anticipate future learning needs and work backward to meet them in the present, and (2) go beyond short-term to long-term perspectives of HRD.

How is this possible? One answer is environmental scanning. But what is it, generally? How is it applied to HRD? What specific methods can be used to carry it out? This chapter addresses these questions.

ENVIRONMENTAL SCANNING: DEFINITION AND DESCRIPTION

Any organization functions in an external environment consisting of two broad components: (1) the general public, consisting of everyone not directly involved in—or affected by—the organization; and (2) external stakeholders, consisting of everyone directly involved in—or affected by—the firm but not working inside it. Strategists determine their organization's environment when they establish business purpose and identify the markets they choose to serve.

However, changes in the external environment over time create unique threats and opportunities for a firm. Managers may approach business as usual and wait for environmental changes to affect the business. This is a *passive strategy*. If external trends are favorable, business conditions improve without requiring any effort to change the organization. Of course, if trends are unfavorable, business conditions will get worse—and bankruptcy may result. As an alternative, managers can try to *anticipate* changes outside their firms and then adjust products or services beforehand so they are attuned to change before it occurs or as it occurs. In other words, managers can spot opportunities for improving the business before they arise, or else head off external threats before they create problems. This is an *active strategy*.

A simple example should illustrate these principles. Think of the funeral business. (It might be somewhat morbid, but the funeral industry *is* involved in business.) When people die, business flourishes; when people continue to live, business is not so good. Now consider: on the whole, the U.S. population is growing older (Dunn, 1985). If long-term demographic trends remain unchanged, the majority of the U.S. population will at least reach retirement age by the year 2020. About 20 percent of the U.S. population is expected to be at retirement age in 1990 (Starling, 1984). While medical science continues to advance and thereby increases average life expectancy, people will eventually die. What, then, are the long-term prospects for the funeral industry? Based solely on population trends, the long-term future looks bright indeed. Barring contrary trends—like a dramatic medical breakthrough that prolongs life—funeral directors can choose a passive strategy and grimly reap the rewards of increasing business.

This general principle holds true for any business: changes taking place externally create unique opportunities and threats. Managers may conduct business as usual and remain helpless pawns of external conditions beyond their control, or they can take active steps to position their organizations so as to anticipate favorable conditions—or avert problems—stemming from environmental change. This ability to anticipate opportunities or threats is the essence of the entrepreneurial spirit (Pinchot, 1985).

Environmental scanning is the name for a structured examination of the future external environment. It "is a systematic procedure for monitoring the world in which the organization receives its sustenance, for the purpose of identifying opportunities and threats" (Shanklin & Ryans, 1985, p. 5). At the heart of modern planning, it is quintessentially anticipatory rather than reactive. Some writers on the subject prefer to break it down into two parts (Glueck & Jauch, 1984): (1) *environmental analysis,* the process by which "strategists monitor the environmental sectors to determine opportunities for and threats to their firms" (p. 95); and (2) *environmental diagnosis,* which "consists of managerial decisions made by assessing the significance of the data (opportunities and threats) of the environmental analysis" (p. 95). Analysis means identifying important sectors of the external environment and systematically monitoring them. It is far easier than diagnosis, which draws conclusions about the *results* of external environmental change. Predicting the effects of change is not as simple as recognizing that change may occur (Gilfillan, 1937; Page, 1982; Utterback, 1979).

THE STATE OF THE ENVIRONMENTAL SCANNING ART IN BUSINESS PLANNING

The environmental scanning art is quite advanced in theory, if not in practice. Jain (1984) conducted a two-year study of corporate environmental scanning practices. Basing his conclusions on interviews with thirty-seven executives in eleven large corporations and a survey of Chief Executives in Fortune 500 firms, he classified scanning into four categories: (1) primitive, (2) ad hoc, (3) reactive, and (4) proactive. These categories represent a continuum through which corporations progress as their size, complexity, and environmental transactions increase. (See Table 4-1 for descriptions of each category.) Jain found that all participating firms in his study with annual sales exceeding $1 billion use a Phase 4, or proactive, approach to scanning. Typically, scanning of this kind is carried out *formally,* both at corporate and business unit levels. In this context, *formally* means in a deliberate, structured, and systematic way.

The focus of environmental scanning varies, depending on the phase in the corporate planning process in which the information is used (see Figure 4-1; see also Kappauf & Falbott, 1982). Each management level faces different environmental demands. As a consequence, "different levels of management experience different needs for environmental analyses. . . ." (Godiwalla, Meinhart, & Warde, 1980, p. 89). Lower-level managers require more information from inside the firm than their top management counterparts. Yet every manager needs to keep an eye on what is happening outside the organization.

Generally, environmental scanning is a highly subjective and creative process. It is likely to become more important as the future grows less like the past and present and as factors external to business firms become more critical to management decision-making. Numerous studies, both theoretical and empirical, have been conducted about environmental scanning. They are worth reviewing, because many of the same principles can be applied to identifying learning needs and delivering instruction. (See Bates, 1985; Diffenbach, 1983; Fahey, King, & Narayanan, 1981; LeBell & Krasner, 1977; Nanus, 1982; Renfro & Morrison, 1983; Roeber, 1973; Sheridan & Monaghan, 1982; Stubbart, 1982; Thomas, 1980; Wilson, 1983).

TABLE 4-1 FOUR PHASES IN THE EVOLUTION OF ENVIRONMENTAL SCANNING

Phase 1	Phase 2	Phase 3	Phase 4
Primitive	Ad hoc	Reactive	Proactive
Face the environment as it appears	Watch out for a likely impact on the environment	Deal with the environment to protect the future	Predict the environment for a desired future
Exposure to information without purpose and effort	No active search Be sensitive to information on specific issues	Unstructured and random effort Less specific information collection	Structured and deliberate effort Specific information collection Preestablished methodology
Scanning without an impetus	Scanning to enhance understanding of a specific event	Scanning to make an appropriate response to markets and competition	Strategic scanning to be on the lookout for competitive advantage

Source: Jain, 1984, p. 118. Reprinted with permission from *Long Range Planning.*

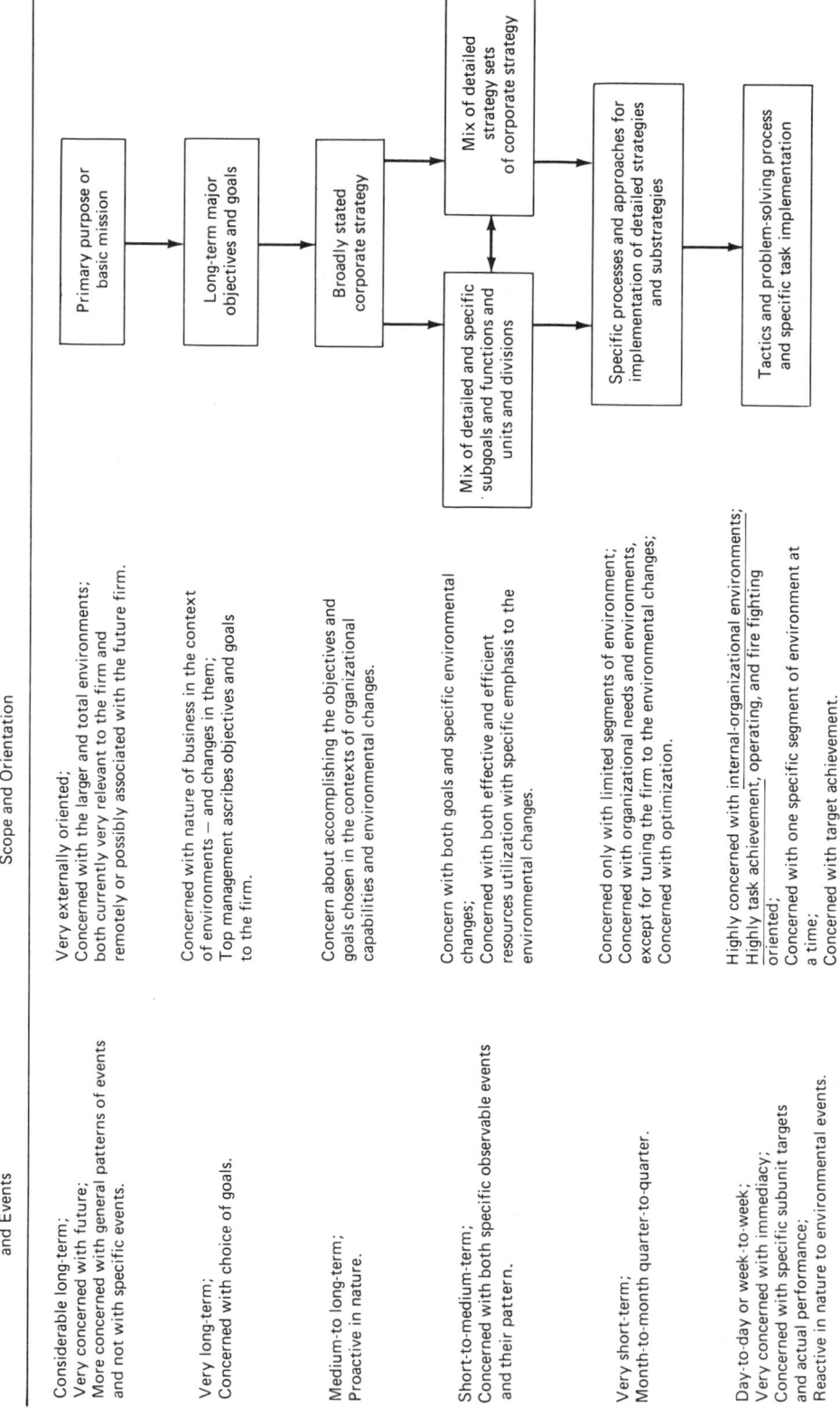

Figure 4-1: The Impact of Total Organizational Environments Upon The Different Phases of Corporate Planning Process. *Source:* Godiwalla, Meinhart and Warde, 1980, p. 90. Reprinted with permission of *Long Range Planning*.

ENVIRONMENTAL SCANNING FOR HRD

Definition

Much like its Strategic Business Planning counterpart, *environmental scanning for HRD is the process of monitoring trends, issues, problems, or events which may create future learning needs as a result of environmental changes.* These changes often require new knowledge and skills among people affected by them. Hence, environmental change may affect the learning needs of the general public, an organization's external stakeholders, members of each work group, individuals preparing for career advancement, or incumbents of each job class.

Importance

The basic purpose of HRD is to prepare people for dealing with the future. In fact, a chief distinction between training, education, and development is *how far into the future* they equip people. Training is traditionally intended for short-term application back on the job (Nadler, 1979); education prepares people for intermediate-term advancement and career movement (Nadler, 1979); and development is long-term and helps individuals become instruments for group or organizational change and learning.

When based on traditional methods of needs assessment, HRD really prepares people only to rectify past performance deficiencies. Traditional needs assessment methods "rely heavily on the examination of past deficiencies or past behaviors as a basis for planning instruction intended to equip learners for meeting future conditions" (Rothwell, 1984d, p. 19). But conditions change, rendering instruction superfluous. Experience, a product of the past, is appropriate for improving future performance *only* when the future will be like the past.

Of course, there *are* situations and problems—and no doubt there always will be some—when the past *is* the best foundation for instruction. That is particularly true in industries facing relatively stable external environments. Heavily regulated industries and government agencies, for instance, often exist in such environments. In short, environments vary widely in how dynamic they are (Emery & Trist, 1965; Katz & Kahn, 1978).

It is increasingly inappropriate to base instruction solely on past problems or on solutions worked out in the past when the environment is unstable or is becoming more unstable. What is needed is a way to *anticipate* future learning needs.

ENVIRONMENTAL SCANNING AND CURRICULUM NEEDS ASSESSMENT

A curriculum is a *long-term instructional plan.* It is a concrete representation of what the future *should* be like. Comprehensive needs assessment identifies long-term, holistic learning needs of various groups, based on differences between actual and desired knowledge and skill in the past and present. When comprehensive needs assessment results are compared to environmental scanning results, future long-term learning needs can be identified. By addressing these needs, managers and employees may avert problems before they arise. They may also pinpoint unique opportunities for improving the performance of job incumbents, achieving individual career objectives, changing the skills represented in a work group consistent with future demands facing the group, improving relations between an organization and external groups, or changing cultural norms of an organization.

STEPS IN ENVIRONMENTAL SCANNING FOR HRD

Environmental scanning for HRD comprises several distinct steps. HRD practitioners and operating managers:

1. classify the external environment into sectors,
2. decide on a time horizon appropriate for their scanning efforts,
3. examine environmental sectors for expected changes over the time horizon they have chosen,
4. try to infer the effects of environmental changes on (a) the general public; (b) external stakeholders; (c) departments or work groups in the organization; (d) individuals; and (e) job requirements,
5. identify future learning needs of (a) the general public; (b) external stakeholders; (c) departments or work groups; (d) individuals; and (e) job requirements, and
6. reassess learning needs by market segment from a future orientation.

Let's consider each step.

Classifying the External Environment

Analysis is the first step in environmental scanning for HRD. It is a process of breaking down the external environment into "sectors" for analysis. *The economic sector* has to do with local, national, and international economic conditions. *The political sector* has to do with government operations at all levels. *The technological sector* has to do with machines, tools, work methods, and other applications of knowledge. *The social sector* has to do with beliefs, attitudes, and values. *The market sector* has to do with the consumers to whom the company sells its goods or provides services and competing firms marketing similar products or services. *The geographic sector* has to do with the movement of key consumers, suppliers, or distributors. *The supplier sector* has to do with firms which supply raw materials or provide essential services. *The distributor sector* has to do with wholesale/retail outlets which sell the organization's products or through which its services are offered to consumers. Strategists may also wish to analyze other sectors focused on the U.S. population, the industry, or the HRD field. Figure 4-2 illustrates the relationship between external environmental sectors and the organization.

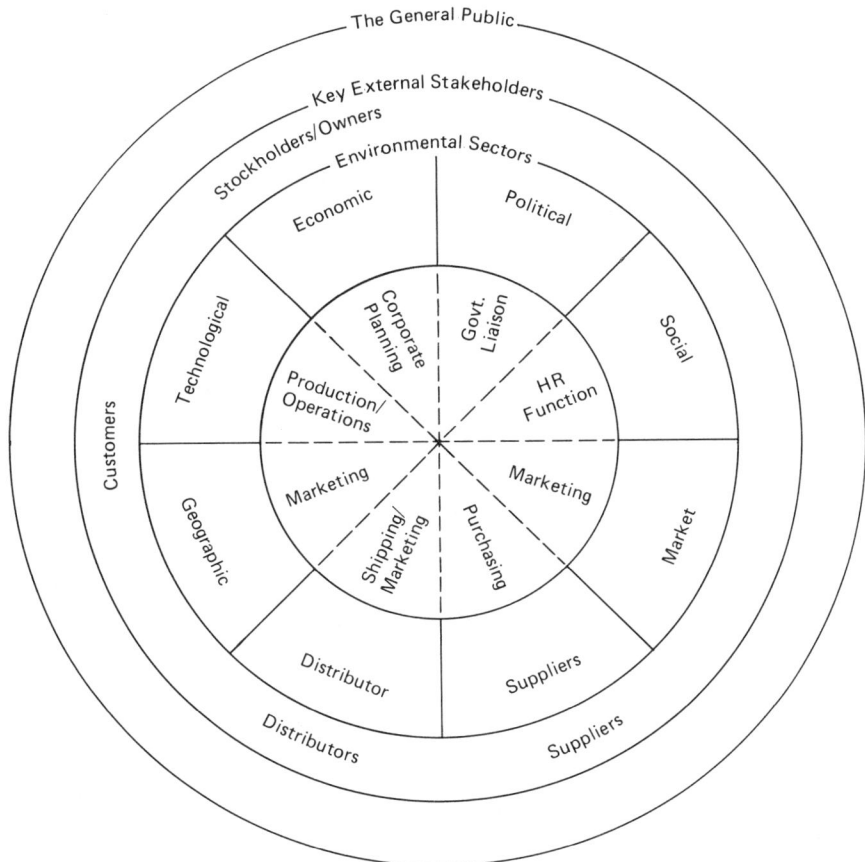

Figure 4-2: Relationships Between Environmental Sectors and the Organization

Deciding on a Time Horizon

How far into the future should the environment be scanned? The second step in the environmental scanning process thus addresses *time horizon,* which is the time encompassed by a plan.

Clarifying time horizon is important for several reasons. First, the accuracy of predictions declines over time. When strategic thinkers try to peer far into the future, they are less accurate in predicting problems and identifying trends or issues. Second, it is easier to set goals when the time period is clear. Managers can then envision where they want to be at a future point and step backward to examine what has to be accomplished in the meantime and how environmental conditions are likely to affect them (See Figure 4-3). Third, when the time horizon is distant, there is less need to pay attention to details; when the horizon is close, there is more need to consider details (Ryans & Shanklin, 1985).

Top corporate managers should generally adopt the longest time perspective. They should be most strategic in their orientation, and focus on the whole organization and environment rather than on specific business functions or work groups.

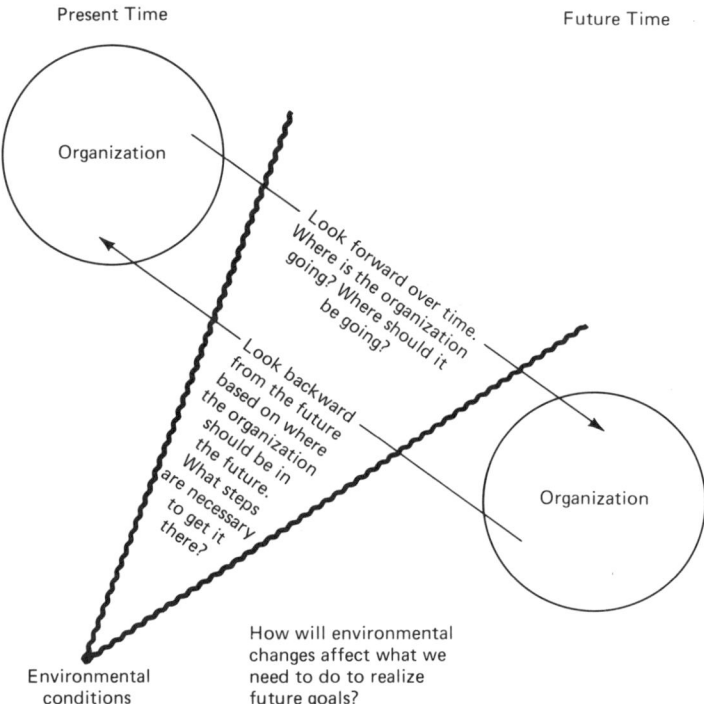

Figure 4-3: Visioning for the Future

Lower-level managers should adopt shorter time perspectives in keeping with their responsibility for achieving shorter-term results. They should focus on functions, work groups, individuals, and job requirements.

Although most writers on Strategic Business Planning usually stress the top management perspective, the basic principles of environmental scanning can be applied at any level—including front-line employees (Leemhuis & Eckblad, 1985). These principles apply over any time horizon—from thirty years to overnight. Doubtless many supervisors, tired of fighting fires, can see the value of applying forethought and of training even nonsupervisors to apply it. In many respects, environmental scanning is just a fancy name for applying forethought *systematically* and *deliberately.*

There is no absolutely right or wrong time horizon. It depends on who is scanning and for what reasons. Top managers need environmental scanning results to conduct corporate or business-level planning. Lower-level managers need scanning results to help them anticipate the future consequences of their present actions as well as trends, issues, or events which may affect goal achievement for their departments or work groups.

Examining Environmental Sectors

Strategists brainstorm about future trends or events once they decide what environmental sectors to examine and over what time horizon. At this point, they should consider what issues or trends will become more important over time. Let's briefly discuss the economic, political, technological, social, market, geographic, supplier, and distributor sectors. Not every organization needs to be concerned about every sector. Appropriate sectors to examine depend on the organization's purpose.

The economic sector. For the most part, businesses deal in free markets. Fluctuations in the business cycle affect sales of company products, the number of people hired or laid off, the willingness of executives to invest in new equipment, and the availability of funds for expansion.

However, changes in economic climate are not felt evenly across all industries. Some—like government—are relatively immune from economic influence. Others are dramatically affected by shifts in interest rates or currency values.

Consider: (1) What are the prospects for recession, depression, recovery, or prosperity over a given time? (2) What is the inflation or deflation rate expected to be? (3) How much will banks and other thrift institutions charge for funds necessary for business expansion and for the purchase of new, updated equipment? (4) Will the U.S. dollar remain stable against foreign currencies? and (5) How much are consumers expected to spend over a given time? What is the aggregate load of consumer debt?

Changes in any of these areas vary in their influence on different firms—and even on work groups or job categories within those firms. In addition, economic conditions affect the demand for (or supply of) labor. Consider: What will the economy probably do over a given period? What trends, events, or issues are likely to become important to a firm? Why are they likely to be important?

Researchers differ in their views about the importance of economic trends or events. Based on an extensive research project of 358 cases over a forty-five-year period, Glueck (1980) found that economic conditions are always a major area of concern to Strategic Business Planners, regardless of industry or stage in the business cycle. Other researchers have not reached the same conclusions. For instance, Wall (1974) found that economic conditions are least important in scanning.

Writers in the HRD field have pinpointed several economic trends which they believe will become more important in the future. There will probably be increasing: (1) profit pressure in the private sector and budget pressure in public and nonprofit sectors; (2) scarcity of all resources; (3) cost of college resulting in a declining percent of the entering work force that will be college-educated; (4) travel costs; (5) population; (6) need for business/industry to operate in an international environment; and (7) average age of people in the work force (*Models for Excellence,* 1983, p. 27. Reprinted with permission). Which, if any, of these trends—or others—will probably become more important in your firm over time? Why are they likely to be important? How are they going to create pressure for change on each work group, in career patterns, and in job requirements?

The political sector. The political sector encompasses the actions of governments at all levels. "For most businesses," notes Steiner, Miner, and Gray (1982), "the government, particularly the federal government, is one of the most significant influences on operations—growth, pricing, production, product quality, competition, wages, profits, investments, markets, interest ratings and capital" (p. 68). Nor is this influence one-way. Business influences the elections and voting patterns of legislators and the actions of other elected officials through sophisticated lobbying efforts.

Think for a moment about the pervasive influence of government on business in each of the following areas:

- government regulation/deregulation of industry
- court decisions
- government in competition with business
- government regulation of safety, environmental pollution, products, and services
- government purchases of goods and services
- tax incentives
- actions of the Federal Reserve Board
- actions of the Securities and Exchange Commission
- platforms of political parties
- investment incentives
- antitrust law and enforcement policies
- federal, state, county and municipal government laws/pending legislation
- tariffs
- trade policy

How many areas will probably be important to one firm over the next few years and the next decade? What other trends in government may affect a firm? How are these trends likely to exert pressure for change in relations with groups outside the firm, on work groups inside the firm, on individuals aspiring to career moves, and on job requirements at each level and in different categories?

Research in the HRD field has pinpointed at least two trends of importance in this area. There will be increased (1) need for business/industry to operate in an international environment, and (2) importance of energy conservation (*Models for Excellence,* 1983, p. 27). To these we can add several more. There will be increasing likelihood that white-collar occupations like accounting, law, and nursing will face mandatory, regulated hours of continuing education as a condition for relicensing at the state level (Knowles, 1986). Similarly, there will be more frequent partnerships between government, business, and educational institutions in economic development—and specifically, HRD. "HRD will contend with increased government influence" (*HRD Tomorrow,* 1984, p. 58). In-house HRD may be subject to future government regulations. Practitioners should already take care to comply with Equal Employment Opportunity and Occupational Safety and Health requirements (Mansfield, 1987). How many of these trends are likely to exert pressure for change in your firm in the future? Why do you think so?

The technological sector. Technology means equipment used in production or service delivery and with the know-how to use it. The introduction of new machinery or tools greatly increases production efficiency, making it less costly to manufacture goods or deliver services. But know-how is by far the most important component of technology. It is embodied in human skills, plant layout and design, computer software, and procedures used in laboratories (Rowe, Mason, & Dickel, 1986, p. 116).

Technology is not equally important to all organizations. In competitive, high technology firms—IBM is a good example—it can be crucial to success. In labor intensive organizations such as government agencies, machine or tool-related technology is not as important as in other settings.

Consider: (1) *State-of-the-art developments* in new equipment and new work methods; (2) *Research and development* efforts and their results; (3) *New markets created by new products* derived through research and development; (4) *New applications of existing technology;* and (5) *The changes required for technological innovation to be applied* in the firm and/or by consumers using new products. How much are these and other technological issues likely to affect specific work groups in a firm, individuals seeking advancement, and job requirements in different job categories? *Why* are these issues likely to be important? How are they likely to affect learning needs?

Research in HRD has pinpointed several technological trends worth thinking about. In the future, there will probably be (*Models for Excellence,* 1983, p. 27): (1) increased accessibility of computer technology; (2) faster/cheaper real time communication, like teleconferencing and electronic mail; (3) more interactive video usable for large-scale learning applications; (4) increased use of cable TV for a broad range of specialized programming; (5) increased visibility and availability of production technology like robotics and office automation; (6) increased use of personal computers; (7) more importance placed on technical and computer competencies; (8) more areas to be studied as a result of technological advances; (9) more knowledge available about human learning and motivation; and (10) more technologies which will facilitate learning. To these, more can be added (*HRD Tomorrow,* 1984, p. 62, reprinted with permission):

- Some jobs requiring no specialized skills will disappear as their functions are performed by automation.
- Some jobs requiring only moderately specialized skills will disappear with the advent of user-friendly software requiring less technical knowledge from the user.
- Pressure will increase on people to become computer literate. Computers in the work place will affect many white-collar workers.
- The development of expert knowledge systems using artificial intelligence will change jobs and improve judgement and intuition.
- Increasing use of computers will cause some people to get too much information to handle or use.
- Automated office systems will alter traditional job duties and relationships drastically. More people will become "telecommuters."

Ask yourself: How many of these trends will be important to your firm in the future? How many will create different learning needs for various work groups, for individuals preparing for career advancement, and for incumbents in different job categories?

The social sector. The social sector encompasses the values, beliefs, and attitudes of (1) *the general public,* about all businesses, the industry of which the organization is part, and the organization itself; (2) *external stakeholders,* about the organization, its management, and its employees; and (3) *employees and managers* of the organization. Clearly, attitudes and expectations can influence sales of a firm's products or services and management practices. To cite one example: employee unionization is, in part, a result of attitudes about company management (Brett, 1980).

Consider future trends relative to

- *corporate social responsibility:* What does the public expect from business? How are attitudes changing about the role expected from business in society and the industry of which one organization is part?
- *company responsibility to consumers:* What do customers expect?
- *company responsibility to investors/stockholders:* What do investors or stockholders expect?
- *work:* What do people think about work? How much is work considered an economic necessity? An outlet for creative expression?
- *leisure:* How do people play? How do they find recreation?
- *marriage:* How do people view marriage? When do people marry? Remarry? Divorce? What prompts marriage? What prompts divorce?
- *family life:* How many children are couples having? When?
- *women working:* How many women are working? How many are heading single-parent families?
- *attitudes about government, companies, politics, the environment, regulations, discrimination in employment, drug abuse, and many more issues:* What do people think about these issues? How does it affect their behavior in the marketplace? In the workplace?

Which of these trends will probably become more important to one firm over time, to specific work groups, to individuals preparing for advancement, and to different job categories? How many other trends will also be important?

Research in HRD has identified several important social trends. There is likely to be more instances of multiple and changed careers, more dual-career families, and greater concern for physical, emotional, and spiritual well-being (*Models for Excellence,* 1983, p. 27). There will be other important future trends: First, the organization's responsibility for an employee's physical, emotional, and psychological well-being will be increasingly emphasized. Second, employees will demand more satisfaction from job and career. Third, people will live longer, the work force will grow older, the typical retirement age will increase, the pool of entry-level workers will shrink, and a new baby boom may occur. Fourth, pregnancy will be delayed more often as the number of women in the work force increases and the number of dual-career couples will increase. Fifth, the proportion of minorities, especially Hispanics, will increase in the U.S. population and work force. Higher numbers of new immigrants will enter the U.S. Sixth, illiteracy will become more pervasive among some groups at the same time that formal education will increase among other groups in the workplace. Lack of adequate preparation for work will be evident. Seventh, job skills will become obsolete rapidly, as manufacturing declines and information and service jobs increase. The workplace will become robotized and automated. Eighth, while the proportion of white-collar jobs increases, middle management positions will decrease. Ninth, mid-life job or career transitions will be more common, as will incidents of burnout. Tenth, more scientists will be employed by the military. Eleventh, businesses will continue to migrate to certain geographic areas (*HRD Tomorrow*, 1984, pp. 64–65). Which trends do you think will become more important to your firm, to specific groups within your firm, to individuals seeking advancement, and to successful performance in different jobs? What learning needs will these trends create? Which trends will create the most important learning needs?

The market sector. The market sector overlaps with the social sector. It encompasses customers and competitors. Most managers appreciate the value of (1) finding out about the people who purchase company products or services, because this information proves useful in designing products and marketing them; (2) identifying key competitors in the current business or in a different business they contemplate entering; (3) gathering information about a competitor's entry to (or exit from) a given market or changes in a competitor's products, advertising methods, or pricing methods; and (4) beating competitors by gaining special relationships with key suppliers, consumer groups, or shippers. Research by Wall (1974), Aguilar (1967), and Keegan (1974) indicates that competitive analysis may be the single most important ingredient in successful environmental scanning.

Key issues or trends to consider in this sector may include (Porter, 1980): (1) *Customer loyalty:* How loyal are customers to a given brand name? (2) *Costs:* What are the relative costs of two or more firms in producing goods/services, distributing, and advertising? What changes are likely? (3) *Strategies:* What are the present strategies of competitors? How are competitors likely to react to increased competition, to entry into new markets, and to changes in production, pricing, distribution, and promotion? (4) *Experience:* Who knows the industry better? Who has the known talent? and (5) *Financial matters:* What is the financial status of key competitors? How much evidence is there that their market share can be eroded?

How important are these issues likely to become for your firm in the future? What learning needs will these trends create in each company work group, for individuals seeking career advancement, and for successful performance in each job?

The geographic sector. This sector of the environment has to do with the present geographical placement and future movements of consumers, competitors, suppliers, and distributors. There is at least one good reason why this sector is worth considering: a firm geographically closer to consumers, suppliers, and distributors is likely to enjoy a significant advantage over competitors in shipping and transportation costs.

In scanning this sector, consider: (1) Are suppliers pulling up stakes to move? If so, where? Are any special trends evident? If so, what are they? (2) Where are distributors heading? Are wholesale and retail outlets opening in some areas faster than others? Why? (3) Are competitors moving to new locations? Are they looking for sites abroad, where labor is often substantially cheaper than in the U.S., or are they opening in domestic population sites of concentrated growth? Are any special trends evident? If so, what are they? and (4) Where are consumers heading? What markets in the U.S. and abroad have the highest concentration of consumers to whom a firm is marketing its products or services? Are changes evident? Are they expected? Which trends may become important in the future for one firm? Why do you think so? What new learning needs will these trends create for people in the organization?

The supplier sector. This sector encompasses organizations which provide raw materials. Clearly, the higher the cost of supplies, the higher the cost of finished goods. Strategists should thus be concerned about any changes in the availability of supplies. They should consider several questions. First, what trends are evident in the availability of supplies? How many companies produce subassembliers, mine needed ores, or manufacture essential machines? Second, what trends are evident in the cost of supplies? Will suppliers face new costs of production as a result of increased regulation and declining availability of *their* supplies? Third, what trends are evident in the firm's relations with its suppliers? Fourth, what companies produce *key* supplies that are absolutely critical to production? What is their status? Of these trends, which ones may be most significant to one firm in the future? How might they create new learning needs? What makes you think so? Are other trends in this sector worth watching? If so, why are they important?

The distribution sector. This sector focuses on firms that relay products to ultimate users. For instance, wholesale and retail stores are distributors for manufacturers. Strategists in any firm should ask themselves several questions about distributors. First, what are the key firms distributing their products or delivering their services? What firms are likely to be more important in the future? Second, what trends are evident at the wholesale or retail level? Third, what trends are generally evident in a firm's relations with its distributors? Fourth, what are the chances that a key distributor is open to takeover by others? Are any of them hostile? Are substitute distributors available? What trends do you believe will be important in this environmental sector for one firm in the future? Why do you think so? How might these trends create new learning needs for work groups in your firm, for individuals seeking career advancement, and for performance requirements for different job categories?

Inferring Effects of Environmental Changes

What will happen as a result of changes in the external environment? This question is very difficult to answer. There are at least two reasons why. First, any trend can exert multiple influences. Second, managers can choose to act in anticipation of an environmental change or can choose to do nothing. About the best that can be hoped for is some educated guesswork about the likely effects of external changes (Anthony, 1985).

Most discussions of environmental scanning usually focus on the effects of external trends on an entire organization. The perspective is appropriate to top management. Little or no attempt is made to deal with the influence of trends on relations with external groups, different work groups, skill requirements in work groups within the firm, job skills needed in different job categories, or the special preparations necessary for individuals seeking career advancement in a changing environment.

The trouble with this viewpoint is that it tends to limit strategic, entrepreneurial thinking to a handful of people at the top. As a consequence:

> The grand vision presented by corporate planners rarely stays long with midlevel managers. They think tomorrow's big picture touches neither their day-to-day work nor their current personal concerns. They sit through a quarterly corporate prognosis assuming action is top management's domain (Leemhuis & Eckblad, 1985, p. 62).

Yet neither strategic thinking nor action should be limited to top managers. Others need to think and act strategically, too.

The effects of environmental change are not limited solely to the organizational-environmental interface. Each work group, each job category, and each individual is affected by external change, even though change is not felt in the same ways by all. A key distinction between lower-level managers and top managers is that the former group is more heavily affected by what is happening *inside* the firm. In some important respects, that makes their jobs more—not less—challenging than their top management counterparts. They have to scan *two* environments: (1) *outside the organization*, particularly sectors most pertinent to activities of their work units or departments, and (2) *inside the organization but outside the departments they head*, particularly Strategic Business Plans imposed from the top and internal policies or procedures affecting their operations. Consider Figure 4-4, which illustrates these two external environments.

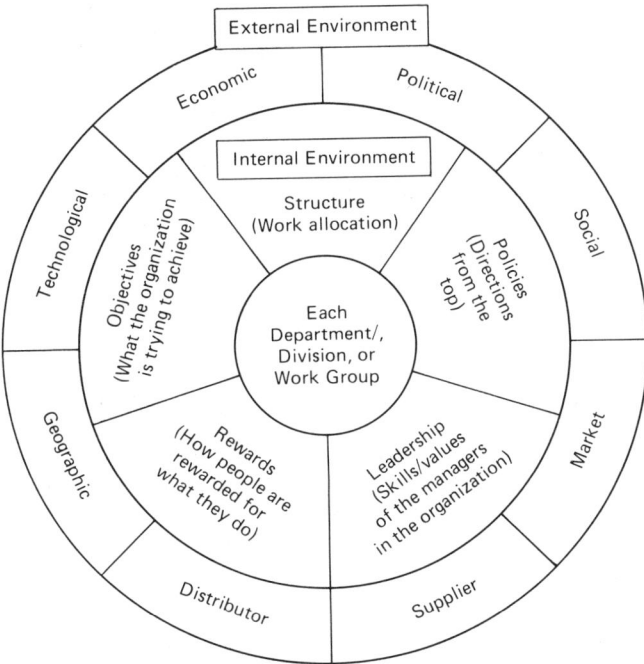

Figure 4-4: The Environmental Context of any Department, Division, or Work Group Inside the Organization

Steps in Environmental Scanning for HRD

Who occupies a better position to assess the effects of external environmental change on activities in one part of the firm than managers and employees working in that part? Top managers have a broad perspective, important in its way but not necessarily helpful for nitty-gritty operations.

Numerous forecasting methods are often suggested for predicting the effects of external trends (a few are summarized in Table 4-2). But training people to think strategically may be more useful than forecasting. Training helps people spot and an-

TABLE 4-2 AN OVERVIEW OF FORECASTING METHODS

To look at (sector)	Use this forecasting method	Brief description
Economic	Economic Forecasting (Econometrics)	• Select variables for consideration (e.g., general economic conditions, consumer prices, wage rates, etc.) • The basis of the model is the assumption that the future is a continuation of the past. • Compare multiple variables over time.
Political	Sociopolitical Forecasting (Scenario Analysis)	• Describe social/political conditions. • Identify the key (critical) indicators. • Identify reasons for changes (sudden catastrophes, crises). • Develop narrative(s)—scenarios—of what will be happening at a future time.
Social	Scenario Analysis	Same as Political
Market	Trend Analysis	• Project past trends into the future on a graph, with one axis showing sales (for example) and the other a time period. Use rate of growth over past time periods as an indicator of growth in the future.
Supplier/Distributor	Same as Market	Same as Market
Geographic	Delphi Procedure	• Identify group of experts. • Prepare list of questions for use on a written questionnaire. • Circulate questionnaire to experts. • Compile expert responses; ask for rating/elaboration. • Repeat until expert opinion converges.
Technological	Brainstorming	• Gather together a group of knowledgeable people. • Ask group members to identify technological developments which are possible/are occurring. • Ask group members to describe how long those developments will require before impacts are felt. • Ask group members to describe how to prepare for (or use) technological advances.

ticipate threats and opportunities to goal achievement, whether originating inside or outside the firm. A good place to start is with environmental scanning, as it can be applied to managing departments, careers, and job activities. Of course, the HRD Effort can—and should—play a central role in this training. At the same time, of course, the HRD Effort is subject to (1) external environmental trends, particularly those having to do with HRD practices; and (2) policies, procedures, and other constraints on HRD inside the organization.

If managers resist planned learning activities and do not see the need for anticipatory thinking, it may take much preparation simply to get them to feel the need. Once managers do feel the need for anticipatory thinking, how do HRD practitioners design instruction on scanning? One approach: (1) introduce everyone in the firm to the basic principles of scanning; (2) provide them with structured opportunities to identify trends pertinent to them and project likely effects of those trends in the future; and (3) afford them an opportunity to establish action plans for anticipating those trends.

Many may object that training on environmental scanning is not necessary, because it is just so much idle crystal-ball gazing. But the following arguments may be convincing:

- The more information collected and applied in strategic decisionmaking, the more likely performance is to be effective (Grinyer & Norburn, 1975).
- As managers increase their awareness of the environment and its effects, their performance improves (Wolfe, 1976).
- The greater the differences in perceptions about the environment among managers, the better organizational performance is likely to be. Conflict breeds creative solutions to problems (Bourgeois, 1978, cited in Glueck & Jauch, 1984).
- A firm's success is highly correlated with an appropriate amount of environmental scanning, given the nature of the environment in which the firm is—or will be—operating (Miller & Friesen, 1977).

It may be risky to extend these assumptions to an HRD Effort. However, there is an intuitive appeal to unlocking the creativity of individual employees and encouraging them to *anticipate,* rather than just *react to,* future threats and opportunities. Training in environmental scanning is one step in this direction.

Identifying Future Learning Needs

The fifth step in environmental scanning for HRD is to anticipate future learning needs based on present trends. Let's begin with a broad overview of the traditional approach to needs assessment and then switch to an overview of future-oriented needs assessment. We'll then show how future-oriented needs assessment can be applied to *external groups* like the general public, consumers, suppliers, and distributors, and *internal groups* like people in work units, individuals seeking advancement, and job categories.

The traditional approach to instructional needs assessment is based on answering four basic questions. First, *what should be?* This question focuses on *criteria*—desired present knowledge or skills. Second, *what is?* This question focuses on *condition*—present knowledge or actual performance. Third, *what are the differences between the actual and the desirable?* This question is usually intended to pinpoint *deficiencies* (poor performance), but it is also capable of pinpointing *proficiencies* (exceptional performance). Fourth and finally, *how much are these differences attributable to lack of knowledge/skills or to some other cause?* This question separates issues that can appropriately be addressed by HRD from those that cannot. These four questions are appropriate to ask when action will be taken to deal with past or present performance strengths and/or weaknesses in a stable environment. They are not appropriate by themselves when the environment is unstable, because changing environmental conditions may produce new and different threats to performance and opportunities for improving it.

Future-oriented instructional needs assessment is a modification of the traditional approach. HRD practitioners and line managers pose five questions that differ from the four questions on which traditional needs assessment is based. First, *what should be in the future?* This focuses on a vision of the future and on desired *future criteria*. What should be the future relationship between the corporation and the general public or key external stakeholders? What skills have to be available in the work group to meet future responsibilities? What do people have to be able to do to prepare for career advancement and future job requirements? Second, *what is the present status?* This question focuses on present conditions. Third, *what will probably be the differences between future criteria and present conditions?* The answer to this question underscores a planning gap between present and future *and* between actual and desired conditions. Fourth, *how much will these differences be attributable to lack of knowledge or skill?* This question helps sort out instructional from noninstructional needs. Fifth and finally, *what learning experiences are necessary to meet future knowledge and skill requirements?* If discrepancies between present and future needs are not attributable to lack of knowledge or skills, then noninstructional strategies will have to be used to deal with them. These strategies include changes in job design, work methods, and organizational structure.

How is future-oriented needs assessment applied? Consider some specific applications.

The general public and its future learning needs. One way to anticipate future problems and opportunities is to devote attention to the future learning needs of the general public. What does the public need to know about the corporation in the future so that relations will be good? If HRD practitioners choose to address this area, they have to add sectors to their analysis during environmental scanning. More specifically, they should consider trends in:

1. *public and/or private education at all levels:* What are the prospects that young people in elementary and secondary school will receive adequate training in basic skills? How adequate are programs in community colleges, universities, and highly specialized technical schools for meeting future labor requirements of a firm?

2. *economic development:* What prospects exist for effective vocational programs for improving skills of the economically disadvantaged and the technologically displaced? Will government retraining funds be available? What requirements have to be met to qualify for them?
3. *attitudes about the industry, firm, or business in general:* How does the public feel about business, about an industry, about one firm? Are there special interest groups opposed to a firm's interests? Are these groups likely to gain popular support and capture media attention?

It can be very worthwhile for a firm to sponsor future-oriented instruction as a means to gain long-term public support or avert long-term public disapproval for its products or services. Some firms do this by adopting schools, for example, and contributing funds and management talent to their improvement. Other firms establish closer ties with colleges and provide them with funds, talent, access to equipment and other facilities. Still other firms champion economic development in communities in which their facilities are located. They establish ties with public sector economic developers and work toward improving the quality of life in the community. Some firms sponsor programs for training the disadvantaged or retraining those displaced by changes in family structure, automation, or plant shutdowns.

How do HRD practitioners know whether all this is necessary? They should consider:

1. *What is the present status of a firm relative to the general public?* What do members of the public know about a firm? How does this knowledge—or lack of it—affect behavior?
2. *What should be in the future?* What should the public know about a corporation and its products or services?
3. *What differences are likely to develop over time between what is and what should be?*
4. *How much will these differences be attributable to knowledge about a firm among members of the general public?* When the public lacks knowledge about the firm, this is a future threat—and a learning need. On the other hand, public awareness of a firm can be a future opportunity—and an indication of unique talent or competency.
5. *What instructional events sponsored by the firm can help avert likely threats and seize future opportunities?* Efforts of this kind increase what representative members of the general public know about a firm, its products, services, and operational requirements.

Key external stakeholders and their future learning needs. Increasingly, HRD activities are directed not just to company employees but also to investors, suppliers, distributors, and customers. Customer training is likely to become more important in the future. As Zemke (1984c) observes, "the number of organizations reporting budgeted training and development funds for customer education programs has increased two-and-a-half times since 1982. . . ." (p. 27).

Why bother meeting future learning needs of key external stakeholders? Consider: the more that investors, suppliers, distributors, and customers know about a firm, the more likely they are to act in ways beneficial to it. There are other benefits as well: HRD activities directed to external groups are likely to be run on a profit basis which can, in turn, fund HRD activities directed to company employees.

It is easy to point to examples of externally-directed HRD activities. Hospitals run wellness programs to help potential clients avert illness. Accounting firms offer training to clients on how to handle the accounting function. These firms meet the needs of external groups while marketing their sevices through instruction. Computer companies are just now discovering what most everybody has long suspected: lack of customer knowledge about computers is a major barrier to computer sales. The same principle applies to all high technology firms. Auto and heavy implement manufacturers have long offered training to the sales and service staffs of dealers. To sell and service a product, dealers must know it inside and out. Goverment agencies sometimes train contractors and vendors about government requirements and expectations. In each case, HRD is anticipatory, geared to meeting the learning needs of customers and other external groups *before they arise.* If a firm is introducing new products or services, future-oriented instruction may be necessary to avert major problems later on—particularly if these new products/services will *change* management's expectations about what suppliers or distributors should do to meet the firm's needs. What should consumers know to use the product? Consider:

1. *What is?* Do customers now get maximum benefit from a firm's products or services? Are suppliers and distributors interacting with the firm as efficiently as possible?
2. *What should be in the future?* What behavior is desired from suppliers, distributors, or customers? In other words, what should they be doing? How can customer knowledge about product use be improved, for example?
3. *What gaps will probably exist between what is at present and what should be in the future?* Given present trends, what is likely to happen over time?
4. *How much will these gaps be attributable to the knowledge or skills of external groups?* Lack of knowledge is a learning need, a threat; extensive knowledge about the firm's products/services among consumers or other groups is a possible future opportunity.
5. *What planned learning activities offered between present and future can help avert potential threats to a firm's sales and other activities?* What planned learning activities can help a firm seize new opportunities by offering new, potentially profitable services to the firm's suppliers, distributors, and customers, and improve efficient operations between members of external groups and the firm?

It is easy to see that major changes of any kind create needs among customers, suppliers, and distributors. As new products or services are offered, managers should consider and plan to act on the future impact of them on groups outside the firm. HRD is one tool that can help.

The organization and its future learning needs. An external trend may create the need for changes in the collective skills needed by a work group to meet its responsibilities to the firm. Organized learning efforts at the work group level often take a long time to succeed, because group norms and culture militate against change. Instruction alone is rarely adequate to change culture (Knowles, 1984). However, planned learning activities can ensure that the work group has the right skills available to carry out its duties.

To apply future-oriented instructional needs assessment to employee development needs at the work group level, HRD practitioners and managers should:

1. *Develop a classification scheme by which to analyze the firm.* (The same one devised during traditional needs assessment may be used.) Break the firm down into work groups.
2. *Analyze present conditions and consider how they may change over time.* What skills are now available in each group? How will the group gradually change over time? What are the present duties of the work group?
3. *Clarify implications of Strategic Business Plans on each work group.* What should each group do in the future? What skills will be needed?
4. *Identify gaps between present and desired future conditions.* What should each work group be able to do in the future? What mix of skills among group members is necessary?
5. *Assess how much these gaps will be attributable to the collective knowledge and skills in each work group.* If the work group is already well-positioned to carry out future responsibilities, it is blessed with an opportunity. If the group lacks adequate skills to meet future demands, it faces a future threat.
6. *Consider what instructional efforts sponsored for work groups can help avert future threats or seize future opportunities.* What planned learning activities can develop the work group so that skills required in the future will be available when needed?

The Individual and Future Learning Needs. The focus of most planned learning is on the individual. The major responsibility for learning rests with the person, not with supervisors or organizations. Employee educational efforts are perhaps best handled in highly individualized ways. People should have a say—if not the *major* say—in experiences designed to help them achieve their own career objectives.

Probably the best way to assess employee educational needs is to begin with a two-fold career program. On one hand, there are present and future careers inside and outside the organization. HRD practitioners and others in the firm should pose such questions as:

1. *What are present relationships between jobs in the firm?* What are career paths in the firm? What education and experience is necessary to move from one job to another?
2. *What should happen to relationships between jobs if management tries to antici-*

pate *changes resulting from new technology or work methods?* How should career paths change if job duties at each level are to be consistent with Strategic Business Plans?

3. *What gaps are likely to exist between the situations considered in items 1 and 2?*
4. *In what ways can individuals prepare themselves for changing career paths/job duties through planned educational experiences?*

On the other hand, each person should consider such questions as:

1. *What are my future career objectives:* What do I want to be capable of doing at a future time?
2. *What trends inside and outside the firm are likely to affect my career progress?* How should I prepare for their potential influence on my career?
3. *What are my present strengths and weaknesses relative to my career objectives?* How well-prepared am I now to assume the future position I desire?
4. *What gaps exist between who I am now and who I want to become?* In short, what do I need to learn to meet my learning needs?
5. *What formal or informal learning experiences can help avert likely threats to my career progress in the future, and seize opportunities to further my career progress?*

Employee educational needs are identified through comparisons of individual career plans and organizational career paths.

Jobs and future learning needs. Of course, jobs cannot "learn." Only individuals can learn. However, requirements in each job category can change as a result of pressures inside and outside the job. Each change in job requirements may create training needs. Future-oriented training may thus be necessary when environmental trends affect *work methods* (how is a job done?), *job duties* (what is expected of a job incumbent?), and *desired results* (what outcomes are needed?).

Training needs should be viewed not just from the standpoint of *each job,* but also from the standpoint of *job categories.* In this way, changes in job requirements at *each* level are also considered *across* levels. To conduct future-oriented training needs assessment, HRD practitioners and operating managers should:

1. *Create a classification scheme for jobs in the organization.* Job categories devised for traditional needs assessment may be relied on.
2. *Consider present and future job requirements.* What is the status of present performance and duties in each job category? What job duties, work methods, and results may change as a consequence of trends?
3. *Clarify implications of business strategy for each job category in the firm.* What job requirements should be established for the future if jobs are to be carried out in ways consistent with Strategic Business Plans?
4. *Identify gaps in the future between what is and what should be.*

5. *Assess how much these gaps will be attributable to lack of knowledge or skills of job incumbents.*
6. *Consider what training offered between present and future can avert future threats to job performance and seize opportunities to improve job performance.*

The results of this assessment produce a general, structured training curriculum that facilitates job performance for each job category. With some modifications, the same approach may be used to focus on meeting the one-time training needs for one group of job incumbents experiencing unique performance problems or opportunities.

Future-oriented training differs from other future-oriented HRD activities in that it is the easiest to "sell" to management. The reason is that the time between need and corrective action is relatively brief. Managers may well feel the need to avert short-term problems by offering training just prior to the installation of new equipment or the implementation of new work methods, for example. They may have a harder time feeling the need to help individuals prepare for future career advancement, develop collective skills of work groups through long-term change efforts, or change group or cultural norms.

Sources of Information for HRD Scanning

It might be helpful to review what we know about sources of information used in environmental scanning based on research by Strategic Business Planning theorists. To summarize their findings (Glueck & Jauch, 1984):

- The most often-used source of information is word-of-mouth.
- The higher a manager's placement within the hierarchy of a firm, the more likely he or she is to rely on word-of-mouth information about the environment.
- The effectiveness of scanning increases as more resources are relied on and more issues are considered.
- In larger firms, information is solicited primarily from people inside the firm. In smaller firms, information about the environment tends to come from outsiders.
- Written information is used more by lower-level than higher-level managers and more by those in stable than in dynamic industries.
- The most important word-of-mouth sources for strategists are personal and professional acquaintances. Information from suppliers is least important (p. 137).

Of what value is this information? First, it suggests that HRD practitioners must somehow gain personal access to top managers if HRD is to have a greater impact on strategy formulation. It also suggests that HRD managers, traditionally "lower-level managers," are more likely to rely on written sources and research studies than their higher level counterparts.

Where can an HRD practitioner go to collect information about general trends in the external environment and specific trends affecting the HRD field? To answer these questions, consult Tables 4-3, 4-4, and 4-5.

These sources of information can be used by HRD practitioners in several ways.

TABLE 4-3 A LIST OF GENERAL SOURCES TO HELP IN IDENTIFYING TRENDS AFFECTING THE ORGANIZATION, ITS PEOPLE, AND ITS JOB CATEGORIES

Economic sector

1. Reports of Predicasts, Inc. (Cleveland, OH)
2. *Statistical Abstract of the United States*
3. *Monthly Labor Review* (Washington, DC)
4. *Survey of Current Business* (Washington, DC)
5. *Economic Indicators* (Washington, DC)
6. *National Economic Projection Series* (Washington, DC)
7. *Regional Economic Projection Series* (Washington, DC)

Political sector

1. Budget of the United States (Annual, Washington, DC)
2. Budget documents published by each state

Technological sector

1. Applied Science and Technology Index
2. National Technical Information Service (Springfield, VA)

Social

1. *Social Indicators* (Washington, DC)
2. *Social Indicators and Social Reporting*
3. Reports by Opinion Research, Inc.
4. *Census of Population* (Washington, DC)
5. Publications of the World Futures Society

Market

1. *Survey of Buying Power*
2. *Guide to Consumer Markets*

Geographic

1. *County and City Data Book*
2. *County Business Patterns*

General sources (periodicals)

- *Business Week*
- *Congressional Digest*
- *Economist*
- *Forbes*
- *Fortune*
- *High Technology*
- *New York Times*
- *Public Opinion*
- *Regulation*
- *Technology Review*
- *Wall Street Journal*
- *Business Periodicals Index*

TABLE 4-4 A LIST OF SOURCES TO HELP IN IDENTIFYING TRENDS AFFECTING THE HRD EFFORT

ALDEN, J. (1982). *Critical Research Issues Facing HRD.* Washington, DC: American Society for Training and Development.

BUTTER, D. (1982). Forecasting the '80s and Beyond—Parts I and II. *Training and Development Journal, 36*(11), 64-66; 68-70.

CARNEVALE, A. (1986). The Learning Enterprise. *Training and Development Journal, 40*(1), 18-26.

DAVIS, S. (1987). *Future Perfect.* Reading, MA: Addison-Wesley.

FEUER, D. (1986). Training in the Fortune 500. *Training, 23*(7), 61.

GILBREATH, R. (1987). *Forward Thinking: The Pragmatist's Guide to Today's Business Trends.* New York: McGraw-Hill.

GORDON, J. (1986). Where the Training Goes. *Training, 23*(10), 49-50, 52-54, 57-60, 62-63.

HALLETT, J. (1987). Worklife Visions. *Personnel Administrator, 32*(5), 56-65.

HARRIS, P. & HARRIS, D. (1983). Twelve Trends You and Your CEO Should Be Monitoring. *Training and Development Journal, 37*(1), 62-69.

HRD Tomorrow. (1984). *Training and Development Journal, 38*(11), 58, 60, 62, 64-65.

HUTCHESON, P. & STUMP, B. (1984). Mining the Future. *Training and Development Journal, 38*(11), 66, 68, 70-72.

LUSTERMAN, S. (1985). *Trends in Corporate Education and Training.* New York: The Conference Board.

MAGNUS, M. (1986, May). Training Futures. *Personnel Journal,* pp. 60-63; 66-71.

MAHONEY, F. (1985). The Future and Human Resources Management. In W. Tracey (Ed.), *Human Resources Management and Development Handbook.* New York: Amacom.

Models for Excellence. (1983). Washington, DC: American Society for Training and Development.

MORGAN, B. & SCHIEMANN, W. (1984). *Supervision in the '80s: Trends in Corporate America.* Princeton, NJ: Opinion Research Corp.

NAISBITT, J. (1982). *Megatrends: Ten New Directions Transforming Our Lives.* New York: Warren Books.

The New Work Force. (1984). *Training, 21*(7), 8, 10-12.

ODIORNE, G. (1985, January). Human Resource Strategies for the '80s. *Training,* pp. 47-49, 51.

PUTMAN, A. & BELL, C. (1984). Projections, Paradoxes, Paradigms. In L. Nadler (ed.), *The Handbook of Human Resources Development.* New York: Wiley.

RALPHS, L. & STEPHAN, E. (1986). HRD in the Fortune 500. *Training and Development Journal, 40*(10), 69-76.

RUKEYSER, L. (1983). *What's Ahead For the Economy.* New York: Simon and Schuster.

The State of Training: Where Are We and Where Do We Go From Here? (1983). *Training, 20*(10), 70-71, 74, 76, 78, 82-92.

SWANSON, R. & MOSIER, N. (1983). Adult Education in America. *Training, 20*(10), 54-55; 58-60; 64; 66; 68.

TOFFLER, A. (1985). *The Adaptive Corporation.* New York: McGraw-Hill.

WEHRENBERG, S. (1983, April). Training Megatrends. *Personnel Journal,* pp. 279-80.

ZEMKE, R. (1987). Training in the '90s. *Training, 24*(1), 40-44, 48-49, 50-53.

TABLE 4-5 A LIST OF SOURCES TO HELP IN IDENTIFYING TRENDS WITHIN THE CORPORATION*

- Published Strategic Plans
- Budget documents
- Management by objectives (MBO) plans
- Speeches by company executives to internal or external groups
- Published articles by company executives
- Annual reports
- Documents circulated by the Corporate Planning department
- Training material

*The best sources are not published. Talk with key executives, and you'll get the best information.

First, they provide a starting point for stimulating the thinking of HRD staff members, operating managers, and even top-level strategists about issues which may imply future instructional needs. Second, they serve as a starting point for future-oriented instructional needs assessments by helping pinpoint key issues or trends for subsequent analysis. Third, they stimulate learners to think about trends which can influence how they can subsequently apply what they learn amid changing conditions. Fourth, they elicit "felt needs" among managers and individuals before a problem is experienced. Fifth and finally, they help frame instructional issues for consideration by top management committees, corporate planners, and HRD managers.

How environmental information is used depends to some extent, at least, on the life cycle stage of the HRD department and organization. Small, newly-formed organizations with correspondingly new HRD departments are likely to approach the environment like entrepreneurs: specific issues will be seized and turned to advantage without much systematic analysis. HRD practitioners, as is common in newly-formed departments (Rothwell, 1983d), will tend to focus inside the organization. As the firm or the HRD department gains maturity, special-purpose committees are often formed in response to specific problems—frequently problems identified by top management. HRD practitioners gradually pay more attention to the external environment, but only for the purposes of identifying instructional needs within the firm. As the firm or HRD department reaches full maturity, HRD practitioners should devote more time to scanning all the environments with which they deal.

Methods for Carrying Out Environmental Scanning for HRD

What methods can be used to scan the environment in order to: (1) begin the process of future-oriented instructional needs assessment when appropriate to head off likely future problems before they arise? (2) create future-oriented experiential exercises for use in training sessions, strategic planning retreats, problem-finding meetings, and other settings? (3) construct future-oriented tests to follow instruction in order to see how present skills will hold up during future changes? (4) give learners opportunities to ponder—or even artificially experience—conditions expected in the future so as to motivate them to do forward-thinking? and (5) create new ideas and new knowledge?

These methods include: job/task analysis; future-oriented employee appraisals; future-oriented assessment centers; group discussions; future-oriented critical incidents; the delphi procedure; and Nominal Group Technique. Many otherwise traditional data collection techniques used in needs assessment can also be modified and used in environmental scanning.

Interviews are widely applied in social science data gathering. They range from highly informal discussions to highly formal, structured surveys. We have already discussed their traditional application to needs assessment in the last chapter.

How are interviews applied to environmental scanning? There are several ways. First, they can identify possible trends outside or inside the organization which can affect external groups, work groups, individuals, or job requirements. Second, they can narrow down possible effects of these trends on work groups, individuals, or jobs. Third, they can help separate instructional from noninstructional needs. Open-ended interview questions are most appropriate for gathering data on these issues. On the other hand, closed-ended questions are appropriately used to prioritize future instructional needs or to gauge the importance of environmental trends.

One round of interviews is rarely sufficient for everything. Several rounds should be used in designing a future-oriented curriculum. As each round of interviews is completed, practitioners will find that they are learning—and discovering—more about future instructional needs.

Where do HRD practitioners start? They should ask executives, managers and supervisors questions such as these:

- What groups—customers, suppliers, distributors, or others—are dealt with regularly?
- What changes in behaviors of these groups over the last year or two are noticeable, if any?
- Given the changes in behaviors, what should the company do now to adapt to these changes? What should be done in the future?
- How might these changes affect your work group in the future?
- What changes in policies or operating procedures in some work units within the company have been noticeable over the last year or two? Describe what has changed or what is changing.
- Given these changes, what does your work group have to do to adapt to these changes?
- What should your work group be doing three years from now if it is to function in a way consistent with company Strategic Business Plans?
- What should be the duties of each position in your work group three years from now? Describe how those duties are changing in each position.
- What problems stemming from environmental change over the next three years will impede desired changes in your work group?
- How will changes affecting the company influence potential for career advancement?
- What changes do you see over the next three years in the responsibilities of such categories as executives, middle managers, and supervisors?

- What organized learning experiences will contribute to heading off problems in the future for your work group and for individuals seeking career advancement?

More detailed questions may focus on specific sectors of the environment, environmental effects, or learning needs. The results of such an investigation should be useful in discovering future threats and opportunities for dealing with the environment.

Surveys can be substituted for interviews. For exploring future environmental change, they usually do not work as well as interviews, which allow follow-up questioning and detailed probing. On the other hand, they are more advantageous than interviews when managers are skeptical about the need for change, and extensive evidence is needed to change their minds. Surveys can be most useful for prioritizing future trends previously identified through interviews. Like interviews, they can dramatize specific environmental threats and opportunities facing the organization, a work group, individuals seeking advancement, or job categories.

Future-oriented job analysis is more concrete than interviews or surveys. There are several ways to analyze jobs. Traditional job analysis describes how work has been done in the past. Each traditional approach to job analysis can be reoriented to a future perspective so that decision-makers can speculate on how work will probably be done or can clarify the way they want it to be done.

Task analysis is similar to, but more specific than, job analysis. HRD practitioners may use it to identify how future changes may alter work tasks. Obviously, it is not possible to observe events in the future which have not yet happened. But they can be simulated by (1) identifying *what* trends may affect work; (2) identifying *how* the trends may affect work; and (3) setting up conditions like those expected or desired in the future—complete with new machines, tools, or work methods—and then observing people perform under simulated conditions. In planning instruction prior to the introduction of new weapons systems in the military or new machines in industrial settings, for instance, before-the-fact task analysis is often a necessity.

Future-oriented employee performance appraisals can provide guidance to individuals in preparing for future jobs. Werther and Davis (1985) distinguish between past-oriented appraisals, that assess how well people have been doing their jobs over the past year, and future-oriented appraisals that evaluate future employee potential or help individuals establish performance goals. Two future-oriented methods they describe are (1) *self-appraisals,* in which individuals set their own goals for work and career achievement, and (2) *management by objectives,* in which individuals and their superiors negotiate goals for a coming year.

However, self-appraisal and management by objectives seldom consider future trends likely to affect individual performance. They should do so. In self-appraisal, the individual should apply strategic career planning to (Rothwell, 1984a; Rothwell & Kazanas, 1988): (1) establish future career goals and objectives; (2) identify personal and professional strengths and weaknesses; (3) examine the environment for trends affecting career progress; (4) compare personal and professional strengths and weaknesses to environmental trends inside and outside the organization; and (5) select a long-term career strategy.

In Management by Objectives, both individuals and their superiors should consider external trends and events that may affect performance as they negotiate annual objectives. There is no need to be fancy here. A simple list of trends should be helpful in formulating and negotiating objectives.

Assessment centers were described in the last chapter. Based on traditional job analysis, they use multiple raters and structured activities to evaluate how well people are likely to carry out job activities. Assessment centers are touted as future-oriented because they assess individual potential. But in reality they are rarely future-oriented, because (1) assessment center exercises are not based on conditions expected in the future, and (2) trained evaluators—usually experienced managers—tend to assess performance from a past rather than a future orientation. To solve these problems, HRD practitioners should base the assessment center on future-oriented job analysis and should rely on evaluators trained to rate employee potential strategically.

Group discussions may be focused on trends in the environment, effects of those trends, instructional versus noninstructional needs, or the importance of environmental issues on a work group, individual, job category, or all. Any group effort is advantageous because groups tend to be more creative than individuals (Campbell, 1968; Fisher, 1980; Hare, 1982; Holloman & Henrick, 1972)—provided that the conformist pressure of groupthink can be avoided (Janis, 1971 & 1973; Moorhead, 1982) and people are willing to voice their true feelings in front of superiors (Bridges, Doyle, & Mahan, 1968).

Zemke and Kramlinger (1982) suggest how to use what they call consensus groups in traditional instructional needs assessment. The idea is to rely on a jury of experts—usually those who are "experienced"—to arrive at a consensus on criteria for assessing job tasks, importance of tasks, or any other issue.

Methods they suggest can easily be applied to environmental scanning. One particularly promising approach is the *priority matrix*. People engaged in environmental scanning: (1) list activities in a job, work group, or profession; (2) set environmental sectors against activity areas in a matrix; and (3) describe in each cell of the matrix any one of the following: likely trends in the environment which may affect the activity; the likely effects of trend(s); the importance of the effects; instructional needs which may emerge in this area; and the appropriate priority for the instructional need. The process of identifying future learning needs may be an iterative one.

Future-oriented critical incidents are based on (1) inferences made about trends in the environment; (2) simulations of future conditions; and (3) observation of simulations. A critical incident is important (*critical*) and an occasion (*incident*). To anticipate future learning needs and changes in the environment, HRD practitioners and/or operating managers should: (1) call together a group of experienced supervisors or job incumbents; (2) explain what critical incidents are and why they are used; (3) provide an example of a critical incident; (4) describe for group members the nature of incidents they are to report and how they should report the incidents; (5) ask group members to describe aspects of their jobs which they believe will be most important for successful job performance at a future time; (6) solicit information about present levels of performance; (7) ask group members to elaborate on levels of performance they expect to be necessary at a future time; and, (8) have group members describe what training/education will be needed from present to future. The same approach can be applied to identifying instructional needs of organizational units, customers, or others dealing with the organization.

Both the *delphi procedure* and the *Nominal Group Technique* are easily applied to: (1) identifying environmental trends; (2) addressing their effects; (3) separating instructional from noninstructional needs; and (4) setting priorities for planned learning. Indeed, these approaches can also be applied during instructional delivery to stimulate creative, future-oriented thinking.

To apply the delphi procedure from a future orientation, HRD practitioners should first select a panel of "experts"—experienced workers, superiors, or people from outside the firm. Second, practitioners should use a small "focus group"—a handful of people—to develop a questionnaire on environmental issues or trends which may affect work groups, individuals, or job requirements in the future. The written questionnaire should then be sent to the panel of experts. Third, practitioners should compile the views of panel members and feed them back. They should ask the panel members to comment on—or rate—the opinions. Fourth, practitioners should continue this process until the panel members' views converge around common conclusions. It may take several different iterations of this process to identify key trends, their effects, instructional needs, and priorities.

To apply the NGT from a future orientation, HRD practitioners should call together a small group of "experts" on a work group, individuals sharing similar career goals/aspirations, and job activities. Practitioners should explain the purpose of the NGT to the experts. The experts should record on slips of paper ideas about any one of the following: key environmental trends/issues; effects of these trends/issues; learning versus nonlearning needs; or learning priorities over time. HRD practitioners should then collect the slips of paper, record the ideas on an overhead or flipchart so that all the participants can see them, allow group members to discuss the ideas, and call for a vote on which ideas are best, most accurate, or most appropriate.

It is thus possible to reorient each traditional approach to instructional needs assessment so that it helps predict future learning needs.

Reassessing Learning Needs by Market or Market Segment

Compiling results is the final step in environmental scanning. These results should be expressed so that they can be compared to the results of a comprehensive needs assessment. Through this comparison, a long-term Organizational Strategy for the HRD Effort can be formulated to unify and provide direction to all HRD activities.

The results of environmental scanning should address two major questions. First, what major threats and opportunities will probably be posed by environmental changes to the firm's dealings with the general public and key external stakeholders, the organization as a whole, each work group, career objectives of individuals, and job performance or job requirements? Second, what should be the future status of the corporation relative to the general public and key external stakeholders, the organization as a whole, each work group, individuals as they progress toward realization of career objectives, and job performance or job requirements? In this context, a *threat* is *any expected deficiency between what is at present and what should be in the future* that stems from lack of knowledge or skill. It is a future learning need, an expected deficiency. An *opportunity* is the opposite of a threat. It is a future talent or competency.

In Chapter 3 we discussed the value of broadly summarizing *present* strengths and weaknesses. There is similar value in broadly summarizing *future* threats and opportunities. Organizational Strategy for HRD is established by comparing strengths, weaknesses, threats, and opportunities.

To derive a summary of threats and opportunities, HRD practitioners should simply compile the results of environmental scanning efforts, and classify the results of each trend as a threat or opportunity. Threats or opportunities may vary in scope. Some may apply to the organization; some apply to specific work groups; some apply to individuals pursuing career goals; and some apply to requirements for performance in a job.

The classification of trends or their effects can be based on the opinions of HRD practitioners, the opinions of strategists, or the opinions of others—key middle managers, for instance. The results of this analysis are recorded on a simple worksheet that provides a simple view of the "big picture"—long-term, broad-scale future learning needs.

Try summarizing threats and opportunities in Activity 4-2 at the end of this chapter.

ACTIVITY 4-1   A Worksheet to Collect Information on Future-Oriented Needs

Directions: Use this activity as the basis for a structured interview guide or an open-ended survey. Ask members of your panel of respondents to answer each question individually. They may continue their answers on additional paper if necessary.

Critical Area

1. What aspect of *(your job/a job category/the work unit's responsibilities and duties/ customer service)** do you believe will be most important to successful performance in *five years?* Describe it.

Reasoning

2. Explain why you believe this aspect will be most important in five years.

Present Performance

3. Describe what you believe to be *exemplary performance* on this aspect at present.

*Choose one and use it consistently throughout the worksheet.

ACTIVITY 4-1 Continued
Desired Future Performance

4. Describe what you believe will have to be exemplary performance on this aspect in five years if the organization's Strategic Business Plans are being implemented successfully.

Instructional Needs

5. Describe the instruction (training/education) which will be necessary to narrow whatever gaps exist between exemplary performance on this aspect at present and desired performance in five years.

ACTIVITY 4-2 Environmental Scanning for HRD: One Approach

Purpose

A future orientation is a quintessential feature of Strategic Business Planning. By thinking about threats and opportunities presented by the environment, HRD practitioners can also anticipate problems which may well affect organizational performance, individual career success, and job performance.

Directions

Use this activity to structure your thinking about the future. Start with the Grid/Matrix. Then turn to the worksheet, which corresponds to each cell on the matrix. Try to think of major environmental trends and their likely future influences on the organization, employees, and jobs. When you finish, summarize your observations on the worksheet at the end.

This activity is intended for top managers, HRD practitioners, operating managers, or any combination of them. It can be used by itself or used in conjunction with a comprehensive examination of an organization's HRD effort. This activity works best for a small group, ranging between five and twelve people.

Master Grid

Directions: Look at the grid below. For each designated cell (e.g., A1, A2, A3), a worksheet can be created to correspond to it. Three worksheets appear on the following pages. Create more worksheets if you wish to do so. For each environmental sector, identify major trends, events, or conditions which can affect the "internal sector." Draw inferences on the worksheets about what effects will be produced by environmental trends and their impact on learning/developmental needs.

External Environmental Sector	Internal Sector		
	Organizational	Individual	Job
Economy	A1	B1	C1
Government	A2	B2	C2
Competitors	A3	B3	C3
Technology	A4	B4	C4
Geography	A5	B5	C5
Society	A6	B6	C6

ACTIVITY 4-2   Continued
Worksheet
Designated Cell: A1
Environmental Sector: Economy
Internal Sector: Organizational
What major environmental trends/events do you expect in the future?
What are the possible effects of these trends/events on the organization? On specific work groups?
What learning and developmental needs do you expect to result from the trends/events? What employee categories/work groups are likely to experience learning needs most acutely?
(Note: Use a similar sheet for the remaining Cells A2–A6.)

Steps in Environmental Scanning for HRD

ACTIVITY 4-2 Continued

Worksheet

Designated Cell: B1

Environmental Sector: Economy

Internal Sector: Individual

What major environmental trends/events do you expect in the future?

What are the possible effects of these trends/events on individuals aspiring to career movement in the organization?

What learning and educational needs do you expect to result from the trends/events listed? How will these trends/events be likely to affect individuals aspiring to career movement inside the organization?

(Note: Use a similar sheet for the remaining Cells B2-B6.)

ACTIVITY 4-2 Continued

Worksheet

Designated Cell: C1

Environmental Sector: Economy

Internal Sector: Job

What major environmental trends/events do you expect in the future?

What are the possible effects of these trends/events on job categories in the organization?

What learning and developmental needs do you expect to result from the trends/events? What employee categories/work groups are likely to experience learning needs most acutely?

(Note: Use a similar sheet for the remaining Cells C2–C6.)

Steps in Environmental Scanning for HRD

ACTIVITY 4-2 Continued

Summary Worksheet

Directions: Use this worksheet to compile your responses from the worksheets prepared for each cell on the grid. Use additional paper if necessary.

What major environmental trends/events do you expect in the future? Over what time horizon?

What are the expected effects of each trend/event? Classify them as threats or opportunities.

Summarize learning/developmental needs on separate sheets of paper. List them on this sheet in order of perceived importance (1 = most important).

ACTIVITY 4-3 A Case Study on Environmental Scanning for the HRD Effort

Directions: Read the case which follows and answer the questions at the end.

The Amorphous Corporation* is an industry leader in retail grocery sales. The Corporation runs over 1,000 grocery stores throughout the U.S. and Canada. It is strongly positioned to capture a greater market share in discount grocery sales. Most of Amorphous's stores are new; most are located in neighborhoods where family incomes average $50,000 a year.

Amorphous has a centralized HRD department in St. Louis, Missouri. New store managers receive one month of intensive training at the new corporate training center in a St. Louis suburb. They learn all aspects of store management, including courses in Customer Relations, Store Accounting, Personnel Practices, and much more.

Amorphous's Strategic Business Plan calls for rapid growth. The company will not be able to develop and train enough store managers internally using present methods. The company does not plan for human resources comprehensively, relying instead on locally-hired Assistant Store Managers as the chief source for future store managers.

Questions

1. What trends external to Amorphous are likely to affect it? Identify the trends and then describe their possible effects on Amorphous.
2. What trends external to Amorphous are likely to create new training needs for Store Managers? Explain your reasoning.
3. What threats and opportunities to the HRD Effort are likely to exist in the future for Amorphous?

*A fictitious case study.

PART 3
CHOOSING AND IMPLEMENTING ORGANIZATIONAL STRATEGY FOR HRD

5

CHOOSING ORGANIZATIONAL STRATEGY FOR HRD

Previous chapters treated comprehensive needs assessment and environmental scanning for HRD. Comprehensive needs assessment is the process of identifying present strengths (proficiencies) and present weaknesses (deficiencies) of learner categories. Environmental scanning for HRD is the process of predicting future threats (deficiencies) and opportunities (proficiencies). These two processes are necessary before choosing Organizational Strategy for HRD, which is the subject of this chapter.

CHOOSING ORGANIZATIONAL STRATEGY FOR HRD: DEFINITION AND IMPORTANCE

Definition. Strategic choice for HRD resembles strategic choice in business planning. It "is the decision to select from among alternative grand strategies the one strategy best suited to meeting the enterprise's objectives. The decision involves focusing on a few alternatives, considering selection factors, evaluating alternatives against these criteria, and making the actual choice" (Glueck & Jauch, 1984, p. 270). In Strategic Business Planning, Grand Strategy means "the comprehensive, general plan of major actions through which a firm intends to achieve its long-term objectives in a dynamic environment.... This *statement of means* indicates how the objectives or ends of business activity are to be achieved" (Pearce & Robinson, 1985, p. 60). Grand Strategy traditionally denotes direction for an entire corporation. It guides lower-level strategies of autonomous business units within a corporation and such functions as operations/production, marketing, finance, and personnel. Further, it addresses this question: *given present internal strengths/weaknesses and likely future environmental threats/opportunities, how can a corporation achieve its long-term objectives in a manner consistent with its present or desired future purpose?*

Strategic HRD integrates long-term, intermediate-term, and short-term learning plans designed to cultivate needed talent. It helps meet needs created by Strategic Business Plans and HR plans. *Organizational Strategy for HRD means a comprehensive, general instructional plan—otherwise called a curriculum—which supports achievement of Strategic Business Plans and HR Plans. "Choosing HRD Strategy" means deciding on an Organizational Strategy for HRD, a long-term direction for planned learning activities offered by the organization.* The result of strategic choice for HRD is thus a unified learning plan that integrates such HRD functions as Organization Development, nonemployee development, employee development, employee education, and employee training.

The importance of choosing organizational strategy for HRD. Organizational Strategy for HRD positions the HRD Effort so it supports Strategic Business Plans, work unit plans, individual career plans, and effective job performance. It prioritizes HRD activities, concentrating initiatives where they are most likely to be useful; it encourages long-term, strategic thinking among learners; and it exerts pressure on top managers to consider linkages between long-term Strategic Business Plans and shorter-term HR decisions.

There are other reasons for choosing HRD Strategy. First, top managers want proactive HR practitioners who contribute to the realization of Strategic Business Plans (*Basic HRD*, 1981; Foltz, Rosenberg, & Foehrenbach, 1982). Second, the ability to think strategically is increasingly important in the career success of HRD practitioners (Baird & Meshoulam, 1984). Third, successful firms in all industries deal strategically with their human resources (Misa & Stein, 1983). Fourth, an Organizational Strategy for HRD guides management of the HRD department (Pattan, 1986). Fifth, Organizational Strategy for HRD furnishes information to top managers about employee skills which they should use in Strategic Business Planning (Pattan, 1986; Tregoe & Zimmerman, 1984). Sixth and finally, Organizational Strategy for HRD helps implement changes in Strategic Business Plans, HR plans, and marketing efforts.

PRESCRIPTIONS ABOUT CHOOSING ORGANIZATIONAL STRATEGY FOR HRD

Numerous articles have appeared in recent years on strategic planning for HRD. At this point, it is worth reviewing the advice they provide.

Advice. According to published articles on this subject, HRD practitioners—by themselves or in concert with line managers—should:

- create a vision of what the HRD department or Effort should be at some point in the future (Hulett & Renjilian, 1983; Pattan, 1986; Ward, 1982),

- prepare a purpose statement which clarifies HRD's role in contributing to achievement of corporate objectives and mission (Hulett & Renjilian, 1984; Pattan, 1986; Ward, 1982),
- establish annual planning objectives for HRD and link them to business mission (Pattan, 1986),
- create a database about environmental changes inside and outside the firm (Harvey, 1983; Pattan, 1986; Ward, 1982),
- work for developing a holistic HRD plan (Linkow, 1985; Mirabile, Caldwell, & O'Reilly, 1986),
- make sure HRD plans support Strategic Business Plans (Harvey, 1983; Linkow, 1985),
- convince top managers that any change in business strategy implies a change in future skill needs of people in the business (Desatnick, 1984; Linkow, 1985),
- devise HRD strategic plans even when no corporate Strategic Business Plans exist or when the formal plans that do exist are ignored (Linkow, 1985; Tregoe & Zimmerman, 1984; Ward, 1982), and
- establish checkpoints and periodic updates to assess whether Organizational Strategy for HRD still matches environmental conditions (Harvey, 1983; Ward, 1982).

Relatively little has been written about how to choose Organizational Strategy for HRD. Ward (1982) is one of the few who treats the subject:

> The strategic choice constitutes the decision, in concert with others, on the strategy most likely to improve the department's contribution to the company, its profits and its overall objectives. Selection can begin when all important and significant individuals have been involved in the strategy planning. The chosen HRD strategy must be consistent with HRD competence and immediately available resources and with the limitations of external and internal company conditions (p. 24).

He provides a checklist useful for evaluating alternatives and considering key issues. (See Activity 5-1 at the end of the chapter.)

Critique. Most articles on strategic planning for HRD focus only on *planning for the HRD department,* not on *the role of all HRD activities in the organization.* HRD planning is treated as the functional responsibility of HRD Managers rather than a shared, joint responsibility of all prospective learners. While the reason for this focus is clear—most articles on HRD planning are written solely for an audience of HRD specialists—the unfortunate implication is that HRD managers should just develop plans to manage their departments rather than coordinate organizational adaptation to environmental change through planned learning.

A second tendency in the literature is a failure to place the HRD strategy in the perspective of HR planning. Yet if the aim is to marshal human talent in the future, organized instruction is not the only way to go about that. Indeed, HRD practitioners should know about initiatives in other personnel areas. After all, HRD planning is affected by hiring practices, compensation, career planning, collective bargaining, and much more. Initiatives in other personnel activities influence the kind of people who are available and are experiencing learning needs.

CHOOSING ORGANIZATIONAL STRATEGY FOR HRD: THE PROCESS

The process of selecting Organizational Strategy for HRD resembles problem-finding in several key respects. Practitioners find problems, formulate them, identify appropriate ways to look at them, consider possible solutions, and choose one appropriate solution.

Finding problems. The starting point for choice of strategy is a perception that a gap does exist or will exist between *what is* and *what should be*. It is the point when future problems or opportunities for improvement are recognized. After considering various alternative strategies or solutions, strategists decide on one they feel will help close present or future performance gaps.

In Strategic Business Planning, a strategic choice is made after comparing an organization's *present internal status* and *its expected future external environment*. Strategic choice thus begins with a comprehensive review of factors affecting organizational success. There is no one widely-accepted method for conducting such a review. The reason is that factors affecting organizational success vary widely, depending on the firm's competitive position in the industry, how information is obtained and used, and what strategists desire in the future.

WOTS-UP Analysis is one way to conduct this review. WOTS-UP is an acronym created from the first letters of four words—*w*eaknesses, *o*pportunities, *t*hreats, and *s*trengths. As used in Strategic Business Planning, a weakness is whatever works against a firm in its present competitive efforts. A strength is a present advantage that a firm enjoys over its competitors. A threat is an expected future environmental change that will result in conditions disadvantageous to the firm. An opportunity is an expected future environmental change that will produce possibilities for gaining a competitive advantage.

The same idea may be applied to HRD. Indeed, we have already discussed (1) strengths and weaknesses as results of comprehensive needs assessment (in Chapter 3); and (2) threats and opportunities as results of environmental scanning for HRD (in Chapter 4). In the context of an HRD Effort, weakness is any past or present discrepancy between condition (what is) and criteria (what should be) stemming from lack of knowledge or skill. It is a present learning need. A strength is any past or present talent, proficiency, or competency. It is a state in which condition (what is) is better than criteria (what should be). An opportunity is a talent, competency, knowledge, or skill expected to make condition better than criteria. A threat is the opposite of an opportunity: it is any expected deficiency, stemming from lack of knowledge or skill, between what will probably be and what should be in the future. A threat is thus an expected future learning need resulting from changes in the environment or organization.

In choosing Organizational Strategy for HRD there are four possible markets to analyze: (1) *external groups*, like consumers, suppliers, distributors, and the general public; (2) *internal work groups* or departments; (3) *individuals* aspiring to new positions; and (4) *job* requirements by job category. All four are possible sources of instructional needs. The four markets can be separately analyzed or combined in one overall analysis of needs for the purpose of choosing a unified Organizational Strategy for HRD. The HRD department is one vehicle for meeting these needs; line departments and external vendors are other vehicles for meeting these needs.

The strategy of the HRD Effort depends on its purpose. It is thus important to consider strengths, weaknesses, threats, and opportunities relative to purpose. Consider these questions: (1) What is the purpose of the HRD Effort? What should it be? (2) What is the purpose of the HRD department relative to the HRD Effort? What should it be? (3) What are the responsibilities of line managers and departments in the HRD Effort? What should they be?

Figure 5-1 may help conceptualize relationships between (1) analysis of strengths, weaknesses, threats, and opportunities; (2) the purpose of the HRD Effort; (3) markets for possible HRD activities; and (4) Organizational Strategy for HRD. The point of comparing present needs and talents (weaknesses and strengths) to future needs and talents (threats and opportunities) is to frame the choice of Organizational Strategy for HRD.

Formulating problems. The second step in choosing strategy is formulating problems. At this point, it is important to refine, synthesize, and prioritize problems sensed in the previous step and filter them through the purpose of the HRD Effort. For each present or future learning need, practitioners should consider:

- What is this need exactly? How precisely can it be described?
- Why is it important now? How important is it likely to become?
- What are the effects of this problem now? What are the expected effects of the problem likely to be over time?
- What will probably happen if *no* action is taken to meet the need? What will probably happen by way of unintended side effects if action is taken at present or in the future?
- How important is this need in meeting organizational objectives, individual career objectives, and job requirements?

These questions can then be applied to the raw information obtained in the previous step. The answers to these questions can then be compared to the purpose of the HRD Effort to determine whether they warrant action.

Identifying a way to look at the problems. Once problem areas have been prioritized, HRD practitioners and line managers are ready to look at the problem. Here they should be interested in

- *determining cause*—What created the problem in the first place, or what trends, events, or other future happenings may create new problems?
- *finding a way to consider solutions*—What approaches can be used in problem-solving?

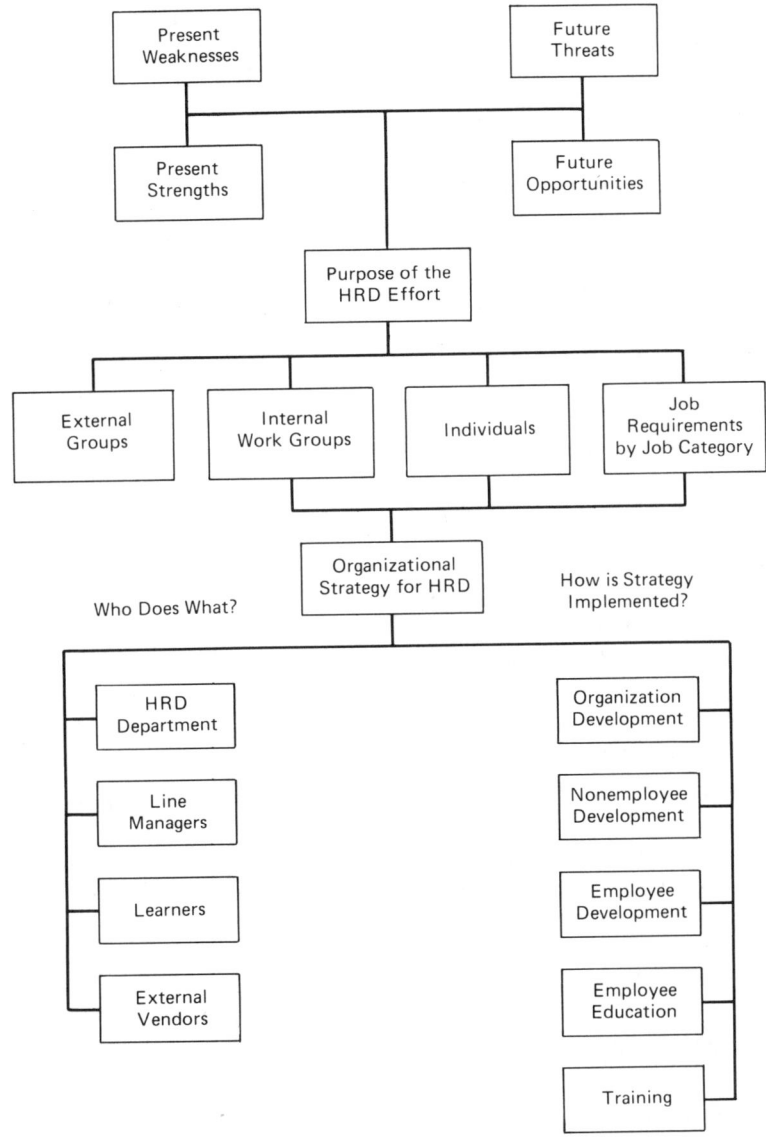

Figure 5-1: Relationships to Consider in Choosing Organizational Strategy for HRD

Determining the cause of a problem is rarely easy, because there may be more than one cause. Does a weakness result solely from a lack of knowledge or a skill? Do threats stemming from these causes seem to be likely in the future? How much do problems which seem to stem from other sources—such as outdated equipment—contribute to lack of knowledge or skill?

Cause is the reason that things have gone wrong or are expected to go wrong in the future. Examples of cause may include any or all of the following:

1. lack of communication
2. negligence
3. poor standards of performance (that is, standards that are obsolete, impractical, or unclear)
4. lack of performance standards
5. decisions to deviate from organizational policies or procedures
6. lack of resources
7. dishonesty
8. departures from common sense or accepted methods of practice
9. sabotage
10. lack of motivation
11. lack of supervision
12. resistance to change
13. breakdowns in equipment or automated systems
14. lack of planning
15. temporary changes in workflow

Finding a way to consider solutions is a link between problem-finding and solution-finding. From what standpoint do practitioners want to think about solutions? There are many. For instance, practitioners may distinguish between

- *repetitive and nonrepetitive needs:* Every time employees enter the organization or change jobs, they face instructional needs stemming from change. These needs are repetitive, though the content of instruction may differ depending on changes in needs over time. Nonrepetitive needs are one-shot occurrences, resulting from the first-time introduction of change. For example, introducing an automated system to employees who have used a manual system creates a nonrepetitive learning need.
- *long-term and short-term needs:* Some weaknesses take a long time to correct; some do not. Likewise, some threats require more time to prepare for than others.
- *critical and not-so-critical needs:* It may be more important to the organization's strategists to focus on a handful of key instructional needs than on all needs. What do they perceive as critical now and in the future? Why?
- *creative versus noncreative needs:* Will old ways of handling problems work well, or will it be more appropriate to create new solutions? Are creative solutions easily recognized through analytical methods like flowcharting a procedure? Or will finding a solution require more innovative methods?
- *instructional versus noninstructional improvement efforts:* Performance of individuals, groups, and organizations can be improved in many ways—not just by

traditional instructional methods. Are other methods likely to be cheaper, more effective, or faster? Consider alternatives to formal instruction such as: (1) job redesign; (2) job aids; (3) feedback interventions; (4) work group redesign; and/or (5) reward system redesign.

Use Activity 5-2 at the end of this chapter to consider these issues.

Another way to think about framing problems is compatible with WOTS-Up Analysis. Recall that WOTS-Up Analysis can be used to summarize strengths, weaknesses, threats, and opportunities of the organization, work groups, departments, individuals, job categories, or external groups. WOTS-Up Analysis can also be linked to distinctive long-term strategies for the HRD Effort, depending on which factors summarized on the WOTS-Up Grid are strongest (see Figure 5-2).

This basic approach has been used to guide strategic choice in Strategic Business Planning (Pearce & Robinson, 1985). For example, a firm enjoying substantial internal strengths and numerous environmental opportunities (Cell 1) is in a very favorable situation. The most appropriate strategy is *growth*. A firm possessing substantial strengths but facing numerous environmental threats (Cell 2) is well-advised to pursue *diversification*, branching out into new and more profitable businesses rather than trying to grow in the present one. A firm in Cell 3 faces critical internal weaknesses and numerous environmental opportunities. The most appropriate strategy is a *turnaround*, a redirection of resources from within. Finally, a firm in Cell 4 contends with both internal weaknesses and major environmental threats. Strategists are well-advised to *retrench*, cutting back on resources and activities while regrouping forces.

In using WOTS-Up analysis as a problem framing method, strategists address a central question that they must consider in strategic choice: "What will be the principal purpose of the grand strategy?" (Pearce & Robinson, 1985, p. 260). In other words, do strategists intend to build on strengths or try to overcome weaknesses? From

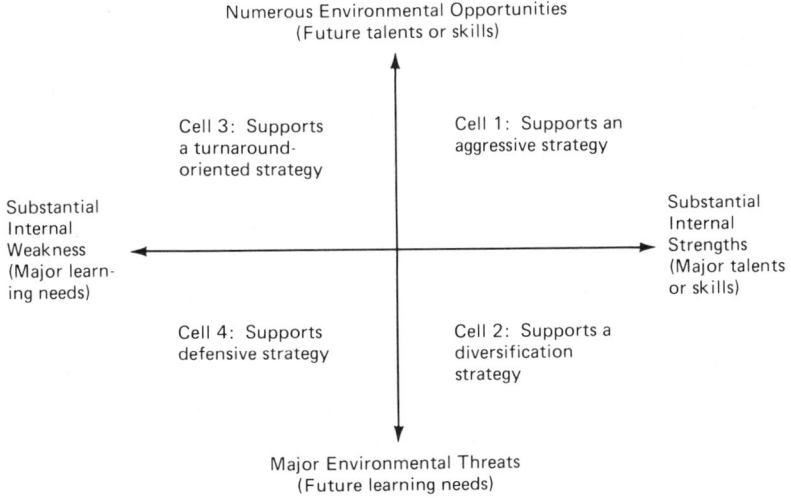

Figure 5-2: WOTS-UP Analysis Profile. *Source:* Pearce and Robinson, 1985, p. 259. Reprinted with permission.

Choosing Organizational Strategy for HRD: The Process

the research which has been conducted, it appears that this approach can yield very useful information for strategic choice (see Hrebiniak & Snow, 1982 [cited in Pearce and Robinson, 1985]).

The same idea, with slight modifications, can be applied to the problem of strategic choice for the HRD Effort. A grid like that shown in Figure 5-2 can be prepared to represent

- *each internal work group or department:* How well does the group meet the present and future needs of the organization? How well is the group presently performing, and how well should it perform in the future?
- *individuals:* How well are people preparing for—or prepared for—future advancement? (Each person can be assessed overall and a dot placed on a grid to represent status.)
- *job categories:* How well-matched to job requirements are job incumbents? (HRD practitioners can then use one dot to represent the *overall* perceived status of the job category.)
- *external groups:* How well do the general public and key external groups understand the business, its products or services, and its operational needs?

The choice of how many grids to use depends solely on whether the emphasis (strategic thrust) is on meeting the needs of external groups, work groups, individuals, or job categories. WOTS-UP analysis provides an overview of the "big picture" of the organization's human skill strengths, weaknesses, threats, and opportunities. It is helpful because, much like its counterpart in Strategic Business Planning, it "provides a logical framework guiding systematic discussions of the business's [human resources skills] situation, alternative strategies and, ultimately, 'choice of strategy' " (Pearce & Robinson, 1985, p. 258).

Considering possible solutions. No strategy is absolutely "right" or "wrong." The range of possible Organizational Strategies for HRD is broad. Should the HRD Effort

1. *grow* by doing *more* of what is already being done? This strategy means adding to planned learning activities sponsored by the organization.
2. *retrench* by doing *less* of what is already being done? This strategy means cutting back on the number or type of planned learning activities sponsored by the organization.
3. *diversify* by *changing* the

    Learners served?

    Needs addressed?

    Emphasis placed on each potential market of learners?

    Projects/services offered?

    Instructional methods used?

    Subjects offered?

    Content treated in each planned learning experience?

4. *integrate* with other efforts by increasing or decreasing HRD's relationship to other functions or activities within the organization? or groups outside the organization? This strategy means tying HRD to other HR functions (like recruitment) or other organizational functions (like marketing).
5. *turn around* otherwise failing HRD activities by first retrenching and then pursuing another HRD Strategy? For example, placing increased emphasis on education rather than training may be a step in a turnaround strategy.
6. *combine* any or all of the preceding strategies by pursuing two or more at the same time? Each group of learners may be the focus of one type of HRD activity more than other groups or types of activities.

Each strategy is possible under *any* environmental conditions. The question is, how appropriate is it? This question leads to the next step.

Choosing organizational strategy for HRD. This step corresponds to the choice of a solution in the problem-finding process. It involves narrowing down possible solutions to one that is: (1) workable and practical; (2) cost effective and cost efficient; (3) likely to be accepted by others; and, (4) likely to overcome weaknesses, build on existing strengths, avert future threats, or seize future opportunities. HRD practitioners and top management strategists rarely have total freedom to pursue what they believe is the "best" or "optimal" choice; rather, they must consider possible strategies for long-term learning efforts based on tests of acceptability.

The Grand Strategy Selection Matrix is one helpful tool in this process (Pearce & Robinson, 1985). Used in Strategic Business Planning, it focuses on two key issues. Should strategists (1) devote attention to overcoming present weaknesses or building on present strengths? or (2) concentrate efforts inside or outside the firm? The Matrix is shown in Figure 5-3.

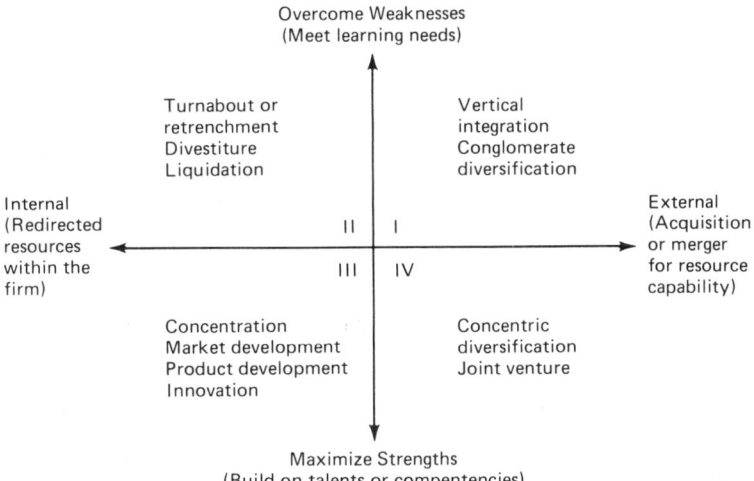

Figure 5-3: Grand Strategy Selection Matrix. *Source:* Pearce and Robinson, 1985, p. 261 with permission.

Each alternative Grand Strategy shown in Figure 5-3 may be translated into HRD terminology. These definitions appear in Table 5-1.

After reviewing the definitions in Table 5-1, look again at Figure 5-3. For HRD practitioners and managers, one choice of long-term strategy is to concentrate on over-

TABLE 5-1 MEANINGS OF DIFFERENT GRAND STRATEGIC CHOICES FOR ORGANIZATIONS AND FOR HRD

Grand strategy	Traditional meaning	Meaning for HRD
Vertical Integration	Purchase businesses which provide a firm with important supplies.	The HRD Effort is tied formally to "suppliers" or distributors of talent within the firm (e.g., the Recruitment/Selection division of Personnel) or outside the firm (e.g., University programs).
Conglomerate Diversification	Purchase another business solely because it is a good investment, not because it is at all related to the business of the purchaser.	Expand into totally new areas of service which are not necessarily related at all to the firm's past HRD Effort.
Concentric Diversification	Purchase another business with markets, technology, or products related to the purchasing firm.	Use the HRD Effort to acquire new markets or customers for the business.
Joint Venture	Two firms pool resources to compete in a given market.	Two or more HRD Efforts are combined in an industry association.
Divestiture	Sell part of the business—or the entire business.	Contract out for major portions of services previously handled by an internal HRD department.
Liquidation	Sell off the assets of the business.	Sell off assets related to, or used in, developing/training employees.
Concentration	Continue to concentrate on the business in which the firm is presently operating.	Continue to meet instructional needs (deal with weaknesses) in ways traditional to the firm's past HRD Effort.
Market Development	Target new customer groups different from those historically served by a firm, and adapt methods of distributing products and advertising to attract them as customers.	Expand planned learning experiences previously limited to one group (e.g., in-house executives) to other groups inside and/or outside the firm.
Product Development	Change the type of product/service of the firm so as to expand the range of potential buyers. "Make an old product new."	Come up with a "new look" for the products/services of the HRD Effort. Use new methods of delivery; different names; etc.
Innovation	Come up with an utterly new approach, a novel idea, which is still compatible with the firm's philosophy of business, purpose, goals, and objectives.	The HRD Effort is tied to stimulation of employee/managerial creativity. It produces new ideas rather than helps people master information derived from experience or comply with company policies and Standard Operating Procedures.

coming present weaknesses (learning needs). That can be accomplished through efforts directed inside or outside the firm. As shown in Cell 1 of Figure 5-3, two choices are possible if strategists want to overcome weaknesses externally: vertical integration or conglomerate diversification.

Vertical integration means tying the HRD Effort more closely to

- internal "suppliers" of talent—such as the recruitment/selection function. Clearly, the kind of people hired affects long-term and short-term learning needs: "Poor selection is the first teetering domino that creates a massive crash down the line. Good selection doesn't guarantee success, but poor selection guarantees failure" (Weiss, 1987, p. 90).
- external "suppliers" of talent—such as university programs which prepare people for jobs in fields critically-needed by the firm. Clearly, education received by potential employees affects their learning needs once employed.
- internal "distributors" of talent—such as major operating departments that hire large numbers of people into entry-level jobs. Clearly, what supervisors in these departments do with their newly-hired workers affects the supply of labor which can be promoted or transferred to other work groups in the firm.
- external "distributors" of talent—such as firms which frequently hire former company veterans who are moving on to "greener pastures." Assuming the firm has conducted research on turnover and managers know where their employees are going, the HRD Effort can be geared in part to improving ties with key company suppliers or distributors. (Some firms deliberately train more new hires than needed because they know that many trainees will be snatched up by company suppliers and distributors, where they may exert influence favorable to the firm which trained them.)

Conglomerate diversification means expansion into totally new areas—regardless of their present benefit to the firm itself. The idea is to maximize profits. One approach is to make HRD a profit center, a relatively autonomous business enterprise. The manager of the department is free to market departmentally-designed materials, products, and services to groups inside and outside the organization. At the same time, line managers in the organization are free to contract for HRD services externally through universities, community colleges, private vendors, or internally through the HRD department. The logic of the marketplace is brought to bear on the HRD Effort. The HRD manager may find external markets more receptive and/or more profitable than internal ones. Indeed, the HRD Effort may be run more for profits obtainable outside than for meeting learning needs inside the organization.

In Cell II of the Grid shown in Figure 5-3, strategists may choose to overcome weaknesses by redirecting resources within the firm. Faced with an unfavorable external environment, they may want to look inward and (1) cut back on HRD activities generally (retrenchment); (2) begin with a retrenchment strategy followed by a redirection of activities (turnaround); (3) cut back on some internal HRD activities by contracting out for selected instruction that can simply be produced cheaper outside, perhaps with help from government funding; or, (4) sell off such HRD-related assets as machines or facilities used in training.

There was a time when HRD was the first target for liquidation when companies, facing unfavorable environmental conditions, reduced spending. That is less true today than it was five years ago. Executives are recognizing that drastic cutbacks in HRD produce dramatically negative long-term side effects. These include: (1) greater difficulty in orienting new hires once the company's environment improves; (2) greater awareness of competitors' moves ("if they don't cut their training staff, we won't either"), (3) greater awareness that the most appropriate time to work for productivity improvement through HRD is precisely when the odds against the firm are most unfavorable; and (4) recognition that employee morale suffers when layoffs occur and HRD activities are necessary to deal with that problem. While there is only a dubious relationship between morale and productivity, they *are* associated among white-collar workers whose expertise may be of greatest value to competitive success (Beach, 1980).

In Cell III of Figure 5-3, notice that strategists who concentrate their efforts on maximizing internal strengths can choose such Organizational Strategies for HRD as:

- concentration, in which HRD activities continue without interruption so as to sharpen the skills of workers who are already performing well,
- market development, in which HRD is geared to new learner groups inside or outside the firm whose needs have not been previously addressed (for example, more clerical instruction or a start-up effort for customer training),
- product development, in which HRD is expanded to offer new products, new services, or new delivery methods (for example, job aids, procedure manuals, OD consulting, and expansion into areas like self-study videotape or computer-based training in addition to classroom instruction)—in this way, otherwise good performance among employees is improved, and
- innovation, in which HRD is directed toward creating new ideas, stimulating strategic thinking, and providing new experience rather than purveying old ideas.

A concentration strategy, sometimes called stable growth (Glueck & Jauch, 1984), is probably what managers would most *like* to do. It is generally associated with swelling profits and staff as well as increasing salaries. Generally, morale improves, too, during growth (Katz & Kahn, 1978). After all, promotions, salary increases, and bonuses tend to occur more often when a firm is growing.

By way of contrast, innovation is the toughest and riskiest of Organizational Strategies for HRD. The aim is to try to create new ideas or to speed up acceptance of state-of-the-art know-how, perhaps even create that know-how, as a means of giving the firm a strong competitive advantage. For practitioners bold enough to blaze this path of championing new ideas, times can be hard. They face resistance to change and should try to harness the conflict implicit in change to generate new ideas. Those pursuing this strategy are the true visionaries and entrepreneurs who recognize, as Schön (1971) has warned, that: (1) generally speaking, the rate of change in the world is increasing; (2) problems of all kinds—including instructional needs—grow more complex as the rate of change increases; (3) solutions take longer to work out as problems grow more complex; and, (4) as the rate of change continues to increase, the life span of an appropriate solution decreases correspondingly. As the life span of a solution decreases, so too does the time available to allow people to participate in decision-making and consider the consequences of action. If old ways of looking at past experiences are followed, people will be even more misled. Yet an HRD strategy of innovation may become increasingly appropriate for all firms as the role of HRD shifts from: (1) problem-solving after the fact to problem-finding before the fact; (2) a tool for socialization of employees, a rite of passage, to one for adaptation to—or even anticipation of—change; and (3) purveying methods based on past experiences, institutional memory, and culture to a means of creating new information and changing culture.

Look now at Cell IV in Figure 5-3. A final choice of Organizational Strategy for HRD is to maximize strengths while focusing outside the firm. Appropriate strategies include concentric diversification or joint ventures. In concentric diversification, the HRD Effort becomes a means for acquiring new markets or potential clientele. Suppose a firm wants to introduce a new line of products. What could be more logical than to go out and buy an HRD consulting firm already offering instruction to this consumer market? If a high-technology manufacturing company that is introducing a new line of personal computers purchases a firm specializing in classroom-based instruction on home computers, then the high-tech firm has acquired a necessary means to reach its new "customers." In joint ventures, HRD activities of several firms are combined for common advantage. This happens occasionally when a group of small businesses, each with a need for HRD but each too small to afford a full-time HRD staff, pools resources to form an industry association that specializes in offering HRD activities for member firms. Both strategies direct resources outside rather than inside the firm, and both strategies add to existing talents rather than meet deficiencies.

SPECIAL ISSUES TO CONSIDER IN CHOOSING ORGANIZATIONAL STRATEGY FOR HRD

Several major issues should be considered when selecting Organizational Strategy for HRD. They include: (1) past strategy; (2) environmental uncertainty; (3) dependence on key groups; (4) attitudes about risk; (5) in-house politics; (6) timing; (7) need for a special focus; (8) available skills; and, (9) relationships to other plans.

Past strategy. Past strategy is a point of departure for planning new strategy. Strategists look at the past and present direction of a firm in order to decide, in light of expected environmental change, whether a new direction or strategy is needed. The greater the perceived gap between actual and desired results in the past, the greater the necessity to choose a radically different strategy in the future.

The same notion can be applied to an HRD Effort. In what ways has HRD been serving external groups, internal work groups, individuals, and job categories? How well has it been meeting past and present instructional needs stemming from

- external stakeholder/public expectations and relations with a firm?
- organizational requirements?

- individual career plans?
- job requirements?

Are HRD experiences, like training courses, generally viewed as "hard work"—or are they viewed in other ways? How often are they treated as "rewards" for good performers? How often are they used solely to remove problem performers from the work setting?

Past HRD strategy is thus important because it establishes expectations about future activities. It is necessary to know what needs the HRD Effort is meeting—and not meeting (Bowman, 1987)—before thinking about future strategy. Consider: will continuation of Organizational Strategy for HRD contribute sufficiently to the attainment of future objectives for the Effort? If so, major changes are not needed; if not, the HRD Effort may require a major change in emphasis. When major change is needed, HRD practitioners must think creatively—and may have to transform the HRD Effort into something utterly different from what it has been in the past.

The degree of environmental uncertainty. Organizations face different kinds of external environments. Some industries—aerospace and computers are notable examples—exist in highly turbulent environments. The more uncertain and dynamic the external environment, the greater the necessity for practitioners to devise flexible strategies in which contingencies have been planned in the event of radical environmental change. This principle is equally applicable to Strategic Business Planning and Organizational Strategy for HRD.

The degree of dependence on key groups. "If a firm is highly dependent on one or more environmental factors," write Pearce and Robinson (1985), "its strategic alternatives and ultimate choice must accommodate this dependence" (p. 268). In short, the greater the dependence of successful Strategic Business Plans on support from key groups inside and outside the firm, the greater the need to anticipate the reactions of these groups before choosing a new strategy. "If external dependence is critical, firms may include representatives of the external factor (government, union, supplier, bank) in the strategic choice process" (Pearce & Robinson, 1985, p. 268). The same principle should hold true for HRD.

Most HRD practitioners will concede that they may serve—potentially, at least—all groups inside a firm and major groups outside it. But the issue of dependence has to do with this question: Who controls the resources? In most organizations, HRD practitioners report to either a Vice President for Human Resources or to a Vice President of HRD who, in turn, reports to the Chief Executive (Rothwell & Kazanas, 1986-1988). In these cases, either the Personnel Chief or CEO controls resources. The HRD Effort competes with other organizational activities for needed resources. It is thus important to base Organizational Strategy for HRD on expectations of those who control resources—or else persuade those people to form new expectations.

However, matters are somewhat different if the HRD Effort extends beyond employees to include customers, suppliers, distributors, or others. If the HRD department is operating as an autonomous enterprise which "sells" products and services to outsiders, it gains greater flexibility of choice. The HRD Manager is an entrepreneur serving two markets—the organization of which the HRD department is part *and* external groups served by the department.

Attitudes about risk. Just how much risk are HRD practitioners and line managers willing to take? According to theorists of Strategic Business Planning, the range of strategic options increases as managers become more inclined to take risks. Risk-taking managers explore opportunities more than their risk-averse counterparts do. This inclination to explore alternative solutions to any problem is particularly important in volatile industries in which technology changes rapidly, posing both threats and opportunities. Research has shown that attitudes about risk affect success in autonomous business units. When general managers view risk in ways matching the firm's strategy, organizational performance is usually better than when their views toward risk do not match strategy (Gupta & Govindarajam, 1984).

The same principle applies to HRD. When HRD managers are willing to take risks in pursuit of outcomes matching the purpose of the HRD Effort, they are likely to perform more effectively than their risk-averse counterparts.

In-house politics. Choice of Organizational Strategy for HRD depends on the ability to influence others. *Power* is equated with the ability to influence; *politics*, related to power, has to do with distributing resources and dealing with special issues that fall outside formal roles and organizational policies.

Strategic Business Planning theorists have long conceded that politics plays an important part in all facets of strategy formulation, implementation, and evaluation. Managers engage in political activity to further their personal and parochial interests. Mutual concerns sometimes lead to the formation of manager coalitions. These coalitions exert influence on decision-making, outcomes of decisions, and methods of evaluating the success of outcomes. Mintzberg, Raisinghani, and Theoret (1976) found through research that managers frequently try to hide the influence of politics in strategic choice. These researchers also found that politics is a crucial factor in decision-making as much as 30 percent of the time. Other writers have traced the influence of politics on strategic choice (Cyert & March, 1963; Fahey & Narayanan, 1983; Macmillan, 1978; Mintzberg, 1979a&b).

Clearly, the HRD Effort can be the focus of considerable political activity when managers view HRD activities as central to the achievement of their goals. Managers may try to control identification of learning needs, the direction of the HRD Effort, choice of Organizational Strategy for HRD, resources provided to HRD, and means of implementing and evaluating HRD strategy. In each case, powerful managers may try to turn the HRD Effort to their own advantage—regardless of the opinions expressed by HRD practitioners or others in the firm. On the other hand, if HRD is not viewed as an activity which contributes to goal achievement, then political maneuvering about it will be minimal because nobody cares.

Obviously, politics may thus exert considerable influence on choice of Organizational Strategy for HRD. HRD practitioners have too often been outgunned by more powerful and politically savvy managers when political maneuvering is an issue (Raia, 1985; Schein, 1983b).

Timing. To underestimate the importance of timing in strategic choice would be foolish indeed, whether the focus is on Strategic Business Plans, HR plans, or HRD plans. Crisis is a powerful stimulant favoring departures from past or present modes of operation (Beer, 1980).

Abell (1978) suggests that managers should take advantage of "strategic windows" in which key competencies of their firm match market requirements for its products or services. The strategic thinker anticipates when these windows will appear and how to match the firm's competencies to market or consumer requirements at given times. These "windows" exist for only brief time periods. Timing is thus crucial to success.

The same principle holds true for HRD. As top management strategists and learners experience problems, they search for solutions. If HRD practitioners anticipate problems before they arise, they improve their chances of gaining acceptance for HRD strategies designed to deal with future problems. Further, if the process of deciding on Organizational Strategy for HRD can be used to focus attention on possible future problems, then it serves an important purpose as a vehicle for environmental scanning.

The need for a special focus. Organizational Strategy for HRD is usually comprehensive in scope. It unifies planned learning intended to anticipate the needs of the organization, external stakeholders, the public, individuals, or job incumbents.

However, it is not always necessary to be so comprehensive in scope. HRD practitioners and line managers may choose to focus *solely* on the long-term learning needs of any *one* of the following:

(1) *organizational culture:* The emphasis is placed on Organization Development.

(2) *external groups:* The emphasis is placed on nonemployee development.

(3) *internal groups:* The emphasis is placed on employee development.

(4) *individuals:* The emphasis is placed on employee education.

(5) *job categories:* The emphasis is placed on employee training.

Moreover, any *one* work unit, type of individual, or job category can be emphasized more than others. For example, Bolt (1985) and Nilsson (1987) feel that executive development is particularly important in matching leadership talents to Strategic Business Planning requirements. For the most part, however, short-term (job-oriented) training has traditionally occupied the greatest attention of HRD practitioners.

When the strategic trust (emphasis) is placed on training, Organizational Strategy for HRD focuses on meeting the learning needs of each major job category in the firm. Line managers and HRD practitioners in the firm decide on a holistic instructional plan for the firm based on job categories and their duties.

When the strategic thrust is on employee education—a rare case—then a separate learning plan has to be negotiated with each employee. Instructional plans are individualized. The time frame is longer than for training. The aim is to help individuals prepare for new jobs and thus achieve their career goals.

When the strategic thrust is on employee development, a group learning plan is prepared for each work unit. It is geared to the collective skill requirements of the organization. The time frame is longer than for education. The HRD Effort becomes a tool for organizational learning.

When the strategic thrust is on nonemployee development, a learning plan is established for one or more external groups. The aim is to improve relations between the organization and that group or meet the learning needs of a group or groups. The time frame is long, though specific training and educational activities undertaken to help realize the plan may have time frames of brief duration.

When the strategic thrust is on Organization Development, learning activities are planned around special issues. The focus is on cultural change at the group or organization levels. The time frame is long.

Available skills. In choosing Organizational Strategy for HRD, another issue to consider is this: Does the organization possess the talent necessary to implement the strategy or, failing that, can the organization obtain that talent externally? In short, are the necessary skills available?

Of course, the HRD department is the first place to look for these skills. Relative to Organizational Strategy for HRD, how well staffed is the department? Are specialists available? If not, are HRD staff members willing to work toward a new long-term learning strategy through new methods? If not, what accounts for *their* resistance to change? How valid are their reasons?

Another place to look for skills is outside the HRD department but inside the firm. Relative to the HRD Strategy, are experts or knowledgeable people available in other departments? How likely is it that they can be—or want to be—involved in implementing a new HRD Strategy? Will these people participate in planning and offering instruction? Will they transfer to the HRD department for extended time periods so they can help? What incentives exist to encourage them to cooperate?

Finally, the environment outside the firm is another place to look for skills matched to HRD Strategy. If skills are not available internally, how likely is it they can be found among potential new-hires for the HRD department, among published authorities in the area, or among vendors and/or other contractors?

It is thus very important to identify precisely what talent will be needed to implement Organizational Strategy for HRD. Is it a question of needing leadership talent, technical expertise, consulting skill, or all of them? If skills are not available internally and are difficult to find externally—or if necessary resources to obtain these skills are lacking—then a proposed Organizational Strategy for HRD may not be feasible.

Relationships to other plans. People involved in choosing Organizational Strategy for HRD should consider its relationship to: (1) corporate-level plans; (2) business-level plans; (3) human resource plans; (4) HRD functions—such as training for different categories of employees; and (5) individual career plans. At each level, issues of key concern differ somewhat.

At the corporate level, managers concern themselves with maintaining a profitable portfolio of organizational assets. Key *corporate* issues and corresponding HRD issues may be summarized as follows:

CORPORATE ISSUES	RELATED HRD ISSUES
What businesses should the corporation be involved in?	What human skills, competencies, and knowledge are equated with success in each business and in all businesses? How can they be obtained through planned learning?
What goals and objectives are appropriate for the corporation?	How should planned learning contribute to the achievement of corporate goals and objectives? How much should planned learning contribute to the choice of corporate goals and objectives?
What distinctive business competencies are associated with success in each business in which the corporation is involved?	What distinctive human skills are related to business competencies? How can they be acquired or improved through planned learning?
What are the long-term prospects for the corporation and for each business?	What changes outside and inside the corporation affect learning needs over the long term, and what changes outside and inside each business affect learning needs over the long term?
What Grand Strategy for the corporation will help it avert threats or seize opportunities in the future?	What long-term learning plan for the corporation will help maximize the skills necessary for organizational success and/or minimize performance problems that may impede organizational success?

Key *business-level* issues and corresponding HRD issues may be summarized as follows:

BUSINESS UNIT ISSUES	RELATED HRD ISSUES
What is the mission of the business unit relative to the corporation?	How can human knowledge and skills help realize the mission and related goals and objectives?
How is it possible to compete successfully in the industry?	What human skills are needed to compete in the industry? How much does the organization possess them? How can it acquire those skills through planned learning?
Who are the consumers? How does the business serve them? How should the business serve them?	What human skills are needed to serve consumers? Does the business possess those skills?

BUSINESS UNIT ISSUES	RELATED HRD ISSUES
	What skills, if any, do consumers need to use the products or services of the business? Do they possess those skills? If not, how can those skills be improved?

Human resource plans encompass the full range of HR activities in the firm. These plans integrate recruitment, HRD, compensation/benefits, labor relations, employee assistance, and other HR functions in a unified effort to close the gap over time between

- the number/types of people needed to achieve strategic business objectives and realize business/corporate plans, and
- the number/types of people available at present.

HRP encompasses all efforts to improve present employee performance and develop future performance potential.

In considering the relationship between HRP and HRD, practitioners should think about such issues as these:

HRP ISSUES	RELATED HRD ISSUES
What is and what should be the long-term role of HR plans in helping realize strategic business plans/objectives?	What is and what should be the role of the HRD Effort relative to organizational goals and objectives? HR plans?
What is and what should be relationships between such HR program areas as recruitment, selection, compensation, benefits, and labor relations?	What is and what should be the relationships between the HRD Effort and other HR activities?
	What is and what should be the relationship between HRP and organization development, nonemployee development, employee development, employee education, and job training?
How can the gap be narrowed between the number/types of people needed by the firm in the future and the number/types the firm presently has on hand?	How can the gap be narrowed between what people know/can do at present and what they should know or be able to do in the future?

HR practitioners have long been criticized for failing to integrate their activities, with the result that these activities have sometimes worked at cross-purposes (Craft, 1980). From the results of one extensive survey conducted in 1985, it appears that some functions in the HR field are working toward integrating their efforts with others. Nkomo (1986) found that "recruitment/staffing, management succession and training and development were the major areas for which strategies and programs were developed as part of the human resource planning process" (p. 78). These HR program areas rated significantly better in this respect than other functions such as health and safety, labor relations, employee benefits, compensation, and affirmative action.

Finally, individual career plans should be considered in the process of selecting Organizational Strategy for HRD. This level is particularly difficult because individuals vary in career orientations (Derr, 1986; Schein, 1978). Key issues pertaining to career plans and corresponding HRD issues may be summarized as follows:

CAREER ISSUES	HRD ISSUES
How well has the organization clarified its career policies?	How clearly are HRD initiatives related to career planning?
How clearly has the organization delineated relationships between jobs/career paths in terms of education, experience, and other requirements necessary for individual mobility?	How much emphasis is placed on employee education? How well is education integrated to other components of the HRD Effort?
How do managers in the firm treat those who do not want more responsibility?	How well-suited are HRD efforts to multiple career orientations and to people with differing values and lifestyles?

HRD practitioners often bear important responsibilities in their firms for establishing career policies and offering instruction to individuals on career planning. It is important to formulate an Organizational Strategy for HRD that is flexible enough to allow growth opportunities for individuals with career orientations different from the traditional upwardly-bound path of increasing responsibility. The need for this flexibility is likely to increase as organizations (1) lay off employees in the wake of increasing automation and corporate downsizing efforts and (2) experience morale problems stemming from baby boomers who, due to sheer numbers, will probably not attain the levels of responsibility they desire (Jones, 1980; Leach & Chakiris, 1985; Spruell, 1985).

PLANNING FOR CONTINGENCIES

Suppose a team of managers, employees, and HRD practitioners develops a unified Organizational Strategy for HRD. Then suppose that something unexpected happens:

1. Two months later, a persistent rumor of a pending merger is publicly confirmed.
2. The firm's most important domestic manufacturing site votes in favor of union representation. (This union has strong views about HRD as a tool for keeping employee skills up-to-date.)
3. A giant in a related industry decides to enter markets presently dominated by this firm.

What should be done in these circumstances? Should a new Organizational Strategy for HRD be formulated from scratch? Should practitioners and others just sit tight and hope the HRD Effort will not be affected by unexpected changes?

This problem underscores the inherent problem of relying on a *programmed* rather than a *contingency* strategy. A programmed plan is inflexible and has to be changed completely when a major change occurs in the environment or when important assumptions made during planning are proven false. Contingency plans allow managers to adjust what they are doing when changing conditions make adjustments essential. Generally, programmed strategies are appropriate only in very stable industries. In all other cases contingency strategies should be used (Glueck & Jauch, 1984).

How is this idea applied to Organizational Strategy for HRD? HRD practitioners should ask knowledgeable people in their organizations about events or trends that were not initially considered in formal planning or that could produce new learning needs. In each case, practitioners should prepare contingency scenarios—that is, short narratives—to describe what to do in case these events do occur or trends produce effects different from what is expected.

CHOOSING ORGANIZATIONAL STRATEGY FOR HRD: THE PRODUCT

The term *curriculum* means "the plan of instruction for learning experiences or events." It is thus synonymous with Organizational Strategy for HRD, the product of strategic choice. Let's discuss *curriculum* in detail.

History. Academic writers have devoted considerable attention to defining curriculum and tracing how the term has been used. Tanner and Tanner (1980) found that "curriculum has been variously defined as: (1) the cumulative tradition of organized knowledge; (2) modes of thought; (3) race experience; (4) guided experience; (5) a planned learning environment; (6) cognitive/affective content and process; (7) an instructional plan; (8) instructional ends or outcomes; and (9) a technological system of production" (p. 36). These definitions can be transformed into nine questions: (1) What has been the sum total of human learning to date? (2) How do we think? (3) What has the human race experienced? (4) How can learners be guided through experience? (5) How can the learners' environment be structured to facilitate learning? (6) What information, facts and feelings are worth knowing and how do learners come to know them? (7) How can learning be organized and prepared? (8) What results are sought from a learning experience? and (9) What tools, methods, and techniques are needed to produce desired learning?

Lewis and Miel (1972) classified definitions of curriculum along similar lines. They found that the term has variously denoted: (1) a course of study; (2) intended results of learning; (3) experiences of learners during instruction; (4) experiences actually provided to learners; and (5) opportunities provided for learning.

On the other hand, Geneva Gay (1980) distinguishes between four different ways of thinking about curriculum. The first is the *academic,* which identifies what should be learned through intensive examination of "learners, society, subject matter disciplines, philosophy and the psychology of learning" (p. 122). The second way of thinking about curriculum is the *experiential,* which "theorizes that personal feelings, attitudes, values, and experiences are critical curriculum content" (p. 126). The curriculum should be a product of inquiry carried out by those who participate in learning. The third way of thinking about curriculum is the *technical,* which "seeks to maximize educational program proficiency and performance through applying the same principles of scientific management and production operating in industry" (p. 132). Fourth and finally, a curriculum can be thought about *pragmatically.* In this sense, practitioners "perceive instructional planning as a particularistic, localized process that is specific to the sociopolitical milieu of the context in which it occurs" (p. 137). While these definitions overlap, the point is that HRD practitioners can choose to focus on learning as it is affected by the outside world (*the academic*), learner desires and experiences (*the experiential*), efficiency and effectiveness in designing instruction (*the technical*), or the unique corporate culture in which the instructional planning process is carried out (*the pragmatic*).

Since publication of the first book on curriculum (Bobbitt, 1918), academic writers have devoted their attention to curriculum issues at primary and secondary school levels. Far less attention has been directed to the university curriculum, inservice training for teachers at any level of public education, or to corporate training, education, or development efforts (HRD). When academic writers discuss HRD, it is not at all unusual for them to make assertions about similarities or differences between public school and HRD curricula. To cite one example, Saylor, Alexander, and Lewis (1981) write:

> The purposes of business and industry training programs are far more specific than the general goals of schools and colleges. In addition, clients, teachers and policy decision makers generally agree on purposes of business and industry training programs (p. 109).

The first statement may be true enough. But the second implies a unity of direction and purpose which simply does not exist in many corporations any more than it does in many communities served by educators. It is true that HRD is usually viewed as a way to increase employee efficiency and effectiveness, just as education is viewed as a way to "prepare young people for life." Beyond that, HRD practitioners find as much agreement about what should be taught and how it should be taught among top managers, line managers, employees, and union representatives as principals and teachers find among parents, civic leaders, representatives of pressure groups, and other members of a community. In many cases, managers and employees base their expectations about HRD on their experiences with public education (Rothwell, 1983b).

For the most part, however, curriculum means the same in HRD settings as it does in public school settings. The differences stem from

- *the kind of learners:* Educators deal primarily with children; HRD practitioners, with adults.
- *the kind of subject matter:* Educators deal with fundamental skills—reading, writing, and arithmetic—and with broad, general information about the world in which we live; HRD practitioners, on the other hand, deal with the applica-

tion of knowledge or disciplines to specific job tasks, career paths, and organizational settings.
- *the kind of setting:* Educators are representatives of society and the community. They select and impart knowledge—and teach youngsters how to think. HRD practitioners are usually representatives of management. Their aim is to select and impart knowledge—and teach workers how to work smarter (more effectively) as well as how to achieve more economical output for the time, labor, and resources expended (more efficiently).

For HRD practitioners—as for educators—"a curriculum is an organized set of formal educational and/or training intentions" (Pratt, 1980, p. 4). It is a comprehensive plan for learning and instruction over time. The plan can cover a five-minute lesson or a series of courses and job rotations lasting several years (Rowntree, 1982).

Curriculum design. Design implies a deliberate effort to establish direction. According to *The Living Webster Encyclopedic Dictionary* (1975), design denotes

> An outline, sketch, or plan, as of a work of art, an edifice, or a machine to be executed or constructed; the combination of details or features . . . intention, purpose, or aim; a plan conceived in the mind; a project; a scheme; sometimes, a hostile plan, or evil, crafty or selfish intention; the object of a plan or purpose; the end in view; the adaptation of means to a preconceived end; a contrivance (p. 271).

Curriculum design is thus "a deliberate process of devising, planning and selecting the elements, techniques and procedures" of learning (Pratt, 1980, p. 5). It is similar to strategy formulation, the process of identifying "major actions or patterns of action for attainment of objectives" (Paine & Naumes, 1974, p. 7). However, strategy is formulated "ahead of time or emerges over time based on ad hoc decisions" (Paine & Naumes, 1974, p. 7).

Curriculum development. Development denotes gradual evolution and growth. The dictionary definition of development makes this meaning explicit:

> The act or process of developing; unfolding; the unraveling of a plot; a gradual growth or advancement through progressive changes (*The Living Webster Encyclopedic Dictionary*, 1975, p. 274).

Development implies implementing a plan. Hunkins (1980) defines curriculum development as "procedures employed in translating general program and instructional objectives, guided by a basic conceptualization of the curriculum, into contents, experiences, and educational environments" (p. 19).

Curriculum is thus an instructional plan; *instruction* is the process of implementing the plan. *Curriculum design* involves coming up with long-term goals and objectives for the HRD Effort; *curriculum development* means implementing activities to achieve those goals and objectives.

In a very important sense, curriculum issues have to do with strategy-making. "When you do curriculum planning in the broad educational sense," explains Patricia McLagan (in Zemke, 1981), "you ask questions about how a program need gets chosen, or why one particular program is built and other apparent needs are ignored. And that's the essence of strategy development in business: making rules for what you will and will not become involved in" (p. 33). For McLagan, the curriculum development process in HRD is synonymous with strategy formulation. It involves considering four key issues: (1) What is the company whose needs HRD is trying to serve? (2) What do managers in the firm think of people generally and people development specifically? (3) What is the present philosophy and assumptions about curriculum development in the organization? and (4) What is the purpose of the HRD Effort in helping external groups, internal work groups, job incumbents, and individuals achieve their learning objectives? Just as Strategic Business Plans provide long-term direction to organizational initiatives, a curriculum provides long-term direction to an HRD Effort.

Consider the following conversation between an external consultant and a Director of Human Resource Development.

Consultant:
"How do you decide what instruction to design and deliver in this organization?"

HRD Manager:
"It is an informal process. It all starts at the plant level. Each training director in each of our plants conducts a needs assessment every year. Training directors vary in how they approach the task. Some sit in their offices and draw up plans without consulting anybody. Some wander through the plant and talk informally to managers—and sometimes to supervisors and employees as well—about what training they would like to see in the coming year. Some make the process more formal by mailing questionnaires to managers, first-line supervisors, and employees. Others develop plans based on staff meetings and formal advisory boards composed of representatives from different levels. In short, they use about any method you can think of."

Consultant:
"You mean that there is no set list of courses—a training curriculum, if you prefer the term—which describes the instruction an employee should have, depending on his or her job category or title or length of time in position?"

HRD Manager:
"No, we have no such thing as that. We do distinguish between 'courses' appropriate for managers, supervisors, certain professional groups—engineers and computer professionals, for instance—and secretaries. By the way, that's an interesting use of the term 'curriculum.' I always thought it referred to the plan of instruction for one course. Sort of like a syllabus."

Consultant:
"Your use of the term 'curriculum' is, I venture to say, rather common. Some people use the term *program planning* in this way. They also use program planning to mean the scheduling of offerings by the HRD department. But I mean something completely different from short-term program planning."

HRD Manager:
"Really? What?"

Consultant:
"I mean a long-term plan of instruction for the entire organization. You look at job categories, individual career plans, organizational or work group and nonemployee needs and then create learning experiences—not just classroom courses, by the way—to meet recurring needs."

HRD Manager:
"Sounds interesting. But I'm not sure it would work here. After the years I've been here, I'm not sure our managers know what they are doing from one minute to the next. They are *really* one-minute managers, because one minute is about as far into the future as they ever plan!"

Consultant:
"I think you are selling them short. Granted, there are times when learning needs are nonrecurring. They are met by nonrecurring instruction—a one-time course offering, for instance. But other learning needs are predictable. They can be met by a long-term learning plan."

As can be seen from this discussion, there is some difference of opinion about the meaning of *curriculum*. The HRD Manager in the dialogue describes the term in a way not significantly different from the practice in many businesses. On the other hand, the consultant uses the same term in a completely different way.

Approaches to Curriculum Planning

How does an HRD practitioner go about planning a curriculum? In what different ways can the practitioner approach the process? This section addresses these questions.

The curriculum planning process. Curricula may differ by

1. Focus—what is to be the basis of the change effort?

2. Scope—how much change is desired?
3. Time horizon—how long is the change effort expected to take?
4. Approach—how can the curriculum be organized and how should the instructional plan be carried out?

Let us look for a moment at the process of planning a training curriculum. We choose training because managers and employees often understand the need for training when they cannot readily see the need for longer-term efforts like employee education or development.

It is important to bear in mind that a training curriculum implies more than just *one* training program or a schedule of "courses" for a one-year period. "The challenge of curriculum design," writes Julia Galosy (1983), "is to build a coherent, sequential plan which will provide structure and unity to the full gamut of . . . training programs" (p. 48). A curriculum is based on recurrent or expected job training needs over time.

According to Galosy (1983), curriculum planning of this type is a six-step process in which HRD practitioners:

1. *formulate goals:* What is the guiding philosophy of the curriculum? What general results are sought? For what purpose(s)?
2. *generate groups:* How can employees be categorized into distinct groups?
3. *determine needs:* What are the recurrent training needs of people in each job category?
4. *differentiate needs:* What are learning needs as opposed to nonlearning needs?
5. *scope and sequence programs:* What instructional experiences will meet recurring needs of employees in each job category? How can instructional experiences be sequenced so learners build from foundational knowledge to advanced knowledge and skills?
6. *design the curriculum:* How are instructional programs organized?

These steps are important enough to warrant elaboration.

The first step, formulating goals, means sorting out the purpose of the instructional effort. As Galosy explains, "goals provide an underlying philosophy, a mission and a values statement to guide design efforts" (p. 48). Coming up with goals can be as simple as articulating what results are sought from training. Goals may reinforce existing company culture, strategy, and values. Alternatively, they may be directed to changing culture, strategy, and values.

The second step, generating groups, means "looking at all divisions and functions and superimposing a logical grouping" (Galosy, 1983, p. 49). In previous chapters we have already described the various markets and market segments to which the HRD Effort can be directed. Decisions about what markets and market segments should be served stem from a sense of the HRD Effort's purpose.

The third step, determining needs, means more than simply identifying what learners should know or do to carry out their jobs. In a curriculum context, the intent is identification of all *critical* learning needs. Historically, what levels of performance exist in the organization? What opportunities exist to improve performance? What performance improvements are necessitated by the Strategic Business Plan? Answers to these questions should produce "a finely tuned but comprehensive list of skills" (Galosy, 1983, p. 49). This is the starting point for designing a curriculum, with training for each job category geared to performance requirements at each level. Remember, "you should approach curriculum design from a holistic viewpoint, not as individual programs" (Galosy, 1983, p. 49).

The fourth step, differentiating training needs, takes up where the previous one ended. In short, what skills are needed for each market segment of learners? HRD practitioners and line managers match up skill requirements to learner markets. Galosy (1983) suggests using a matrix, like that shown in Table 5-2, as an aid in this process. At each level, practitioners decide (1) how the "subject" or "skill" needs to be treated, and (2) how previous treatments should influence future ones. For instance, first-line supervisors may need "decision-making" treated in one way to match their job requirements. Middle managers may also need exposure to the same subject, but the treatment has to be modified to match up to their job requirements and build on instruction they previously received as supervisors.

The fifth step, scoping and sequencing instructional programs, means deciding

- how much emphasis to place on specific subjects at each level, and
- how to sequence subjects so that learners are exposed to topics in a logical way.

How much emphasis to place on subjects is a strategic issue. It affects future capabilities of learners. Traditionally, HRD practitioners make decisions about how much to emphasize a subject by first determining the subject's importance for successful job performance. Important subjects are emphasized more and are reinforced several times across courses. How to sequence subjects depends on curriculum goals. Are they intended to: (1) *present distilled experience from the past?* In that case, a logical se-

TABLE 5-2 MANAGEMENT NEEDS MATRIX					
Management dimension	Supervisor	Middle managers	Executive	Officers
Appraisal	X	X	X	
Building Teams		X	X	
Coaching/Counseling	X	X		
Communication	X	X	X	X
Conducting Meetings			X	X
Conflict	X	X		
Delegation	X	X		

Source: Galosy, 1983, p. 50. Reprinted with permission from The American Society for Training and Development.

quence from simple to complex subjects is appropriate. (2) *pool experience of learners?* In that case, a sequence based on how learners perceive the importance of different issues may be appropriate. (3) *create new experience and new knowledge?* In that case, a sequence beginning with an upending event/situation—such as simulation of a never-before-encountered problem—may be appropriate. For the most part, however, "it is difficult to find a basis for correct sequencing of the entire set of topics for a course or set of courses other than a kind of 'common-sense' logical ordering" (Gagné & Briggs, 1979, p. 140).

The sixth and final step, curriculum design, produces a list of courses—and other planned learning experiences—which constitute the curriculum. "At this point, you are breaking down the matrix you built and recombining the . . . dimensions into individual [instructional] programs" (Galosy, 1983, p. 51). The result is a learning plan for each job class or job category in the organization. It can then be communicated to employees and line managers as a simple list of courses or as a course matrix (see examples in Table 5-3 and Figure 5-4).

The steps in planning a training curriculum can be modified in planning organization development, nonemployee development, employee development, and employee education. Differences may exist in what groups are served, how needs are identified, how needs are addressed, what planned learning experiences are offered to what groups, and how those experiences are offered. Yet all these planned learning initiatives are unified through a common direction—that is, through an Organizational Strategy for HRD.

Alternative approaches to curriculum planning. No doubt the previous section will lead many readers to believe there is only *one* right way to go about curriculum planning. That is not so. There are at least *four* major ways to go about it (Sredl & Rothwell, 1987): (1) *the course-centered approach;* (2) *the experience-centered approach;* (3) *the goals-centered approach;* and (4) *the learner-centered approach.* This figure can be doubled from four to eight by distinguishing between curricula intended to *distill* past experience and knowledge from those intended to *create* new experience and knowledge.

The most familiar approach is the course-centered. "Historically and currently, the dominant concept of the curriculum is that of subjects and subject matter therein to be taught by teachers and learned by students" (Saylor, Alexander, & Lewis, 1981, p. 4). HRD practitioners—and managers as well—often associate "courses" with "curriculum" because they base their expectations about HRD on their own experiences with grade schools, high schools, and colleges. In schools, "the term curriculum has been and still is widely used to refer to the set of subjects or courses offered. . . ." (Saylor, Alexander, & Lewis, 1981, p. 4).

Designing a course-centered curriculum is not very complicated. The HRD practitioner only needs to (Rothwell, 1984e): (1) "ask subject matter specialists what should be included; (2) arrange the content in a logical sequence, and (3) install it" (p. 41). Subject matter specialists may include top managers, line managers, experienced employees, published authorities, or members of a work group. Typically, the result will be a list of *course titles.* The content of any single course offering—here

TABLE 5-3 A REPRESENTATIVE TRAINING CURRICULUM ORGANIZED BY COURSE TITLES: LIST FORMAT

Job class	Course number	Course title	Length
Auditor I			
Entry			
	1	Orientation	2 Hours
	2	Orientation Self-Study (Same as Developmental Reading Assignments)	
Middle and Advanced			
	•	Same as Auditor II	
Auditor II			
Entry			
	3	Introduction to the Industry	1 Day
	4	Audit Interviewing	1 Day
	5	Developing Audit Findings	1 Day
	6	Audit Workpapers	1 Day
Middle			
	7	Legal Research	1 Day
	8	Library Research	1 Day
	9	Introduction to EDP Auditing	2 1/4 Days
	10	Sampling	
Advanced			
	11	Report Writing	1 Day
	12	Statistics	2 Days
	13	Fundamentals of Supervision	1 Day
Auditor III			
Entry			
	•	Same as Auditor II Advanced	
	14	Audit Planning	1 Day
Middle			
	15	Training Employees	1 Day
	16	Oral Presentation Skills	1 Day
Advanced			
	17	Advanced Supervision/Project Mgmt.	
	18	Audit Contracting	
	19	Advanced EDP Auditing	Varies
Audit Manager			
Entry			
	•	Same as Auditor III Advanced	
Middle and Advanced			
	•	Continuing Professional Education as desired, needed, and approved	

OFFICEWIDE TRAINING CURRICULUM

CORE COURSES	ENTRY			MIDDLE			ADVANCED		
AUDITOR I	**ALL** ○ Orientation ○ Orientation Self-Study ○ Introduction to the Industry ○ Legal Research ○ Library Research ○ Flowcharting			**ALL** ○ Report Writing			**ALL** ○ Logic ○ Legal Evidence ○ Introduction to EDP Auditing ○ Advanced State Government Accounting ○ Advanced EDP Auditing		
	COMPLIANCE ONLY	PERFORMANCE ONLY		COMPLIANCE ONLY	PERFORMANCE ONLY		COMPLIANCE ONLY	PERFORMANCE ONLY	
	○ Division Orientation (E) ○ Interviewing ○ Developing Audit Findings ○ Workpapers	○ Division Orientation ○ Interviewing ○ Developing Audit Findings ○ Workpapers		○ Sampling	○ Survey Methods ○ Sampling ○ Introduction to State Government Accounting			○ Statistical Inference ○ Introduction to Statistical Package for the Social Sciences	
AUDITOR II	**ALL** ○ Same as Auditor I Advanced			**ALL** ○ Training Employees ○ Employee Performance Appraisal ○ Oral Presentation Skills			**ALL**		
	COMPLIANCE ONLY	PERFORMANCE ONLY					COMPLIANCE ONLY	PERFORMANCE ONLY	
	○ Audit Planning & Management	○ Audit Planning & Management					○ Audit Contracting	○ Audit Contracting	
AUDIT MANAGER	**ALL** ○ Same as Auditor II Advanced			**ALL** ○ General Management Colloquium ○ Other Courses as Needed, Requested, or Desired					
				COMPLIANCE ONLY		PERFORMANCE ONLY			
				○ Audit Management Colloquium		○ Audit Management Colloquium			

Figure 5-4: A Representative Training Curriculum Organized by Course Titles: Matrix Format

"offering" means each time the course is given—depends on preferences of instructors and, to a lesser extent, on learner needs at the time when the course is delivered.

Perhaps a simple example will clarify how this process works. Suppose a consultant is asked to develop a curriculum for employees of a large personnel department. All new employees enter as corporate recruiters or trainers. After completing a six-month probation in which they receive training, new employees are rotated to other parts of the department.

The consultant would begin the curriculum design process in the training and recruitment divisions. The consultant asks managers—and perhaps experienced employees of each division as well—what newcomers "need to know about" during their first six months. The consultant then compares their responses, identifies areas of agreement, labels each "area of agreement" with a course title, and arranges these titles in a logical sequence. The final step is to feed back the list of titles to the department manager for comments or suggestions. The ambitious consultant might even ask: (1) What topics should be treated in each "course"? (2) How soon after date of hire should newcomers attend each "course"? (3) What delivery method—for example, individual study or classroom-based—is desirable for each course? Why? A similar approach can be used to identify instructional needs *beyond entry* as employees prepare for rotations to new divisions within the department, enter new, temporary jobs in the new division, or settle into semipermanent jobs presumably different from those to which they have previously been rotated. The same process is repeated in every *department* of the firm so each department has its own curriculum.

The course-centered approach can be modified to anticipate the future rather than distill experiences from the past. To design a curriculum of this kind, the HRD practitioner should first assess the goals of instruction (Rothwell, 1984e). In short, what is the focus and purpose of the curriculum? Second, examine trends in the environment outside the organization. How are they likely to affect nonemployee groups, work groups, individuals, and job categories? Third, appraise present strengths and weaknesses inside the organization. What are the deficiencies and proficiencies of work groups, individuals, and job categories? Fourth, decide on a curriculum prioritized by critical issues having to do with expected future learning needs. Fifth and finally, install the curriculum. These steps are illustrated schematically in Figure 5-5.

The future-oriented approach to course-centered curriculum design differs significantly from its traditional counterpart. In the future-oriented approach, courses are selected for the curriculum on the basis of *anticipated future needs*. In contrast, the traditional approach selects courses from *needs identified through experience*.

Simplicity is the chief advantage of the course-centered approach. It should not take much time or effort to poll a few people about repetitive learning needs of new employees in one job category. Yet this process provides the basis for making simple instructional plans to meet common training needs on a regular basis.

A chief disadvantage of the course-centered approach is that it does not focus on outcomes. The curriculum is just a list of course titles—with no indication of what learners will be able *to do* once they have completed a course. In fact, the content of each course may vary—depending on who the instructors and learners are and what their preferences happen to be at the time a course is offered.

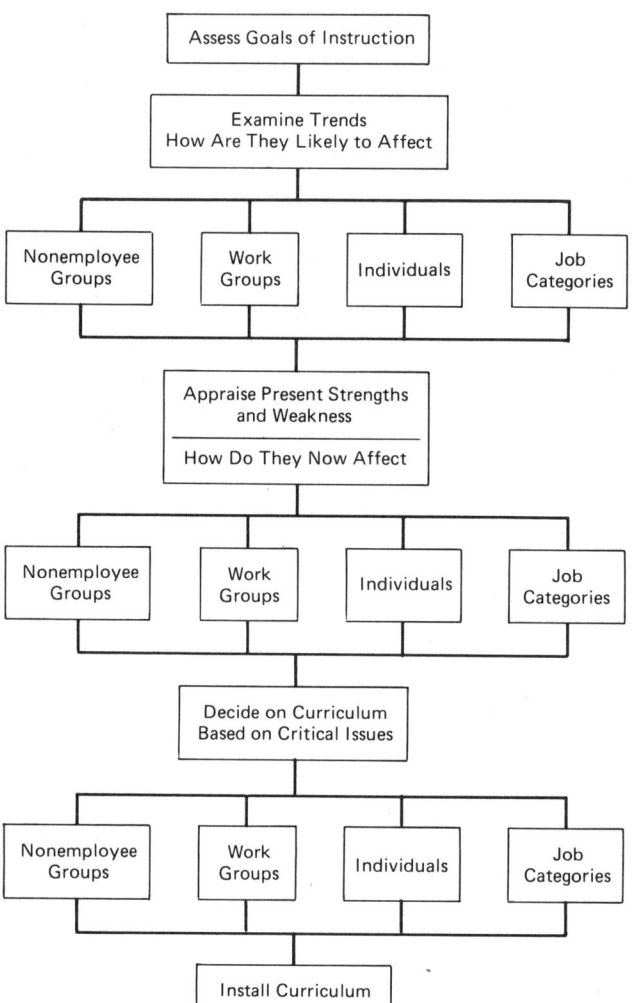

Figure 5-5: Steps in a Strategic, Course-Centered Approach to Curriculum Planning

A second way to approach curriculum design, different from the course-centered approach, is based on what learners experience during the learning process. This is the experienced-centered approach. It assumes that individuals vary in how they perceive events. People "see" things in different ways because their prior experiences, backgrounds, education, and beliefs vary. "Every perceiver is, as it were, to some degree a nonrepresentational artist, painting a picture of the world that expresses an individual view of reality" (Krech, Crutchfield, & Ballachey, 1962, p. 20).

Individuals thus "interpret" unspoken rules of organizational culture in different ways. When this interpretation is faulty, other people let them know through remarks such as "hey, that's not the way we do things here," or "don't you know we're supposed to. . . ." If an individual persists in behavior that violates cultural norms, he or she is ostracized by the work group or disciplined by a superior.

Action Research, sometimes called the basis of Organization Development, provides one way to think about developing an experience-centered curriculum. Managers sense a need for cultural change. They contract with an internal or external change agent—a consultant—to assist with the change effort. The consultant then: (1) collects information about the "problem," including what it is, how prevalent it is, and how people feel about it; (2) feeds back the information to decision-makers and people who provided information about the problem; (3) helps participants in the change effort establish objectives for change; (4) gathers information as action is taken; and (5) periodically feeds back information to participants in the change effort, helping them establish new plans for change. These steps comprise a cyclical change process, which replaces one-shot learning experiences with continuous learning.

The experience-centered approach is instrumental in initiating and bringing about change through learning

- *in the organization:* The focus is usually on cultural change, helping intact work groups in the organization adopt new norms of behavior.
- *with individuals:* The focus is on stimulating individual insight, helping each person discover new ideas or new approaches.
- *across job categories or within them:* The focus is on hierarchical relationships between supervisory and nonsupervisory employees or between members of the same occupation within the firm.

The impetus for the learning effort is usually crisis. Destructive conflict between work groups is frequently a symptom that signals a need to reexamine goals, work methods, and results.

Curriculum theorists have long noted that potential disparities may exist, too, between what curriculum planners say they are doing and what, in fact, others perceive they are doing. It is thus possible to distinguish between the curriculum plan as it is (Saylor, Alexander, & Lewis, 1981):

- documented in writing or discussed by curriculum planners (*formal curriculum*),
- perceived by instructors (*perceived curriculum*), and
- viewed by external observers or by learners attending instructional events (*experienced curriculum*).

The difference between formal curriculum and perceived curriculum "is symptomatic of separating means and ends in education. The ends . . . are responses to the question, 'What shall be taught?' while the means of education are responses to the question, 'How shall it be taught?' When means are separated from ends, the curriculum experienced may vary from the curriculum planned" (Saylor, Alexander, & Lewis, 1981, p. 5). This difference between planned and experienced learning is similar to differences between *espoused theory* and *theory-in-use* (Argyris & Schön, 1974 & 1978). *Espoused theory* is what decision-makers and others say should be; *theory-in-use* is how they actually behave. "Individuals may or may not be aware of the incompatibility of the two theories" (Argyris & Schön, 1974, p. 7). By using the action research model illustrated in Figure 5-6, HRD practitioners and others in the organization reveal discrepancies between curriculum intentions and results.

To transform experience-centered curricula to a future orientation, HRD practitioners must mobilize support for change. To do that, they collect information from people inside and outside the organization about future threats and opportunities likely to affect external stakeholders, work groups, the organization, individuals, and job categories. This information is fed back to decision-makers to *create* impetus for change. Another way is to identify dissatisfied people in the firm and collect information from them to create a "picture of reality" that will shock decision-makers out of complacency, because it is radically at odds with what they believe (Rothwell, 1984a). A third way is to bring together groups in conflict and let them confront each other (Beckhard, 1967). These methods stimulate long-term planning for future-oriented change. Organized learning activities are tools for engineering change.

Comprehensiveness is a chief advantage of the experience-centered approach to curriculum design. It makes the HRD Effort a tool for *cultural* change, not solely *individual* change.

A chief disadvantage of this approach is the difficulty of measuring long-term change. When productivity increases or measures of employee morale show improvement, how can it be determined for certain that the cause is attributable to these change efforts? It is difficult to measure effects that stem from large-scale, long-term change initiatives. However, attempts have been made to do so—some rather success-

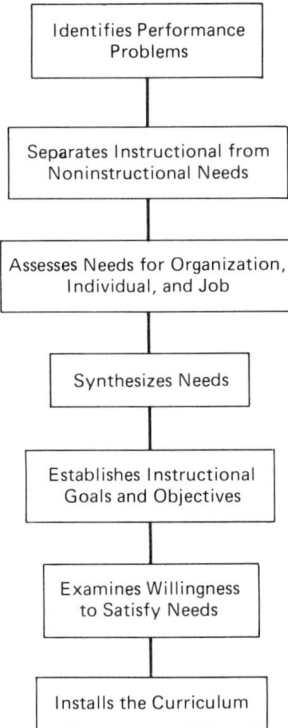

Figure 5-6: Steps in a Simplified Model of Steps in Developing a Performance-Based Curriculum

fully (for example, Marrow, Bowers, & Seashore, 1967; Porras & Berg, 1978; Porras & Wilkins, 1980).

A third approach to curriculum design is goal-centered. Public education has been profoundly influenced by the notion of curriculum as results (outcomes) to be achieved through instruction (Saylor, Alexander, & Lewis, 1981). Through the writings of Robert Mager (1975), the goal-centered approach has had perhaps an even greater influence on HRD. The reason is that its bottom-line, results orientation appeals to HRD practitioners and line managers.

There are essentially two ways to design a goal-centered curriculum (Davis & McCallon, 1974; Rothwell, 1983b, 1983c, 1984e & 1984f; Sredl & Rothwell, 1987): (1) based on performance; and (2) based on competencies.

The curriculum planner using the performance-based approach thinks of the HRD Effort as a tool for satisfying learning deficiencies. The starting point for curriculum planning is a *problem* with individual performance which is wholly or partly attributable to lack of knowledge or skill (Gilbert, 1967). The planner (Rothwell, 1984f): (1) identifies performance problems by job class, work unit, or individual; (2) identifies training, education, and development needs by separating them from other problems not attributable to lack of knowledge or skill; (3) assesses training, education, and development needs from the standpoint of the group, individual, and/or job; (4) synthesizes needs; (5) establishes instructional goals and objectives to correct the needs; (6) examines the willingness of key decision-makers to satisfy needs; and (7) installs the curriculum through instructional activities. These steps are illustrated in Figure 5-6.

The starting point for planning a performance-based curriculum is an examination of recurring or critical problems in

- the environment—HRD practitioners look at problems between the organization and its suppliers, distributors, customers, and others.
- the organization—Using an organization chart, practitioners identify work groups and then examine each group, asking this question: What performance problems are common at this time in this group?
- individuals—Practitioners categorize individuals into groups, such as "new entrant to the job," "stable tenured employee," or "promotable tenured employee," and then consider common performance problems, if any, among employees in each group.
- job categories—Practitioners classify employees by job categories. They then ask: "What performance problems are common in each category?"

This examination produces four separate, but related, lists of learning needs. Each list provides a foundation for preparing behavioral objectives describing what learners should be able to do upon completion of a planned learning experience. Objectives are grouped together logically as the foundation for planned learning experiences.

The chief advantage of the performance-based approach is its strong emphasis on results. It is especially appealing to decision-makers, whose interests it serves.

Learning needs are linked directly to problems; instructional objectives are linked directly to solving problems.

The chief disadvantage of the performance-based approach is that it relies on past problems as the basis for future learning. Problems must be experienced before they prompt action. This approach is sometimes defended on the grounds that adults are highly motivated to learn while grappling with a problem (Knowles, 1984).

The trouble is that future conditions may turn out utterly unlike those experienced in past or present (Rothwell, 1984d). Anticipating the future—and thus engaging in future-oriented curriculum planning—requires a different approach, one that prepares learners *before* or *as* they encounter problems. Unfortunately, "it is hard to imagine an adult's deciding to engage in paradigm shifting, perspective transformation, or the replacing of one meaning system with another purely on his or her own volition. What will induce this exploration . . . is some kind of external event or imperative" (Brookfield, 1986, pp. 49–50). A present or impending crisis is often necessary to stimulate change through learning.

To transform the performance-based approach to a future orientation, the HRD practitioner should be a catalyst for change who creates occasions when "context shifting" can occur. "Context shifting" means giving learners and decision-makers opportunities to place themselves artificially at a future point in time, think about problems likely to be encountered, and then retrace their footsteps to the present in order to determine future learning needs (Lefkoe, 1985). This is more than just "blue sky" forecasting: it puts people on the spot to function in conditions they themselves believe will occur in the future. The result is a new, firsthand awareness of future learning needs. "The assumption is," writes Brookfield (1986), "that if you are successful in changing adults' perceptions of the world in which they live, you will not need to *teach* adults to acquire new skills and knowledge—they will be eager to discover these for themselves" (p. 248).

To do this, HRD practitioners may try: (1) helping learners scan the environment to detect future trends or issues which may affect them in the future; (2) giving learners opportunities to pinpoint, through simulations and other artificial exercises set in the future, problems that are likely to come up; (3) separating future training, education, and development needs from noninstructional needs stemming from other sources; (4) assessing future needs by stepping back to the present but looking to what performance will be needed at a future time; (5) establishing instructional goals or objectives that, if satisfied, will meet future learning needs; (6) helping learners and decision-makers identify instructional methods and resources for satisfying their learning needs; and, (7) installing the curriculum through instructional activities—but planning for contingencies if future conditions do not turn out as expected. These steps are illustrated in Figure 5-7.

The competency-based approach to curriculum planning differs in a few key respects from its performance-based counterpart. Unfortunately, *competency* is a term which has been used in several different ways (Davies, 1973; Klemp, 1979; Olson & Freeman, 1979; Zemke, 1982a). As a consequence, some confusion exists about what it means. Some writers do not consider competency as different from *behavior*. Others define it as *performance* (results of behavior). Perhaps the best definition is Klemp's (1979):

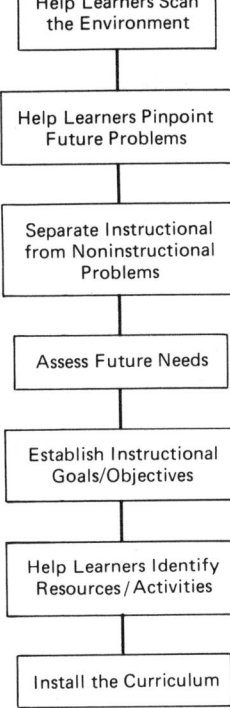

Figure 5-7: Simplified Model of Steps in Developing a Performance-Based Curriculum: A Future Orientation

A competency is a generic knowledge, skill, trait, self-schema or motive of a person that is causally related to effective behavior referenced to external performance criteria, where:

- *Knowledge* is a set of usable information organized around a specific content area.
- *Skill* is the ability to demonstrate a set of related behaviors or processes.
- *Trait* is a disposition or characteristic way of responding to an equivalent set of stimuli.
- *Self-schema* is a person's image of himself or herself and his or her evaluation of that image.
- *Motive* is a recurrent concern for a goal state or condition which drives, selects, and directs behavior of the individual (p. 42 as cited in Boyatzis, 1982).

Competency is thus an *underlying characteristic,* one manifested in many ways (Boyatzis, 1982).

To plan a competency-based curriculum, the HRD practitioner (Rothwell, 1984e; Sredl & Rothwell, 1987):

1. Designs a competency model for each work unit, job category, or other group by: (a) asking a panel of experienced practitioners to identify crucial outputs of the work unit, job category, or group; (b) asking a second panel of practitioners to

synthesize major outputs; (c) reviewing past studies of work units, job classes, or other groups so as to develop a tentative list of competencies necessary to succeed; (d) preparing a list of tentative competencies, reviewed and approved by experienced members of each work unit, job category, or other groups; (e) assigning priorities to identified competencies; (f) developing, for each competency, "behavioral anchors"—narrative descriptions of behavior associated with a competency. These descriptions are arranged in a three- or four-step continuum from basic to advanced levels of proficiency.

2. Analyzes the current level of performance. In other words, what competencies are now evident in the work unit, job category, or other group? What competencies are not evident? How proficient are members of the work unit/job category/group in each competency area?
3. Specifies desired levels of performance. In other words, what competencies are desirable in the future? What competencies are not desirable? How proficient should each work unit, job category, or other group be in the future?
4. Compares present to desired future competencies.
5. Prepares instructional objectives to narrow gaps between present and desired future competencies.

These steps are illustrated in Figure 5-8.

Unlike its performance-based counterpart, this approach to curriculum development "is not primarily concerned with what is wrong but with what is possible. As such it lends itself to the pursuit of new opportunities" (Davis & McCallon, 1974, p. 32). To put it another way, competency "models"—descriptions of human characteristics underlying performance—can be future-oriented. In using the competency-

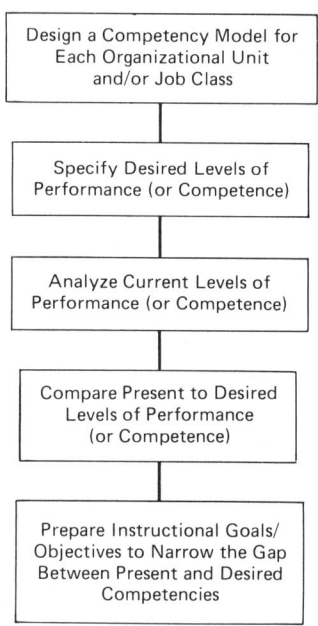

Figure 5-8: Steps in a Simplified Model for Competency-based Curriculum Planning

based approach, curriculum planners start out with a model that (1) describes exemplary performance, but (2) exists nowhere in the organization, group, or job category at present. Instructional objectives are geared to creating "super performers," despite vagaries about environmental conditions in the future. The performance-based approach, however, begins with *either* minimum or desired job standards. Present performance is then compared to standards established in the past. When actual performance differs from standards, and this difference results from lack of individual knowledge or skill, then instruction is one way to address the problem.

The difference is important. The performance-based approach tends to focus on *nonrecurring problems*, often brief shortfalls between desired standards and actual results. Since standards are developed in the past, present results are compared to past requirements. The competency-based approach may focus on *recurring problems* or *future expectations*. As a consequence, it helps people cope with future requirements.

Performance-based curriculum planners find it difficult to establish long-term instructional plans, because they use HRD as a "fix-it" tool. This satisfies managers, who want immediate justification for instructional expenditures, but does not help avert future performance problems before they occur. On the other hand, competency-based curriculum planners establish long-term instructional plans. Moreover, they *may* identify future-oriented rather than past-oriented competencies. This is, in fact, the chief advantage of the competency-based approach. However, not *all* competencies are necessarily future-oriented. If managers list competencies based on their estimations of past performance, then the curriculum will *not* be future-oriented. To ensure that a competency-based curriculum is future-oriented, HRD practitioners must base competencies on the results of environmental scanning efforts.

A competency-based curriculum is time-consuming and expensive to develop. Nor is it an undertaking which any novice can begin or end successfully. Even experts in HRD disagree about the meaning of "competency-based," so wide variations in instructional planning activities are possible.

The learner-centered approach is the fourth, and final, approach to curriculum design. It rests on the belief of some adult educators—most notably Malcolm Knowles (1984), perhaps its most vocal advocate in HRD circles—that adults differ from children in how they learn. Knowles is an articulate champion of the adult as a self-directed learner. As Brookfield (1986) explains:

> The development of self-directed learning capacities is perhaps the most frequently articulated aim of educators and trainers of adults. . . . Self-directed learning is defined as a process in which individuals take the initiative in designing learning experiences, diagnosing needs, locating resources, and evaluating learning (p. 40).

The learner-centered approach to curriculum design stresses the desire of individuals to participate in the process of identifying—and meeting—their own learning needs. As Greene (1977) explains, "Curriculum, to me, ought to be a means of providing opportunities for the seizing of a range of meanings by persons open to the world" (p. 283). In short, learning helps individuals become more of what they are capable of becoming.

Malcolm Knowles (1984) fervently believes in *androgogy,* the "art of teaching adults." It is founded on several key assumptions (Knowles, 1984). First, adults need to see a reason for learning before they will be motivated to make the effort. In this respect, adults are unlike children. Second, adults are self-directing; they want to take charge of their learning and their lives. Many adult educators believe that their chief purpose is to help learners achieve a state of self-directedness (Evan, 1982). Third, adults view learning through the filter of experience. As people mature, "they increasingly define themselves in terms of the experiences they have had" (Knowles, 1984, p. 58). Fourth, adults are motivated to learn while grappling with immediate problems confronting them. Timing is thus crucial for learning. As Knowles points out, though, "it is not necessary to sit by passively and wait for readiness to develop naturally" (p. 59). There are ways to create readiness to learn—including (as Knowles points out) modelling of behavior, counseling, and simulation. Fifth, adults tend to be problem-centered in their orientation to learning. They "are motivated to devote energy to learn something to the extent that they perceive that it will help them perform tasks or deal with problems that they confront in their life situations" (Knowles, 1984, p. 59). These ideas, central to the notion of learner-centered curriculum development, have been widely examined and criticized. Brookfield (1986) found research results which seem to be at odds with Knowles' assertions: (1) not all adults are self-directed learners, nor should they be (Witkin, 1949), and (2) adults proceed in their learning more by accident than by deliberate planning (Brookfield, 1980; Danis & Tremblay, 1985).

To develop a learner-centered curriculum, the HRD practitioner:

1. identifies learners as members of work groups, as individuals with their own career aspirations, and as representatives of various job categories,
2. helps learners explore present problems and surface new ideas worthy of exploration, and
3. guides learners to people, activities, situations, and other sources which will help them meet their learning needs or identify new issues worth exploring.

Alternative models of curriculum development appropriate to the learner-centered approach have been suggested by, among others, Houle (1972), Rothwell (1984e), Sredl and Rothwell (1987), and Verduin (1980).

In developing a curriculum using the learner-centered approach, the HRD practitioner categorizes learners according to their work group affiliation, individual life stage and career interests, or job concerns. The HRD practitioner then helps learners identify and explore problems they have experienced—or expect to experience in the future—within the organization, their careers, and their jobs. More than that, HRD practitioners assist learners so that they arrange experiences that help them become more aware of future problems worthy of exploration.

Finally, HRD practitioners serve as advisors and brokers who connect resources for learning with individuals desiring them. Practitioners scan the environment inside and outside an organization for people, events, and situations that can facilitate learning.

The learner-directed approach to curriculum design is well-suited to anticipatory thinking. Such techniques as inquiry-oriented instruction—widely advocated by Jerome Bruner (1961) and John Dewey (1938)—rely on questioning, "context shifting," simulations, and other techniques which produce knowledge. In this respect, the learner-directed approach lends itself to the creation of new ideas rather than the distillation of experience.

RESULTS OF CURRICULUM PLANNING AND CHOICE OF ORGANIZATIONAL STRATEGY FOR HRD

The result of curriculum planning and choice of Organizational Strategy for HRD is a comprehensive instructional plan for: (1) groups outside the corporation or business; (2) work groups or departments inside the organization; (3) individuals aspiring to new jobs; and (4) job categories. Organizational Strategy for HRD and the curriculum are synonymous. This long-term instructional plan integrates and unifies organization development, nonemployee development, employee development, employee education, and training.

ACTIVITY 5-1 A Checklist for HRD Strategy and Planning

Directions: Top management in many organizations expects HRD programs to be as much profit-oriented as they are people-oriented. Complete this checklist and plan for implementing an HRD strategy that can help HRD managers do their part to affect the bottom line. Use this checklist to rate your HRD Effort.

The Strategy	Yes	No
*Can HRD management define what an organizational strategy is?	☐	☐
*Does HRD have a "strategic profile"[1]?	☐	☐
*Has a "strategic forecast"[2] been completed?	☐	☐
*Has a "resource audit"[3] been completed?	☐	☐
*Has a "test of consistency"[4] evaluation been completed?	☐	☐
*Have alternative strategies been developed?	☐	☐
*Has a "strategic choice" been based on facts, results, and experience?	☐	☐
*Is the strategy identifiable and has it been made clear either in words or practice?	☐	☐
*Does the strategy take full advantage of resources and opportunities?	☐	☐
*Is the strategy consistent with HRD competence and resources, both present and projected?	☐	☐
*Are the major provisions of the strategy and the program of major policies of which it is comprised internally consistent?	☐	☐
*Is the chosen level of competency feasible in institutional and personal terms?	☐	☐
*Is the strategy appropriate to the personal values and aspirations of the key participants?	☐	☐
*Is the strategy appropriate to the desired level of contribution to the main organization?	☐	☐
*Does the strategy constitute a clear stimulus to HRD effort and commitment?	☐	☐
*Are there any early indications of the responsiveness of the company to the strategy?	☐	☐

ACTIVITY 5-1 Continued

The Plan

*Have the results of present HRD planning been identified? Has it been successful? Does it work? If so, why? If not, what policy elements need to be reevaluated and perhaps changed? ☐ ☐

*Are the plans appropriate, given the environment, resources, organization, and time frame? Are objectives internally consistent with each other? Are they consistent with the company personality and the personal objectives of the principal participants in the company? Have Company members participated in the development of objectives that concern them and in which their participation is appropriate? Can the objectives be clearly expressed to and supported by all appropriate personnel in the company? ☐ ☐

*Have enough feasible strategic alternatives been considered and the most suitable ones selected? ☐ ☐

*Is the time span appropriate to attain the objectives set forth? ☐ ☐

*Have HRD's major strengths and weaknesses been identified? Is it known from what sources these arise? ☐ ☐

*Is the central HRD plan clear enough to provide a criterion for results evaluation? ☐ ☐

*Have better combinations of resources and competencies been identified to make for continual improvement? ☐ ☐

[1] For Ward, a "strategic profile" describes the mission/purpose of the HRD department, identifies its available expertise which can be used to advantage, clarifies that the philosophy of the department is to be anticipatory rather than reactive, and identifies the broad goals and measurable objectives of the department.

[2] A "strategic forecast" identifies trends in the external environment which can influence HRD efforts inside the firm.

[3] A "resource audit" identifies the present strengths/weaknesses of—and the future opportunities/threats confronting—the HRD department.

[4] A "test of consistency" is an examination of a proposed HRD department strategy intended to determine whether it can realistically implement the strategy successfully.

Source: Ward, 1982, pp. 22-23. Reprinted with permission from *Training*.

ACTIVITY 5-2   A Worksheet for Problem Framing

Directions: In the spaces below, describe the performance problem in the first box. Then consider each question, relative to that problem, in succeeding boxes. Remember, you are focusing here on employee performance problems only.

WHAT IS THE PROBLEM? (Describe it. Be sure to clarify what is [*current condition*] and what should be [*desired status or criteria*].)

IS THE PROBLEM REPETITIVE OR NONREPETITIVE? (Does it appear—or can it appear—at regular intervals? If so, explain the circumstances. If not, explain what you think *caused* this problem.)

IS THE PROBLEM SHORT-TERM OR LONG-TERM? (Will this problem require some time to correct, or can it be corrected in a relatively brief time period?)

IS THE PROBLEM CRITICAL OR NOT SO CRITICAL? (How important is this problem? Explain why it is or is not important.)

ACTIVITY 5-2 Continued

DOES THE PROBLEM CALL FOR CREATIVE OR NONCREATIVE SOLUTIONS? (How well will tried-and-true methods work in correcting the problem? What could happen in the future which would render those solutions inappropriate?)

WILL INSTRUCTIONAL OR NONINSTRUCTIONAL IMPROVEMENT EFFORTS BE MOST APPROPRIATE FOR DEALING WITH THE PROBLEM? (Is formal instruction the only way to solve the problem? What alternatives exist? What are the relative advantages and disadvantages of each one?)

ACTIVITY 5-3 Case Study on Organizational Strategy for HRD*

Directions: Read over the case which follows and answer the questions at the end.

The Texarkana Office of Auditor General is a State agency employing 120 people. Its annual budget is $12 million. The agency conducts financial, compliance, management, and program results audits of all State agencies in Texarkana.

By State law, financial and compliance audits must be conducted at least once every four years. On the other hand, management and program results audits are only undertaken when the Texarkana Office of Auditor General is directed to do them by the State Legislature.

The structure of the agency is a simple one: there are only five divisions (see Table 5-4). As the Table illustrates, four are related directly to audit work. A fifth division supports audit activities. Job classes are nearly as simple as the agency structure. There are only twenty-three job titles in the agency (see Figure 5-9).

*This case is fictitious.

TABLE 5-4 LIST OF JOB TITLES AND THE CHIEF RESPONSIBILITIES OF EACH JOB IN THE TEXARKANA OFFICE OF THE AUDITOR GENERAL

Job title	Chief responsibility
1. Agency Head	directs the operations of the agency
2. Director, Financial Audits	directs the financial audit division
3. Director, Compliance Audits	directs the compliance audit division
4. Director, Management Audits	directs the management audit division
5. Director, Program Audits	directs the program audit division
6. Director, Support Operations	directs the support operations division
7. Financial Audit Manager	manages a group of financial audits
8. Financial Audit Senior	directs the work of financial audit juniors on a daily basis
9. Financial Audit Junior	conducts audit tests; documents results
10. Compliance Audit Manager	manages a group of compliance audits
11. Compliance Audit Senior	directs the work of compliance audit juniors on a daily basis
12. Compliance Audit Junior	conducts compliance audit tests; documents results
13. Management Audit Manager	manages a group of management audits
14. Management Audit Senior	directs the work of management audit juniors on a daily basis
15. Management Audit Junior	conducts audit tests; documents results
16. Program Audit Manager	manages a group of program audits
17. Program Audit Senior	directs the work of program audit juniors on a daily basis
18. Program Audit Junior	conducts audit tests; documents results
19. Internal Accountant	"keeps the books" of the agency
20. Personnel Officer	recruits/trains agency employees
21. Legal Technician	helps auditors with legal issues arising from their work
22. Secretary I	provides basic clerical support for auditors
23. Secretary II	provides more demanding clerical support than the Secretary I

Recently, top managers met to formulate the agency's Strategic Plan. While "conducting audits" is an activity required by law, how the agency approaches this process is left to managers and employees of the agency. The top managers commissioned a survey of agency staff and legislators. (Legislators use audit results when deciding on budget allocations for State agencies in Texarkana.) Based on survey results and on the wishes of top managers, it was decided that the agency would work in the future to improve the coverage of State agency computer operations and personnel practices in State audits. The agency would also simplify the presentation of audit results so that, instead of being reported in the jargon of accountants, they would be reported in a way that nontechnical decision-makers like legislators could understand.

From these general initiatives, top managers decided it was important to plan for staff skills necessary to bring these goals into reality. The personnel records and career planning documents of employees were examined. The results were that the agency possessed only nine of ninety auditors whose computer skills were deemed adequate for carrying out intensive reviews of computer operations; only three of ninety auditors were adequately skilled in personnel practices. Not one auditor had ever prepared an audit report in "lay language."

Agency turnover averages 10 percent or less each year. In most cases, entry-level auditors are 80 percent more likely to leave the agency than those in higher-level positions. Extensive recruitment of needed skills from outside the agency is not an appropriate staffing strategy to acquire desired expertise at this time. Nor does top management want to add unnecessary personnel—that is, people whose hiring cannot be justified solely on the basis of work load—in order to obtain necessary skills from outside. External consultants cannot be used in lieu of permanent staff, either.

The only way to acquire the skills necessary to realize the agency's strategic plan is to cultivate those skills among staff already employed in the Texarkana Office of Auditor General.

Questions

1. How would you go about designing and developing a course-centered curriculum in this agency?
2. How would you go about designing and developing an experience-centered curriculum in this agency?
3. How would you go about designing and developing a goal-centered curriculum in this agency? (Answer this question both for a performance-based *and* a competency-based curriculum.)
4. How would you go about designing and developing a learner-centered curriculum in this agency?
5. How would you ensure that, for each approach to curriculum design/development used, some provision is made to (a) build computer skills? (b) build expertise in personnel matters? and (c) help learners produce audit reports in "lay language"?
6. Assume that the agency's strategic plan covers a six-year time horizon. What time horizon should the curriculum cover?
7. What nonemployee development needs do you feel should be considered? How can agency top managers see to it that those needs are assessed and that instruction is planned accordingly?

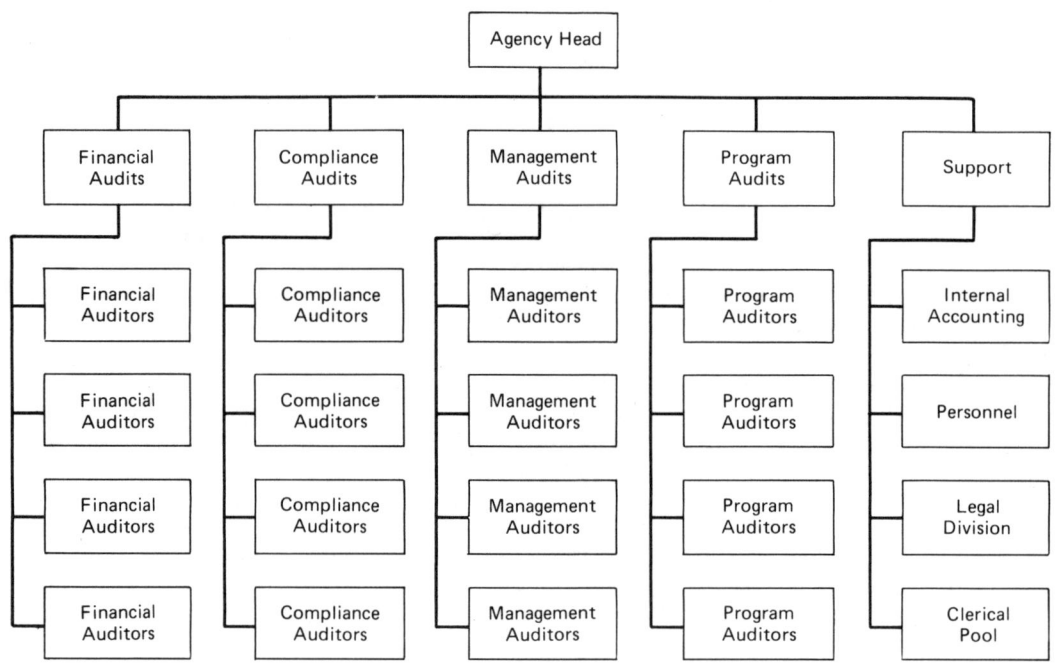

Figure 5-9: Organizational Structure of the Texarkana Office of Auditor General

6

IMPLEMENTING ORGANIZATIONAL STRATEGY FOR HRD

Implementation is the process of turning plans into actions. As in Strategic Business Planning, implementation of Organizational Strategy for HRD is perhaps the single most important step. Without careful forethought about what actions to take, when to take them, and who should take them, no strategy will ever be successful.

Implementation is commonly cited as the weakest link in Strategic Business Planning (Keichel, 1982). One reason is that successful implementation takes a long time. Ackerman (1975) studied two organizations and concluded that changes initiated by top managers required about six years to implement. Dramatic changes at odds with organizational culture may take longer. A second reason is that resistance to any new strategy is likely to be pronounced—especially when a proposed change differs radically from traditions. Resistance stems from such causes as the time required for people to learn how to act in new ways consistent with new business plans; different perceptions about what a change "means"; financial costs of change; distrust of others' motives; simple anxiety about change; confusion about what to do; and vested interests in the status quo (Calish & Gamache, 1981; Odiorne, 1981; Stanislao & Stanislao, 1983). Both the length of time required for successful implementation and resistance to change itself are not problems limited solely to Strategic Business Planning. In fact, both can affect the implementation of Organizational Strategy for HRD.

STEPS IN IMPLEMENTING ORGANIZATIONAL STRATEGY FOR HRD

Think of implementation as a series of steps in which HRD practitioners and line managers

1. establish operational objectives for the HRD Effort,
2. review and revise HRD policies,
3. examine leadership in the corporation or business,
4. review the structure of the organization, HRD department, and learning experiences sponsored by the organization,
5. review reward systems,
6. budget for resources to implement strategy,
7. communicate about Organizational Strategy for HRD, and
8. develop HRD functional strategies.

ESTABLISHING OPERATIONAL OBJECTIVES FOR THE HRD EFFORT

The importance of objectives is repeatedly emphasized in literature on Strategic Business Planning and HRD. Objectives provide guidance for the outcomes sought from any undertaking.

Business planners often advocate a Management by Objectives (MBO) approach to implementation because it is results-oriented. It matches resources to priorities during annual budgeting. MBO also builds commitment through participation at lower levels in the corporate hierarchy, because objectives should be negotiated at every level. It clarifies priorities, evaluates individual performance, allocates rewards based on predefined criteria, and prepares individuals in ways directly tied to long-term, intermediate-term, and short-term requirements of the organization, work groups, and jobs.

When MBO is used in Strategic Business Planning, top managers usually establish objectives for the entire organization and then for their respective areas of responsibility. Within each top manager's area of responsibility, objectives are allocated to different departments. Mid-level managers then negotiate objectives with superiors and subordinates. "Since the setting and splitting of objectives continues until the lowest level of management is reached, the end result is that the objectives set forth at each level of the organization are closely interrelated" (Meidan, 1981, p. 36). Objectives are established all the way down to front-line employees. In this way, everyone has an opportunity to negotiate objectives for their jobs. Periodically, managers at each level meet with subordinates to discuss their progress toward meeting objectives.

Typically, an MBO program is geared to meeting *annual* objectives. However, longer-term objectives can be established for five or more years. These objectives reflect action toward implementing Strategic Business Plans.

Despite the advantages of an MBO approach to implementation of strategy, it is by no means foolproof. Good objectives are time-consuming to write and negotiate (see Table 6-1 for characteristics of good objectives). They require skill to prepare and

TABLE 6-1   CRITERIA FOR A GOOD OBJECTIVE

1. relates directly to a strategic thrust[1]
2. relates to mission of the organization
3. is clear, concise, and understandable
4. is stated in output or results terms
5. begins with "to" and an action verb
6. specifies a date for accomplishment
7. deals with one major subject or outcome
8. ties in with upper- and lower-level objectives[2]
9. ties in with lateral objectives[3]
10. is quantifiable

[1] These are major goals which help chart the direction of the firm and which are expressed as part of a mission or purpose statement.
[2] Those for units above or below this hierarchical level.
[3] Those for units at the same hierarchical level.
Source: Anthony, 1985, p. 89. Reprinted with permission from Quorum Books.

monitor. When thrust on employees without give-and-take negotiation, they create hostility and frustration. Several writers have pointed out other problems with MBO (for example, Kondrasuk, 1981; Levinson, 1970).

Instructional objectives are more limited than the *organizational* objectives prepared in MBO. They are widely advocated and used in HRD. They link learning needs and the instruction designed to meet those needs (Cummings, 1986). Instructional objectives were popularized in the 1960s.

A good instructional objective answers three fundamental questions (Mager, 1975): (1) What will the learner be able *to do* upon completion of a learning experience? (2) *Under what circumstances* and/or *with what tools or equipment* will the learner be able to perform? and (3) *How well* will the learner be able to perform? It is not always necessary to address the second question—sometimes circumstances are understood—but the other two questions should always be addressed.

Not all objectives deal with the same issues. In fact, Benjamin Bloom and his colleagues distinguish between three learning "domains": (1) *the cognitive,* having to do with thinking and knowledge; (2) *the affective,* having to do with feeling and values; and (3) *the psychomotor,* having to do with physical skill. Each domain is arranged in hierarchical order from least to most complex (see Figures 6-1, 6-2, and 6-3). More complete treatments of them can be found in Bloom and others (1956), Krathwohl, Bloom, and Masia (1964), and Simpson (1969). For more information on objectives see Dillman and Rahmlow (1972), Mager and Beach (1967), Odiorne (1971), and Popham (1968). Another way to classify objectives, distinct from the approach of Bloom and his colleagues, can be found in Gagné (1965).

Just as organizational objectives vary by the time horizons they encompass, so

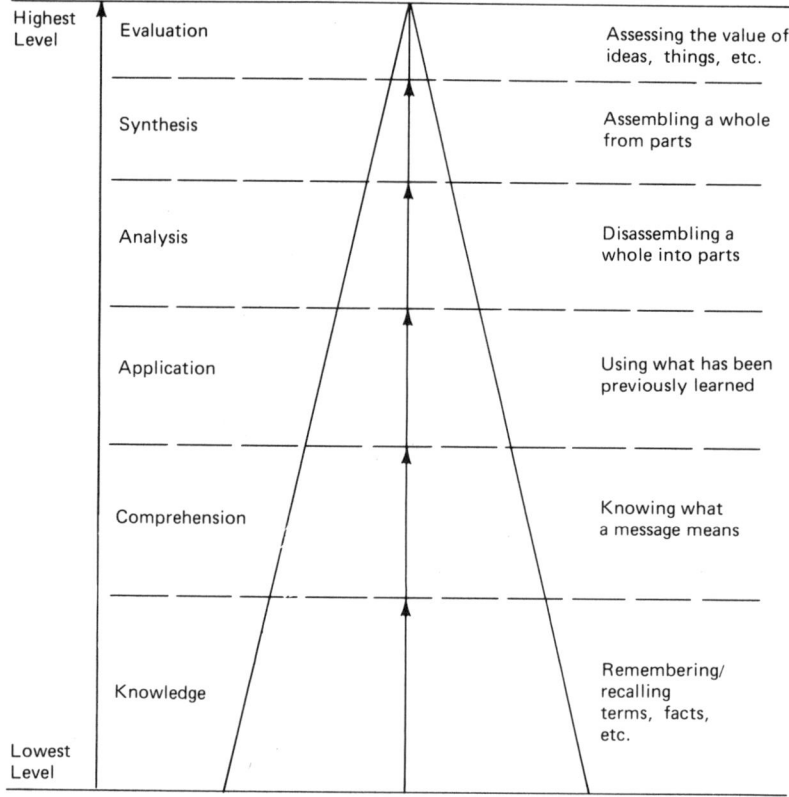

Figure 6-1: Levels of Objectives in the Cognitive Domain

too do instructional objectives. They can be viewed as (Briggs, 1970): (1) *long-term:* reflecting desired change that occurs throughout life; (2) *medium-term:* reflecting desired change that occurs from formal learning; (3) *course:* reflecting desired change that results from a single, discrete learning experience; (4) *unit:* reflecting desired change that results from a section of a "course," a group of related lessons; (5) *lesson:* reflecting desired change that results from a single portion of a course section; and, (6) *specific behavior:* reflecting desired change that results from going through one lesson. Other writers have also suggested that objectives can be viewed according to (1) time horizon, and (2) type of change desired (see, for example, Brakken & Bernstein, 1982; Hamblin, 1974; Warr, Bird, & Rackham, 1970).

This idea has profound implications for implementing Organizational Strategy for HRD. Top managers, HRD practitioners, and others may establish different kinds of instructional objectives to specify desired changes to be achieved through different but related learning experiences. For instance, objectives should be established in a comprehensive Organizational Strategy for HRD to bring about change in

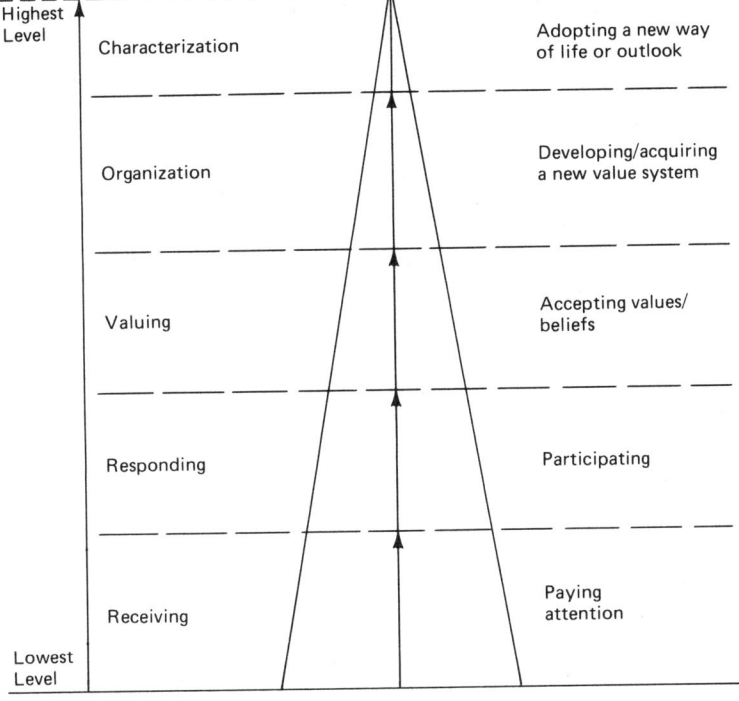

Figure 6-2: Levels of Objectives in the Affective Domain

1. what knowledge, skills, and values are implicit in organizational procedures and in the interactions of groups/people within the firm (the intent is to influence the organization),
2. what the general public knows about the corporation and its products or services (the intent is to influence the broad external environment),
3. what key external stakeholders—such as consumers/clients, suppliers, and distributors—know about the corporation and its products/services (the intent is to influence key stakeholders),
4. what people are available to meet the collective skill needs of each work unit (the intent is to influence the mix of available talents in each work unit),
5. what people are available for what new jobs (the intent is to influence the direction of individuals' careers), and
6. what knowledge and skills people can apply on their present jobs (the intent is to influence present job performance).

These objectives form a taxonomy in their own right (see Figure 6-4). At the highest level is cultural change in the organization. This takes time and is the most difficult to achieve. Below that is change relative to the external environment, which corresponds

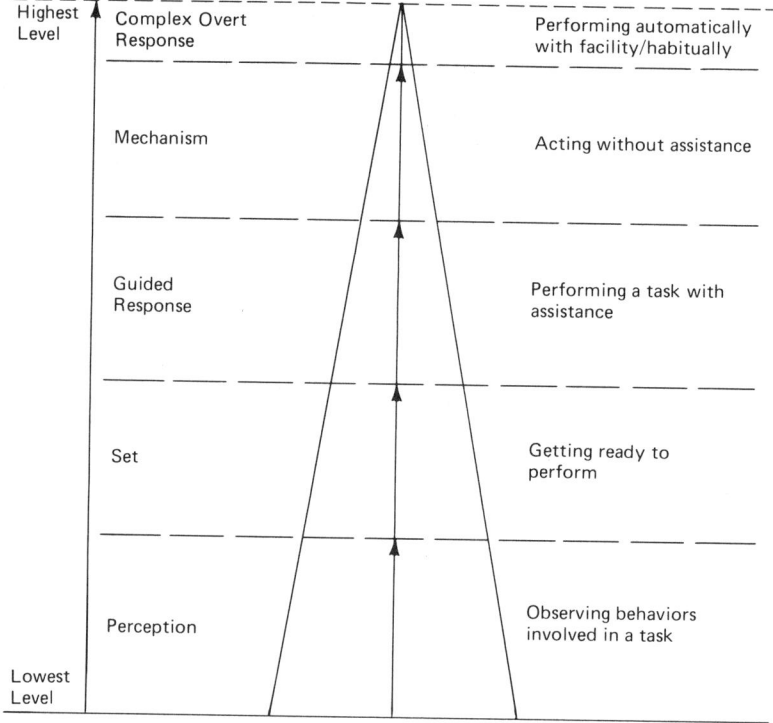

Figure 6-3: Levels of Objectives in the Psychomotor Domain

to nonemployee development. At the center of the hierarchy is change in the work unit, which corresponds to employee development. At the lowest levels are objectives focused on changing individuals (employee education) and job performance (training). The lowest-level objectives take less time to achieve than higher-level objectives.

A further distinction between objectives can be made on the basis of *change direction*. Is the intent to narrow a gap between what is and what should be at present *or* between what is and what should be in the future? In other words, is planned learning intended to solve past performance problems or to anticipate future performance threats or opportunities? The choice of change direction depends entirely on the nature of Organizational Strategy for HRD. A strategy focusing on correcting past weakness usually requires little dramatic change. In contrast, a radically new Organizational Strategy for HRD calls for utterly new knowledge and skills to be cultivated over time.

Establishing objectives for each type of change is a key to formulating Organizational Strategy for HRD, and following those objectives is a key to successful implementation of that strategy.

There are several ways that objectives can be used in implementing Organization Strategy for HRD. One method is to prepare HRD objectives to correspond to each

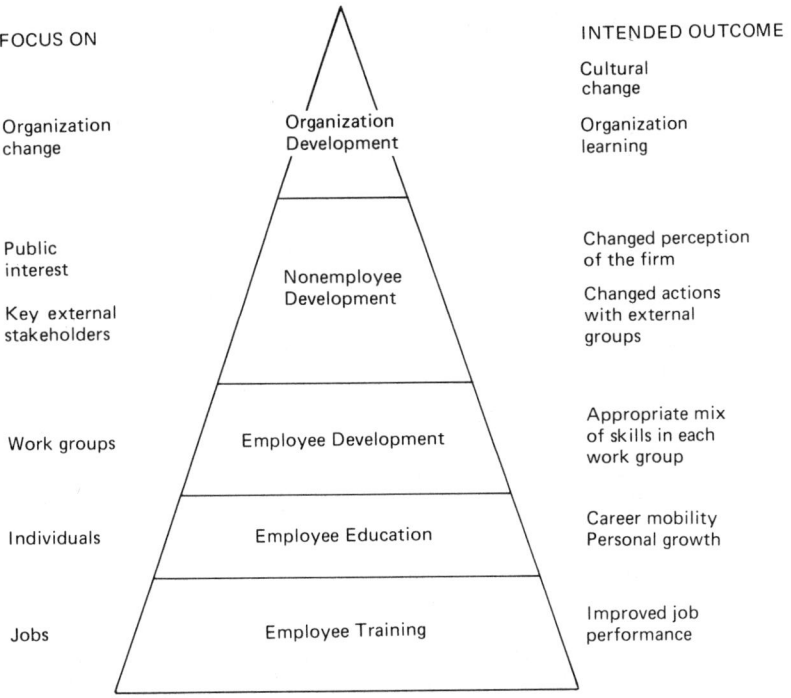

Figure 6-4: Objectives by Type of Change

strategic business objective. After all, human knowledge, skills, and attitudes are necessary to achieve strategic business objectives. As strategists formulate business objectives, they should also think about corresponding learning objectives.

Another method is to separate strategic business objective-setting from instructional objective-setting, but preserve continuity by involving the same people in each process. Managers at each hierarchical level establish strategic business objectives and then, in a parallel process, establish corresponding objectives for training, education, employee development, organization development, and nonemployee development.

After objectives are established for the organization, corporate planners schedule periodic meetings to compare notes on progress and pinpoint problems associated with achieving them (O'Connor, 1980b). The same approach can be used in monitoring progress on HRD objectives. HRD practitioners can schedule meetings with managers to report progress and identify problems. Alternatively, both planners and HRD practitioners can work together so that one meeting provides feedback on achievement of business objectives *and* HRD objectives. In this way, results of action are fed back to the managers who set objectives in a way reminiscent of the Action Research Model popularized by Organization Development practitioners. In Action Research, feedback and further problem-solving efforts follow objective-setting and action in a continuous, long-term cycle. For more on using objectives in implementing Organizational Strategy for HRD, see Activity 6-1 at the end of this chapter.

Establishing Operational Objectives for the HRD Effort

CREATING, REVIEWING, AND REVISING HRD POLICIES

Policies are formal pronouncements intended to guide behavior. They ensure that decisions made at lower levels conform with desires at higher levels, and that actions taken conform with Strategic Business Plans and objectives. Most organizations have at least some formal policies, which reflect organizational experience.

Written policies have distinct advantages when compared to unwritten ones. According to Leonard Nadler and Garland Wiggs (1986) written policies: (1) ensure that directives are communicated in the original language of policymakers; (2) are more easily transmitted from person-to-person and preserved over time than unwritten policies; and (3) demonstrate commitment. Policymakers seldom waste time writing about matters they do not consider important. In addition, the process of writing helps clarify issues among policymakers, flushing out areas of disagreement for discussion and resolution.

Clearly, policies should always be reviewed upon choice of a new strategy. After all, it does not make sense to expect people to behave one way if policies, intended to guide behavior, lead them to behave another way.

Many corporations have HRD policies on such matters as: (1) delivering speeches to associations, groups, or societies about the activities of an employer; (2) preparing articles for publication about the employer; (3) serving in professional societies or civic groups; (4) receiving reimbursement for college tuition, workshop/seminar, or conference fees, and for professional accreditation fees; and (5) receiving training, both off-the-job and on-the-job. Policies state the employer's philosophy and sometimes provide procedures for getting approval for training, education, or other improvement efforts.

Large corporations may also have policies governing HRD practice. Policies of this kind describe how HRD practitioners should approach needs assessment and instructional design, delivery, and evaluation.

A third type of policy is more rare but is also important. Some corporations, government agencies, and not-for-profit enterprises establish formal policies about the HRD responsibilities of supervisors and employees. Policies of this kind clarify precisely what the supervisor should do and what employees should do in the HRD process. Few firms, however, establish a predetermined number of hours per year to be devoted to formal learning (Roth, 1986).

From what little research has been done on HRD policy in organizations, it appears that HRD is (Spector, 1985 cited in Nadler & Wiggs, 1986): (1) rarely planned; (2) usually considered important only for some but not all job categories or customer groups; and (3) provided upon job entry but rarely planned in any structured way thereafter. As a consequence, HRD initiatives tend to be more reactive than proactive and lack adequate management oversight (Nadler & Wiggs, 1986). Not surprisingly, then, HRD is rarely considered an appropriate vehicle by which to help an organization achieve operational objectives, much less strategic ones (*Human Resources*, 1982).

It is important to formulate a written HRD policy and review it for possible modification whenever there is a change in the: (1) purpose of the HRD effort or HRD department; (2) Organizational Strategy for HRD; (3) higher-level strategy of the organization; and/or (4) HR (personnel) practices generally. Use Activity 6-2 at the end of this chapter to evaluate the comprehensiveness of an organization's HRD policy and/or to consider issues to be covered in a policy to be prepared for top management review. For more on the general subject of HRD policy see Nadler and Wiggs (1986), Newman (1980), Sredl and Rothwell (1987), and Tracey (1984).

EXAMINING LEADERSHIP

Leadership is "an attempt at influencing activities of followers through the communication process and toward attainment of some goal or goals" (Fleishman, 1973, p. 3). If there is one thing which can make or break successful implementation of any strategy—whether for an organization (Glueck & Jauch, 1984), human resources or staffing activities (Rothwell & Kazanas, 1988), or HRD (Sredl & Rothwell, 1987)—it may well be this. Successful implementation depends on appropriate leadership because strategy is, quite simply, a human manifestation requiring human guidance (Rock & Eisthen, 1983).

In examining leadership's importance in the implementation of Organizational Strategy for HRD, HRD practitioners should ask: (1) *Who* are the key decision-makers in the firm? (2) *What* do they value? (3) *What* do they think of HRD generally? and (4) *What* do they think of HRD as a tool for improving relations with the general public, corporate suppliers, customers, and distributors, for developing both the organization as a whole and specific work groups, for helping realize corporate/business strategic plans, for preparing individuals for career mobility, for helping individuals realize their career plans, and for improving job performance? Organizations with strong value systems, ideologies, and cultures tend to attract and retain individuals—and leaders—who embody those value systems, ideologies, and culture (Glueck & Jauch, 1984). When HRD's importance is not presently emphasized in the culture or supported by top managers, building support for it—or for changes in Organizational Strategy for HRD—will be difficult.

The most important leader to analyze is the Chief Executive, who is the chief organizational strategist. The CEO's role is so important that, in a study of conditions essential to integrating Strategic Business Planning and HR efforts, Nininger (1982) concluded that the CEO's support is one of seven conditions *required* for success. HRD practitioners should thus pose such questions as these: (1) How much does the CEO believe an HRD Effort is worthwhile? (2) How much does the CEO believe an HRD Effort can contribute to successful implementation of Strategic Business Plans? and (3) How much *real* support does the CEO provide to HRD? Does the CEO take an active interest in HRD—and encourage others to do so? Undoubtedly, the greater the CEO's interest in HRD, the greater the likelihood it will attract attention from others. Moreover, when the CEO actively encourages a change in Organizational Strategy for HRD—through both public and private statements—the greater the likelihood is that the change will also attract attention from others.

Lower-level managers also exert influence on the success or failure of Organizational Strategy for HRD. In fact, in Nininger's (1982) study mentioned previously, Nininger concluded that another condition essential to effective integration of Strategic Business Planning and human resource management is that "the organization at all levels establishes responsibility and accountability for human resource management" (p. 9). The role of lower-level managers is to give support, provide resources, and reward HR efforts.

But what should HRD practitioners do when leaders of their organization do *not* see the relevance of HRD initiatives to their needs or those of the business? One answer, of course, is for practitioners to look for employment elsewhere. But for those too stubborn to give up without a fight, here are a few suggestions:

1. *Start small.* Tackle one highly visible problem successfully. Collect anecdotes stemming from success in dealing with the problem and use every channel of information available to emphasize the value of HRD as demonstrated by this case.
2. *Build a following.* Start with the most powerful clientele that can be approached and work on satisfying *their* needs and concerns. Expand gradually beyond that clientele.
3. *Insert information about HRD activities in company publications.* Build lower-level support if top management is hard to reach.
4. Use every occasion that problems come up to show how HRD activities could have prevented them—and how present HRD activities can help rectify them.

Practitioners will have to work on building support for HRD over time, often over many years. This "strategy" can be successful if approached with persistence, diligence, and patience.

But what about resistance to changing Organizational Strategy for HRD, assuming support already exists for HRD generally? A good starting point is diagnosis. *Why* are people resistant to change? Think about such possible causes as (Kotter & Schlesinger, 1979): (1) *self-interest*—Do people think that they will lose something of value as a result of change? If so, what? (2) *confusion*—Do people understand what the change means, or have they somehow gotten the wrong impression? (3) *mistrust*—Do managers/employees doubt the motives of those advocating change? If so, what is the source of their concern? and (4) *lack of knowledge or skills*—Sometimes people resist change simply because they do not know what they are to do or how they should do it. Each problem listed may require a different solution. To overcome concerns about self-interest, HRD practitioners should work on showing the benefits of change; to overcome confusion or lack of knowledge/skills, practitioners should offer training and provide opportunities for discussions; and to overcome mistrust, practitioners should work on building trust and openness through appropriate Organization Development efforts.

Use Activity 6-3 at the end of this chapter to consider the values of the present leaders, their receptiveness to changing Organizational Strategy for HRD when such change is appropriate, and ways of building support for that change.

REVIEWING STRUCTURE

Structure has long been viewed as important in Strategic Business Planning. Chandler (1962), the first writer on strategy, hypothesized that decision-makers in any firm adjust structure once strategy is chosen. Later researchers have shown that matters are not as simple as Chandler's early hypothesis suggests. Indeed, structure can constrain strategic choice (Galbraith & Nathanson, 1979).

Structure means "a relatively stable framework of jobs and departments that influences the behavior of individuals and groups toward organizational goals" (Gibson, Ivancevich, & Donnelly, 1985, p. 418). It affects behavior in several ways. First, structure implies allocation of job tasks, duties, and responsibilities in the organization. Each task requires specific knowledge/skills from individuals and requires interactions with people in related jobs. Second, structure affects who reports to whom and thus how many and what types of people are grouped together. The numbers and types of people grouped together affect how much people communicate with each other, how close together they feel, and how creative they are. Third, structure affects the level of conflict present in the work group or organization. Conflict results when two work groups are interdependent, differ in goals, or differ in perceptions about what is important. There is little doubt that structure affects both organizational and individual performance. What is less clear is *how* structure affects performance (Cummings & Berger, 1976; Dalton, Todor, Spendolini, Fielding, & Porter, 1980; Oldham & Hackman, 1981).

Structure is obviously important in implementing Organizational Strategy for HRD. It can be viewed on three levels: (1) organizational; (2) departmental; and (3) instructional. Organizational structure means the pattern of reporting relationships and duties allocated to departments in the organization. Department structure is similar, referring to reporting relationships established *within* a work group and work duties allocated within the group. Instructional structure connotes relationships between learning experiences sponsored by the firm.

Any change in organizational structure may create new learning needs. It is entirely possible that a radical reorganization will make all prior instructional planning obsolete. There are several reasons why. First, a reallocation of tasks changes job duties and thus training appropriately focused on jobs or job categories. Second, as relationships between jobs change, employee education based on prior career paths is affected. Third, as old work groups are disbanded and new ones are formed, individuals find they have to learn not just new tasks but also how to interact with new people and how to deal with a new group purpose. Fourth and finally, as duties are shifted work groups begin to serve external groups in new ways. The effect of a corporate reorganization on the HRD Effort is much like throwing a stack of cards up in the air. Not all changes can be predicted, nor will all changes be desirable.

Less radical reorganizations should be analyzed to determine what tasks, duties, and responsibilities will be affected and over what time period effects will be evident. Employees may be trained in anticipation of change so that they know what to do and when they are expected to do it. They can also be counseled about changes in their career prospects. Reorganizations of any kind open up new career paths even as old ones fade away. Clearly, if a work group is being changed, team building—a special type of Organization Development intervention—is in order from the outset (see Dyer, 1977). The important point to remember is that any change in organizational structure—including downsizing—creates new learning needs before, during, and after the change (Allevras & Frigeri, 1987; Newell, Redfoot, & Sotar, 1987).

Radical reorganizations are traumatic for employees and fraught with potential dangers for managers. For this reason, they are rarely appropriate—even in failing firms. An alternative is to begin with the replacement of key personnel—for example, the CEO and his or her immediate subordinates—and then follow that up with gradual retrenchment. Research by Bibeault (1982) suggests that a successful turnabout strategy requires an average of $7^{1}/_{2}$ years to implement. Rather than face this long-term prospect, some corporate managers prefer more drastic alternatives—selling assets of a failing division (*liquidation*), spinning off a failing firm (*divestment*), or selling a division to another firm (also called *divestment*). Smaller divisions are more likely to be sold off so that the corporation can use the cash resulting from a sale to find a better return on investments elsewhere (Duhaime, 1981). Successful divestments occur more often when managers in the division participate in the process than when the decision comes as a surprise to them (Duhaime, 1981).

Dramatic changes in organizational structure are rarely appropriate if the intent is to introduce a radically new product or service requiring methods utterly unlike those handled previously by the firm. Perhaps the best approach is to create a parallel organization or at least isolate sites where change is being introduced. Human resistance to change is so great that radical changes work best when a new unit is created, people are socialized in it, and the culture develops separate from that of the sponsoring organization (Hage, 1980; Heller & Monahan, 1977; Mintzberg, 1979a).

Structural changes within the organization require a review of the HRD department's structure. For example, a shift from a centralized and functionally-structured firm to a decentralized, regionalized firm may well create the need for reorganizing the HRD department. There are many alternatives:

1. Decentralize and regionalize HRD, too. (In effect, eliminate the corporate-level HRD department.)
2. Create informal or formal liaisons in each region who communicate regularly with the centralized HRD department.
3. Separate the duties of a centralized HRD department from duties of "one-person operations" in each facility or from duties of small bands of itinerant HRD "marauders" who move from site to site in each region.
4. Create a field operations chief at the corporate level whose job involves travelling to different regions and reporting back to the corporate level HRD department.
5. Create a separate but smaller HRD department within each division or region which interacts with "one-person operations" in the field on one hand and with the corporate HRD department on the other hand.

Matters can become even more complicated if the organization's change in strategy calls for the introduction of a new project or matrix structure. A project structure is characterized by temporary work teams assigned to one-time efforts like product start-ups. Matrix structures are similar, except that project managers are equal to division chiefs in status and are not, as in a pure project structure, of lower status (Davis & Lawrence, 1977). Project structures are common in turbulent environments or in temporary job assignments requiring tight control from beginning to ending. Many professionals—engineers, accountants/auditors, research scientists, and even physicians—frequently work in project structures. A structure of this kind is also common in the start-up of a new venture—a new product, a new service, or a new plant or production facility.

A project environment differs radically from a functional or divisional one. Each project team works on an issue or assignment utterly unlike anything which is currently being worked on by others and, in some cases, utterly unlike what has been worked on before or will be worked on again. Scheduling HRD activities in the classroom is difficult because each team—ranging from two or three people to as many as several thousand in rare cases—is at a different stage of progress. Time out for the classroom disrupts work schedules within or between teams.

If a project structure is introduced, HRD practitioners may find they need to reexamine every facet of their work. If the organization is large enough, classroom efforts may continue—but they will not be enough. They will tend to attract team members when they are at a "low point" on a project, not necessarily when they need instruction. For this reason, it may be appropriate to create outreach efforts so that HRD practitioners call on project teams *while they work*. Alternatively, HRD practitioners may be assigned to project teams. Instructional delivery methods will have to be geared more to individualized learning such as programmed instruction, computer-based, and on-the-job training so that team members receive instruction at the work site during slack periods. New hires should be trained *before* they are assigned to projects, lest training be sacrificed for pressing work assignments.

Finally, any change in organizational structure or in Organizational Strategy for HRD will also require a review of how learning experiences are sequenced (that is, how the curriculum is structured).

There are different, albeit appropriate, methods of sequencing training, education, and development. Likewise, different methods of sequencing are appropriate depending on whether the curriculum is subject-centered, goal-centered, experience-centered, or learner-centered. On one level, the issue of sequencing seems simple enough: learners should be introduced to subject matter or skills in a common sense ordering from the known to the unknown. Each instructional lesson should thus build on what precedes it and prepare learners for what follows it. This approach works well enough for most cognitive (knowledge) instruction. The HRD practitioner analyzes, for example, a work task and considers three questions: (1) What behaviors have to be performed? (2) How well does each behavior have to be performed? and (3) What does the learner already have to know or be able to do before exhibiting the behavior? Answering these questions will help construct a *learning hierarchy*, a depiction of what skills or knowledge should precede others. Hierarchies are useful in sequencing instruction (Gagné & Briggs, 1979). Learners are then tested prior to instruction to determine their *entry-level skills*.

The notion of the learning hierarchy is a powerful one, especially for manual and technical training at a detailed level. It is not as well nor as easily applied for: (1)

white-collar workers—analysis of their work requires other methods, different from task analysis (Zemke & Kramlinger, 1982); (2) *large blocks of learning*—the preparation of a learning hierarchy requires massive amounts of work; and (3) *employee education or development*—both take place over much longer time spans than training does.

When HRD practitioners are faced with sequencing large blocks of instruction over long time periods, they find that much of the literature in the HRD field is no longer very helpful or relevant. It tends to be too detailed, designed around task-oriented instruction. It also tends to be biased toward a bottom-up approach to instructional design, in which the sequence of activities in each job task is analyzed as the basis for instruction. Of course, this approach is past-oriented, in that it assumes the ways tasks have been performed will be appropriate for the future. However, people may find that new, utterly different tasks are not just necessary but are required.

How, then, is it possible to sequence large blocks of instruction—say, a dozen "courses" or a five-year planned group of learning experiences? There are several ways (Kowles, 1984; Sredl & Rothwell, 1987):

1. from simple to complex—begin with job "basics" and keep adding,
2. from particular to general—start with examples of job duties or activities and then draw conclusions to reach generalizations,
3. from tangible to intangible—begin with concrete examples and progress to abstractions,
4. from one activity to another, related activity, and so on—treat related tasks or duties in order,
5. from whole to part—start with an overall model of job performance and then treat each part in isolation, and
6. from a brief and incomplete treatment of one topic to a more complete treatment of another topic to a more in-depth treatment of the first and so on, in a cyclical pattern in which topics are selectively introduced and reintroduced over time. (This is called a spiral curriculum.)

Each approach to sequencing is appropriate under particular circumstances. Descriptions of other methods can be found in Romiszowski (1981).

The question is, will strategic change affect appropriate sequencing of instructional experiences over time? If there is a change in Organizational Strategy for HRD—the way employees and other learners are prepared over time—a change in the sequencing of instruction may also be necessary.

REVIEWING REWARD SYSTEMS

Behavioral scientists have long stressed the importance of *reward systems,* the ways and means by which managers allocate tangible and intangible rewards according to employee performance, longevity, or other factors. Clearly, reward systems are important because people do what they are rewarded for doing and slight or ignore what they are not rewarded for doing (Lawler, 1984; Morse & Martin, 1983). Managers do not pay close enough attention to the consequences of reward systems in their organizations (Kerr, 1975; Whyte, 1955). Even before implementation of any change, the reward system should be analyzed to determine whether it will facilitate or impede change (Lawler, 1977). If it will impede change, then the reward system itself may have to be redesigned before implementing the strategy.

Types of rewards. To diagnose reward systems, it is first necessary to understand what they are. Rewards fall into two broad categories (Burke, 1982): (1) *extrinsic,* stemming from actions of other people (examples of extrinsic rewards include salary increases, achievement awards, and promotions), and (2) *intrinsic,* stemming from work or activity itself (examples of intrinsic rewards include pride of accomplishment, increased self-esteem, satisfaction with a job well-done, and joy at seeing results of one's handiwork).

Intrinsic rewards result from interaction between the individual and work. Important intrinsic factors include (1) meaningfulness, (2) responsibility, and (3) awareness of results (Hackman & Oldham, 1975). *Meaningfulness* denotes how much individuals view their work as important. *Responsibility* is associated with how much individuals feel accountable for work results. *Awareness of results* refers to feedback individuals receive on their performance. To produce satisfaction, a job must rate high on all three factors (Hackman & Oldham, 1975). It should require varied activities, produce identifiable results, and should influence others. These factors are linked to meaningfulness. The job should also lead to independence. This factor is linked to responsibility. Finally, the job should yield feedback on results. This factor is linked to awareness of results.

Extrinsic rewards should meet five criteria described by Lawler (1977) and Burke (1982). The first is *significance.* Employees must value the likely rewards stemming from their efforts. The second is *flexibility.* Since individuals vary in what rewards they desire, a successful reward system must allow for individual differences. The third is *frequency.* The more often rewards are given and the sooner they follow behavior, the more effective they are likely to be. Of course, some rewards lose their value when awarded frequently. The fourth is *visibility.* Rewards are enhanced when other people know about them. The fifth is *expense.* Can the organization afford to give out the reward?

Learning and rewards. People learn for different reasons. It is important to understand why people learn if they are to be motivated and rewarded for it.

In a classic study, Houle (1961) classified adult learners into three general categories: (1) *goal-oriented,* people who undertake learning to achieve clear results (for example, solve a problem); (2) *activity-oriented,* people who seek social contact through learning; and (3) *learning-oriented,* people who think of learning as an end in itself. These categories have been supported by later writers (for example, Cross, 1981; Knowles, 1978).

Reviewing rewards and changes in organizational strategy for HRD. The two previous sections have described types of rewards and reasons for learning. Use them as a starting point to consider several questions:

1. How much does your organization presently reward learning in general? How does your organization specifically reward people for achieving desired results from training, for preparing for advancement and career mobility through employee education, for improving the work group, department, and organization through planned development, and for improving relationships between the organization and outside groups?
2. How much *should* your organization encourage learning in general? How much should the organization reward people in the future for achieving desired results of training, for preparing for advancement and career mobility through employee education, for improving the work group, department, and organization through planned development, and for improving relationships between the organization and outside groups?
3. What gaps exist between the conditions discussed in items 1 and 2?
4. What extrinsic and/or intrinsic rewards can help narrow the gap and thus help implement the Organizational Strategy for HRD?
5. What distinctions can be made in the allocation of these rewards based on different individual orientations to learning and styles of learning?

Use Activity 6-4 at the end of this chapter to brainstorm about these issues.

HRD Practitioners should be aware that traditional compensation systems are not always best for implementing radical changes in Organizational Strategy for HRD. One promising alternative is *skill-based pay,* which compensates people "for learning new job knowledge and skills regardless of their position or length of service with the company" (Feuer, 1987, p. 57). Learning activities are planned by job category, by work group, and by career intentions. They are organized in "skill blocks," and employees are rewarded on the basis of speed and level of mastery. While there are disadvantages to skill-based pay—including difficulties in linking productivity increases to learners, in using this incentive system for white-collar workers, and in dealing with people who master all "skill blocks" available to them (Feuer, 1987)—it is an idea worth pursuing when implementing radical changes in Organizational Strategy for HRD.

BUDGETING FOR NECESSARY RESOURCES

The ultimate test of management commitment to any plan is the extent to which resources are allocated to it. Budgeting is thus an important tool in implementing any strategy. It is the process of converting objectives into resource requests necessary to achieve them. Budgeting typically takes place annually, though some expensive items—buildings or high-cost equipment—may have to be budgeted for over several years.

The aim in this discussion is not to provide a primer on how to prepare an annual budget for the HRD department. For this information, see Clark and Perlman (1985), Laird (1985), Sredl and Rothwell (1987), Tracey (1984), West (1986), and Willard (1986). Practitioners who are interested in industry benchmarks—how much organizations in different industries budget for HRD—should see Feuer (1986b).

The point of this discussion is that an annual budget should stem from an Organizational Strategy for HRD and from long-term HRD objectives (see Figure 6-5). For this reason, it is important to look beyond annual budget horizons and consider several questions. First, what is going to be the complete cost of achieving a strategic HRD objective over the full time horizon of the strategy—five years, for example? Second, what estimates can be made now of the company's financial position over that time period? Will it probably erode over that time span due to external conditions like new competitors or a weak market position? Will the HRD Effort be affected heavily or not so heavily by cutbacks and growth? Why? Third and finally, would it make more sense to put higher priorities on some strategic objectives in early annual budgets in a five-year sequence so that cutbacks later will not be felt so much? If so, what should be emphasized early on, and what should be emphasized later?

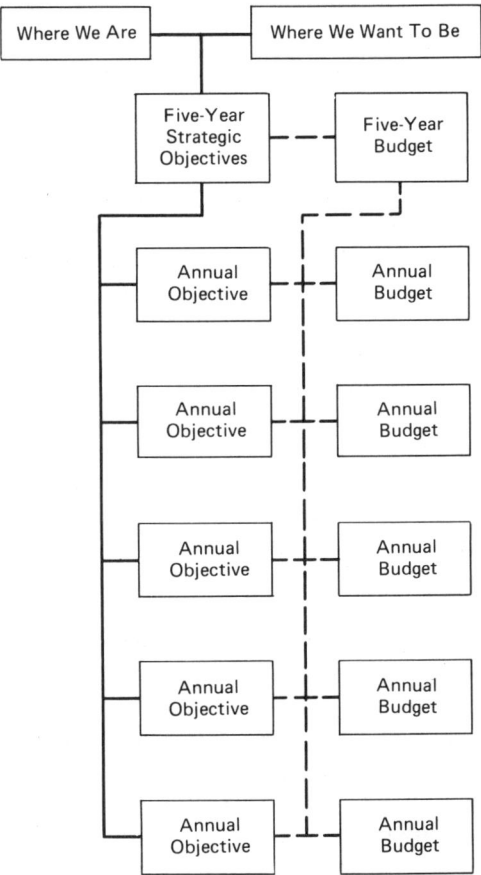

Figure 6-5: The Relationship Between Strategic Objectives and Annual Budgets

Some HRD practitioners may object that questions like these are not very useful for them, because they must live with budgets imposed from above. In some organizations that may be true: higher-level managers handle budgeting. This is called a *nonparticipative budget process*. However, it is probably more the exception than the norm: most firms allow at least some negotiation in the process. Use Activity 6-5 at the end of this chapter to structure issues having to do with budgeting for the HRD effort and to consider improvements for budgeting methods currently being used in a firm.

COMMUNICATING ABOUT STRATEGY

"A major reason for the failure of many planning systems is the lack of sufficient communication to make the system work" (Lewis, 1983, p. 24-10). For this reason, it is essential to consider communication when implementing Organizational Strategy for HRD. *In this context, communication means conveying information and building support.*

Clearly, communicating about Organizational Strategy for HRD is easiest when the firm has a coherent and unified communication policy to inform employees and supervisors about such matters as ongoing activities of the corporation; corporate, business, and HR plans; and sensitive or controversial matters (Sigband, 1969).

Without a unified organizational communication policy, there is a tendency for controversial issues to be skirted or questions about them to be handled inconsistently by different managers (Sigband, 1969). With such a policy, HRD practitioners and line managers have clear guidance on how to communicate about HRD generally, how to address supervisory and employee concerns about changes in training, employee education, and employee development practices, and how to use various media to communicate about HRD. In organizational settings in which HRD is considered an important matter, communicating changes about it can easily affect subsequent employee acceptance or rejection.

A key goal of an organized communication effort is to overcome the many barriers to effective communication which may exist in the firm (St. John, 1981). Multiple channels of communication are frequently used, because they are more likely than a single channel to reach the intended audience and to overcome barriers. Representative downward channels include placing advertisements or articles of interest on bulletin boards; sending direct mail to employees or supervisors at home; sending memos to employees or supervisors at work; placing articles or announcements in company newsletters and magazines; inserting information in personnel handbooks; issuing special publications like training catalogs or brochures; holding meetings; holding one-on-one discussions; and enclosing notices with paychecks. Upward channels of communication include receiving information from in-house suggestion systems; meetings; attitude surveys; one-on-one discussions with supervisors; and questions posed by employees through union representatives. HRD activities are also important components in the in-house communication process and useful tools in communicating about business plans and employee performance. After all, "changes and improvements in the capacities of human beings to do their work . . . are changes and improvements in communication" (Pace, 1983, p. 2).

Use Activity 6-6 at the end of this chapter to brainstorm about: (1) how well HRD issues are currently being communicated to supervisors and employees in your organization; (2) how well these issues should be communicated in the future; (3) what HRD-related issues are most important to communicate about; and (4) how these issues should be communicated.

Three specific communication methods can be used most effectively in implementing Organization Strategy for HRD: (1) meetings; (2) training sessions; and (3) advisory/oversight committees.

Meetings. One way to communicate about strategy is through meetings. As Lorange and Vancil (1977) observe:

> In our view, the most critical design feature for a strategic planning system is the schedule of planning meetings, not the documents to be presented at those meetings. A well-designed planning calendar specifies when a meeting is to be held, which executives are to be there, what the agenda is to consist of, and how much time is to elapse until the next meeting. . . . Attempting to structure how the work is to be performed is far less important than assuring that the right cast of characters has been assembled at the right point in time to discuss the issues (p. xiii).

The results of a 1980 Conference Board survey revealed that 82 of 109 responding firms use meetings to prepare their managers for corporate or business-level planning (O'Connor, 1980a).

Meetings have several purposes. First, they are vehicles for informing managers and supervisors about company strategy. Second, meetings garner support and motivate participants. Third, meetings provide guidance to managers at all levels in the hierarchy. Fourth and finally, meetings allow participation in planning processes and provide an avenue for feedback to strategic managers about specific problems impeding progress at the operational level.

HRD can be included on the agenda as an issue for discussion during Strategic Business Planning meetings. Managers and supervisors can then be asked what training education or development would contribute to the implementation of Strategic Business Plans by building employee skills necessary to implement those plans. HRD priorities can be set and action plans can be established at that time, so that the link between HRD activities and company plans is indisputable.

As an alternative, meetings on Organizational Strategy for HRD can be arranged to parallel meetings on Strategic Business Plans. The advantage of this approach is that more time and effort will be devoted to HRD than when business plans and HRD are considered together. The disadvantage is that it may be difficult to keep participants on target in matching up business needs and the skills and training necessary to meet those needs when skills are treated separate from business plans.

Meetings devoted exclusively to the HRD Effort may also be scheduled regularly with managers and supervisors at different levels and locations. They are useful for identifying future trends or issues affecting the HRD Effort *or* specific training, education, or development needs. Meetings also provide supervisors with opportunities to discuss relationships between instructional methods and Organizational Strategy for

HRD. Supervisors can brainstorm on problems they encounter as they try to implement Organizational Strategy for HRD. A major advantage in holding meetings of this kind is that they raise consciousness at all hierarchical levels about the importance of business planning *and* HRD. Meetings also emphasize the value of a unified Organizational Strategy for HRD, allowing discussion about it and possible modification to it. When HRD activities are not accepted in the organizational culture, meetings can be a starting point for a long-term cultural change effort to make HRD part of the culture (see Rogers, 1981).

Training. Some Strategic Business Plans fail because people do not possess the necessary skills to make them work, or because managers themselves lack appropriate skills or experience (Keichel, 1981). For this reason, some firms sponsor training soon after the choice of a new business strategy, to build the new skills people need to begin implementation. "When the initial [training] program is over, the solutions worked out are put in practice on the job, and brief follow-up sessions assist with modifying or fine-tuning the approaches developed by managers in the workshops and refined on the job" (Stonich, 1982, p. 82).

Training may also facilitate the implementation of Organizational Strategy for HRD. Several kinds of training may be appropriate. Each serves a different purpose (O'Connor, 1980a). *Orientation programs* focus on questions like these: What is Organization Strategy for HRD? How does it help operating managers? What are their responsibilities? *Implementation programs* focus on methods of implementing Organizational Strategy for HRD and on objectives for Organization Development, employee and nonemployee development, education, and training. *Simulation programs* identify what future conditions will be like inside and outside the organization and assess learning needs based on artificially-simulated experience with the future. *General training on planning* focuses on issues like the nature of Strategic Business Planning. How is it used in the company? What are company plans at present? What is the role of HRD—among other functions—in the process of implementing business strategy?

Training may be developed in-house, jointly developed by company HRD staff and outside consultants, or developed solely by outside consultants. (For sources of possible training see the *Marketplace Directory,* 1986-1987.) Steps in designing training of this kind are no different from those in any other type of instruction: (1) identify purpose, (2) assess needs, (3) establish objectives, (4) prepare tests (if appropriate), (5) develop instructional materials or modify those available from other sources, (6) pilot test the training, (7) make final revisions to material, (8) offer the training on a large scale, and (9) evaluate results. We are not aware of any published off-the-shelf training packages on Strategic Planning for HRD. Several exist on Strategic Business Planning, however. Perhaps the best is by Pfeiffer, Goodstein, and Nolan (1986).

Advisory or Oversight Committees. Another fruitful way to build support for Organizational Strategy for HRD is to create a standing advisory committee on employee training, education, and development—or separate committees at different hierarchical levels or in different departments. School systems have long used "committees" in a similar way. In a sense, a school board is a committee, though it governs like a board of directors. Curriculum committees have been established at many schools. Similar committees are used to administer Federal training programs for economically disadvantaged or technologically displaced workers. Curriculum committees are also widely used in higher education.

Similar committees have been suggested for HRD (Kruger, 1983). They structure participation in setting HRD priorities. They make HRD activities more visible, underscore the responsiveness of HRD practitioners to needs at many levels, set priorities while allowing for many perspectives and viewpoints, settle jurisdictional issues, and coordinate activities when solutions are difficult to arrive at, many specialties may be needed, and broad, long-term support is desirable. Operating best in organizations with clearly defined department structures, advisory or oversight committees prove useful in interpreting needs assessment results, designing curricula at different levels and locations, and setting priorities (*Win New Allies,* 1982). Members of these committees are likely to find committee work useful for their own development.

There are many ways to establish and run an HRD committee. Nor is it necessary that a committee be specially commissioned, though that is typical. For example, it is possible to form a committee consisting of all top managers—the Chief Executive and his or her immediate reports. They meet to establish the long-term direction of the HRD Effort so that organized learning is tied directly to Strategic Business Plans. Alternatively, HRD issues can be treated during top-level management planning meetings and retreats. Similar committees may be formed at other hierarchical levels in the firm to ensure that the HRD Effort is responsive to needs at those levels.

In establishing a committee, HRD practitioners should take care to: (1) *Clarify its purpose and objectives from the outset.* A written charter is helpful (see Table 6-2). (2) *Select members with great care, consistent with the committee's purpose.* (3) *Establish a way of maintaining some continuity on the committee while, at the same time, ensuring that there is a regular infusion of new members so that the group does not stagnate;* and (4) *Find ways to feed back information for decisions to the committee and feed back results of prior decisions or recommendations of the committee.* The most important point is to build member involvement while not burdening members with so many demands and so much information that they become unable or unwilling to participate in decision-making.

Committees on HRD should be kept relatively small—between five and nine members are best. Members may be (Kruger, 1983)

- temporary or permanent,
- insiders, outsiders, or some combination,
- asked to make decisions, offer recommendations, or simply generate ideas, and
- representatives of different groups or limited to people at the same hierarchical level, from the same location, or in the same occupation.

Most committees will be chaired by a member, not by an HRD practitioner. Chairpersons should be selected for such special skills as the ability to (Kruger, 1983): (1) lead discussions; (2) create and preserve a psychologically comfortable climate conducive to group member interactions; (3) select members; (4) attend to administrative de-

TABLE 6-2 HRD ADVISORY COMMITTEE

Statement of policy and procedures: an example

Basic Purpose

The purpose of the HRD Advisory Committee (HAC) is to establish priorities and guidelines for the selection, scheduling, development, and evaluation of all staff training, education, and development. It shall provide the Director of HRD with advice on selection and scheduling of formal and informal learning experiences, assist in reviewing and developing instructional content and form, recommend time frames for delivery of experiences, and evaluate the effectiveness of the HRD Effort. As an ongoing *advisory* committee, its recommendations need to be approved by upper management before being formally adopted for the entire organization.

Membership

Selection of Members: The HAC shall consist of four regular members. Department heads shall nominate *four* staff people to serve on the HAC. The Senior Executive V.P., in conjunction with the HRD Director, shall review nominations and make final appointments of the regular HAC members. In addition, the Senior Executive V.P. (or his/her designee) shall serve as an *ex officio* member. At least one regular member shall be appointed from each department. Each of the three major work sites shall also be represented.

Term: Of the first four regular members, two shall serve two-year terms and two shall serve one-year terms. The Senior Executive V.P. shall determine the terms of service for the members who serve on the first HAC. Subsequent appointments will be for two-year terms.

Structure: The HAC members shall choose a Chairperson and Secretary. The Senior Executive V.P.'s designee shall serve as the Committee's Top Management Liaison.

Conflicts between the HAC, HRD Director, and the Senior Executive V.P.'s designee shall be resolved by the Senior Executive V.P.

Evaluation of HAC Members: Each member shall be evaluated annually on his or her performance on the HAC. This evaluation should be conducted by his or her immediate superior with input from the HRD Director. Such evaluations shall figure into the employee's annual salary review.

Frequency of Meetings

The HAC shall meet at least four times each year, with the HRD Director or his/her designee present. Meetings shall be open to other interested parties.

Roles and Responsibilities of HAC

The Chairperson, working closely with the HRD Director, schedules meetings as needed, but at least four (4) meetings will be scheduled each year. The Chairperson conducts the HAC meetings, acting as discussion leader. One primary job of the Chairperson is to facilitate discussion by all people present at a meeting. The Chairperson should strive to keep an open and balanced conversational flow and protect individuals and their ideas from destructive criticism.

The Secretary prepares written minutes of the meetings and distributes copies to the members. The Secretary will maintain a file of all important documents for the HAC.

The Top Management Liaison will report HAC activities, conclusions, and recommendations to top management and will advise the HAC of concerns or directives from top management.

All HAC members shall be responsible for carrying out the tasks of the Committee. Committee member duties are ongoing and members do not need a formal HAC meeting to proceed.

The HAC's duties include the following:

1. *General Policy Statement:* The HAC will adopt a general policy statement regarding the HRD Effort of the organization.

> **TABLE 6-2** Continued.
>
> 2. *General Oversight of the HRD Effort:* The HAC will provide oversight of the HRD Effort, developed by the HRD Director and others. The HAC will evaluate the effectiveness of the HRD Effort in meeting the organization's needs. The HAC will recommend necessary revisions to the Effort, in consultation with the HRD Director.
> 3. *Selection of Experiences:* The HAC works with the HRD Director each year to select and schedule training, educational, and developmental activities attuned to organizational needs.
> 4. *Scheduling of Learning Experiences:* The HAC works with the HRD Director to schedule the offering of learning experiences to members of job categories, individuals sharing common career aspirations, and to some work groups in which developmental needs have been planned. The HAC may recommend time frames for the development and scheduling of planned learning activities.
> 5. *Developing Specifications for Learning Experiences:* The HAC advises the HRD Director in developing specifications for learning experiences based on staff needs. Such specifications will include: the purpose of the experience, objectives stated in terms of what employees will be able *to do* after completion; methods to be used in delivering the experience(s); and minimum acceptable qualifications for those chosen to lead training courses, serve as career mentors, or guide developmental efforts.

tails; (5) prepare meeting agendas; and (6) schedule meetings. Members should be selected on the basis of their (1) willingness to serve, (2) representativeness, relative to the purpose of the committee, and (3) competence (Kruger, 1983).

It is unwise to rush into establishing advisory committees without first assessing how much support they will receive and, once the idea is accepted, without "training" members. Nothing can be so frustrating to committee members as to propose an idea and learn later than HRD practitioners were unable to accept their advice because it was not approved by higher-level management or because necessary resources were not available. It is also unreasonable to expect managers or employees to advise on HRD issues which they know little about. A good "briefing" on the HRD Effort and the practices of the HRD department is a necessary first item in any kickoff meeting of a committee. Further, if committee members are to provide input on future-oriented learning needs, they will undoubtedly require instruction on strategic thinking skills.

Advisory committees are important. In many respects, they can serve in the same capacity as Strategic Business Planning committees. They can identify present strengths/weaknesses of an organization's long-term learning efforts, compare them to expected future demands, and set priorities for planned learning. These are not matters of minor consequence, nor should they be treated as such, because they can yield support to guide implementation of the Organization's Strategy for HRD in line with business and staffing plans.

DEVELOPING FUNCTIONAL STRATEGIES FOR HRD

As traditionally discussed in Strategic Business Planning, "*a functional strategy* is the short-term game plan for a key functional area *within* a company" (Pearce & Robinson, 1985, p. 297). Functions include production/operations, marketing, finance, and personnel. The purpose of a functional strategy is to "translate grand strategy at

TABLE 6-3 STEPS AND ISSUES IN HUMAN RESOURCES STRATEGY DEVELOPMENT AND IMPLEMENTATION

Step	Key issues
1. Human Resources Goal Identification	■ What demands do the mission and strategic plans place upon the organization's climate and human resources? ■ What kind of people, with what skills and performance capabilities, does the organization require? How many and how soon? ■ What leadership styles and management skills will be needed for each relevant division, location, or business group?
2. Situation Diagnosis	■ What are the present status and nature of the organization's culture, people, human resources systems, and personnel programs? ■ What is the existing inventory of managerial and specialized skills? ■ What is the prevailing leadership style and management profile?
3. Needs Assessment	■ What gaps exist between the organization's future requirements for its human resources and working climate and the status quo? ■ What are the key needs in terms of management abilities, technical skills, staff size and experience, management succession, problem-solving skills, organizational values and styles, performance levels, productivities, and so on?
4. Developmental Plans	■ What developmental steps or actions need to be implemented in order to bring the organization's people and culture to the level and nature of strength required by the mission and strategic plans? ■ What priorities, costs, resources, and probabilities of success are associated with meeting these developmental needs?
5. Plans Implementation	■ How must the enterprise design, communicate, phase in, and gain individual commitment to the various pieces of its human resources development plan?
6. Implementation Control and Corrective Action	■ How is progress toward human resources strategy goals to be measured? ■ What level of actual performance shall constitute acceptable progress in each development plan area? ■ What obstacles threaten fulfillment of the human resources strategy, and how should they be addressed? ■ What remedial actions are necessary? ■ How must the basic strategy be modified through experience?

Source: Roberts & Wolf, 1983, p. 15-6 [Figure 15-2]. Reprinted with permission from McGraw-Hill Book Company.

TABLE 6-4 SBU/STRATEGIC MANAGEMENT IMPLICATIONS FOR HUMAN RESOURCES STRATEGY

Process	Phase in life cycle		
	Invest to grow	Earn and protect	Harvest and divest
Resource allocation	Strategic investment	Protective investment	Minimized investment
Marketing strategy	Product differentiation	Selling-system differentiation	Individual selling and distribution
Organization structure	Flat Minimum organization	Highly supportive Complex	Centralized Hierarchical
Job design	High freedom to act Innovation encouraged	Interdependent Team-oriented	Highly controlled Task-oriented
Climate and culture	Highest urgency	Paced urgency	High loyalty Routine Security
Management style	Entrepreneurial Few formal processes	Sophisticated management processes	Sophisticated control processes
Staffing	Aggressive Risk oriented Top quality people predominate	Broad specialists Challenge-oriented Above average people predominate	Narrow specialists Security-oriented People of a broad range of abilities
Reward systems	High total compensation Modest base High incentive compensation Big risks—big rewards	High to average total compensation Average base Above average incentive compensation Moderate risk—moderate reward	Low to average total compensation Above average base Modest incentive compensation Low risk—low reward

Source: Roberts & Wolf, 1983, p. 15-7 [Figure 15-3]. Reprinted with permission from McGraw-Hill Book Company.

the business level into action plans for subunits of the company" (Pearce & Robinson, 1985, p. 289).

We have written elsewhere about the importance of establishing functional strategies within personnel (Rothwell & Kazanas, 1988). It is essential to integrate (Alpander, 1982): (1) overall HR Grand Strategy* with organizational strategy so that personnel initiatives support business plans; and (2) the strategy for each "activity area" within HR with that of the overall strategy of the HR function so that each activity area of personnel supports others. These "activity areas" include hiring/selection/recruitment, training, compensating, and dealing with organized labor. The purpose of HR Grand Strategy is an important one: "it ensures that the organization's human resources will be capable of fulfilling the stated business mission" (Roberts & Wolf, 1983, p. 15-2). Steps in formulating HR Grand Strategy resemble those in formulating strategic business plans (see Table 6-3) and appropriate HR goals depend on business goals (see Table 6-4).

Organizational Strategy for HRD is an important component of HR Grand Strategy because plans for equipping people with appropriate skills and knowledge for the future are closely related to plans for ensuring that the right people are in the right places at the right times and that they possess the right skills.

But within Organizational Strategy for HRD there can also be *functional strategies*. They differ in purpose because they focus on different kinds of change. They also focus on different learners. These functions are:

1. *organization development*, a long-term effort for changing the culture of an organization or group,
2. *nonemployee development*, a long-term effort for improving relations between a business, the general public, or external stakeholders,
3. *employee development*, a long-term effort for matching up the collective skills of a work group and the responsibilities assigned to the group by the organization,
4. *education*, an intermediate-term effort for helping individuals achieve their career objectives, keep abreast of changes in their occupations, and gain new insights about themselves, and
5. *training*, a short-term effort for helping job incumbents meet their responsibilities.

Each function is a component of a unified Organizational Strategy for HRD. Each contributes, in its own way, to the implementation of that Organizational Strategy for HRD. Yet each can be distinct from other functions and can be guided by separately-prepared objectives, policies, and activities. Part Four of this text focuses on each function.

---

*We use the term HR Grand Strategy to mean plans for all personnel activities.

ACTIVITY 6-1 Objective-Setting for Implementing Organizational Strategy for HRD

Directions: Use this activity to do some brainstorming. For each issue listed in column 1, describe in column 2 what long-term outcomes are to be achieved over a five-year time period. Then describe in column 3 what specific, measurable outcomes are to be achieved through organized HRD activities in one year. It might be helpful to diagram, on separate sheets, the relationship between long-term objectives (in column 2) and short-term objectives (in column 3).

Column 1 Issue	Column 2 What Long-Term Outcomes Are To Be Achieved Over A Five-Year Period?	Column 3 What Specific Measurable Outcomes Are To Be Achieved in a One-Year Period?
changes in what the general public knows about the corporation and its products/services		
changes in what key external stakeholders know about the corporation and its products/services		
changes in the organization, its departments, or work groups through learning		
changes in individuals so that they are ready for movements between jobs		
changes in what individuals know about their present jobs		

Developing Functional Strategies for HRD

ACTIVITY 6-2 Evaluating the Comprehensiveness of an Organization's HRD Policy

Directions: In column 1 you will find a number of issues which should be covered in an organization's HRD policy. In column 2, check (✔) whether your firm's present policy addresses the issue. In column 3, describe what *changes* in HRD policy are appropriate in light of any changes in Organizational Strategy for HRD.

Column 1	Column 2		Column 3
	Response		
Does your organization's HRD policy cover:	Yes (✔)	No (✔)	What changes in HRD policy are appropriate in light of the change in HRD Grand Strategy?
1. The purpose of the HRD Effort as it relates to			
a. the general public?	( )	( )	
b. key external stakeholders?	( )	( )	
c. work groups/departments?	( )	( )	
d. individuals and their careers?	( )	( )	
e. job categories?	( )	( )	
2. The relationship between the HRD Effort and organizational purpose, goals, and objectives?	( )	( )	
3. Responsibilities of			
a. managers at each level for HRD?	( )	( )	
b. employees for HRD?	( )	( )	
4. Under what circumstances HRD policy should be changed?	( )	( )	
5. The needs to be met through the HRD Effort?	( )	( )	
6. How to finance the HRD Effort?	( )	( )	
7. How to staff activities conducted for HRD?	( )	( )	
8. How top managers should be involved in the HRD Effort?	( )	( )	
9. How managers and employees at lower levels should participate in planning for the HRD Effort?	( )	( )	

ACTIVITY 6-2 Continued		
Column 1	Column 2	Column 3
Does your organization's HRD policy cover:	Response Yes No (✓) (✓)	What changes in HRD policy are appropriate in light of the change in HRD Grand Strategy?
10. Other matters? List other important issues: _____ _____ _____ _____ _____ _____ _____ _____ _____	( ) ( )	

ACTIVITY 6-3 Leadership and Implementation of Organizational Strategy for HRD

Directions: As in the two previous activities, use this activity to do some brainstorming. In column 1, consider: who are the key leaders? In column 2, consider: how receptive are these leaders to changing Organizational Strategy for HRD? In column 3, consider: how can these leaders be persuaded of the value of a new Organizational Strategy for HRD? Write notes to answer these questions in the space below each question.

Column 1	Column 2	Column 3
Who are the key leaders?	How receptive are these leaders to changing Strategy for HRD?	How can these leaders be persuaded of the value of a new Organizational Strategy for HRD?

ACTIVITY 6-4 Rewards and Implementing Organizational Strategy for HRD

Directions: Use this Activity to think about rewards and Organizational Strategy for HRD. Go through each of the following sections and answer the questions. Use additional paper.

I. Present Rewards

1. How much does your organization presently reward learning (generally) and each of the following (particularly)?
    A. achieving desired results from training
    B. preparing for career mobility through *planned* employee education
    C. improving the work group through *planned* development
    D. improving relations between the organization and external groups

II. Future Rewards

2. In the future, how should your organization encourage:
    A. achieving desired results of training?
    B. preparing for career mobility through *planned* employee education?
    C. improving a work group through *planned* development?
    D. improving relations between the organization and external groups?

III. Identifying Gaps

3. What gaps exist between the conditions discussed in items 1 and 2?

IV. Rewards

4. What extrinsic and/or intrinsic rewards can help implement Organizational Strategy for HRD? Who should be rewarded? How?

ACTIVITY 6-5 Budgeting and Organizational Strategy for HRD

Directions: Answer the questions in each section. Use additional paper if necessary.

I. The Complete Cost

1. Have you considered the *long-term* costs of implementing Organizational Strategy for HRD? If not, prepare a five-year budget for the HRD Effort. (Use additional paper if necessary.)

II. External Conditions

2. What estimates can you make of the company's financial position over a five-year time period?
   A. Will this position erode? If so, why?
   B. How will the HRD Effort be affected by the company's financial position? Why do you think it will be affected (if at all)?

III. Priorities

3. What priorities should be assigned to each initiative described in the budget?

ACTIVITY 6-6   Communicating about Organizational Strategy for HRD

Directions: Answer the following questions. Use additional paper if necessary.

I. Present Communication

1. How well do you feel issues associated with the HRD Effort are presently being communicated to supervisors and employees in your organization?

II. Future Communication

2. How do you feel issues associated with the HRD Effort should be communicated to supervisors and employees in your organization in the future?

Part III.   Important Issues

3. What HRD issues are most important to communicate about in the future? To whom should this communication be directed?

Part IV.   Channels

4. Through what channels should information about HRD-related issues be communicated in the future? Why?

Developing Functional Strategies for HRD

ACTIVITY 6-7   A Case Study on Implementing Organizational Strategy for HRD

Directions: Read the following case and answer the questions at the end.

The Worthington Corporation* is a fully diversified, multinational manufacturing firm which produces consumer electronics goods like televisions, compact disc players, videotape machines, and cassette tape recorders. Worthington's largest manufacturing facilities are located in Taiwan and Korea. Marketing, research and development, and finance are handled through the firm's large corporate headquarters complex in Duluth, Minnesota.

Worthington established a corporate-level HRD Department at the Duluth headquarters only ten years ago. The firm has historically leaned toward decentralization. Prior to 1977, all HRD activities were handled on-site (plants or corporate headquarters).

Worthington employs thirty-five professional HRD practitioners at corporate headquarters. Most of them hold doctorates in HRD or Instructional Technology. Corporate headquarters offers management, executive, engineering, and other high-level training seminars in a new $6 million training complex. In addition, the corporate-level HRD department produces professional videotapes, computer-based training software, and other instructional resources for use in company plants abroad.

Though the corporate-level HRD department offers the highest-cost seminars on-site, each plant is staffed by at least one experienced HRD practitioner. Typically reporting to a plant's Personnel Manager, each HRD practitioner at a company facility prepares an annual training and development plan for the facility. Coordination between line managers and HRD practitioners at all levels is essential to avoid expensive overlapping of training.

Worthington does not conduct comprehensive HR Planning. No attempt is presently made to integrate company recruitment, HRD, compensation/benefits, or other HR activities.

Worthington does plan strategically at the corporate level. However, the chief focus of these plans is on future markets, company financial condition, and product lines. No attempt is made to draw conclusions about human skills needed or available to carry out these plans.

Worthington faces stiff competition from foreign firms, some of which enjoy substantially lower labor costs on goods produced. However, Worthington possesses a well-known corporate name worldwide. Company management plans to expand and automate manufacturing facilities, increase expenditures on marketing and research and development, and decrease labor costs. The corporate HRD department will receive more resources and staffing—perhaps as much as 50 percent more resources over the next few years. That is most unusual in a firm which is (generally) decreasing its staffing levels worldwide.

Assume that you are hired as an external consultant by Worthington's corporate-level HRD department to help establish an Organizational Strategy for HRD.

ACTIVITY 6-7 Continued

Questions

1. Prepare a list of questions about the purpose of the HRD Effort to use in an initial interview with the corporate-level Director of HRD. What would you want to know about purpose?
2. What problems are created by the lack of a company Strategic Business Plan and comprehensive HR Plan? What can be done to overcome these problems, assuming the corporation will not change its planning methods?
3. How can you develop a comprehensive list of HRD-oriented strengths/weaknesses and threats/opportunities facing Worthington? Discuss *how* you would prepare such a list.
4. Consider the range of Organizational Strategies for HRD available to Worthington. List *what they are* and *discuss what each one means*.
5. What problems, if any, can you foresee in attempting to formulate and implement an Organizational Strategy for HRD in the Worthington Corporation? How do you suggest handling each problem?

*A fictitious name for a well-known company.

PART 4
FUNCTIONAL STRATEGIES FOR HRD

7

ORGANIZATION DEVELOPMENT

This chapter deals with preparing *groups* of people for the future by changing organizational culture or group norms. This process of change is called Organization Development (OD).

DEFINITION OF ORGANIZATION DEVELOPMENT

OD connotes more than its literal meaning of "fostering long-term growth of an organization and people within it." Instead, it is

> a top-management-supported, long-range effort to improve an organization's problem-solving and renewal processes, particularly through a more effective and collaborative diagnosis and management of organization culture—with special emphasis on formal work team, temporary team, and intergroup culture—with the assistance of a consultant-facilitator and the use of the theory and technology of applied behavioral science, including action research (French & Bell, 1984, p. 17).

Distinguishing features of OD thus include a focus on long-term change (1) compatible with top management desires, (2) in the context of work groups or work teams, (3) carried out by an external consultant as a catalyst for change, and (4) using specialized techniques drawn from behavioral sciences such as sociology, psychology, and cultural anthropology.

HOW IS ORGANIZATION DEVELOPMENT DISTINGUISHABLE FROM OTHER CHANGE METHODS?

There are three very general approaches to change in any organization (Chin & Benne, 1969; French & Bell, 1984). The first approach is *persuasion*. Convince people to change because there is some benefit to them by doing so. Since people act out of self-interest, they will change. The second approach is *coercion*. Make people fear what will happen if they do not change. Out of fear, they will change. The third approach is *education*. Teach people new ways to behave and instill new attitudes, and they will change.

OD is directed to bringing about long-term change through planned learning in group contexts. It is thus based on an educational approach to change. Unlike employee development, it is directed to changing culture—the elusive, often inarticulated and taken-for-granted standards and norms of appropriate behavior in an organizational or group setting.

WHAT IS THE RELATIONSHIP BETWEEN ORGANIZATION DEVELOPMENT AND ORGANIZATIONAL LEARNING?

The essence of strategic planning and thinking is the awareness of how future conditions may affect present decisions or past actions. Strategy-making helps avert problems or seize opportunities that may arise at a future time and that are consequences of external trends, events, or conditions over which managers in one organization have little control. In short, strategic planning is based on adapting to—even anticipating—external environmental change.

Learning is one means, though not the only means, for individuals and groups to adapt to external change. While HRD practitioners typically devote most of their attention to such individually-oriented change efforts as employee training and education, it is clear that organizations and work groups also "learn." Though neither organizations nor groups "learn" in precisely the same way as individuals, they are human institutions and are influenced by phenomena, like learning, to which individuals are subject (Bedeian, 1984).

It is time that HRD practitioners begin to adopt a broader conception of their role—indeed, a strategic view—that they are agents who facilitate learning for organizations and work groups as well as individuals. Viewed from this broader standpoint, OD is any planned learning activity intended to help groups adapt to future external environmental demands.

The work group. The work group consists of an employee, the employee's immediate supervisor, and other employees who work together. They share common work space and are placed in close enough physical proximity to interact socially. French and Bell (1984) call this the *family group*, the intact and relatively permanent team consisting of employees and their immediate superior.

A substantial amount of attention has been devoted to individual performance in team settings and, more generally, to *group dynamics*. The latter term refers to the interactions of individuals in a group. Many influential thinkers in the behavioral sciences stress that group change is a means of facilitating individual and organizational change. For instance, Lewin (1951) pointed out that *work group norms*—the unspoken and often unexamined beliefs about how individuals should behave—pose barriers to change. The reason is that if individual behavior is at odds with group norms, the individual will be pressured by group members to conform to accepted practices. When individuals do not conform, they are punished or ostracized by peers. Chris Argyris (1962) discussed the relationship between individual and organization, asserting that the hierarchical nature of most groups and organizations forces individuals into passive and dependent roles. In frustration they may leave the organization, seek freedom through acquisition of more power, withdraw mentally from the job, or form new groups, like unions, to fight for their interests.

The nature of work groups varies substantially, depending on how tasks are carried out in the organization. In some settings, individuals work closely with others for a common goal. For example, a product manufactured on an assembly line is handled by many people. Nor is team work restricted to blue-collar settings: it is common enough among doctors, lawyers, and accountants. On the other hand, some work is highly individualized—like that of the medical research scientist.

A second important issue has to do with organizational structure. Managers in most organizations have considerable freedom to determine how work will be divided among various groups and, indeed, what kinds of groups and how many of them will exist. Beyond that, jobs *within* each group may vary widely and contribute to pressures favoring or impeding cooperation.

Groups share common characteristics (Gibson, Ivancevich, & Donnelly, 1985). First, individuals are accorded *status* within a work group based on the authority associated with their positions and such individual characteristics as educational level, experience, age, and relationships with superiors. Second, groups vary in *cohesiveness*, a force pulling members together as a group and away from other groups. Third, all groups have *norms*. These are standards of conduct that are rarely articulated but are pervasive in their influence. They arise as groups are formed and are sustained through socialization, the process by which new members are inducted to a group. To remain a group member, an individual must behave in ways consistent with group norms. Fourth, all groups manifest three types of leadership behavior: behavior concerned with task accomplishment; behavior concerned with preserving good interpersonal relations between group members; and behavior not relevant to group needs (Benne & Sheats, 1948). How leaders behave exerts considerable influence on group performance and morale (Fiedler, 1972; Tannenbaum & Schmidt, 1973). Fifth, members of any group adopt roles, patterns of behavior associated with their jobs and with group allegiance. Individuals receive messages from others about how they are expected to behave and, in turn, send messages about roles through words and deeds (Katz & Kahn, 1978). Behavior inconsistent with the role expectations of others excites comment and, perhaps, sanctions by the work group or its leader. Individual performance in jobs affects group performance which, in turn, affects organizational performance (Gibson, Ivancevich, & Donnelly, 1985).

Work groups, like individuals and organizations, progress through predictable life cycle stages in which some concerns dominate others. A group's stage of development is important because it affects productivity and the learning experiences to which the group is susceptible. Stated rather simplistically, the stages are: (1) creation, (2) communication, (3) production, and (4) fixation (Gibson, Ivancevich, & Donnelly, 1985). In the first stage, new members meet for the first time. They are not necessarily familiar with either the work task confronting them or with each other. In the second stage, group members interact to deal with the task confronting them. They often rebel against the task and against authority figures. They "sort things out"—both how to deal with the task and with each other. In the third stage, group members resolve initial problems with *what should be done* and *how group members should get along with each other*. They devote their energies to the task/problem and cooperate with each other. In the final stage, group members become fixated on certain ways of doing things and ways of interacting. Norms regulate group member behavior, often to the point that fresh approaches are stifled. Indeed, members may be subject to *groupthink,* a general unwillingness to innovate when it means increasing intragroup conflict (Janis, 1973).

The stages of group development are most keenly felt in organizations characterized by (1) a project or matrix structure, in which heterogeneous teams are formed temporarily; (2) rapid turnover in leadership; or (3) start-up efforts of any kind. As Table 7-1 illustrates, some change efforts are particularly appropriate in each stage of group development.

Organizational learning. There are some key similarities and differences between individual and organizational learning. An individual has limited experiences and finite knowledge, skills, and memories. On the other hand, an organization is characterized by (1) a broad store of experiences composed of aggregate individual

TABLE 7-1 APPROPRIATE GROUP DEVELOPMENT EFFORTS BY PHASE OF GROUP

Group phase	Brief description of group phase	Group development effort
Creation	• Members meet for the first time. • Productivity is predictably low because group members are uncertain of what to do and how to act.	• The supervisor should focus attention on what is to be done and provide specific, concrete directions as much as possible.
Communication	• Members of the group learn how to interact with each other. • Members of the group focus on what they are to do and how they are to do it.	• The supervisor and/or change agent should facilitate group interaction and help members of the group establish roles/work methods.
Production	• This phase of group development is characterized by the highest level of productivity.	• The supervisor and/or change agent should allow group members to participate, to the extent they wish, in decisions affecting them.
Fixation	• Group norms are fixed and may suffocate innovation.	• The supervisor and/or change agent should initiate team-building and team development efforts and foster constructive reviews of existing group interaction and work methods.

experiences over time—not just present employees but all past employees who have "left their mark"; (2) a much broader store of knowledge and skills than possessed by one person; and (3) an institutional memory comprised of a "hard component" embodied in job descriptions, organizational structure, policies, and procedures, and a "soft component" embodied in stories, myths, and legends about what works and what does not (Bedeian, 1984). An organization is relatively permanent and possesses a history distinct from that of individuals. Work groups share this characteristic with organizations.

However, there are two similarities between individual and organizational learning. First, learning stems from a preception of need, a sense that something is not as it should be or that something will change in the future; and second, learning is influenced by past experience. For organizations and groups, needs pinpointed by managers provide a basis for action. Not all needs have to do with the knowledge or skills of individuals—but many do. That is why Organizational Strategy for HRD, focused on learning needs, is important in Strategic Business Planning. However, experiences guide assessments of need and interpretations of what is worth knowing or doing. Like individuals, organizations "adjust their activities based on past experiences. . . ." (Bedeian, 1984, p. 261). Organizational or group *culture* is the embodiment of experience. It is the sum total of what has been learned. It influences how individuals behave and how they are socialized as they become members of the organization.

OD efforts are geared to changing culture and thus to facilitating organizational learning. Since Strategic Business Plans may require cultural change for successful implementation, OD efforts are capable of facilitating organizational and group change in line with strategic needs.

Methods Associated with Organization Development

OD is based on *action research*. Different OD change efforts, called *interventions*, stem from it, chosen on the basis of need.

Space here does not allow for an exhaustive treatment of these subjects, but they are important for HRD practitioners to know about. One reason is that implementation of a large-scale, integrated Organizational Strategy for HRD may be treated as an OD intervention. Another reason is that implementation of Strategic Business Planning methods generally (and one strategic plan specifically) may require cultural change of the kind handled best by OD (Lewis, 1983; Rogers, 1981).

Action research. Both an approach to change and to organized learning, action research is a process comprising a specific, ongoing chain of events. It is a method of problem-solving (French & Bell, 1984).

Action research stems from work of John Collier and Kurt Lewin (French & Bell, 1984). Collier learned from experience that cooperation is essential to success in any change effort. Lewin believed that research of value to practitioners is very important, a way of linking action and reflection or linking creative problem-solving to work activities.

Action research is a cyclical process, one "with the focus on new or advanced problems as the client group learns to work more effectively together" (French, 1969,

p. 26). The first step is a perception that change is needed. This perception is often triggered by crisis. The second step is a realization that outside consultants—drawn from another part of the firm or from outside the firm—are needed to facilitate the change effort. Outsiders are chosen because they are not bound by the chain of command in the same way as insiders. From that point on, the steps in action research are clear enough:

1. *defining the problem:* What is it that needs to be changed?
2. *collecting information:* What facts can be found about the problem? How do people feel about it?
3. *providing feedback:* What information has the consultant collected about the problem? How can it be fed back to managers and employees to help them diagnose the problem and take corrective steps?
4. *planning action collaboratively:* What plan of action, based on feedback, can managers, employees, and the consultant agree on?
5. *taking action:* What steps are taken to correct the problem previously diagnosed?
6. *assessing results:* What outcomes resulted from the action?
7. *providing feedback:* What information has the consultant collected about the problem and about the results of steps taken to correct it?
8. *planning action:* What further steps should be taken?

These steps continue indefinitely, as shown in Figure 7-1.

Action research is fundamentally an approach to experiential learning (Kolb, 1984). The Lewinian action research model uses "immediate concrete experience as the basis for observation and reflection. These observations are assimilated into a 'theory' from which new implications for action can be deduced. These implications then serve as guides in acting to create new experiences" (Kolb, 1984, p. 21). Group learning results from collective or individual experiences.

For more information on action research, see Cooperrider and Srivastva (1987), Corey (1953), Frohman, Sashkin, and Kavanaugh (1976), Jenks (1970), Lippitt, Langseth, and Mossop (1985), Neilsen (1984), Shepard (1960), and Whyte and Hamilton (1964).

OD interventions. An intervention is a change effort. Psychologists use intervention to mean a *therapeutic* change effort. Chris Argyris (1970) provides the classic definition: "To intervene is to enter into an ongoing system of relationships, to come between or among persons, groups or objects for the purpose of helping them" (p. 15). OD interventions are undertaken to produce desired change in line with objectives for change established by members of the organization and are "designed to improve the organization's functioning through enabling organization members better to manage their team and organization cultures" (French & Bell, 1984, p. 120).

There are several ways to think of OD interventions. They may be classified on the basis of first, *what is to be changed:* According to one typology, the least complex OD interventions are directed to changing elements of the formal (public, rational,

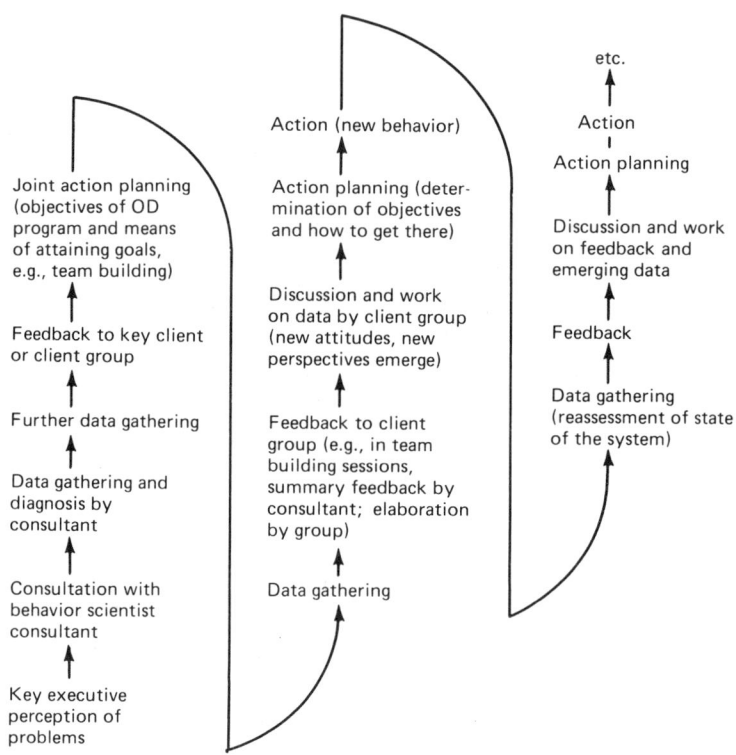

Figure 7-1: Action-Research Model for Organization Development. *Source:* French, 1969, p. 26 with permission of *California Management Review*.

and observable) organization such as structure, policies, employee appraisal, and management attitudes/skills. More complex interventions are directed to changing the informal (private, affective, and unobservable) organization such as behavior within or between groups or between individuals (see Selfridge & Sokolik, 1975). Second, OD interventions can be classified by *who is to be changed*. Some interventions focus on individuals; some on groups of two or three people; some on teams or groups; some on relations between teams or groups; and some on an entire organization (French & Bell, 1984). Third, interventions can be classified by *what methods of change are emphasized*. Some interventions rely on feedback; some on changing norms; some on improving communication; some on working through differences using confrontation; and some on training or employee education (French & Bell, 1984).

Many OD interventions can support change and help meet objectives planned to bring it about. They include: (1) the role analysis technique; (2) interpersonal peacemaking; (3) process consultation; (4) team-building; (5) survey-guided development; (6) the organizational mirror; and (7) strategic planning interventions.

The role analysis technique (RAT) deals with group performance problems in which members face unclear or conflicting role expectations from their colleagues. A role is, of course, the behavior associated with a job or position in a group or organization.

Roles arise naturally in group settings as members learn how to approach work tasks and interact with each other. During the early stages of group development, the roles of all members are unclear. Productivity is predictably low until both task and group process issues are worked out. New group members confront a similar problem, in that existing group roles have already been established, but newcomers do not know what they are. For example, an individual trained in accounting has a general idea of what to do, but is not necessarily aware of specific job requirements or the modes of interaction between people in one organization.

Individuals enter work settings with their own expectations about their roles and the roles of others. How they behave and what they say about their jobs send *role messages* to other people, who respond by providing *feedback* about those messages which may subsequently influence behavior (Katz & Kahn, 1978). When the role incumbent's behavior clashes with the expectations of others, he or she is sure to hear about it. Some individuals will then modify their behavior to match the expectations of others; some will try to change the expectations of others; and some will ignore or misperceive role feedback at odds with their expectations. Generally, aggressive or self-satisfied individuals will not modify their role behavior to satisfy others (Katz & Kahn, 1978).

To apply the role analysis technique, a role incumbent lists role expectations in a group setting. Then group members list what they expect from the incumbent. They negotiate the lists, arriving at consensus. The process is continued in round robin fashion until each role incumbent in the group has been discussed. (For more on this, see Burke [1982].)

An alternative to face-to-face group discussion is a modified delphi procedure in which individuals are surveyed about the roles of other group members and themselves. Of course, there are practical limitations to this method: it will not work for groups exceeding eight or nine people, because large groups produce voluminous data, and those data are difficult to feed back.

If the role problem stems from a difference in perceptions between the individual and the supervisor, then it can be handled during the employee appraisal process. Using the job description, the supervisor and the individual separately prepare narratives about what the individual is *to do*. They then meet to compare notes and work out differences.

The value of the RAT in implementing Organizational Strategy for HRD should be apparent. A long-term change in Strategic Business Plans may require the creation of new groups, changes in individual role behavior, and changes in role behaviors within existing groups. The RAT may thus be used to compare present with desired future roles as a tool for pinpointing individual and group learning needs.

Interpersonal peacemaking is a fancy name for a process of resolving *destructive* conflicts between two, three, or more individuals. On occasion, it is also appropriately used in resolving destructive conflicts between two or more *groups*.

Note the emphasis on the word *destructive* in the previous paragraph. Not all conflict is necessarily destructive. Indeed, constructive conflict is an important ingredient in individual—and organizational—learning and innovation, but only if it occurs in a mutually supportive and nonthreatening environment.

Walton (1969) has described interpersonal peacemaking at length. The change agent (1) brings together two or more conflicting individuals or groups; (2) focuses on the feelings of individuals or group members, encouraging them to explain the sources of their feelings; (3) summarizes, underscores, and encourages feedback; and (4) helps individuals establish common grounds for future understanding and interaction. By drawing attention to the importance of interpersonal relations and providing a structure by which to improve relations between conflicting groups or individuals, this intervention can be an important tool for OD practitioners.

In implementing Organizational Strategy for HRD, there may be a use for interpersonal peacemaking when relations between two individuals—particularly two supervisors or managers—negatively affect the achievement of organizational goals. In some cases, a manager resists plans when a rival advocates them. In such cases, an interpersonal peacemaking intervention may be in order.

Process consultation is an OD intervention focusing on how people interact. *Process* simply means *ways of interacting between two or more individuals or groups*. It is distinct from work methods, what people do to get the work out. Interactions between people clearly affect work methods, just as work methods influence interaction. In short, how people interact influences their productivity and their willingness to be open and honest.

Think about a meeting. If interpersonal relations are poor, there is a good chance the meeting will not be productive. People sit around in silence, not wishing to provoke confrontation. One person may dominate the discussion, interrupting others or undercutting what they say. If a supervisor leads the discussion, he or she may dominate it and may think that silent listeners acquiesce.

In process consultation, change agents participate silently in group activities. They observe what is going on and how group members interact. A passive consultation strategy involves (1) providing feedback about what consultants observe during the group experience *after* it occurs; (2) helping group members focus their attention on their behaviors in dealing with others; and (3) helping participants establish their own plans for improvement. In short, consultants silently monitor activities but focus group attention on process issues at the end.

An active process consultation strategy is somewhat different. Consultants participate fully in group activities but focus their attention on group interaction during those activities. They may call a "time out" during a task and ask group members to express how they are feeling about themselves, their behavior, the task, the group, or something else which seems to be impeding progress.

Process consultation helps produce behavioral change through immediate and concrete feedback. Some process consultants may go further and (1) model or demonstrate appropriate behavior for group members, (2) coach participants, or (3) ask group members to role play.

Process consultation can modify behavior when interpersonal relations are inconsistent with requirements for interdepartmental cooperation in line with Strategic Business Plans. Process improvement techniques may prove useful in settings like Strategic Planning or HRD planning meetings in which group interaction influences outcomes and decisions. (For more on process consultation, see Edgar Schein's classic book [1969].)

Team building, sometimes called *team development*, is the general name for a whole range of OD interventions. Geared to change at the work group level, it is perhaps the single most important OD intervention. The work group is crucially important in establishing norms of behavior which can facilitate or impede individual change. Team building, while often a term in search of a meaning (Guest, 1986), is undertaken to improve group performance and identify the contributions of each group member (Hughes, Rosenbach, & Clover, 1983; Woodman & Sherwood, 1980).

Team building can only be used in group settings where members share at least one common goal and cooperative group behavior is essential to individual achievement (Burke, 1982). Moreover, there must be an up-front determination by managers that a problem in group performance stems from group interaction rather than a lack of individual motivation or knowledge (Kilcourse, 1984). As Dyer (1977) explains in a classic treatment, "a program should not begin unless there is clear evidence that a lack of effective teamwork is the fundamental problem. If the problem is an intergroup issue, a technical difficulty, or an administrative foul-up, team building would not be an appropriate change strategy" (p. 35). Generally, team building is appropriate for any newly-formed group. With existing groups it is also useful in clarifying member roles, establishing priorities, examining or improving patterns of member interaction, examining or improving group decision-making and problem-solving, allocating tasks, improving work operations, and planning learning experiences for people in the work group.

Assuming a team development effort is needed and managers are willing to devote adequate time and resources to it, the first step is the choice of a change agent to facilitate the process. While every supervisor is in a sense a change agent (Kirkpatrick, 1985; Varney, 1977), not all supervisors are ideally suited to lead team development efforts or, for that matter, any OD intervention. One reason is that they may not possess the necessary skills. Another reason is that they are associated with the existing organizational hierarchy of authority, group culture, and status quo. For both reasons, an external change agent—drawn from another department or from outside the organization—is probably appropriate in most cases (Baker, 1979; Patten, 1979b).

After a consultant is chosen, the intervention begins with a meeting in which group members discuss the organization, hear from the consultant about team building in general, and formulate a vision of the group's future which they would like to work toward bringing about (Mahoney, 1982a). From there, they establish change objectives and, over a long time period, focus on solving problems and implementing solutions (Mahoney, 1982b; 1982c). These steps parallel those in the group life cycle.

While the approach recommended by Mahoney is comprehensive, not all group problems require it. Shorter-term interventions may be carried out to achieve a single purpose, such as setting goals or priorities, allocating work, examining and improving specific team procedures or processes, and clarifying role relationships between team members (Burke, 1982). In these instances, one meeting may suffice to rectify a problem.

Team building is a powerful OD intervention. It can be used in several ways which are related to Strategic Business Planning and Organizational Strategy for HRD.

Top managers should operate as a team. The Chief Executive and immediate subordinates constitute a work group. A team building effort carried out with this group can have far-reaching consequences, including improved relations and a greater willingness to work together effectively. These changes can ripple throughout the firm and contribute to increased creativity, improved cooperation, and more effective organizational planning.

Team building efforts can have similar benefits at all levels of a firm if handled properly. Indeed, there is potential to use team building to generate new ideas of use as the future unfolds in the present, foster joint planning among group members for HRD activities, and provide a structure to help identify and work toward realizing new individual and group roles in line with Strategic Business Plans. In these ways, team building may serve as a tool for formulating and implementing Organizational Strategy for HRD and Strategic Business Plans. For more on team building, see DeMeuse and Liebowitz (1981), Mahoney (1981a; 1981b; 1982a; 1982b; 1982c; 1982d; 1982e), Patten (1979a), and Woodcock (1979).

Survey-guided development is useful in changing the culture of an entire organization or any component of it, but is not generally applicable to individual change efforts. Survey-guided development stems from the work of Rensis Likert (1967). He found that employee attitude surveys are not useful by themselves to create an impetus for organizational or group change unless they are paired with feedback and joint planning efforts (Burke, 1982).

One of Likert's important contributions to OD was a technique called the *interlocking conference.* This technique is simple but powerful. The results of an attitude survey are fed back to members of the organization through special meetings. A change agent meets first with the Chief Executive and his or her immediate subordinates to summarize survey results, help participants in the meeting pinpoint areas requiring action and prioritize those areas, and lead meeting participants to devise concrete action plans for organizational improvement. Following this initial meeting, subsequent meetings are held at successively lower levels—but always in work groups consisting of supervisors and their immediate subordinates. The meetings are "interlocking," in that all supervisors are members of two groups: one consisting of their superior and peers and a second consisting of their subordinates. Through these meetings, plans made at higher levels are factored into plans at lower levels in a collaborative, long-term, and far-reaching improvement process.

While survey-guided development takes a long time, it improves problem-solving, because groups tend to do better than individuals in solving complex problems (Rosenberg, 1983), increases participation of employees in decisions affecting them, and clarifies the direction of organizational efforts. These benefits are quite important for establishing and implementing Strategic Business Plans and long-term Organizational Strategy for HRD. Planning is an activity from which all can benefit (Leemhuis & Eckblad, 1985). For more on survey-guided development, see Bowers and Franklin (1972; 1976), Hausser, Pecorella, and Wissler (1977), and Nadler (1977).

The *organizational mirror* is another OD intervention, primarily useful for departments or work groups (Fordyce & Weil, 1971). Information is collected and fed back to group members about how others in the organization perceive them. The organizational mirror can also reveal how group members perceive themselves. In short, it reflects group image so that group members can use that information as a starting point for corrective action.

Several approaches can be used in carrying out this intervention. People in the organization are contacted about their perceptions of one work group or department through written questionnaires, phone surveys, or selected interviews. Surveys may be scaled or open-ended.

One place to begin is with the group or department being examined. Group members are asked such general, open-ended questions as these:

- What is the primary purpose of your group?
- How does your group contribute to achieving organizational objectives?
- In your opinion, what are the chief strengths of your group? What are its chief weaknesses?
- What trends outside the organization will have the greatest impact on your group in three to five years?
- What trends inside the organization but outside the work group will probably have greatest impact on your group in three to five years? Why do you think so?
- What should your group do to take advantage of future opportunities stemming from trends outside the organization, and to avert future threats stemming from trends outside the organization?
- What should your group do to take advantage of future opportunities stemming from trends inside the organization but outside your work group, and to avert threats stemming from trends inside the organization but outside your work group?

As an alternative, questions may focus on the quality of group decision-making, communication, problem-solving, and conflict resolution methods. Both group members and those outside the group are separately surveyed. The results are used to stimulate planning.

The organizational mirror gives group members a means to compare their view of the group to the way it is viewed by others. Major differences stimulate insights and interest in taking corrective action.

Sometimes differences in viewpoint stem from conflict. Any two groups in an organization may be in conflict. As the level of conflict increases, group members close ranks and exhibit the characteristics of highly cohesive groups (Janis, 1973): first is the *development of an ideology*. Group members moralize about what they do and how much better it is than the behaviors of others. Second is *stereotyping*. People in other groups are seen as a mass rather than as individuals. Third is *low tolerance for self-criticism or new ideas*. Members grow intolerant of internal group conflicts, even constructive ones, while engaged in conflict with external groups.

Conflicts stem from many causes. Generally, any group is in conflict with all others with which it comes in contact, a principle called the "law of interorganizational conflict" (Downs, 1968). Common sources of conflict stem from *interdependence*, the degree to which two groups must rely on each other, and from differences in *goals*, the results sought by each group.

While some conflict is desirable because it prompts innovation, much conflict is counterproductive to organizational performance and morale. Degrees of acceptable conflict differ across groups and organizations. When conflict becomes too great, symptoms may include increased turnover, strident complaints, union grievances, and perhaps even sabotage.

The organizational mirror uses conflict as a starting point for change. The change agent's role in this process is an important one, because group members may become defensive, hostile, and unwilling to accept viewpoints conflicting with their own idealized images of the group. They must be led by others to accept responsibility for who they are and how they are viewed. A change agent begins this process by reporting the perceptions of others, both good and bad.

The organizational mirror can initiate and implement change in line with Strategic Business Plans and Organizational Strategy for HRD. There are several ways to do so. First, OD practitioners can focus the mirror on strategy, top management perceptions of a department, and department members' perceptions of themselves. In what ways do top managers believe a group has been contributing to the organization's mission? How has it not been contributing? What are the group's strengths and weaknesses? What are its prospects for the future? The same questions can be posed to group members separately and then the results can be compared. Second, OD practitioners can focus the mirror on group learning needs. Others in the organization are asked to describe the learning needs of different work groups. The answers are compared to the results of a separate but similar assessment of group members themselves. These results serve as a starting point for devising a group action plan, developed through joint planning with group members. Through these and other approaches, the organizational mirror stimulates change in line with Strategic Business Plans, identifying and pinpointing long-term HRD needs.

Strategic planning interventions are the last group of OD change efforts we shall discuss here. The introduction of strategic planning in an organization which has never before used it calls for (1) specialized skills, knowledge, and information; (2) interaction between members of the top management group, and; (3) a "culture" that supports key assumptions of Strategic Business Planning. These conditions do not come about on their own. It is apparent from the number of firms which have trouble implementing Strategic Business Planning methods that too little attention is paid to these issues (Keichel, 1982). It is also apparent from recent survey data that corporate planners, as a group, would like to see broader participation in strategy formulation than is the case at present (Rothwell & Kazanas, 1986–1988).

The action research model provides guidance for what to do in a start-up planning effort. The first step is a perception that change is needed. The second step is consideration of who should facilitate the change effort: should it be someone from inside or outside the organization? Additional issues are worth raising: Where can people be found who know about strategic planning and group interaction? Is the expertise already available in the organization, or will an outsider—or team of outsiders—be necessary? Another issue: are funds available for this purpose? If not, then an insider, such as a member of the HRD or corporate planning staff, may have to be used.

Assuming that top managers perceive a need for Strategic Business Planning and locate someone who can help introduce it, subsequent steps in an intervention of this kind are based on the action research model (see Figure 7-2). As the Figure shows,

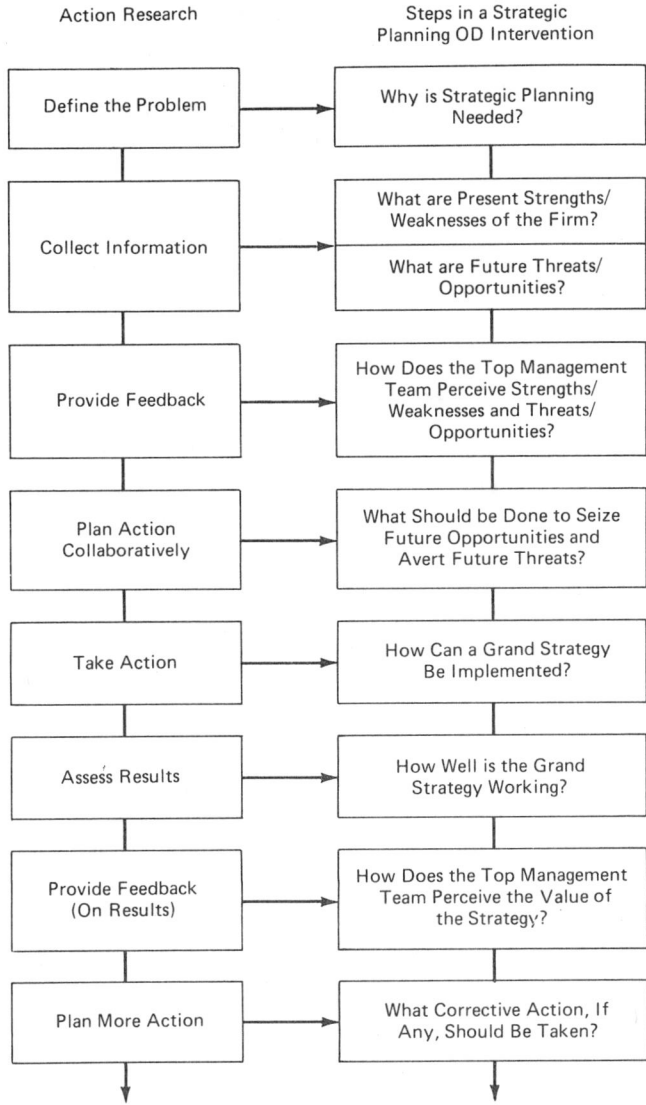

Figure 7-2: Steps in a Strategic Planning Intervention Based on Steps in Action Research

the consultant helps strategists define the problem and collect information. Using this method, top managers are able to develop a genuinely effective planning process which influences future organizational performance.

Of course, specific interventions may also be used in tandem with this general approach. The role analysis technique (RAT) can assist top managers, lower-level managers, and employees in defining their respective roles in establishing and implementing Strategic Business Plans. Interpersonal peacemaking helps iron out personality conflicts, particularly between top managers, before they begin group planning efforts. Techniques from process consultation are useful during strategic planning meetings. Team building interventions are appropriate before, during, and after strategy formulation sessions. Survey-guided development can surface important ideas from lower-level employees as a starting point for planning (Rothwell & Kazanas, 1986–1988). An organizational mirror can contribute to improved relations between groups and may be used before, during, and after strategy formulation.

There are other interventions that we shall not discuss in this chapter. For more information on them, see Francis (1982), French and Bell (1984), Harvey and Brown (1982), and Huse and Cummings (1985). More expansive treatments of organizational change can be found in Alderfer (1977), Friedlander and Brown (1974), Goodman and Kurke (1982), and Levy and Merry (1986).

PROBLEMS ASSOCIATED WITH TRADITIONAL ORGANIZATION DEVELOPMENT INTERVENTIONS

There are problems with traditional OD efforts. To mention a few, managers:

- are sometimes unaware of OD's purpose,
- do not always realize how much organizational culture and/or group norms can affect productivity,
- have trouble seeing the contribution of OD to bottom-line considerations like profitability, return on investment, or market share,
- feel the need for OD most in crisis, so that OD interventions are often undertaken as a reaction to problems rather than in anticipation of them,
- expect immediate, and sometimes dramatic, results from OD,
- refuse to participate in OD efforts (they may see an intervention as a "quick fix strategy" geared to their subordinates only),
- associate OD with a few controversial intervention methods, like sensitivity training, and
- view OD efforts as ends-in-themselves rather than as part of a more comprehensive, unified Organizational Strategy for HRD.

For these reasons it may be necessary for HRD practitioners to demonstrate the value of OD by training others in their organizations about it.

Some HRD practitioners have found it best to start on a modest scale with a simple, relatively short-term OD intervention in response to some pressing operational problem at a relatively low level. From this modest beginning, practitioners can demonstrate the value of OD. After its value has been demonstrated, more elaborate interventions can be gradually undertaken.

STRATEGIC ORGANIZATION DEVELOPMENT

Unlike traditional OD, strategic OD is: (1) comprehensive, (2) future-oriented, and (3) integrated with other components of Organizational Strategy for HRD.

Conceptualizing strategic OD. Think of strategic OD as consisting of a series of steps in which managers and employees

1. identify what group norms and organizational culture *should* exist to facilitate implementation of Strategic Business Plans,
2. assess future pressures favoring change,
3. assess existing pressure impeding change,
4. compare present and future pressures, and
5. carry out OD interventions to deal with future pressures favoring change and existing pressures impeding it.

Identifying norms that should exist. The study of norms is really the study of culture. As Berger (1986) points out, this study is difficult because "culture" is hard to define. Units of analysis are not always easy to pinpoint. Work groups within firms differ in norms, creating subcultures. An appropriate methodology for researching corporate culture is difficult to find, because meanings are implicit and are not easily revealed through such common data collection methods as surveys, interviews, observations, and document reviews. The problem is further complicated, in that group or organizational members may be unaware of prevailing norms, having taken them for granted.

If it is hard to identify *present* norms and culture, it is even harder to envision what they *should be in the future* (Albert, 1985). Think of this issue from another standpoint. When confronted with a problem, managers can pursue at least two possible courses of action: (1) they can examine it from the perspective of past beliefs, ideas, and theories or through interpretations of prior observations, or (2) they can question their basic assumptions, based on past beliefs or past observations, and thereby create a new understanding of the problem itself. The first course of action is related to what Argyris and Schön (1978) call *single-loop learning,* in which "members of the organization respond to changes in the internal and external environments . . . by detecting errors which they then correct so as to maintain the central features of organizational theory-in-use" (p. 18). (In this context *theory-in-use* refers to interpretations of observations, what observers see when they watch managers. It is distinct from *espoused theory,* what managers talk about.) The second course of action is akin to what Argyris and Schön call *double loop learning,* "those sorts of organizational inquiry which resolve incompatible organizational norms by setting new priorities and weighings of norms, or by restructuring the norms themselves together with associated strategies and assumptions" (p. 24).

It is difficult to stimulate double-loop learning and thus identify new norms which should exist in the future (Argyris, 1982). Several specific methods can be used. One method is *visioning.* Members of a work group are asked to imagine what the future will be like and then step back into the present. Transition teams are developed to help bring into reality the future that is envisioned. A shared image of the future leads group members to their own normative change (Boulding, 1976; Markley & Harman, 1982; Polack, 1973). A second method is *changing the purpose of the organization or group.* This change is followed by others in such areas as work methods, politics, and culture (Tichy, 1983). A third method is *creating new, alternative organizations or work groups* rather than trying to change the existing system (Levy & Merry, 1986). The development of new norms is a long-term, torturous, and expensive process. Hence, the greater the difference between present and desired future norms, the greater the length of time needed for change and the greater the potential for failure.

Assessing future pressures favoring change. Pressures favoring change stem from many sources (Levy & Merry, 1986): (1) *external crisis,* such as recessions, technological innovations, changes in laws or regulations, or competitive maneuvers by other firms; (2) *internal crisis,* such as reorganization, management reshuffling, or the departure of a key member of top management; (3) *external opportunities,* such as new markets or new and unexpected financial resources; and (4) *internal opportunities,* such as task forces, problem-solving groups, and freestanding committees. In most cases, the impetus for organizational change comes from a single visionary manager (Levy & Merry, 1986), what some call an "idea champion," because he or she takes up a cause and fights for it (McCall & Kaplan, 1985). This manager is brought into the organization from outside and is thus relatively immune from the dampening effects of socialization and existing culture (Levy & Merry, 1986). However, it is also possible to tap progressive groups in an organization and use their energy to create the impetus for change (Mason & Mitroff, 1981).

To assess future pressures favoring change, HRD practitioners and line managers should examine factors influencing (1) the organization as a whole, and (2) each department or work group. Strategic Business Planning methods are adequate for the first of these.

To examine each work group or department, however, HRD practitioners and managers need some means of classifying them. There are, of course, several ways to classify work groups: (1) by reporting relationships; (2) by location; (3) by tasks or types of activities; and (4) by the length of time the group members must stay together in working on a common goal. An organization chart is one place to start. It should depict employees reporting to each supervisor. In small, centralized firms, all work groups may be classified solely by the reporting relationship. But if the firm is large and decentralized, it may also be necessary to identify groups by location. Employees may share the same supervisor but are scattered geographically. If the work group is heterogeneous—comprised of employees involved in different lines of work—an alternative classification scheme may be developed using activity as the focus. Finally, some groups are relatively permanent, like those on assembly lines; other groups, like start-up teams and project groups, are not. As a result, it is necessary to consider the duration of the work group's existence as a basis for developing a classification scheme.

A classification scheme is important because it provides a more specific framework for analysis than the entire organization, and it draws attention to unique norms and conditions affecting individual performance. To assess future pressures favoring change, members of each work group can be surveyed regarding their relative level of satisfaction with present conditions (Rothwell & Kazanas, 1986–1988). When dissatisfied groups and individuals are identified and their ideas are fed to higher-level management, the potential for widespread change is increased. Use Activity 7-1 at the end of this chapter to assess pressures favoring change in an organization.

Assessing existing pressures impeding change. Any organization is essentially a dynamic field in which some forces favor change and others impede it (Lewin, 1951). There are many reasons why members of an organization might resist group change consistent with Strategic Business Plans. Failures in OD stem from these and other sources—including low commitment of top managers to change and poor rapport between the change agent and members of the organization (Mirvis & Berg, 1977). Use Activity 7-2 at the end of this chapter to brainstorm about factors impeding progressive change in each work group of an organization.

Comparing pressures favoring and impeding change. The basic assumption underlying Lewin's force field analysis is that a comparison of forces favoring change and forces impeding change can pinpoint areas in which to take action. Organizational change occurs when forces favoring change are strengthened or those impeding change are weakened. Generally, Lewin favored weakening forces impeding change because the alternative tends to increase resistance (Burke, 1982). Use Activity 7-3 at the end of this chapter to compare forces favoring and forces impeding change.

Carrying out OD interventions. The final step in Strategic OD is to carry out OD interventions so as to narrow the gaps between what exists at present and what should exist in the future. In short, OD facilitates the implementation of strategic change through efforts designed to (1) strengthen forces favoring progressive, long-term change, (2) weaken forces impeding such change, or (3) both strengthen forces favoring change and weaken those impeding it.

OD thus becomes a tool for changing cultural norms in line with future needs. When HRD activities geared to changing individuals are paired with OD activities geared to cultural change, the combined effects can produce individuals possessing the knowledge, skills, and creative ability to perform in ways that help realize Strategic Business Plans, and (2) work groups characterized by greater openness so that what individuals learn may be more readily accepted by the groups in which they work. The result should thus be greater progress toward implementing Strategic Business Plans and gradual, evolutionary change in corporate or work group culture.

ACTIVITY 7-1 A Worksheet for Identifying Forces Favoring Change in an Organization

Directions: Use this activity to brainstorm about forces favoring changes in line with strategic needs in an organization. Answer the questions in the sections which follow. There are no right or wrong answers. Use additional paper if necessary.

External Forces

1. What forces outside the organization are driving it toward change? Describe them. (Some examples: increased competition, technological advancement.)

2. Are any work groups, departments, or divisions of the firm facing more external pressures favoring change than others? If so, describe which groups are so affected and why.

Internal Forces

3. What forces within the organization, if any, are creating pressure for change? (Some examples: new top managers; strong groups within the firm.)

ACTIVITY 7-1 Continued

4. Are any work groups, departments, or divisions within the firm facing more internal pressures favoring change than others? If so, describe the groups affected and why they are under pressure.

Assessment of Strength

5. What forces inside and outside the firm are exerting the most pressure favoring change? List them. Start with the strongest forces first.

External	Internal

Strategic Organization Development

ACTIVITY 7-2   A Worksheet for Identifying Forces Impeding Change in an Organization

Directions: Use this activity to brainstorm about forces impeding or restraining change in an organization. Answer the following questions. There are no right or wrong responses. Use additional paper if necessary.

External Forces

1. What forces outside the organization (if any) are keeping it from changing? Describe them. (Some examples: substantial market share, commanding leadership in the industry.)

2. Are any work groups, departments, or divisions of the firm facing more pressures impeding change than others? If so, describe which groups are so affected and why.

Internal Forces

3. What forces inside the organization, if any, are keeping change from occurring? (An example: top management philosophy/attitudes.)

ACTIVITY 7-2 Continued

4. Are any work groups, departments, or divisions inside the firm facing more internal pressures impeding change than others? If so, describe the groups affected and why they are affected.

Assessment of Strength

5. What forces inside and outside the firm are exerting the most pressure *against* change? List them. Start with the strongest forces first.

External	Internal

ACTIVITY 7-3 A Worksheet for Comparing Forces Impeding and Favoring Change

Directions: Use this activity to compare forces impeding and favoring long-term change in line with Strategic Business plans. Answer the following questions. There are no right or wrong answers. Use additional paper if necessary.

Strategic Plans

1. Describe the long-term direction of the firm. What specific changes are sought?

Forces Favoring and Impeding Change

2. What forces are favoring and impeding changes in line with Strategic Business plans? List them. Start with the strongest forces first.

Forces Favoring Change	Forces Impeding Change

Role of OD

3. How can a long-term OD intervention be planned to weaken forces impeding change? (What other actions may also be taken, and how can OD help in taking those actions? Consider: structural reorganization; changes in leadership; changes in rewards; and changes in policies.)

8

NONEMPLOYEE DEVELOPMENT

HRD has traditionally focused on meeting learning needs inside an organization. It is easy to see, then, why HRD has often been confused with employee training. However, it is not necessary to limit HRD to employees alone. As a matter of fact, there are good reasons for designing and delivering instruction to those *outside* the organization. Yet the literature of the HRD field offers surprisingly little advice about preparing instruction to meet existing—let alone anticipated—learning needs of external groups. No doubt one reason is that "organizations do not naturally adopt an external . . . orientation. The persistent tendency is to be inner directed and to give unbalanced emphasis to internal aspirations and short-run efficiency considerations" (Day, 1984, p. 3). Another reason is that many HRD practitioners are often placed in Personnel departments, where the natural emphasis is on employees rather than external groups.

However, a strategic orientation to HRD implies that HRD practitioners—as well as managers and employees—bear a responsibility to look outside their firms, not just inside, for learning needs. A strategic orientation emphasizes the external environment (Day, 1984). Present performance weaknesses and future opportunities for performance improvement are not found solely inside a firm. They exist outside, too. Consumers who do not know how to use a product will not buy it. Stockholders who do not know about the firm in which they have invested will not be inclined to invest more. Suppliers who remain unaware of a firm's unique production or service delivery needs will have a tough time meeting them. Retailers unfamiliar with products will not be inclined to stock them for long—and will not be knowledgeable enough to do a credible job of selling them to consumers if they do. Legislators who pass laws or government officials who create regulations will not be able to make informed decisions if they are unaware of conditions faced by business.

In all these cases, people outside a firm experience learning needs. The HRD Effort can be used to meet these needs at present and anticipate those arising in the future. Managers and strategists can thus step beyond efforts to adapt the firm to changes taking place externally. Indeed, they can change the environment itself through organized, externally-directed HRD activities. We call activities of this kind *nonemployee development* to emphasize that the orientation is different from employee-oriented learning activities. This chapter focuses on nonemployee development, describing each step in a model of it.

STEPS IN NONEMPLOYEE DEVELOPMENT

Think of nonemployee development as consisting of a series of steps in which HRD practitioners and operating managers:

1. classify members of the public and external stakeholders by their general interests or concerns,
2. analyze existing relationships between the business and each group identified in the external environment whose learning needs managers wish to address,
3. determine what these relationships are at present and should be in the future,
4. pinpoint
    a. discrepancies between what is and what should be with each group at present,
    b. opportunities for narrowing anticipated gaps between what is and what should be in the future,
5. separate HRD from non-HRD needs,
6. decide what changes should occur in relationships between the corporation and external groups,
7. design HRD activities consistent with desired changes,
8. select instructional content and delivery methods, and
9. follow up, over time, to meet new instructional needs or maintain efforts intended to meet the continuing needs of external groups.

CREATING CLASSIFICATION SCHEMES

People outside a firm vary in what they need to know and what they are interested in knowing about. In analyzing learning needs, managers and HRD practitioners thus find it helpful to classify external groups by needs or interests. This process is akin to what market specialists call *segmentation*. It "is the division of a market into those subgroups which have special needs and preferences and which represent sufficient pockets of demand to justify separate marketing strategies" (Buell, 1984, p. 66).

The general public. Any individual, group, organization, or community which "affects or is affected by the corporation and over which it has no control and, at best, little influence" is part of its general public (Ackoff, 1981, p. 90). The nature of a corporation's general public depends on its *scope of operations* and *its purpose.* The scope of a small business is limited. Its public and consumers may be restricted to one town or city. The scope of a large corporation is not limited and may be affected by different national cultures and correspondingly different consumer preferences. The purpose of the firm, as defined by top managers, implies the consumers, suppliers, distributors, and government agencies with which the firm is or will be dealing.

Two key points are worth remembering, however. First, every business is dependent on its external environment—even when no business is transacted with particular individuals, groups, or organizations. Second, every business is increasingly viewed by American society not just as a profit-making enterprise but also as a tool for implementing public policy and effecting social change (Toffler, 1980). The manager who ignores public concerns will tread perilously and will be unable "to avoid those missteps that, while seeming to be minor, in effect generate an inordinate amount of bad publicity and do considerable damage to the firm's efforts to build credibility" (Diebold, 1982, p. 15). Past business abuses—whether real or imaginary—lead to the enactment of laws and regulations which impose burdensome requirements on business.

To analyze dealings with the general public, managers need some framework suitable for that purpose. Most writings about interactions between the organization and the environment adopt a sociological perspective. The organization is viewed in relation to institutions and, to a lesser extent, special interest groups. Depending on the geographical scope of business operations, different levels of institutional-environmental interaction may exist (see Figure 8-1).

As Figure 8-1 illustrates, top managers tend to deal with broad, large groups of the general public; lower-level managers deal more often with narrower groups, like one community. There may be exceptions. The opening of a large, new plant in a community may stimulate interactions between the corporate level and local governments. Most interactions between business and the public take place at the local level. Yet a major occurrence at a local facility—a disaster, for instance—may prompt national and even international attention. For the most part, however, the highest corporate levels tend to deal with the federal government, special interest groups, and large numbers of people through the mass media. Managers of local company facilities more often interact with (1) city, township, and county governments, (2) local pressure groups, and (3) local groups of people, often through methods other than mass media.

While corporate and national issues are important, there can be little doubt that the public image of business is more often apparent—and crucial—at the community than at the national level. As explained by one influential source, "*A community is a miniature of the national public. This is where national opinions are born*" (Cutlip & Center, 1982, p. 312). It is in the community where the otherwise faceless monolithic bureaucracy of a large corporation takes on the face of a neighbor, friend, or fellow citizen employed by the company.

Needs of communities differ substantially by type and degree. Communities range from large metropolitan cities, to suburbs, to medium-sized cities, to small

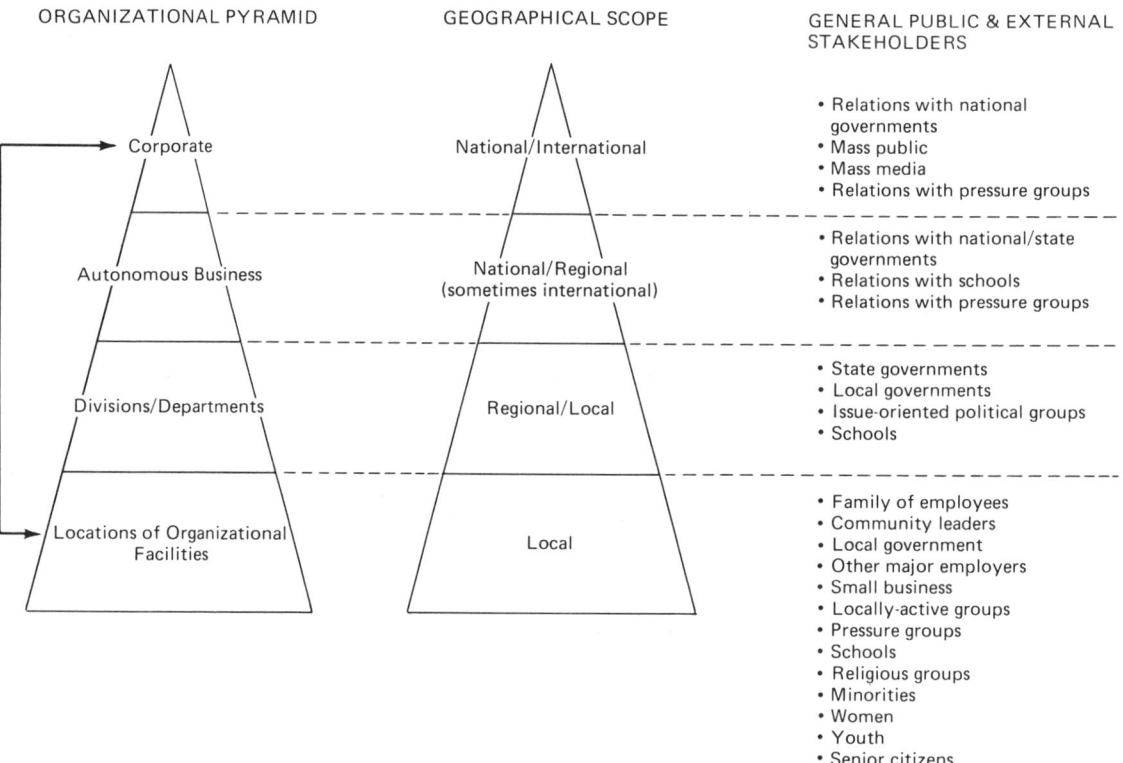

Figure 8-1: Relationships Between the Organization's Hierarchy of Authority, Geographical Scope, and the Primary Groups with which Managers come in Contact

towns. In each setting, people interact in different ways. That is the key to community relations and development: determining "how people live together and meet their functional needs through community social institutions" (Gilbert, 1975, p. 103).

Regardless of the community, some issues are of common interest at the local level. Will an employer expand and hire more people or close down and throw people out of work? Is the employer acting in a socially responsible manner, taking care to avoid unnecessary environmental pollution and discrimination in employment?

Use Activity 8-1 at the end of this chapter to brainstorm about key institutions and concerns at the community level. This activity can serve as a starting point in classifying the general public into groups at the community level. For more information on community development, see Archer, Kelly, and Bisch (1984), Biklen (1983), Blakely and Schutz (1979), Levy and Merry (1986), Moles (1979), Rothman (1974), Rothman, Erlich, and Teresa (1976), Spiegel (1979), and Voth (1979).

External stakeholders. External stakeholders are "individuals, organizations, and institutions with which the corporation interacts directly" (Ackoff, 1981, p. 90). They include suppliers, distributors, competitors, investors, consumers, and employees' families. (We exclude employees from this discussion, since they are internal stakeholders and later chapters focus on them.)

Special relationships between an organization and its stakeholders call for special communication between them. Each stakeholder group has unique needs and interests. For instance, *investors* want to know about company financial performance. Are investments safe? Is the company making or losing money? What accounts for profits or losses? *Suppliers* want to know what can be done to get more business. How well-satisfied is a corporate customer with the supplier's products or services? How well are the supplies furnished by one vendor meeting customer needs? Is there a chance of securing more business? What problems, if any, exist between the supplier and customer? *Distributors (retailers) or sales agents* want to know about products they sell so they can answer questions posed by consumers. At the same time, distributors may wonder: How well-satisfied is the corporate supplier with product display and with promotion? What corporate changes are likely in product design, warranties, and advertisement? *Consumers* have special needs in using the firm's products or services, maintaining those products, or even deciding prior to purchase whose products or services will best meet their needs. They may also want to know about new products to be marketed by the firm in the future, improvements in existing products, and any other information of potential value. *Employees' families* are silent partners in the business. What happens in the business affects their well-being and that of the family member employed by the firm. They are rightfully curious about the firm.

Much has been written about identifying different consumer categories with which a firm does business. (A few categories are shown in Table 8-1.) Less has been written about examining suppliers, distributors, investors, or employees' family members.

There are several ways to structure examinations of stakeholders: (1) by product or service type and those interested in them; (2) by geographical areas and consumers located within these areas; and (3) by types of stakeholders—for example, institutional versus individual. Use Activity 8-2 at the end of this chapter to identify key external stakeholders of a firm and their probable interests or concerns. This activity can help classify external stakeholders.

ANALYZING RELATIONSHIPS BETWEEN THE CORPORATION, ITS PUBLIC, AND ITS STAKEHOLDERS

What is the current relationship between a corporation and members of the general public, and between a corporation and external stakeholders? In other words, how well is the corporation presently meeting the needs of the individuals, groups, and organizations with which it transacts business, and with which it does not transact business but which may influence business operations in some way? Answering these questions involves analyzing existing relationships between the corporation and its general public and/or external stakeholders.

HRD practitioners may think of this step as part of learning needs assessment and may use any data collection method commonly applied to needs assessment to find out about the learning needs of external groups. Professionals in fields outside HRD advocate similar starting points for their efforts. *In public relations* it is important to begin with fact-finding (Aronoff & Baskin, 1983). What problems exist in rela-

TABLE 8-1 EXAMPLES OF CONSUMER MARKET SEGMENTS

Geographic	
• location of population (i.e., by country, region, urban, suburban, rural) • climate	• topography • water • soil characteristics • political

Demographic	
• sex • age • race • ethnic origin • religion • education	• personal status (i.e., single, married, unmarried but living together) • health • physical characteristics (i.e., height, weight, complexion)

Economic	
• personal income • family, household income • occupation • income source	• savings • assets • price

Social and psychological	
• social class • reference group • lifestyle	• stage of family life cycle • personality

Reference and use	
• usage rate (light user, heavy user) • use application • quality (performance)	• benefits sought • aesthetic • brand loyalty

Source: Buell, 1984, p. 71. Reprinted with permission from McGraw-Hill Book Company.

tions between the public and an organization? Using systematic research rather than intuition to answer this question distinguishes public relations from publicity. *In marketing,* professionals research types of buyers, buying decisions made by consumers, and factors influencing consumer buying behavior (Buell, 1984). This information is a starting point for decisions about future marketing strategies. *In organizational communications,* broad analysis of current status precedes efforts to pinpoint specific problems, solutions, and actions worth taking in the future (Pace, 1983). *In community development,* diagnosis is an early step in which practitioners "obtain data on the beliefs, goals, roles, norms, and sanctions in the community and relevant information on the power structure, influence system and shared community goals" (Blakely, 1979, p. 141).

These similarities of approach are really not all that surprising: data gathering and analysis are fundamental to rational problem-solving. Managers begin problem-solving by (1) identifying or clarifying a problem, and (2) collecting information about it. Before problem identification, managers experience a felt need, a desire to find out why something is going wrong—or is not going as expected or desired. *Felt need* is a vague irritation with the present status of things (Mason & Mitroff, 1981).

However, HRD should not be confused with public relations, marketing, organizational communications, or community development. HRD activities are geared to identifying and solving problems that stem from lack of knowledge or skill. They help groups external to a firm learn how to interact better with the firm, and they sensitize employees to the needs and issues affecting external groups.

Use Activity 8-3 at the end of this chapter to brainstorm about existing relationships between a corporation, its public, and its external stakeholders.

It is unwise to rely solely on perceptions of business executives about corporate relationships with the public and external stakeholders. Likewise, it is unwise to rely solely on a plant manager's perceptions about the relationship between a local facility and the surrounding community. In both cases, information collected from inside a firm is suspect. High-level executives are socially insulated. They are difficult to reach by members of the public or even by key suppliers or distributors. As a consequence, they remain unaware of prevailing consumer or public beliefs until too late—often until a major crisis occurs. To rely on their perceptions of public opinion will be like staring at a brushed photograph: all blemishes are removed.

How, then, can accurate information be collected? There are several ways. The firm's managers should

1. establish a formal method to monitor the public and stakeholders at every level. That may include
   a. monitoring international, national, and local mass media—television, radio, and newspapers—for stories about the company, industry, or issues associated with them or which will affect them, and
   b. monitoring issues and concerns at the community level—that is, at every major business site. Establish community "focus groups" or advisory councils composed of representatives from different socioeconomic classes to deal with relations between the business and community.
2. Commission consultants to conduct in-depth studies of external groups periodically. While expensive, these studies furnish useful information for subsequent business, marketing, and HRD-related planning.
3. Establish *formal* methods of obtaining feedback from consumers, suppliers, distributors, and investors about what they think of the company, its products/services, and its methods of doing business. What improvements do they suggest—and why?

Methods of collecting data include:

- national opinion polls for corporate use
- community polls for use by managers at major company facilities
- surveys included with company products, annual reports, bills sent to consumers/distributors, and payments sent to suppliers

- follow-up phone calls to suppliers or distributors to find out how interactions between the two companies can be made more efficient or effective
- follow-up calls to randomly-selected consumers to find out how well they are satisfied with new products or with the services they receive
- open meetings, seminars, and conferences for consumers, suppliers, distributors, investors, and/or members of the community
- corporate "open house" for the public: citizens—and family members of employees—are invited in to see how products are made.
- tours of company facilities with follow-up discussions.

As an alternative to these methods of data collection, managers—or third-party consultants—can undertake a comprehensive *social audit,* which reviews an organization's general contributions to society and/or communities in which company facilities are located. There is no standardized approach: some audits are mere catalogs of company social programs (Aronoff & Baskin, 1983); some are detailed examinations, conducted by external consultants or special in-house management committees, of corporate social responsibility and actions stemming from it. For more on this subject, see Anshen (1980), Bauer and Fenn (1973), Corson and Steiner (1974), and Hay (1975). Information collected from these and similar efforts can help identify a company's *present* strengths and weaknesses in dealings with the public and external stakeholders.

Use Activity 8-4 at the end of this chapter to brainstorm about ways to collect information from members of the general public and key external stakeholders for use in subsequent decision-making.

ANALYZING PRESENT AND FUTURE CRITERIA

What are strategists' current objectives regarding desired relationships with the public and external stakeholders? How should those objectives be changed in the future in light of changing external trends? The first question focuses on present criteria; the second, on future criteria. These issues have to do with what company executives or HRD practitioners would like to see at a future time, not necessarily with what actually exists at present.

In many treatments of problem-solving, criteria are assumed. Yet just about everyone acknowledges that problems—and opportunities—do not exist in isolation; rather, managers must recognize a difference of some kind between what is (condition) and what should be (criteria). When actual conditions are not as good as desired ones, a discrepancy exists which prompts corrective action.

It is worthwhile in its own right for managers to think about such issues as these:

- What are corporate social responsibilities?
- What is the role of business in society?
- What may account for public dissatisfaction with business and with an industry of which an organization is part?

- What should be the "public image" of a corporation at the national/international level, regional and state level, and community level?
- What objectives are worth establishing in corporate relationships with the public and with stakeholders?
- How can achievement toward these objectives be measured?

(Use Activity 8-5 at the end of this chapter to consider these issues.)

By thinking about these questions, managers clarify how they want their firm to interact with external groups, individuals, and organizations. Answers to these questions are particularly important for such externally-oriented functions as marketing and public relations. They are also important for the organization's HRD Effort, which is one tool for correcting present problems or heading off future problems attributable to the public or stakeholder knowledge about a business, its operations, or its products or services.

However, conditions in the world do not remain static. Americans have learned how to mobilize organized opposition to government and business actions which they oppose. Vietnam protestors were able to amass a million angry people in Washington in the early 1970s. Examples of organized opposition are easy to find among consumer advocates, environmentalists, civil rights activists, opponents of abortion, and proponents of "free choice." Whole industries face such opposition—as managers at nuclear reactor sites and in petroleum firms know too well. Pressure groups have learned how to capture and even manipulate mass media attention, use courts and other government agencies to block business activities, and influence law-making through funding and campaign support during elections.

The question is: What social concerns will dominate in the future? Clearly, the corporation which anticipates and acts on these concerns ahead of time will enjoy a substantial advantage over competitors and may benefit through increased public credibility. Answers to this question may furnish valuable new ideas about future business objectives. In this sense, objectives are geared to closing a gap between what is (present condition) and what should be at a future time (future criteria). These objectives may reveal initiatives for corporate programs—among which HRD activities should rightfully play a key part in dealings with people outside the corporation.

How are such social concerns or trends detected? Sociopolitical forecasting is one approach (Wilson, 1974). There are several ways to devise such forecasts, including some previously discussed in Chapter 4. *Social monitoring* is one way not previously treated. It involves examination of what is happening in such bellwether states as New York, Massachusetts, and California. Trends apparent in these locales usually appear later in other parts of the U.S. (Starling, 1984). Issues arise after business abuses that are widely publicized. They elicit public outrage and calls for reform, subsequently making their way into public policy through laws, court rulings, and regulations.

Do some research. Identify pressing issues in New York, Massachusetts, and California. Analyze the content of leading newspapers and pending legislation in those states. Record your observations on the worksheet provided in Activity 8-6 at the end of this chapter. Then summarize these trends and establish corporate-level and community-level objectives on these issues.

PINPOINTING DISCREPANCIES

What differences exist between the actual and the desirable relationship of the corporation, the general public, and external stakeholders? Answers to this question help pinpoint present discrepancies that may require immediate, short-term action. What differences, on the other hand, exist between the actual and the desired future relationship of the corporation, the general public, and external stakeholders? Answers to these questions help pinpoint issues requiring long-term action. Use Activities 8-7 and 8-8 at the end of this chapter to structure your thinking on present strengths and weaknesses and future threats and opportunities.

SEPARATING INSTRUCTIONAL FROM NONINSTRUCTIONAL NEEDS

Why are there discrepancies in relationships between the corporation and its general public and between the corporation and its key external stakeholders? In other words, from what causes do differences between *what is* and *what should be* stem? (A discrepancy is, of course, any difference between *what is* and *what should be*.).

Discrepancies stem from many causes. Only some lend themselves to correction through organized learning geared to managers/employees inside the corporation or people outside it. Instruction is not appropriate for dealing with problems stemming from lack of:

1. *motivation*—Managers/employees feel no need to improve external relations with the public or with stakeholders such as customers, suppliers, distributors, or owners/stockholders; those outside the firm feel no need to find out more about the firm or its products and services.
2. *feedback*—Managers/employees hear little from members of the public or from stakeholders.
3. *structure for organizing feedback*—Front-line employees receive consistent or pervasive feedback from consumers, suppliers, distributors, and/or people in the community, but have no way to channel this information up the chain of command to be used in subsequent top-level decisions.
4. *consequences*—Managers/employees do not see the effects of their actions. This problem is particularly acute at the highest corporate levels. For example, the decision to close a plant in a small community may make good business sense—but can also have a devastating effect on a small, local economy and produce a public embittered with one firm for a long time.

If managers—particularly top managers—see no need to improve relations with the public, then it is not very likely that one-shot instructional efforts will contribute much to effective external relations. Likewise, if members of the public and stakeholder groups see little need for improving relations with the corporation, then it is not too likely that one-minute television commercials or full-page newspaper ads will keep the public informed, because citizens feel no need to listen.

For corporate managers and HRD practitioners interested in improving external relations, there are several places to begin analyzing deficiencies:

- *by community:* What concerns dominate in each community in which the firm has major production or service facilities? How well is the firm perceived to be meeting its responsibility as a good corporate citizen in dealing with those community concerns?
- *by product or service line:* What are the chief concerns of product users and service recipients? How well is the firm dealing with these concerns?
- *by market segment:* Different types of consumers have different needs which are met by a product or service. How well is the firm meeting each different need?
- *by type of interaction with the corporation:* Political activists and concerned citizens who do no business with the firm have very different needs from consumers, suppliers, distributors, or shareholders. What are the needs of each group? How well is the organization meeting them?

In each case it is important to consider what people in each group *need to know*. What *are* their interests? How has the firm been responding to them in the past? What changes is the firm contemplating in the future? By focusing on these questions, managers can pinpoint areas in which HRD can help meet the learning needs of nonemployee groups.

Of course, it is difficult to answer these questions if managers have no information available. For this reason, they should select some means to systematically assess the instructional needs of various external groups. A few methods for doing so are briefly summarized in Table 8-2.

The act of assessing needs may raise the consciousness of each external group about the corporation and its products or services. It can also demonstrate how much the corporation's managers and employees care about the needs of those with whom they transact business at present and, potentially, in the future. In short, the process of needs assessment can itself serve as a useful tool in building good external relations and meeting some informational needs about the firm.

DECIDING WHAT CHANGES SHOULD OCCUR

What is to be changed? By how much? These questions are the focus of the sixth step in nonemployee development.

Change efforts can be directed:

- *outside the corporation:* The aim is to improve what those external to the corporation know about it and its products or services.
- *inside the corporation:* The aim is to improve what managers or employees know about the needs of the community, product or service users, market segments, or specialized groups so that these needs can be better served in the future.

TABLE 8-2 SYSTEMATIC METHODS FOR ASSESSING INSTRUCTIONAL NEEDS OF VARIOUS GROUPS

To assess instructional needs of	Use such methods as:
A Community	• written/phone surveys • call-in shows on local TV/radio stations • surveys published in newspapers • "focus groups" composed of community leaders/representatives • door-to-door interviews
Product/Service Users	• surveys enclosed with products/advertisements • direct-mail appeals • phone follow-ups on filed warranties • names collected during promotion campaigns • random interviews • random phone surveys
A Market Segment	• Same methods as used with product/service users but restricted to special market segments
Special Groups • Public • Suppliers • Distributors	• same as for community (above) • same as for product/service users (above) • surveys/interviews/logs of problems in dealing with each major supplier kept by purchasing staff • surveys/interviews/logs of problems in dealing with major distributors kept by marketing staff
Pressure Groups	• monitoring local news • monitoring national news • management task forces

Instruction directed outside the corporation can range from long-term to short-term change efforts. It is possible to view the influence of the HRD Effort on a grid in which one axis represents the time horizon and another axis represents the type of change desired (see Figure 8-2). HRD activities directed inside the organization can be viewed in much the same way (see Figure 8-3).

There is no right or wrong direction; rather, the questions are: (1) What changes are desirable? and (2) Why are they desirable? By addressing these questions, corporate decision-makers can set priorities and appropriate time horizons. Use Activity 8-9 at the end of this chapter to think about these issues.

It may be difficult for managers and employees to envision alternatives to existing relationships between the corporation and external groups. In these instances management meetings, training seminars, and brainstorming sessions can help formulate innovative approaches to promoting better external relations and meeting the present or possible future learning needs of the public and external stakeholders. Use Activity 8-10 at the end of this chapter to consider this issue.

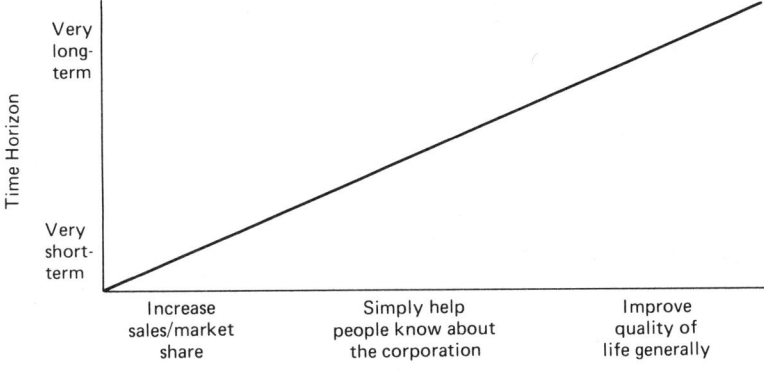

Figure 8-2: A Grid Representing the Type of Change and Expected Time Horizon for Changing Relationships with the General Public and Key External Stakeholders

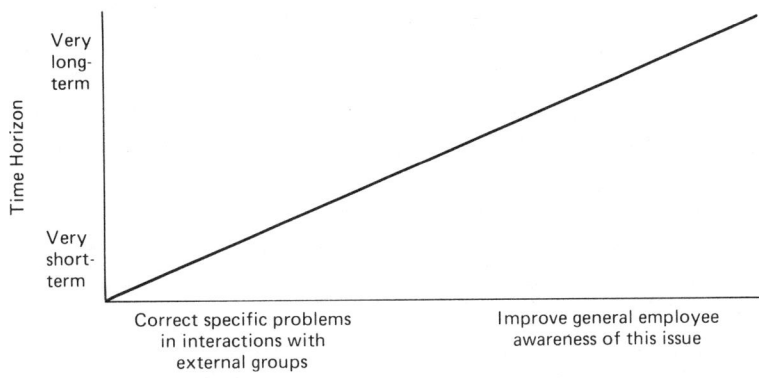

Figure 8-3: A Grid Representing the Type of Change and Time Horizon for Changing Employee Perceptions of the Needs of Outside Groups

DESIGNING INSTRUCTION CONSISTENT WITH DESIRED CHANGES

While approaches to designing instruction may differ, instructional design typically involves:

1. identifying a past performance problem—or an opportunity for averting possible future performance problems before they arise,
2. clarifying actual conditions (what is?),
3. clarifying desired conditions (what should be?),
4. comparing actual to desired conditions so as to pinpoint instructional needs (discrepancies between what is and what should be that stem from lack of knowledge or skill),

5. establishing learning objectives that, when met, will close the gap between actual and desired conditions,
6. creating tests, linked to instructional objectives, to measure achievement of objectives,
7. designing tailor-made instructional materials or selecting content from existing sources (in compliance with copyright laws) that will help learners meet objectives,
8. selecting delivery methods appropriate for the content and learners,
9. preparing and delivering instruction, and
10. evaluating results.

We have already discussed the first four steps of instructional design as they may be applied to individuals, groups, or even entire organizations outside the corporation. To some extent, we have also discussed change objectives, though Activity 8-11 at the end of this chapter provides an opportunity to consider instructional objectives in more detail.

Formal testing has limited applicability to most instruction designed for individuals, groups, and organizations outside a firm. It can be used, of course, when

- consumers participate in organized training, seminars, and workshops in product use (tests can be administered, for example, to newly-trained computer operators or to secretaries trained on a word processing package);
- distributors participate in organized training on a product they will sell or service (indeed, service personnel, for example, can be given paper-and-pencil tests or can be asked to diagnose the cause of a machine breakdown and then repair the machine); and
- disadvantaged workers, sponsored by various governmental training programs, can be tested for their abilities at the end of an apprenticeship effort.

In most cases, however, externally-directed instruction will not lend itself to formal testing. In community development and other long-term change efforts, the only way to "test" may be to conduct a full-scale social audit before, during, and after a change effort to assess the value added to the community or to society by planned learning activities sponsored by a firm.

SELECTING CONTENT AND DELIVERY METHODS

What information will help targeted learners meet instructional objectives? What methods of delivering that information will be most efficient and effective? These questions focus on the eighth step of instructing the public and/or key external stakeholders.

It is difficult to deal in the abstract with issues of instructional content and delivery for different groups of learners and different instructional objectives. For example, members of the community may have needs quite different from those of consumers, suppliers, or distributors. The nature of a corporation's business and the intentions of its managers may also have much to do with what instruction should be offered, what content should be chosen, and what methods should be used to deliver it.

A simple illustration may help clarify what we mean here. When you have a chance, investigate the community service offerings of a local hospital (the bigger the hospital, the more likely it is to have such courses). These can be very instructive for HRD practitioners in business, industry, or government. Hospitals typically go beyond employee training/education and even patient (consumer) training, adopting a holistic view of their community presence. They are quite likely to offer a range of workshops, some oriented to preventive health care (for example, "Keeping Fit," "Eating Right," and "How to Stop Smoking"), and some oriented to the specialized needs of the community (for example, "Parent Training," "Becoming a New Father," "Becoming a Big Sister," "Dealing with a Family Member Who is an Alcoholic").

Community colleges also run such workshops, typically for no credit, minimal fees, and with instructors drawn from the community rather than the college. These courses are offered for fun, not for a degree, and range from the serious (for example, "Fixing Your Car," "Building Your Own House," and "Finding a Job: A Course for Displaced Homemakers"), to the lighthearted (for example, "Aerobics," "Growing Plants," and "Making Home Movies").

While some managers may point out that few hospitals or community colleges run for profit and thus enjoy considerable flexibility in what they can do, the point is that there is no reason—apart from management values to the contrary—which prevents businesses from offering similar community service seminars.

As a matter of fact, there might be sound business reasons for doing so. Consider the advantages of public seminars. They:

1. increase the visibility and credibility of a firm in the community, perhaps spurring interest in—and purchases of—its products,
2. may easily become money-making ventures in their own right, perhaps subsidizing employee training and education (Feuer, 1984), and
3. may serve as a means to teach consumers about company products or services before they need to buy them.

In many cases, the "best minds" are not found in colleges but rather in businesses. Who is better than a successful bank president to teach people about investments? Who is better than a successful contractor to discuss home remodeling? Who is better than an owner of a computer store to teach people about computers? In short, HRD activities can become distinct marketing tools—or even services worthy of being marketed in their own right.

On one end of a continuum, some externally-oriented instruction may be geared solely to improving the quality of life in the community. Business leaders can lead seminars and participate in efforts to improve management of schools, public agencies, churches, and civic groups. They may also be prominent in community development efforts to attract industry, promote tourism, and lead popular social reform movements to improve the plight of minorities, women, and the economically disadvantaged.

On the other end of a continuum, they may choose to devote their energies to activities with more obvious bottom-line relevance. In such cases they may want to offer seminars pertinent to actual or prospective consumers. Though the nature of such seminars may differ by the type of business and the type of consumers it serves, business leaders may want to structure instruction around (1) product adoption and use, (2) product repair, and (3) specialized product needs or concerns of distinct market segments. Some representative course titles might include: "Using and Maintaining Your Home Computer," "Making Simple Repairs to Your Computer," and "Choosing a Computer System Appropriate for Farmers" (or other groups). If needs are extensive enough—as sometimes happens in the computer industry, for instance—an entire curriculum consisting of related courses can be designed to meet consumer needs.

The choice of what instruction to offer depends on present problems—or those expected in the future. Consider:

1. Is there anything consumers absolutely must know before they can use the product or service? Is it worth offering instruction on this prerequisite knowledge?
2. What are the most common problems confronting a first-time product or service user?
3. What future changes in product design may lead to problems in product use by consumers?

Similar questions can be posed about suppliers and distributors and considered when selecting instructional content for them. Use Activity 8-12 at the end of this chapter for that purpose.

Choice of delivery methods depends on who is to be reached, what instruction is to be delivered, and what level of behavioral change is desired. For example, the methods used in dealing with members of the community may have to be oriented to mass media or personal contact unless the firm's managers are willing to be more innovative in approach. Public seminars can be offered to most groups: members of the community, suppliers, distributors, and others. Exotic delivery methods may also be used with groups like suppliers or distributors with which the firm does business. Such methods may include teleconferencing, video-assisted or video-based instruction, audio-assisted or audiocassette-based instruction, computer-assisted or computer-based instruction, and programmed instruction. Use Activity 8-13 at the end of this chapter to brainstorm about appropriate delivery methods and their relative advantages and disadvantages.

FOLLOWING UP ON INSTRUCTIONAL NEEDS

How well are the instructional offerings of a firm helping to narrow the gap between what is and what should be, concerning corporate relations with the general public and external stakeholders? These questions center on the ninth step in the process of instructing external groups. They involve following up on needs *after* instruction to assess whether—and how much—instructional objectives were achieved.

This step is relatively simple if the focus of instruction is on a change effort with a discrete beginning and ending. Public seminars are examples. HRD practitioners can (1) test knowledge at the end of seminars to determine how well participants mastered the material, and (2) follow up with participants several months after they attend a seminar to determine how effectively instruction changed their behaviors or attitudes.

Other long-term change efforts, on the other hand, may be more difficult to assess. How is it possible, for instance, to determine whether corporate-sponsored community development efforts are successful? If the aim is as broad as improving quality of life, success may also be hard to measure. Perhaps the best method is to (1) identify attributes associated with instructional objectives at the outset of the process—that is, during the establishment of instructional objectives, and (2) measure achievement toward these attributes. At the community level, company managers may link their objectives to existing community development plans. When they contribute to realization of those plans, their own may be deemed successful. Use Activity 8-14 at the end of this chapter to brainstorm on how to judge the relative value of instructional efforts in meeting the needs of the community, product/service users, market segments with which the firm deals, the general public, suppliers, and distributors.

THE RELATIONSHIP BETWEEN ORGANIZATIONAL STRATEGY FOR HRD AND THE HRD EFFORT PLANNED FOR GROUPS OUTSIDE THE ORGANIZATION

Offering instruction to external groups is important because it (1) heightens awareness of managers and employees about the needs of the general public and external stakeholders, (2) creates pressure, via external groups, for change within the corporation, (3) removes barriers to efficient and effective interactions between the corporation, the general public, and external stakeholders, and (4) provides information to consumers about the corporation's products or services. The last reason has made customer education the fastest growing area of HRD practiced (see Table 8-3).

How can nonemployee development contribute to the implementation of Strategic Business Plans? How can nonemployee development contribute to Organizational Strategy for HRD? There are no absolutely right or wrong answers to either question. In fact, the best answers depend on the organization and on the environment in which it resides. For this reason, consider the questions as they apply to your organization. Use Activities 8-15 and 8-16 at the end of this chapter for this purpose.

TABLE 8-3 GROWTH IN CUSTOMER EDUCATION

Study Year	% Reporting	% Growth
1982	17.0%	0.0%
1983	26.3%	54.7%
1984	42.7%	62.3%

Reported customer education activities by industry

	Transportation, Communications, Utilities	Health Services	Manu-facturing	Finance, Insurance, Banking	Wholesale/ Retail Trade	Educational Services	Public Admin.	Across Industry Average
Percent Reporting	53.0%	47.7%	47.7%	41.6%	39.1%	30.0%	21.0%	42.4%

Employee size category by customer education activities

	50–99	100–499	500–999	1,000–2,499	2,500–9,999	More than 10,000	Across Industry Average
Percent Reporting	44.4%	38.3%	43.0%	44.8%	41.1%	53.8%	42.4%

Source: Zemke, 1984, p. 30. Reprinted with permission from *Training*.

ACTIVITY 8-1 Pinpointing Key Institutions and Issues at the Community Level

Directions: Use this activity to structure your thinking about key institutions and key issues in each community in which your firm does significant business (for example, the firm operates a plant at the site). If you are unable to complete the activity without more information, then identify what information you need and collect it before beginning the activity. (The discovery that you need information is important in its own right.) Use additional paper if necessary.

I. Community Presence

1. At what locations does your firm do such significant business that conditions at the community level could have an impact on operations? Identify major sites of your firm.

II. Institutions

2. In each location you pinpointed in response to question 1, identify the major institutions which exert significant influence on life in the community (for example, employers, family, government, schools, religious organizations).

III. Importance of Institutions

3. In each community, which institutions listed in response to question 2 seem to be *most* important? *Least* important?

ACTIVITY 8-1 Continued

IV. Key Issues at the Community Level

4. In each community, what issues seem to be of greatest concern (for example, the economy in a depressed farm community; government issues; economic development; flight of the able-bodied to other locations, etc.)?

V. Importance of Issues

5. In each community, prioritize the most important issues. Start with the most important.

ACTIVITY 8-2 Pinpointing External Stakeholders

Directions: Use this activity to structure your thinking about the relative importance of external stakeholder groups. Use additional paper if necessary.

I. Key External Stakeholders

1. List the most important external stakeholders of your corporation (for example, shareholders/owners, consumers, important suppliers, important distributors).

II. Importance of Each Stakeholder Group

2. Not all managers value different groups and their opinions equally. List, in order of priority, the corporation's stakeholder groups. (Think about groups discussed frequently by top executives. That should serve as an indication of which groups are considered most important.) List the most important ones first.

III. Issues by Stakeholder Group

3. What appears to be the major issues of concern to each stakeholder group you identified in response to item 1?

ACTIVITY 8-2 Continued
IV. Importance of Issues by Stakeholder Group

4. List, in order of importance (where 1 = greatest importance), issues of greatest concern to each stakeholder group. Begin with the most important group (as identified in item 2).

ACTIVITY 8-3 The Relationship Between the Corporation, General Public, and External Stakeholders

Directions: Use this activity to brainstorm about relationships between the corporation and outside groups. There are no right or wrong answers. Use additional paper if necessary.

I. The Corporation and the General Public

1. Generally, what is the relationship between the corporation and the general public? More specifically, in what ways is the corporation presently viewed positively by the public? How do you know? In what ways is the corporation viewed negatively? How do you know?

2. What problems, if any, are created for the corporation by lack of public knowledge about it?

II. The Corporation and External Stakeholders

3. Generally, what is the relationship between the corporation and such external stakeholders as consumers, major suppliers, major distributors, shareholders/owners, and so on? More specifically, in what ways do you think the corporation is viewed positively by members of each group? Negatively? How do you know?

ACTIVITY 8-3 Continued
II. The Corporation and External Stakeholders

4. What problems, if any, are created for the corporation by lack of knowledge about it among
   a. consumers?
   b. major suppliers?
   c. shareholders/owners?
   d. other important groups outside the corporation?

ACTIVITY 8-4 Collecting Information

Directions: Use this activity to think about ways of collecting information from outside groups about the corporation. Use additional paper if necessary.

I. The General Public

1. How can the corporation's managers systematically collect information about the general public? Consider such possible sources as: communities in which the firm does significant amounts of business; social activists; professional groups/associations, etc.

II. Key External Stakeholders

2. How can the corporation's managers systematically collect information about shareholders/owners, consumers, major suppliers, and major distributors? (Consider each group separately.)

ACTIVITY 8-5 Clarifying the Role of the Corporation in Society

Directions: Use this activity to structure your thinking. Answer each question. Use additional paper if necessary. Of course, there are no right or wrong answers.

I. Corporate Social Responsibility

1. What are the responsibilities of a corporation to the society of which it is part?

II. Role of Business in Society

2. Why do you think the general public may be dissatisfied with business in general?

3. Why do you think the general public may be dissatisfied with the industry of which your firm is part?

ACTIVITY 8-5 Continued

III. Public Image of the Corporation

4. What do you think the "public image" of your corporation *should be* at the national level (and, when appropriate, international level)?

5. What should be the public image of your corporation at the regional or state level? (Are there good reasons to work for a different image at this level than at the national or local levels?)

6. What *should be* the public image of your corporation at the community level? (Are there good reasons to work for a different image at this level than at the national or state/regional levels? Should a different image be cultivated at some locations but not at others?)

ACTIVITY 8-5 Continued

IV. Objectives

7. What objectives should be established to improve corporate relations with the general public through planned learning activities?

8. What objectives should be established to improve corporate relations with external stakeholders through planned learning activities? (Prepare separate objectives for consumers, major suppliers, major distributors, owners/shareholders, and other groups.)

V. Evaluation

9. How can the achievement of objectives be measured?

ACTIVITY 8-6 A Worksheet for Social Monitoring

Directions: Collect information about conditions/issues over the last two years in such bellwether states as California, New York, and Massachusetts. (Use newspapers, magazines, government reports, pending legislation, and discussions with anyone residing in these locales.) Then answer the following questions. Of course, there are no right or wrong answers. Use additional paper if necessary.

I. Trends

1. What social trends are noticeable in California, New York, and Massachusetts? Explain why you think so. How can planned learning activities help prepare employers for changes likely to occur as these trends are felt?

II. Objectives

2. What corporate objectives should be established in anticipation of the trends listed in question 2?

ACTIVITY 8-7 Pinpointing Weaknesses and Threats in Relationships Between the Corporation and External Groups

Directions: Use this activity to brainstorm about present weaknesses and future threats to relationships between the corporation and external groups. Use additional paper if necessary. Answer each question in the space provided.

I. What Is?

1. What is the present relationship between the corporation and the general public? (Describe it.)

2. What are the present relationships between the corporation and such external stakeholders as consumers, shareholders, major suppliers, and distributors? (Describe the relationships.)

II. What Should Be?

3. What should be the relationship between the corporation and the general public? (Describe it.)

ACTIVITY 8-7 Continued

4. What should be the relationships between the corporation and such external stakeholders as consumers, shareholders, major suppliers, and distributors? (Describe the relationships.)

III. What are the Weaknesses and Threats?

5. Describe present weaknesses and future threats to relationships between the corporation and the general public.

6. Describe present weaknesses and future threats to relationships between the corporation and such external stakeholders as consumers, suppliers, distributors, or shareholders.

ACTIVITY 8-8 Pinpointing Strengths and Opportunities Between the Corporation and External Groups

Directions: Use this activity to brainstorm about present strengths and future opportunities in relationships between the corporation and external groups. Use additional paper if necessary.

I. What Is?

1. What is the present relationship between the corporation and the general public? (Describe it.)

2. What are the present strengths in relationships between the corporation and such external stakeholders as consumers, shareholders, major suppliers, and distributors? (Describe the strengths.)

II. What Should Be in the Future?

3. What should be the relationship in the future between the corporation and the general public? (Describe it.)

ACTIVITY 8-8 Continued

4. What should be the future relationship between the corporation and such external stakeholders as consumers, shareholders, major suppliers, and distributors? (Describe opportunities for improvement.)

III. What are the Strengths and Opportunities?

5. Describe present strengths in relationships between the corporation and the general public. Describe future opportunities to improve those relationships.

6. Describe present strengths in relationships between the corporation and such external stakeholders as consumers, shareholders, major suppliers, and major distributors. Then describe future opportunities to improve those relationships.

ACTIVITY 8-9 Types of Change Sought Through an HRD Effort

Directions: Use this activity to organize your thoughts about what changes in relations between the corporation and external groups should be the result of planned instructional (HRD) efforts. Answer the questions which follow. Use additional paper if necessary.

I. Types of Changes

1. What changes in relationships between the corporation and the general public are being sought through instructional efforts? (Describe.)

2. What changes in relationships between the corporation and external stakeholders are being sought through instructional efforts? (Describe.)

II. Rationale

3. Why are these changes appropriate?

4. Why are instructional efforts appropriate for helping bring about these changes?

ACTIVITY 8-10 Providing Instruction to External Groups Through Innovative Approaches

Directions: Read the brief introduction to creative problem-solving which follows. Then answer the questions in the boxes. Use additional paper if necessary.

An Introduction to Creative Problem-Solving

According to Arthur Koestler (1964), the essence of creativity is *bioassociation.* This is the process of bringing one body of knowledge into a totally different, and seemingly unrelated, line of inquiry. An example: bringing ideas, techniques, or methods from (say) physics to bear on a problem-solving activity in history, business, or economics. In short, creativity involves combining two unrelated ideas to produce a new idea.

The process of creative problem-solving is reasonably predictable. It begins with *basic training*—that is, some familiarity with the field of inquiry. In other words, people who have no knowledge of a subject will be unable to provide contributions to it. The second step in the process is a *felt need,* a vague irritation with the way things are. The creative person feels that something is not as it should be. The third step is *deliberation,* the process of rolling over a problem in the mind—perhaps for years. The fourth and final step is *affirmation,* the belief that some otherwise unrelated subject area provides ideas that shed light on the problem at hand. The individual then elaborates on his or her ideas—or those of other people.

For more on creativity, see Aiken and Alford (1970), Aiken and Hage (1971), Brightman (1980), de Bono (1972), and Osborn (1953).

I. Present Methods

1. What methods, if any, are presently being used to identify and meet the instructional needs of the general public?

2. What methods, if any, are presently being used to identify and meet the instructional needs of external stakeholders?

ACTIVITY 8-10 Continued

II. Creative Methods

3. Apply the following list of verbs to the methods described in your answers to questions 1 and 2. Explain how each verb can be used to *change* the methods listed.
   a. substitute methods
   b. rearrange methods
   c. combine with methods used in public relations, marketing, personnel, or other functions
   d. reverse methods

ACTIVITY 8-11 Establishing Instructional Objectives for External Groups

Directions: Use this activity to help you clarify and formulate instructional objectives for groups outside a corporation. Answer the following questions. Use additional paper if necessary.

I. Conditions

1. What should *members of the general public* know about the corporation and/or its products/services upon completion of the instructional effort?

2. What should *each group of key external stakeholders* know about the corporation and/or its products/services upon completion of the instructional effort?

II. Time Frame

3. Describe the time horizon for bringing about the change cited in item 1.

4. Describe the time horizon for bringing about the change cited in item 2.

ACTIVITY 8-11   Continued
III. Criteria
5. How will successful progress be measured for item 1?
6. How will successful progress be measured for item 2?

ACTIVITY 8-12 Deciding What Instruction to Offer to External Groups

Directions: Use this activity to brainstorm about what instruction to offer to external groups. Answer each question in the space provided.

1. Is there anything the consumer *must* know before being able to use the corporation's products (or services)?

2. Is it worthwhile to offer instruction to consumers, particularly those who are first-time product users?

3. What are the most common problems of first-time product users?

4. What future changes in product design (or service offerings) may lead to problems in consumers' use of company products or services?

5. How can instruction improve the future ability of consumers to use the products/services?

ACTIVITY 8-13 Deciding How to Deliver Instruction to External Groups

Directions: Use this activity to brainstorm about the best ways to reach appropriate learners. Answer the questions in the space provided.

1. In what ways does your corporation *presently* interact with potential learners outside the organization?

2. How can instructional delivery methods be geared to the means by which your corporation presently interacts with potential learners?

3. What other delivery methods can be used to reach potential learners? What are the relative advantages and disadvantages of each method?

ACTIVITY 8-14 Deciding on Evaluative Methods
Directions: Use this activity to brainstorm on the means to evaluate instruction offered to external groups. Answer the questions in the space provided.
1. How can progress be measured in achieving instructional objectives relative to *communities?*
2. How can progress be measured in achieving instructional objectives relative to *product* or *service users?*
3. How can progress be measured in achieving instructional objectives relative to *consumers?*
4. How can progress be measured in achieving instructional objectives relative to *major suppliers? Major distributors?*

ACTIVITY 8-15   Integrating Corporate Grand Strategy and Instruction for External Groups

Directions: Use this activity to brainstorm on how instruction for external groups can support corporate grand strategy—or suggest new strategies for the organization. Answer the questions in the space provided.

1. How can HRD activities, geared to the general public, support implementation of corporate Grand Strategy?

2. How can HRD activities, geared to external stakeholders, support implementation of corporate Grand Strategy?

3. What new Grand Strategies are suggested by any past HRD activities geared to external groups?

ACTIVITY 8-16 Integrating Organizational Strategy for HRD and Instruction for External Groups

Directions: Use this activity to brainstorm about the relationship between Organizational Strategy for HRD and externally-oriented instructional efforts. Answer the questions in the space provided.

1. What is the role of instruction directed to the general public in implementing Organizational Strategy for HRD?

2. What is the role of instruction directed to external stakeholders in implementing Organizational Strategy for HRD?

3. What should be the *future* role of instruction geared to the general public in implementing Organizational Strategy for HRD?

4. What should be the *future* role of instruction geared to key external stakeholders in implementing Organizational Strategy for HRD?

9

EMPLOYEE DEVELOPMENT

Employee development is an extension of externally-oriented instruction, because it helps employees of an organization adapt to changes taking place externally. As the environment of the organization changes, employees are affected. Employee development prepares people for these external changes. Employees and managers of any firm are *internal* stakeholders in organizational survival and success. Thus they have vested interests in organizational performance. Among these interests, employees are particularly concerned about present job security and future advancement.

This chapter defines employee development, explains how to identify ED needs, and summarizes special methods associated with ED. Finally, problems with traditional ED are explained and a new strategic approach to ED is described.

DEFINITION OF EMPLOYEE DEVELOPMENT

Employee development cultivates employees in line with organizational, departmental, and/or work group needs. As Nadler (1979) explains, "employee development is concerned with preparing employees so that they can move with the organization as it develops, changes and grows" (p. 88). It thus makes individuals agents for organizational and group change.

Differing from employee education and training in key respects, ED is not always directly tied to observable, behavioral change. It cultivates individuals so that their organization and work group collectively possess the knowledge and skills necessary to meet present, and prepare for future, responsibilities. ED "is concerned with the future of the organization and the individual in directions which are not [always] clearly definable" (Nadler, 1979, p. 88). For this reason, ED is hard to justify solely for immediate return on investment.

Employee development efforts are widespread but are seldom well-planned. Most managers can think of a few occasions when they sent an employee off to a professional conference, assigned work, or otherwise tried to "broaden" an individual or improve the mix of skills available in the work group. ED encompasses these efforts. Since ED is often combined with work assignments—temporary rotation to other jobs is a frequently-mentioned method of development (Moore, 1982)—it is hard to distinguish from work itself. As a result, not enough information is available about successful and not-so-successful employee development methods.

Nor is enough emphasis placed on employee development: it is easily lost in the shuffle of daily work activities. In many organizations, as Hall (1984) points out, "training and development (T&D) activities may be characterized as 'big T and little D' . . . (i.e., much training and little development)" (p. 160). There are several reasons why this is so. First, too little effort is made to identify long-term skill needs and think through means of acquiring them. Second, too much time is spent trying to demonstrate immediate, short-term payoffs from HRD activities to hard-eyed skeptics, with the result that long-term developmental efforts are neglected. Third and finally, too many managers do not understand the purposes of HRD activities. While they may give lip service to employee development, they are unsure of what it is—and are sometimes reluctant to commit resources to it when they are.

IDENTIFYING ED NEEDS

A planned ED program means that HRD practitioners and operating managers should:

1. identify each work group in the organization,
2. clarify the group's actual purpose, activities, and responsibilities,
3. plan changes to group purpose, activities, and responsibilities so that they match the desired purpose, activities, and responsibilities of the work group,
4. determine how many and what kind of people are presently available in the work group,
5. plan how many and what kind of people are needed to change group purpose, activities, and responsibilities in line with desired group purpose, activities, and responsibilities,
6. compare desired human resources (HR) to available supplies,
7. establish long-term action plans for each work group to narrow gaps between desired and available HR supplies through planned ED.

This model resembles HR planning, "the process of analyzing an organization's human resource needs under changing conditions and developing activities necessary to satisfy these needs" (Walker, 1980, p. 5). This resemblance is no accident: ED should be one tool for implementing HR plans. Unfortunately, it rarely is because ED is seldom planned.

Identifying each work group. A work group consists of all employees reporting to one supervisor. These groups should be easy to identify with an organization chart.

Clarifying the group's purpose, activities, and responsibilities. Why does the group exist? What does it do? Which other groups, inside and outside the business, interact with it and depend on it for materials? By answering these questions, supervisors clarify the present purpose, activities, and responsibilities of their work groups.

Planning changes in group purpose, activities, and responsibilities. Any change in an organization or its leadership implies that at least some, if not all, activities of the work group should also change. From the standpoint of executives and managers, why should the work group exist? What should it do? Why? What other groups depend on it, and in what ways? By answering these questions, supervisors clarify the desired purpose, activities, and responsibilities of their work groups. (Managers can apply the same approach to determine what others in the organization expect of a department. Executives can similarly apply the approach for several departments.)

Determining how many and what kind of people are available. How well is the work group performing? How well is it serving the purposes other people want it to serve? What kind of people—and how many—are presently available in the group? By answering these questions, supervisors examine the strengths and weaknesses of their work groups. They match production (output) levels to numbers of people available; they match quality of work to skills available.

Four methods are traditionally used in assessing HR supplies. The first method is a *comprehensive HR Information System*. It takes stock of skills available among an organization's work force. Typically computerized, it contains information about employee education, experience, skills, performance appraisals, career interests, and much more. It can be tailored to the unique needs of one firm or can be purchased from outside vendors to meet general needs (Frantzreb, 1986). The second method is an *HR audit*. It is usually carried out to assess how well the personnel department is functioning (Odiorne, 1972). The third method is *succession planning*. It identifies replacements for key executives. The fourth method is a *combination of the others*.

Each method can be modified to assess *available HR supplies*—that is, the actual numbers and skills of employees—in a work group. Supervisors create a skill inventory by listing the major tasks of the work group and then rating each employee work group relative to it. Supervisors carry out HR audits to identify special performance problems (deficiencies) and talents (proficiencies) of the work group. Supervisors plan for succession by identifying a "back-up" for each worker except those carrying out the simplest duties. Each method helps identify available HR supplies in the work group.

Planning how many and what kind of people are needed. What changes should be made to the work group so that it will perform in ways consistent with what other people desire? What kind and how many people are needed to serve a desired purpose for the group, carry out desired activities, and meet desired responsibilities? These questions focus on identifying *desired HR supplies*, the needed number and skills of employees for the work group.

To determine desired HR supplies, supervisors should discuss with other people what changes should be made to the activities of the work group. Supervisors must first address *what should be the activities and results of the work group* before they can address *what number and type of people are needed to carry out the activities and achieve desired results*. One way to go about this process is to flowchart activities that must be carried out by the work group to achieve desired results. Each step on the flowchart requires special skills, some of which may not be available presently in the work group.

Comparing desired to available HR supplies. How many and what kind of people are presently available in the work group? How many and what kind of people are needed in the work group to meet desired group responsibilities? By answering these questions, supervisors identify gaps between available and desirable staffing. This comparison should be made regularly to pinpoint differences between HR supplies and demands.

One way to answer these questions is by comparison. Supervisors list actual group activities and then list those which other people want their group to carry out at present. They list all employees in the group. Finally, they rate each employee on the ability to perform each activity and each activity on the number of people needed for it. Discrepancies are revealed through this method.

Another way to answer these questions is by estimate. Supervisors determine what the work group should be doing and what people will be needed to do it. They can then compare that to their present output and staffing to identify discrepancies between how many and what kind of people are needed. Instead of making estimates by activity, they simply make a general estimate.

Establishing action plans. Employee development is one way to narrow gaps between what the group is actually doing and what others want it to be doing. It is appropriate when three conditions are met. First, supervisors must prefer investing in the firm's employees rather than hiring externally. Second, high levels of trust must exist between employer and employees. Supervisors must not fear that developing individuals will increase turnover as more skilled employees are snatched up by competitors. Third, supervisors must believe that neither external contractors nor recruitment from outside will do as well as employee development in producing the skills needed in work groups. When these conditions exist, ED is appropriate to cultivate talent in work groups.

An ED program encourages the preparation of individuals for meeting the collective requirements of a work group or department. Supervisors in each work group establish measurable objectives, or at least articulate goals, so that the numbers and skills of employees match up to what the work group should be doing at present. In each work group, individuals are then developed *in a planned way* through one or more methods.

SPECIALIZED METHODS FOR EMPLOYEE DEVELOPMENT

Objectives for employee development can be achieved through such methods as (1) long-term, informal mentoring programs; (2) long-term, formal mentoring programs; (3) long-term, formalized transfer or exchange programs across organizations, divisions, departments, work units, or jobs; (4) short-term rotation programs; (5) special job assignments; (6) field trips; (7) professional conferences; (8) behavior modelling; and (9) "think tank" experiences (Nadler, 1979).

Long-term, informal mentoring programs. Mentoring remains a popular buzzword in the HRD field. A *mentor* is a more experienced and often higher-placed individual who establishes a special relationship with others, called *protégés*. It is possible to establish such relationships between two people of equal organizational status in which one is more experienced than the other. (The latter is called a *buddy program* and has been used successfully in orienting and socializing newcomers [see Werther & Davis, 1985]).

The classic mentoring relationship develops informally through the initiative of the protégé, not through planned pairings of individuals. It satisfies a protégé's need for specialized guidance by a significant other, who becomes a role model. It also satisfies a mentor's need to pass on knowledge and experience the intrinsic satisfaction of helping others realize their potential (Roche, 1979).

Some authorities contend that truly effective mentoring relationships cannot be engineered. All true development, they contend, is really self-development (Gardner, 1963; Hague, 1974, 1978; Pedler & Boydell, 1980). There is some truth to this notion, because successful people are motivated from within rather than from without.

Yet even if HRD professionals take no active part in matching up people at lower levels with prospective mentors at higher levels, they can

- exert moral persuasion on decision-makers so that they see the benefits of mentoring to their organizations,
- raise the consciousness of employees and managers alike about the advantages to be gained through mentor-protégé relationships, and
- offer training, when requested, on mentoring skills.

Through these and other approaches, HRD practitioners create a climate which encourages helping relationships between aspiring employees and their more experienced counterparts. These relationships can be the starting point for planned employee development.

Long-term, formal mentoring programs. One way to develop employees is to establish a formalized mentoring program for *all* employees. Such programs—sometimes called formal *sponsorship* programs—have been used in management development (London, 1985). But when a true employee development philosophy prevails, the same logic is applied throughout the firm—not just for the benefit of high potential junior executives.

A formal mentoring program is established by the direct pairing of individuals (London & Stumpf, 1982). HRD practitioners identify experienced people who act as mentors, and provide training to them on how to coach their protégés, protect them, offer them challenging work assignments, provide them with advice and feedback, and expose them to higher-placed people who can positively affect their career progress. HRD practitioners also identify inexperienced people who need mentoring and meet with them to explain what mentoring is and why it is important. The final step is the direct matching of mentors and protégés. To be successful, a formal mentoring program should be based on the belief that preparing future leaders and technical workers is important to the business.

Use Activity 9-1 at the end of this chapter to consider how to develop a formal mentoring program in an organization.

According to Lawrie (1987), formalized mentoring programs are particularly useful for people whose jobs involve large investments and exert substantial influence on customer relations. Lawrie believes that prospective mentors should be recruited on the basis of their interest in coaching or teaching others—as evidenced by their interest in helping roles, like off-the-job community activities. Mentors are often able to relate stories enthusiastically about the help they received from others early in their own careers. They view mentoring as an enriching activity for themselves as well as for others (Zey, 1988).

Mentoring programs are beneficial for improving succession planning, reducing the induction period of the newly hired or promoted, reducing turnover, and increasing communication. However, their success depends on overcoming barriers created by senior management, tradition, and organizational culture (*Mentoring in the U.S.A.*, 1986).

The HRD practitioner's role in a formal mentoring program is as a linking pin, coordinating interactions between learners and mentors. The practitioner takes special care to assess individual needs and help learners meet them. Learning is highly individualized. To be part of an organized ED program, such learning should be guided by the collective needs of the work group in which the individual is positioned.

Long-term, formalized transfer programs. Another way to foster employee development is by long-term, formal transfer programs in which individuals are rotated for long periods to other organizations, departments, divisions, work groups, or jobs. Such transfers may last several months or years. Some firms participate in exchange programs in which they trade employees with other firms.

Exchange programs build bridges between a corporation and institutions exerting broad influence—such as schools, colleges, government agencies, major suppliers, distributors, or institutional customers. Exchange programs increase communication between a corporation and its stakeholders, serving a three-fold purpose in developing individuals, strengthening ties with external groups, and furnishing the individual with knowledge and skills of value to the work group.

Some firms actively promote exchange programs with universities. For example, "Executive in Residence" programs enable universities to draw on the expertise of real executives, thereby enriching student exposure to "real-world" thinking and problems. At the same time, the corporation is able to develop the executive through exposure to new ideas, approaches, and challenges. Of course, the executive also represents the corporation to students. Depending on the executive's success as a role model and resource, he or she may (1) attract talent to the corporation, thereby promoting recruitment, and (2) influence faculty—and perhaps even future academic offerings—so that the university serves effectively to prepare students for the future.

Transfer programs can also be established for a company's sales agents, product dealers, or employees of key suppliers, distributors, and institutional customers so that they can learn firsthand about a firm with which they are conducting business. Quite apart from the increased efficiency and effectiveness which may result from the presence of a firsthand liaison, the experience broadens individuals in liaison roles. Alternatively, employees of the business may be sent to spend time at a supplier, distributor, or institutional customer. Employees return with firsthand knowledge of problems encountered by the firm's key supplier, distributor, manufacturer, or other group. More than a few firms, for example, recruit their Sales Trainers from the ranks of successful salespeople. They enjoy instant credibility with trainees—and learn more about the operations of the company while on transfer from the field.

Transfer programs may also be established internally between divisions, departments, or work groups. Much like externally-oriented exchange programs, they increase communication between two groups. The individual transferred to another unit serves thereafter as a linking pin and liaison. The individual's knowledge, skills, and experience are also broadened through exposure to a different part of the organization, which in turn provides a source of information for the individual's work group.

Job transfers often stem from pressing organizational needs—such as lack of talent in one location but a surplus of talent in another. But no individual should be transferred without taking into account the needs of the whole person. Managers who rose through corporate ranks by moving from one work site to another should not necessarily expect unquestioning acceptance of geographical transfers from all new workers of the 1980s, who may refuse transfers if too disruptive to their spouse's careers, children's education, or homeowner obligations (but see Blomquist, 1982). For this reason, contemplated transfers should always be preceded by a frank discussion between employee and supervisor. This discussion should deal with such issues as these:

- *intended benefits of the transfer:* What will the company and the individual's work group gain from the transfer? How will the employee gain from it?
- *what objectives, both instructional and noninstructional, will be established?* In short, what outcomes are expected?
- *barriers:* What problems will a move pose for an employee, his or her spouse, his or her children, and others, like elderly relatives, for whom the employee is responsible?

- *degree of company support:* What, if anything, can the company do to make a geographical transfer easier? Some firms offer extensive help in relocation; others do not (see Estrin, 1985; Walsh & Anderson, 1985).
- *consequences of decisions made about a transfer:* What will happen if an employee refuses transfer? If he or she agrees? Will it influence future advancement? Will concern about these issues prompt the employee to look for employment elsewhere?

The handling of a transfer is thus quite important, providing an opportunity for employee and superior to discuss the individual's long-term development and the organization's needs.

In preparing managers for increased responsibilities, long-term rotation programs are common. They are rarely formalized. They should be formalized, however, so as to clarify the purpose and desired outcomes for individuals and for their sponsoring work groups. To develop special skills, managers may be assigned to (1) start-up efforts (new ventures); (2) problem departments (turnabout efforts); (3) line positions (if the manager will become a staff manager); (4) staff positions (if the manager will become a line manager); (5) overseas jobs (if there is a need to develop cross-cultural sensitivity); and, (6) other, special long-term assignments. Each cultivates important skills that prepare the individual for future advancement. In the meantime, the individual carries back to the original work group new skills and knowledge that enrich the collective talents of the group.

Short-term rotation programs. Job rotation, the short-term movement between jobs, first received attention in assembly line work. It was used to reduce worker ennui and expand an individual's repertoire of tasks. Short-term rotations can range from a few minutes to a few months.

Many organizations use short-term rotations for management employees, particularly during orientation (Fresina & Associates, 1987). Individuals are rotated from department to department, sampling the work and learning firsthand about the organization's activities, people, and culture (Pascale, 1984). At the end of the orientation period individuals are either permanently assigned to one unit or are asked to choose the department or work group in which they want to work on a long-term basis.

It is not a good idea to rotate people without any instructional plan whatever; rather, HRD professionals must approach rotation as a form of instruction. That means they should

- *establish long-term learning objectives for the rotation experience:* What should learners know at the end of the entire rotation program? What should they be able to *do*?
- *establish human support and continuity:* How can newcomers be made to feel welcome? Amid rotations, how can individuals establish long-term interpersonal ties for the future?
- *establish objectives for each phase of rotation:* What should employees, temporarily transferred, know about the department when they leave it?

- *structure the experiences:* A line manager or HRD practitioner should meet with learners before rotation to focus attention on the purpose of the impending experience. Has the experience been structured in some way? Are there planned activities in which learners are expected to take part? If so, what are they? Why are they being provided? (HRD practitioners should assist line managers in developing outlines or lesson plans to structure rotation programs so that each phase is planned and produces results for which learners can be held accountable.)
- *reinforce the experience:* Individuals vary in their styles of learning (Brookfield, 1986). Several different ways should be used to present information and structure experience during a rotation.
- *provide for debriefing:* Just as meetings before rotations help learners understand the purpose of rotation experiences in which they participate, meetings afterward tie together—and reinforce—experiences.

In an orientation, for example, learners may participate in classroom training, which is then followed by rotation to the work setting. Before the rotation, learners are told how it relates to the classroom instruction. During rotation, the supervisor emphasizes the task on which the classroom instruction was focused. After rotation, learners are asked to interpret what happened. They also receive concrete feedback about their performance during the rotation experience.

Perhaps a description of such a program will help clarify what it is and how it works. In one large company, a downsizing effort unexpectedly robbed the organization of experienced middle managers, many of whom had accepted attractive early retirement offers. Stepped up recruitment produced a flood of management trainees. The company was not prepared for them because it never had a planned HRD program or centralized HRD department.

An experienced HRD practitioner was hired from outside. She immediately formed a management development advisory committee (MDAC), consisting of experienced supervisors and managers from different levels of the hierarchy and from different departments. Though new to the firm herself, she was still able to organize a planned job rotation program for management trainees in short order.

Her approach was simple enough. She asked members of the MDAC to identify key experiences to which management trainees should be exposed during their first six months of employment. She then asked committee members for the names of people in the company who could discuss each topic and supervise each experience. At this point she developed a simple questionnaire (see Figure 9-1) and surveyed the "experts" about issues that should be discussed with trainees in short, informal, one-on-one discussions. She compared responses—at least two people were designated as experts for each topic—and identified common issues. The survey results provided a foundation for on-the-job lesson plans to ensure that each newcomer would consistently receive certain basic information regardless of who discussed it. Specific, planned rotation experiences were designed to follow each discussion.

Job rotation programs do not have to mean a stint in every department. Nor do they have to be elaborate. They can be restricted to movement between groups in one department or jobs in one work group. Nor do they have to be limited to orientation. They can be tied to job posting programs or used by themselves to foster

- *cross-training within a work group,* so everyone has at least some familiarity with the jobs and tasks of their peers (cross-training is more important in some settings than in others. The chief barrier to it is the unwillingness of some operating managers to schedule for it);
- *long-term preparation for advancement,* so individuals are gradually prepared for greater responsibility or increasing technical competence (this aids succession planning); and
- *retraining,* so employees are familiarized with recent advances in their fields or occupations and can apply this new information.

Use Activity 9-2 at the end of this chapter to prepare a plan for a structured short-term rotation program for new employees.

Special job assignments. Special assignments may mean: (1) researching a problem or issue; (2) developing a solution or recommendations for dealing with a special problem or issue; or (3) assuming responsibility for a project. Assignments like these resemble what Tough (1979) calls *independent learning projects.* A key difference is that, for Tough, independent learners identify their own projects and resources for learning, while a special job assignment is structured and planned by an organizational superior.

For example, suppose that a department is experiencing excessive downtime, scrap rates, or some other performance problem. Rather than look into the matter, the department manager calls in an employee and says something like this: "We've been experiencing a problem with __(manager provides description)__ . Would you look into the matter for me, find out the nature of the problem, and bring me a list of one or more recommended solutions within __(some specific time period)__ ? Write up the results in a memo that is short and succinct. State the problem(s), proposed solution(s), reasons for selecting the solution(s), costs associated with the solution(s), and any problems that may stem from consequences of implementing solution(s)."

An assignment like this gives an employee an opportunity to develop skills and exercise responsibility. Astute superiors plan *many* occasions like this *over time* to develop their employees. If superiors do their jobs as developers well enough, many employees are eventually prepared to accept higher levels of responsibilities, and the collective skills of the work group are broadened. Table 9-1 lists specific methods of developing employees through increased delegation.

Some superiors approach such broadening assignments in a relatively unplanned way, letting them stem from problems encountered spontaneously in the course of daily work activities. Others plan these assignments in advance as part of an annually negotiated Management by Objectives agreement or a short-term Personal Performance Contract with each employee (Fritz, 1987). Some managers deliberately prepare a plan of informal experiences or job assignments for each employee to ensure the systematic, planned development of *all* employees in the work group. (The latter approach is a true employee development program when explicitly matched to work group purpose, objectives, and duties.) Refer to Activity 9-3 at the end of this chapter and describe how to transform each critical incident into a developmental experience.

TOPIC: _____

YOUR NAME: _____

<u>Directions</u>: You have been designated by the Management Development Advisory Committee as a top performer in the topic area above. In the future, we'll ask you to meet briefly with each newcomer for a one or two-hour discussion of this topic. To help us organize this effort, would you please complete this survey and return it to the Director of Management Training?

<u>Question 1</u>: Assume you have only one or two hours to speak on your designated topic to newly-hired employees during their first six months of employment. What should they <u>know or be able to do</u> at the end of this discussion with you?

<u>Question 2</u>: List topics you will discuss with newcomers in the order you plan to discuss them. (Again, assume you have only one or two hours.) Underline topics which you plan to emphasize.

<u>Question 3</u>: What matters would you want to discuss if you had the luxury of delivering a day-long, classroom-based treatment of this topic? What additional activities, if any, would you want trainees to experience in a classroom-based treatment of this topic?

Figure 9-1: A Survey for New Employee Orientation

Question 4: Assume that the new employee will <u>not</u> go through a classroom-based treatment of this topic and will have only the benefit of your one-or two-hour discussion as a <u>formal</u> preparation to do work in this area. What <u>additional</u> activities on your topic do you recommend for newcomers which can help bring them "up to speed" as fast as possible? Describe the <u>preferred sequence</u> of activities, starting with the first in the sequence.

ACTIVITIES:

Question 5: What other comments would you like to make?

THANK YOU FOR YOUR COOPERATION!

Figure 9-1: Continued

TABLE 9-1 DELEGATION AS A FORM OF VERTICAL JOB LOADING

Job loading principle	Guide for effective delegation
1. Remove some controls while retaining accountability.	1. Give employees freedom to pursue tasks in their own way, while establishing agreed-upon results and standards of performance.
2. Increase the accountability of individuals for their own work.	2. Encourage an active role on the part of employees in defining, implementing, and communicating progress on tasks.
3. Give people a complete natural unit of work.	3. Entrust employees with completion of whole projects or tasks whenever possible, or at least explain tasks' relevance to larger projects or to department or organization goals.
4. Grant additional authority to employees in their activities.	4. Give employees the necessary authority to accomplish tasks and allow them to do jobs in their own ways.
5. Make periodic reports directly available to workers themselves rather than to their supervisors.	5. Allow employees access to the information, people, and departments which may not ordinarily be directly available to them to accomplish their tasks.
6. Introduce new and more difficult tasks not previously handled.	6. Assign tasks that move employees beyond their current level of skill; provide training, instruction, and guidance as necessary to complete tasks.
7. Assign individuals specific or specialized tasks, enabling them to become experts.	7. Assign tasks based on employees' needs and interests.

Source: Vinton, 1987, p. 66. Reprinted with permission from American Society for Training and Development.

Field trips. Any journey undertaken as a learning experience is a field trip. Elementary school pupils take trips to see zoos, amusement parks, and historical sites. In college, students take trips related to their academic majors: business students tour corporate offices and factories; history students visit historical landmarks; drama students visit theaters; and HRD students visit HRD departments. In a training program on machine operation, an instructor may use a field trip to show trainees a real machine in operation.

In recent years, field trips have become a popular method of fact-finding. American executives go abroad to learn firsthand about management practices, production methods, and cultural matters in Japan, Taiwan, Korea, China, the Philippines, Australia, the Soviet Union, and other countries. U.S. economic development and government officials do likewise. In turn, the U.S. hosts itinerant emissaries from abroad, many interested in learning about such specific American industries as health care, higher education, agriculture, or government.

Developmental field trips need not be restricted to high-level executives. Indeed, they can be used by any supervisor to give employees brief exposure to other sites in the organization, stimulate new insights and creativity, and motivate them to learn more.

Much like special job assignments, field trips can stem from immediate problems in the work setting or can be planned well in advance, perhaps as part of an annually negotiated Management by Objectives program or a group learning plan tied to work group duties. If a field trip is planned on short notice, the supervisor simply asks employees to visit a specific location and report back with ideas, observations, and (perhaps) solutions to identifiable problems. On the other hand, if the trip is planned long in advance, the supervisor has leisure to reflect on this question: What should the employee know when he or she returns? The superior prepares a list of skills related to the skill needs of the work group, and systematically plans specific field trips in which employees can observe a skill being applied—and practice it as well. Trips are planned for their value in furnishing guided learning activities as part of an organized employee development program.

To use a field trip for maximum advantage, the supervisor should meet with employees beforehand and pose broad questions to be answered upon their return. Employees may also be asked to keep a diary or log during the experience to record insights, feelings, and ideas (James-Neill, 1982; Porter, 1982). The act of writing down thoughts clarifies them, as well as preserves them for future reference. Laird (1985) suggests that a field trip should be treated like an "Easter egg hunt" in which employees search for answers to specific questions. Supervisors use field trips to focus employee attention, stimulate thinking, direct individual experience, and expand the mix of skills available in the work group.

Professional conferences. Many professional societies, industry groups, and vendors offer professional conferences each year. They range from product exhibits to lectures on state-of-the-art services, equipment, and issues in a field or industry. The annual conference of the American Society for Training and Development exemplifies a typical large conference. There are different "tracks" of speakers delivering talks concurrently in different rooms; a large exhibit hall provides participants with opportunities to see new products and hear about new services; social networking activities are planned so participants can meet people sharing similar interests; and special events—like film shows and computerized learning exhibits—are abundantly offered for the curious.

Sending employees to professional or industry conferences is a developmental activity intended to (1) update skills and knowledge, (2) evoke new insights and fresh ideas, and (3) provide for social networking opportunities so that attendees can hear about practices in other organizations. Conferences resemble field trips. Conferences are typically located at some distance from the work site, and often the conference outcomes are difficult to plan in advance. As with field trips, supervisors and HRD practitioners help conference participants take maximum advantage of the learning opportunity by providing them with a list of questions in advance to be answered upon their return. Employees may be asked to keep a diary or log of experiences. Other methods for maximizing the value of the experience include (1) having participants brief their colleagues orally on conference highlights, (2) circulating to colleagues literature or handouts collected at the conference, and (3) asking participants to write up a report on the conference for circulation to coworkers. When sending individuals to a conference is carried out as a means of meeting the present or future needs of a work group, it is a tool for employee development.

Behavior modelling. Just like it sounds, behavior modelling involves a two-step process of (1) demonstrating appropriate behavior, and then (2) asking students to demonstrate it. Behavior modelling has been widely advocated for teaching some skills in classroom settings. Trainees observe behaviors enacted on videotape, on film, or by an instructor. This approach works particularly well in training supervisors how to give orders, interview prospective employees, carry out disciplinary counseling, and conduct employee appraisal interviews.

Behavior modelling may also be a more subtle, long-term development method. By rotating employees to exemplary supervisors or performers, they learn through observation how to think and behave like the *role models* with whom they are paired. As in many developmental efforts, specific outcomes from a learning experience may be difficult to plan ahead of time. But learners are encouraged to pay special attention to the exemplary performers to whom they are rotated.

Behavior modelling is grounded solidly on the social learning theory of Bandura (1971, 1977; Bandura & Walters, 1963). For Bandura, people learn through observation of others and by imitation of their examples. The effects of observation can be powerful. For example, if one employee successfully manipulates a supervisor or gets away with infractions of rules, other employees observe and then imitate the same behavior. The key, then, is to be selective in exposing employees to appropriate role models over a long time period and reinforcing, through praise and other rewards, employee imitation of desired behavior. For more information about behavior modelling, see Robinson (1982; 1985) and Zemke (1982c).

"Think tank experiences." A "think tank" is an organization or group formed for the purpose of devoting special attention to a specific problem or group of related problems. Nadler (1979) defines it as "an environment in which production is secondary, except the production of new ideas" (p. 104). He predicts that "the day can be foreseen when such centers will . . . proliferate, but not for many years to come" (p. 105). Nadler identifies it with employee development, as he does some other approaches described in this chapter so far.

Think tanks were originally stand-alone institutions. The most famous was established by the Rand Corporation to study military problems. Since the creation of the first think tank, many others—devoted to a wide range of different issues—have sprung up.

Think tank experiences are characterized by certain key conditions (Delbecq, 1967):

- open communication between group members,
- willingness, even eagerness, to participate in problem-finding and problem-solving,
- clear separation between generating and evaluating ideas,
- relaxed relations in the group,
- courtesy between group members,
- support for creativity,
- a nonauthoritarian point of view,

- appreciation for humor, playfulness, and exploration of seemingly bizarre notions, and
- a desire for consensus but a willingness among group members to accept majority rule.

These conditions should characterize a single problem-solving or problem-finding effort or else characterize the climate of a creative and participative work group, department, or division. Use Activity 9-4 at the end of this chapter to assess the developmental climate of a group.

"Think tank" employee development experiences include: (1) management or employee retreats; (2) task forces; (3) freestanding employee committees; (4) quality circles; (5) staff meetings; (6) impromptu problem-solving groups; and (7) confrontation meetings. Developmental "think tank" experiences like these serve an important purpose: "Involving grass-roots employees on participative teams with control over their own outcome helps the organization to get and use more ideas to improve performance and increase future skills. Whether called 'task forces,' 'quality circles,' 'problem-solving groups,' or 'shared-responsibility teams,' such vehicles for greater participation at all levels are an important part of an innovating company" (Kanter, 1983, p. 241). They may also broaden the existing mix of skills available in the work group.

Each type of "think tank" experience has its own uses and contributes in its own ways to employee development.

A *management or employee retreat* is usually held off-site, somewhere other than the work setting. A *management retreat* gives executives or managers an opportunity to reflect, as a group, on past company performance—and on prospects for the future. Retreats are frequently used as settings for Strategic Business Planning (see Cathcart, 1986). An *employee retreat* serves a similar purpose. Members of a work group step back from the pressures of immediate work demands and reflect on past problems or future opportunities for improving group performance. It is a growth experience for individuals, allowing them to exercise creativity, contribute to increased productivity, and improve relations with coworkers. It is a tool for employee development because it equips participants with new ideas about what they do and how they interact as a group.

A *task force* is a committee formed to deal with a special issue or problem. Very often a task force represents different hierarchical levels and work groups. Usually temporary in nature, it exists just long enough to investigate a specific problem. Task force experiences give employees opportunities to exercise creativity and gain new insights about organizational operations. Supervisors control who is developed, because they choose people assigned to a task force. Task forces serve the needs of employee development when linked to the problems or issues confronting the individual's work group, and when they produce new knowledge which somehow benefits the work group.

Freestanding employee committees are similar to task forces, but are enduring rather than temporary. Individual members rotate on and off, but the committee remains. One example is an HRD committee, formed to provide advice to HRD practitioners about company training, education, and development efforts. Other committees may be permanent: new product committees; budget committees; sales promotion committees; and, committees composed of representatives from the community, industry, or sales force. Service on a committee develops individuals, because it gives them a chance to exercise creativity.

Quality circles gained great popularity in recent years. While there are signs that this popularity is fading (Geber, 1986), they can be most useful nevertheless. Members of a work group are assembled to focus on specific problems encountered by them and to recommend ideas for production improvement. By encouraging individuals in work groups to pool their insights, quality circles tap the collective problem-solving skills of the group and improve the interaction of group members.

Staff meetings are a tradition in many organizations. Their primary purpose is to organize and schedule work. They also give supervisors an opportunity to communicate with all members of a work group at once. They become developmental experiences if group members are encouraged to air suggestions, raise problems, or cooperate on solutions.

Impromptu problem-solving groups are less formal than task forces, freestanding committees, or even staff meetings. When a problem comes up, the supervisor calls in a few handpicked individuals for a short brainstorming session about it. Members are chosen for what they know about the problem and what contributions they can make in solving it. By allowing for individual participation in decision-making, these groups foster individual growth and serve a developmental purpose.

Confrontation meetings stimulate creativity. First described by Beckhard (1967), meetings of this kind bring together two groups with conflicting views on an issue. Group members state their ideas and then argue them out to promote greater understanding.

These "think tank" experiences contribute to employee development by giving individuals opportunities to hear about new ideas, experience new insights, and improve interpersonal skills. As individuals are enriched, they provide new talents and skills to be tapped by their work units. The developmental value of these experiences can be increased if (1) they are guided by some kind of systematic improvement plan for the work unit and individuals in it; (2) they are preceded by a discussion between employee and superior to clarify what an employee should learn during the experience and why it is worth learning; (3) individuals are encouraged to keep a log or diary during the experience so that they may record observations and insights; and (4) they are followed up by a debriefing, in which employee and superior discuss what was learned, why it is important, and how it is related both to individual and work unit improvements.

Use Activity 9-5 at the end of this chapter to identify the issues or problems confronting an organization, department, or work group which could benefit from a "think tank" experience. Then consider how such an experience can contribute to employee development.

The developmental methods described in this part of the chapter are not the only ones that can be used. In fact, many other methods can help match the collective skills of a work group to its activities. For example, employee performance appraisal and on-the-job coaching can also be used.

PROBLEMS WITH TRADITIONAL EMPLOYEE DEVELOPMENT PROGRAMS

Traditional employee development programs suffer from several problems. First, they are rarely planned. The process, if something as informal can be called that, works in most companies as one top HR executive described it in her firm:

> Our supervisors watch their subordinates and those reporting to other supervisors. When a promising person comes along, a supervisor will think "now there's a person I can use someday." Supervisors talk over the matter among themselves and arrange for an exchange. Then they talk to a union steward. One day, the employee is told to "report to so-and-so today and come back when you are told to."

No attempt is made to think through the collective skill needs of each work unit. Individuals are not told the reasons for developmental experiences in which they are asked to participate. Lack of planning results from an inability of supervisors to project skill needs. Individuals are kept in the dark about the reasons for developmental experiences because, as one executive explains it, managers are afraid of the possible consequences. Why? As the executive explained:

> If we told the person why he or she was chosen to participate, we might find ourselves saddled with someone with a "swelled head." The person would think a promotion was looming just over the horizon. We might find ourselves facing blackmail at raise time or else constant questions about when a promotion or transfer would take place. To avoid all that, we prefer to keep employees ignorant of our plans for them. We don't always *have* plans in any case.

Developmental experiences are rendered less effective than they might otherwise be as a consequence of trying to avoid problems which might not even come up. To employees, these experiences may be unsettling and frustrating. "Does the boss want to get rid of me?" they secretly wonder. Then, too, experiences will not be maximally effective, because the need for secrecy will rule out a frank talk about what the individual should try to learn during the experience, why it is worth learning, and what knowledge or skills the employee should try to acquire during the developmental experience. Nor will it be possible to debrief employees after experiences, because debriefings may raise unrealistic employee expectations about the future.

A second problem is that, too often, employee development is viewed more as a reward for individual behavior than as a vehicle for obtaining future knowledge and skills needed by a work group or an organization. HRD practitioners should closely examine requests for professional conferences or other developmental activities which do not, on the surface, appear to mesh with the long-term objectives of a unit.

A third problem with employee development programs is that they tend to perpetuate past traditions only. It is easy to see how that happens: employees are rotated to performers who proved themselves in the past rather than rotated to performers whose progressive views mesh with Strategic Business Plans; employees are given broadening job assignments which perpetuate traditions rather than raise questions about them; and employees are sent off to conferences to bring back information about state-of-the-art innovations rather than to think about how to apply those innovations to the tasks facing the work group.

There are, of course, instances when such past-oriented approaches to employee development are appropriate:

- when the work unit's environment is relatively stable,
- when the organization does not face competition,
- when the organization's Strategic Business Plan calls for slow, stable growth without radical changes, and
- when the future HR demands of a work group do not differ significantly from existing HR supplies.

On the other hand, a future-oriented approach is necessary when

- the work group's external environment is volatile,
- competitive advantage is sought by the firm and is essential to long-term organizational survival and success,
- the Strategic Business Plan calls for long-term, radical change—particularly in some work groups or departments more than others, and
- future HR demands at the work group level differ significantly from existing HR supplies.

STRATEGIC EMPLOYEE DEVELOPMENT

Strategic employee development (SED) adopts an approach different from its traditional counterpart. Unlike traditional employee development, it should be

- explicitly linked to a long-term Organizational Strategy for HRD, which in turn supports the plans of the organization and HR generally,
- distinctly future-oriented,
- based on a comprehensive, long-term view of organizational—and work group—needs,
- planned explicitly and deliberately for *each* work group and *each* department, and
- treated as part of Strategic Business Planning efforts.

Conceptualizing strategic employee development. Much like traditional employee development, strategic ED begins with questions about long-term HR needs and demands. Think of it as a series of questions:

1. What competencies will be needed by the organization to implement Strategic Business Plans?

2. What competencies will be needed *by each department or work group* to carry out new duties or meet new responsibilities stemming from Strategic Business Plans?
3. What competencies exist at present in the organization and in *each* department or work group?
4. What discrepancies exist between competencies needed in the future and those already present in the organization and in *each* department or work group?
5. What long-term employee development methods can be planned to rectify the discrepancies identified in question 4?

The focus is on identifying and meeting the *future* collective skill needs of each work group and department. While external recruitment and/or external contracting can potentially help meet these needs, development is another means of meeting needs. In this context, *competency* means "ability to perform." Strategic planners generally accept the notion that organizations have distinctive competencies, proven abilities to perform successfully in certain areas of the business and/or with certain product lines (Glueck & Jauch, 1984). Use Activity 9-6 at the end of this chapter to identify the present and desired future competencies of an organization; use Activity 9-7 to identify the present and desired future competencies of each work group or department in an organization. Then use Activity 9-8 to identify discrepancies between the present and desired future competencies of each work group or department which are suitably addressed through ED efforts.

SPECIALIZED EMPLOYEE DEVELOPMENT METHODS FOR MEETING LONG-TERM ORGANIZATIONAL NEEDS

Each employee development method described in the previous part of the chapter can be treated from a future-oriented rather than a past-oriented perspective. These methods include: (1) long-term, formalized mentoring programs; (2) long-term, informal mentoring programs; (3) long-term, formalized transfer or exchange programs; (4) short-term rotation programs; (5) special job assignments; (6) field trips; (7) professional conferences; (8) behavior modelling; and (9) "think tank" experiences. When these methods are used to prepare people for meeting the future responsibilities of their work groups, they are tools for strategic employee development. Let's discuss long-term planning of related developmental experiences, and selecting, planning, and following up each experience.

Long-term planning of related experiences. Unlike the relatively unplanned approach characteristic of traditional employee development efforts, strategic employee development requires planning for general change objectives for the organization and its departments or work groups. In short: (1) What competencies should be found in the organization in five years? and (2) What competencies should be found in each department or work group in (say) five years? HRD practitioners and/or supervisors can choose many different methods to evoke individual insights and develop individual skills in line with strategic needs at the group level.

Selecting experiences. Selectivity is the key to using developmental experiences strategically. Consider: (1) What experiences will elicit individual insights and develop skills needed by the work unit in the future? and (2) What people and/or other resources can be identified which will provide those experiences? The idea is to pinpoint progressive people, events, or situations that can serve developmental ends. Use Activity 9-9 at the end of this chapter to help pinpoint resources which can serve in this way.

Planning each developmental experience. What supervisors do to prepare employees for developmental experiences affects outcomes dramatically. If supervisors say nothing, employees are left to draw whatever interpretations seem appropriate. Of course, these interpretations may not be appropriate.

In traditional employee development efforts, the supervisor can guide individual experience by providing a list of questions in advance. As a consequence, a structure is imposed on otherwise inchoate aspects of reality. Open-ended questions prompt learners to make discoveries on their own.

Questions of this kind can be keyed to the past, present, or future. If past-oriented, they lead learners to focus on successful practices as proven by experience. For

---

TABLE 9-2 FUTURE-ORIENTED QUESTIONS

- What problems do you expect to come up in the future?

- What future trends may affect work methods?

- How can future problems in this area be averted before they arise?

- Can you describe how you see this unit functioning in, say, five years? What makes you think it will function in this way?

example, learners can be directed to ask such questions as: (1) What methods have proven especially successful in the past? and (2) Why are these methods so successful? In contrast, present-oriented questions focus on current methods, problems, and issues. These help learners familiarize themselves with the state of the art.

Future-oriented questions direct learner attention to anticipating possible future problems and issues. If these questions are asked of supervisors in other parts of one organization—or in other organizations—they may stimulate supervisory creativity and planning as well. A sample list of questions is shown in Table 9-2.

Following up each experience. It is just as important to follow up after each developmental experience as it is to build employee expectations beforehand.

Supervisors and/or HRD practitioners should use a debriefing to:

- hear from the employee about information gathered during the developmental experience,
- impose order on employee insights by careful questioning, designed to maximize insights gained through the experience, and
- expand on—and enlarge—key points and issues.

Questioning is a key skill because it guides learners by eliciting new insights and discoveries. For more on this subject, see Friedman and Yarbrough (1985).

Strategic employee development is anticipatory, designed to avert problems or seize improvement opportunities before they come up. Each developmental experience should be planned for its value in anticipating the collective knowledge or skill needs of a work group. In this way, individuals are guided to learn so as to improve the aggregate talents of the organization and their work groups.

ACTIVITY 9-1 Developing a Formal Mentoring Program in Your Organization: A Brainstorming Exercise

Directions: Use this activity to brainstorm about matters essential to establishing a mentoring program in your organization. Answer the questions which follow. There are no right or wrong responses. Use additional paper if necessary.

Part I—Purpose

1. What is the primary purpose to be served by a mentoring program? Is it to (1) ensure a supply of talent needed to meet long-term organizational requirements? (2) to improve morale? (3) to involve managers and supervisors at all levels in long-term preparation of their employees in a formal way? and (4) to meet some other need? *(Specify.)*

Part II—Objectives

2. What method or methods can be used to demonstrate results from this program? In other words, how can achievement be measured?

Part III—Conditions Favoring the Program

3. What existing conditions in the organization favor establishment of a *formal* mentoring program? (Consider: philosophy of management; recent problems created by lack of necessary human resources; stability of tenure among managers or supervisors at all levels.) How can these conditions be turned to advantage?

ACTIVITY 9-1 Continued

Part IV—Conditions Not Favoring the Program

4. What existing conditions in the organization do not favor establishment of a *formal* mentoring program? (Consider: major emphasis on short-term results; no rewards or recognition associated with long-term grooming of employees; recent scandals about management/supervisory relations with employees.) How can these conditions be corrected?

Part V—Design and Delivery

5. Describe formal elements of the mentoring program which will be needed. Consider such matters as: (1) how mentors/protégés will be matched up; (2) for how long these formal relationships are intended to last; (3) on what basis these relationships can be dissolved; (4) third-party conflict resolution between mentors-protégés; (5) necessary restrictions (if any) on which people are eligible as mentors and as protégés; (6) a description of the mentoring program (that is, a policy); (7) roles of the mentor and the protégé (that is, what are they expected to do?); (8) how developmental experiences are to be selected/negotiated; (9) how expected developmental experiences are to be documented (that is, written down or otherwise clarified); (10) what, if anything, mentors should do during developmental experiences; and (11) how results of developmental experiences are to be used (that is, required debriefings).

ACTIVITY 9-2 Designing a Short-Term Rotation Program for New Employees

Directions: Answer the following questions in the space provided.

Part I—Purpose

1. Clarify the purpose of the rotation program. What is its primary reason for being? What results do you—or other managers—hope to see from this effort?

Part II—Constraints

2. Clarify existing constraints. Consider such matters as: (1) amount of time that can be counted on for new employees (how long are they available? can this time frame be counted on for sure?), (2) degree of support (how much do managers throughout the firm agree with the purpose of this effort? understand it?), (3) degree of cooperation (can everyone be counted on to participate?), and (4) other constraints that you can think of which need to be planned for or considered at the start.

Part III—Objectives

3. What long-term results are sought from this program for each work group and for the organization? How can the relative success of this program be demonstrated over time? (Although you may wish to establish measurable outcomes, you do not have to restrict them to end-of-program outcomes for a program of this kind. In fact, a questionnaire follow-up six months or a year *after* the program may provide better indications of long-term results.)

ACTIVITY 9-2 Continued

Part IV—Program Design

4. Describe the rotation program, including: (1) what departments, work groups, or job sites new employees should be exposed to; (2) how long each of these experiences should last; (3) to whom the employee should be assigned at each site; (4) what special experiences the employee should participate in while at the site; (5) in what order the departments, groups, or sites should be rotated; (6) what special outcomes or results are sought by exposing the employee to these sites; (7) what preparation the employee should receive prior to a new rotation; (8) what special coaching the employee should receive while at each site; and (9) what follow-up or debriefing the employee should receive at the end of each rotation.

Part V—Linkages

5. How will this rotation program link up to classroom-based training efforts and on-the-job training following rotation? Are some linkages between the program and other types of training/education especially desirable? If so, describe what the linkages should be and why they are important.

Part VI—Differences by Employee Type

6. Should some differences in the rotation program exist for employees entering some but not all job classes/positions? If so, describe what additional or specialized experiences should exist for various groups of employees (for example, clerical/secretarial, technical, professional, managerial).

ACTIVITY 9-2   Continued
Part VII—Follow-Up

7. How will the value of the rotation program be demonstrated? Describe how follow-up after the rotations will be planned so as to collect information about its (1) value to newcomers; (2) effects, if any, on subsequent job performance/employee morale or job satisfaction; (3) strengths of the rotation program itself; and (4) weaknesses of the rotation program.

| ACTIVITY 9-3 Critical Incidents ||

Directions: For each critical incident described in the left column, describe in the right column how a supervisor can use the occasion as a developmental experience for an employee. There are no right or wrong answers.

Critical Incident	How Can the Incident be Used for Employee Development?
1. The employee makes a major mistake.	
2. An employee asks about the job duties of another employee.	
3. The work group faces a problem which it has never experienced before.	
4. The supervisor has to be away from work for several hours.	
5. The supervisor confronts a major problem.	
6. The supervisor wants to delegate work.	
7. The employee faces a problem in his or her job which he or she has never experienced before. The employee asks the supervisor for help.	
8. Several new employees enter the work group and need to be "shown the ropes."	
9. A new machine is being introduced to the work site.	

Specialized Employee Development Methods

ACTIVITY 9-4 Assessing Developmental Climate

Directions: Use this activity to assess the general developmental climate of a work group, department, or division. For each characteristic listed in the left column, rate your sense of its presence in the middle column. Then in the right column, describe what should be done to improve the characteristic in the group. Use additional paper if necessary.

Characteristic	To What Extent is the Characteristic Apparent? Not at all To a great extent 0 1 2 3 4 5 6 7	What Can be Done to Improve the Degree to Which the Characteristic is Evident?
1. Open communication exists between *all* members of the group.	0 1 2 3 4 5 6 7	
2. Group members are willing to participate in finding problems before they come up.	0 1 2 3 4 5 6 7	
3. Group members are willing to participate in finding problems after they come up.	0 1 2 3 4 5 6 7	
4. Group members are willing to participate in solving problems after they come up.	0 1 2 3 4 5 6 7	
5. Group members clearly separate the processes of generating and evaluating ideas.	0 1 2 3 4 5 6 7	
6. The group climate is relaxed.	0 1 2 3 4 5 6 7	
7. Group members are courteous to each other.	0 1 2 3 4 5 6 7	
8. Group members support creative ideas.	0 1 2 3 4 5 6 7	

ACTIVITY 9-4 Continued

Characteristic	To What Extent is the Characteristic Apparent? Not at all To a great extent 0 1 2 3 4 5 6 7	What Can be Done to Improve the Degree to Which the Characteristic is Evident?
9. The group maintains a nonauthoritarian point of view.	0 1 2 3 4 5 6 7	
10. Group members are playful in their attitudes when they are coming up with new ideas.	0 1 2 3 4 5 6 7	
11. Group members are open to "crazy ideas."	0 1 2 3 4 5 6 7	
12. Group members strive for consensus.	0 1 2 3 4 5 6 7	

ACTIVITY 9-5 Identifying Problems, Issues, or Challenges Confronting the Work Group

Directions: Use this activity to structure your thinking about problems, issues, or challenges confronting a work group which could benefit from "think tank" experiences. Answer the following questions. Use additional paper if necessary.

Part I—Present Problems

1. What problems, issues, or challenges are confronting the work group, department, or division *at present?* List major ones.

Part II—Future Challenges

2. What problems, issues, or challenges will probably confront the work group, department, or division in the future? List major ones.

Part III—Priorities

3. Prioritize the problems listed in response to questions 1 and 2. List the most important problems first.

Present Problems	Probable Future Problems

ACTIVITY 9-5 Continued

Part IV—Identifying Experiences

4. Which of the priorities, listed in response to question 3, best lend themselves to "think tank" experiences? Explain why you think they lend themselves to such experiences and what kind of think tank experiences they lend themselves to.

Part V—Action Plan

5. Prepare an action plan for a series of planned "think tank" experiences over time for each work group. Tell what should be done, by whom, when, and what outcomes are desired.

ACTIVITY 9-6 A Worksheet for Identifying/Summarizing Present and Desired Future Competencies of an Organization

Directions: Use this worksheet to structure and organize your thinking. Describe in the first part the key competencies of an organization at present. In what ways is it strong relative to other firms in the industry? What is the organization able to do better than any other? Tell why you think it possesses these competencies. Then in Part II, describe the organization's future plans. Finally, in Part III, describe what competencies will be needed to realize these plans.

Part I—Present Competencies

1.

Part II—Future Plans

2.

Part III—Needed Future Competencies

3.

ACTIVITY 9-7 A Worksheet for Identifying/Summarizing Work Group/Department Competencies in Your Organization

Directions: In the left column, list each major department of a firm and, under each department, the units which comprise it. (Example: Personnel department; HRD unit; Compensation unit; Benefits unit; Recruitment unit, etc.) Then in the right column, explain the key competencies of each department/work unit. In short, what makes the unit/department special? How does it contribute, if it does, to key strengths/competencies of the organization as a whole? Simply describe. Use additional paper if necessary.

Departments/Work Units	Key Competencies

ACTIVITY 9-8 A Worksheet for Identifying Appropriate Employee Development Efforts in an Organization

Directions: Answer the questions which follow.

I—Discrepancies

1. What discrepancies exist between the present competencies of the firm and those needed/desired in the future? Describe them.

2. What discrepancies exist between the present and desired future competencies of each department and each work group in the firm? Describe them.

Department/Work Group	Discrepancies Between Present/ Desired Future Competencies

ACTIVITY 9-8 Continued

II—Employee Development Efforts

3. What employee development efforts are appropriate in each work group or department to narrow gaps between *present and desired future competencies?* Describe them.

Department/Work Group	Appropriate Employee Development Efforts

ACTIVITY 9-9 Pinpointing Resources to Meet Strategic Employee Development Needs

Directions: For each work group or department in the organization, summarize appropriate employee development needs in line with long-term Strategic Business Planning requirements, and then identify people or other resources—inside or outside the organization—which can help satisfy those requirements and meet those needs. (If none, write "none.") Use additional paper if necessary.

Department/Work Group	Employee Development Needs	Resources

ACTIVITY 9-10 A Case Study on Employee Development

Directions: Read over the case which follows and answer the questions at the end.

Larkin Memorial Hospital* is a full-service regional medical facility in a medium-sized city.

Larkin recently hired a management consulting firm to conduct an attitude survey of hospital employees. Among the results of that survey: Larkin should establish a comprehensive HRD program with particular emphasis on supervisory and management training, education, and development.

Larkin has long offered Staff Development activities to such professionals as nurses, medical technicians, and physicians. However, it has not offered in-house courses on supervision. The hospital administrator once summed up the reason why: "Let them go out to the local university if they want to learn about that." Clearly, employees did not agree with that sentiment, so hospital administrators grudgingly decided to hire a full-time Management Development Coordinator.

Larkin, like some Midwestern hospitals, has had difficulty recruiting professionals—particularly nurses. Those hired are typically assigned to special units like Intensive Care, the Emergency Room, and others. Each unit is led by a Head Nurse, who is on duty eight hours a day during a forty-hour work week. The remainder of the time, a Charge Nurse is responsible for the unit. Charge Nurses are selected from experienced staff in the unit. They rotate—different people take turns in this capacity. Charge nurses receive no training, informal or formal, to carry out their duties.

The Management Development Coordinator hired at Larkin will be asked to set up a comprehensive HRD program for nurses at the hospital. It will combine classroom-based training, organized employee education, and employee development.

Questions

1. What problems, if any, do you suppose are created by the present Charge Nurse system at Larkin?
2. How can the Charge Nurse system be used to advantage—as a developmental activity, for example? What should be done to convert it from its present form to a valuable developmental experience?

*A fictitious name for a real organization.

Specialized Employee Development Methods

10

EMPLOYEE EDUCATION

Imagine for a moment that you are a supervisor on a highly automated assembly line. Eleven people work on it—yourself, a mechanic, a supplier, four machine operators, three packaging operators, and one laborer. Your responsibility is to keep the line in operation. The mechanic makes repairs; the supplier transports raw materials to the line, finished goods from the line, and makes light repairs to machines; machine operators operate equipment; packaging operators watch trouble spots on the line; and the laborer serves as janitor. The plant is not unionized.

One day you arrive at work to find that the mechanic, line supplier, and one machine operator have called in sick. You waste little time contacting the production manager. But you are told, "tough luck—you'll have to work with the crew you have." "But," you begin, "they don't know each other's jobs." What do you do?

If this problem strikes a responsive chord, then you should appreciate the value of employee education. This chapter defines employee education, emphasizing its relationship to career planning activities of individuals and career planning programs sponsored by organizations.

WHAT IS EMPLOYEE EDUCATION?

According to Nadler (1984), employee "education is learning to prepare the individual for a different but identified job" (p. 1.19). It can mean preparation for a promotion or transfer permanently or only for a day or so; it can mean preparation for one specific job or for any one of a group of related jobs (Nadler, 1984). The point is that employee education focuses on changing *individuals*. In this respect, it is unlike employee development, which focuses on changing the collective knowledge and skills of a work group or an organization; it is unlike training, which focuses on job requirements. Employee education is a tool for *anticipatory socialization*, the process by which an individual acquires information about—and experience in—a job or role prior to entry to it (Feldman, 1976 & 1981).

Traditionally, employee education prepares people for future work. However, it is not truly future-oriented, because most educational efforts perpetuate notions based on the experiences of others and on conventional wisdom about "right" and "wrong" ways of "doing things around here." Education thus passes on cultural norms from one generation of job incumbents to the next. It is for this reason that radical changes—major departures from past group and organizational traditions—frequently require leaders brought in from outside (Glueck & Jauch, 1984). There is a large and growing body of information about the leadership skills necessary to effect change, particularly countercultural or transformational change, in organizations (for example, Deal & Kennedy, 1982; Harrison, 1984; Kanter, 1983; Kiefer & Stroh, 1984; Vaill, 1982).

To be effective, traditional and thus culturally-bound employee education must be based on a comprehensive career program. While it is possible to "groom" individuals for new jobs without considering career issues, such short-term planning is often counterproductive if individuals are given no opportunity to participate in decisions affecting their future. Why? Consider: there is already evidence that employees and managers alike perceive career advancement opportunities to be severely limited in their organizations (see Table 10-1). Long-term trends in the demographic composition of the work force lend credence to this view, because the crowded cohorts of the baby boom generation are competing for dwindling numbers of higher-level jobs (Leach & Chakiris, 1985; Spruell, 1985). Without long-term attention to career issues, "current feelings about advancement . . . are not likely to offset managers' concerns

TABLE 10-1 PERCEPTIONS ABOUT ADVANCEMENT OPPORTUNITIES

Question: How would you rate your company on opportunity for advancement?

	Very Good/Good	
	1980–1982	1983–present
Manager	49%	44%
Exempt	35%	30%
Nonexempt	19%	22%

Source: Morgan & Schiemann, 1986, p. 104. Reprinted with permission from *Personnel Journal*.

about lower job security and increased work pressure. Instead, they are likely to act in conjunction with other negative feelings to increase the likelihood of departure and to decrease loyalty and commitment" (Morgan & Schiemann, 1986, p. 104).

Career programs that make employee education genuinely effective have two components: *organizational* and *individual* (Sredl & Rothwell, 1987). What individuals do in planning their careers should be matched by different but corresponding organizational efforts (Walker, 1973). After all, "every employee is influenced by management actions at each step of his or her career" (Walker, 1980, p. 251). Hence, employee education stems from career programs in which individuals plan what they want to do and who they want to become. At the same time, managers should plan how many people and what kinds of skills they need over time. Employee education is one vehicle for realizing individual career aspirations.

A *career* means all jobs held by a person in the course of his or her life span (Werther & Davis, 1985); *career planning* is the process of identifying career goals and the means of achieving them (Werther & Davis, 1985); *career development* connotes activities undertaken by an individual to realize career aspirations (Werther & Davis, 1985); *career management* is the process of charting out and describing relationships between jobs in an organization; *career education* consists of learning experiences which enrich individual understanding of career issues; and *career counseling* means helping individuals sort out career issues and make career decisions.

CAREER PLANNING: SOME CONSIDERATIONS

Employee education is rarely adequate by itself to ensure promotion or other career moves. Individuals must, for example, maintain at least adequate—and quite often above average—job performance in their present jobs to be considered for advancement (Werther & Davis, 1985). Additional elements may also be important:

- *visibility:* How well-known is an employee to superiors and to supervisors in units to which the employee would like to move? Does an employee's name come up if somebody says, "who is ready to be promoted?"
- *willingness to move:* Is the employee willing to leave the present work group to further his or her career? If the answer is no, the employee's potential for growth is restricted (Magnus & Dodd, 1981; Sinetar, 1986).
- *mentors:* How successfully has an individual identified and established mentoring relationships with people who can further his or her career?
- *luck:* How lucky has the individual been? Has he or she been at the right place at the right time? While luck should not be relied on, it can be an important element in career progress (*Choosing a Career,* 1982).

By way of background prior to a more detailed treatment of employee education, let's discuss career planning in organizations and individual career planning.

CAREER PLANNING IN ORGANIZATIONS

A good place to begin when thinking about career planning from the organization's perspective is with the distinction between internal and external labor markets. According to labor economists, the *external labor market* consists of people *outside* the firm or craft. The *internal labor market* consists of people *inside* the firm or craft. To be more specific, "the internal labor market is defined as an administrative unit, such as a plant, office, or construction site, within which the pricing and allocation of labor are determined primarily by a set of prescribed rules rather than by impersonal market forces" (Marshall, Briggs, & King, 1984, p. 336). Managers inside a firm enjoy much flexibility in setting wage scales, structuring work into jobs, and creating jobs. While such decisions are affected by external labor demands, managers exercise considerable control over who they choose to promote, prepare for other jobs, or compensate for work performed.

A related issue is the *dual labor market theory*. Economists have long emphasized the existence of primary and secondary markets outside organizations. The aim of programs created by the Manpower Development and Training Act of 1962, the Comprehensive Employment and Training Act of 1973, and the Job Training Partnership Act of 1983 has been to lift disadvantaged individuals from the secondary to the primary labor market through government-sponsored training efforts and government-subsidized employer incentives.

Primary and secondary labor markets may also exist *inside* organizations (Doeringer & Piore, 1971; Marshall, Briggs, & King, 1984). Some people enter jobs after careful screening. The jobs require unique skills, such as specialized academic training or prior experience. Workers of this kind are in line to receive more training, education, and development. This part of the organization's labor force is the *primary labor market*. In contrast, people hired into the firm after less rigorous screening to carry out jobs not requiring advance preparation comprise the *secondary labor market*. The latter group is often comprised of inordinately large numbers of women and minorities. As a result, much attention has been focused in recent years on special career programs to bridge gaps between secondary and primary labor markets within firms (Brimmer, 1982; Doll, Sullivan, Simmonetti, & Erwin, 1982; Flanders & Anderson, 1973; Gray, Loeffler, & Cooper, 1982; Harley & Koff, 1980; Hammer, 1983; Lee, 1986; Raudsepp, 1983; Robson, 1983; Stewart & Gudykunst, 1982; Stinson, 1983; *Women are Moving,* 1983).

Formalized career planning may serve any number of different purposes—and some more emphatically than others. These purposes include (Werther & Davis, 1985): (1) developing employees who are ready for short-term or permanent movement to different jobs; (2) reducing absenteeism and turnover (Hinrichs, 1980); (3) cultivating realization of individual potential; (4) motivating employees to establish their own career objectives and act on them; (5) increasing management awareness of available talent within the firm; (6) helping satisfy employee needs for advancement, recognition, and achievement; (7) contributing to organizational preparation for long-term trends which might pose threats to, or opportunities for, strategic success; and (8) meeting Affirmative Action goals. Without management support for any or all these purposes, however, no formalized career program is likely to be successful.

Steps in Establishing a Formal, Organizational Career Planning Program

To establish a formal, organizational career planning program, HRD practitioners and line managers in the firm should:

1. develop a climate conducive to career planning,
2. establish a career policy in line with Strategic Business Plans, HR plans, individual career plans, and Organizational Strategy for HRD,
3. analyze work, including jobs and career paths/ladders,
4. analyze the work force, including data on groups and individuals, and
5. identify future needs for work and the work force.

Developing a climate conducive to career planning. Managers play important parts in career planning. First of all, top managers set the tone. How much are they committed to a formal career planning program in the firm? If the answer is "not much" or "they'll only pay lip service to it," then the career program faces a problem from the start. In all likelihood, a career planning program cannot succeed if it lacks complete top management support and is not linked to, and supported by, other planning initiatives. Quite simply, top managers must see some point to the whole effort before they will back it. In many cases, it is up to HRD practitioners and line managers to make the case for a formal career planning program.

A good place to start is with career planning for supervisors and managers. Results of several surveys reveal that a lack of sufficient numbers and kinds of leaders to meet future organizational needs is an issue top managers are concerned about (*Basic HRD,* 1981; Foltz, Rosenberg, & Foehrenbach, 1982; Nkomo, 1986). If a career planning program begins as a means to deal with the problem of management succession planning, it may well garner real support from top managers. In time, career planning efforts can be expanded to include all employees.

Top managers are not the only ones whose support is crucial to the successful implementation of a career planning program. Support from immediate supervisors is essential. There are several reasons why. First, immediate superiors exert tremendous influence over subordinates. Effective superiors advise employees about handling job tasks and dealing with organizational politics. Supervisors influence employee career progress by influencing individual work habits, work assignments, and developmental or educational opportunities to which individuals are exposed (Bronikowski, 1983).

An employee's peers also influence the success of career planning programs. Without trust in management and faith in organizational practices, they may sabotage the implementation of such programs. They affect how much people are willing to participate in career planning.

Use Activity 10-1 at the end of this chapter to assess the climate for formal career planning in an organization.

Establishing career policy. A career policy is an official pronouncement by an organization's management which articulates the organization's stance on career issues. It puts the organization on the record regarding company responsibilities for career matters. Specific issues should be covered in such a policy. They include:

- *purpose of the program:* What is the major purpose of the program? Are there limitations on its scope?
- *responsibilities of the individual:* What is the role of the individual in the program? What should the individual *do?*
- *responsibilities of the organization:* What are the responsibilities of the organization and its managers? What should they *do?*
- *methods of administering the program:* Who does what? Are one or more special committees appropriate for administering the program? If so, what committees? What are they to do? Why?
- *methods of carrying out the program:* What features of a career planning program are to be used by an individual?
- *provisions (if any) for special groups or needs:* How much does management want to gear specialized career programs to meet the unique problems experienced by women, minorities, the handicapped, the functionally illiterate, or other groups?
- *Relationships between career planning and*
  —*strategic business plans:* How does career planning contribute to the realization of Strategic Business Plans and company purpose?
  —*HR plans:* What relationships should exist between career plans and other HR efforts? How does a career program contribute to the realization of HR plans?
  —*HRD Effort:* What should be the relationship between career planning policy and HRD policy? Between career planning and employee development, education, and training?

A sample career policy is shown in Table 10-2.

Career planning policy provides direction to career planning efforts. Without unified direction, employees in one work group or department will probably receive treatment entirely different from those in other departments. Some managers may even try to "hoard" good people and thus thwart individual career advancement so as to make their own jobs easier. This practice stifles individual growth and is not beneficial to the company in the long run. A formal career policy provides a foundation for consistent and equitable practices across the organization.

Once adopted, a career policy should be relatively enduring. As Nadler and Wiggs (1986) note, "policies, like an organization's charter (its constitution and by-laws), should be relatively stable, but they should not be written in concrete and difficult to change if and when the need arises" (p. 19). Remember that an individual's career can span an entire lifetime, from kindergarten through retirement. Even in one firm an individual may hold many different jobs in a career spanning a thirty or forty year period. "Estimates show that during his or her career, the average 47-year-old manager will take on a new managerial position between three and nine times" (*A*

TABLE 10-2 A SAMPLE CAREER POLICY
Purpose
To make the best use of the human resources of the [organization] and to identify and accommodate compatible career objectives of employees, it is essential that the [organization] state its position on career planning.
General policy
The [organization] is committed to the idea of helping individuals achieve their career objectives within the [organization], provided that employees (1) accept responsibility for their own learning and growth; and (2) make every effort to improve their job performance and prepare for future growth, including vertical *and* horizontal advancement in their jobs.
Procedures

The [organization] will:
 	
1. Sponsor a voluntary seminar on general career planning principles each year.
2. Make available, in self-study form, instructional materials on individual career planning.
3. Maintain a formal career planning program, distinct from past-oriented employee performance appraisals, in which each employee and his/her supervisor* will:
   a. Discuss the employee's potential in the [organization] as that potential relates to the needs of the [organization].
   b. Negotiate annual career objectives.
   c. Negotiate an action plan to achieve the annual career objectives of the individual through a combination of any or all of the following:
     • External training, education, or conferences.
     • Internal training/education seminars.
     • Self-study learning projects, both formal and informal.
     • Planned job assignments for developmental purposes.
     • Assigned reading.
     • College courses.
     • Other methods of learning.
4. Ensure that all career action plans are forwarded to the HRD Department to help in locating resources, seminars, and other events which will provide the means for employees to meet their career objectives.
5. Provide a means for employees to share the benefits of their learning insights with others, particularly those with similar learning and career objectives. Methods for this may include:
   a. Informal briefings to other employees about their insights/learning experiences—particularly when gained through attendance at external conferences, seminars, and workshops.
   b. Formal in-house training courses in areas of general organizational need.

*Supervisors may attend a voluntary seminar each year to help them learn how to identify training needs and how to serve as career counselors.

Myth, 1987, p. 8). Changes in career policy, while appropriate when business plans or Organizational Strategy for HRD are changed, should not be undertaken lightly. The reason is that changes in career policy may well be interpreted by employees as affecting their chances for advancement or career mobility. The general idea is to align career planning processes and outcomes to be consistent with Strategic Business Plans. However, *radical* changes may well give a signal to individuals that career opportunities are not as good as they once were. A predictable result is turnover, as employees preparing themselves in line with one set of career expectations suddenly find that those expectations no longer apply, and move to another firm where prospects appear brighter.

Employee education and strategic business plans. Employee education, like other HRD efforts, can serve as a tool for helping to (1) equip managers with skills needed to formulate Strategic Business Plans in problem-solving groups or meetings; and (2) implement Strategic Business Plans when used to prepare employees for their next jobs or series of jobs.

Many large corporations formulate their strategic plans, and follow up periodically on performance linked to those plans, in meetings and retreats (O'Connor, 1980a & 1980b; Rothwell & Kazanas, 1986). To a major extent, group performance in these settings depends on the willingness and ability of members to interact (Schein, 1969). Climate is influenced by leader and situation (Fiedler, 1967); the willingness and ability of members to interact are influenced by the interpersonal skills of the members themselves. Leaders can be trained to run more effective and creative meetings (Lewis, 1975), and members can be educated to improve their interaction (Schein, 1969). In these ways, then, *employee education can be instrumental in formulating Strategic Business Plans.*

By the same token, *educational efforts can help implement plans.* Remember that education is geared to preparing people for the skills they will need "for a different but identified job" (Nadler, 1984, p. 1.19). Often it is used in preparation for a promotion. That is not necessarily its sole use. It can also help prepare people for lateral transfers, demotions, retirement, outplacement, or enrichment of a present job.

But for implementing strategy, educational efforts for promotion are crucial. The reason is that leadership at all levels must be consistent with business strategy. Particularly at the highest levels, it is important to make sure that managers have appropriate attitudes and skills to make strategy work. While individuals find it difficult to change (Staw, 1976), they can be groomed at lower levels for promotion in ways calculated to ensure that they possess skills consistent with future organizational needs. In this way, employee education can help implement Strategic Business Plans.

Employee education and HR plans. Employee education helps narrow gaps between present HR supplies and future HR demands. Talent within the firm can be tapped and educated to meet pending or existing HR needs. Employee education also prepares people for movement to specific jobs or job categories over time.

Employee education and career plans. Career planning is the responsibility of the individual. However, it is also the responsibility of managers and HRD practitioners to ensure that the foundation is laid for meaningful planning by describing relationships between jobs in a firm. *Employee education is a means by which to prepare individuals for movement along a career path.*

Employee education and organizational strategy for HRD. Recall that Organizational Strategy for HRD is the direction for all planned learning activities in the organization over time. While not driven solely by business or HR plans, Organizational Strategy for HRD should be compatible with them. Employee education is an intermediate-term change effort, much like coordinative planning is intermediate-term when compared to Strategic Business Plans. The primary thrust of employee education is not in determining what should be offered in the way of planned learning, an issue considered in strategy formulation; rather, *the thrust is in the appropriate deployment of resources/activities to support efforts in line with organizational and individual needs.*

In the framework of an integrated Organizational Strategy for HRD, employee education focuses on individual learning objectives. It helps meet individual career objectives and organizational objectives on an intermediate-term basis extending from one to three years. Of course, employee educational efforts should be integrated with other HRD initiatives—such as development and training—so that the cumulative effect of the HRD Effort is greater than the sum of its individual parts.

Work analysis. The starting point for implementing a formal CP program is work analysis and career path analysis (see Burack & Mathys, 1979; Rothwell & Kazanas, 1988; Walker, 1980).

According to Walker (1980), "work analysis is a process of gathering and examining information on the principle work activities" in a position and the qualifications (skills, knowledge, abilities, and other individual attributes) necessary to perform these activities" (pp. 144-45). Work analysis addresses two specific questions: (1) What are the activities/outcomes of each job? and (2) What knowledge, skills, and attitudes (KSAs) are needed by a job incumbent to carry out those activities or achieve those outcomes?

Work analysis is a logical starting point for career planning. It is necessary to know what people are presently doing and what knowledge, skills, and attitudes they presently possess before it is possible to assist them in planning for their next job or career move or to identify how their knowledge or skills may be most appropriately used in the future to help narrow gaps between present HR supplies and the future HR demands of the organization. In any case, a present job is the point of convergence between the individual and the organization (Walker, 1980). It thus represents a place to start in planning.

There are many approaches to work analysis. Depending on how detailed they are, work analysis is synonymous with job, activity, or task analysis. No single approach is satisfactory for all uses; rather, each is more appropriate for some uses more than for others.

It is not our intention to describe all work analysis methods here. That exceeds the scope of this section. It is, in any case, treated by us elsewhere (Rothwell & Kazanas, 1988).

The focus of work analysis is traditionally on the present job. It is most appropriately used in planning *training,* a topic treated in the next chapter. However, work analysis must be carried out before it is possible to identify *career paths,* "descriptions of the possible alternative sequences of jobs that an individual may hold in an organizational career" (Walker, 1980, p. 151). The latter is the appropriate focus of employee education and a necessary requirement in formal career planning/programs.

For more information on work analysis, see Levine, Ash, Hall, and Sistrunk (1983), McCormick (1979) and Markowitz (1981).

Career path analysis. A career path is an "explicit description of possible alternative sequences of jobs that an individual may hold in an organizational career" (Walker, 1980, p. 151). This definition is not universally accepted—some writers prefer to consider paths leading outside a firm as well as those inside it (for example, Werther & Davis, 1985). But it serves our purposes.

There are two types of career paths: (1) *formal,* made explicit by the organization; and (2) *informal,* made explicit by examining historical movements of employees. *Career path analysis* is literally the process of analyzing career paths. There are two different but related types: (1) *prescriptive,* detailing logical relationships between jobs and logically-related knowledge and skills necessary to qualify for movement from one job to the next; and (2) *descriptive,* detailing historical employment experiences of individuals who have moved through the ranks over time.

If we lived in a perfect and stable world, there would never be a difference between formal and informal career paths. But the world is not perfect. Career progression does not depend solely on qualifications nor on fairness. Ample evidence proves that more elusive elements play a part; among them in-house politics, personal favoritism, visibility, timing, luck, family influence, ethnic background, and race (Dalton, 1951). It is not too surprising, then, that neither managers nor employees are certain of performance requirements on the present job, let alone requirements for advancement to a new job (Bernardin & Abbott, 1985; Chinoy, 1955; Goldner, 1970; Kanter, 1977; Vroom & MacCrimmon, 1968).

Establishing *formal* career paths is not difficult, at least in theory. They can be based on

- *work activities:* An activity is what people do to meet job requirements.
- *work behaviors:* Behaviors are observable actions taken to carry out work activities.
- *work perceptions:* Perceptions are what people believe.

To base career paths on work activities, managers must have access to current information about job duties. They (Walker, 1980):

1. collect data about activities involved in each job, how important these activities are, and how much time is devoted to them,
2. infer from job information what knowledge and skills are necessary for incumbents to perform each activity,

3. group jobs together in "families" or "clusters" based on common knowledge and skills,
4. pinpoint logical patterns of movement between jobs, based on similarities in knowledge and skills required, and
5. assemble results of all such analyses for the entire organization.

It is not necessary to undertake a time-consuming study of jobs to assemble career paths of this type; rather, job titles are simply listed in logical progression. It is even possible, using this approach, to identify so-called *dual career ladders* in which individuals can choose between increasing technical competence *or* increasing responsibility for supervising other people. The latter is associated with vertical movement on the chain of command; the former is associated with horizontal movement to higher levels of skill proficiency in the present job.

To base career paths on work behaviors rather than activities, managers go beyond job titles or job descriptions. They focus instead on relationships between actual behaviors or work outcomes/results in different jobs. This analysis is more time-consuming, but is potentially more useful than activity analysis.

There are two different, though related, ways to carry out career path analysis based on behaviors. One is called the *discrepancy method;* the other is the *competency-based method.*

The discrepancy method assumes that the highest-level jobs are terminal ones, at least from the standpoint of the internal labor market. (Of course, it is possible to make a career move to another organization, but that possibility is not emphasized.) Instead, top-level jobs are viewed as terminal steps in possible career paths. Managers then:

1. analyze each highest-level job in terms of skills, knowledge, and behaviors equated with successful performance,
2. examine jobs immediately below these highest-level ones,
3. compare each high-level job to those immediately below it to identify differences between behaviors/skills required for successful performance at each level,
4. compare differences at each hierarchical level between jobs,
5. continue the process from the top to the bottom of the organization's hierarchy of authority, and
6. identify instructional needs (differences between jobs) which have to be satisfied by individuals desiring to move vertically, horizontally, or diagonally to other jobs.

Figure 10-1 helps clarify these distinctions.

The competency-based method is more challenging. For each activity carried out in each job, the analyst: (1) identifies tangible outputs or outcomes traditionally associated with it; (2) describes behaviors—not one but several—associated with successful performance; (3) pinpoints critical behaviors linked to successful performance; and (4) develops clusters of related jobs, regardless of titles or placements within departments. This method is based on key results sought in each job.

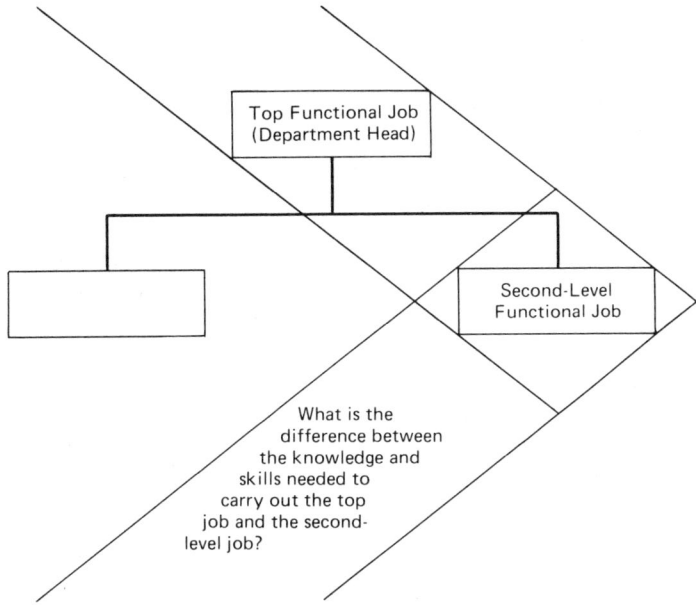

Figure 10-1: An Illustration of the Discrepancy Method of Career Path Analysis

To base career paths on work perceptions and experiences, managers rely on common interpretations of many people. Managers:

1. ask experienced people to describe their past jobs, past assignments, and other matters that people feel have contributed to their career progress,
2. ask these people to advise lower-level employees about what future jobs to prepare for, what future assignments to seek, and what educational opportunities to take advantage of, and
3. identify any similarities between these stories.

Through these steps, HRD practitioners can answer such questions as: Are there common historical patterns in career paths? What are they? Are they still applicable? If so, why? If not, why not?

This description of career paths has been necessarily brief. For more on this topic see Burack and Mathys (1979), Rothwell and Kazanas (1988), and Walker (1980).

Work force analysis. The counterpoint of work analysis is work force analysis, the process of taking stock of the numbers and kinds of people employed by the organization at present and expected to be needed in the future. The work force can be analyzed by focusing on individuals, positions, occupational groups, or by departments, divisions, or work groups. Each focus is useful in its own ways.

Work force analysis by individual. There can be a considerable difference between two individuals functioning in the same job.

Most organizations hire numerous people into a few entry-level jobs. Each person occupies one position, but there may be any number of positions sharing the same job title and the same general job description. To cite a simple example: both the Production Manager's secretary and the Training Director's secretary share the same title. Technically, they function at the same level and in common jobs. Yet each position really has different duties.

At the same time, no two individuals fill the same job or position in precisely the same ways. Each person has his or her own role expectations, strengths and weaknesses, and unique aspirations for the future. As a consequence, distinct differences may exist in how two individuals carry out the same job.

One way to analyze individuals is by their backgrounds. For example, they may be asked to describe their education, prior experience outside the firm, prior experience inside the firm, training programs completed, specialized knowledge of foreign languages, and familiarity with computer languages.

Another way to analyze individuals is by their performance appraisal ratings. How well have they been rated by superiors? Are historical patterns discernible? Have they done better in some capacities than in others?

A third way to analyze individuals is by *aspirations* (what they want to be) or *expectations* (what they believe they will be). This information reveals important clues about motivation. It can be cross-checked with work history. Have they been willing to undertake difficult tasks or activities in their lives? If so, how well have they fared?

Work force analysis by position. What people occupy jobs in the organization at present? What kind *should* be occupying those jobs in the future? These questions are addressed by work force analysis when it is conducted position-by-position.

Perhaps the most common example of this type of analysis is succession or replacement planning, which is usually restricted to upper echelons of the management hierarchy. In reality, it is a form of disaster planning. Suppose the Chief Executive suddenly dies of a heart attack. Who takes over? Succession plans answer this question, providing for orderly transition until a permanent replacement can be selected.

Nothing prevents succession or replacement planning from being extended all the way down the organization. Of course, that would not be as simple as it sounds. Since turnover is highest at the lowest organizational levels (Wanous, 1980), succession plans would have to be updated frequently so as to be kept current. That would of course require much staff time and effort, neither of which is inexpensive. Hence, concentrated attention on succession planning would have to be explicitly linked to organizational and departmental objectives and plans to prove worthwhile.

Succession planning also helps identify long-term staffing issues or problems warranting attention. In one organization, for example, personnel practitioners discovered through succession planning that the firm's entire top management team would retire over a ten-year period. Of course, information of that kind is useful in preparing for predictable losses in personnel talent, dramatizing the need for employee development *and* employee education adequate to avert future problems.

Of course, work force analysis by position need not be limited solely to replacement planning. In some job categories, it is important to plan for a mix of skills not restricted to specific academic training or professional experience. In fact, many different backgrounds may be deliberately sought to create constructive conflict rather than the conformist thinking which arises in groups where all members share identical academic training and similar work experience.

To analyze the work force by position, group together everyone with the same job titles. Then, by individual, list pertinent facts. These facts may be about academic training/degrees by field, prior experience, length of services, and other factors deemed relevant. This list is a snapshot of the work force as it currently exists. The next step involves making value judgements. What individuals *should* be in those positions? Why?

Work force analysis by occupational group. An occupational group is a related cluster of jobs. For example, everyone in a firm may be classified into such groups as management/administrative, technical, professional, clerical/secretarial, skilled, and unskilled labor (Gordon, 1986). Each group comprises two or more job titles sharing common characteristics. People occupying those groups are then examined much as they are by position.

Work force analysis by department, division, or work group. A final and more or less obvious method of work force analysis is by structural unit—department-by-department, work group-by-work group.

There are two ways to do this: (1) by position or job title, and (2) by skill. It is simple enough to list all job titles in a department. In many cases, that can be done in a few minutes. It requires nothing more than an organization chart.

It is not such a simple matter to inventory skill. There may be no problem at all in listing such indicators as individual education, prior jobs inside and outside the organization, hobbies and avocations, and knowledge of foreign languages. Yet these are not really "skills," defined by *Webster's Dictionary* as "developed proficiency or dexterity in some art, craft . . . deftness in execution or performance." They may *indicate* that skills exist, but they are not skills *themselves*. To gather skill information at a detailed level, the supervisor—and perhaps individuals as well—have to log relative performance on each work task and then develop some inventory of who can do what and how well they can do it.

Naturally, such an effort is time-consuming and may not be worth the effort. Yet it does furnish detailed information about the skill required for each work activity performed by each department or work group. That might be important to know when there is a need to prepare another person for job tasks or to consider the job incumbent for promotion. It is also helpful to know who the best performers happen to be, because they are often the most appropriate role models, mentors, and (sometimes) on-the-job instructors for others about to move into similar positions.

Identifying future needs for work and the work force. No task, work activity, job, or even career path remains the same forever. Nor do individuals remain the same. Under the influence of environmental changes, organizations change what they do. Similarly, changes eventually occur in tasks, activities, jobs, and even career paths. As individuals change what they do, their skills also change.

A simple example may help clarify this point. Suppose a large, prominent manufacturer of baby food analyzes the environment and discovers that birth rates in the U.S. are declining. Demand for baby food will probably level off, as will sales. Top managers must then decide what to do. One choice, of course, is to do nothing. Management simply acknowledges that the market itself is stagnating or even declining. Perhaps they may choose to increase their commanding lead in market share by cutting into the business of their competitors. Other choices are possible: (1) increasing efficiency and thus profitability by preserving the same level of output but reducing inputs (for example, reducing the number of workers); (2) developing new markets by expanding in foreign countries where birth rates *are* on the rise; (3) diversifying into new, more promising product or service lines; or (4) integrating with suppliers of critical raw materials or distributors through purchases, mergers, or takeovers.

Each strategy has unique advantages and disadvantages. The point is that some choices—like increasing efficiency—may lead to actions within the firm which change *how work is done* and *what skills are needed to do that work*. Choices like foreign expansion imply that skills probably not existing within the firm at present will have to be found.

To identify future needs for work and the work force, managers and/or HRD practitioners should scan the future to determine how work will probably be done and what skills will probably be needed to do it (Rothwell & Kazanas, 1988). There are four steps in this process:

1. clarifying the present status of the organization, work, work force, and relationships (career paths) between jobs,
2. identifying what environmental changes will affect the organization, work, work force, and relationships between jobs,
3. envisioning what the future will probably look like or what managers want it to look like, and
4. stepping back into the present to plan for the future.

We have already treated the first step, clarifying present status. Traditionally, that is as far as most writers on this subject take it.

Subsequent steps have already been treated at greater length elsewhere. Scanning the environment was discussed in Chapter 4 of this text; identifying future work, work force and career paths was treated in another text (Rothwell & Kazanas, 1988).

Once these steps are completed, it is possible to shift perspective back to the present and plan for the future.

Employee education is one means by which to prepare individuals for the future, both in terms of their own career movement, and in terms of changes wrought by external conditions.

CAREER PLANNING: INDIVIDUAL ISSUES

Career planning is a joint responsibility of the organization and the individual. Managers, as agents of the organization, should clarify career paths, provide a climate conducive to career planning, encourage time spent in cultivating individuals, and make resources available so people can achieve their career objectives. On the other hand, individuals should take advantage of opportunities provided to them and accept responsibility for managing their careers.

Purposes of Career Planning

From the individual's standpoint, formalized career planning:

1. establishes direction for occupational pursuits,
2. establishes time frames and objectives against which to measure individual career progress,
3. motivates the individual to act and assume responsibility for his or her career,
4. dramatizes emerging conflicts between career objectives and personal objectives of an individual's life, and
5. points up the value of training, education, and employee developmental efforts as tools for helping individuals achieve their career objectives.

Some people also value career planning for its usefulness in discovering their *career anchors*—"patterns of self-perceived talents, motives and values [which] serve to guide, constrain, stabilize, and integrate a person's career" (Schein, 1978, p. 127)—such as the need for security, autonomy, creativity, technical competence, or the need for power, status, and advancement.

A Model of Individual Career Planning

Many self-help books are available on individual career planning (for example, Adams, 1975; Albrecht, 1983; Bolles, 1986; Hagberg & Leider, 1982; Schmidt, 1983). To carry out planning, individuals should:

1. clarify their personal values and identities,
2. make some decisions about the kind of people they would like to become in the future and the kind of jobs in which they would like to work,
3. assess present personal strengths and weaknesses,
4. scan the future environment and pinpoint threats and opportunities affecting career progress, and
5. establish a long-term career strategy.

This model resembles Strategic Business Planning—and it is intended to (Rosenthal, 1983; Rothwell, 1984b).

Clarifying personal values and identity. Career planning efforts start with the clarification of personal values and identity. Too often people make no effort to do this until they encounter a personal crisis—or expect one in the near future (Janis & Mann, 1977; Remer & O'Neill, 1980). In this respect, personal values clarification is much like organizational planning, which is also stimulated by crisis (Beer, 1980).

Individuals can clarify their values and identity on their own or with special counseling. Many instruments exist which can aid in this process, helping provide feedback to individuals about their own interests and values (Isaacson, 1985).

Making decisions. It is not enough just to clarify present identity and values. Individuals should also envision what kind of person they would like to become and the career or job in which they would like to work. Much like organizational planning, this process works best when people envision their idealized selves or idealized jobs and then gradually work toward the realization of this ideal (Ginzberg, 1972).

Assessing personal strengths and weaknesses. At first glance it may seem that assessing personal strengths and weaknesses is really the same as clarifying personal values. That is not true, because assessment of needs has to be made in comparison with something else. Once individuals are aware of their occupational interests, they are ready to consider how well their present skills match up to what is necessary for entry to and advancement in a specific occupation. Whatever characteristics tend to improve their chances for entry to a field or advancement in a career are *strengths;* conversely, whatever characteristics tend to detract from their chances for entry or advancement are *weaknesses.*

Scanning the future environment. Conditions do not remain the same forever. They change. Just as strategists scan the environment to identify trends which may pose threats to or opportunities for accomplishment of stated organizational objectives, so should individuals scan environments inside and outside their employing firm and occupation. Key trends to consider include: the economy, technology, the labor market in the occupation, social trends, and noticeable geographical movement of practitioners and businesses. How will these affect achievement of career objectives?

Establishing a long-term career strategy. Business strategists compare organizational strengths/weaknesses to environmental threats/opportunities as a basis for establishing long-term plans. Individuals should also compare their present career strengths/weaknesses to future environmental threats/opportunities as a basis for career strategy.

Employee education is a tool to

- build on present strengths,
- rectify present weaknesses,
- take advantage of future opportunities,
- minimize the effects of future environmental threats, and
- narrow gaps between actual/present and desired/future knowledge, skills, and abilities.

Of course, a key difference between organizational and individual career planning is that individuals routinely can—and do—consider available opportunities outside one organization or occupation. In contrast, not many organizations provide advice about movements to other firms—except perhaps in outplacement programs or large-scale decruitment connected with a plant or facility shutdown (Krajci, 1987).

EMPLOYEE EDUCATION

"Education," write Gutteridge and Hutcheson (1984), "is the portion of HRD that is generally associated most closely with career development" (p. 30.22). Assuming that managers have laid out career paths in an organization and established other key components of a career planning system, and that individuals have planned for their careers, they are ready to plan employee education.

But how are employee education efforts planned from the organization's standpoint and from an individual's standpoint? How is employee education delivered? How are educational efforts tied to Organizational Strategy for HRD? This section addresses these questions.

Planning Educational Efforts: The Organizational Component

There are three ways to plan educational efforts: (1) by occupational group; (2) by special groups or needs; and (3) by stage of individual socialization or career.

By occupational group. When managers make career paths explicit, they lay the foundation for planned education by occupational groups.

Perhaps the most common method of doing so is the *pyramid model.* Individuals start their careers in an organization at the lowest rung of the occupational ladder and move upward gradually. Since pyramids narrow from bottom to top, there are always fewer high-level than low-level jobs. Movement up the pyramid involves pairing technical knowledge, which is most important upon entry, with interpersonal and conceptual skills. The highest level positions in any organizational pyramid are always management ones, which require well-developed conceptual and interpersonal skills (see Figure 10-2 for an illustration of the pyramid).

Another way to think of occupational groupings makes use of the spiral concept popularized by Bruner (1960). This approach has been applied by Bortz (1981), who correlates two related "spirals": the *long-range employment spiral* and the *long-range curriculum spiral.* The first "is the conceptual model used to organize the occupations of a functionally related group of occupations" (p. 27); the second "is an organizational concept that complements the employment spiral and adds educational dimension to it" (p. 28). Each dot in a curriculum spiral configuration represents a learning objective; each dot in an employment spiral configuration represents a task. See Figure 10-3 for an example of the employment-curriculum spiral.

The spiral concept integrates education and occupational requirements over time. As Bortz (1981) points out, it provides an organized way to think about vertical mobility (up or down) and horizontal mobility (across the functional work groupings of the organization).

However, the spiral concept preserves the pyramid notion. It is primarily organized around functional specialities. There is less opportunity for horizontal mobility than there appears to be, because movement is assumed to be upward.

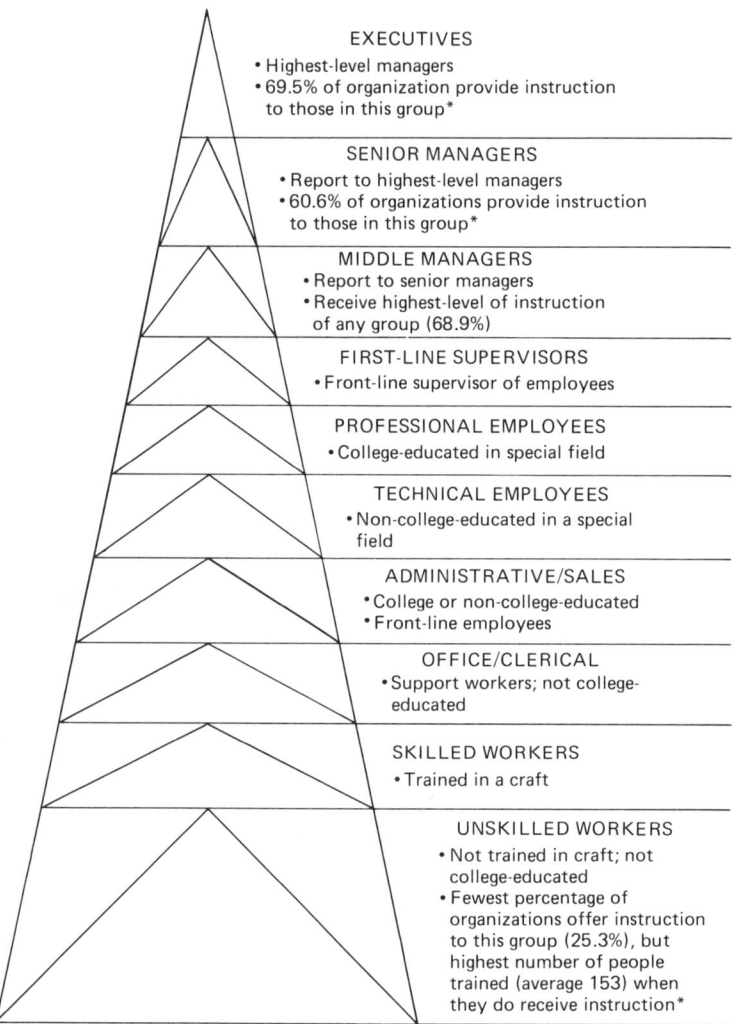

Figure 10-2: The Pyramid Model by Occupational Group

The assumption that career progress should always be upwardly bound and tied to increasing management responsibility creates problems for employers. For one thing, not everyone is interested in management careers; for another, demographic trends, organizational practices, and a host of other conditions are leading to slowdowns in upward mobility for many people in the U.S. (see Byrne & Konrad, 1983; Spruell, 1985).

For these reasons, it is increasingly appropriate to rely on another method of describing career paths as a basis for planning education by occupational group (Danforth & Alden, 1983)—the *dual-career pathing method*. This assumes individuals enter an organization with a technical specialty, but can choose to grow into either managerial *or* technical positions at higher levels. Rather than *one* career path, *two* exist side-by-side. Employee education is planned accordingly, with choices at each step.

Figure 10-3: A Long-Range Employment-Related Occupations for Money Distribution and Management-Related Occupations. *Source:* Bortz, 1981, p. 26. Reprinted with permission of Allyn and Bacon, Inc.

By special group or needs. Substantial attention has been focused in recent years on the long-term needs of special groups within corporations, specific needs stemming from legislation and regulation, social issues affecting the workplace, and a trend toward educating the "whole person."

First, it is clear that women, minorities, and the disabled face special career problems. Members of these groups are often denied the support and mentoring provided to men and nonminorities (Stinson, 1983). Though nearly a third of all management positions are presently held by females, for example, only 2 percent of top executives are females (Lee, 1986). In the 1970s, many specialized programs were offered to meet the unique needs of women and other groups. Today the trend is toward making no formal distinction between training/educational offerings for women, minorities, and others—but toward ensuring that they *are* accorded equal access to such offerings so that employers satisfy Equal Employment Opportunity laws, rules, and regulations. For more on the educational needs of special groups, see Brown, Brown, and Collins (1984), Doll, Sullivan, Simmonetti, and Erwin (1982), Hammer (1983), and Rambo (1976).

Legal and regulatory requirements should be considered in employee educational planning. Employees should be prepared for career movement in part through exposure to laws, rules, and regulations influencing performance in positions to which they aspire. More than 65 percent of all decisions in organizations are presently affected by *external* requirements (*The Road Ahead for HRD,* 1983). Firms must now sponsor instruction on hazardous materials to comply with legislation on occupational health and safety. Failure to do so can increase a firm's chances of subsequently being penalized in legal settlements amounting to millions or billions of dollars. As people

Employee Education

progress, they *must* have a grasp of the legal issues that will affect them when they enter the new job.

It should not be difficult to plan such instruction. HRD practitioners and managers need only

1. identify legal and regulatory matters constraining company actions,
2. pinpoint requirements contributing to legal/regulatory compliance at each job level in the firm,
3. identify issues about which employees at each level and in each occupational group should receive instruction,
4. assess how well instruction is presently contributing to legal/regulatory compliance, and
5. plan instruction at each level in anticipation of career moves to other levels.

Use Activity 10-2 at the end of this chapter to identify critical legal/regulatory matters and identify what needs to be done to educate employees about them.

There may, of course, be company policies and procedures which also influence job performance. One example is labor agreements. Employees being groomed for promotion to first-line supervision may need education on labor contract administration so that they will perform in ways attuned to current company policy. They may also need information about specific provisions of existing labor agreements.

Special social issues also require employee education. Some issues may not be tied to specific future jobs, but may be important nevertheless. Some examples are instructional programs on employee drug abuse, alcoholism, personal crisis counseling, and AIDS. While professional programs are available to provide in-depth counseling to employees suffering from such problems, supervisors and peers may be able to (1) spot symptoms early on, and (2) refer individuals to appropriate sources of help. At minimum, employees should be educated about company policies on these matters. Supervisors require additional education so that they will know how to spot problems, open up dialogue with troubled individuals, handle work-related implications of these problems, and make referrals to professional help when necessary.

Programs of the kind just mentioned go a long way toward educating the "whole person." Some observers believe that trends in the HRD field are headed away from strict job-specific and even career-specific instruction (*Models for Excellence*, 1983). It does not make much sense to segregate an individual's personal (off-the-job) and occupational/organizational (on-the-job) interests, needs, and concerns into neat but artificial compartments. Each person spends about 2,000 hours a year on the job and 6,700 hours a year off the job. The 20 percent of a person's life at work affects the 80 percent at home—and vice versa. Stresses at work affect family, drug use, and sick time; stresses at home can—and do—affect job performance and relations with co-workers (Dennis, 1987; Friedman, 1987; Sekaran, 1986; *Work and Family*, 1986).

Quality of work life programs (QWL) go beyond job-specific performance improvement efforts to involve employees—and sometimes their families—in learning how to live better. Such programs need not be limited to Quality Circles or other specific programs with which QWL has often been closely associated. Rather, they may add to job-specific and career-specific instruction efforts to (1) improve the whole person through instruction not tied specifically to work, and (2) tap employee creativity for solving organizational, individual, and even community problems.

Wellness programs are also being sponsored by corporations. They take a broad perspective of individual learning needs, one transcending mere job-related needs. Employees are viewed as having physical, spiritual, emotional, social, and other needs. Consistent with this line of thinking, employers are providing planned learning experiences on such issues as the following:

- curbing drug and alcohol abuse,
- dealing with stress and hypertension,
- preventing cancer, heart disease, and other common killers,
- instructing employees how to be physically fit,
- teaching employees about proper nutrition and dieting,
- assisting expectant mothers by offering prenatal education,
- counseling individuals with personal, financial, legal, or marital problems, and
- exercising due care to avoid accidents and to deal safely with dangerous substances.

While these programs are often undertaken by employers to reduce employee time lost due to illness and to reduce insurance and disability claims, they underscore just how far away from a strict job-related perspective employers have been moving in their efforts to sponsor planned learning experiences (see Bellingham & Cohen, 1987).

By stage of individual socialization or career. Another way to plan employee education is by an individual's stage in socialization and/or career. Effects of socialization are most pronounced when there are significant differences between expectations raised prior to job entry and actual experiences occurring afterward. This phenomenon is called *reality shock*. It occurs during transition from outsider (job applicant) to insider (entry-level job incumbent). Much has been written about it, especially as it affects job satisfaction and turnover rates of college graduates first entering professional jobs (for example, Dean, 1983; Dean, Ferris, & Konstans, 1985; Feldman, 1976, 1981).

However, there is no need to speak of socialization solely in terms of organizational entry. Nor is reality shock limited to the first job: it may occur upon promotion or transfer whenever actual experiences prove significantly different from expectations. One reason for employee education is to control expectations in anticipation of future career moves. See Table 10-3 for a brief description of how to base employee education on socialization stages.

Another way to plan employee education is by individual career stage. From seminal work by Erik Erickson (1959), theorists of HRD and career planning have shown that individuals progress through predictable career stages (Dalton, Thompson, & Price, 1977; Hall, 1976). Not all authorities agree on what those stages are (see Burack, 1984). But most authorities do agree that each stage is characterized by a

TABLE 10-3 BASING EMPLOYEE EDUCATION ON STAGES OF SOCIALIZATION

Socialization Stage	Primary Interest	Education
Self-Selection	• Preparing for entry to an occupation • Job-search	• Provide "realistic job preview"
Introduction	• Learn the work task • Learn people • Learn culture	• Speed up the employee's introduction to culture
Encounter	• Learn culture	• Help employee think about, and cope with, conflicts between work and personal life
Metamorphosis	• Resolution of conflicts between work and personal life	• Prepare individual for movement (self-selection) into the next job (stemming from promotion/transfer)

central crisis which must be resolved before an individual can progress to the next stage. In addition, each stage, because it is characterized by a central crisis, makes some issues of particular concern. Individuals are especially motivated to learn when instruction is a tool for coping with this central conflict (Knowles, 1984). The general stages of the Dalton, Thompson, and Price model and their influence on employee education are summarized in Table 10-4.

TABLE 10-4 SUMMARY OF STAGES IN THE DALTON, THOMPSON, AND PRICE MODEL

Stage	Focus	Affects employee education
Apprentice	• performs technical work • deals with authority • learns from others about work and about dealing with others	• interest in techniques and technical issues • interest in dealing with others
Colleague	• begins to specialize • regarded as competent • makes contacts	• interest in maintaining professional competence
Mentor	• provides leadership • develops more contacts • demonstrates ability to get things done	• interest in guiding/influencing others
Sponsor	• initiates programs • guides others • continues to develop contacts	• interest in exerting long-term impact by influencing "up-and-coming" people

Planning Educational Efforts: The Individual Component

Not every educational experience offered by an organization is appropriate for everyone. The idea of preparing people for different jobs implies that individual needs differ, not only because jobs are not the same, but also because each person brings to bear his or her own unique strengths and weaknesses to a job. Consequently, HRD practitioners "can no longer afford to take a 'one-size-fits-all' approach" (Gee, 1987).

There are at least three ways by which to plan individually-oriented educational efforts: (1) by employee appraisal; (2) by individual learning contract; and (3) by organizational offering.

By employee appraisal. Most organizations have some kind of formal employee performance appraisal to review patterns in individual performance on the present job, assess present strengths and weaknesses, and negotiate areas warranting improvement in the future. Appraisal results are used to: (1) provide a basis for wage/salary increases; (2) identify instructional needs for short-term training and intermediate-term employee education; and (3) provide information for decisions about promotions, terminations, and transfers.

Unfortunately, not all appraisal systems are equally good for all purposes. Employees often expect criticism when they enter an appraisal interview. The appraisal process may have little impact—or even a negative impact—on performance. Some authorities believe that appraisals should *not* be used for dealing with career planning—or employee education—due to significant problems in administering such systems (Johnson & Rohan, 1982).

Despite these problems, it is possible to use a Management by Objectives (MBO) approach to negotiate not only short-term training plans for improvement on a present job (a year at a time) but also medium-term educational/career plans in preparation for movement to a future job (for one- to three-year time spans). While it is true that external environmental conditions may change over that time period, and that managers should avoid making promises which they may not be able to keep, a negotiated and individualized educational plan establishes benchmarks and time frames by which to prepare individuals for the future. Since MBO plans are negotiated, individuals participate in the planning process. As a result, they are more committed to the realization of the plan.

By individual learning contract. An individual learning contract is a learning agreement. For many reasons it may be the best approach for helping individuals plan their own learning. As Knowles (1986) explains, a "contract may have as its purpose the accomplishment of the objectives of particular units or projects of a course or of a whole course, of a staff-developmental program, of a clinical experience or internship, of a total degree program, or of a personal development project" (p. 38). A contract may be self-initiated and self-monitored; or it may be negotiated between an individual and others—such as a supervisor, instructor, trainer, or a committee (Knowles, 1986).

Most learning contracts specify at least (Knowles, 1986):

- *objectives*—what are the desired outcomes of learning?
- *resources*—what materials and people will be needed to achieve desired objectives?
- *methods*—how will the individual go about achieving objectives?
- *time frame*—what time period will be necessary to achieve objectives?
- *evaluation*—how will the relative success of the learning experience be measured? In short, how well were learning objectives achieved?

Contracts may also justify a learning project or series of projects by showing the relationship between the proposed project(s) and (1) organizational plans/objectives; (2) individual career plans/objectives; (3) HR plans; (4) department, division, or work group plans/objectives; and/or (5) the individual's present job content and job performance. In short, the learning contract approach is very flexible.

For more on learning contracts, see Avakian (1974), Caffarella (1983), Knowles (1986 & 1987), and Sredl and Rothwell (1987). Figure 10-4 illustrates a sample Career Action Plan that can be used as a learning contract.

By organizational offering. Some people have trouble doing any planning. They do nothing until they see an instructional offering which strikes their fancy. They handle career planning in the same way—with no organized effort at all. When a promotion or other career opportunity opens up, they scurry around madly at the last minute trying to pick up whatever instruction they can find which may improve their chances for promotion or transfer.

There will always be those who are passive, even lazy, learners. They exist in every firm. About the only way to motivate them is to offer as much instruction as possible, as often as possible, and as conveniently packaged and presented as possible. These learners will participate in experiences that happen to coincide with their own problems and career interests.

Kinds of Employee Educational Programs

What kinds of programs may be offered to meet employee educational needs? They include: (1) adult basic education; (2) career education; (3) continuing education; (4) occupational education; and (5) cooperative education.

Adult basic education. There is a chronic literacy problem in the U.S. This problem is particularly ironic when advancing technology demands highly literate workers for an increasingly information-oriented society (Naisbitt, 1982). Between forty-seven and seventy-two million people in the U.S. cannot read or figure simple arithmetic problems. The ranks of the illiterate are swelling by two million each year (Schoultz, 1986). The cost of illiteracy to industry is estimated at $20 billion annually (Kozol, 1986). However, that figure does not indicate the real loss in human potential or the suffering caused, directly or indirectly, by illiteracy. (Is it coincidental that a

Directions: (To Employee) The purpose of this action plan is to negotiate your career development over the next year. Complete your part first, then forward to your supervisor. He or she will then negotiate the plan with you--or will appoint someone for that purpose. If you need more room to detail your plan, attach additional paper.

(To Supervisor) Review this employee's proposed career plan for the year, complete your section below, and then meet with the employee to negotiate a plan for the year that will strike a balance between individual career objectives and organizational needs. If you need more space, attach additional paper. Forward the final plan to the Training or HRD Department so that it can be used in locating learning resources to support the plan.

Employee Name _____

Job Title _____ Today's Date _____

For Fiscal Year: _____ Cost Center _____

EMPLOYEE OBJECTIVES (To be completed by employee)

1. What learning/work experiences do you hope to have over the next year? What skills and knowledge do you hope to acquire? Improve?

Figure 10-4: A Sample Learning Contract

ORGANIZATION NEEDS (To be completed by supervisor)

2. What learning/work experiences would you like to see this employee have over the next year? What skills/knowledge would you like to see the individual acquire? Improve? What skills/knowledge are <u>crucial</u> for this person in order to prepare for promotion <u>or</u> increasing specialization?

PRIORITIES

3. (To be completed jointly by employee and supervisor. The priorities established in this section should be the product of a frank, two-sided, give-and-take discussion.) List below, in order of priority, the experiences/skills/knowledge which the employee should seek over the next year. (Continue the list on the next page.) The top priority should appear first.

EXPERIENCES/SKILLS/KNOWLEDGE

1.

2.

Figure 10-4: Continued

PRIORITIES (Continued)

3.

4.

5.

6.

OTHER REMARKS

APPROVALS

This contract accurately describes our agreement.

_____   _____
     (Employee's signature)   (Date)

_____   _____
    (Supervisor's signature)   (Date)

Return the completed plan to the HRD Department. Be sure to keep a copy!

Figure 10-4: Continued

high proportion of imprisoned criminals are illiterate?) Without basic skills, illiterate workers are placed at a great disadvantage for entering the work force or receiving advanced training or education. Their potential for career advancement is severely restricted. In addition, they may also suffer in more personal ways—low self-respect, low aspiration levels, and general feelings of inadequacy.

What can be done about this problem? Adult basic education is one solution. It includes instructional activities intended to produce people who can read, write, and use simple arithmetic. Organizations can:

- offer basic education in-house: According to the results of a *Training* survey, about 4.8 percent of 2,550 responding organizations provide basic education in-house *only* (Gordon, 1986, p. 54);
- offer basic education through outside groups (for example, local school programs). In the *Training* survey, about 4 percent of responding firms use external providers only;
- combine both internal and external sources to furnish basic education;
- give people time off with or without pay to attend off-site basic education programs full-time;
- encourage attendance at "night school"—and reimburse employees for some or all of the cost.

These possibilities are probably not being used as much as they could be. In fact, of all types of instruction listed in the results of the *Training* survey, basic education was offered by the lowest percentage—14.8 percent—of all responding firms (Gordon, 1986, p. 54). In contrast, over 75 percent of all firms offer management skills instruction.

This issue will not disappear in the near future. As the numbers of illiterates increase in the work force, employers will need to pay more attention to the problem (Stoker, 1987). One way to address the problem is to establish an organized educational effort (*Job-related Basic Skills*, 1987).

Career education. To help meet both organizational and individual needs, many firms offer special career education programs. They are designed to help individuals understand career issues better. They may also serve organizational ends by motivating people to prepare for career movements within the firm and by directing management attention to career matters generally.

The most common component of a career education program is organized instruction on career planning. The desired outcomes of such instruction vary widely. Group workshops are offered to help individuals plan their own careers without guidance of any kind from the firm's management; conversely, workshops are highly specific to the sponsoring firm and provide concrete guidance for employees establishing career plans. Some firms simply make available off-the-shelf training packages for individualized use. Others design their own individualized, highly firm-specific workbooks.

There is no right or wrong approach in any absolute sense. It all depends on how much career education is valued by managers—and employees—of the firm. Ask yourself: is career education, in the sense of formal instruction, a worthwhile endeavor for your firm? If so, why? If not, why? If it is worth offering, what end results should be sought from it? How should it be offered? When? For whom? Use Activity 10-3 at the end of this chapter to consider these questions. For more on this subject, see Crites (1981), Gutteridge and Otte (1983), Hanson (1981, 1982), Leibowitz and Schlossberg (1981), and Meckel (1981).

Continuing education. Not many years ago, most people assumed that their lives consisted of two distinct phases: schooling and working. That point of view no longer makes much sense. The rate of change is so great that the skills of most people are in serious danger of obsolescence. In short, people need to think of *lifelong learning* and *continuing education.*

The problem of skill obsolescence is particularly acute in information-dependent professions like medicine, law, accounting, engineering, and even management. Without awareness of current methods, doctors will watch patients die unnecessarily, lawyers will lose cases to more up-to-date practitioners, accountants will get their clients in trouble with various federal agencies, engineers will miss out on applications of new technology, and managers will find themselves placed at a significant disadvantage with more savvy competitors.

The stakes are higher than they seem. As Knowles (1986) reports, "consumers of professional services have become so concerned that their providers of professional services keep up to date that a number of state legislatures have passed laws mandating continuing education as a basis for relicensing" (p. 180). The trouble is, it is difficult to control the quality and measure the outcomes of continuing education, and costly for taxpayers to fund state-run monitoring. Often, relationships between education and job improvements are hard to demonstrate.

Continuing education is likely to become more—not less—of an issue in years to come. A related issue is *worker retraining,* necessitated by changing technology and labor demand. Once associated only with efforts to upgrade the skills of production workers displaced due to automation or plant relocations, retraining is now being carried out even for white-collar professionals (Morano & Deets, 1985).

Continuing education courses are offered by universities, community colleges, private vendors, professional societies, and work organizations. HRD practitioners who want to find courses to meet specific needs have their work cut out: while there are large-scale computerized data bases and published reference books, they are by no means complete. One way to find out about special courses is to get on the mailing lists of continuing education vendors and sponsors. To do that, join professional societies. In many cases, they sell their mailing lists to vendors. Another way is to survey local universities and community colleges—and perhaps other sources of education as well—about available (off-the-shelf or on-demand) courses. The survey results are then used to compile a Directory of Continuing Education courses or an on-line data base tailored to the specific needs of one firm (Rothwell, 1987). Individual needs are matched up to course offerings uncovered by the survey. See Activity 10-5 at the end of this chapter for a tested survey instrument which may be used for this purpose.

The second problem is quality, which varies widely in continuing education. Practitioners may need to do extensive advance research to determine course content and instructor quality. Costs vary as much as quality. A one-day session can add up to more than $2,500 at this writing when fees, travel costs, lodging, and other expenses are figured in.

But for planning purposes, consider: what professions are especially sensitive to change? Are certain issues in the industry of special importance for some members of the organization to know about? How important are continuing education efforts relative to (1) each other?, or (2) other possible instructional initiatives?

Occupational education. As its name implies, occupational education is geared to meeting the special needs of specific job groups, families, or clusters. It implies *instruction intended to facilitate movement within or between job or occupational categories.* Employees in each category have their own distinct learning needs in their present jobs (a training issue) and in preparing for movement to new, future jobs (an educational issue).

What education is presently being offered to members of each occupational category in your organization? What education should be offered to them in the future? For what purposes? Use Activity 10-6 at the end of this chapter to consider these issues.

For more information on occupational education, see Barney (1984), Birnbrauer (1985), Bittel (1987), Connell (1984), Daly (1976), Desid (1987), Eastburn (1987), Fenn and Matthews (1987), Ives (1976), Kinn (1976), Kirkpatrick (1985), Mahler (1976, 1985), McCarthy (1985), Pouliot (1984), Ramsey (1985), Rebedeau and Tagliere (1976), Saltzman, Moly, and Hartshorn (1976), and Sellers (1985).

Cooperative education. The common meaning of *cooperative education* is clear enough: "programs under which students spend some time at school and some time at work" (Saltzman, Moly, & Hartshorn, 1976, p. 25-8). They have been popular for over three quarters of a century (Whitlock, 1976). Sometimes used in recruitment programs, they give students an opportunity to acquire real-world experience, and they give employers an opportunity to try out prospective newcomers before hiring them.

There are other ways to apply this idea of alternating work and structured learning. In the last chapter we describe long-term developmental activities, in which individuals are transferred to—or exchanged with employees of—other firms, departments, divisions, or work groups. On a shorter-term basis, employees may be temporarily promoted or transferred to new jobs while receiving informal mentoring/coaching and formal job instruction. The advantage of this approach is that individuals are especially motivated to learn when already placed in, and working to remain in, a job.

Methods of Delivering Employee Educational Programs

How can employee educational programs be delivered? There are several ways. They include:

- in-house, formal group instruction,
- in-house, informal group instruction,

- in-house-sponsored, externally-designed instruction,
- external instruction sponsored by senior universities,
- external instruction sponsored by community colleges,
- external instruction sponsored by vendors,
- correspondence study,
- external degree programs, and
- other methods.

Each delivery method has its own advantages and disadvantages. The appropriate choice depends on costs versus benefits and on the most likely means of achieving desired outcomes. Each is a way of preparing people for promotion, transfer, or other career moves.

In-house, formal group instruction. Similar to organized training, in-house, formal group instruction is defined as a group of people assembled for a structured, organized purpose designed and delivered by staff of the organization at the organization's work site, to prepare participants for promotion or other career movement. It is this emphasis on future career change which distinguishes in-house education from training.

Chief advantages of in-house programs include:

- cost efficiency gained through group, rather than individual instruction,
- consistency of treatment for those on similar career paths, and
- possibility of increased personal contacts and improved social interaction between people with similar career aspirations within the firm.

Disadvantages include: (1) the possibility that in-house trainers are not as good as external trainers; and (2) the costs of designing and delivering instruction may be greater than when external trainers are hired on a short-term basis.

In-house, informal group instruction. This delivery method is similar to, but not precisely the same as, formal group instruction. HRD practitioners and line managers identify people in line for promotion or transfer. These people are encouraged to form a study group and, in cooperation with each other and their superiors, draw up a learning plan to guide preparation for career movement. They meet on or off company property; they may request guest speakers; they can meet during the days or evenings. Such groups may endure even after members are promoted or transferred.

This method places responsibility for learning on the learners. They are free to set their own learning objectives and meet them. The group setting provides learners with support—other people like themselves from whom they can learn and with whom they can interact. However, this method depends heavily on the participation of members. Not all group members *will* participate, particularly when they see others as competitors for scarce openings.

In-house-sponsored, externally-developed instruction. This method is virtually the same as in-house, formal group instruction, except that educational materials are developed and delivered by outsiders. These outsiders may be faculty members from local universities or community colleges; they may be experienced HRD consultants specializing in training for particular audiences—like new or prospective supervisors, managers, or technical specialists.

In some organizations, consultants have been called in to offer instruction for such reasons as the following:

- in-house HRD practitioners lack credibility with line managers, who assume anybody from outside is always an "expert,"
- decision-makers find an experienced instructor who requires less time to develop a planned learning event than in-house trainers,
- the consultant's quoted rates compare favorably to the costs of in-house presenters when cost-benefit analysis is used, and
- in-house HRD staff members are few and far between. They are already overburdened with duties, so temporary external consultants are used when extra HRD staff members are needed for short-term projects.

External instruction sponsored by universities. Many senior-level universities offer extensive continuing education and special workshops. Some seminars are offered to the public regularly; others are tailor-made to meet the specific needs of one organization. Topics range from pure self-improvement to basic training on a range of topics.

For HRD practitioners who set out to meet a specific organizational need by this method, the best advice is to find out the names of Directors of Continuing Education at local universities. Get on mailing lists and, when workshop brochures arrive, post them on bulletin boards or contact specific individuals who should attend. Better yet, organize a summary of many brochures and circulate it to those who have learning needs. Research the school, its offerings, and the specific programs in advance *before* sending people. Ask for detailed course outlines. Check the reactions of employees who attend.

Senior-level universities are also appropriate sources for consultants. The major problem is finding them, especially if the university is a large one. Some schools have computerized skill inventories of faculty research interests and publications. Find out what schools in the area have faculty skill inventories and then learn how to use them. They may come in handy when consultants are needed in the future.

External instruction sponsored by community colleges. Local community colleges are also a source of instruction. Many have designated units to assist business. Government funding for training or retraining is sometimes available. Community colleges should be handled in much the same way as senior-level institutions. Start by finding out names; then determine what needs they can help meet and how well they can help meet them.

External instruction sponsored by vendors. There are thousands of HRD consultants and vendors in the U.S. They range from one-person, local operations to large, international firms. As with universities, the practitioner who wishes to find a good vendor faces a major challenge. Some common methods of locating vendors include: word-of-mouth referrals; directories; and reviews of people who have published on the topic.

It may help to develop your own skill inventory of consultants over time. That way, you have a base of proven people on which to draw.

What about seminars and workshops offered by vendors? Handle them as you would university offerings. Look carefully at brochures announcing seminars to see if they match up to the needs of your firm or specific people. Look for course purpose, objectives, instructional strategies, content, instructor qualifications, cost, and location (Laird, 1985). If this information is not listed—or if the course outline is vague—contact the vendor directly. Try to find several sources of instruction on the same subject. Compare them. Ask for names of past students, call them, and inquire about the course. See Figure 10-5 for a checklist that is helpful in evaluating external seminars.

Computerized data bases can also help. The American Society for Training and Development operates one, for which a fee is paid to "subscribe." It lists 100,000 seminars. Other data bases are also available. Some are industry-specific; some are privately owned.

Correspondence study. According to Ruth Salinger (1976), "correspondence study is a systematic method of training in which an exchange of materials and examinations, usually by mail, is the main means of interaction between the student and the source of instruction" (p. 38-1). In 1972 there were approximately 700 institutions offering correspondence study and 188 were fully accredited; in 1982, 375 institutions offered correspondence study and 70 were accredited (Baker, 1985). The trend is toward growth, rather than decline, of these schools. About two million people are presently enrolled in correspondence programs (Baker, 1985).

Correspondence study offers major advantages. It is flexible, individualized, and usually cheaper than other methods. College credit is awarded through accredited institutions, offering an additional incentive for some learners. Of course, there are disadvantages: the burden of learning is heavily on the learner; feedback on exercises and homework may not be as prompt as in other settings; and instructors as well as institutions may vary greatly in quality.

For HRD practitioners who want to use correspondence study as a means to meet learning needs, the first challenge is finding an appropriate source. In this respect, published directories are helpful. It is also worthwhile to contact the National Home Study Council in Washington, DC. Assemble information on similar courses available through several correspondence schools and compare them on the basis of content. Evaluate them in the same way as external vendors. Prior to enrolling learners, you may wish to negotiate a learning contract with them. Be sure to provide a way for them to get help with any problems they encounter during individualized study.

External degree programs. The so-called external degree program is a means by which employed adults earn college credit or even college degrees—ranging from the two-year Associates' to the Doctorate. Costs, residency requirements, quality, and topics (majors) vary widely (Sullivan, 1983). In many respects they resemble correspondence programs, though there may be additional requirements.

PART I--CHECKLIST

<u>Directions to Part I</u>: Use this checklist to evaluate an external seminar to which you are planning to send a company employee. For each item listed in the left column below, check (/) yes or no in the middle column. (<u>If you check no to any item, consider carefully how important it is that you have this information and deal with this issue in your meeting with the employee in Part II</u>. Write your remarks in the right column and use them in Part II to plan a meeting with the employee before the seminar.

ITEM	YES	NO	REMARKS
DOES THE SEMINAR BROCHURE:	(√)	(√)	
1. Tell you exactly what participants will be able <u>to do</u> when they complete the seminar?	( )	( )	
2. Describe who should attend the seminar?	( )	( )	
3. Describe the maximum number of people who will attend the seminar?	( )	( )	
4. Out topics to be treated in detail?	( )	( )	
5. Describe how the training will be delivered?	( )	( )	
6. Tell how participant knowledge or skills will be assessed at the end of the seminar?	( )	( )	

Figure 10-5: A Checklist for Evaluating External Seminars and Planning Meetings About Them

ITEM	YES	NO	REMARKS
DOES THE SEMINAR BROCHURE:	(√)	(√)	
7. Explain who the speaker will be?	( )	( )	
8. Show how the trainer is qualified to deliver instruction on this subject?	( )	( )	

<u>PART II--MEETING PLANNER</u>

<u>Directions to Part II</u>: Use the following questions to plan meetings with an employee who is attending an outside seminar. Hold a meeting <u>before</u> the employee attends the seminar and another <u>after</u> the employee returns.

A. ISSUES FOR DISCUSSION WITH EMPLOYEES BEFORE THEY ATTEND AN EXTERNAL TRAINING SEMINAR

1. Why is <u>this</u> employee going to <u>this</u> seminar? (Discuss your answer with the employee.)

2. What should the employee <u>know or be able to do</u> upon returning from the seminar? (Discuss your answer in terms directly applicable to the employee's job. List these <u>learning objectives</u> below in order of importance. The highest priority should be listed first.)

Figure 10-5: Continued

3. What subjects described in the seminar brochure are particularly important for <u>this</u> employee at <u>this</u> time? (Explain to the employee.)

4. What other issues, covered on the checklist, should be covered before the employee attends the seminar?

B. ISSUES FOR DISCUSSION WITH EMPLOYEES AFTER THEY ATTEND AN EXTERNAL TRAINING SEMINAR

1. How well did the seminar help the employee achieve the learning objectives established <u>before</u> the seminar? (Ask the employee.)

2. What methods were used in the seminar to help the employee <u>apply</u> what was learned? (Ask the employee.)

Figure 10-5: Continued

3. How can the employee apply on the job what was learned in the seminar? (Work toward planning specific changes with the employee.)

4. Would the employee recommend this course for other company employees in the future? Why or why not?

Figure 10-5: Continued

For HRD practitioners looking for ways to educate employees, external degree programs are one option. They should be evaluated in the same ways as external vendors and correspondence schools.

Other delivery methods. There are countless other ways by which to deliver employee education. In fact, delivery methods are limited only by the imagination of learners and HRD practitioners. Consider a few other delivery options in addition to those already discussed:

- *off-the-shelf training packages* sold by book publishers, vendors, and others: They can greatly reduce the time needed for course development, though they have to be treated in compliance with existing copyright laws.
- *computer-based and computer-assisted instruction:* They offer great flexibility and individualized instruction.
- *books:* especially college texts, can be used as self-study packages.
- *articles published in professional and academic journals:* They can be circulated to people in the organization to contribute toward their continuing education.
- *informal speakers' bureaus:* Identify knowledgeable people in the organization or community and ask them to meet with those who have special needs. The setting need not be formal. Consider "brown-bag lunch discussions," for instance.

No doubt you can think of other methods, too. For more information on this subject see Cantwell, Hosterman, and Shelton (1976), Chakiris and Fornaciari (1985), and Hope, Hope, & Hope (1987). See Table 10-5 for useful sources.

Tuition reimbursement programs. Though not a delivery method, tuition reimbursement programs are important inducements for employee education. Of course, "A tuition-aid plan is a formal company plan that provides financial assistance to employees who take credit courses. . . ." (McQuigg, 1985, p. 1263). Though often associated with college courses attended on the employee's own time, tuition may also be reimbursed for virtually any external education—including pursuit of a GED certificate, attendance at public seminars or conferences, or degree or nondegree-related college coursework.

Estimates of the number and size of such programs vary widely. There really are no reliable figures. A 1977 study estimated that nearly 90 percent of large firms offer at least partial tuition reimbursement for some external education (Lusterman, 1977). At that time, it was projected that 7,500 firms were spending about $2 billion per year on direct reimbursement, not counting such indirect costs as time away from work (Lusterman, 1977).

Individuals participate in external instruction for many reasons. Among the most common reasons are to advance in a career; to enrich personal knowledge; to socialize with other people; and to learn how to be a better citizen (Channer, 1979; Cross, 1981). Employers sponsor such programs to meet specific HR needs, comply with negotiated labor agreements, and improve employee job satisfaction and morale.

TABLE 10-5 SOURCES OF INFORMATION

As you search for courses or specialized expertise to help meet employee educational needs, consider the following sources of information.

BARD, R., BELL, C., STEPHEN, L. & WEBSTER, L. (1987). *The Trainer's Professional Development Handbook.* San Francisco: Jossey-Bass.

BEAR, J. (1982). *How to Get the Degree You Want: Bear's Guide to Non-traditional College Degrees* (8th ed.). Berkeley: Ten Speed Press.

BURKE, R. (1983). *CAI Sourcebook.* Englewood Cliffs, NJ: Prentice Hall.

EPIE Annotated Courseware Provider List. (1986, annual). Water Mill, NY: EPIE Institute.

HAPONSKI, W., & HAPONSKI, S. (Eds.) (1985). *Directory of External Degrees from Accredited Colleges and Universities.* Clayville, NY: ETC Associates.

The Independent Study Catalog. (1986–1988). Princeton, NJ: Peterson's Guides. (NUCEA Book Order Department, Box 2123, Princeton, NJ 08540.)

Index to Computer Based Learning. (1986, annual). Milwaukee, WI: University of Wisconsin.

In-house Training and Development Programs. (1981). Detroit, MI: Gale Research.

JONES, J. (1984). *The Correspondence Educational Directory* (3rd ed.). Oxnard, CA: Racz Publications.

NADLER, L., & FETTEROLE, E. (Eds.). (1987). *The Trainer's Resource 1987: A Comprehensive Guide to Packaged Training Programs.* Amherst, MA: Human Resource Development Press.

National Guide to Credit Recommendations for Noncollegiate Courses. (1986, annual). Washington, DC: American Council on Education, 1 Dupont Circle, Washington, DC. Phone: (202) 833-4920.

National Information Center for Educational Media. (1980). *Index to Educational Video Tapes* (5th ed.). Columbia, SC: University of South Carolina.

National Information Center for Educational Media. (1983). *Index to 16 mm Educational Film* (8th ed.). Columbia, SC: University of South Carolina.

SMART, J. (1984). *Guide to Five Thousand Home Study Diploma-Certificate Programs.* Rockport, MO: Smartco.

SULLIVAN, E. (Ed.). (1983). *Guide to External Degree Programs in the U.S.* Washington, DC: ACE.

Trainet, American Society for Training and Development, P.O. Box 1433, 1630 Duke St., Alexandria, VA 22313. Phone: (703) 683-8100.

Training Video Directory: Management, Organization, and Career Development Programs. (1985). Alexandria, VA: American Society for Training and Development.

Training Video Directory: Technical and Skills Training Programs. (1985). Alexandria, VA: American Society for Training and Development.

The Video Source Book (6th ed.). (1984). Syosset, NY: National Video Clearinghouse.

WASSERMAN, R., et al. (1982). *Learning Independently: A Directory of Self-Instruction Resources* (2nd ed.). Detroit, MI: Gale Research.

A program of this kind is usually treated as an employee benefit (Werther & Davis, 1985).

It is a good idea to develop a written company policy on tuition reimbursement and procedures for obtaining it. The policy should stipulate the purpose of the program, employee eligibility, types of courses (or other experiences) qualifying for reimbursement, extent of support (100 percent or only partial), the intended relationship (if any) between the program and job-related performance improvement, and the intended relationship between external and internal HRD activities.

At the time this text is going to press, changes in federal tax law affect employer reimbursements for tuition. Generally speaking, employers must treat reimbursements as part of individual income and withhold tax accordingly. If employees can demonstrate that a course maintains or improves their skills on the present job, they may be able to deduct withholding taxes on their individual tax returns.

Internally-sponsored educational efforts should be closely tied to organizational culture, policies, and expectations. Externally-sponsored educational efforts are more appropriate for giving employees the chance to gain new insights and hear about practices in other firms. Procedures should clarify *how* to obtain reimbursement: for example, voucher preparation, minimum grade (like C) necessary for reimbursement, documents which must be furnished as proof of course completion, travel policy, and approvals which may be necessary. For more on tuition reimbursement programs, see McQuigg (1985).

TYING EMPLOYEE EDUCATION TO ORGANIZATIONAL STRATEGY FOR HRD

While employee education is geared toward individual improvement and preparation for advancement, it should be integrated with a larger, integrated Organizational Strategy for HRD.

HRD practitioners, line managers, and even learners themselves should consider such questions as these at regular intervals:

- What is the purpose—or purposes—of employee education programs?
- How are these programs contributing to the realization of Organizational Strategy for HRD, HR strategy, individual career plans, and Strategic Business Plans?
- How consistent are these programs with other learning initiatives? What causes any inconsistencies? How can inconsistencies be corrected?
- How do outcomes of employee educational efforts affect employee development and training for specific jobs? How should they be related?
- What employee education policy should be established? How should it play an integral part of HRD policy?

By addressing these questions and acting on them, HRD practitioners can tie employee education to a long-term HRD plan for the entire firm. Use Activity 10-7 at the end of this chapter to consider these questions.

ACTIVITY 10-1 A Questionnaire to Assess the Climate for a Formal Career Planning Program

Directions: For each factor listed in the left column, circle a number in the right column to indicate how much the factor is *presently* evident in the organization. Use the following scale:

1 means "to a very small extent"
2 means "to a small extent"
3 means "to some extent"
4 means "to a great extent"
5 means "to a very great extent"

Factors*	Degree to Which the Factor is Evident		
	To a Very Small Extent	To Some Extent	To a Very Great Extent
1. Company managers feel obliged to provide a lifetime career plan for every employee.	1 2	3	4 5
2. Company managers believe employees should make a career choice by age thirty.	1 2	3	4 5
3. Company managers believe employees can change to a better job after age fifty.	1 2	3	4 5
4. Company managers generally believe they should be able to guide subordinates.	1 2	3	4 5
5. Company managers feel that individuals do not need to inform them of career aspirations.	1 2	3	4 5
6. Promotions should be made on the basis of strict rules.	1 2	3	4 5

Tying Employee Education to Strategy for HRD

ACTIVITY 10-1 Continued

Factors*	Degree to Which the Factor is Evident		
	To a Very Small Extent	To Some Extent	To a Very Great Extent
7. Transfers should be made on the basis of strict rules.	1 2	3 4	5
8. Extremely good performers should not be promoted.	1 2	3 4	5
9. Company managers feel they should have final say about career choices of their subordinates.	1 2	3 4	5
10. Company managers do not feel they have enough input in promotion decisions.	1 2	3 4	5
11. Company managers feel they are obliged to help their subordinates make career progress.	1 2	3 4	5
12. Company managers believe the organization should clarify career paths.	1 2	3 4	5

*Adapted from Burack & Mathys, 1979, pp. 20-21, with permission from Brace-Park Press.

ACTIVITY 10-2 An Activity to Identify and Plan for Employee Education on Legal and Regulatory Matters

Directions: Use this activity to structure your thinking about employee education needs. In short, what does an employee need to know about legal/regulatory matters *before* he/she is promoted or is transferred into a new position? Answer the questions which follow.

Crucial Legal/Regulatory Matters

1. What are the *most important* legal and/or regulatory matters with which the firm must comply? List them in order of importance (where 1 = most crucial).

Issue by Level and for Preparation to that Level

Column 1	Column 2	Column 3
Level	What do Employees at Each Level Have to Know About Each Legal Issue?*	
1. Executives	1.	Now move issues listed in column 2 into education at the next lower level
2. Senior Managers	2.	1.
3. Middle Managers	3.	2.
4. First-Line Supervisors	4.	3.
5. Professional Employees	5.	4.

Tying Employee Education to Strategy for HRD

ACTIVITY 10-2 Continued

Column 1	Column 2	Column 3
Level	What do Employees at Each Level Have to Know About Each Legal Issue?*	
6. Technical Employees	6.	5.
7. Administrative/Sales	7.	6.
8. Office/Clerical Workers	8.	7.
9. Skilled Workers	9.	8.
10. Unskilled Workers	10.	9.
		10.

*Fill out a separate sheet for each issue. Then summarize them for each occupational category.

ACTIVITY 10-3 Tying Employee Educational Efforts to Career Stages

Directions: Use this activity to brainstorm about the means to link employee educational efforts to career stages. For each stage listed in the left column, describe in the right column how educational efforts may be able to help individuals cope with the stage. There are, of course, no right or wrong answers.

Career Stage*	How can Educational Efforts Help Individuals Cope with Each Stage?
Apprentice	
Colleague	
Mentor	
Sponsor	

*Based on the model of Dalton, Thompson, and Price, 1977.

ACTIVITY 10-4   Continuing Education

Directions: Use this activity to structure your thinking about continuing education. Simply answer the questions which follow in the space provided.

Special Needs

1. What professions/occupations in the organization are especially sensitive to change? List them.

Issues

2. Are certain issues in the industry of special importance for employees to know about? If so, list them.

Importance

3. How important are these efforts relative to (a) each other? and (b) other initiatives to which the organization could devote time and effort?

ACTIVITY 10-5 A Questionnaire on Continuing Education Workshops, Resources, and Facilities*

Directions: Use this questionnaire to collect information about the continuing education offerings of local universities and community colleges. *(Use this information to supplement national data bases.)* Obtain a mailing list from the applicable state agencies which administer high education. Compile results on a computerized data base or in written form. Update annually.

CONTACT PERSON: _____ DATE: _____

TITLE: _____ PHONE: _____

SCHOOL: _____

MAILING ADDRESS: _____

	YES (✓)	NO (✓)
1. Does your university or community college:		
a. Offer short courses/workshops that would be pertinent to training people who are employed?	( )	( )
b. Have available one or more short courses/workshops that are regularly offered on demand (for example, basic computer training; basics of supervision)?	( )	( )
c. Possess unique experience with specialized areas of employee training or continuing education which may distinguish your institution from most others in the state (for example, CAD/CAM training)?	( )	( )
d. Contract to design instruction for employees?	( )	( )
e. Rent films, videotapes, audiotapes, or other instructional aids to organizations for them to use in their own employee training efforts?	( )	( )
f. Loan films, videotapes, audiotapes, *or* other instructional aids to organizations for them to use in their own employee training efforts?	( )	( )
g. Rent meeting space, when available, to employers for their use in training employees?	( )	( )
h. Loan meeting space, when available, to employers for their use in training employees?	( )	( )

ACTIVITY 10-5 Continued

2. Please describe briefly any short courses/workshops that your college/university does (or could) *offer regularly on demand*. (Exclude courses which are only *tailor-made* for one employer on a contractual basis. Exclude courses that are for *individual improvement* only without job training value [for example, aerobics; basket weaving].)* Attach additional sheets if necessary. (Skip this question if your answer to item 1.b. was no.

   COURSE TITLE: _____
   BRIEF DESCRIPTION: _____

	YES (✓)	NO (✓)
a. Available to the general public on demand?	( )	( )
b. Available to employers for their employees on demand?	( )	( )
c. Scheduled and offered at least once a year?	( )	( )
d. Classroom-based?	( )	( )
e. Charge per person?	( )	( )
f. Charge by group?	( )	( )

   DESCRIBE FORMAT (Classroom; individualized): _____

   NUMBER OF SESSIONS: _____ LENGTH (Hours or days): _____
   DESCRIBE CHARGE FOR COURSE (Dollar amount): _____

   DESCRIBE INTENDED PARTICIPANTS: _____

3. COURSE TITLE: _____
   BRIEF DESCRIPTION: _____

	YES (✓)	NO (✓)
a. Available to the general public on demand?	( )	( )
b. Available to employers for their employees on demand?	( )	( )
c. Scheduled and offered at least once a year?	( )	( )
d. Classroom-based?	( )	( )
e. Charge per person?	( )	( )
f. Charge by group?	( )	( )

   DESCRIBE FORMAT (Classroom; individualized): _____

   NUMBER OF SESSIONS: _____ LENGTH (Hours or days): _____
   DESCRIBE CHARGE FOR COURSE (Dollar amount): _____

   DESCRIBE INTENDED PARTICIPANTS: _____

ACTIVITY 10-5 Continued

4. COURSE TITLE: _____
   BRIEF DESCRIPTION: _____
   _____

	YES ($\checkmark$)	NO ($\checkmark$)
a. Available to the general public on demand?	( )	( )
b. Available to employers for their employees on demand?	( )	( )
c. Scheduled and offered at least once a year?	( )	( )
d. Classroom-based?	( )	( )
e. Charge per person?	( )	( )
f. Charge by group?	( )	( )

   DESCRIBE FORMAT (Classroom; individualized): _____
   _____

   NUMBER OF SESSIONS: _____ LENGTH (Hours or days): _____
   DESCRIBE CHARGE FOR COURSE (Dollar amount): _____

   DESCRIBE INTENDED PARTICIPANTS: _____
   _____

5. COURSE TITLE: _____
   BRIEF DESCRIPTION: _____
   _____

	YES ($\checkmark$)	NO ($\checkmark$)
a. Available to the general public on demand?	( )	( )
b. Available to employers for their employees on demand?	( )	( )
c. Scheduled and offered at least once a year?	( )	( )
d. Classroom-based?	( )	( )
e. Charge per person?	( )	( )
f. Charge by group?	( )	( )

   DESCRIBE FORMAT (Classroom; individualized): _____
   _____

   NUMBER OF SESSIONS: _____ LENGTH (Hours or days): _____
   DESCRIBE CHARGE FOR COURSE (Dollar amount): _____

   DESCRIBE INTENDED PARTICIPANTS: _____
   _____

6. Please describe any *unique* experience with *highly specialized* areas of employee training or continuing education that probably distinguishes your college or university from most others in [your state]. (Such experience will typically result from a long-standing [two or more years] contractual arrangement with a local employer for training which is of unique value to that employer.) Attach additional sheets if necessary. (Skip this question if your answer to item 1.c. was no.)

ACTIVITY 10-5 Continued

   a. What are the specialized areas?
   b. How was the experience obtained?
   c. When was the experience obtained?
   d. Who at your institution can be contacted for more information on each specialized area listed in (a)?
7. Regarding loan or rental of instructional aids (skip this question if your answer to item 1.e. was no):
   a. What daily rate, if any, is charged for rental of films, videotapes, audiotapes, and other aids?
   b. How can someone from outside your institution access your collection of films and media?
      (1) Does your college/university publish a film catalog?
      (2) If your school publishes a film catalog, how is one obtained?
   c. Who should be contacted for more information on loaning or renting instructional aids?
   d. What restrictions, if any, are imposed by your college/university in renting or loaning instructional aids (for example, films may only be used on the university campus by local employers)?
8. Regarding loan or rental of meeting space when it is available (skip this question if your answer to 1.f. was no):
   a. What rate, if any, is charged for classroom/meeting room space on a daily basis to employers wanting to conduct training?
   b. Who at your institution should be contacted by outside groups for information about reserving space?
   c. Does the university *guarantee* space, once arrangements are made?
   d. Do you have food service available? If so, please describe it briefly.
9. Please add any other comments you wish.

THANK YOU FOR YOUR COOPERATION!
Please return this survey in the envelope enclosed

---

*From Rothwell, 1987.

*Survey researcher reserves the right to exclude any item from a directory or data base compiled from results of this survey.

ACTIVITY 10-6 Occupational Education			
Directions: Use this activity to structure your thinking about occupational education. Answer the following questions in the space provided.			
Occupational Group*	What Education is Presently Being Offered to Members of this Category by the Organization?	What Education Should be Offered to Members of this Category in the Future?	Why Should this Education be Offered to Members of this Category in the Future?
Executives			
Senior Managers			
Middle Managers			

Tying Employee Education to Strategy for HRD

	ACTIVITY 10-6 Continued		
Occupational Group*	What Education is Presently Being Offered to Members of this Category by the Organization?	What Education Should be Offered to Members of this Category in the Future?	Why Should this Education be Offered to Members of this Category in the Future?
First-Line Supervisors			
Professional Employees			
Technical Employees			
Administrative/ Sales			

ACTIVITY 10-6 Continued			
Occupational Group*	What Education is Presently Being Offered to Members of this Category by the Organization?	What Education Should be Offered to Members of this Category in the Future?	Why Should this Education be Offered to Members of this Category in the Future?
Office/Clerical Workers			
Skilled Workers			
Unskilled Workers			

*Based on groups listed in Gordon, 1986.

ACTIVITY 10-7 Tying Employee Education to Organizational Strategy for HRD
Directions: Use this activity to structure your thinking about how to tie employee education to Organizational Strategy for HRD. Simply answer the questions which follow in the space provided.

Purpose
1. What is the purpose of employee education? Purpose(s)?

Linkages

2. How are employee educational programs contributing to realization of
   a. organizational strategy for HRD?
   b. HR strategy?
   c. individual career plans?
   d. Strategic Business Plans?
3. How consistent are employee educational programs with
   a. formal training?
   b. developmental efforts of all kinds?

Occupational Groups	
Group*	What educational efforts should be offered to members of each occupational group to contribute to implementation of Organizational Strategy for HRD?
Executives	

ACTIVITY 10-7 Continued

Occupational Groups
Senior Managers
Middle Managers
First-Line Supervisors
Professionals
Technical Employees

ACTIVITY 10-7 Continued	
Occupational Groups	
Group*	What educational efforts should be offered to members of each occupational group to contribute to implementation of Organizational Strategy for HRD?
Administrative/Sales Employees	
Office/Clerical Workers	
Skilled Workers	
Unskilled Workers	

*Based on groups listed in Gordon, 1986.

11

EMPLOYEE TRAINING

Employee training is most frequently associated with HRD. It should produce immediate changes in job performance so that supervisors and trainees themselves are able to see the difference between job performance before and after training. Its effects are thus more immediate than development or education.

This chapter defines traditional training and explains its relationship to job performance. It describes each step in a model for designing and delivering training. Finally, traditional training is distinguished from its strategic counterpart, and steps in a model for strategic training are described.

WHAT IS EMPLOYEE TRAINING?

According to Leonard Nadler (1984), "training is defined as learning related to the present job" (p. 1.18). It narrows the gaps between what individuals know or can do and what they should know or do. As a short-term change effort for improving present job performance, the traditional approach to training is unlike employee education, which prepares individuals for future jobs, and employee development, which contributes to organizational learning by cultivating the collective skills of individuals in group settings. The major benefits of training are listed in Figure 11-1.

How Training Benefits the Organization

- Leads to improved profitability and/or more positive attitudes toward profit orientation.
- Improves the job knowledge and skills at all levels of the organization.
- Improves the morale of the work force.
- Helps people identify with organizational goals.
- Helps create a better corporate image.
- Fosters authenticity, openness and trust.
- Improves the relationship between boss and subordinate.
- Aids in organizational development.
- Learns from the trainee.
- Helps prepare guidelines for work.
- Aids in understanding and carrying out organizational policies.
- Provides information for future needs in all areas of the organization.
- Organization gets more effective decision making and problem solving.
- Aids in development for promotion from within.
- Aids in developing leadership skill, motivation, loyalty, better attitudes, and other aspects that successful workers and managers usually display.
- Aids in increasing productivity and/or quality of work.
- Helps keep costs down in many areas, e.g., production, personnel administration, etc.
- Develops a sense of responsibility to the organization for being competent and knowledgeable.
- Improves labor-management relations.
- Reduces outside consulting costs by utilizing competent internal consulting.
- Stimulates preventive management as opposed to putting out fires.
- Eliminates suboptimal behavior (such as hiding tools).
- Creates an appropriate climate for growth, communication.
- Aids in improving organizational communication.
- Helps employees adjust to change.
- Aids in handling conflict, thereby helping to prevent stress and tension.

Benefits to the Individual Which in Turn Ultimately Should Benefit the Organization

- Helps the individual in making better decisions and effective problem solving.
- Through training and development, motivational variables of recognition, achievement, growth, responsibility and advancement are internalized and operationalized.
- Aids in encouraging and achieving self-development and self-confidence.
- Helps a person handle stress, tension, frustration and conflict.
- Provides information for improving leadership knowledge, communication skills and attitudes.
- Increases job satisfaction and recognition.
- Moves a person toward personal goals while improving interaction skills.
- Satisfies personal needs of the trainer (and trainee!).
- Provides trainee an avenue for growth and a say in his/her own future.
- Develops a sense of growth in learning.
- Helps a person develop speaking and listening skills; also writing skills when exercises are required.
- Helps eliminate fear in attempting new tasks.

Benefits in Personnel and Human Relations, Intra and Intergroup Relations and Policy Implementation

- Improves communication between groups and individuals.
- Aids in orientation for new employees and those taking new jobs through transfer or promotion.
- Provides information on equal opportunity and affirmative action.
- Provides information on other governmental laws and administrative policies.
- Improves interpersonal skills.
- Makes organization policies, rules and regulations viable.
- Improves morale.
- Builds cohesiveness in groups.
- Provides a good climate for learning, growth, and coordination.
- Makes the organization a better place to work and live.

Figure 11-1: Why Have Training?

WHAT IS JOB PERFORMANCE?

Definition

"Performance is defined as the *result* of a pattern of actions carried out to satisfy an objective according to some standard" (Bailey, 1982, p. 4). It is not the same as behavior, which is observable action. Appropriate job behavior may—or may not—result in good job performance. Performance is equated with *results;* behavior is equated only with *actions taken.*

Job performance consists of three interrelated elements (Bailey, 1982): (1) the *individual* (who?); (2) the *activity* (what?); and (3) the *context* (where?). Individual performance is influenced by *ability* (what are the individual's capacities to perform?) and *motivation* (how much does the person feel inclined to perform?) (Cummings & Schwab, 1973). To improve job performance, change must occur for the individual, the activity, the context, or some combination of the three. For more information on performance, see Bailey (1982), Cummings and Schwab (1973), Geis (1986), Nash (1983), and Swanson and Gradous (1986).

WHAT IS THE RELATIONSHIP BETWEEN TRAINING AND JOB PERFORMANCE?

Training can improve job performance by (1) improving individual abilities, (2) stimulating motivation, (3) matching individual ability to activity requirements, and/or (4) matching the individual to contextual requirements. However, it cannot change job activities or work context. It changes individuals by furnishing them with new knowledge and skills pertaining to the work.

HOW IS TRAINING RELATED TO PLANNING?

Training contributes to the realization of Organizational Strategy for HRD, HR Plans, and Strategic Business Plans.

Training and Organizational Strategy for HRD

To formulate Organizational Strategy for HRD, managers and employees must have a firm grasp of present strengths and weaknesses in job performance. The reason is that planning should begin with information about present conditions. Training needs assessment provides detailed information about present conditions.

Training and HR Planning

One way to narrow a gap between present labor supply and future labor demand is to improve the present productivity of job incumbents. In this sense, then, training helps implement HR plans by improving the productivity of people already employed in the firm. In short, training makes better use of existing employee talent.

Training and Strategic Business Planning

Training contributes to the realization of Strategic Business Plans in two ways. First, it furnishes people involved in formulating plans with skills necessary to do it. Second, it provides new knowledge and skills to employees at each organizational level, so they can go about their jobs in ways leading to the realization of long-term plans.

A MODEL FOR DESIGNING AND DELIVERING TRAINING

The Model

There are almost as many ways to conceptualize training design and delivery as there are authors on the subject. Variations exist because authors do not agree on the same philosophy of instruction or learning (Sredl & Rothwell, 1987). For the purpose of this discussion, the traditional performance-based model of training design is a good starting point. It is commonly accepted in the HRD field (Rothwell, 1983), and many famous people in the HRD field are associated with it (for example, Gilbert, 1978; Harless; 1975; Mager & Pipe, 1970).

To apply this model, the HRD practitioner*:

1. identifies opportune occasions to apply it,
2. assesses learner needs,
3. clarifies key characteristics of learners which affect how they should be trained,
4. analyzes work and instructional settings, taking them into account as training needs are identified,
5. carries out detailed work analysis to determine what individuals do in their jobs,
6. prepares training objectives designed to narrow gaps between what trainees *actually* know or do and what they *should* know or do,
7. creates tests and other ways of measuring performance,
8. arranges training objectives in an appropriate sequence,
9. identifies appropriate instructional delivery methods, and
10. prepares and selects appropriate content to match objectives.

Following these design steps, training is delivered and evaluated.

Identifying Occasions to Use the Approach

Training is one solution to a performance problem. When individuals cannot perform due to lack of knowledge or a skill, then they experience a training need. On the other hand, when they are able to perform and choose not to do so, they experience a non-training need requiring corrective action other than training (Mager & Pipe, 1970).

---

*This model is based on the instructional design steps described in *Instructional Design Competencies: The Standards*. (1986). Iowa City, IA: International Board of Standards of Training, Performance, & Instruction. Used with permission of the Board.

Of course, problems in the real world rarely appear in a straightforward way. More often they are complicated and appear in random order (McCall & Kaplan, 1985). Managers and HRD practitioners must analyze problems so that corrective action addresses causes rather than symptoms. An HRD practitioner who confronts a job performance problem should ask several questions about it.

First, *what should employees be doing?* Have work standards—the "right ways of doing things" (Laird, 1985)—been established and communicated? Employees can hardly be expected to perform when minimally acceptable work methods or outcomes have not been clarified. Nor can they perform appropriately when they have not been informed about those requirements.

Second, *what are employees actually doing?* How are employees presently carrying out their jobs? What results are they getting? It is hard to identify a problem when present status is unknown. Are some employees performing better than others? If so, why?

Third, *what differences exist between what employees should be doing and what they are doing?* Can HRD practitioners pinpoint particular "trouble spots" in work methods or in results achieved? Are these trouble spots common among groups of people or only for individuals?

Laird (1985) distinguishes between macro and micro training needs. The latter "exists for just one person, or for a very small population"; the former exists "in a large group of employees—frequently in the entire population with the same job classification" (p. 49). New employees, upon entry to the firm, possess macro needs; problem employees, who have trouble performing some facet of their jobs but are already experienced, possess micro needs. However, not *all* problems stem from training needs.

Fourth, *how important are discrepancies between what employees should be doing and what they are doing?* There is little point to wasting time correcting unimportant discrepancies. In fact, it is frustrating to employees to have their work "nit-picked." An effective manager knows when to intercede—and when not to. If job performance discrepancies cost more than it costs to solve them, however, they are important enough to warrant corrective action. Training is one such action.

Fifth, *assuming discrepancies are important and cannot be tolerated, what causes them?* Do employees know how to perform appropriately? Do they possess the necessary skills to do so? Or do performance problems result from other causes?

Sixth, *what should be done about nontraining needs?* If a performance problem stems from a cause other than lack of individual knowledge or skill, HRD practitioners need to determine that cause. They can begin by looking at:

- *allocation of work duties:* Are duties inappropriately allocated across departments or jobs? To solve problems stemming from poor or inappropriate allocation of work duties, job or work group redesign—not training—should be used.
- *policies:* Are company policies interfering with job requirements or with realities of the work place? If so, review policies and change them as necessary. Then train people to perform in ways consistent with the new policies.
- *rewards:* Are rewards, supposedly based on one set of behaviors or outcomes, really based on others? Examine incentives for—and against—people perform-

ing as desired. Change incentives if necessary. Training will not solve a problem stemming from incentives that are at odds with desired performance.

- *leadership:* How much do supervisors agree with goals and objectives established at higher levels? Team-building and key changes in leadership should be used to deal with leadership problems. Training should not be used when leadership issues or politics are the real causes of a performance problem.
- *feedback:* How well, how often, and how clearly do individuals receive feedback about their performance? From whom do they receive it? The frequency of feedback should be increased or its quality should be improved to correct problems stemming from poor feedback. If performance problems stem from lack of feedback, employee training will not solve them.
- *group norms:* How well do desired work methods and outcomes match up to traditions among co-workers? Organization Development interventions, not training, should be directed to problems stemming from group norms.
- *practice:* Are individuals asked to perform a task often enough to gain proficiency? If not, they should be given planned opportunities to practice on the job. Training should be used to provide practice only as a last resort, because it is too expensive to remove workers from the job just to give them practice.
- *motivation:* Do individuals believe their performance will lead to achieving the rewards or outcomes they desire? Do they value those rewards or outcomes? If not, training will not induce them to behave in desired ways, because incentives are lacking.
- *ability:* Is the individual mentally or physically able to perform as desired? If a job performance problem exists for one person even after corrective action, consider job transfer or termination. If it exists for everyone, consider automating the work or redesigning the job.

Use the structured interview form in Activity 11-1 at the end of this chapter to analyze the cause of performance problems.

Seventh, *what should be done about training needs?* Most people outside the HRD field associate "training" with classroom-based instruction. Even many within the field do, too (Zemke, 1985). However, there are many alternatives to it.

Classroom training is an expensive solution. It is costly to develop and deliver. HRD staff are tied up for long time periods; instructional materials cost tidy sums to develop; line employees must offer assistance during instructional design and are away from work during instructional delivery. In most cases employees are not producing, but are being paid while receiving instruction.

For these reasons, HRD practitioners should consider alternatives to classroom training before designing it. There are a few specific issues to consider: (1) *the problem(s) to be solved:* Do they lend themselves to solutions other than classroom training? (2) *time frame(s):* How much time is there to develop and deliver formal training to solve the problem? If sufficient time is not available, what alternatives exist? (3) *expertise:* Is the requisite knowledge available in the organization to design and deliver training to solve the performance problem? If not, can it be located externally? (4) *re-*

sources: What resources are available for dealing with the performance problem? Are they adequate to fund training design and delivery? (5) *importance:* Just how important is the problem to the organization? (6) *scope of the problem:* How many individuals are affected? One? A group? Everyone in the department, division, or organization? (7) *need for consistency:* Is there a special need for imposing consistency on the application of policies and/or procedures? Classroom training is appropriate only when the performance problems lend themselves to no other solutions, time frames are adequate, expertise is available, resources are adequate, the problem is important, many people are affected, and the need for consistency is great.

Alternatives to classroom training include:

- *job aids:* Can instructions be simplified and handed out for on-the-job use? If so, a job aid is appropriate. A job aid is any tool or set of instructions which can be used on the job. For more on this subject, see Finnegan (1985), Harless (1986), and Probot (1985).
- *decision aids:* Similar to a job aid, a decision aid provides situation-specific instruction on what to do when certain circumstances exist. It answers this question: "What should be done if all the following conditions hold true?" Obviously, decision aids are appropriate only for relatively common problems. Checklists are decision aids (Joinson, 1982).
- *individualized instruction:* Can training needs be met through individualized instruction offered by computer, by written text, or by film or videotape?
- *on-the-job training* (OJT): Can the training needs of people be met through instruction delivered by peers or supervisors on the job? If so, OJT is appropriate (Broadwell, 1986; Jacobs & McGiffin, 1987; Sullivan & Miklas, 1985).

Use Activity 11-2 at the end of this chapter to consider alternatives to classroom-based training.

If HRD practitioners still believe classroom instruction is warranted after reviewing alternative approaches, then they should continue with subsequent steps in the performance-based model of instructional design and delivery.

Assessing Learner Needs

When it is apparent that a performance problem exists, that it is caused by the lack of appropriate knowledge and/or skill, and that it lends itself to a training solution, then HRD practitioners should focus on the problem in a more detailed manner. In short, they should assess learner needs. As traditionally defined, a *learning need* is synonymous with a discrepancy between *what employees should know or do* and *what they actually know or do*. A *training need* is more specific: it is a *job performance discrepancy resulting from lack of knowledge or skill on the present job.*

This step in designing training is crucial. If needs are improperly identified, no amount of instruction will meet them. As a consequence, all subsequent steps in the design process will prove fruitless (Sredl & Rothwell, 1987).

Think of learner needs assessment as a flexible process. First, HRD practitioners decide how to carry out needs assessment. They ask themselves these questions:

- *What are the goals/objectives or desired outcomes of the assessment process?* What results are sought from it?
- *Whose needs are being assessed?* Is assessment focused on one job class or on all of them?
- *How will information be collected?* What approaches to data collection are appropriate, given constraints on time, resources, and conditions in the organization?
- *What specific guidelines should be established in advance about data collection methods?* In other words, should special care be taken in using surveys, interview guides, work observations, or other methods of data collection? If so, why?
- *What analytical techniques should be used to interpret the results of needs assessment, once data have been collected?*

Use Activity 11-3 at the end of this chapter to consider these questions.

Second, HRD practitioners carry out the needs assessment. They implement the plan established in the prior step. They should take care to avoid getting sidetracked on issues unrelated to needs initially pinpointed for examination. Only rarely should a needs assessment plan be altered during the assessment process. Departure from the needs assessment plan is appropriate only when new information comes to light that changes the assumptions on which the initial assessment plan was based (Sredl & Rothwell, 1987).

Third, *clarify the precise nature of performance problems which are to be solved by training.* Following completion of needs assessment, HRD practitioners should clarify just what problems they plan to address through training. When they also uncover information about nontraining needs, they should relay it to executives so that additional corrective action can also be taken in areas unrelated to knowledge or skills.

The choice of how to approach a needs assessment depends on the skills of HRD practitioners and the assumptions made about training by line managers, employees, and top executives. Cost is often touted as the single most important issue. Yet it may not be as important as it is made out to be. What often matters most is what practitioners or line managers prefer—and how committed they are to solving a problem.

Research conducted on training needs assessment suggests that formal approaches are rarely used in even the largest corporations (Digman, 1980; Feuer, 1986a; Roth, 1986). Instead, informal approaches—brief talks, meetings with line supervisors, interviews and observation—are more common. They are less time-consuming than formal studies, and HRD practitioners are often under pressure to act quickly in a way that makes detailed front-end analysis difficult. In addition, informal approaches do not raise expectations for improvement among many people in the same way that highly visible surveys tend to do. That is often an advantage. Unmet expectations create frustration among line managers and employees and eventually damage the HRD department's credibility.

Clarifying Key Characteristics of Learners

Who are the learners? What are their characteristics? How will those characteristics affect training? These questions should be considered after needs assessment, but before preparation of instructional objectives.

In most cases, HRD practitioners start out with a general idea of who will receive the training (Dick & Carey, 1985). In some cases, the task of identifying important characteristics of learners is easier than in others. For example, newly-hired employees with no prior work experience share some common characteristics: (1) they do not know the organizational culture; (2) they have a limited store of personal experiences on which to draw; (3) they know relatively little about specific jobs, though they may have had formal education in the general field; and (4) quite often—but not always—they are in the same general age group and stage of personal development.

More experienced workers may share characteristics of their work group. For example, members of one work group may (1) share the same attitudes, (2) have considerable familiarity with tasks in their group, (3) have undergone similar socialization experiences, and (4) have been influenced in their job performance by expectations of the same superior. They may also be classified in roughly the same age group and career stage.

For HRD practitioners, information of this kind is valuable for gearing training to solve common problems, address common interests, and deal with individual concerns of a target trainee group.

Three questions about learner characteristics are important to consider prior to specifying training objectives. First, what learner characteristics will generally affect training on a particular activity, task, or job duty? Second, what learner characteristics will affect training on job activities, tasks, or duties for a specific group of people at a specific time? Third and finally, how can these characteristics be planned for? Long-term, general characteristics of learners are influenced by organizational selection, recruitment, and promotion practices; short-term, specific characteristics of one group are influenced by special problems or issues on the job which affect performance and which may also affect interests and expectations. Figure 11-2 illustrates this concept.

Use Activity 11-4 at the end of this chapter to consider learner characteristics.

How do HRD practitioners deal with individual differences? Several strategies are possible. First, *identify prerequisites for all training and screen out those who do not meet selection criteria.* To minimize the influence of individual differences, restrict access to training. People who do not meet selection criteria for training—that is, possess prerequisite knowledge or skills—are given remedial instruction to prepare them for it.

There are two ways to establish prerequisites (Dick & Carey, 1985). One way is by trial-and-error. Offer training to employees. Then follow up with them later to find out what they think they should have known prior to training. Another way is by inference. For each need area, identify what learners must know before they can begin the training.

Second, *be prepared to modify instructional objectives, context, and delivery*

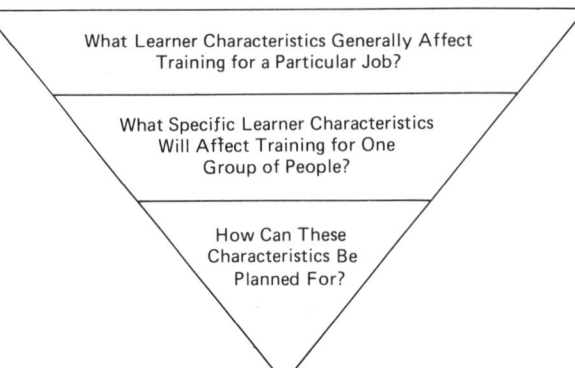

Figure 11-2: Key Issues to Consider About Learner Characteristics

methods. Develop instruction in small segments and give individuals the flexibility to skip segments when they already possess necessary skills.

Third, *identify different ability levels of employees who are to attend training, and establish different training for each level.* This approach is similar to "ability grouping" in secondary schools. Trainees are divided into three categories, and training programs are geared to the needs of learners in each category.

For more on this subject see Goldstein (1986) and Hoover (1982).

Analyzing the Setting

Training should not be planned in a vacuum. It makes sense to analyze up front the settings in which (1) training will subsequently be applied, and (2) training is to occur. Not surprisingly, training conducted in a setting resembling the work site is more likely to influence subsequent, post-instructional job performance than training conducted in a setting not resembling the work site.

What conditions face an employee in the work setting? Consider: (1) *physical conditions:* Are they adequate? Safe? (2) *tools/resources:* Are they up-to-date? Easily accessible? Appropriate to the work? (3) *group norms:* What work methods are acceptable to coworkers? What work methods are unacceptable? (4) *supervisory expectations:* What do supervisors expect from trainees? (5) *employee expectations:* What do employees expect from the work and from training? Much like learner characteristics, work setting conditions affect the subsequent willingness of, and opportunities for, people to apply training.

What conditions face a trainee in the instructional setting? Consider: (1) *physical conditions:* How much do they resemble the work setting? Can they be made similar? (2) *tools/equipment:* How closely do the tools and equipment used in training resemble those used in the work setting? (3) *resources:* Is there adequate time, money, and staff to carry out training effectively? (4) *philosophy/beliefs:* Are employees exposed to a radically different philosophy in training than they are exposed to on the job?

Use Activity 11-5 at the end of this chapter to consider the work setting and the instructional setting.

Carrying Out Detailed Work Analysis

When the need for training is justifiable and when learner characteristics and work/instructional settings have been analyzed, the HRD practitioner is ready to carry out a detailed work analysis to determine (*Instructional Design Competencies,* 1986): (1) job duties, activities, and tasks; (2) their importance; (3) the order in which they should be enacted; (4) the frequency of their performance; and (5) background knowledge, skills, and attitudes necessary to carry out those duties, activities, or tasks. The purpose of work analysis is to clarify the most *appropriate* way to do the work. "Appropriate" can mean: (1) the way an *experienced* worker performs the task, activity, duty, or job; (2) the way the *best worker* actually performs the task, activity, duty, or job; or (3) the way the task, activity, duty, or job should be *ideally* performed.

Regardless of how "appropriate" is interpreted, the usual starting point for work analysis is the task level. A task is a discrete activity, one with a definite beginning and ending (*A Handbook,* 1973). Many tasks, grouped together, comprise a position occupied by one person in an organization. A job is the generic name for many positions with the same title. An occupation comprises similar jobs in different organizations.

Task analysis is a detailed examination of every discrete component of a job or position. There are at least twenty-five ways to go about the process (Gibbons, 1977). The basic steps are simple enough: (1) break down the job into component tasks; (2) describe how each task is carried out; (3) identify which tasks are most important, difficult to learn, and most difficult to carry out; (4) sequence tasks as they are performed on the job; and (5) determine what the worker must know or be able to do to carry out each task. Task analysis is appropriate for blue-collar jobs and manual trades in which work behaviors are easily observed. Alternative approaches are usually more appropriate for white-collar occupations. For more information on work analysis see Jackson (1986), Goldstein (1986), McCormick (1979), Rothwell and Kazanas (1988), Sredl and Rothwell (1987), and Tracey (1984).

Preparing Training Objectives

"A [training] objective is a description of a performance you want learners to be able to exhibit before you consider them competent" (Mager, 1975, p. 5). Objectives are obtained from work analysis and needs assessment. From work analysis, HRD practitioners obtain information about *what must be done in order to achieve desired performance;* from needs assessment, practitioners find out *what people are actually doing and where discrepancies exist.*

Instructional objectives clarify outcomes to be achieved by the end of a training experience. *Terminal objectives* are outcomes sought by the end of a planned learning event; *enabling objectives* are outcomes sought during the learning event to help the learner achieve terminal objectives. In short, terminal objectives express the desired outcomes of a course; enabling objectives express the desired outcomes at different points during a course. Enabling objectives are thus rationally related to—and supportive of—their terminal counterparts.

Instructional objectives are blueprints for training design. Trainees who achieve objectives demonstrate they can perform a job's activities or tasks. As Figure 11-3 illustrates, objectives should be linked directly to job activities. Achievement of objectives should demonstrate ability to perform tasks or activities (Cummings, 1986).

There are different levels of objectives. In training, a terminal objective is specific. It describes what the learner can do, what tools or other requirements are necessary for the performance, and a way of measuring the quality of performance (Mager, 1975). In employee education, a terminal objective is not as specific as in training. It clarifies what the learner can do and under what conditions, but not necessarily how well the learner can perform. It is too general to provide a criterion for performance. In employee development, a terminal objective is expressed for a work group—not, as in training or education, for individuals. The objective may specify what the group can do, under what conditions, and how well. Terminal training objectives are enabling objectives for employee education, as individuals prepare for performance at higher levels of technical competence or responsibility. Likewise, terminal objectives of training and employee education are enabling objectives for employee development (see Figure 11-4).

Several guidebooks are available to help novice HRD practitioners write training objectives (for example, see Dillman & Rahmlow, 1972). The basic format is not difficult to master. A typical objective takes the following form (Mager, 1975):

Upon completion of this [course, unit, or lesson], the trainee will be able to

- do what?
- how well?
- using what tools or other resources? Under what conditions?

Creating Tests

In performance-based training, test items are derived from objectives. They are prepared after objectives, before decisions are made about delivery methods and instructional content (Dick & Carey, 1985). Tests are the basis for decisions about delivery and content; test items are built-in benchmarks to measure trainee achievement during and after instruction.

Job Task
What task must be performed on the job?

Instructional Objective
What must an employee know or be able to do to perform the job task?

Figure 11-3: The Relationship Between Job Task and Instructional Objective

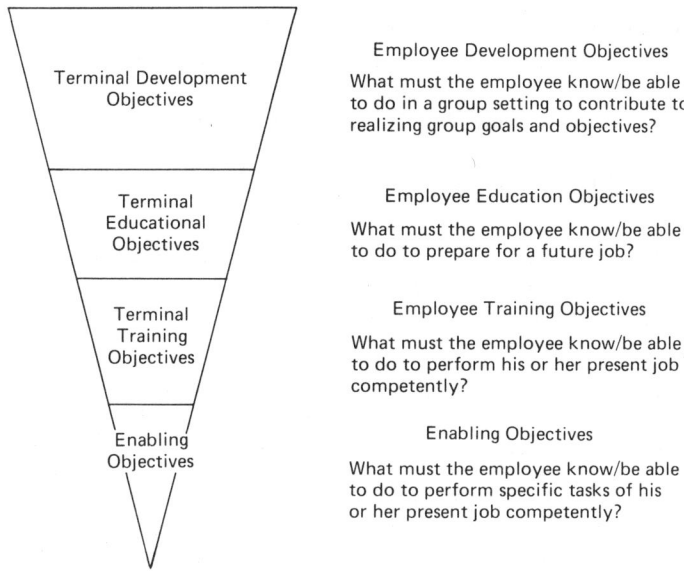

Figure 11-4: The Relationship Between Instructional Objectives in Training, Employee Education, and Employee Development

According to Mager (1973), "the development of criterion items that test for an objective is straightforward and a simple matter for those whose objectives are derived from task analyses and are well stated.... One merely has to prepare items that ask the student to demonstrate the performance called for by the objective, under the conditions called for by the objective" (p. 3). A criterion is a measure of what should be. A test item "calls for a single response or set of responses to a single stimulus or stimulus pattern" (Mager, 1973, p. 7).

The relationship between job task, instructional objective, and test item is thus quite close. The task is what the person is to do on the job; the objective is an instructional outcome linked to the task; and a test item measures how well the objective has been achieved or is being achieved (see Figure 11-5).

There are several kinds of tests: (1) *oral,* administered by voice; (2) *written,* administered by written text; and (3) *performance,* administered by having a trainee demonstrate a task or an activity required on the job.

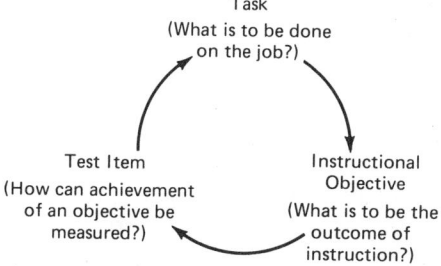

Figure 11-5: The Relationship Between Job Task, Instructional Objective, and Test Item

A Model for Designing and Delivering Training

Oral and written tests take different forms—multiple choice; fill-in-the-blank, true-false, essay, and matching. The point worth emphasizing is that each form is more appropriate for measuring some objectives than others (Dick & Carey, 1985). For more on this subject see Blank (1982), Denova (1979), and Mager (1973).

Arranging Objectives in Sequence

Sequencing objectives means arranging them so that they will provide a foundation for designing and delivering instruction. There are several approaches to sequencing. Objectives may be arranged (Knowles, 1980):

1. *from simple to complex:* Begin with simple ideas and progress to increasingly complicated ones. "Simple ideas" have few parts or distinctions; "complex ideas" have many parts, distinctions, or exceptions to rules.
2. *from known to unknown:* Base sequencing on prerequisites. Each idea, concept, or objective is a building block for later ones. The HRD practitioner begins with what learners know and progressively moves into unknown areas.
3. *from whole to part:* Begin with a simplified model of all steps or tasks in a job, introduce trainees to it, and then proceed to explore each part. With this sequencing method, trainees can place each part of the training experience in the context of the whole course or job.
4. *from past to present to future:* Begin historically, focusing on time. This method is appropriate when instruction is geared to contrasting past, present, or future methods.
5. *from simple to complex treatments of alternating subjects:* This is the "spiral approach" to organizing instruction. Several topics or issues are treated at a simple level. Later, they are treated again at a more complex level. Thus, "content topics are systematically reintroduced at periodic intervals. Two purposes are served by such a scheme. First, the previously learned knowledge of the topic is given a review, which tends to improve its retention. And second, the topic may be progressively elaborated when it is reintroduced, leading to broadened understanding and transfer of learning" (Gagné & Briggs, 1979, p. 141).
6. *in other ways:* These five sequencing methods are by no means the only ones. There are others, including (Romiszowski, 1981): (1) *the pyramid*, in which some objectives are covered with all learners but other objectives are only covered with some learners; (2) *the doughnut*, in which a common core of instructional objectives is surrounded by specialized ones for some employee groups; and (3) *the network*, in which some objectives are related to others in a grand scheme.

Philosophy of sequencing. The basic principle of sequencing is that prerequisite knowledge should always be treated first. "The only justifiable reason for *forcing* a particular sequence on students is if a task happens to be an essential prerequisite that is needed to master another task" (Blank, 1981, p. 140). Adults resist learning sequences imposed on them, especially when they believe a different sequence is more appropriate to suit their needs or cope with immediate job problems (Brookfield, 1986).

Identifying Appropriate Delivery Methods

Choice of delivery methods follows sequencing of objectives. At this point, HRD practitioners make decisions about *what media to use*—for example, classroom, videotape, or individualized text. But what are some delivery methods? What media should be used for delivery?

Instruction can be delivered by:

- Lecture
- Independent Reading
- Panels
- Buzzgroups
- Exercises
- Case studies
- Incident Process
- Role Play
- Behavior Modelling
- Demonstration
- Simulations/Games

Of course, this list is by no means exhaustive. There are other choices (see Eitington, 1984; Holmes, Morgan, & Bundy, 1976; Laird, 1985; Malasky, 1984; Spaid, 1986; and Tracey, 1984). In fact, Huczynski (1983) lists and describes 350 delivery methods. Some are appropriate for lengthy instructional experiences; most are useful only for a portion of a course.

Lecture. Despite the increasing availability of computer-based and video-based instruction, lecture remains the most popular and frequently used training delivery method (see Figure 11-6). A lecture is a speech delivered in a classroom setting. Lecture can also be delivered by videotape or by teleconference to large groups at scattered locations.

Pure lecture is one-way communication: the instructor speaks and trainees listen. The burden rests with the instructor. Trainees are passive recipients of information. Since the average speed of thought is over 400 words per minute, but the average speed of talking is around 100 words per minute (Lambert, 1986), trainees have a tough time keeping their attention fixed on the lecturer. They grow bored quickly.

Fortunately, HRD practitioners need not restrict themselves to pure lecture. They can include visual aids to reinforce and dramatize what they say. They can also solicit questions and comments from their audience. Other techniques are also used to liven up lectures. Here are a few tips (Lambert, 1986; Thiagarajan, 1986):

- Talk as fast as you please. Trainees can easily keep up.
- Vary the pitch and volume of your voice.
- Ask questions. In fact, try for one question every three minutes.
- Call people by name. That's an attention-getter.
- Be active. The more energetic and enthusiastic the presenter, the more lively the learners are likely to be.

- Use fill-in-the-blank. Give trainees handouts with key words missing. As you talk, tell them what words to insert in the blanks. Use the same approach with visual aids. Put them up on a blackboard or an overhead projector only half-done. Complete them as you talk.
- Pair the lecture with other methods—exercises, case studies, and role plays—so trainees can participate and have to apply what they learn.
- Use lecture to do more than present information. Stimulate ideas and new lines of thought. Take advantage of small-group problem-solving methods.

In all likelihood, the lecture is here to stay. It will probably always exist in some form.

Independent reading. Independent reading can be tied to other, related learning experiences or can stand alone.

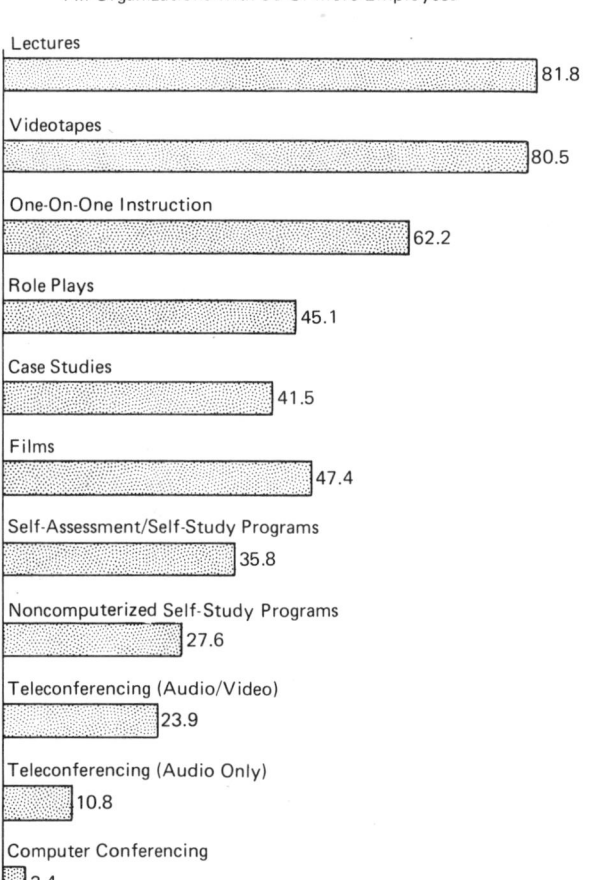

Figure 11-6: Instructional Methods*

412 Employee Training Chap. 11

Independent readings can be assigned before, during, or after classroom training or tutorials. Reading is appropriate for (1) providing necessary background information which is too time-consuming to cover in a lecture, (2) adding information to a topic treated briefly in a lecture, or (3) giving the learner resources for future, self-directed learning (Sredl & Rothwell, 1987).

It does not make sense to assign too much advance readings. The authors know of training situations in which learners were given hundreds of pages to read before class. Trainees ignored most of it. If that much background is needed, then a course should precede the training.

A better approach is to limit advance reading to less than twenty pages. Give readers instructions about what to focus on while they read. Laird (1985) recommends building in accountability for learners by announcing that advance reading will be discussed or used in a class exercise. Any approach which motivates learners to read the material is good. If necessary, build in objectives and a follow-up test so that readers treat advance reading as part of the course.

Reading can also stand alone. It may substitute for a lecture or a training course. Stand-alone reading is associated with off-the-shelf individualized training packages, assigned readings out of college texts or technical manuals, and programmed instruction.

Off-the-shelf packages—purchased from publishers or professional societies—vary greatly in quality. Some are short; some are hundreds of pages long. They are useful if reviewed and tailored to the organization by HRD practitioners and line managers before they are given to inexperienced trainees. (For a good source of these packages, see Nadler and Fetteroll, 1987). Instructions should accompany them in order to clarify what the reader should pay special attention to and why the material is important. In most cases, readers should be asked to complete exercises included in the package. A face-to-face follow-up should be planned after completion so that learners can go over their answers to exercises with a subject matter expert who can check them and reemphasize important points from the training material.

Assigned readings should be treated like advance reading assignments: they should clarify what the learner should pay attention to and should build in learner accountability with tests, exercises, or guided activities.

Programmed instruction (PI) is a special kind of reading assignment. Much used prior to the advent of computer-based training, it is a written text that gives learners the chance to evaluate their own progress. The text is prepared in *frames*, short segments no longer than a paragraph. At the end of each frame is a question on content. Answers are placed in the margin so learners can cover them up, answer questions, and check their own answers. Special skills are required to write PI. Some vendors offer classroom instruction that will teach HRD practitioners how to write frames.

Reading assignments are advantageous because they reduce training time and guide learners quickly through background material. They are especially useful in small organizations or in those with a small HRD staff or slow movement into or out of some job classes. They are disadvantageous because they may require substantial tailoring to work effectively in unique organizational settings.

Panels. A panel is a group of people, usually subject experts, assembled to discuss a topic. Panels may be highly structured and focused on one or more topics; they may be unstructured and cover many topics. In a structured format, each speaker on the panel—there are usually six or less—has a strict time allotment. In a focused format, each speaker addresses a different facet of a topic.

Panel discussions often resemble short lectures. Audience participation is discouraged. Question and answer sessions are structured after each speaker or after all of them. Few panel discussions encourage active interaction between panelists and audience.

To design a panel, simply decide on the learning objectives in advance and then select speakers who can help achieve them. The choice of moderator is most important, because the moderator controls time use by speakers, encourages questions between audience and panelists, and guides panel members as they discuss a subject (Laird, 1985).

Panels are appropriate when participants bring open minds to the learning experience (Laird, 1985). They are also useful for exploring problems or issues for which pat answers are not available. Variations of the expert panel include learner panels made up of trainees; manager panels made up of trainees' supervisors; and open forums geared to freewheeling exploration of a problem or issue.

Buzzgroups. A buzzgroup is a small group assembled to work on a problem and report solutions back to a larger group. They are frequently used in classroom training. They may also be used in simple problem-solving. Hanson (1981) argues that "experiential learning is best accomplished through the use of small work groups as the basic learning units through which workshop events are processed" (p. 194). He believes they provide individuals with maximum opportunity for participating in problem-solving activities, experiencing involvement in the learning event, accepting responsibility for results, receiving feedback on what they have learned in a supportive environment, and observing group phenomena. He recommends a group size of six people.

To arrange a buzzgroup experience, the HRD practitioner: (1) selects group members or provides a means to do so like counting off or drawing numbers out of a hat; (2) clarifies the task confronting the group and the results expected from the group; (3) makes clear any constraints (for example, "I'll give you fifteen minutes"; "Don't look at your notes"); and (4) provides special instructions or materials. Group members may be asked to do almost anything: work on a case study, role play, or other exercise together; discuss an issue, problem, or common concern; define a term; classify information; or answer questions. Buzzgroups stimulate creativity on a relatively structured problem or issue, particularly one just discussed in training. They are not appropriate when individual, independent mastery of subject matter is the aim of instruction. After all, it is hard to tell how much each person contributed to a group solution.

Exercises. This is a broad category of methods. Anything requiring learners to practice knowledge or skill is an exercise. Perhaps the simplest is a list of questions which learners answer individually or in groups. Other exercises include case studies, critical incidents, and role plays.

Case study. Case studies are narrative descriptions of problem situations. Though often printed, they can be described orally by an instructor. Typically, the description is at least adequate to identify a problem and issues affecting it.

Case studies should have a real-life feel. They should excite interest and stimulate discussion. They are quite flexible. A case study can introduce a learning event, thereby serving to disorient trainees and dramatize their need for instruction. A case study is more often used in the middle or at the end of a longer discussion to illustrate a point, underscore the importance of a problem, or apply a principle.

There are six steps in preparing a case study. The instructor (Boyd, 1980):

1. decides what outcomes are desired from the case study experience and the general ideas that are to be illustrated,
2. creates a fictitious situation or identifies a real one that serves the instructional purpose of the case,
3. adds details related to, or symptomatic of, the problem,
4. creates a cast of characters,
5. writes up the case, and
6. may place questions at the end to focus learner attention on key points raised by the case

The chief disadvantage of the case study is that learners are not actually involved in the problem. For this reason, they sometimes give unrealistic answers.

For more on case studies see Boyd (1980), Ford (1970), Kelly (1983), and Pigors (1987).

The incident process. Sometimes called the critical incident method, the incident process is a greatly condensed version of a case study. Trainees are given a one- or two-sentence problem situation and are asked to describe what action to take. Alternatively, the trainer may describe the problem situation and allow learners to pose questions for more information.

To write critical incidents, HRD practitioners follow the same basic steps as in preparing case studies. Alternatively, they may collect information about common problem situations confronting job incumbents and then provide critical incidents during training based on these problems. As a result, learners are exposed to the proper handling of real-life problems. A major advantage of the incident process is that it allows the instructor to cover much ground in a relatively short time. A major disadvantage is that trainees sometimes have trouble responding to incidents without more details.

The role play. Role play is a range of methods in which trainees put themselves in dramatic situations and act out scenes like actors in a play. I. L. Moreno, a psychiatrist, is credited with the first use of role play in 1911. It was synthesized with case study and adapted for use in training by Norman R. F. Maier at the University of Michigan (Wohlking & Weiner, 1981).

There are essentially two kinds of role play: structured and spontaneous. Structured role play helps individuals become more productive in some aspect of their work.

Spontaneous role play helps individuals understand how they interact with others (Wohlking & Weiner, 1981).

Structured role play is based on a case study. Participants receive instructions about a situation, the roles they are to play, and some goal to achieve during the role play. Preparing a structured role play involves most of the steps taken in preparing a case study: (1) decide what outcomes are desired; (2) create or identify a situation; (3) add details; and (4) create a cast of characters. From this point, the writer creates a separate role to be played by each "actor" in a "live case."

Spontaneous role plays are based on momentary experiences. For example, an instructor asks participants to trade organizational roles, explain how they feel, put themselves in the place of another person, act out the part, imitate the behavior of one person in the group, or speak only one word at a time to voice their spontaneous feelings.

Preparation of spontaneous role play is informal. It relies entirely on spur-of-the-moment arrangements made by instructors. They prepare participants by polling the group for common problems, concerns, and issues. A brief description of role play is then provided. Instructors may even "model" a role play in front of the group, either by themselves or with handpicked confederates. In contrast, structured role plays are usually preceded by lecture, discussion, case analysis, exercises, films, videotapes, or other "warm-up" experiences. They are then followed by a description of role play. Like any experiential exercise, role play should be followed by a discussion of key points and participant insights to reinforce learning. The chief disadvantage of role play is that participants may experience difficulty in making the situation feel realistic and may resent being put on the spot to act a part or reveal their feelings in a group. If handled well, however, a role play can be very effective in stimulating insight or demonstrating a skill.

For more on this approach see Cooke (1987), Maier, Solem, and Maier (1975), Molloy (1982), Shaw, Corsini, Blake, and Mouton (1980), and Van Ments (1983).

Behavior modeling. "Reduced to its base essence, behavior modeling involves learning by watching and practicing" (Robinson, 1982, p. 2). It is founded on social learning theory, whose proponents believe most learning occurs by observing others and imitating what they do (Bandura, 1977). To prepare a training experience using behavioral modeling, the HRD practitioner: (1) clarifies what results are sought; (2) analyzes behaviors of particularly effective *and* ineffective performers; (3) describes these behaviors; (4) acts out the behaviors to see if they are, in fact, related to appropriate and inappropriate performance; (5) develops methods to illustrate models of appropriate and inappropriate behavior (for example, on films or videotapes); (6) asks learners to practice or imitate the good performance model they observed; (7) provides feedback about how well learners exhibited desired performance; and (8) asks learners to repeat the process until they adequately demonstrate desired performance. Modeling is especially effective in supervisory training. In the latter case, instructors often choose to concentrate on interpersonal behaviors—how to get along with and lead others. For more on this subject see Robinson (1985), Robinson (1982), and Zemke (1982b).

Demonstration. Demonstration resembles modeling. Trainers show learners how to perform tasks or operate equipment. In many respects it is perhaps the most common approach to *on-the-job training* (OJT), defined as planned and structured, albeit informal, instruction delivered by a supervisor to a worker at the job site. Laird (1985) defines demonstrations as "merely illustrated lectures or presentations" (p. 135).

To prepare a demonstration, the supervisor or HRD practitioner begins by (1) determining what outcomes are desired; (2) assembling necessary tools or materials; and (3) preparing a simple outline so that the process/work activity can be broken down into steps and then demonstrated. Subsequent steps are the same as those in job Instruction Training (JIT), made famous by C. R. Allen in the 1920s. The supervisor or HRD practitioner thus (McCord, 1976):

1. prepares the worker to receive instruction by putting the person at ease, determining what the employee knows already, motivating the individual to learn the task by explaining why it is important, and placing the individual in the correct position near equipment;
2. presents the process (that is, gives the demonstration) by telling the worker what to do, showing the worker what to do, illustrating all steps, questioning the worker on key points, and emphasizing important points;
3. allows the worker to demonstrate performance by asking the worker to tell what is done, having the worker demonstrate the process or steps one-by-one, asking the worker questions, and correcting any errors; and
4. follows up by making the worker subsequently responsible for performing the task/process, telling the worker who to see for more help if needed, checking up on performance frequently at first but less as time goes on, and encouraging questions.

While other approaches to demonstration and on-the-job training (OJT) have been discussed, Allen's basic four-step model has withstood the test of time for seventy years. For more on the demonstration, see Broadwell (1986).

Simulations/games. A simulation resembles a lengthy role play in which many people participate; a game is a ritualized simulation, often modeled after key aspects of a work setting, in which teams compete while following preestablished rules.

Simulations take much time to prepare, test, and administer. They are appropriately used to (Coppard, 1976): (1) explore the elements of a large system, like an organization, because the nature of simulation allows *process*—system dynamics—to be brought into the training situation; (2) test a course of action in situations when information is unreliable or hard-to-come-by; (3) stimulate conversation on otherwise controversial matters; (4) enliven boring material; (5) provide instruction in a context similar to that on the job—assuming the simulation replicates key features of the job environment; (6) provide an anchor for subsequent discussion of theory and concepts (or alternatively, a means to test theories and concepts previously discussed); and (7) substitute for real experiences, providing learners with opportunities to learn by experience without the attendant costs and detrimental side effects of making mistakes in real settings.

To prepare a simulation, HRD practitioners should probably begin by researching the thousands of simulations already available. It is easier to modify an existing simulation than to start from scratch. One reference guide for this purpose is by Horn and Zuckerman (1980).

For more intrepid practitioners who prefer to design their own simulations, the basic steps in the process appear to be deceptively simple:

1. Establish objectives. What are the intended outcomes?
2. Describe the setting. Is it to be a work site, work group, department, organization, community, or some other entity?
3. Develop a story line. Who are the key actors and actresses in the setting? What are they doing? Why?
4. Develop role descriptions. What does each actor/actress do in the setting?
5. Create the foundation for the simulation by (a) clarifying how actors/actresses are to interact; (b) establishing rules of the "game" or "simulation." Do any procedures have to be clarified? Does a structure have to be imposed on group interaction? and (c) creating a means for decisions to have consequences. Will players or teams be awarded points or be given feedback on how well or poorly they are performing?
6. Test the simulation or game.
7. Revise it to fix any problems revealed through testing.

These steps are, of course, somewhat oversimplified. To find out more on the issue of design, see Adair and Foster (1972), Duke (1978), Ellington, Addinall and Percival (1982), Keiser and Seeler (1987), McLean (1978), and Zemke (1982a).

The chief disadvantages of simulations have to do with time and cost. It takes much time to develop a good simulation, especially one complicated enough to portray a complex process or setting. Nor is this likely to be cheap. Yet these factors may be outweighed by the value of representing processes for training purposes.

What delivery method should be used to present instruction? The answer to this question has to do with media selection. It is one of two fundamental issues in instructional design. The other has to do with preparation or selection of content.

Over the years, instructional delivery methods have become increasingly sophisticated. Trainers have realized that individuals vary in learning styles (Smith, 1982 & 1983). Some media are more appropriate than others for specific learning situations, trainees, and objectives (Kemp, 1971). There is still much to be learned on these matters. The state of the art is not that advanced (Levie & Dickie, 1973).

Many attempts have been made to develop *media models,* decision aids to help HRD practitioners select appropriate and cost-effective means of delivering instruction. One of the best is Anderson's (1983). It is comprehensive and covers most key issues in the selection process. These issues include: (1) *mandates:* Has somebody mandated what delivery method to use? (2) *purposes:* What are the intended outcomes? Is the primary purpose to inform, instruct, entertain, or persuade? (3) *constraints:* How much time, money, staff, effort, and equipment are available for designing instruction and for delivering it? (4) *cost benefits:* Are some methods more cost beneficial than others? (5) *flexibility:* Is there a great need to build in the possibility for easy revision at a later time? For instance, group instruction is appropriate when management requests it; more than one person has a need for instruction; adequate people, time, and money are available; and the need for flexibility is high. Individual instruction, on the other hand, is perhaps most appropriate when only one person has a need or when there is a good instructional reason to allow for individual differences.

For more information on the subject of media, see Hartley (1985), Heinich, Molenda, and Russell (1985), Kemp (1980), Percival and Ellington (1984), Romiszowski (1981), and Spector (1984).

Preparing or Selecting Content

There are three ways to develop content from instructional objectives: (1) HRD practitioners can prepare instructional content themselves; (2) they can select content from published or unpublished material and modify it for the uses at hand; or, (3) they can prepare part of the content on their own and select the remainder from material prepared previously or available commercially. This choice is a make-or-buy decision, and costs are usually the deciding factor.

How are objectives transformed into lessons, units, courses, or other formats? What alternatives to this approach exist? This section addresses these questions.

The process of transforming objectives into instruction begins after sequencing them appropriately and selecting media. There are three major steps: (1) creating a syllabus, (2) grouping objectives together into courses, units, and lessons, and (3) preparing or selecting content at each level.

A syllabus is a list of objectives. Objectives are sequenced in a way deemed minimally essential so that learners have adequate preparation to perform tasks or undertake learning objectives requiring background knowledge. In many cases, sequence may be based on actual steps taken in performing a job task (Blank, 1982). Using the syllabus, HRD practitioners group together related objectives to create training curricula, courses, units, and lessons.

All *courses* needed to teach employees to perform their jobs to minimal competency levels constitute a *training curriculum* (Sredl & Rothwell, 1987). A training curriculum is an organized and sequenced plan for training by job class. A curriculum "requires that we view the whole fabric of training in its totality; individual training (courses) are created from this perspective" (Galosy, 1983, p. 48). Without regard to specific titles, job classes are grouped together according to common characteristics. These groupings cut across the organization horizontally (see Figure 11-7). Each group has some relatively predictable needs. A separate training curriculum is designed for each job grouping, though all training curricula are interrelated (Sredl & Rothwell, 1987). As a result, an employee preparing for promotion may begin basic training for the next higher job grouping.

A *course* is an organized learning experience with a discrete beginning and end-

Figure 11-7: Job Groupings for Training Curricula

ing. Though typically associated with classroom training, courses do not have to be formal. In fact, they can be delivered on the job or in a college classroom off-site. Each training course focuses on a major task, activity, or responsibility associated with the job group.

Each course, in turn, comprises instructional *units* and *lessons*. A unit is a "chunk" of instruction (Posner & Rudnitsky, 1982). Its scope is smaller than a course, consisting of at least two units, and larger than a lesson, of which at least two are required to comprise a unit. As Hoover (1982) explains, "the basic element of a . . . unit consist of a number of related concepts, grouped together for instructional purposes" (p. 23). Each concept is, in turn, the basis of a *lesson plan*—a more detailed description of instructional activities than a unit.

Figure 11-8 illustrates relationships between a job curriculum, a course, a unit, and a lesson plan. Note that this relationship is one of increasing specificity, with job curriculum most general and lesson most specific. Use Activity 11-6 at the end of this chapter to consider the training curriculum of your organization.

Each lesson focuses on *one* instructional objective. Frequently, that objective enables the learner to prepare for achieving a terminal or end-of-course objective. It is thus rationally related to, but narrower in scope than, a terminal objective.

Many books and articles are available to provide guidance to trainers in preparing lessons and units. Units are usually scoped out in broad terms, describing: (1) the relationship of the unit to terminal course objectives; (2) the enabling objectives of the unit itself; (3) the lessons comprising the unit; and (4) the exercises or tests to reinforce

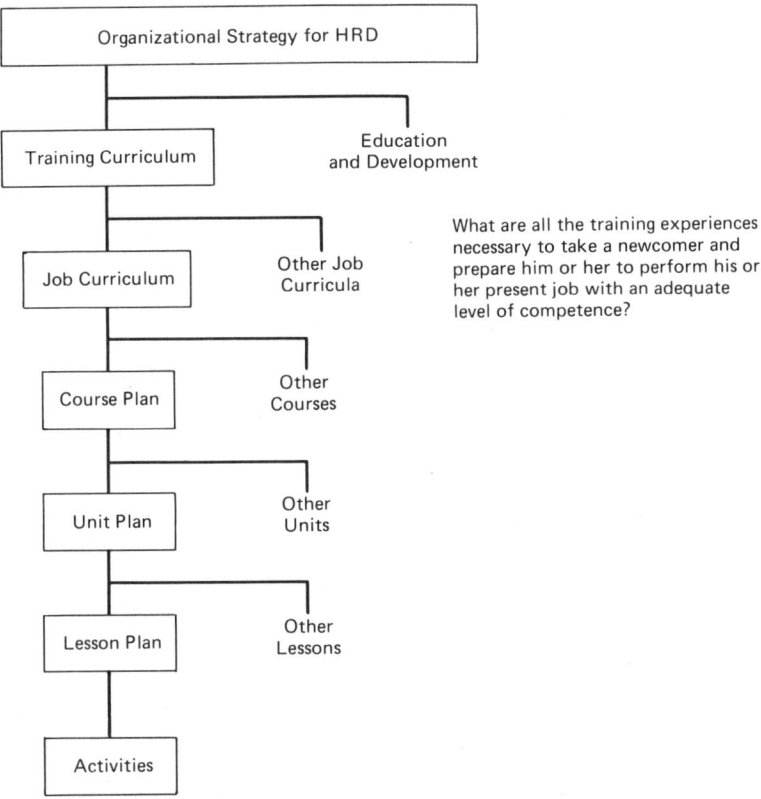

Figure 11-8: Relationships Between Organizational Strategy for HRD and Training Curriculum, Job Curriculum, Course Plans, Unit Plans, Lesson Plans, and Instructional Activities

principles. Hoover (1982) suggests that unit planning should clarify initiating, developing, and culminating activities. *Initiating activities* identify what learners will be able to do upon unit completion, and set forth major concepts presented in the unit (Hoover, 1982). *Developing activities* identify how the unit is structured and what methods are used to present concepts (Hoover, 1982). *Culminating activities* test or measure learner achievement (Hoover, 1982).

Lesson plans are more specific. They lay out in concrete terms what information to present, who should present it, and how to measure learner achievement (Hoover, 1982). Figure 11-9 illustrates the format of a sample lesson plan. This format is not meant to be representative of the *only* right way to lay out a lesson; rather, it is *one* way to do so.

Lessons, units, and syllabi are combined in an *instructor's guide* for each training course. It is part of an *instructional package* for a course which contains the trainee guide, instructor's guide, course tests, and instructions on using the entire package (Dick & Carey, 1985; Ribler, 1983). The trainee guide can be prepared before or after the instructor's guide. It contains a course outline, notes, exercises, copies of

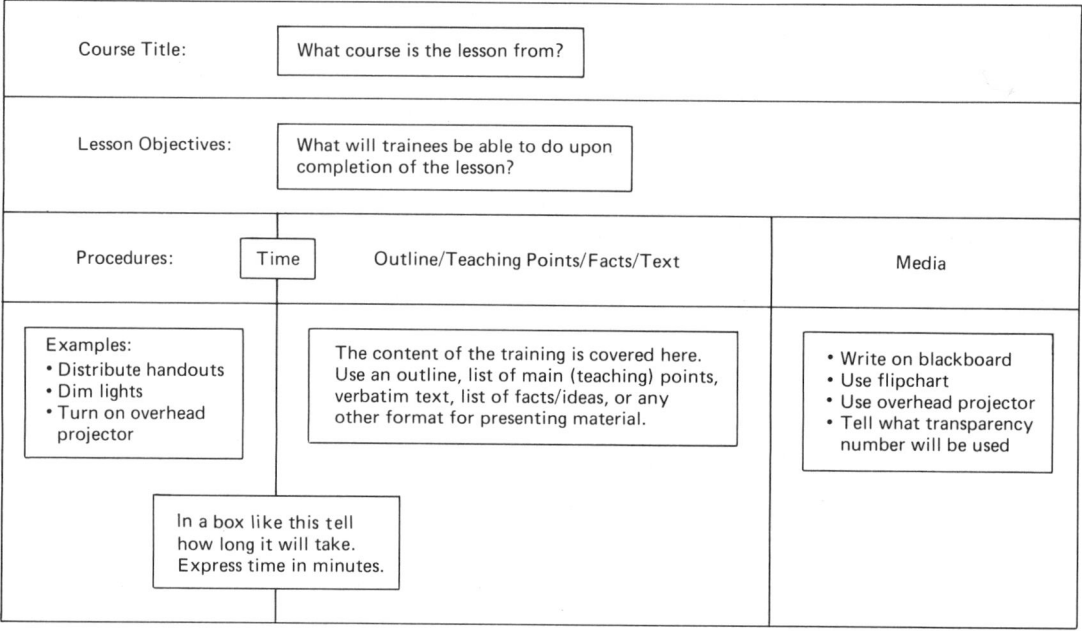

Figure 11-9: A Sample Format for a Lesson Plan

visual aids, and such additional resources as supplementary reading or a bibliography of pertinent books and articles.

Thus far, it seems that developing content from objectives is primarily a top-down process, beginning with course or curriculum development and culminating in unit and then lesson plans. However, the process can work the other way—from bottom up. HRD practitioners may begin with lesson planning, proceed to grouping related lessons into units, and in turn grouping related units into courses (Sredl & Rothwell, 1987). The danger of this approach is that it may result in poor overall planning.

In some corporations, HRD practitioners do not prepare formal lesson plans from behavioral objectives. The steps in the performance-based training design model are used in some instructional planning—for technical training, for instance—but are not used in management and executive-level training.

There are three major alternatives to developing instruction from objectives: (1) skeletal outlining; (2) detailed outlining; and (3) guided questioning or discovery learning (Sredl & Rothwell, 1987).

Skeletal outlining assumes that presenters are already versed in the subject matter. They need only a brief outline to list topics to be discussed in a training session. Otherwise, instructors "wing it." HRD practitioners provide, in addition to a skeletal topic outline, a list of instructional objectives to clarify what results are sought from the training.

A detailed outline is more complete, but not as thorough as lesson plans or instructional scripts. Basing the outline on a thorough needs assessment and work analysis, HRD practitioners furnish subject-matter-experts-turned-presenters with outlines of topics and subtopics, recommendations about how much time to spend on each topic, and tests or exercises to measure and reinforce learning.

The source of the guided questioning approach is the Socratic method, made famous in the *Dialogues* of Plato. There are two ways to use it. The first is *deductively,* in which instructors begin with a broad, general principle and guide trainees to specific conclusions. The second is *inductively,* in which instructors begin with specific details and guide trainees through skillful questioning to reach broad, general, but tentative conclusions.

In the first instance, the instructor will most likely guide trainees to "discover" what they already know and share it with other learners. The HRD practitioner has to analyze, in advance, every task and develop questions that will lead trainees to predetermined conclusions.

In the second instance, instructors are coinquirers with the learners. There are no "right" or "wrong" answers; rather, questions are designed to stimulate insights and create new information. The starting point is a series of participant problems, issues, or concerns. Instructors solicit a list of work-related problems from participants. They then (1) write the problems or issues on a blackboard, flipchart, or overhead so that all participants can see them; (2) group them into logical categories; (3) summarize each category with an open-ended question (that is, a question beginning with *who, what, when, where, how, could,* or *for what reason*); and (4) use the questions to begin a process of inquiry in which group members mutually explore issues, seeking new knowledge together (Knowles, 1980). Once decisions have been made about instructional content, the training design process is complete. The training is then tested prior to widespread delivery, modified based on the test results, and offered to targeted trainees.

PROBLEMS WITH THE TRADITIONAL MODEL OF TRAINING

The model of training design and delivery described in the previous part of this chapter assumes that job performance is *always* improved by (1) analyzing how a job is presently being performed; (2) assessing how well individuals are carrying out the job; and (3) designing instruction to encourage individuals to conform to present ways of performing the job. The assumption is that individuals *must* perform in ways consistent with traditional practices and historical job requirements. In many cases, of course, that is true.

On the other hand, there are cases when training should help anticipate future job requirements utterly unlike those that have existed in the past. Instead of narrowing gaps between actual and desired job performance at present, the focus should be on gaps between (1) present, actual performance, and (2) future, desired performance. Figure 11-10 illustrates this concept.

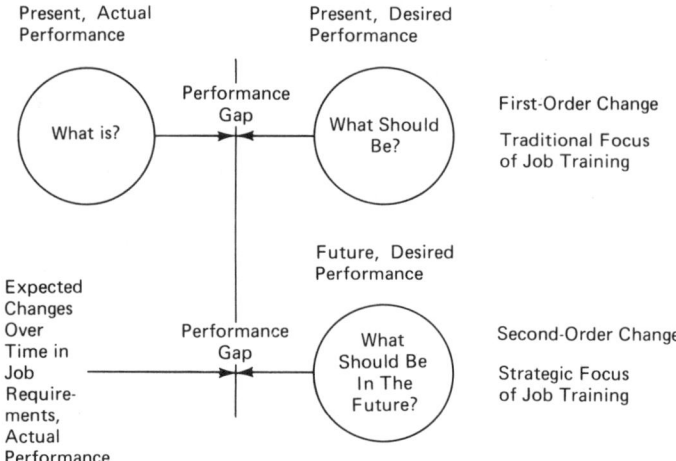

Figure 11-10: Differences in Focus Between Traditional and Strategic Training

The distinction, illustrated in Figure 11-10, really has to do with whether training should initiate first- or second-order change. First-order change is maintenance-oriented. Individuals learn existing work methods and steep themselves in organizational culture. Individuals adapt their behavior to organizational requirements. As Archer, Kelly, and Bisch (1984) explain:

> [First-order change] is brought about in a system without the system itself being changed. The basic rules are not changed, nor is the system's structure altered. The assistance given clients under the heading of "helping them to work the system," is first-order change. Despite the best of intentions, all one is really doing is helping clients to make the best of a less than desirable situation. They, not the system, adjust and conform (p. 44).

In this sense, training thus serves as a *maintenance system* as the term is used by Katz and Kahn (1978). It preserves an existing system by teaching people how to conform to policies, procedures, methods, and rules. At best, it fosters consistency by obtaining uniform behavior regarding policies and procedures intended "to formalize or institutionalize all aspects of organizational behavior" (Katz & Kahn, 1978, p. 86).

On the other hand, second-order change "seeks new ways to do things: new approaches and innovative structures and ideas" (Archer, Kelly, & Bisch, 1984, p. 45). It requires system change as well as individual change. When used in this way, training becomes an *adaptive system*. It "tends to achieve environmental constancy by bringing the external world under control" (Katz & Kahn, 1978, p. 89). Instead of bringing individual performance into compliance with organizational policies, procedures, work methods, and cultural requirements, training becomes a vehicle for anticipating future environmental requirements. As environmental conditions change, the organization *and* individuals gradually learn how to behave so as to meet new requirements created by those changing conditions.

STRATEGIC TRAINING

Strategic training prepares employees for changes in job requirements wrought by external environmental conditions or by organizational policies, procedures, plans, or work methods. It is based on predictions of future job requirements stemming from strategic necessity. Strategic training requires HRD practitioners and managers to envision what future job performance should be under future conditions and prepare people for those conditions. In this sense, then, training is a method of changing the "organizational paradigm," the culture or metarules governing behavior in the firm. It is a vehicle for realizing a vision of what individual performance should be under relatively uncertain future conditions. Hence, strategic training is a tool for organizational and individual transformation, renewal, and creativity (Levy & Merry, 1986). Its focus is on working smarter, not working harder.

HOW IS STRATEGIC TRAINING RELATED TO PLANNING?

Much like its traditional counterpart, strategic training contributes to formulating and implementing Organizational Strategy for HRD, HR Planning, and Strategic Business Planning. However, strategic training is useful in ways different from its traditional counterpart.

Strategic Training and Organizational Strategy for HRD

To formulate Organizational Strategy for HRD, managers and employees must envision the future. What are job conditions going to be in one year, two years, five years, and as business plans change? If people anticipate the future, they are positioned to take advantage of opportunities and avert threats posed by the changes it brings. This principle applies as much to individuals in their jobs as it applies to organizations in their interactions with the external environment.

To formulate Organizational Strategy for HRD, managers and employees need training to envision the future and plan in anticipation of it. Since future conditions are not fixed, like the past, envisioning them is a highly creative and subjective process. Future training needs are identified in the context of a vision of what future job requirements will be or should be.

Implementing Organizational Strategy for HRD is also highly creative and subjective. Since the future may not unfold as expected, HRD practitioners must plan for contingencies to cope with otherwise unexpected problems. To plan for contingencies, both HRD practitioners and operating managers may need instruction in the principles of contingency planning.

Strategic Training and HR Planning

To narrow the gap between present labor supply and future demand, managers can do more than just make better use of available supply. They can also: (1) change the allocation of work, which may affect the numbers and skills of people needed in the future; (2) automate; or (3) change the kind of people recruited into the firm. There are other strategies too: reduce turnover and absenteeism; change the distribution of full-time and part-time employees; and introduce innovative practices like job sharing or flexible work hours.

Any of these strategies will, of course, influence job training needs. In fact, HRD practitioners and managers may need to predict the likely future effects of each change, so as to anticipate future training needs. Strategic training is necessary to avert future shortfalls in the supplies of skilled people. Examining past requirements or projecting past needs into the future are equally inadequate for this purpose.

Implementation of HR plans calls for action on several fronts at once: recruitment of skills from outside the organization; contracting for skills on a short-term basis; and training employees for skills they will need to implement Strategic Business Plans.

Strategic Training and Strategic Business Planning

Strategic training contributes to Strategic Business Planning in two ways. First it furnishes new, perhaps better, methods of doing work. Second, it prepares employees at each organizational level to carry out their jobs in ways consistent with future job requirements. The process of formulating strategic training may reveal issues appropriate for consideration in formulating business strategy. The process of implementing strategic training may also produce new information of value in subsequent organizational strategy-making.

WHEN SHOULD STRATEGIC TRAINING BE USED INSTEAD OF TRADITIONAL TRAINING?

Use strategic training to: (1) train people for anticipating new job requirements stemming from changes in organizational plans, work methods, policies, procedures, or structure; (2) come up with new, innovative, ways to perform jobs or work tasks; (3) create new information or ideas; or (4) evaluate future job conditions and provide individuals with artificial experience in performing under those conditions. For this training to transfer back to the job, it has to be linked to other change strategies as part of a long-term organizational improvement effort (Knowles, 1984). Innovative methods are rarely accepted easily or painlessly.

A MODEL OF STRATEGIC TRAINING

The Model

The model of strategic training we propose is similar to the traditional performance-based model of instructional design and delivery. However, it differs from the traditional model in key respects. To apply the model, the HRD practitioner:

1. identifies opportune occasions to use it based on *problem-finding* rather than *problem-solving*,
2. assesses learner needs based on predictions of future conditions,
3. clarifies key characteristics expected of future learners,
4. analyzes the future setting in which training will be delivered and applied,
5. carries out future-oriented work analysis,
6. prepares strategic instructional objectives to narrow gaps between what learners know and do at present and what learners should know and do in the future if they are to perform their jobs in ways consistent with Strategic Business Plans,
7. creates strategically-oriented tests and other performance measures,
8. arranges objectives in sequence,
9. selects and uses appropriate delivery methods,
10. prepares and selects content for strategic training, and
11. delivers training.

Identifying Occasions to Use the Approach

The HRD practitioner who expects future changes to influence employee job performance should ask several key questions.

First, *what should employees be doing in the future?* Strategic Business Plans imply behavior and skills at every level of the organization's chain of command. If a plan calls for stable growth, employees may not need training. Past work methods may be appropriate.

On the other hand, dramatic changes in business strategy or external environmental conditions require utterly new duties and activities at every level of the firm. For example, the introduction of word processing in an office requires operators to learn how to use the equipment, people interacting with operators to learn how to deal with them under new conditions, and supervisors to learn new skills. The same is true, albeit on a larger scale, when Strategic Business Plans are changed.

Second, *what are employees actually doing?* This question elicits information about present performance, knowledge, and skills of employees.

Third, *what differences exist between what employees should be doing in the future and what they are actually doing?* Are performance problems *likely to arise in the future?* Are these problems likely to affect entire job classes or only individuals? What differences exist between knowledge, skills, and abilities *needed to perform a job competently at present* and those that *will be required in the future* to perform the same job competently? Changes in future job requirements can either be mandated or evolutionary. If mandated, managers tell people how they should perform; if evolutionary, change is introduced gradually.

Fourth, *how important are these differences?* Can training priorities be established to avert problems expected in the future? If problems are important enough to prevent successful implementation of Strategic Business Plans, for instance, then they are worth dealing with in advance through training or other methods.

Fifth, *what will be the cause of these differences?* Scan short-term conditions affecting job performance. What, if any, changes are likely to result from

- *new products* being introduced by the firm or new services being offered by it?
- *new policies* of the organization?
- *new procedures* or work methods?
- *new supervisors* with expectations different from past supervisors?
- *new technology* introduced in the work setting?
- *trends in work flow?* Will it increase, decrease, remain the same, or change in type or in form?
- *new methods of allocating work?* Will changes be made to organizational, departmental, divisional, or work group structure?
- *new methods of measuring job performance?* How will people be evaluated? What will be evaluated?
- *new methods of rewarding performance?* How will people be rewarded for what they do?

Changes like those listed provide the impetus for training to head off future problems.

Sixth, *what should be done about nontraining needs expected in the future?* Future performance problems may stem from causes other than knowledge or skill deficiencies. For example, a change in business plans may require changes in policies, procedures, leadership, structure, and rewards (Glueck & Jauch, 1984). No amount of training, for example, will solve problems resulting from improper allocation of work, inappropriate policies, reward systems which do not provide incentives in line with business strategy, lack of leadership, failures to provide individuals with feedback about their performance, group norms that are resistant to changes in line with Strategic Business Plans, lack of motivation to prepare for the future, or lack of ability. Admittedly, it may be difficult to anticipate and head off future problems stemming from *all* these causes, but it is worth the effort to try.

And seventh, *what should be done about strategic training needs?* Classroom-based instructional experiences are admittedly expensive. Nor are they the only means by which information can be gathered about future problems and solutions, or by which training can be delivered in anticipation of future needs.

Alternatives to traditional training can sometimes be substituted for strategic training. They include:

- *job aids:* Can future problems be averted by simple instructions to employees about what to do if a problem arises in the future? Job aids can be prepared and handed out in advance.
- *coaching:* Can future problems be averted by coaching employees individually about trends in the work or changes in their jobs which they need to prepare for?
- *work simplification:* Can future problems be averted by siphoning off special problems to management or employee committees, task forces, or other groups established to deal with them before they come up?

- *OD data gathering:* Can future problems be averted by polling experts inside or outside the organization about problems likely to come up in the future and by devising action plans needed to avert those problems? (See Nadler, 1977.)
- *creative problem-finding techniques:* Can innovative approaches to finding and averting future problems be used? These approaches include: the delphi procedure and Nominal Group Technique. Of course, these approaches may also be used to identify strategic training needs and to deliver creative, strategically-oriented "training" sessions.

However, if special benefits are associated with group training—such as the desirability of social interaction or the significant advantages to creative problem-solving which can be realized in group settings—then they may outweigh the high cost in lost production time of group training. In addition, these settings may be used to simulate future conditions, so that learners experience them and can thus be motivated to prepare for them in advance.

Assessing Strategic Training Needs

Historically, "there has been little explicit linkage between organizational planning modalities and training needs decisions" (Moore & Dutton, 1978, p. 533). One reason is that traditional training needs assessment tends to "rely heavily on the examination of past deficiencies or past behaviors as a basis for planning instruction intended to equip learners for meeting future conditions" (Rothwell, 1984, p. 19). Of course, the future does not always resemble the past. Experience is not always an appropriate guide for grappling with changing future conditions.

Traditional training needs assessment identifies past or present discrepancies between *what employees actually know or do* and *what they should know or do.* Instruction is then designed to narrow this gap between *what is* and *what should be.* On the other hand, strategic needs assessment identifies possible future discrepancies between what employees know or do at present and what they should know or do in the future. Instruction is then designed to anticipate future discrepancies between *what is at present* and *what should be in the future.*

The real difference, then, between traditional and strategic needs assessment has to do with *criteria.* Present criteria are what managers and other employees expect by way of job performance from a job incumbent at this time. If job standards have been established, they are the criteria by which to assess present performance. Future criteria are what managers expect after job requirements and standards have been affected by changing conditions inside and outside the firm. To predict future criteria, HRD practitioners and others should determine what major changes will affect the organization, and how those changes should affect job standards or job performance requirements.

The process of predicting future criteria is tentative and highly subjective. It is based on environmental scanning for each job class. During this process, it is relatively easy to link up Strategic Business Planning to training needs. HRD practitioners need only ensure that performance implications of Strategic Business Plans are considered while planning the training for each job class in the firm.

What data collection approaches are appropriately used for strategic training needs assessment? The answer is many of the same used in traditional training needs assessment. The most commonly used traditional approaches are (Beaudin & Dowling, 1985): (1) management requests; (2) record and report reviews; (3) informal group discussions; (4) questionnaires; and (5) observations/interviews. The key difference between traditional and strategic training needs assessment approaches really has to do with *what questions are asked,* not so much with *what data are collected.*

Management requests are usually past-oriented. By the time supervisors perceive a training need, performance problems have surfaced already. One way to handle this problem is to create an organizational training advisory committee for the purpose of identifying possible *future* performance/training problems before they come up. The HRD practitioner gathers information from various levels in the firm, presents the results to members of the committee, and listens to their opinions about which problems are likely to have the greatest future impact. Training needs are then identified *before* they are perceived in bottom-line, dollars-and-cents losses.

Systematic reviews of reports and records provide a source of information for this purpose. So, too, may informal meetings at various levels in the firm. The important point to bear in mind is this: the focus of data collection efforts should remain on future trends at the job level, their potential importance relative to Strategic Business Plans, and how these trends can be dealt with before they cause problems. In addition to surveys, interviews, observation, and record reviews, many other data collection approaches associated with futures research may help identify possible future performance problems. They include: the delphi procedure; nominal group technique; scenario development and analysis; cross-impact analysis; and many more (see Helmer, 1983; Rothwell & Kazanas, 1988; Schwartz, Svedin, & Wittrock, 1982; Wagschall, 1983). The same techniques used to assess strategic training needs may also be used to deliver strategic training.

Clarifying Key Characteristics of Future Learners

Who will receive strategic training? What characteristics will be common to them? This section addresses these questions.

Two primary groups of people who will be affected by strategic training are (1) *present job incumbents:* They are called the *horizontal market* of trainees because they occupy a job class at present; and (2) *future job incumbents:* They are called the *vertical market* of trainees because they do not occupy a job class yet but may well enter it before, during, or after future changes affect the job class (Sredl & Rothwell, 1987). Figure 11-11 illustrates differences between these two "markets" for training.

Incumbents of the horizontal market are gradually prepared for changes in job requirements. However, only some remain in the job category by the time changes are felt. Others are promoted, retired, transferred, terminated, or otherwise leave the organization. In contrast, incumbents of the vertical market require *employee education* because they have not yet entered the job but will do so eventually.

Employees presently working in a job may well be affected by changes in job duties and performance requirements resulting from changes in business strategy or

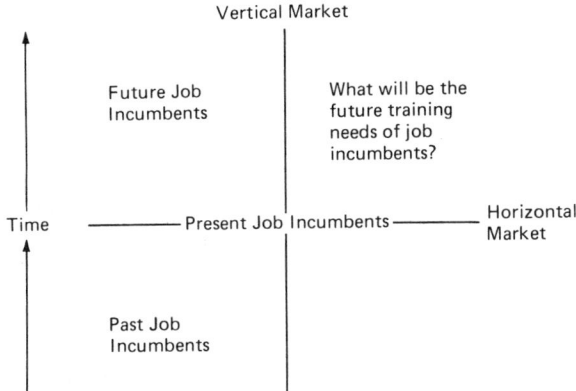

Figure 11-11: The Horizontal and Vertical Markets for Training

external environmental conditions. But if the emphasis is on the future, some employees are gone—moved out of the job class—by the time changes are felt. Other employees will be moving into the job class.

It is thus necessary to predict who the learners will be. There is little reason to devote substantial time and money to preparing employees for future changes in jobs when they will not experience those changes. In addition, it may be possible to reduce the need for strategic training if hiring and promoting procedures are coordinated with it so as to include consideration of *future* job requirements. In short, HRD practitioners reduce the need to train people in anticipation of future job changes if they select for hiring or promotion people already possessing knowledge and skills needed in the future.

Planning for future learners is related to HR planning—not instructional planning. Since strategic training calls for a relatively short time horizon—anticipatory training is best carried out shortly before a change is about to occur so that learners do not forget needed skills—the issue is less pertinent to training for present job incumbents than for preparing future ones through employee education. Yet it should be considered for planning training nevertheless (see Rothwell & Kazanas, 1988).

What learner or trainee characteristics will influence appropriate instructional design for strategic training? Consider:

- *ability:* Do trainees have the ability to learn in anticipation of need?
- *motivation:* How motivated are learners to prepare for future changes on the job? Are they likely to accept or reject training? Why or why not?
- *necessary base of skills:* How much do learners possess necessary background knowledge and skills? For example, it will be pointless to try to train people for technological changes when they lack basic skills in reading, writing, or arithmetic.
- *strategic thinking skills:* How much do learners possess the ability to peer into the future and work to anticipate it? This skill is learned. In some job classes,

individuals may never need such a skill—especially when their work allows little latitude for individual discretion. What can be done to prepare people to think ahead when their jobs do allow for discretion?

Are other learner characteristics worth taking into account when planning strategic training?

Analyzing the Future Setting

In traditional instructional design, HRD practitioners analyze work and instructional settings in advance. The closer the match between them, the better: when training is delivered under conditions resembling the work environment, it is more likely to be transferred to that setting. In strategic training, the HRD practitioner has to visualize the future job or work environment and create an instructional environment to simulate it. The idea is to use the instructional setting to simulate future, but not yet existing, job conditions, so that learners gain experience without incurring the costly consequences of doing so in a real setting. Mistakes and confusion in training, while not desirable, are at least less costly or significant than on the job.

What conditions will exist on the job in the near future? Consider: (1) *tools:* Will new tools or technology be introduced? What kind? (2) *physical conditions:* What will the job environment be like? (3) *work methods:* What methods will be used? (4) *policies/procedures:* What organizational policies and procedures will influence the job? and (5) *group norms:* What will coworkers say and do? How might their beliefs influence job conditions in the future? Obviously, the future work setting will affect employee job performance. Can it be simulated for instructional purposes?

Carrying Out Future-Oriented Work Analysis

Since training is geared to improving job performance, it makes sense to analyze job or task requirements. For this reason, work analysis is an essential component of any instructional design process. Once the HRD practitioner knows what a job incumbent is expected to do, training is designed to help learners master the knowledge or skills associated with successful job performance. In designing strategic training, the HRD practitioner goes beyond the analysis of present work to determine what a job incumbent should be doing if performance is to be consistent with Strategic Business Plans at a future time. This process we call strategic work analysis.

Perhaps the simplest method of strategic work analysis is based on job descriptions and job specifications. Of course, a *job description* simply summarizes major duties and responsibilities of a job. A *specification* lists minimum education and experience necessary to learn the job. Traditional work analysis yields a description of what job incumbents should be doing and what education and experience is necessary to do it. By way of contrast, strategic work analysis describes what job incumbents should be doing in the future and what education and experience will be necessary for them to do it. Discrepancies between traditional and strategic work analysis, as evident in job descriptions and specifications, constitutes a *planning gap* that subsequent, strategically-oriented training is designed to close (Wissema, Brand & Van der Pol, 1981).

Preparing Strategic Instructional Objectives

Instructional objectives express what learners will be able to do upon completion of a learning experience. They are traditionally intended to close a performance gap between *what employees know or do* and *what they should know or do.*

Strategic instructional objectives are no different. Like their traditional counterparts, they are designed to close a performance gap. However, the gap is different. Instead of expressing a discrepancy between what is and what should be at present, a strategic instructional objective is based on a discrepancy between *what is at present* and *what should be in the future.* When a strategic objective is met, a *planning gap* is closed.

In all other respects, strategic instructional objectives resemble their traditional counterparts. *Terminal objectives* express outcomes to be achieved by an entire course or other discrete learning experience; *enabling objectives* express outcomes to be achieved during a learning experience to measure progress toward terminal objectives.

Creating Strategically-Oriented Tests

There is little difference between creating traditional and strategic test items. For each strategic objective, the HRD practitioner prepares at least one test item to measure achievement. Each item links measurement to instructional outcomes and to *future* work tasks/activities, as shown in Figure 11-12. Strategically-oriented tests are administered in writing, orally, or by demonstration.

Arranging Objectives in Sequence

The arrangement of objectives in strategic training depends on the purpose of "instruction." There are two major purposes. *Nondirective training* produces new information. It fosters the sharing of insights, ideas, and innovative techniques among learners. *Directive training* is designed and delivered in anticipation of a future need, one which is soon going to be felt on the job. These purposes are not mutually exclusive; rather, they form a continuum. A training event may combine the two (see Figure 11-13).

If the purpose is directive, instructional objectives are sequenced exactly as they are in traditional training. The HRD practitioner makes sure that instruction follows

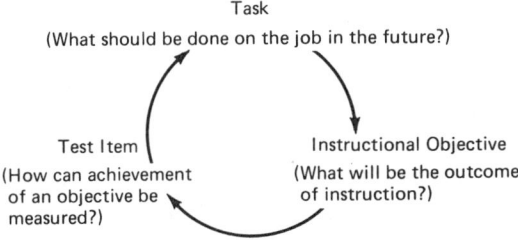

Figure 11-12: The Relationship Between Future Job Tasks, Instructional Objectives, and Test Items

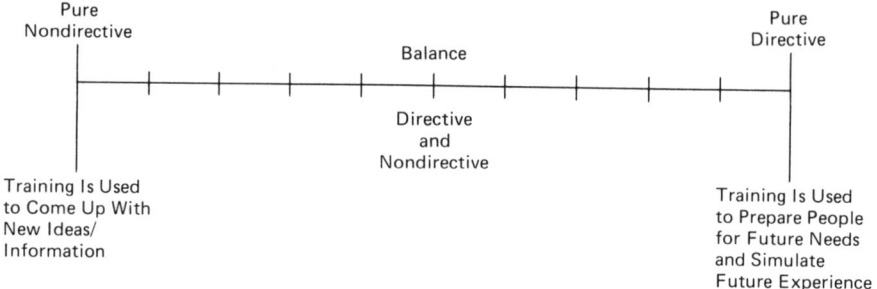

Figure 11-13: The Continuum of Instructional Purposes in Strategic Training

a sequence from what the learner already knows to what he or she does not know. In other words, prerequisite information must be provided first. Quite often this order is chronological: from what people now do to what they should do in the future.

On the other hand, if the purpose is purely nondirective, sequencing should depend on learner interests and concerns. As Knowles (1980) suggests:

> Early in the session there would be a problem census or a diagnostic exercise through which the participants would identify the specific problems they want to be able to deal with more adequately. This is not to suggest that a good adult-learning experience ends with the problems the learners are aware of in the beginning, but that is where it starts. (p. 54)

Additional issues may be suggested by the group leader. The learners, in cooperation with the group leaders, then sequence the topics or objectives in the order they wish to treat them. The sequence may thus be based on perceived importance rather than on logical groupings.

Selecting and Using Appropriate Delivery Methods

The selection and use of appropriate delivery methods depends on the purpose of strategic training. When the purpose is purely directive, specific outcomes are desired. The choice of delivery methods is based on the same issues which are important in traditional training: cost, time, skills of HRD staff, and available materials. If the purpose is purely nondirective, specific outcomes are not necessarily fixed. The learning event is a discovery session where new ideas are created and new learning needs are identified.

For either purpose, however, many delivery methods can be used to provide information, reinforce learning, evoke new insights or new ideas, and simulate future job conditions or problems. Some of these methods have been discussed earlier in the chapter and are capable of being modified to help anticipate future needs as well as meet present ones. They are summarized in Table 11-1.

TABLE 11-1 ADAPTING TRADITIONAL TRAINING METHODS TO STRATEGIC TRAINING

Method	Brief description	Traditional use	Strategic use
Lecture	a lengthy talk delivered to trainees	deliver information to trainees	tell trainees about what changes are likely to affect their jobs as a result of trends inside and outside the organization
Independent Reading	reading intended to provide background information for training or to substitute for classroom-based instruction	(1) provide background information (2) substitute for live lecture	(1) provide information about trends likely to affect future job performance and their effects (2) substitute for live lecture
Panels	a group of people assembled in front of trainees to discuss an issue or problem	stimulate thinking of trainees about present (topical) issues	stimulate thinking of trainees about future issues which influence job tasks/performance
Buzzgroups	a small group (five to six people) assembled to work on a common problem and report a solution to a larger group	problem-solving in classroom training sessions	(1) identify future problems (2) suggest solutions to future problems before the problems come up
Exercises	broad category of methods; anything which requires learners to apply their knowledge or skill	focus on job-oriented problems which are common at present or have been common in the past	discuss job-oriented problems likely to come up in the future
Case Studies	narrative descriptions of a problem situation, usually ranging from a paragraph to several pages	focus on improving trainee problem-solving skills by analyzing problems which are common at present or have been common in the past	describe features of the future job environment; focus attention on anticipating future problems and solving them before they arise
Incident Process	a short (one- to two-sentence) description of a problem situation	similar to case study	similar to case study
Role Play	a dramatic enactment between two or more people intended to represent a situation	act out a role to experience insights	simulate future conditions or situations

A Model of Strategic Training

TABLE 11-1 Continued

Method	Brief description	Traditional use	Strategic use
Behavior Modeling	acting out the "right way" to behave—that is, show someone how to act	demonstrate, concretely, how an individual should behave at present	demonstrate, concretely, how an individual should behave under expected future job conditions
Demonstration	showing the learner how to perform a task/activity or how to operate equipment	illustrate steps in a job task or work process, usually as it should be carried out at present	using a machine not yet installed in the work setting, illustrate how to carry out steps in task or work process in the near future (e.g., after installation of the machine in the work setting)
Trips	take learners to see something for themselves	What are work conditions like at present?	What are work conditions like in settings where a new innovation (e.g., new technology) has been introduced?
Simulation/ Games	similar to a lengthy role play involving several participants intended to represent a work (or problem situation), often as completely as possible	act out a part similar to that played in the present job setting	• illustrate/dramatize future conditions • motivate trainees to learn • give trainees a chance to gain experience before it is possible to do so in the work setting

There are others:

- Brainstorming
- Brainwriting
- Crawford Slip Writing
- Phillips 66
- Delphi Procedure
- Nominal Group Technique
- Force field analysis
- Cross impact analysis
- Scenario analysis

- Multiple scenario analysis
- Morphological analysis
- Checklists
- Microsimulations
- Lateral thinking
- Devil's advocate
- Group advocate

Nor are these the only ones (see Spaid, 1986; Van Gundy, 1981; 1982; 1984). Each of the 350 delivery methods described by Huczynski (1983) can be reoriented to a strategic use.

Brainstorming is perhaps the simplest way to unleash group creativity to deal with problem-finding and solving. Rawlinson (1981) defines it simply as "a means of getting a large number of ideas from a group of people in a short time" (p. 36). He identifies six stages in the process: (1) "state the problem and discuss"; (2) "restate the problem"; (3) "select a basic restatement and write it down"; (4) "warm-up session"; (5) "brainstorm"; and (6) "wildest idea" (p. 40). These stages are largely self-explanatory: during the first stage, the problem is stated and discussed; in the second stage, the problem is restated and possible solutions are considered; in the third stage, one restatement of the problem is selected to stimulate discussion of solutions; in the fourth stage, participants warm up by generating ideas in rapid fire for no more than five minutes; in the fifth stage, the process continues but in a more serious vein, and the group leader writes down ideas for group members to see; and in the sixth and final stage, the wildest idea is taken from the previous stage and used to stimulate more serious ones.

Much has been written about brainstorming (Bouchard, 1971; Coon, 1976; Madsen & Finger, 1978; Street, 1974; and Terry, Berry, & Block, 1958). It continues to be applied in many settings to generate new ideas and approaches. Of course, it can be applied to identifying (1) training needs in each job class which may result from Strategic Business Plans; (2) new work methods and innovative approaches; and (3) performance problems before they arise.

Brainwriting is a modification of brainstorming. Two variations are common (Van Gundy, 1981): (1) the brainwriting pool, and (2) battelle-bildmappen-brainwriting (BBB). In the first approach, a problem is read to a small group (six is a good number). After group members brainstorm on the problem aloud, they are given several photographs or drawings unrelated to it. They then write down ideas suggested to them by the pictures. Solutions are read to the group and used to stimulate more ideas. In the second approach, a problem is read to a group. Individuals scribble ideas on a piece of paper. After several ideas are listed on the paper, it is placed in a pool at the center of the group. Individuals remove different sheets, record new ideas on them, and place them back in the pool. This process continues for thirty or forty minutes.

Brainwriting, like brainstorming, can also be used in strategic training. It serves as a means to identify future training needs likely to stem from business plans or environmental changes. Similarly, it can unleash group creativity relative to future problems likely to confront job incumbents, or methods for solving those problems.

Crawford Slip Writing is a variation of brainwriting. Charles Clark (1978) has described the approach in detail. The approach can be modified for strategic training. The HRD practitioner:

- gives each participant a pad of paper (3" x 5") with at least twenty-five sheets,
- reads a question to the group, such as (a) What problems are likely to confront you on the job in the next year? (b) What knowledge/skills do you feel you will need over the next year to solve problems you expect to come up on your job? (c) How can the organization deal with a major strategic issue?,

- asks group members to write an idea on each slip of paper,
- asks group members to stop writing after five or ten minutes,
- collects the slips of paper,
- appoints a task force to evaluate ideas, sorting slips of paper into categories based on importance or practical use, and
- uses the ideas to identify future training needs or content for future-oriented instruction.

The value of the approach should be apparent.

The Phillips 66 Technique is a way to stimulate ideas and identify future job-related problems, training needs, or issues for subsequent exploration.

To apply the approach to strategic training, the HRD practitioner:

- divides a large group into smaller groups of no more than six people each,
- encourages group members to get acquainted,
- asks each group to select a leader and a secretary,
- reads a carefully-worded statement or question to the groups about a problem or issue to be considered by them,
- asks each group to come up with one brief statement about (a) an issue of strategic import to the organization; (b) an issue of strategic import to a division, department, or work group within the organization; (c) a trend inside or outside the organization which will change job duties, tasks, or work methods; (d) a future training need; or (e) a solution to a future problem,
- gives the groups a time limit of five to fifteen minutes to come up with a short, single answer (or question), and
- asks a representative from each group to report at the end of the agreed-on time limit.

The Phillips 66 technique can thus help generate new ideas, identify future training needs, suggest new approaches to handling work, and recommend specific content to meet future training needs.

The Delphi Procedure is a method for "obtaining the most reliable consensus of opinion of a group of experts . . . by a series of intensive questionnaires interspersed with controlled opinion feedback" (Dolkey & Helmer, 1963, p. 458). It is used to scan the environment to identify possible changes, their effects, training needs, new work methods and approaches, and issues worth exploring. For more on the Delphi see Linstone (1978), Linstone and Turoff (1975), and Van de Ven and Delbecq (1974).

The *Nominal Group Technique* can be used to identify likely future problems, training needs, and issues worthy of exploration. It "combines a silent time for idea generation . . . with the social reinforcement of an interacting group setting" (Ulsehak, Nathanson, & Gillan, 1981, p. 86). Like the Delphi, it has already been described in an earlier chapter of this book.

Force field analysis is the creation of Kurt Lewin (1947). The HRD practitioner asks participants in a small group to

- identify any of the following: (a) a major trend in the external environment likely to affect job performance in the future; (b) a major trend in the internal environment—that is, inside the organization—likely to affect job performance in the future; (c) effect(s) of a major trend in the external or internal environment; (d) training need(s) resulting from major trends or their effects; or (e) training content adequate to anticipate and meet future needs,
- identify forces which (a) inhibit a trend, its effects, training needs, or efforts to anticipate and meet those needs; and (b) facilitate a trend, its effects, training needs, or efforts to anticipate and meet those needs, and
- plan action steps to: (a) weaken forces inhibiting change; (b) strengthen forces facilitating change; (c) strengthen forces inhibiting change; (d) weaken forces facilitating change; or, (e) some combination of these.

Force field analysis is most useful as a needs assessment method, though it can also be used as the basis for experiential learning exercises to pinpoint possible future job performance problems and the training needed to deal with them.

Cross impact analysis examines when "the occurrence of an event will affect the likelihood that other events will occur" (Stover & Gordon, 1978, p. 302). A matrix is developed to summarize possible events and their relationships. To apply this technique to strategic training, HRD practitioners (Stover & Gordon, 1978): (1) identify possible events which might occur; (2) estimate probabilities of each event; (3) estimate possible linkages *between events;* and, (4) come up with action plans to deal with likely events.

Probabilities are initially established by experts. Of course, when it comes to possible future events affecting job duties, incumbents may well be the best "experts." Predictions stemming from such analysis identify future training needs and instructional content adequate to anticipate those needs.

Scenario analysis is a quintessential tool in Strategic Business Planning. The term *scenario* comes from drama, where it means a plot outline. In concrete terms, that is precisely what a scenario is—an outline, story, or flowchart of events. It is a plausible description of the future. To apply scenarios to strategic training, the HRD practitioners may use (1) a "training" session to develop one or more scenarios of conditions affecting incumbents of a job class, organization, division, department, or work group; (2) scenarios to stimulate thinking about future training needs or simulate future conditions so that learners can draw conclusions about their own training needs; or, (3) scenarios to reinforce principles brought up in strategic training.

Developing a scenario sounds easy, but it is not. The instructional designer, manager, or group participant confronted with the task must: (1) *Identify boundaries and scope.* Will the scenario encompass the organization, a division, department, work group, job class, community, or some other "unit"? (2) *Clarify time horizon.* For training, use periods of a year or two. Longer time frames are appropriate for strategic planning and employee education, but not for short-term training. (3) *Identify key elements.* What trends, problems, or issues are likely to exert influence and be important to future job performance, are highly unlikely to exert influence and are unimportant to job performance, and are somewhere in between? (4) *Adopt assumptions.*

What will be the likely future effects of a problem, issue, or trend? and (5) *Use "hard" or "soft" methods to generate the scenario.* Soft methods are intuitive; hard methods are strictly logical. See Heydinger & Zentner (1983), Mandel (1983), and Wilson (1978).

Multiple scenario analysis uses between two and four scenarios. Each is a plausible, albeit different, view of the future. "Very often, each scenario reflects a different perspective, a different set of assumptions, and a different logic about the future" (Mandel, 1983, p. 10-5). By planning for alternatives, trainees gain different perspectives about future trends/problems/environmental conditions, possible effects of them, and training needs.

Morphological analysis "is an eclectic, forced-relationship approach that consists of dividing a problem into its major parameters or dimensions and then subdividing these into different possible forms of the original dimensions" (Van Gundy, 1981, p. 244). Morphology also lends itself to examining trends, issues, and events.

To apply the approach to strategic training, HRD practitioners and/or trainees (Van Gundy, 1981): (1) identify a problem, trend, or likely environmental change; (2) identify several dimensions of the problem, trend, or change; (3) generate a list of characteristics for each dimension; (4) create a two- or three-dimensional matrix; (5) list dimensions and characteristics on the matrix; and (6) use the matrix to identify solutions and effects. The basic idea is illustrated in Figure 11-14.

Morphological analysis, like other approaches described in this section of the chapter, helps trainees generate new ideas to deal with future problems before they come up, identify future training needs, and develop content for strategic training. For more on the subject see Allen (1962) and Zwicky (1969).

Checklists help generate new ideas by comparing items on a preexisting checklist to a given problem or a situation. This technique to problem-solving has often been applied to marketing as a way to identify new products or new consumer markets for development. For instance, Osborn (1963) suggests that managers ask the following questions when considering the development of a new product from an old one:

- What other product is similar? (Is adaptation possible?)
- How can a product be changed? (Is modification possible?)
- How can additions be made to the product? (Is magnification of existing features a possible alternative?)
- How can features be taken away from the product? (Is minification an alternative?)
- What could be used instead of this product or portions of it? (Is substitution of features possible?)
- What alterations in the product could be made? (Is rearrangement a viable alternative?)
- How could the needs which the product is designed to meet be turned around? (Is reversal possible?)
- What features of two or more existing products could be assembled into one new product? (Is combination possible?)

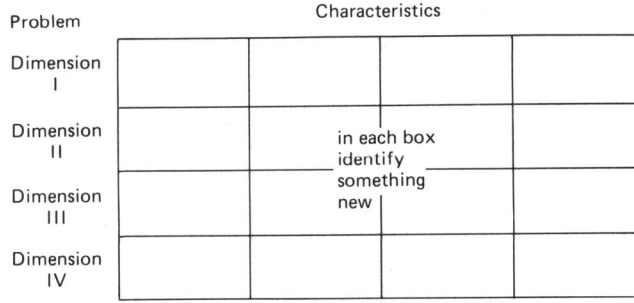

Figure 11-14: Preparing a Problem Matrix

The same approach can be applied to work tasks, work methods, performance problems, future training needs, or even future training content. Use Activity 11-7 at the end of this chapter to apply this approach.

Microsimulations are short, relatively informal practice sessions carried out under conditions anticipated in the work setting in the near future. They are slightly more lengthy than role plays, which they resemble, and use such "props" as new equipment to support the simulation. Trainees perform under these artificial conditions. Their experience is artificial but does furnish a means to (1) motivate trainees to learn about new equipment by proving to them the need to do so; (2) train them in new skills not yet needed in the work setting; (3) let learners practice in a setting where mistakes will not prove to be too expensive; and (4) develop instructional content for future training.

Lateral thinking "is not so much a formal technique as it is a method for developing new attitudes to apply to the thinking process" (Van Gundy, 1981, p. 234). Developed by Edward deBono (1970), it is meant to be distinct from traditional, logical thinking. Lateral thinking seeks new perspectives and ideas; avoids value judgments about "right" or "wrong"; welcomes unusual, chance intrusion of unrelated information; attempts to find the unique or different rather than the obvious; and progresses illogically through patterns of free association.

Three major activities are used in lateral thinking: (1) *awareness*, used to change definitions and clear up current thinking; (2) *alternatives*, used to stimulate new ways of looking at problems or issues; and (3) *provocative methods*, used to develop new ideas (Van Gundy, 1981). In the awareness stage, five different areas are looked at; in the alternatives stages, any one of seven techniques can be used; in the provocative methods stage, any one of seven techniques can be used. Activity 11-8 at the end of this chapter summarizes the five areas of the awareness stage and the seven techniques associated with the alternatives and provocative methods stages. Each can be applied in strategic training to stimulate new ideas and identify and anticipate future problems and instructional needs.

The *devil's advocate* method assumes that the best way "to deal with a complex problem is rendered in the context of opposition" (Mason & Mitroff, 1981, p. 37). Conflict sharpens thinking about problems, issues, or solutions. Too often managers try to suppress conflict because they view it negatively, as a destructive rather than

A Model of Strategic Training

potentially constructive phenomenon (Hensey, 1983). Indeed, there is a tendency to reduce conflict on interpersonal matters—"personality conflicts"—rather than recognize that conflict can stem from different goals, perspectives, and role requirements (Kolb & Glidden, 1986).

The devil's advocate approach has been used in Strategic Business Planning and can also be applied in strategic training. Trainees work up a solution to a problem—or identify an issue which they believe will increasingly pose a job performance problem in the future—and present it to their instructor or a panel of peers. The instructor or panel then deliberately adopts the role of critic, attacking ideas presented in the solution. Trainees defend their ideas. The assumption is that good ideas will survive stiff challenge. This process trains employees how to anticipate and plan for these challenges.

One variation of the devil's advocate approach is to place a special handicap on challengers: every time they attack an idea, they must present a reasonable alternative to it. If they attack a solution on the basis of practicality, then they *must* present a more practical alternative; if they attack a solution on the basis of cost, then they *must* present a cheaper but equally effective alternative. An advantage of this variation is that it forces progressive thinking. It gets around the chief disadvantage of a pure devil's advocate approach: "if the censure prevails and the plan is rejected, there is nothing to replace it" (Mason & Mitroff, 1981, p. 129).

The *group debate method* examines an issue or problem from different points of view. Trainees are divided into at least two groups. They are then presented with an issue or problem. For example, they might be asked to begin with any one of the following questions: (1) What trends inside or outside the organization do you believe will influence your ability to do your job in the next year? (2) What problems do you expect to come up in your job in the next year? Why do you think they will come up? (3) What knowledge or skills will you need over the next year or two to anticipate work-related problems before they come up and to deal with those problems before they arise? Each group answers the question. If their answers differ significantly, group members are arranged in two panels and debate their ideas and solutions. Through opposition, they eventually arrive at a synthesis or consensus about (1) problems likely to come up, (2) actions needed to anticipate them, (3) training needs associated with likely future problems, and (4) instructional content for future training that is designed to provide employees with knowledge or skills before they are needed.

Delivery methods described in this section of this chapter can be used in settings other than training. Indeed, they can serve as useful learning tools during Strategic Business Planning retreats, meetings of training advisory committees, and problem-identification or problem-solving meetings of work groups, departments, or divisions. When properly applied, these methods can help people anticipate problems rather than react to crises.

Preparing and Selecting Content for Strategic Training

If strategic training is directive, then instructional content is prepared in-house or selected from externally-prepared training materials in precisely the same way that traditional instruction is prepared. Instructional objectives are elaborated into courses, units, and lessons. Great emphasis is placed on experiential methods to simulate future job conditions and prepare individuals for performing in them.

On the other hand, nondirective training produces new information, stimulates new insights, motivates trainees to prepare for the future, provides a means to simulate future conditions, and gives trainees a chance to gain experience before it is needed. Nondirective training is dependent on the skills of the group facilitator, who stimulates group thinking. Content stems from the "training" session and is a function of group interaction and methods used to elicit new ideas.

Delivering Training

In directive training, whether traditional or strategic, effective delivery is synonymous with good public speaking. The instructor bears the chief burden and must use good "platform skills." Much has been written on this subject (see Snyder & Ulmer, 1972). Most of it boils down to a few key principles: (1) speak clearly; (2) use good eye contact; (3) vary tone and modulation of voice; (4) watch the audience and respond to nonverbal cues; (5) use questions to increase audience participation; and (6) reinforce ideas and enliven the presentation with visual aids.

In nondirective strategic training, most of the burden for delivery rests with participants rather than with the instructor. The group leader is a facilitator—one who stimulates thinking—rather than pure subject-expert or instructor.

Good questioning skills are important for instructors, but are essential for successful group facilitators (Sredl & Rothwell, 1987). Questions control discussions, stimulate thinking, and identify problems and solutions.

There are two types of questions. *Closed-ended questions* elicit "yes" or "no" responses. They begin with words like "do" or "is." For example: "Do you believe that is correct?" or "Is that true?" *Open-ended questions* are difficult to answer with one word. They begin with words like "who," "what," "when," "where," "why," "how," "how much," "could," and "would." For example: "What are some reasons?"; "When would it be appropriate to do that?" Closed-ended questions control discussion because a "yes" or "no" response closes off further discussion. That is not always true, of course, because some trainees may object to a simple response. But it is generally true. Open-ended questions, on the other hand, stimulate further discussion. They invite talk, provoking problem-finding and problem-solving efforts. They can be used to prompt (Hennings, 1975):

- data gathering, such as (a) defining; (b) fact-finding; (c) providing or eliciting examples; and (e) prompting judgments,
- data processing, such as (a) noting relationships; and (b) comparing or contrasting ideas, and
- abstracting, such as (a) drawing conclusions; (b) coming up with generalizations; and (c) predicting what will or may happen.

For more on questioning, see Friedman and Yarbrough (1985), Hunkins (1972), and Micali (1982).

ACTIVITY 11-1 A Structured Form for Analyzing Human Performance Problems

Directions: Use this form to structure your thinking about any problem having to do with people or events in a firm. Answer the following questions.

I—The Problem

1. Describe the problem. Explain, as clearly as you can, what it is, when it first manifested itself, how it manifested itself, who is involved with it, where (part of the firm or location) it is most noticeable, and why it or its consequences are important.

II—Cause

2. To what extent does the performance problem stem from *lack of individual knowledge or skill?* To what extent does the problem stem from some other cause? Describe the principal cause(s) of the problem.

3. To what extent is the problem caused by a *poor allocation of work duties?* If that is a major cause of the problem, what changes in work duty allocation can solve the problem?

ACTIVITY 11-1 Continued

4. To what extent is the problem caused by *inappropriate policies?* If a policy (or policies) contributes to a problem, what changes in policy can help solve the problem?

5. To what extent is the problem caused by *reward systems* which are not consistent with desired employee performance? What changes in reward systems can contribute to solving the problem(s)?

6. To what extent is the problem caused by *leaders at lower levels who do not agree with goals/objectives* established at higher levels? What can be done to solve problems stemming from leadership?

7. To what extent is the problem caused by *lack of feedback* to employees about their performance? How do they hear about their mistakes? What can be done to improve feedback to employees about their work performance?

ACTIVITY 11-1 Continued

II—Cause

8. To what extent is the problem caused by *group norms?* Do employees, as a group, seem to support changes? What can be done to improve performance when problems stem from group norms?

9. To what extent are *individuals able to practice their skills and apply their knowledge* on a regular basis? To what extent do performance problems stem from lack of practice? What can be done to increase opportunities for practice?

10. To what extent do performance problems stem from lack of individual motivation? Do employees know what results they are to achieve? Do they associate getting results with consequences important to them? What can be done to correct problems stemming from lack of motivation?

ACTIVITY 11-1 Continued

11. To what extent do performance problems stem from lack of individual ability? Are individuals capable of performing correctly? If not, what can be done to correct the problem?

12. To what extent do performance problems stem from causes other than those listed in this activity? List some possibilities and consider them.

ACTIVITY 11-2 Alternatives to Classroom-Based Training

Directions: Use this activity to structure your thinking. Consider: does the training you contemplate lend itself to alternatives other than formal, classroom-based experiences? Answer the questions which follow.

I. Description

1. What training needs are you intending to meet? Describe them.

II. Alternatives

2. Would any or all of the needs described in item 1 lend themselves to instruction other than classroom-based training? Consider each of the following.

   a. Job aids?
   b. Decision aids?
   c. Individualized instruction?
   d. On-the-job training?
   e. Another method? (Describe it.)

III. Costs

3. Prepare an estimate of how much it will cost to deliver training using each delivery method listed in Part II. (Be sure to consider the cost of time spent away from work, including lost production and salary expense.)

ACTIVITY 11-2 Continued

IV. Special Considerations

4. Are there special considerations which might outweigh cost? List the relative advantages and disadvantages of each method in Part II. Then compare them to the advantages and disadvantages of classroom-based training.

V. Conclusions

5. What delivery method(s) should be used to meet training needs?

A Model of Strategic Training

ACTIVITY 11-3 Carrying Out Needs Assessment

Directions: Use this activity to structure your thinking about important issues in carrying out the needs assessment. Answer the questions which follow.

I. Goals/Objectives

1. What are the goals and objectives of the training needs assessment process? What general results are you hoping to achieve? What specific outcomes are desired? Are there secondary goals, such as (1) building interest in a change effort? (2) raising expectations for performance improvement? and (3) improving employee morale?

II. Target Group

2. Whose needs are being assessed? Define the target group.

III. Data Collection

3. How will information about the training needs of the target group be collected? Are some approaches to data collection better than others?

ACTIVITY 11-3 Continued

IV. Special Guidelines

4. What special guidelines should be established, in advance, regarding the use of data collection methods?

V. Analysis

5. What analytical techniques should be used to interpret the results of needs assessment efforts? Why should those techniques be used rather than others?

ACTIVITY 11-4 An Activity on Learner Characteristics

Directions: When planning for training, consider learner characteristics. Use this activity to do some brainstorming on this issue. Answer the following questions.

I. Training Need

1. Describe the need that the training will be designed to meet.

II. General Characteristics

2. What learner characteristics generally affect training for a particular job?

3. How can these general characteristics be planned for?

ACTIVITY 11-4   Continued
III. Specific Characteristics
4. What characteristics of learners will be especially pertinent to training at a given time? Consider: topical issues affecting the job, the work group, the department, the division, or the organization.
5. How can these characteristics be planned for during training design?

ACTIVITY 11-5 The Work Setting and the Instructional Setting

Directions: It is important to consider, during the planning of training, the work setting in which the training is to be subsequently applied. Generally, the more the instructional setting resembles the work setting, the greater the likelihood that training will transfer successfully back to the job. Use this activity to consider the key features of the work setting, the instructional setting, and ways to make the instructional setting resemble the work setting. Answer the following questions.

I. Work Setting

1. Describe important features of the setting in which the individual will apply training. Be sure to cover physical conditions, tools/resources, group norms, supervisory expectations, and employee expectations. *(If you can't describe these features, research them.)*

II. Instructional Setting

2. Describe important features of the setting in which training is to be delivered. Be sure to cover physical conditions, tools/equipment, resources, and philosophy/beliefs.

III. Ways to Make the Instructional Setting Like the Work Setting

3. How can the instructional setting be made to resemble the work setting?

ACTIVITY 11-6 Designing a Traditional Training Curriculum

Directions: Using your own employer, list job titles in column 2 which correspond to the general categories in column 1. Then, for each job grouping, note the most important duties in column 3. For each major duty listed in column 3, list a corresponding instructional objective or series of objectives in column 4. Finally, for each objective listed in column 4, list a course title for training in column 5. If necessary, continue your answers on other sheets.

Column 1	Column 2	Column 3	Column 4	Column 5
Job Groupings*	Jobs	Key Duties	Instructional Objectives	Training Courses or Experiences
Executives				
Senior Managers				
Middle Managers				
First-Line Supervisors				
Sales Personnel				
Professionals				
Administrative Employees				
Clerical Support				
Skilled Production Workers				

A Model of Strategic Training

ACTIVITY 11-6 Continued					
Column 1	Column 2	Column 3	Column 4	Column 5
Job Groupings*	Jobs	Key Duties	Instructional Objectives	Training Courses or Experiences
Unskilled Production Workers				
Customer Service Representatives				
Others				

*Based on job groupings found in Gordon, 1986.

ACTIVITY 11-7	A Checklist for Creative Reconsideration of Work Activities/ Job Tasks		
Directions: Answer the questions in the two parts which follow for a work activity or job task of your choice.			
I. Description of Present Status			
1. Describe a job task or a work activity. What is it? How is it carried out? When is it performed? Why is it important? Who performs it or is involved with it? List steps in the task, or flowchart stages of carrying it out.			
II. Reconsideration of Status			
How can the job task or work activity be changed?		Describe the change	What are the advantages/ disadvantages of the change over present methods?
2. What other tasks/ work activities are *similar?* (Is it possible to handle this task or activity like a different one?)			
3. How can the tasks/ work activities *be changed?* (Is modification possible?)			

A Model of Strategic Training

ACTIVITY 11-7 Continued

II. Reconsideration of Status

How can the job task or work activity be changed?		Describe the change		What are the advantages/ disadvantages of the change over present methods?
How can *additions* be made to the task or work activity? (Is magnification of existing features a possible alternative?)				
How can features be *taken away* from the task or activity? (Is simplification of features possible?)				
What other tasks/ activities can be *used instead of* this task/activity or portions of it?				
What *alterations* to the task/activity could be made? (Is rearrangement of steps a possible alternative?)				

ACTIVITY 11-7 Continued			
II. Reconsideration of Status			
How can the job task or work activity be changed?	Describe the change		What are the advantages/ disadvantages of the change over present methods?
Is it possible to *reverse steps* in the task/work activity?			
What features of two or more existing tasks or work activities could be *combined* to create one new overall task/ activity?			

A Model of Strategic Training

ACTIVITY 11-8 Lateral Thinking and Its Uses in Strategic Training

Directions: For each area listed in column 1, column 2 summarizes the key question or issue with which it is associated. In column 3, describe how *you* could use this area/issue in (1) identifying future job performance problems which could come up, (2) solving those problems, (3) identifying future training needs, and (4) meeting future training needs.

Column 1	Column 2	Column 3
Area*	Key Question	Application to Training
Dominant Ideas	How is the problem or issue presently being viewed?	
Tethering Factors	What factors are typically overlooked when considering a problem or issue?	
Polarizing Tendencies	How much does the problem/issue tend to produce "either/or thinking" about solutions?	
Boundaries	What perceptions limit the ways people think about a problem/issue? Consider organizational culture.	
Assumptions	What assumptions are being made about a problem or issue? Do they suggest new ideas? How valid are they?	
Avoidance Devices	Can old ideas be intentionally ignored in a quest for new ones?	

ACTIVITY 11-8 Continued		
Column 1	Column 2	Column 3
Rotation of Attention	Can the traditional focus of attention in a problem/issue be intentionally ignored in favor of a different focus?	
Change of Entry Point	Can a fresh perspective be gained by working backward in problem-solving, from impacts or consequences?	
Quota of Alternatives	Could a new perspective on a problem or issue be gained by imposing an artificial quota on the number of alternatives to consider?	
Concept Changing	Could a concept change shed new light on a problem?	
Fractionation	What subdivisions or subparts can a problem/issue be broken down into?	
Bridging Divisions	Could two unrelated ways of looking at a problem/issue be combined to produce a new way of looking at it?	
Reversal	Could a problem or issue be turned around to suggest an innovative solution?	
Distortion and Exaggeration	Could one feature of a problem/issue be distorted so as to suggest a new way of looking at solutions/alternatives?	

	ACTIVITY 11-8 Continued	
Column 1	Column 2	Column 3
Area*	Key Question	Application to Training
Exposure	Could unrelated items be randomly introduced during problem-solving or problem-finding to stimulate new ideas/approaches?	
Cross-Fertilization	Could experts from utterly unrelated fields be asked for their opinions about how to solve a problem—or about what future problems to look for?	
Problem Switching	Could new perspectives be gained by rapidly switching from considering one problem/issue to another and then back again?	
Analogies	Could new perspectives be stimulated by changing the problem/issue into an analogy? ("This situation is like another in which . . . .")	
Random-Word Stimulation	Could tables of randomly-selected words be brought to bear on a problem/issue to suggest new ideas, solutions, approaches?	

*The areas are based on the work of Edward de Bono (1970) as described in Van Gundy (1981).

ACTIVITY 11-9 Case Study on Employee Training

Directions: Read over the case which follows and answer the questions at the end.

The Washington General Insurance Company* is an industry leader. The Training Department at Washington just completed a needs assessment for a training course on Customer Relations. Company trainers surveyed managers, supervisors, and wage-earning employees about this issue. The trainers then followed up the survey with intensive interviews of randomly-selected supervisors and hourly employees.

Among the findings:

1. Customers (policyholders *and* sales agents) are often bounced around from one department to another when they call in with questions. The reason: nobody is sure who handles some issues.
2. Telephone etiquette of wage-earning employees leaves much to be desired. Customers often complain that they are made to feel like they are bothering the person who is supposed to be helping them.
3. Letters from customers are not always answered promptly. In some cases, over two months elapse between the time a letter is received at the Home Office and it is answered.
4. Supervisors feel that, if a customer relations "problem" exists, its cause has less to do with training needs than with lean staffing.
5. Older employees believe that younger employees are simply "less polite."

Company managers are concerned that employees need training on customer relations. The Washington's training staff is therefore planning to offer a one-day seminar on the topic for *all* employees. It will cover telephone etiquette, letter writing, and other matters.

In the meantime, a task force of company executives is investigating the possible creation of a special Customer Service Center. All incoming calls and letters will be directed to the Center, which will be staffed with specially-trained employees drawn from work units in the company. They will handle all problems until resolved to the customers' satisfaction.

Questions

1. How might the creation of a special Customer Service Center affect appropriate *present* training of employees on customer relations?
2. How might creation of a special Customer Service Center affect appropriate *future* training of employees on customer relations?
3. Should training staff members at the Washington General Insurance Company handle the issue of customer relations training from a traditional or strategic standpoint? Why do you think so?

*A fictitious company.

PART 5
EVALUATING HRD

12

EVALUATING HRD

Evaluating the HRD Effort means collecting and using information to make effective decisions about the choice, implementation, and follow up of all development, education, and training efforts of an organization. It is part of a comprehensive appraisal of an organization. It is the culmination of evaluative activities having to do with choice, modification, or follow up of each planned learning experience. This chapter defines HRD evaluation, summarizes its importance, describes some ways of thinking about it, and provides information about evaluating training, education, development, and the entire HRD Effort.

WHAT IS EVALUATION?

According to the *Living Webster Encyclopedic Dictionary,* evaluation means "ascertaining the value of something" and "appraising worth carefully." To a considerable extent, evaluation of HRD is in the eyes of the beholder. What does the "beholder" value? How well do HRD activities match up to those values? These questions are of central importance in evaluating anything.

In a classic definition, Rokeach (1973) defines a *value* as "an enduring belief that a specific mode of conduct [read 'behavior'] or end-state of existence [read 'outcome'] is personally or socially preferable to an opposite or converse mode of conduct or end-state of existence" (p. 5). Rokeach (1973) distinguishes between two types of values—*terminal* and *instrumental*. Terminal values are worth achieving for their own sake. Instrumental values are desirable because they contribute to achieving terminal values. "A knowledgeable, skilled employee" is valued by a supervisor for the employee's instrumentality; "an effective, growing firm" is valued for its own sake.

HRD activities are usually valued for their instrumentality. They lead to changes in individual performance or capabilities that are, in turn, associated with desirable ends. HRD is thus a means to an end. Managers favor HRD when they believe it leads to improved job performance, increased compliance with organizational policies and procedures, or greater profits. Individuals favor HRD when they believe it leads them down a path toward their career goals.

Why are values important? The answer should be obvious. Managers evaluate the HRD Effort relative to its perceived contribution to fostering the values they prize in employees and realizing desired organizational goals. Of course, matters are rarely this simple. There are several reasons why. First, individual values and desired organizational goals vary. Second, perceptions about what is important vary across levels of supervision. As a result, HRD practitioners have to begin evaluative efforts by defining values and goals that are prized in the organization most, and determining how much they are prized at different levels. By doing so, they can identify bottom-line concerns by level and gear evaluation to assessing how much HRD contributes to the concerns or the key stakeholders they serve.

Research results underscore just how much variation exists about values and goals. Schmidt and Posner (1982) surveyed over 1,400 managers about values. The results were revealing: managers prefer *responsible* and *honest* people the most. These instrumental values "were mentioned 20 percent more often than the next choice—*capable*—which was selected by about two-thirds of the managers, while *imaginative* and *logical* were cited by about one-half" (Schmidt & Posner, 1982, p. 33). A summary of results is depicted in Figure 12-1. Of course, cultivating responsible and honest behavior tends to be emphasized less by HRD practitioners than improving human capability.

From a list of organizational goals, managers preferred *effectiveness* and *high productivity* the most. (Effectiveness means accomplishing desired results.) However, not all managers value these goals to the same degree. Generally, executives feel they are more important than supervisors do. Supervisors value *high morale* and *efficiency* more than executives. (Efficiency means getting more done with fewer resources.) See Table 12-1 for a summary of results. See also Activity 12-1 at the end of this chapter.

WHY IS EVALUATION WORTHWHILE?

In the most general sense, evaluation of HRD is worthwhile because it

- provides information which can be used to improve planned learning, making it more effective in meeting needs, solving past performance problems, and anticipating future opportunities for performance improvement,

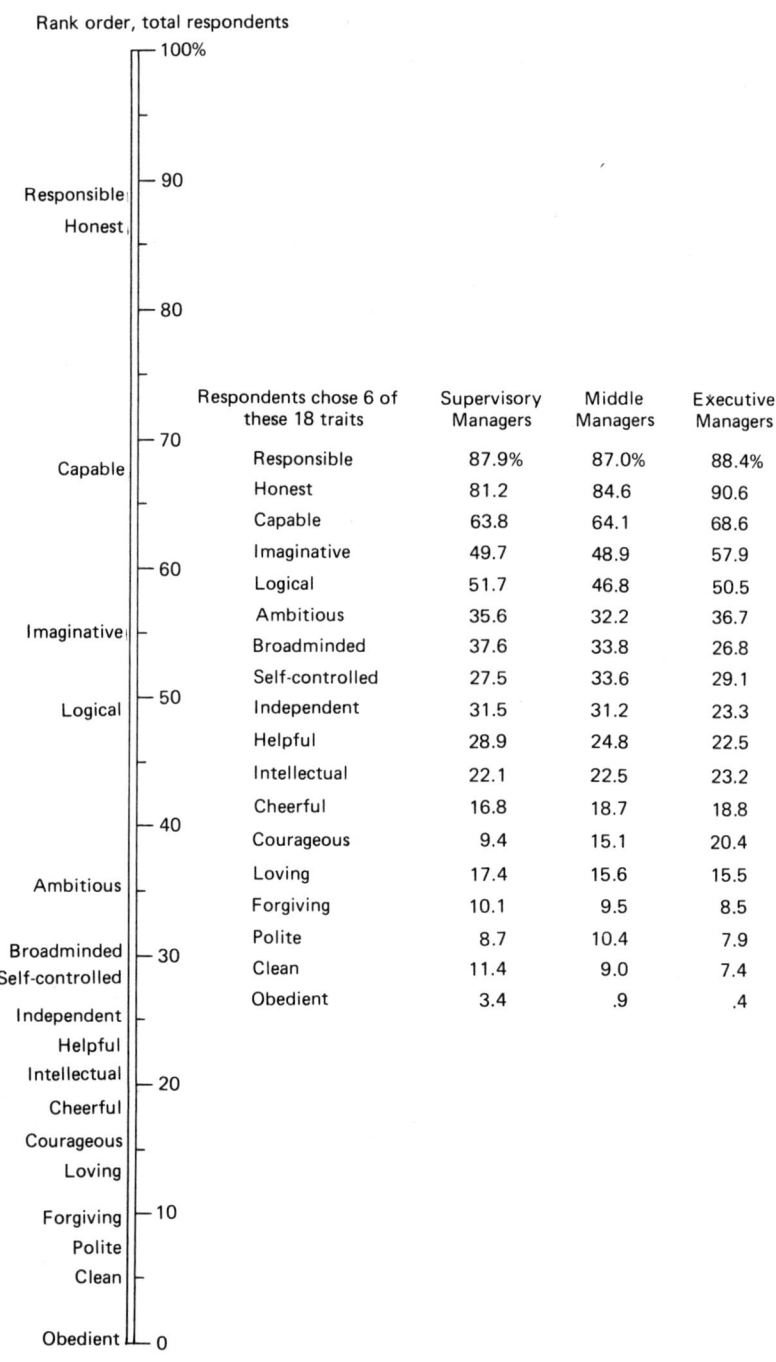

Figure 12-1: Personal Qualities that are Generally Admired in the Workplace. *Source:* Schmidt and Poser, 1982, p. 34. Reprinted with permission from the American Management Association.

TABLE 12-1 THE IMPORTANCE OF VARIOUS ORGANIZATIONAL GOALS

Average ratings are listed below. Respondents used a seven-point scale. N = 1,460 respondents

Organizational goals	Total sample	Supervisory managers	Middle managers	Executive managers
Organizational effectiveness	6.24	6.13	6.22	6.26
High productivity	6.11	5.97	6.02	6.16
Organizational leadership	6.09	5.90	6.12	6.11
High morale	6.02	6.03	6.04	6.01
Organizational reputation	5.98	5.76	5.93	6.04
Organizational efficiency	5.95	5.98	5.96	5.93
Profit maximization	5.22	4.53	4.98	5.44
Organizational growth	5.14	4.96	5.05	5.20
Organizational stability	5.12	5.14	5.07	5.13
Organizational value to community	4.87	4.82	4.92	4.82
Service to the public	4.80	4.99	4.92	4.68

Source: Schmidt & Posner, 1982, p. 38. Reprinted with permission from The American Management Association.

- sheds light on problems of all kinds, both those stemming from lack of individual knowledge or skill and those stemming from other causes,
- makes people accountable for HRD activities,
- points up results of HRD activities, demonstrating how well they are working, and
- stimulates improvement generally, providing feedback which triggers additional plans and actions.

As Phillips (1983) observes, evaluation of HRD is important because it (1) makes good economic sense to assess the value of planned learning; (2) prevents budget cutbacks on HRD expenditures; (3) demonstrates results to top managers; (4) leads to greater satisfaction among HRD staff members because they receive feedback on results; and (5) promotes increased professionalism in HRD.

WHAT ARE SOME WAYS OF THINKING ABOUT EVALUATION?

In evaluating planned learning, HRD practitioners should begin by thinking about six fundamental questions: (1) Who wants to know? (2) Who is doing the evaluating? (3) What is the real focus of interest? (4) When should evaluation be carried out? (5) Why is evaluation necessary? and (6) How will the evaluation be conducted? These questions have to do with the stakeholders, evaluator, content, timing, purpose, and method of evaluation. (Consider them in Activity 12-2 at the end of this chapter.)

Stakeholders. To be useful, an evaluation must meet the needs of stakeholders, those decision-makers and interested groups or individuals who want the results of an evaluation. However, needs of different audiences vary substantially, as Table 12-2 illustrates. Generally, the broader the audience of stakeholders whose interests are to be addressed by an evaluation, the more complex the evaluation needs to be. Broad audiences vary in interests, and an evaluation needs to be comprehensive to answer the questions of more people.

Evaluator. Who will conduct the evaluation? This question is important because, no matter how carefully designed and executed an evaluation, stakeholders inevitably "consider the source." Credibility is thus essential. Evaluation results are discounted when evaluators are perceived to be biased or poorly qualified. It is essential to choose evaluators who are credible in assessing the subject, capable in assessing instruction, and competent in using methods selected for collecting and analyzing data.

Content. What do evaluators want to know about? This question focuses on *content*. Unlike research, which is carried out *to create new knowledge*, evaluation is carried out *to provide information for subsequent decision-making* (Brandenburg & Smith, 1986). This means that evaluation has to be judged according to *usefulness* or *practicality* rather than *form* or *rigor of research design and execution*. By way of contrast, research is judged more by its form than by its usefulness.

TABLE 12-2 INTERESTS OF STAKEHOLDERS	
Stakeholder	Interests
Top Managers	• Is HRD contributing to the bottom-line? • Is HRD producing an adequate supply of managers?
Middle Managers	• Is HRD contributing to the bottom-line? • Is HRD producing an adequate supply of supervisors?
First-Line Supervisors	• Is training/education/development making the work unit more productive? • Is HRD improving employee morale?
Employees	• Is HRD contributing to better job performance? Improved employee appraisal? Will participation in HRD activities lead to a raise? a promotion? achievement of some other goal that is important to the individual?
HRD Practitioners	• Is HRD improving performance? • How can HRD activities be improved? • Is HRD accepted by people in each group?

Many content issues may be examined (see Table 12-3). Generally, the more issues which are included in an examination, the more comprehensive, costly, and time-consuming the evaluation must be.

Timing. When is evaluation appropriate? This question focuses on *timing*. If evaluation is to provide information for decision-making, then appropriate timing depends on what decisions are to be made. For example, it is important to have information about problems before deciding whether learning needs exist distinct from other needs. Likewise, information about the value of training materials is needed before they are used on a broad scale.

Evaluation may be conducted before, during, or after decisions are made about planned learning. The essential point is to determine *when* that information is needed, depending on the purpose of the evaluation.

Purpose. Why is evaluation conducted? This question is undoubtedly the single most important one. There are, of course, several major reasons which may prompt an evaluation. They include:

- deciding whether formal instruction is the most appropriate strategy for meeting a need,
- deciding whether instructional materials will produce desired results,
- deciding whether instruction is worth continuing or a program is worth repeating, and
- assessing how well instruction is being delivered and how well learners are mastering desired knowledge/skills during instruction.

Method. How will the evaluation be carried out? This question has to do with planning the evaluation. *An evaluation plan* sets forth precisely what to evaluate and how to evaluate it. An evaluation plan resembles a research plan except that, as noted earlier, research creates knowledge while evaluation creates information useful for decision-making (Brandenburg & Smith, 1986). A typical evaluation plan consists of five parts: (1) problem; (2) hypothesis *or* objectives; (3) research design; (4) sample; and (5) methods for analyzing and interpreting data.

The problem component of an evaluation plan sets forth the question which the evaluation study is designed to answer. It is a purpose statement phrased as a question. As we shall see later in this chapter, differences exist between evaluations of training, education, development, and the entire HRD effort. Nevertheless, a common problem is to measure how much and what kind of change occurred before and after planned learning experiences.

The hypothesis is appropriate only when evaluators seek statistical evidence that some change occurred as a result of instruction. An *evaluation hypothesis* sets forth what evaluators expect to find and why they expect to find it. A *null hypothesis* is what evaluators actually test. It is an arbitrary convention proposing that changes did *not* occur or, if they did, that they are attributable to chance or some other variable out of the researcher's direct control. When evaluators seek evidence different from that

TABLE 12-3 CONTENT ISSUES FOR EVALUATION

Issue	Brief description of issue	Key questions
Purpose of Instruction	the reason for offering the instruction	What performance problem is to be solved by training? What career objectives are to be met by employee education? What organizational objectives are to be supported by developmental activities?
Linkage to Needs	the relationship between training, education, or development and the needs to be met by them	Are instructional objectives clearly linked to identified needs? Are objectives for training linked to job performance problems? Are objectives for education linked to staffing plans? Individual career plans? Are objectives for development linked to long-term organizational strategy?
Marketing	the way the instruction is promoted/communicated to stakeholders	Are stakeholders clearly identified? Are their interests clear? Is instruction promoted to them based on their interests and needs?
Objectives/Goals	the general outcomes to be met by instruction; the specific outcomes to be met by a training course, educational experience, or developmental intervention	Are the instructional goals for each program stated? Are instructional objectives for each program, lesson, and unit clearly stated?
Desirable Outcomes	the desired impact of training on the job; the desired impact of education on career mobility; the desired impact of development on a part of the organization, the culture, or a stakeholder group.	Are the desired on-the-job effects of instruction clarified? Is someone held accountable for transfer of learning from the instructional setting to the work setting?
Assessment of Outcomes	the way the outcomes of training, education, or development will be measured	Is it clear how participant reactions to instruction will be measured? Is it clear how learning outcomes will be measured? Is it clear how behavior will be measured? Is it clear how on-the-job effects will be measured?
The Setting	where instruction will be carried out; where evaluation will be carried out	What is special about the instructional setting? What is special about the evaluation setting?
The Learners	the people for whom the instruction is intended	What assumptions are made about the learners? What prerequisite skills are needed?
Instruction	the subject matter to be delivered	Does the subject matter match objectives? Is the subject matter selected/prepared appropriately?
Provision for Differences	planning for differences between learners	How are differences between learners recognized? How are differences between learners dealt with during instruction?

TABLE 12-3	Continued	
Issue	Brief description of issue	Key questions
Logistics	planning for delivering the instruction	Are the resources available for carrying out instruction? Planned for?
Testing of Instruction	how learning will be measured at the end of instruction	Are test items clearly linked to instructional objectives? Have tests been tested?
Implementation of Instruction	how the instruction will be carried out	Do presentation methods match objectives and are appropriate for them?
Application	how instruction will be applied on the job	What on-the-job application is desired? How will on-the-job application be measured?
Effects	the results of instruction in improved productivity, cost savings, improved quality of work life, improved morale	What effects are possible? What effects are desired? What effects are being achieved?
Use of Information about Effects	how information about the effects of instruction will be used	Who wants to know about training? Education? Development? What decisions will be based on the information?

yielded by statistics, they establish *objectives* instead of hypotheses. Objectives describe what results are to be achieved by the evaluation study.

An evaluation design is a description of procedures to be followed in the evaluation study. Its meaning is the same as *research design*—"that is, a description of the procedures to be followed in testing the hypotheses" or in achieving the study's objectives (Ary, Jacobs, & Razavieh, 1979, p. 84). Evaluation designs fall into three general categories: (1) *descriptive;* (2) *quasi-experimental;* and (3) *experimental.* The choice of which one to use depends on what is to be evaluated, evaluator purposes, and the working environment (Phillips, 1983).

Descriptive evaluation designs, as the name implies, are set up to *describe* existing phenomena. They cannot be used to test hypotheses. No attempt is made to control conditions. Evaluators simply describe what they see.

Quasi-experimental evaluation designs are more rigorous than descriptive evaluation. They are appropriate for imposing at least partial control over experimental conditions and the assignment of individuals to groups. In experimental research, individuals are randomly placed in two or more groups—*control groups,* which do not receive benefits of planned learning, and *experimental groups,* which do receive those benefits. Other differences between groups are held constant. The idea is to set up, for comparative purposes, two groups that are essentially the same. Change through planned learning is sought in one group but not in the other. Evaluators then compare groups to find differences in attitudes, learning, behavior, or results *before* the change effort is begun and *after* it has been administered.

In quasi-experimental designs, evaluators make every effort to preserve existing work groups, but select at least two that are essentially the same—though perhaps not identical. Baseline measurements of both groups are taken. These measurements may be yielded from results of attitude surveys, pre-tests, structured observations of on-the-job behavior, examinations of production data, or some combination. Attitude surveys measure feelings; pre-tests measure knowledge; behavioral observations measure what people do; and examinations of production data focus on work outputs. Members of one group are then provided with planned learning experiences, while members of another group are not. After planned learning events—so-called *experimental treatments*—measures are again taken of attitudes, knowledge, behavior, or results. Statistically significant differences in measures of the groups are attributed to the learning events.

Experimental designs are more rigorous. Participants in each group are assigned at random; all other conditions affecting performance are held constant. Baseline measurements are taken of both groups before learning events. Only the experimental group receives planned learning. Then measurements are taken again. Differences are attributed to learning events.

It is possible to use other, more sophisticated, quasi-experimental or experimental designs. More sophisticated designs remove threats to *internal validity* (that is, "in this situation, did instruction make a difference which is not attributable to such possible problems as unplanned events before and after training, the aging of participants, etc?") and *external validity* (that is, "can the results of this evaluation study be reasonably generalized as true for other, similar groups?"). For more on evaluation design see Campbell and Stanley (1963), Cook and Campbell (1976, 1979), Goldstein (1986), Isaac and Michael (1971), Miller and Barnett (1986), Phillips (1983, 1984), and Spector (1981). For an example of a descriptive design, see Golembiewski and Carrigan (1970); for an example of quasi-experimental design, see Komaki, Heinzmann, and Lawson (1980); and for an example of an experimental design, see Goodacre (1955).

Practically speaking, experimental rigor is rare in organizational settings. Practical considerations—like the need to make all workers maximally productive—make it difficult to offer learning experiences to some people while not offering it to others. Differential treatment may also create morale problems. People who do not receive the benefit of learning experiences may feel slighted (Goldstein, 1986). In fact, such feelings may influence performance and thus distort evaluation results (Hand & Slocum, 1972). Participants in evaluation must not feel they are being manipulated like puppets (Argyris, 1968).

The sample is the fourth component of an evaluation plan. It describes a group to be studied. Sampling is used when a large group, perhaps the entire organization, is to be studied. Sampling economizes effort, so that a relatively small group can be studied and the results can be inferred to apply to all people affected. Sampling also reduces bias. Random sampling—that is, assigning participants to control or experimental groups on a random basis—holds differences between participants constant.

Sampling is not always used in evaluation studies. For instance, in a case study of a training program, the evaluator may describe the entire organization, one department, one work group, or one individual. In descriptive studies of this kind, however, the evaluator is obliged to clarify the *unit of analysis*—literally, the person, group, or structural component of an organization to be analyzed (Stake, 1981).

When using sampling in quasi-experimental and experimental designs, evaluators find some kinds of samples more appropriate than others. *Simple random sampling* is common with relatively small populations. People are assigned to control and experimental groups through random number tables or random number generators. *Stratified random sampling* is appropriate for larger populations or those in which wide variations exist among participants. The aim is to ensure representativeness in the sample to preserve the distribution of such variables as age, location, and educational background found in the population. *Systematic random sampling* is appropriate for the largest populations. All employees are listed and chosen on some systematic basis—for example, every sixth person is included in the study. Finally, *simple cluster sampling* is also appropriate for the largest populations. Prospective participants in the evaluation are clustered on some basis—by operating unit, location, supervisor, or another means—and only some "clusters" are used for drawing a sample.

For more on sampling, see Fitzgibbon and Morris (1978) and Phillips (1983).

Methods to be used in analyzing and interpreting data are described in the last section of an evaluation plan. It is important to specify in advance of data collection how information will be organized and subsequently examined (Sredl & Rothwell, 1987). In fact, it helps if evaluators think ahead to the time when results will be presented to decision-makers. By doing so, they can anticipate questions—and what information will be needed to answer them.

If statistical methods will be used for analysis, evaluators should clarify in advance of data collection precisely what statistical tests they will apply to the data. In this way, evaluators can make sure they collect the data necessary for performing those tests. Nothing is more embarrassing than to have to backtrack to collect data because no advance thought was given to how the data would later be analyzed.

If nonstatistical, qualitative research methods are used for analysis and interpretation, then evaluators still need to think ahead. How will descriptive information be organized and presented? These questions *must* be answered before information is collected.

For more on analyzing and interpreting evaluative data, see Isaac and Michael (1971), Jacobs (1985-1986), Lincoln and Guba (1985), Murphy (1980), Stake (1978, 1981), and Weiss (1972, 1983).

What is the State of the Art in HRD Evaluation?

HRD practitioners usually associate evaluation with *training*. There is good reason for that: few HRD departments progress beyond training. Indeed, many practitioners are philosophically attuned to running "company schoolhouses" (Zemke, 1985b)—not to examining present, or averting future, performance problems. Nor do practitioners give much attention to systematic planning for long-term change efforts like employee education or development. Research by Faris (1983) and Digman (1980) indicates that HRD practitioners, on the whole, do not do a very good job of identifying instructional needs. This conclusion is supported independently by the research of others (Feuer, 1986a). It is scarcely surprising, then, that practitioners are unable to evaluate how well they have satisfied needs.

The results of a small-scale survey conducted by Dale Brandenburg in 1981 revealed that the primary purpose of most training evaluations is to improve training, not demonstrate the bottom-line dollar impact of instructional results (see Table 12-4). Open-ended comments and written surveys are the most commonly used data collection techniques (see Table 12-5).

A more recent study of 756 responding firms revealed that only half use formal methods to evaluate training (*Employee Training*, 1986). Those that do use formal evaluation methods tend to be larger, more innovative firms.

Transfer of learning from formal instruction to on-the-job application is a major problem. The two chief reasons are that no rewards are given for applying what was learned, and there is not enough time to spend on training people (see Table 12-6).

From published accounts, it is possible to construct a profile of state-of-the-art practices in training evaluation even if it is more difficult to do so for education or developmental activities. In general: (1) between 50 to 70 percent of all training is evaluated in some way (Ball & Anderson, 1975; Brandenburg & Smith, 1986; *Employee Training*, 1986); (2) improving instruction is the primary purpose of most evaluation (Ball & Anderson, 1975; Brandenburg, 1982; Brandenburg & Smith, 1986); (3) evaluation is usually carried out by HRD practitioners, not by others inside or outside a firm (Ball & Anderson, 1975; Brandenburg & Smith, 1986); (4) paper-and-pencil tests are most frequently described in published accounts as a method of evaluating training (Brandenburg & Smith, 1986), but participant surveys are most commonly used by practitioners (Brandenburg, 1982); and (5) published accounts suggest

TABLE 12-4   EVALUATIVE FUNCTIONS

Listed below are a number of functions that may be linked to the evaluation of training activities. Please rate the priority of each function as it relates to your organizational unit. (Scale: High, Medium, Low, Never)

Evaluative Function	Group			
	Sales		SIG	
	Mean	Rank	Mean	Rank
1. cost analysis of activities	3.0	5	2.6	7
2. improve the training program	4.0	1	3.6	2
3. provide feedback to program planners or management	3.8	2	3.7	1
4. gain knowledge of employee skill levels	3.3	4	3.1	3
5. identify future organizational leaders	2.6	7.5	2.2	8
6. provide information for performance appraisal	2.2	9	2.1	9
7. placement of employees into units where they most benefit organizational goals	2.1	10	1.9	10
8. provide feedback to program participants	3.5	3	3.0	4
9. study employee effectiveness	2.6	7.5	2.7	6
10. build status or prestige for the training unit	2.9	6	2.8	5

Note: in this and other tables, means were calculated to a third significant digit before ranks were assigned.

Source: Brandenburg, 1982, p. 16. Reprinted with permission from the American Society for Training and Development.

TABLE 12-5 DATA COLLECTION TECHNIQUES

In conducting evaluations of training, whether before, during, or after the activities, how frequently are the following data collection techniques used by you or your operational unit? (Scale: Very Often, Fairly Often, Once in a While, Never)

	Group			
	Sales		SIG	
Techniques	Mean	Rank	Mean	Rank
1. objective questionnaire or survey	3.6	2	3.0	2
2. open-ended comments or reactions	3.9	1	3.4	1
3. multiple-choice (or similar) achievement measures	3.0	4	2.5	3
4. essay (open-ended) achievement measures	1.9	12	1.9	10.5
5. participant self-assessment	2.9	5	2.3	6.5
6. task performance measures (e.g., simulation, role playing)	3.1	3	2.5	4.5
7. observation or anecdotal record	2.7	6	2.5	4.5
8. use of videotape	2.5	7.5	1.7	12
9. structured interviews	2.4	9	2.3	6.5
10. later on-the-job performance appraisal	2.5	7.5	2.1	8
11. indirect follow-up studies	2.2	10	2.0	9
12. collection of cost analysis information	2.0	11	1.9	10.5

Source: Brandenburg, 1982, p. 16. Reprinted with permission from the American Society for Training and Development.

TABLE 12-6 WHY TRAINING FAILS

Reason for failure	Percent who mentioned
no on-the-job rewards for behaviors and skills learned in training	58%
insufficient time to execute training programs	55%
work environment does not support new behaviors learned in training	53%
lack of motivation among employees	47%
inaccurate training needs analyses	40%
training needs changed after program had been implemented	35%
management does not support training program	30%
insufficient funding of training program	21%

Source: Employee Training, 1986, p. 37. Reprinted with permission from The American Society for Training and Development.

that HRD practitioners use sophisticated evaluation designs, employing "control" and "experimental" groups (Campbell, Dunnette, Lawler, & Weick 1970; DeMeuse & Liebowitz, 1981; Smith, 1984). However, surveys of practitioners do not support this view (Ball & Anderson, 1975; Brandenburg, 1982; Catalanello & Kirkpatrick, 1968).

EVALUATING TRAINING

What should be evaluated? Training is traditionally designed to produce immediate change in employee job performance. Its focus is on the job. The purpose of training is to narrow gaps between what job incumbents should know or do and what they actually know or do. Training is a very short-term change effort.

Evaluation pervades all aspects of training. It guides decisions to use training to correct a performance problem rather than use some other improvement strategy. This is called front-end analysis. It influences the preparation of test items matched to instructional objectives. It is used in field-testing instruction before and after widespread adoption, and even during instruction. However, evaluation is perhaps most often associated with post-instructional assessment.

Front-end evaluation (FEA): the traditional approach. FEA is "the bridge between recognizing a need and deciding what to do about it" (Datta, 1978, p. 13). Harless (1987) explains the goals of FEA succinctly. They are to (1) isolate performance problems that have potentially high economic "worth"; (2) isolate precise performance deficiencies within the problem area that account for the greatest loss; (3) increase the probability that the solution to a given problem is effective by matching the cause of the problem to the appropriate type of remedy; (4) increase the probability that the solution selected is the most cost effective; (5) isolate the root cause of the performance problem; and (6) increase the probability that there is a match between the precise performance deficiency and the individuals who have the deficiency (p. 8, reprinted with permission). It is thus intended to correct the most glaring human performance problems in the most cost-effective manner.

As Harless (1987) emphasizes, it is necessary to clarify the precise nature of the performance problem, its cause(s), appropriate solutions, and costs of appropriate solutions. These issues are important, because not all problems should be addressed by training. The costs of solutions are worth considering because training is expensive: it means lost work time and substantial investments in materials and design. There is no point in wasting money: some problems can be solved through means other than training—such as job aids, automation, or job redesign. The cheapest alternative should, of course, be favored.

To clarify the nature of a performance problem and possible solutions, practitioners should ask such questions as (Harless, 1987, p. 8, reprinted with permission): (1) Do we have a problem? (2) How will we know when the problem is solved? (3) What is the performance problem? (4) What is the range of possible causes of the problem? (5) What is the precise probable cause of the problem? (6) What general solution is indicated? (7) What are the relative costs, effects, and development times of each solution? (8) What are the constraints? and (9) What are the overall goals? Answers to these questions help clarify whether training is an appropriate solution.

In sorting out instructional from noninstructional needs, HRD practitioners should apply four acid tests: (1) *management commitment:* Do managers view a problem as important enough to warrant attention? (2) *resources:* Are adequate resources available to meet the need? If not, are managers willing to provide funds, staff, time, and materials? (3) *skills:* Do HRD practitioners possess necessary skills to meet the need? If not, can they identify people who do possess the skills from inside or outside the organization? Are they free to contract for needed skills? and (4) *costs versus benefits:* Will costs of solving a problem produce greater benefits than alternatives, like taking no action or selecting a different solution?

Of these tests, cost-benefit analysis is most important—and most difficult. It is important because HRD practitioners are often faced with the necessity of convincing managers that training is worth the costs associated with it. A cost is understood to mean both (1) *direct* expenditures such as funding required to analyze a problem, develop, deliver, and evaluate instruction, and (2) *indirect* expenditures on salaries, lost production time, and facilities rental. Benefits are estimates of increased production or cost savings. They can be calculated per employee and then multiplied over the number of trainees. Calculating cost-benefit ratios is difficult because they are simple estimates that are easily challenged. It is not all that clear what cost or benefit categories should be used, since even experts differ on this point (see Cullen, Sawzin, Sisson, & Swanson, 1978; Deming, 1979; Mirabel, 1978; Smith & Marcinuk, 1982; Spencer, 1984; Weinstein, 1982).

If the results of front-end analysis reveal that training is an appropriate and cost-beneficial solution to a performance problem, then HRD practitioners may complete an intensive needs assessment and begin instructional design.

Front-end evaluation: the strategic approach. One major problem exists with the traditional approach to FEA: it assumes that any performance problem can be judged using information about *present* conditions and *present* cost-benefits. That assumption is not always valid. Changes inside or outside an organization may gradually increase or decrease the importance of a performance problem—or even alter the nature of it.

Consider a simple example. Suppose that production output is below standard in one work group. Upon further analysis, HRD practitioners determine that the problem is attributable to lack of employee skills. For simplicity's sake, assume that new machines are being introduced gradually. Even experienced workers do not know how to use them. A simple front-end analysis of this problem may or may not demonstrate a present need for training. However, common sense dictates that production levels will probably remain below standard until all new machines are introduced and, assuming no formal training is provided, workers learn through trial and error how to use the machines.

In this example, a traditional approach to FEA does not tell the whole story. The performance problem is not severe at present—but it may well become more severe as new machines are introduced. Experience is not an adequate gauge for judging how long it will take for production levels to reach or exceed normal, unless similar machines were introduced on a similar production line at another company facility some time before.

If HRD practitioners wait around for this performance problem to reveal itself, valuable production output will be lost. Nor will it be easy to estimate how much output will be lost. Even supervisors may not be convinced under present conditions that training is necessary.

What then? Is HRD forced into a reactive mode, unable to respond until the performance problem is apparent to everyone and managers are willing to support organized instruction on new machines?

The answer to these questions is "not at all." The HRD practitioner has to demonstrate beforehand that the problem will exist, will affect production, and will lend itself to solution through training.

How is this accomplished? There are several ways: (1) *through direct persuasion:* HRD practitioners can go to the people affected by the problem—the production manager, the foreperson, and workers—to discuss the problem; (2) *through indirect persuasion:* Practitioners can find analogous situations. They can remind managers of historical events and point out similarities between them and the problem at hand; or (3) *through simulation:* Practitioners can set up a demonstration and show supervisors or managers what the problems are. If this is not possible, they can shoot a videotape and show it to key decision-makers.

The purpose of future-oriented FEA is to anticipate future performance problems before they come up and determine the most effective means of averting them. To undertake a future-oriented FEA, HRD practitioners:

1. scan trends in work flow and work methods at the operational level,
2. isolate areas in which changes are likely to occur,
3. pinpoint changes which are likely to be most costly in the future,
4. separate noninstructional from instructional needs,
5. consider alternative strategies for averting a performance problem,
6. isolate root causes of anticipated problems—such as changes in technology, job, or work group redesign, new products, or job duties, and
7. point out the likely problem to managers and supervisors, gaining their support to avert future performance problems.

If these steps are followed, HRD practitioners will find that their mode of operation is proactive. Planned learning activities will anticipate and help avert problems before they arise. (See Activity 12-3 at the end of this chapter.)

Testing: the traditional approach. Traditionally, a major purpose of testing is to measure how well trainees achieved terminal objectives upon course completion. It can also be used to screen trainees to ensure that they possess the necessary prerequisite skills to receive training or to measure their progress during training.

Criterion-referenced tests are, however, most important because they measure trainee mastery of course objectives. They take their name from explicit linkage to objectives. Objectives are stated in measurable terms, and achievement of them is intended to close a performance gap. Test items are prepared from objectives and linked to them.

There are numerous types of test items, such as true-false, multiple choice, essay, matching, and many others. Each is more appropriate for measuring some objectives than others. Recall that objectives can be classified in three broad domains—affective or feeling-oriented, cognitive or knowledge-oriented, and psychomotor or movement-oriented.

For more on testing see Denova (1979), Dick and Carey (1985), and Kemp (1985).

Testing: the strategic approach. There are two major problems with traditional testing. First, it tends to focus solely on terminal *course* objectives. When tests are geared to measuring end-of-unit (enabling) objectives or end-of-course (terminal) objectives alone, trainees are only held accountable for formal instruction. Testing which focuses on objectives of this kind makes trainers accountable for doing a good job, no doubt, but does not really hold trainees accountable for applying on the job what they learned in training (Wheeler, 1988).

A more useful approach is to express instructional objectives on several levels, including not just end-of-course mastery but also on-the-job behaviors and results. Testing can be—and sometimes is—carried out back on the job. In this way, trainees are held accountable for making sure that change occurs on the job, where it really counts.

The second problem with traditional testing is that it does not take into account changes in job conditions occurring over time. In fact, most training is purely maintenance-oriented, intended to bring the performance of inexperienced workers in line with experienced ones. HRD practitioners look at historical standards and tried-and-true methods. This technique works well in settings where job conditions do not change much. It is not, however, appropriate under fast-paced, rapidly-changing conditions. In such cases, practitioners should prepare instructional objectives based on *predictions* of future job conditions. When that is done, test items have to be prepared accordingly.

This is admittedly risky business, because job conditions may not change as expected. But in fast-paced, dynamic settings it is *more* appropriate than waiting around to design tests until some future time when conditions become more settled.

The format of future-oriented test items need not differ much from their traditional counterparts. However, it may be more appropriate under some conditions to rely on experiential exercises such as case studies, role plays, simulations, and critical incidents instead of paper-and-pencil testing to assess how well trainees will fare in expected future job conditions. Testing should be handled longitudinally, with pre-programmed follow-ups on the job to assess performance under future conditions.

Formative evaluation: the traditional approach. Michael Scriven (1967) was the first to suggest rigorous, advance testing of instructional content and presentation methods before widespread use of them. Formative evaluation takes its name from using evaluation to *form* instruction (Gagné & Briggs, 1979).

Formative evaluation is conducted in many different ways and is often carried out rather informally. Think of it as a special kind of market test in which the product (the instructional materials) is tried out on all its possible consumers (instructors, trainees, supervisors, and perhaps others). A whole range of issues may be considered in this process (see Figure 12-2).

Formative evaluations can be as complicated or as uncomplicated as HRD practitioners wish them to be. However, extensive testing is probably worthwhile under the following conditions: (1) when opinions on the issue are sharply divided within the firm, the occupation/discipline, or between managers or supervisors or prospective trainees; (2) when HRD practitioners are using methods or media with which they are unfamiliar; (3) when targeted trainees vary widely in skills, knowledge, or attitudes; or (4) when the instruction is a first attempt to satisfy a need.

Table 12-7 describes some ways of conducting a formative evaluation. Any or all may be used, depending on preferences of evaluators and time and money available. For more information on this subject see Bloom, Hastings, and Madaus (1971), Dick and Carey (1985), and Gagné and Briggs (1979).

Formative evaluation: the strategic approach. One problem with the traditional approach to formative evaluation is that it is based on the fundamental assumption that instructional materials can be made more effective in the future if they are revised on the basis of tests in the present or past. If requirements are stable, this assumption is valid enough. If they are unstable, however, results of past tests will do nothing to improve instruction, especially when the subject matter itself is also past-oriented.

A simple example should illustrate this point. Suppose an HRD practitioner is orienting entry-level auditors to their job requirements. The auditors possess appropriate entry-level knowledge of accounting basics. What they do not possess is organization-specific knowledge of policies and procedures. They know from college courses

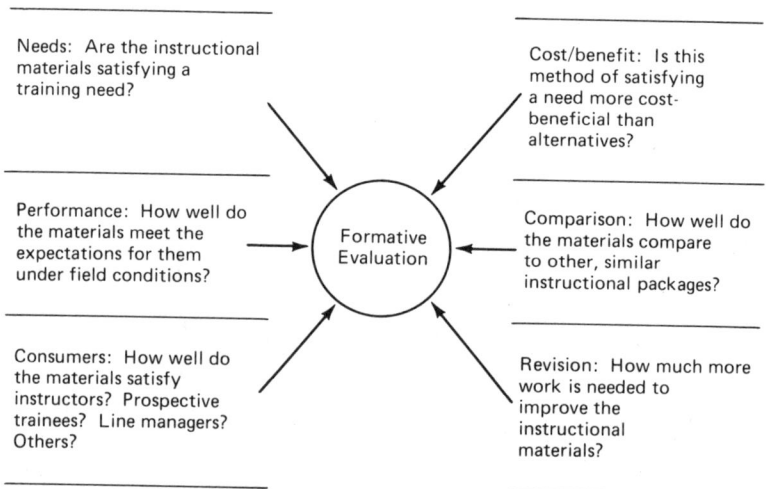

Figure 12-2: The Range of Issues for Consideration in Formative Evaluation

TABLE 12-7 METHODS OF CONDUCTING FORMATIVE EVALUATION

Method	When?	Description
Individualized Testing	upon completion of the training materials	Treat the instructional materials to intensive field-testing with only one person. Go through the materials with the individual, attempting to identify anything which is unclear.
Small-Group Testing	upon completion of individualized testing	Go through the instructional materials in a small-group setting. Identify any problems with the material.
Field Testing	upon completion of small-group testing	Offer instruction under real conditions—but on an experimental basis.
Expert Testing	upon completion of field testing	Ask subject experts/supervisors to review materials.

what a workpaper is; they do not know the kind of workpaper requirements that exist in one public accounting firm. On the latter issue, they need training. HRD practitioners can design a program to teach them organizational workpaper requirements. It can be evaluated formatively. If workpaper requirements in the firm do not change, then the results of formative evaluation will be appropriate for revising instruction to increase its effectiveness.

But suppose that policymakers decide to change the organization's policies on workpapers, perhaps as a result of attending a rehearsal of training on present policies. Then what? Will training have to be redesigned and retested accordingly? The answer is yes, particularly if the change in policy is a radical departure from past practices.

In some instances, however, HRD practitioners may be aware that such a change is likely. When they are, it makes no sense for them to develop and test instructional materials based on a workpaper policy about to be changed. Some practitioners will argue that, in such a case, the sensible course of action is to wait around until a new workpaper policy has been formalized. Then training can be designed and tested.

The trouble is that this wait-and-see method makes HRD practitioners purely reactive. When policy changes, instruction lags long after. By that time, many otherwise unnecessary on-the-job mistakes have been made.

The point is that formative evaluation should be carried out under conditions that closely match the conditions expected to exist when trainees are ready to apply what they learned. If radical changes are expected, then HRD practitioners should simulate those conditions when they test instructional materials. Admittedly, that may be easier said than done. But if formative evaluation is to be effective, it has to be carried out in this way. If not, trainees will be instructed the wrong way—and future job performance will not be as effective as it could have been.

Summative evaluation: the traditional approach. Michael Scriven (1967) considered formative evaluation only a first step in testing instructional materials. He believed that it should be followed at a later time by summative evaluation, which takes its name from using *summed effects* of instruction for evaluative purposes. Dick and Carey (1985) observe that "sometimes it is almost impossible to distinguish between a formative evaluation field trial and a summative evaluation" (p. 258). Unlike a formative evaluation, however, summative evaluation seeks "to determine the value of the present materials for a defined target group or a particular target setting or both" (Dick & Carey, 1985, p. 258).

To conduct a traditional summative evaluation as described by Dick and Carey (1985), an HRD practitioner:

1. examines all instructional materials after they have been revised in light of formative evaluation results—do they appear to do what they are supposed to do?,
2. observes an instructor delivering the materials—do learners respond as expected? Does the instructor adequately present the material?,
3. administers a post-test to measure trainee achievement of objectives,
4. administers an attitude survey to find out how well participants liked the course and felt it met their needs, and
5. compares subsequent job performance of (a) those who received training, and (b) those who did not receive the training (or else benefited from a different kind of performance improvement strategy).

In traditional school settings, summative evaluations are sometimes undertaken *before* a course, lesson, or unit is added to the curriculum (Gagné & Briggs, 1979). In training departments they are rarely undertaken at all (Brandenburg & Smith, 1986).

Summative evaluation: the strategic approach. The same problem which plagues formative evaluations also affects their summative counterparts. Will present or past evaluation results be appropriate for judging the future? Traditionally it is assumed they will be.

As in formative evaluations, this assumption is valid only when job conditions and learners' entry characteristics or skills remain stable. If work methods or organizational policies change, then the results of *past* summative evaluations will be inappropriate for judging instruction based on *present* conditions or *present* needs. Likewise, if entry characteristics of learners change because the organization recruits workers with different backgrounds, then summative evaluations carried out in the past will no longer be valid.

What can be done, then? Will new summative evaluations have to be carried out? Perhaps. It all depends on *how much* future conditions will change. HRD practitioners have to scan the environment to foresee changes likely to have a future impact either on trainees selected for instruction or on job requirements. Consider: is there a chance that the kind of workers recruited in a job class will differ significantly from those entering that class in the past? Is there a chance that work methods, technology, company policy, or some other characteristic will change substantially?

If the answer to either question (or both) is yes, then HRD practitioners will have to (1) identify what changes they expect; (2) predict what impact they expect those changes to have on work methods and corresponding training needs; (3) modify present training in line with predictions; and (4) test the training under simulated conditions like those expected on the job in the future.

Concurrent evaluation: the traditional approach. A concurrent evaluation is undertaken during training delivery. It is thus *concurrent* with the instruction it is intended to evaluate. It may be undertaken as part of a summative study, or it may stand alone.

A third-party evaluator, someone other than the instructor, can call a time-out during a course or at the end of a course unit. An attitude survey is then administered to trainees to assess their feelings at that point. They are asked to describe their reactions to the instructor, presentation methods, progress to that point, and group interaction.

Tests may also be administered during a training course to measure trainee achievement relative to enabling objectives. In this way, trainee progress can be assessed during the training. If test results reveal inadequate progress, individuals can then be targeted for remedial attention, or training methods can be altered when group progress collectively falls below expectations.

Structured observation by a third party, another method of concurrent evaluation, is typically carried out by a peer or supervisor who sits in on training. The evaluator does not rely on vague, subjective impressions about the quality of delivery; rather, the evaluator completes a structured observation form during the presentation. This form, developed in advance, lists critical dimensions of instructor performance and corresponding behaviors along a continuum. The evaluator notes how often these behaviors are exhibited by the instructor. The results are later discussed as a starting point to improve delivery.

Unstructured naturalistic observation also requires a third-party evaluator. However, the evaluator does not record observations on a form prepared in advance. Instead, the evaluator *is* the instrument of inquiry and relies on observation of the classroom setting, personal impressions, and perhaps follow-up interviews with instructor and/or participants to arrive at conclusions about strengths and weaknesses of the instructor's presentation methods. These are, in turn, fed back to the instructor as a stimulant for improvement. Naturalistic inquiry, as used in this setting, is "a guiding model that inquirers use to help them order and understand real-world complexities" (Jacobs, 1985–1986, p. 25). It is, of course, applicable to uses other than examining instructional delivery (Lincoln & Guba, 1985).

Electronically-enhanced feedback is a fancy phrase for something simple: using videotapes to show the instructor precisely what behaviors are being exhibited during delivery. There are two kinds: (1) simultaneous feedback, occurring during delivery; and (2) delayed feedback, occurring after delivery. Imagine aiming a television camera on an instructor during delivery with a television monitor placed so the instructor can see it. Feedback occurs as the delivery is made. The instructor, at once observed and observer, can then modify behavior as events occur. (For some instructors, this creates stage fright that was not apparent before.) Delayed feedback occurs after delivery: the instructor watches the presentation, noting behaviors and their effects on participants. This feedback is the starting point for self-modeling, in which the instructor notes areas for future improvement in delivery methods.

Concurrent evaluation: the strategic approach. It is difficult to anticipate conditions in group training before they occur. Each group has its own chemistry, stemming from the individuals comprising it and from interactions between people.

One approach that helps anticipate problems that may occur in a group setting is to poll participants in advance. Ask them questions like those appearing in Activity 12-4 at the end of this chapter. At the beginning of the training session, read through the returned surveys as a "warm-up." In this way, the hidden agenda of an individual is revealed and dealt with up front. While this approach does not always work, it sometimes serves as a lightning rod for releasing pent-up feelings or problems.

The best advance preparation for delivery of instruction is, of course, practice. It never hurts any presenter, even the most experienced, to rehearse an entire training program before delivery. Dry-runs have beneficial side effects, especially if interested parties—like supervisors or executives—are invited to attend. The instructor benefits from their suggestions, while supervisors are exposed to the training their subordinates receive and are thus informed enough to hold subordinates accountable later for on-the-job application.

Post-instructional evaluations: traditional approaches. Post-instructional evaluations are conducted, as their name suggests, after a training course or program has been delivered. They overlap with other forms of training evaluation which have already been discussed.

Donald Kirkpatrick (1959, 1960) conceptualized a classic way of viewing post-instructional evaluations by arranging possible results of training on a four-level hierarchy of change (see Table 12-8). In ascending order, these levels are:

1. *reactions:* How much did trainees like a course? How much do they feel it will help them improve their job performance?
2. *learning:* How much knowledge or skill change resulted from a course? How well did participants achieve the terminal objectives of the course?
3. *behaviors:* What changes in job behaviors resulted from training? How much are workers applying what they learned in a way that is measurable and observable?
4. *results:* What changes in job results are attributable to training? How much more productive are trained than untrained workers? What differences in productivity levels stem from training?

Reactions are undoubtedly measured most frequently (Brandenburg, 1982), often by means of attitude surveys—so-called participant evaluations—handed out at the end of courses or sessions. Participants are typically asked to respond to questions

TABLE 12-8 DONALD KIRKPATRICK'S EVALUATION HIERARCHY

Reactions	Learning	Behavior	Results
How well do learners like the training?	How well do learners score on tests at the end of training?	How well do learners apply on the job the behaviors they learned in training?	How well does the productivity of learners improve on the job?

like those shown in Activity 12-5 (at the end of this chapter). While reaction surveys may indicate *feelings*, they do not really address bottom-line *results*.

Another way to evaluate reactions is to send trainees a survey about one to six months after their participation in a training program. Sometimes their views change as they acquire more experience or reflect on course content.

Learning, the second step in Kirkpatrick's hierarchy of change, is measured by tests. During instructional design, one test item—or more than that—is written to correspond to each instructional objective. After test items are developed, instructional content (subject matter) and delivery methods (means of presentation) are chosen. The result is a direct link between intentions for end-of-course change as expressed in terminal objectives and test items for measuring them.

Most people think of *written* tests, which are sometimes called paper-and-pencil tests. However, tests may also be administered orally or through demonstration of knowledge or skills. What could be a better way to prove mastery of learning objectives than to perform what was learned? Frequently, demonstration involves assembling or disassembling machinery—or some other physical object. To demonstrate skill or knowledge mastery with data (as in mathematics), trainees may be asked to solve a problem. To demonstrate skill or knowledge mastery with people, trainees may be asked to participate in an experiential exercise—a simulation, a role play, or a case study.

Tests need not be administered only at the end of a course, though that is appropriate if the intent is to measure *end-of-course* learning. They may also be given to trainees before instruction to measure entry knowledge or skills. Sometimes *pretests* are used for screening purposes to ensure that learners possess adequate entry skills, meaning that they have satisfied prerequisites. Tests may also be given periodically during a course to determine how well learners are progressing.

Behaviors, the third level in Kirkpatrick's hierarchy of change, are measured *on the job* rather than *at the end of a course.* This distinction is important, because trainee job behavior is affected by much more than instruction. It is also affected by individual motivation, peer pressure exerted by coworkers, expectations of supervisors, and much more. It is possible for a trainee to complete training successfully—and never change behavior on the job.

There are several ways to assess changes in job behaviors produced by training, what some call simply *transfer of learning.* To list a few: (1) ask the learners, their coworkers, supervisors, or subordinates if training has influenced job behavior; (2)

show up at the work site and ask former trainees to demonstrate how they are using what they learned in training; (3) observe former trainees at work both before and after training, noting any changes in observable work methods; and (4) compare job behaviors of former trainees and a control group of similar but randomly-selected non-trainees using predetermined criteria. To phrase it another way, behavioral change on the job can be measured through the opinions of trainees or other people, through tests of learning conducted at the job site, through work sampling of behaviors, or through evaluation design. Obviously, the first method is the easiest but least valid and reliable, because opinions are not necessarily accurate. The fourth method is most valid and reliable, but is also the most costly and time-consuming.

Results, the fourth level of Kirkpatrick's hierarchy of change, are also (like behaviors) measured on the job rather than at the end of instruction. Results are the real bottom-line: did training change on-the-job output or quality? To address this difficult question, HRD practitioners must identify before training (1) *what results* they will attempt to change, (2) *how much change* they will try to achieve, and (3) *how* they will analyze and interpret change.

Depending on the performance problem which training is intended to solve, *what results* are sought can vary. Table 12-9 lists so-called hard measures of results; Table 12-10 lists soft measures. "Hard data," as Jack Phillips (1984) explains, "are the primary measurement of improvement, presented as rational, undisputed facts, easily accumulated" (p. 12.7-12.8). On the other hand, "soft data . . . are more difficult to collect and analyze. They are used when hard data are not available" (Phillips, 1984, p. 12.8). Improvements are measured using these data.

Post-instructional evaluations: the strategic approach. It is difficult to predict post-instructional outcomes of training. For this reason, practitioners should improve an area they have too often neglected during instructional design—analysis of the work context.

Before training is delivered and during needs assessment, practitioners should carefully examine the work setting. Just what are the accepted norms of behavior? What does a supervisor believe his or her employees need to know? What rewards or punishments are likely to affect application of new methods on the job?

Once these questions have been addressed, practitioners should gear their efforts as closely as possible to conditions likely to exist when trainees return to the job. If barriers to application exist, they should be identified *during* training. Trainees will have to be furnished with methods to help them eliminate the barriers or apply instruction *despite* barriers. While this is quite difficult—especially when trainees attend from a cross-section of work groups rather than only one—it is not impossible. HRD practitioners should enlist the support of others back on the job site, such as experienced workers who have attended training in the past or supervisors who have a stake in performance improvement. These supporters serve as on-the-job coaches who facilitate application of training.

Comprehensive reviews of training. There is little point in distinguishing between traditional and future-oriented approaches to comprehensive reviews of all training courses. There are two good reasons why. First, few organizations develop a

TABLE 12-9 HARD DATA FOR EVALUATING RESULTS OF TRAINING

OUTPUT	TIME
Units Produced	Equipment Downtime
Tons Manufactured	Overtime
Items Assembled	On-Time shipments
Money Collected	Time to Project Completion
Items Sold	Processing Time
Forms Processed	Supervisory Time
Loans Approved	Break-in Time for New Employees
Inventory Turnover	Training Time
Patients Visited	Meeting Schedules
Applications Processed	Repair Time
Students Graduated	Efficiency
Tasks Completed	Work Stoppages
Output Per Man Hour	Order Response
Productivity	Late Reporting
Work Backlog	Lost Time Days
Incentive Bonus	
Shipments	QUALITY
	Scrap
COSTS	Waste
Budget Variances	Rejects
Unit Costs	Error Rates
Cost By Account	Rework
Variable Costs	Shortages
Fixed Costs	Product Defects
Overhead Cost	Deviation From Standard
Operating Costs	Product Failures
Number of Cost Reductions	Inventory Adjustments
Project Cost Savings	Time Card Corrections
Accident Costs	Percent of Tasks Completed Properly
Program Costs	Number of Accidents
Sales Expense	

Source: Phillips, 1984, p. 12.9. Reprinted with permission from Wiley-Interscience.

long-term learning plan or training curriculum by job class (Rothwell & Kazanas, 1988). Second, evaluation is relatively rare (*Employee Training,* 1986). In short, there is no training curriculum and little evaluation.

Before a comprehensive review of training can be conducted in an organization, several preconditions must be met. First, a curriculum must exist. That means that HRD practitioners have succeeded in planning for long-term training needs in each job class. Second, the purpose of the training curriculum must be stated. Why does it exist? Third, the goals must also be stated. What results are sought from training for each job class and for all job classes taken together? Fourth, each training program must be systematically planned and evaluated (Saylor & Alexander, 1966, p. 243). Fifth, each training program should simultaneously reflect: (a) job requirements for its targeted learners; (b) organizational requirements and priorities; and (c) Organizational Strategy for HRD. Sixth and finally, the evaluation results of each training pro-

TABLE 12-10 SOFT DATA FOR EVALUATING RESULTS OF TRAINING

WORK HABITS	NEW SKILLS
Absenteeism	Decisions Made
Tardiness	Problems Solved
Visits to the Dispensary	Conflicts Avoided
First Aid Treatments	Grievances Resolved
Violations of Safety Rules	Counseling Problems Solved
Number of Communication Breakdowns	Listening Skills
Excessive Breaks	Reading Speed
	Discrimination Charges Resolved
WORK CLIMATE	Intention to Use New Skills
Number of Grievances	Frequency of Use of New Skills
Number of Discrimination Charges	
Employee Complaints	DEVELOPMENT/ADVANCEMENT
Job Satisfaction	Number of Promotions
Unionization Avoidance	Number of Pay Increases
Employee Turnover	Number of Training Programs Attended
	Requests for Transfer
FEELINGS/ATTITUDES	Performance Appraisal Ratings
Favorable Reactions	Increases in Job Effectiveness
Attitude Changes	
Perceptions of Job Responsibilities	INITIATIVE
Perceived Changes in Performance	Implementation of New Ideas
Employee Loyalty	Successful Completion of Projects
	Number of Suggestions Submitted
	Number of Suggestions Implemented

Source: Phillips, 1984, p. 12.10. Reprinted with permission from Wiley-Interscience.

gram should be collected and stored (a) program-by-program; (b) learner-by-learner; and (c) job class-by-job class.

Perhaps the most important preconditions are the first, fourth, and sixth. A curriculum must exist before a comprehensive review of training can be carried out. Each training course or other planned instructional event must be planned and evaluated so that information is available about each program. This information must be recorded in a way that allows data to be compared and aggregated over time.

To carry out a comprehensive review of training, practitioners should begin by setting a policy that such reviews will be conducted at periodic intervals—every year or two. A training advisory committee, composed of representatives from the HRD department, line management, top management, and trainees, can be especially useful. This committee directs studies, participates in them, and/or receives results and makes recommendations for corrective action.

Regardless of who is involved, however, it will be necessary to (1) clarify the purpose, goals, and objectives of the review, (2) select people who possess the skills necessary to carry it out, (3) establish an evaluation plan, and (4) clarify precisely what will be done with the results once they are received.

In most respects, a comprehensive training review is approached like any evaluation study. The only key difference between it and most studies has to do with focus. It focuses on the overall training plan for each job class or all job classes in the organization.

Evaluating Employee Education

What should be evaluated?   Employee education grooms individuals for specific future jobs (Nadler, 1984), keeps people current and up-to-date in their fields, or stimulates new ideas by exposing people to practices in other organizations. Each purpose is somewhat different. Hence, evaluation of education varies in methods and approaches, depending on purpose.

Think of evaluative methods for employee education as analogous to, but not the same as, those for training. The methods thus include: front-end analysis for employee education; advance counseling; evaluation of educational materials; concurrent evaluation; post-educational follow-up; and comprehensive reviews of employee education.

Front-end analysis for employee education.   FEA for employee education is different from its training counterpart. Its purpose, from a manager's standpoint, is to plan for future staffing needs; from an individual's standpoint its purpose is to plan for realizing immediate career objectives—advancement to a higher position, transfer to a different career line, or some other objective. The idea is to negotiate these objectives so that the supervisor and the employee share a common goal for the employee's next career step.

The essence of FEA for education is best summarized through a series of questions. Supervisors should ask: (1) What will be the most critical future staffing needs of the unit, department, or organization? (2) How can those needs be met in the most cost-effective means—through external education, external recruitment, internal transfer, internal education and transition into the new position, or external contracting? (3) If external education is selected, what is the best source or group of sources of education to meet future staffing needs?

Individuals should consider a parallel and similar series of questions: (1) What skills are essential in a targeted future position? (2) What skills does the individual possess at present? (3) What differences exist between the individual's present skills and those needed in the future for the targeted position? and (4) How can needed skills be acquired? What sources are available to meet needs?

When supervisors and individual negotiate answers to these questions, then they can arrive at a plan for employee education which will satisfy—or at least strike a balance between—both individual and organizational needs. It is wise to express this plan in terms of educational objectives, which can be negotiated through a Management by Objectives plan or a learning contract.

Evaluation of educational sources.   There are, of course, many ways to meet an educational need. Individuals can be sent to external seminars, directed through externally-produced materials, sent to college courses, or sent to programs delivered by external consultants but presented in-house.

Each alternative should be considered according to cost, convenience, and relevance to educational objectives, as well as constraints on time, funding, and available information. Once a prospective source is chosen, it should be evaluated carefully in advance. Methods of doing that may vary, depending on source.

If an external seminar or college course is a possible source, the HRD practitioner should research it carefully before sending people to it. A good place to start is with the course brochure (Laird, 1985). What does it say about the course? What objectives are stated for it? For what kind of people is it intended? Is an outline available and, if so, what subject matter will be covered? By what methods? It also helps to contact past participants—the vendor should be willing to give that information. What do past participants say about the course's strengths and weaknesses? What is the general reputation of the vendor? If these questions yield satisfying answers, then consider how many people in the organization share the same educational need. If many do, it might be worthwhile for the HRD practitioner to attend the course and/or send a few experienced employees to attend and bring back a report.

If the educational source is a package available for purchase, HRD practitioners can request it on a trial basis. They can look it over. They should ask subject matter experts in the firm to do likewise.

If an external consultant is to be hired, practitioners should check out his or her education and experience in advance. What about recommendations from previous clients?

If HRD practitioners consider meeting educational needs in-house, they should be as rigorous in their up-front assessments as they are in evaluating external sources. Does the HRD department possess the resources and expertise to meet a specific educational need? If not, can these resources be acquired? Can expertise be obtained through temporary transfers from other departments? Will the in-house costs of meeting needs be cheaper *and* more effective than alternatives?

Advance counseling. Before sending employees through educational experiences, advance counseling is crucial and is essential to success. Employees should understand why they are going through an experience, what they should be able to do upon completion, and why the experience is important. It is helpful to counsel individuals prior to their participation in education. Such counseling sessions can be handled by the HRD practitioner, the employee's supervisor, or both.

Concurrent evaluation. Some educational experiences take a long time. A college course may last up to sixteen weeks, for example. Some in-house programs may last even longer.

Concurrent evaluation is performed during educational experiences. On the simplest level, the HRD practitioner arranges to speak with employees periodically as they progress through education. These sessions are usually informal, intended to check on progress. If an individual is experiencing difficulties, this is the time to discuss them and arrange for help.

Post-educational follow-up. Each educational experience should be evaluated after the individual has completed it. Much like training, an employee educational experience can be judged according to (1) *reactions:* Do employees feel that the experience contributed to preparing them for career advancement? Do supervisors feel the experience contributed to meeting future staffing needs? (2) *learning:* Can employees demonstrate the skills they learned during the educational experience? (3) *behavior:* Can employees apply, upon promotion, the skills they learned through employee education? and (4) *results:* How well are employees able to perform under future conditions in their new position? Reactions are measured through surveys and interviews; learning is measured by tests; behavior is measured by observation, employee appraisals, and long-term follow-up; and results are measured by availability of talent and/or expressions of individual satisfaction with career progress.

Comprehensive reviews of employee education. A comprehensive review of employee education is similar to a comprehensive review of training, except that its focus is on the entire range of educational offerings sponsored by an organization. The purpose for carrying out such a review is precisely the same as it is for reviewing training comprehensively. It helps managers consider the value of employee education in contributing to the achievement of goals pertinent to business strategy, staff strategy, individal career mobility, organizational profitability, HRD strategy, and quality of work life.

Several preconditions are necessary before a comprehensive review of employee education can be carried out:

1. Employee education must be planned according to a formal, deliberate process.
2. The purpose(s) of employee educational efforts must be stated.
3. The goals of employee education must be stated. What results are sought?
4. Each educational effort must be related to a personalized, negotiated plan for each individual.
5. Each educational effort must be formally planned and evaluated.
6. Each educational activity should simultaneously reflect (a) career objectives of individuals; (b) staffing requirements of the organization, department, or work unit; and (c) the Organizational Strategy for HRD.
7. Evaluation results, by individual, should be maintained in a Human Resource Information System.

Perhaps the most appropriate way to approach a comprehensive review of employee education is from the standpoint of formal career planning for individuals (on one hand) and formal HR planning for the organization (on the other hand). Consider:

1. *evaluation of career paths:* Have decision-makers in the firm clarified educational, experience, and other requirements for each position and for movement between positions?

2. *evaluation of staff planning:* Have decision-makers clarified the organization's future staffing needs?
3. *evaluation of educational sourcing:* How well is the organization identifying sources for meeting educational needs? Does the HRD department systematically collect and store such information?
4. *evaluation of educational management:* How well is the organization managing employee educational efforts and tracking them?
5. *meta-evaluation:* How is the organization evaluating educational efforts?

A comprehensive review of employee education is carried out much like a comprehensive review of training. In fact, they may be carried out together as well as separately.

EVALUATING DEVELOPMENT

What should be evaluated? Development is a long-term change effort carried out to change the collective skills of people in group settings.

Employee development activities are difficult to plan, let alone evaluate, because the odds are stacked against them: supervisors have trouble defining the mix of employee skills needed to match up to group needs; and top managers, whose tenure in U.S. corporations averages around four years (Naisbitt, 1982), tend to view human skills as acquired easily enough externally so that long-term internal development efforts are unnecessary.

Organization development is valued by managers at all levels—once they know what it is. Most experienced managers know how difficult it is to overcome resistance to change. Top managers realize that changes in organizational direction or strategy grow more difficult as they run counter to past tradition, culture, and group norms. OD encourages cultural change but is by no means a "quick fix."

Nonemployee development is rarely approached systematically through organized HRD activities. Managers sometimes have difficulty recognizing immediate payoffs from these activities. In the U.S., however, business leaders can hardly overlook increasing pressure on business to take an active role in improving community life. Nor can leaders easily dismiss that, as products and services become more complex technologically in response to consumer demand, there is a growing need to help consumers learn how to use the sophisticated goods and services they buy. Indeed, lack of knowledge among consumers may be the greatest barrier to future sales growth for some high-technology firms.

While methods of development may differ, evaluation methods are not unlike those used in employee education or training. It occurs before, during, or after the implementation of a development strategy. When it occurs beforehand, it is front-end analysis or field testing; when it occurs during implementation, it is concurrent evaluation; when it occurs at the end, it is post-developmental follow-up. Since development is long-term, however, after-the-fact evaluation is not as useful as in training or education. Objectives should be articulated for each type of development and used as a basis for evaluation.

Front-end analysis of development. To conduct front-end analysis for employee development, the HRD practitioner must work in tandem with other managers in the organization to decide on long-term objectives to satisfy the staffing needs for each work unit. The purpose of FEA for employee development is to pinpoint the most critical long-term staffing needs of each work group in line with Strategic Business Plans.

To carry out FEA for employee development, HRD practitioners should begin with information about organizational staffing plans. In concert with other managers in the firm, they should deliberate over such questions as these: (1) What skills will be needed over three to five years to meet needs of the organization? (2) What skills are presently available? and (3) How can gaps between skills needed in the future and those available at present be narrowed?

Once supervisors answer these questions, they need to consider sources. *How can individuals be groomed over the long term for the benefit of the work group?* Sources include: long-term mentoring programs; transfer or exchange programs; special job assignments; field trips; professional conferences; behavior modeling; and "think tank" experiences. Each must be weighed not so much for cost as for effectiveness: How useful will it be in meeting the long-term staffing needs of the work unit?

When is an OD intervention appropriate? This question has to do with FEA for OD. OD is appropriate when someone desires change because conditions differ from expectations, top managers support change, problems stem from interactions between individuals or groups, cultural norms are at odds with desired change, and there is sufficient time and other resources to enact change. Unlike most HRD activities, OD facilitates *group* learning and *group* change.

When OD practitioners are asked to lend assistance, they begin by collecting information about the problem which prompted the call for help. This process works very much like FEA for training. However, there is one key difference: in OD, data about problems are fed back to participants in data collection and to decision-makers to stimulate problem-solving and decision-making; in HRD, data are used to separate training from nontraining needs.

In OD, managers and employees set objectives for change and, with the help of a consultant typically from outside the unit or organization experiencing trouble, choose an appropriate OD intervention.

When is community and/or stakeholder development appropriate? This question has to do with FEA for nonemployee development. Progressive decision-makers believe nonemployee development efforts are *always* appropriate, because business firms should strive for improved relations with the communities in which their facilities are located and with the society in which they do business. Improved relations with suppliers, consumers, distributors, and other key stakeholder groups produce significant advantages to the firm. The more that stakeholders understand the unique needs of the business, the more effectively the firm will be able to sell its products or services, obtain necessary supplies, and produce goods or deliver services.

To conduct FEA for community/stakeholder development, HRD practitioners should work with managers in the firm. There are four questions to ask. First, what future relationships are desirable with each external stakeholder group? Second, what is the nature of the present relationships between the organization and each major group outside it? Third, how can HRD help improve relations between the organization and external groups? Fourth and finally, what efforts stand the best chance of improving relations over time?

By systematically addressing these questions; managers and HRD practitioners establish a unified direction for nonemployee development efforts.

Field testing development. The old adage, "start small but think big" is appropriate for any development effort. It is a way of field testing. To field test employee development, start with one work group or department in the firm. Establish a model for employee development in the department or work group that is appropriate to it. Enlist the support of managers, supervisors, and employee opinion-leaders in planning, implementing, and periodically following up on it.

Once a model of employee development has been successfully used in one work group or department, it can be extended gradually into the remainder of the firm.

Use exactly the same approach with OD and nonemployee development. Start with one group, devise a successful means of developing the group, scan the environment for changes, and implement the development effort gradually.

Concurrent evaluation of development. Concurrent evaluation controls development efforts against initial objectives to ensure that activities are in line with intentions.

The HRD department should hold periodic meetings for interested parties to assess the progress of developmental efforts and identify areas requiring corrective action. Meetings can be held in groups participating in employee development programs or OD interventions. Advisory groups, much like marketing focus groups, can be assembled to represent external stakeholders, and meetings can be held with these groups to evaluate nonemployee development activities.

Post-development follow-up. Use post-development follow-up only when there is a need to *change* employee, organization, or nonemployee development initiatives. Change is appropriate when there is a major shift in Strategic Business Plans, environmental conditions, staffing strategy, or Organizational Strategy for HRD.

Post-development follow-up begins with data collected through surveys or interviews. Results are then presented in meetings, along with information about the successes and failures of each development effort. This information sets the stage for establishing new development objectives and new action plans to meet them.

EVALUATING THE HRD EFFORT

Definition of strategic evaluation. Strategic evaluation (SE) of the HRD Effort monitors how well:

- *Results match intentions.* Have the consequences of an Organization's Strategy for HRD been working as desired?

- *Organizational Strategy for HRD is being implemented in line with long-term objectives.* Is the organization practicing operationally what was preached strategically?
- *Organizational Strategy for HRD is attuned to environmental conditions as the future unfolds in the present.* Were expectations about the future accurate, and do they still furnish a reliable guide for HRD activities?

Strategic evaluation of the HRD Effort is a comprehensive examination of how well human resources in the organization have been, are being, and will be developed over time. It is the culmination of separate but comprehensive reviews of training, education, and development. Its purpose is to take stock of how well Organizational Strategy for HRD has worked, is working and will probably work in the future.

When is strategic evaluation appropriate? Strategic evaluation (SE) is appropriate before, during, and after implementation of Organizational Strategy for HRD. When a proposed HRD Strategy is examined before implementation, it is instrumental in making a *strategic choice;* when the chosen HRD Strategy is evaluated during implementation, it is called *strategy review* or *concurrent evaluation;* when HRD Strategy is evaluated as decision-makers are contemplating a change, it is called *summative evaluation.*

SE prior to strategic choice. According to Schendel and Hofer (1979), the purpose of evaluating *organizational* strategy is to

> answer two basic questions. First, will the organization's *existing* strategy lead to the achievement of its goals and objectives (intended results), subject to the environmental conditions it is expected to encounter? If not, then it will be necessary to change the existing strategy. Second, will any *proposed strategy* alternate lead to the achievement of these goals and objectives subject to the expected environmental conditions? (pp. 189-90)

For the same reasons, SE is helpful in choosing Organizational Strategy for HRD.

To carry out SE prior to strategic choice, decision-makers should address five key issues (Schendel & Hofer, 1979):

1. *goal consistency:* How much are the goals/objectives of the existing—and any proposed—Organizational Strategy for HRD internally consistent? In short, is the direction unified across proposed activities and integrated with Strategic Business Plans and HR plans?
2. *design process:* How well-designed was the process used to formulate the Organizational Strategy for HRD?
3. *strategy implementation:* How well can the Organizational Strategy for HRD be implemented? Will operating managers do their share? Will the HRD department do its share? How well-matched to proposed Organizational Strategy for HRD is structure, leadership, policies, and rewards?
4. *early indicators:* How well has Organizational Strategy for HRD been working? Have indicators been established to provide feedback about the effectiveness of

HRD strategy in the early stages of implementation? Will time allow tentative, small-scale tests of strategy in some plants or regions without committing all resources to an unproven strategy?

5. *strategy content:* How well does existing or proposed Organizational Strategy for HRD meet the needs and conform to the values of key stakeholders inside and outside the organization (Mintzberg, 1979)? How well does it meet tests for completeness, consistency, resource requirements, environmental accuracy, and goodness of fit with environmental assumptions?

By addressing these questions, decision-makers can choose an Organizational Strategy for HRD that is appropriate to the organization and its environment.

Strategy review. Once a unified Organizational Strategy for HRD has been chosen and implemented, decision-makers need some way to find out whether it is working out as intended. As Rothschild (1976) observes, "you can't guarantee that a strategy will produce its promised results until it is implemented. . . ." (p. 201). Action is the fire-test of strategy.

A strategy review is a periodic examination of how well HRD Strategy is working out. It can be included as an item on the agenda of a Strategic Business Planning review meeting, or it can be the topic of a meeting all its own. Meetings of this kind should be scheduled on some regular basis—monthly, quarterly, semiannually or annually. Often the frequency of review meetings is a function of hierarchical level. Corporate officers may meet only once or twice a year; business, functional, and divisional officers usually meet more frequently.

Rothschild (1976) suggests that a review of Strategic Business Plans is best handled by someone outside the firm. The reason is that a review "requires a critical, unbiased look at what you say you will do and why. . . . It can't be done by someone who has his mind already made up or an ax to grind" (p. 201). In short, objectivity is essential. This principle applies as much to HRD Strategy review as to Strategic Business Planning.

What issues are appropriately addressed during a review of Organizational Strategy for HRD? First, consider *progress to date.* Assuming that long-term objectives have been established to measure achievement, how well is Organizational Strategy for HRD contributing to organizational learning and adaptation, to preparation of individuals for movement to future jobs, and to performance improvement on present jobs? Second, review *responsiveness to stakeholders.* How well is Organizational Strategy for HRD meeting needs and conforming to values of top managers, middle managers, first-line supervisors, nonsupervisory employees, and customers, suppliers, distributors, and community members? Third, review the *adequacy of original assumptions.* As Rothschild (1976) notes, strategies are built on assumptions of the future. As the future unfolds, assumptions may remain valid, but strategy implementation may not necessarily follow the original course charted for it. On the other hand, assumptions may prove faulty and may require reconsideration. Are assumptions still valid? Are they congruent with implementation? Fourth, review *realism.* Was the original Organizational Strategy for HRD realistic? In short, was it ever capable of being implemented, or did it call for too much change in too short a period of time?

Fifth and finally, check the *availability of skills*. Are the skills needed to implement Organizational Strategy for HRD available to the organization? Do line managers, supervisors, and HRD staff members possess the necessary skills to do what is required of them? By addressing these questions periodically, decision-makers control actions against intentions and pinpoint areas needing correction or attention. (See Activity 12-6 at the end of this chapter.)

Summative evaluation. For most HRD practitioners, summative evaluation connotes a process "usually undertaken when development of an instructional entity is in some sense completed, rather than on-going. Its purpose is to permit conclusions to be drawn about how well the instruction has worked" (Gagné & Briggs, 1979, p. 293). It is backward-looking because it judges the value of past instruction; it is forward-looking because these judgments are used to make decisions about adopting a planned learning experience on a broader scale. The word *summative* connotes evaluation intended to "sum up" the value of planned learning (Gagné & Briggs, 1979).

When applied to strategic evaluation, the summative approach aims to identify and underscore the need for a change in Organizational Strategy for HRD. In this sense, it closes the circle begun when the purpose, goals, and objectives of an organization's HRD Effort were established.

What issues are appropriately addressed during a summative evaluation of Organizational Strategy for HRD? First, does the purpose of the HRD Effort match up to Strategic Business Plans, HR plans, and the needs and expectations of key stakeholders inside and outside the organization? Changes in business strategy, major HR plans, or leadership of the firm may require alterations to the purpose of the HRD Effort. Second, does the existing Organizational Strategy for HRD match up to the external environment of the organization? Major changes outside the firm may require a complete review of Organizational Strategy for HRD so that people are being developed in line with present and future needs. Third and finally, does the existing Organizational Strategy for HRD build on strengths within the firm and minimize weaknesses?

The most appropriate time to carry out a summative evaluation is during Strategic Business Planning efforts. Future organizational initiatives imply human skills to carry them out (Rothschild, 1976; Schein, 1978). When these skills are *not* already available, decision-makers should think twice before choosing a strategy calling for them; when untapped human skills *are* available, decision-makers should think about how this organizational strength can be put to best competitive use. While the development of human resources from within the firm is only one way to meet future skill needs—recruitment from outside, short-term and long-term outside contracting, and transfer from inside are alternatives—it is clear that the HRD Effort should support Strategic Business Plans. Evaluation helps determine how much it does—and when a new Organizational Strategy for HRD is needed.

ACTIVITY 12-1 Importance of Goals in Instructional Evaluation

Directions: Use this activity to consider the relative importance of various organizational goals to different groups in your organization. For each goal and each job grouping, describe (1) how important you believe it is to focus on the goal during instructional evaluation, and (2) your thoughts on the best ways to carry out instructional evaluation on the goal. There are no right or wrong answers.

Goal*	Job Group			
	Top Managers	Middle Managers	First-Line Supervisors	Employees
Organizational Effectiveness				
High Productivity				
Organizational Leadership				
High Morale				
Organizational Reputation				
Organizational Efficiency				
Profit Maximization				
Organizational Growth				
Organizational Stability				
Organizational Value to the Community				
Service to the Public				

Source: The goals are from Schmidt & Posner, 1982, with permission.

ACTIVITY 12-2 Fundamental Issues to Consider in Instructional Evaluation

Directions: Reflect on instructional evaluation in your organization. Use this activity to brainstorm on evaluation. Answer the questions which follow.

Stakeholders

1. Who are the primary stakeholders of planned learning activities in your organization? Who are the primary stakeholders of instructional evaluation?

Evaluators

2. Who are the primary evaluators of instruction in your firm? *Why* are they the evaluators?

Content

3. What is the primary focus of instructional evaluation in your organization? Describe it.

ACTIVITY 12-2   Continued

Timing

4. Is timing of evaluation important? Is it particularly important that the results of evaluation be compiled and communicated at any specific time?

Purpose

5. Why is instructional evaluation carried out in your organization?

Method

6. How is instructional evaluation carried out in your organization? (Describe the methods that are used.)

ACTIVITY 12-3 Strategic Front-End Analysis of Training

Directions: Use this activity to structure your thinking about the need for training. Answer in the right column each question posed in the left column.

Questions	Answers
1. What trends in work flow and work methods are most likely to be felt over the next year?	
2. In what specific work areas is change most likely to occur?	
3. What changes are likely to be most costly in the future?	
4. What knowledge/skills can help employees prepare for changes in the future?	
5. What methods *other than* formal, classroom-based training can help prepare employees for changes in the future?	
6. What will be the causes of anticipated future problems?	
7. How can supervisors and managers be convinced of the need to prepare for anticipated future problems?	

ACTIVITY 12-4 Advance Survey of Participants

Directions: Use this survey to gather information from participants *before* a training course. Mail this survey to them in plenty of time to get a response before the first training session.

1. What are you hoping to learn in the training session?

2. What "gripes" do you have about this subject?

3. What problems have you noticed in this organization that are pertinent to this subject?

ACTIVITY 12-5 Participant Evaluation

Directions: Give this survey to trainees immediately *after* a training course.

1. What did you like most about this training course?

2. What did you like least about this training course?

3. Did the trainer(s) do a good job of presenting this course?

4. What aspects of this course could be improved?

Evaluating the HRD Effort

ACTIVITY 12-5   Continued

5. How well were visual aids used in this course?

6. Did participants interact effectively?

ACTIVITY 12-6 Reviewing Organizational Strategy for HRD

Directions: Use this activity to structure your thinking about Organizational Strategy for HRD in your organization. Answer the following questions in the space provided.

Progress to Date

1. How well is Organizational Strategy for HRD contributing to

    a. organizational learning and adaptation?
    b. the preparation of individuals for movement to future jobs?
    c. improving performance on jobs at present?

Responsiveness to Stakeholders

2. How well is Organizational Strategy for HRD conforming to the values of

    a. top managers?
    b. middle managers?
    c. first-line supervisors?
    d. nonsupervisory employees?
    e. other stakeholders?

Adequacy of Assumptions

3. Have the original assumptions on which Organizational Strategy for HRD was based remained valid?

ACTIVITY 12-6   Continued
Realism

4. Was the original Organizational Strategy for HRD realistic?

5. Are the skills needed to implement Organizational Strategy for HRD available in the organization? Do managers, supervisors, and HRD staff members possess the necessary skills to implement the Strategy?

REFERENCES

ABELL, D. (1978, July). Strategic Windows. *Journal of Marketing, 42,* 21-26.

ABELSON, M. & WOODMAN, R. (1983, Spring). Review of Research on Team Effectiveness. *School Psychology Review,* pp. 125-36.

ACKERMAN, R. (1975). *Managing Corporate Responsibility.* Boston: Harvard University Press.

ACKOFF, R. (1981). *Creating the Corporate Future: Plan or Be Planned For.* New York: John Wiley.

ADAIR, C. & FOSTER, J. (1972). *A Guide to Simulation Design.* Tallahassee, FL: Instructional Simulation Design, Inc.

ADAMS, E. (1975). *Career Advancement Guide.* New York: McGraw-Hill.

AGUILAR, F. (1967). *Scanning the Business Environment.* New York: Macmillan.

AHUMADA, M. & HEFFERLIN, J. (1986). Sources of Assistance. In P. Callan (Ed.), *Environmental Scanning for Strategic Leadership.* San Francisco: Jossey-Bass.

AIKEN, M. & ALFORD, R. (1970, August). Community Structure and Innovation. *American Sociological Review,* pp. 650-65.

AIKEN, M. & HAGE, J. (1971, January). The Organic Organization and Innovation. *Sociology,* pp. 63-82.

AJIMAL, K. (1985). Force Field Analysis: A Framework for Strategic Thinking. *Long Range Planning, 18*(5), 55-60.

ALBERT, M. (1985). Assessing Culture Change Needs. *Training and Development Journal, 39*(5), 94; 97-98.

ALBERT, M. (1987). Transmitting Corporate Culture through Case Stories. *Personnel, 64*(8), 71-73.

ALBRECHT, K. (1978). *Successful Management by Objectives: An Action Manual.* Englewood Cliffs, NJ: Prentice Hall.

ALBRECHT, M. (1983). *Careers in Business: Exercises and Cases.* New York: Wiley & Sons.

ALDERFER, C. (1977). Organizational Development. *Annual Review of Psychology, 28,* 197-223.

ALLEN, M. (1962). *Morphological Creativity.* Englewood Cliffs, NJ: Prentice Hall.

ALLEVRAS, J. & FRIGERI, A. (1987). Picking Up the Pieces After Downsizing. *Training and Development Journal, 41,* (9), 29-31.

ALPANDER, G. (1982). *Human Resource Management Planning.* New York: Amacom.

ANDERSON, R. (1983). *Selecting and Developing Media for Instruction* (2nd ed.). New York: Van Nostrand Reinhold.

ANDERSSON, B. & NILSSON, S. (1964). Studies in the Reliability and Validity of the Critical Incident Technique. *Journal of Applied Psychology, 48,* 398-403.

ANSHEN, M. (1980). *Corporate Strategies for Social Performance.* New York: Macmillan.

ANTHONY, W. (1985). *Practical Strategic Planning: A Guide and Manual for Line Managers.* Westport, CT: Quorum Books.

ARCHER, S., KELLY, C. & BISCH, S. (1984). *Implementing Change in Communities: A Collaborative Process.* St. Louis: C. V. Mosby Company.

ARGYRIS, C. (1962). *Interpersonal Competence and Organizational Effectiveness.* Homewood, IL: Dorsey Press.

ARGYRIS, C. (1970). *Intervention Theory and Method.* Reading, MA: Addison-Wesley.

ARGYRIS, C. (1982). How Learning and Reasoning Processes Affect Organizational Change. In P. Goodman & Associates (Eds.), *Change in Organizations: New Perspectives on Theory, Research and Practice.* San Francisco: Jossey-Bass.

ARGYRIS, C. (1968). Some Unintended Consequences of Rigorous Research. *Psychological Bulletin, 70,* 185-97.

ARGYRIS, C. & SCHÖN, D (1974). *Theory in Practice.* San Francisco: Jossey-Bass.

ARGYRIS, C. & SCHÖN, D. (1978). *Organizational Learning: A Theory of Action Perspective.* Reading, MA: Addison-Wesley.

ARMSTRONG, J. (1982). The Forecasting Audit. In S. Makridakis & S. Wheelwright (Eds.), *The Handbook of Forecasting: A Manager's Guide.* New York: John Wiley & Sons.

ARONOFF, C. & BASKIN, O. (1983). *Public Relations: The Profession and the Practice.* St. Paul, MN: West Publishing.

ARY, D., JACOBS, L. & RAZAVIEH, A. (1979). *Introduction to Research in Education* (2nd ed.). New York: Holt, Rinehart and Winston.

ASCHER, W. (1978). *Forecasting: An Appraisal for Policy Makers and Planners.* Baltimore, MD: Johns Hopkins University Press.

AVAKIAN, A. (1974). Writing a Learning Contract. In D. Vermilye (Ed.), *Lifelong Learners: A New Clientele for Higher Education.* San Francisco: Jossey-Bass.

BAILEY, R. (1982). *Human Performance Engineering: A Guide for System Designers.* Englewood Cliffs, NJ: Prentice Hall.

BAIRD, L., & MESHOULAM, I. (1984, January). Strategic Human Resource Management: Implications for Training Human Resource Professionals. *Training and Development Journal,* pp. 76-78.

BAKER, E. (1980, July). Managing Organizational Culture. *Management Review,* pp. 8-13.

BAKER, H. (1979, June). The Hows and Whys of Team Building. *Personnel Journal,* pp. 367-70.

BAKER, J. (1985). Correspondence and Home Study. In W. Tracey (Ed.), *Human Resources Management and Development Handbook.* New York: Amacom.

BAKKE, E. (1953). *The Fusion Process.* New Haven: Yale University.

BALL, S. & ANDERSON, S. (1975). *Practices in Program Evaluation: A Survey and Some Case Studies.* Princeton, NJ: Education Testing Service.

BANDURA, A. (1971). *Psychological Modeling: Conflicting Theories.* Chicago: Aldine-Atherton.

BANDURA, A. (1977). *Social Learning Theory.* Englewood Cliffs, NJ: Prentice Hall.

BANDURA, A. & WALTERS, R. (1963). *Social Learning Theory and Personality Development.* New York: Holt, Rinehart & Winston.

BARNEY, D. (1984). Technical Programs. In L. Nadler (Ed.), *The Handbook of Human Resource Development.* New York: Wiley-Interscience.

BARTHOLOMEW, D. & FORBES, A. (1979). *Statistical Techniques for Manpower Planning.* Chichester, UK: John Wiley.

BARTUNEK, M. & MURNINGHAM, J. (1984, September). The Nominal Group Technique. *Group and Organization Studies,* 417-32.

BASIC HRD, not Productivity, is CEO's Top T&D Concern. (1981). *Training, 18*(2), 69.

BATES, C. (1985). Mapping the Environment: An Operational Environmental Analysis Model. *Long Range Planning, 18*(5), 97-107.

BAUER, R. & FENN, D. (1973, January-February). What is a Corporate Social Audit? *Harvard Business Review,* pp. 37-48.

BEACH, D. (1980). *Personnel: the Management of People at Work* (4th ed.) New York: Macmillan.

BEATTY, R. & SCHNEIER, C. (1981). *Personnel Administration: An Experiential Skill-Building Approach* (2nd ed.). Reading, MA: Addison-Wesley.

BEAUCHAMP, G. (1981). *Curriculum Theory* (4th ed.). Itasca, IL: F. E. Peacock.

BEAUDIN, B. & DOWLING, W. (1985). Data Collection Methods Used to Determine Training Needs in Business and Industry. *Performance and Instruction, 24*(8), 28-30.

BECK, L. (1983). Assessment Centers. In F. Ulschak (Ed.), *Human Resource Development: The Theory and Practice of Need Assessment.* Reston, VA: Reston Publishing.

BECKHARD, K. (1967). The Confrontation Meeting. *Harvard Business Review, 45*(2), 149-55.

BEDEIAN, A. (1984). *Organizations: Theory and Analysis* (2nd ed.). Chicago: The Dryden Press.

BEER, M. (1980). *Organization Change and Development: A Systems View.* Santa Monica, CA: Goodyear.

BEER, M. & DRISCOLL, J. (1977). Strategies for Change. In J. Hackman and J. Suttle (Eds.), *Improving Life at Work: Behavioral Science Approaches to Organizational Change.* Santa Monica, CA: Goodyear.

BELBIN, R. (1982). The Discovery Method. [rpt. from November 1973 *Training.*] In *Adult Learning in Your Classroom,* Minneapolis, MN: Lakewood Publications.

BELL, C. (1984). Building a Reputation for Training Effectiveness. *Training and Development Journal, 38*(5), 50-52, 54.

BELLINGHAM, R. & COHEN, B. (Eds.). (1987). *The Corporate Wellness Sourcebook.* Amherst, MA: Human Resource Development Press.

BENNE, K. & SHEATS, P. (1948). Functional Roles of Group Members. *Journal of Social Issues, 4,* 41-49.

BERGER, M. (1986). Research on Corporate Culture: The Agony and the Ecstacy. In J. Glidewell (Ed.), *Corporate Cultures: Implications for Human Resource Development.* Alexandria, VA: American Society for Training and Development.

BERNARDIN, H. & ABBOTT, J. (1985). Predicting (and Preventing) Differences Between Self and Supervisory Appraisals. *Personnel Administrator, 30*(6), 151-52, 155-57.

BIBEAULT, D. (1982). *Corporate Turnaround.* New York: McGraw-Hill.

BIKLEN, D. (1983). *Community Organizing.* Englewood Cliffs, NJ: Prentice Hall.

BILES, G. (1986). Auditing HRM Practices. *Personnel Administrator, 31*(12), 89-94.

BILES, G. & SCHULER, R. (1986). *Audit Handbook of Human Resource Management Practices.* Alexandria, VA: American Society for Personnel Administration.

BIRNBRAUER, H. (1985). Technical Training. In W. Tracey (Ed.), *Human Resources Management and Development Handbook.* New York: Amacom.

BITTEL, L. (1987). Supervisor Development. In R. Craig (Ed.), *Training and Development Handbook* (3rd ed.). New York: McGraw-Hill.

BLAKE, R. & MOUTON, J. (1978). *Making Experience Work: The Grid Approach to Critique.* New York: McGraw-Hill.

BLAKELY, E. (1979). The Community Diagnostic Method: An Approach to the Application of Community Development Research. In E. Blakely (Ed.), *Community Development Research: Concepts, Issues and Strategies.* New York: Human Sciences Press.

BLAKELY, E. & SCHUTZ, H. (1979). A Policy Systems Approach to Community Development Research and Action. In E. Blakely (Ed.), *Community Development Research: Concepts, Issues and Strategies.* New York: Human Sciences Press.

BLANK, W. (1982). *Handbook for Developing Competency-based Training Programs.* Englewood Cliffs, NJ: Prentice Hall.

BLESSING, B. (1986). The Muscles Behind the Smiles. *Training, 23*(10), 85-94.

BLESSING, B. (1986). Career Planning: Five Fatal Assumptions. *Training and Development Journal, 40*(9), 49-51.

BOBBITT, F. (1918). *The Curriculum.* Boston: Houghton Mifflin.

BOLLES, R. (1986). *What Color is your Parachute?* Berkeley, CA: Ten Speed Press.

BOLT, J. (1985, November-December). Tailor Executive Development to Strategy. *Harvard Business Review,* pp. 168-76.

BLOMQUIST, C. (1982). Study Shows Relocation Resistance Reversing. *Personnel Administration, 27*(12), 55-58.

BLOOM, B., and others, (1956). *Taxonomy of Educational Objectives, Handbook I: Cognitive domain.* New York: David McKay.

BLOOM, B., HASTINGS, J. AND MADAUS, G. (1971). *Handbook on Formative and Summative Evaluation of Student Learning.* New York: McGraw-Hill.

BORTZ, R. (1981). *Handbook for Developing Occupational Curricula.* Boston: Allyn & Bacon.

BOUCHARD, T., JR. (1971). Whatever Happened to Brainstorming? *Journal of Creative Behavior, 5,* 182-89.

BOULDING, E. (1976). Learning to Image the Future. In W. Bennis, K. Benne, R. Chin, & K. Corey (Eds.), *The Planning of Change* (3rd ed.). New York: Holt, Rinehart and Winston.

BOULMETIS, J. (1981). *Job Competency: Adult Vocational Instruction.* Belmont, CA: Pitman Learning.

BOURGEOIS, L. (1978). The Environmental Perception of Strategy Makers and their Economic Correlates. Published working paper. [Cited in Glueck & Jauch, 1984]. Pittsburgh: University of Pittsburgh.

Bove, R. (1985). Should HRD Directors Have a Training Background? *Training and Development Journal, 39*(1), 28-30.

Bowers, D. & Franklin, J. (1977). *Data-Based Organizational Change.* LaJolla, CA: University Associates.

Bowers, D. & Franklin, J. (1978). *Survey-Guided Development I, II, and III.* LaJolla, CA: University Associates.

Bowers, D. & Franklin, J. (1972). Survey-Guided Development: Using Human Resources Measurement in Organizational Change. *Journal of Contemporary Business, 1,* 43-55.

Bowers, D. & Franklin, J. (1976). *Survey-Guided Development: Data Based Organizational Change.* Ann Arbor, MI: Institute for Social Research.

Bowman, B. (1987). Sins of Omission: The Missing Link in Evaluation. *Training, 24*(5), 45-48.

Boyatzis, R. (1982). *The Competent Manager.* New York: Wiley-Interscience.

Boyd, B. (1980). Developing Case Studies. *Training and Development Journal, 34*(6), 113-117. [Reprint of a 1964 article.]

Brache, A. (1986, April). Strategy and the Middle Manager. *Training,* pp. 30-32, 34.

Brakken, D. & Bernstein, A. (1982, August). A Systematic Approach to Evaluation. *Training and Development Journal,* pp. 44-48.

Brandenburg, D. (1982). Training Evaluation: What's the Current Status? *Training and Development Journal, 36*(8), 14-19.

Brandenburg, D. & Smith, M. (1986). *Evaluation of Corporate Training Programs.* ERIC monograph, TME report 91. Princeton, NJ: Educational Testing Service.

Brett, J. (1980, Spring). Why Employees Want Unions. *Organizational Dynamics,* pp. 432-52.

Bridges, E., Doyle, W. & Mahan, D. (1968, Fall). Effects of Hierarchical Differentiation on Group Productivity, Efficiency, and Risk-Taking. *Administrative Science Quarterly,* pp. 305-39.

Briggs, L. (1970). *Handbook of Procedures for the Design of Instruction.* Pittsburgh, PA: American Institutes for Research.

Brightman, H. (1980). *Problem-Solving: A Logical and Creative Approach.* Atlanta: Georgia State University.

Brimmer, A. (1982, September). The Patience Factor: Management Careers in Corporate Enterprise. *Black Enterprise,* p. 30.

Broadwell, M. (1986). *The Supervisor and On the Job Training* (3rd ed.). Reading, MA: Addison-Wesley.

Bronikowski, R. (1983, April 7). Are you Promotable? Part 4: Relating to your Supervisor. *Machine Design,* pp. 56-60.

Brookfield, S. (1980). *Independent Adult Learning.* Unpublished doctoral dissertation. University of Leicester.

Brookfield, S. (1986). *Understanding and Facilitating Adult Learning.* San Francisco: Jossey-Bass.

Brown, L., Brown, L., & Collins, V. (1984). Special Populations. In L. Nadler (Ed.), *The Handbook of Human Resource Development.* New York: Wiley-Interscience.

Bruner, J. (1960). *The Process of Education.* New York: Vintage Books.

Buell, V. (1984). *Marketing Management: A Strategic Planning Approach.* New York: McGraw-Hill.

Burack, E. (1984). The Sphinx's Riddle: Life and Career Cycles. *Training and Development Journal, 38*(4), 52-61.

Burack, E. & Mathys, N. (1979). *Career Management in Organizations: A Practical Human Resource Planning Approach.* Lake Forest, IL: Brace-Park Press.

Burke, W. (1972, September). The Role of Training in Organization Development. *Training and Development Journal, 26*(9), 30-34.

Burke, W. (1982). *Organization Development: Principles and Practices.* Boston: Little, Brown and Co.

Byars, L. (1984). *Strategic Management: Planning and Implementation.* New York: Harper & Row.

Byrne, J. & Konrad, W. (1983 July). The Fast Track Slows Down. *Forbes,* pp. 77-78.

Caffarella, R. (1983). Fostering Self-Directed Learning in Post-Secondary Education: The Use of Learning Contracts. *Lifelong Learning, 7*(3), 7-26.

Calish, I. & Gamache, R. (1981, October). How to Overcome Organizational Resistance to Change. *Management Review,* pp. 21-28, 50.

Callahan, R. (1962). *Education and the Cult of Efficiency.* Chicago: University of Chicago Press.

Calvert, R. (1985). Training America: The Numbers Add Up. *Training and Development Journal, 39*(11), 35-40.

Campbell, J. (1968, June). Individual Versus Group Problem-Solving. *Journal of Applied Psychology, 52,* 205-10.

Campbell, J., Dunnette, M., Lawler, E., & Weick, K., Jr. (1970). *Managerial Behavior, Performance and Effectiveness.* New York: McGraw-Hill.

Campbell, D. & Stanley, J. (1963). *Experimental and Quasi-Experimental Designs for Research.* Chicago: Rand McNally.

Cangelosi, V., & Dill, W. (1965). Organizational Learning: Observations Toward a Theory. *Administrative Science Quarterly, 10*(2), 175-203.

Cantor, J. (1971). *Pragmatic Forecasting.* New York: American Management Association.

Cantwell, J., Hosterman, D., & Shelton, H. (1976). Using External Programs and Training Packages. In R. Craig (Ed.), *Training and Development Handbook: A Guide to Human Resource Development* (2nd ed.). New York: McGraw-Hill.

Careers in Training and Development. (1983). Washington, D.C.: American Society for Training and Development.

Carey, A. & Varney, G. (1983). Which Skills Spell Success in OD? *Training and Development Journal, 37*(4), 38-40.

Carkhuff, R. & Fisher, S. with Cannon, J., Friel, T., and Pierce, R. (1984). *Instructional Systems Design II: Evaluating the Instructional System.* Amherst, MA: Human Resource Development Press.

Carnevale, A. (1986). The Learning Enterprise. *Training and Development Journal, 40*(1), 18-26.

CARNEVALE, A. & GOLDSTEIN, H. (1983). *Employee Training: Its Changing Role and an Analysis of New Data.* Washington, D.C.: American Society for Training and Development.

CARUTH, D. & MIDDLEBROOK, B. (1981, July). How to Make a Better Decision. *Supervisory Management,* pp. 13-17.

CASCIO, W. (1982). *Costing and Human Resources: The Financial Impact of Behavior in Organizations.* Boston: Kent.

CATALANELLO, R. & KIRKPATRICK, D. (1969). Evaluating Training Programs—the State of the Art. *Training and Development Journal, 22,* 2-9.

CATHCART, J. (1986). How to Conduct a Strategic Planning Retreat. *Training and Development Journal, 40*(5), 63-65.

CHAFNER, I. (1979). Lifelong Learning and the World of Work. *Interdisciplinary Perspectives, 10*(2-3), pp. 21-26.

CHAKIRIS, B., & FORNACIARI, G. (1985). Self-Development. In W. Tracey (Ed.), *Human Resources Management and Development Handbook.* New York: Amacom.

CHALOFSKY, N. & LINCOLN, C. (1983). Up the HRD Ladder: A Guide for Professional Growth. Reading, MA: Addison-Wesley.

CHANDLER, A. (1962). *Strategy and Structure: Chapters in the History of American Industrial Enterprise.* Cambridge, MA: M.I.T.

CHARLES, D. (1986). National Issues and HRD: What's the Connection? *Training and Development Journal,* 40(6), 26-30.

CHICKERING, A. (1977). *An Introduction to Experiential Learning.* New Rochelle, NY: Change Magazine Press.

CHIN, R. & BENNE, K. (1969). General Strategies for Effecting Changes in Human Systems. In W. Bennis, K. Benne, & R. Chin (Eds.), *The Planning of Change* (2nd ed.). New York: Holt, Rinehart and Winston.

CHINOY, E. (1955). *Automobile Workers and the American Dream.* New York: Random House.

CHOOSING A CAREER—The Agony and the Ecstasy. (1982, March 15). *Forbes,* pp. 138-44.

CLARK, C. (1978). *The Crawford Slip Writing Method.* Kent, OH: Charles H. Clark.

CLARK, G. & PERLMAN, J. (1985). Budgeting for Human Resource Systems. In W. Tracey (Ed.), *Human Resources Management and Development Handbook.* New York: Amacom.

CLELAND, D. (1981). The Cultural Ambience of the Matrix Organization. *Management Review, 70*(11), 24-39.

The Coming Battle: Who'll Control the Training? (1983). *Training, 20*(3), 7-8.

Competency Analysis for Trainers: A Personal Planning Guide. (1979). Toronto: Ontario. Society for Training and Development.

CONNELL, H., III (1984). Sales Programs. In L. Nadler (Ed.), *The Handbook of Human Resource Development.* New York: Wiley-Interscience.

COOK, T. & CAMPBELL, D. (1976). The Design and Conduct of Quasi-Experiments and True Experiments in Field Settings. In T. Bouchard, Jr., Field research methods. In M. Dunnette (Ed.), *Handbook of Industrial and Organizational Psychology.* Chicago: Rand McNally.

COOK, T. & CAMPBELL, D. (1979). *Quasi-Experimentation: Design and Analysis Issues for Field Settings.* Chicago: Rand McNally.

COOKE, P. (1987). Role playing. In R. Craig (Ed.), *Training and Development Handbook* (3rd ed.). New York: McGraw-Hill.

COON, A. (1976). Brainstorming—a Creative Problem Solving Technique. In R. Cathart & L. Samovan (Eds.), *Small Group Problem Solving: A Reader.* New York: Brown.

COOPERRIDER, D. & SRIVASTVA, S. (1987). Appreciative Inquiry in Organizational Life. In R. Woodman & W. Pasmore (Eds.), *Research in Organizational Change and Development.* Vol. I. Greenwich, CT: JAI Press.

COPPARD, L. (1976). Gaming Simulation and the Training Process. In R. Craig (Ed.), *Training and Development Handbook* (2nd ed.). New York: McGraw-Hill.

COREY, S. (1953). *Action Research to Improve School Practices.* New York: Teachers College, Columbia University.

CORSON, J. & STEINER, G. (1974). *Measuring Business Social Performance: The Corporate Social Audit.* New York: Committee for Economic Development.

CRAFT, J. (1980). A Critical Perspective on Human Resource Planning. *Human Resource Planning, 3*(2), 39-52.

CRITES, C. (1981). *Career Counseling: Models, Methods and Materials.* New York: McGraw-Hill.

CROSS, K. (1981). *Adults as Learners.* San Francisco: Jossey-Bass.

CROSS, L. (1982, November). Career Development—A Critical Look. *Training and Development Journal,* pp. 58-60.

CULLEN, J., SAWZIN, S., SISSON, G., & SWANSON, R. (1978, January). Cost Effectiveness: A Model for Assessing the Training Investment. *Training and Development Journal,* 24-27, 29.

CUMMINGS, D. (1986). Objectives: The Link Between Needs Assessment and Results. In H. Birnbrauer (Ed.), *The ASTD Handbook for Technical and Skills Training.* Alexandria, VA: American Society for Training and Development.

CUMMINGS, L. & BERGER, C. (1976, Autumn). Organization Structure: How Does it Influence Attitudes and Performance? *Organizational Dynamics,* pp. 34-49.

CUMMINGS, L. & SCHWAB, D. (1973). *Performance in Organizations: Determinants and Appraisal.* Glenview, IL: Scott, Foresman and Co.

CUTLIP, S. & CENTER, A. (1982). *Effective Public Relations* (5th ed.). Englewood Cliffs, NJ: Prentice Hall.

CYERT, R. & MARCH, J. (1963). *A Behavioral Theory of the Firm.* Engelwood Cliffs, NJ: Prentice Hall.

DALKEY, N. (1969). *The Delphi Method.* New York: McGraw-Hill.

DALKEY, N. & HELMER, O. (1963). An Experimental Application of the Delphi Method to the Use of Experts. *Management Science, 9*(3), 458.

DALTON, D., TODOR, W., SPENDOLINI, M., FIELDING, G. & PORTER, L. (1980, January). Organizational Structure and Performance: A Critical Review. *Academy of Management Review,* pp. 49-64.

DALTON, G., THOMPSON, P., & PRICE, R. (1977, Summer). The Four Stages of Professional Careers: A New Look at Performance by Professionals. *Organizational Dynamics,* pp. 19-42.

DALTON, M. (1951). Informal Factors in Career Achievement. *American Journal of Sociology, 56,* 407-445.

DALY, A. (1976). Management and Supervisory Development. In R. Craig (Ed.), *Training and Development Handbook: A Guide to Human Resource Development* (2nd ed.). New York: McGraw-Hill.

DANFORTH, T. & ALDEN, A. (1963, Summer). Dual Career Pathing: No Better Time, No Better Reason. *Employment Relations Today*, pp. 189-201.

DANIS, C. & TREMBLAY, N. (1985). *Critical Analysis of Adult Learning Principles from a Self-Directed Learner's Perspective*, no. 26. Tempe, AZ: Arizona State University.

DATTA, L. (1978, Spring). Front-end Analysis: Pegasus or Shank's Mare? *New Directions for Program Evaluation, 1*, 13-30.

DAVIES, I. (1973). *Competency-Based Learning*. New York: McGraw-Hill.

DAVIS, G. (1973). *The Psychology of Problem Solving*. New York: Basic Books.

DAVIS, L. & MCCALLON, E. (1974). *Planning, Conducting and Evaluating Workshops*. Austin, TX: Learning Concepts.

DAVIS, S. (1985). *Managing Corporate Culture*. Cambridge, MA: Ballinger.

DAVIS, S. & LAWRENCE, P. (1977). *Matrix*. Reading, MA: Addison-Wesley.

DAY, G. (1984). *Strategic Market Planning: The Pursuit of Competitive Advantage*. St. Paul, MN: West Publishing.

DEAL, T. & KENNEDY, A. (1982). *Corporate Cultures: The Rites and Rituals of Corporate Life*. Reading, MA: Addison-Wesley.

DEAN, R. (1983). Reality Shock: The Link between Socialization and Organizational Commitment. *Journal of Management Development, 2*(3), 55-56.

DEAN, R., FERRIS, K., & KONSTANS, C. (1985). Reality Shock: Reducing the Organizational Commitment of Professionals. *Personnel Administrator, 30*(6), 139-40, 142, 147-48.

DEBONO, E. (1970). *Lateral Thinking: Creativity Step by Step*. New York: Harper & Row.

DEEGAN, A. III (1986). *Succession Planning: Key to Corporate Excellence*. New York: John Wiley.

DELBECQ, A. (1967, December). The Management of Decision Making Within the Firm: Three Strategies for Three Types of Decision Making. *Academy of Management Journal*, pp. 334-35.

DELBECQ, A., VAN DE VEN, A., & GUSTAFSON, D. (1975). *Group Techniques for Program Planning*. Glenview, IL: Scott, Foresman.

DEMEUSE, K. & LIEBOWITZ, S. (1981, September). An Empirical Analysis of Team-Building Research. *Group and Organizational Studies*, pp. 357-78.

DEMING, B. (1979, November-December). A System for Evaluating Training Programs. *Personnel, 56*, 33-41.

DEMING, B. (1982). *Evaluating Job-Related Training: A Guide for Training the Trainer*. Washington, D.C.: American Society for Training and Development.

DENNIS, S. (1987). Is Work a Family Matter? *Personal Administrator, 32*(8), 50-57.

DENOVA, C. (1979). *Test Construction for Training Evaluation*. New York: Van Nostrand Reinhold.

DERR, C. (1986). *Managing the New Careerists*. San Francisco: Jossey-Bass.

DESATNICK, R. (1984, February). What Makes the Human Resource Function Successful? *Training and Development Journal*, pp. 41-44, 46.

DESIO, R. (1987). Engineers and Scientists. In R. Craig (Ed.), *Training and Development Handbook* (3rd ed.). New York: McGraw-Hill.

DEWEY, J. (1938). *Experience and Education*. New York: Collier Books.

DICK, W. & CAREY, L. (1985). *The Systematic Design of Instruction* (2nd ed.). Glenview, IL: Scott Foresman.

DIEBOLD, J. (1982). *The Role of Business in Society*. New York: Amacom.

DIFFENBACH, J. (1983). Corporate Environmental Analysis in Large U.S. Corporations. *Long Range Planning, 16*(3), 107-16.

DIGMAN, L. (1980, Winter). Determining Management Development Needs. *Human Resource Management*, pp. 12-17.

DILLMAN, C. & RAHMLOW, H. (1972). *Writing Instructional Objectives*. Belmont, CA: Lear Siegler.

DIRECTOR, S. (1985). *Strategic Planning for Human Resources*. Work in America Institute Studies in Productivity, Report 42. New York: Pergamon Press.

Directory of Academic Programs in T&D/HRD. (1983-1984). Washington, D.C.: American Society for Training and Development.

The Directory of Accredited Home Study Schools. (1987, annual). Washington, DC: National Home Study Council.

DOERINGER, P., & PIORE, M. (1971). *Internal Labor Markets and Manpower Analysis*. Lexington, MA: Lexington Books.

DOLL, W., SULLIVAN, D., SIMMONETTI, J., & ERWIN, J. (1982, May-June). Fast Tracks to Success for Women in Personnel. *Personnel*, pp. 12-22.

DOWNS, A. (1968). *Inside Bureaucracy*. Boston: Little Brown.

DUHAIME, I. (1981). *Corporate Divestment*. Unpublished doctoral dissertation. Pittsburgh, PA: University of Pittsburgh.

DUKE, R. (1978). Simulation Gaming. In J. Fowles (Ed.), *Handbook of Futures Research*. Westport, CT: Greenwood Press.

DULL, J. (1986). Helping Employees Cope with Merger Trauma. *Training, 23*(1), 71-73.

DUNN, S. (1985). What the 90s Labor Shortage will Mean to You. *Training, 22*(6), 39-43.

DYER, L. (1982). Human Resource Planning. In K. Rowland & G. Ferris (Eds.), *Personnel Management*. Boston: Allyn & Bacon.

DYER, L. (1984). Linking Human Resource and Business Strategies. *Human Resource Planning, 7*, 79-84.

DYER, L. (1977). *Team Building: Issues and Alternatives*. Reading, MA: Addison-Wesley.

DYER, L. (1983, Fall). Bringing Human Resources into the Strategy Formulation Process. *Human Resource Management, 22*, 257-71.

EASTBURN, R. (1987). Management development. In R. Craig (Ed.), *Training and Development Handbook* (3rd ed.). New York: McGraw-Hill.

EASTERBY-SMITH, M. & DAVIES, J. (1983). Developing Strategic Thinking. *Long Range Planning, 16*(4), 39-48.

EGAN, K. (1978). What is Curriculum? *Curriculum Inquiry, 8*(1), 65-72.

EITINGTON, J. (1984). *The Winning Trainer.* Houston, TX: Gulf Publishing.

ELLINGTON, H. (1985). *Producing Teaching Materials: A Handbook for Teachers and Trainers.* New York: Nichols Publishing.

ELLINGTON, H., ADDINALL, E., & PERCIVAL, F. (1982). *A Handbook of Game Design.* New York: Nichols Publishing.

EMERY, F. & TRIST, E. (1965). The Causal Texture of Organizational Environments. *Human Relations, 18,* 21-32.

Employee Training in America. (1986). *Training and Development Journal, 40*(7), 34-37.

EPIE Annotated Courseware Provider List. (1986, annual). Water Mill, NY: EPIE Institute.

ERICKSON, E. (1959). *Identity and the Life Cycle.* New York: International Universities Press.

ESTRIN, D. (1985). Selecting a Van Line? Not Me! *Personnel Administrator, 30*(4), 35-42.

ETZIONI, A. (1964). *Modern Organizations.* Englewood Cliffs, NJ: Prentice Hall.

EVAN, M. (1982). Adapting Cognitive Style Theory in Practice. *Lifelong Learning: The Adult Years, 5*(5), 14-16, 27.

FAHEY, L., KING, W., & NARAYANAN, V. (1981, February). Environmental Scanning and Forecasting in Strategic Planning—The State of the Art. *Long Range Planning, 14*(1), 32-39.

FAHEY, L. & NARAYANAN, V. (1983). The Politics of Strategic Decision Making. In K. Albert (Ed.), *The Strategic Management Handbook.* New York: McGraw-Hill.

FARIS, J. (1983). Employee Training: The State of the Practice. *Training and Development Journal, 37*(11), 85-93.

FARMER, R. (1973, February). Looking Backward at Looking Forward. *Business Horizons, 16*(1), 21-28.

FEINGOLD, S. (1983). Tracking New Career Categories will Become a Preoccupation for Job Seekers and Managers. *Personnel Administrator, 28*(12), 86-93.

FELDMAN, D. (1976, Autumn). A Practical Program for Employee Socialization. *Organizational Dynamics,* pp. 64-80.

FELDMAN, D. (1981, June). The Multiple Socialization of Organization Members. *Academy of Management Review,* pp. 309-18.

FENN, R. & MATHEWS, R. (1987). Office and Clerical Skills. In R. Craig (Ed.). *Training and Development Handbook* (3rd ed.). New York: McGraw-Hill.

FEUER, D. (1984). Taking your In-House Training to Market. *Training, 22*(1), 41-46.

FEUER, D. (1985). Where the Dollars Go. *Training, 22*(1), 45-46, 48, 50-51, 53.

FEUER, D. (1986a). Training in the Fortune 500. *Training, 23*(7), 61.

FEUER, D. (1986b). Training Budgets. *Training, 23*(10), 32-48.

FEUER, D. (1987). Paying for Knowledge. *Training, 24*(5), 57-58, 60, 61-66.

FEUER, M. (1983). From Environmental Scanning to Human Resource Planning: A Linkage Model Applied to Universities. *Human Resource Planning, 6*(2), 69-82.

FEUER, M., NIEHAUS, R., & SHERIDAN, J. (1984). Human Resource Forecasting: A Survey of Practice and Potential. *Human Resource Planning, 7*(2), 85-98.

FIEDLER, F. (1967). *A Theory of Leadership Effectiveness.* New York: McGraw-Hill.

FIEDLER, F. (1972, Autumn). How do you Make Leaders More Effective? *Organizational Dynamics,* pp. 3-8.

FINK, A. & KOSECOFF, J. (1985). *How to Conduct Surveys: A Step-By-Step Guide.* Beverly Hills, CA: Sage.

FINKEL, C. (1984). The Learning Environment: Its Critical Importances to Successful Meetings. In L. Nadler (Ed.), *The Handbook of Human Resource Development.* New York: Wiley—Interscience.

FINNEGAN, G. (1985). Job Aids: Improving Employee Performance in Healthcare. *Performance and Instruction, 24*(6), 10-11.

FISHER, B. (1980). *Small Group Decision-Making* (2nd ed.). New York: McGraw Hill.

FITZ-ENZ, J. (1984). *How to Measure Human Resource Management.* New York: McGraw-Hill.

FLANDERS, D. & ANDERSON, P. (1973, April). Sex Discrimination in Employment: Theory and Practice. *Industrial and Labor Relations Review,* pp. 938-955.

FLEISHMAN, E. (1973). Twenty Years of Consideration and Structure. In E. Fleishman & J. Hunt (Eds.), *Current Developments in the Study of Leadership.* Carbondale, IL: Southern Illinois University Press.

FLEISHMAN, E. & QUAINTANCE, M. (1984). *Taxonomies of Human Performance: The Description of Human Tasks.* Orlando, FL: Academic Press.

FOLTZ, R., ROSENBERG, K., & FOEHRENBACH, J. (1982). Senior Management Views the Human Resource Function. *Personnel Administrator, 27*(9), 37-51.

FORD, L. (1970). *Using the Case Study in Teaching and Training.* Nashville, TN: Broadman.

FORDYCE, J. & WEIL, R. (1971). *Managing with People.* Reading, MA: Addison-Wesley.

FOX, D. (1986). The Internal Sale. *Training and Development Journal, 40*(9), 29-30.

FRANCIS, G. (1982). *OD: A Practical Approach.* Reston, VA: Reston Publishing.

FRANTZREB, R. (1984). *Case Studies in Human Resource Planning: An Annotated Bibliography.* Roseville, CA: Advanced Personnel Systems.

FRATZREB, R. (1986). *Microcomputers in Human Resource Management.* Roseville, CA: Advanced Personnel Systems.

FRENCH, W. (1969, Winter). Organization Development: Objectives, Assumptions and Strategies. *California Management Review, 12,* 23-34.

FRENCH, W. & BELL, C., JR. (1984). *Organization Development: Behavioral Science Interventions for Organization Improvement* (3rd ed.). Englewood Cliffs, NJ: Prentice Hall.

FRESINA, A. & ASSOCIATES. (1987). *The Identification and Development of High Potential Managers.* Palatine, IL: Executive Knowledgeworks.

FRIEDLANDER, F. & BROWN, L. (1974). Organization Development. *Annual Review of Psychology, 25,* 313-41.

FREIDMAN, D. (1987). Work vs. Family: War of the Worlds. *Personnel Administrators, 32,* (8), 36-38.

FREIDMAN, P. & YARBROUGH, E. (1985). *Training Strategies from Start to Finish.* Englewood Cliffs, NJ: Prentice Hall.

FRITZ, R. (1987). *Personal Performance Contracts: The Key to Job Success.* Los Altos, CA: Crisp Publications.

FROHMAN, M., SASHKIN, M., & KAVANAGH, M. (1976, Spring-Summer). Action-Research as Applied to Organization Development. *Organization and Administrative Sciences, 7*(1&2), 129-161.

GAGNÉ, R. (1965). *The Conditions for Learning.* New York: Holt, Rinehart & Winston.

GAGNÉ, R. & BRIGGS, L. (1979). *Principles of Instructional Design* (2nd ed.). New York: Holt, Rinehart and Winston.

GALBRAITH, J. & NATHANSON, D. (1979). The Role of Organizational Structure and Process in Strategy Implementation. In D. Schendel & C. Hofer (Eds.), *Strategic Management: A New View of Business Policy and Planning.* Boston: Little Brown.

GALOSY, J. (1983). Curriculum Design for Management Training. *Training and Development Journal, 37*(1), 48-51.

GARDNER, J. (1963). *Self-Renewal: The Individual and the Innovative Society.* New York: Harper and Row.

GATEWOOD, R. & GATEWOOD, E. (1983). The Use of Expert Data in Human Resource Planning: Guidelines from Strategic Planning. *Human Resource Planning, 6*(2), 83-94.

GAVIN, J. (1984). Survey Feedback: The Perspectives of Science and Practice. *Group and Organization Studies, 9*(1), 29-70.

GAY, G. (1980). Conceptual Models of the Curriculum Planning Process. In A Foshay (Ed.), *Considered Action for Curriculum Improvement.* Alexandria, VA: Association for Supervision and Curriculum Development.

GEBER, B. (1987). The Who, How and Why of Training. *Training, 24*(9), 80.

GEBER, B. (1986). Quality Circles: The Second Generation. *Training, 23*(12), 54-62.

GEE, J. (1987). Training Program Haute Couture. *Personnel Administrator, 32*(5), 69-70, 72.

GEIS, G. (1986). Human Performance Technology: An Overview. In M. Smith (Ed.), *An Introduction to Performance Technology.* Washington D.C.: The National Society for Performance and Instruction.

GENTILMAN, R. & NELSON, B. (1983). Futuring: The Process and Implications for Training and Development Practitioners. *Training and Development Journal, 37*(6), 30-32; 36-38.

GEPSON, J., MARTINKO, M., & BELINA, J. (1982). Nominal Group Techniques: A Diagnostic Strategy for Training Needs Analysis. *Training and Development Journal, 35*(4), 78-83.

GERSTEIN, M. & REISMAN, H. (1983). Strategic Selection: Matching Executives to Business Conditions. *Sloan Management Review, 24*(2), 33-49.

GIBBONS, A. (1977). *A Review of Content and Task Analysis Methodology.* San Diego: Courseware, Inc. (ERIC Document ED 143 696).

GIBSON, J., IVANCEVICH, J., & DONNELLY, J., JR. (1985). *Organizations: Behavior, Structure, Processes* (5th ed.). Plano, TX: Business Publications.

GILBERT, T. (1967, Fall). Praxeonomy: A Systematic Approach to Identifying Training Needs. *Management of Personnel Quarterly,* p. 20.

GILBERT, T. (1978). *Human Competence: Engineering Worthy Performance.* New York: McGraw-Hill.

GILBERT, W. (1975). *Public Relations in Local Government.* Washington, DC: International Management Association.

GILFILLAN, S. (1937). The Prediction of Inventions. In *Technological Trends and National Policy.* Washington, D.C.: U.S. Government Printing Office.

GILLEY, J. & GALBRAITH, M. (1986). Examining Professional Certification. *Training and Development Journal, 40*(6), 60-61.

GILMORE, F. & BRANDENBURG, R. (1962, November-December). Anatomy of Corporate Planning. *Harvard Business Review, 40*(6), 62-65.

GINSBURG, S. (1983). Selecting and Managing Management Consultants. *Training and Development Journal, 37*(1), 76-80.

GINZBERG, E. (1972). *Career Guidance.* New York: McGraw-Hill.

GLUCK, F. (1985). Vision and Leadership in Corporate Strategy. In J. Ryans, Jr. & W. Shanklin (Eds.), *Strategic Planning: Concepts and Implementation.* New York: Random House.

GLUECK, W. (1978). *Personnel: A Diagnostic Approach* (rev. ed.). New York: McGraw-Hill.

GLUECK, W. (1980). *Business Policy and Strategic Management* (3rd ed.). New York: McGraw-Hill.

GLUECK, W. & JAUCH, L. (1984). *Business Policy and Strategic Management* (4th ed.). New York: McGraw-Hill.

GODIWALLA, Y., MEINHART, W. & WARDE, W. (1980, October). Environmental Scanning—Does it Help the Chief Executive? *Long Range Planning,* pp. 87-99.

GOLDNER, F. (1970). Success vs. Failure: Prior Managerial Perspectives. *Industrial Relations, 9,* 453-74.

GOLDSTEIN, I. (1986). *Training in Organizations: Needs Assessment, Development and Evaluation* (2nd ed.). Monterey, CA: Brooks/Cole Publishing.

GOLEMBIEWSKI, R. (1982). Individual Choice about Change: Four Useful Models. In L. Porter & B. Mohr (Eds.), *Reading Book for Human Relations Training.* Arlington, VA: NTL Institute.

GOLEMBIEWSKI, R. & CARRIGAN, S. (1970). Planned Change in Organization Style Based on the Laboratory Approach. *Administrative Science Quarterly, 15,* 79-83.

GOODACRE, D. (1955). Experimental Evaluation of Training. *Journal of Personnel Administration and Industrial Relations, 3,* 143-49.

GOODLAD, J. & Associates. (1979). *Curriculum Inquiry: The Study of Curriculum Practice.* New York: McGraw-Hill.

GOODMAN, P. & KURKE, L. (1982). Studies of Change in Organizations: A Status Report. In P. Goodman & Associates (Eds.), *Change in Organizations: New Perspectives on Theory, Research, and Practice.* San Francisco: Jossey-Bass.

GORDON, J. (1986). Where the Training Goes. *Training, 23*(1), 49-50, 52-54, 57-60, 62-63.

GORDON, J. & ZEMKE, R. (1986, May). Making Them More Creative. *Training,* 30-34, 39-45.

GOULD, R. (1985). Conjoint Executive Assessment for Strategic Planning. *Personnel Administrator, 30*(4), 51-52, 54-56.

GRAY, B., LOEFFLER, D., & COOPER, R. (1982). *Every Woman Works.* Belmont, CA: Lifetime Learning Publications.

GREENE, C. (1979, March). Questions of Causation in the Path-Goal Theory of Leadership. *Academy of Management Journal,* pp. 22-41.

GREENE, M. (1977). The Artistic-Aesthetic Curriculum. *Curriculum Inquiry, 6,* 283-84.

GREENLAW, P. & KOHL, J. (1986). *Personnel Management: Managing Human Resources.* New York: Harper & Row.

GREINER, L. (1967, May-June). Patterns of Organization Change. *Harvard Business Review,* pp. 119-28.

GRIDLEY, J. (1986, May). Who Will be Where When? Forecast the Easy Way. *Personnel Journal,* pp. 50-58.

GRINYER, P. & NORBURN, D. (1975). Planning for Existing Markets: Perceptions of Executives and Financial Performance. *Journal of Royal Statistical Society, 138,* 70-97.

GUEST, R. (1986). *Work Teams and Team Building.* Report no. 44. New York: Pergamon Press.

GUPTA, A. & GOVINDARAJAN, V. (1984, March). Build, Hold, Harvest: Converting Strategic Intentions into Reality. *Journal of Business Strategy,* pp. 34-47.

GUTTERIDGE, T. & HUTCHESON, P. (1984). Career Development. In L. Nadler (Ed.), *The Handbook of Human Resource Development.* New York: Wiley-Interscience.

GUTTERIDGE, T. & OTTE, F. (1983). *Organizational Career Development: State of the Practice.* Washington, DC: American Society for Training and Development.

Hackman, J. & OLDHAM, G. (1975). Development of the Job Diagnostic Survey. *Journal of Applied Psychology, 60,* 159-170.

HAGBERG, J. & LEIDER, R. (1982). *The Inventurers.* Reading, MA: Addison-Wesley.

HAGE, J. (1980). *Theories of Organizations.* New York: John Wiley.

HAGUE, H. (1974). *Executive Self-Development: Real Learning in Real Situations.* New York: Macmillan.

HAGUE, H. (1978). Tools for Helping Self Development. *Journal of European Industrial Training, 2,* 3-5.

HALES, L. (1986, July). Training: A Product of Business Planning. *Training and Development Journal,* pp. 65-66.

HALL, D. (1976). *Careers in Organizations.* Pacific Palisades, CA: Goodyear.

HALL, D. (1984). Human Resource Development and Organizational Effectiveness. In C. Fombrun, N. Tichy & M. Devanna (Eds.), *Strategic Human Resource Management.* New York: John Wiley & Sons.

HAMBLIN, A. (1974). *Evaluation and Control of Training.* London: McGraw-Hill.

HAMMER, N. (1983, June). Companies must Communicate their Commitment to Promoting Women. *Personnel Administrator,* pp. 95-98.

HAND, H. & SLOCUM, J., JR. (1972). A Longitudinal Study of the Effects of a Human Relations Training Program on Managerial Effectiveness. *Journal of Applied Psychology, 36,* 412-17.

Handbook for Designers of Instructional Systems. (1973). Washington, D.C.: Headquarters, USAF.

HANNUM, W. (1980). Task Analysis Procedures. *NSPI Journal, 19*(3), 16-17.

HANSON, M. (1981). Training Employees and Managers for their Roles in Career Development. In *Career Management: Implications for Organizations and Individuals.* Washington, DC: American Society for Training and Development.

HANSON, M. (1982). Career/Life Planning Workshops as Career Services in Organizations—Are they Working? *Training and Development Journal, 36*(2), 58-63.

HANSON, P. (1981). *Learning Through Groups: A Trainer's Basic Guide.* San Diego, CA: University Associates.

HARE, A. (1982). *Creativity in Small Groups.* Beverly Hills, CA: Sage.

HARLESS, J. (1986). Guiding Performance with Job Aids. In M. Smith (Ed.) *Introduction to Performance Technology.* Washington, D.C.: The National Society for Performance and Instruction.

HARLESS, J. (1987). An Analysis of Front-End Analysis. *Performance and Instruction 26*(2), 7-9.

HARLESS, J. (1975). *An Ounce of Analysis (Is Worth a Pound of Objectives).* Newman, GA: Harless Performance Guild, Inc.

HARLEY, J., & KOFF, L. (1980, April). Prepare Women Now for Tomorrow's Managerial Challenges. *Personnel Administrator,* pp. 41-42.

HARRISON, R. (1984). Leadership and Strategy for a New Age. In J. Adams (Ed.), *Transforming Work.* Alexandria, VA: Miles River Press.

HARRISON, E., PETRI, P., & MOORE, C. (1983). How to Use Nominal Group Technique to Assess Training Needs. *Training, 20*(3), 30-35.

HARTLEY, J. (1985). *Designing Instructional Text* (2nd ed.). New York: Nichols Publishing.

HARVEY, D., & BROWN, D. (1982). *An Experiential Approach to OD* (2nd ed.). Englewood Cliffs, NJ: Prentice Hall.

HARVEY, L. (1983, October). Effective Planning for Human Resource Development. *Personnel Administrator,* pp. 46-48, 50, 52, 112.

HAUSSER, D., PECORELLA, P., & WISSLER, A. (1977). *Survey-Guided Development II: A Manual for Consultants.* San Diego: University Associates.

HAX, A. (1985, May). A New Competitive Weapon: The Human Resource Strategy. *Training and Development Journal,* pp. 76, 78-80, 81-82.

HAY, R. (1975, December). Social Auditing: An Experimental Approach. *Academy of Management Journal,* pp. 872-74.

HAYES, R. & ABERNATHY, W. (1980). Managing Our Way to Economic Decline. *Harvard Business Review, 58,* 67-77.

HEDBERG, B. (1981). How Organizations Learn and Unlearn. In P. Nystrom & W. Starbuck (Eds.), *Handbook of Organizational Design,* vol. 1. New York: Oxford University Press.

HEIDRICK & STRUGGLES, INC. (1981). *Mobile Manager 1981.* Chicago, IL: Heidrick & Struggles.

HEINICH, R., MOLENDA, M. & RUSSELL, J. (1985). *Instructional Media and the New Technologies of Instruction* (2nd ed.). New York: John Wiley.

HELLER, K. & MONAHAN, J. (1977). *Psychology and Community Change.* Homewood, IL: Irwin-Dorsey.

HELMER, O. (1983). *Looking Forward: A Guide to Futures Research.* Beverly Hills: Sage.

HENDERSON, B. & ZAKON, A. (1983). The Growth-Share Matrix in Corporate Growth Strategy. In K. Albert (Ed.), *The Strategic Management Handbook*. New York: McGraw-Hill.

HENNINGS, D. (1975). *Mastering Classroom Communication*. Pacific Palisades, CA: Goodyear Publishing.

HENSEY, M. (1983). Conflict: What it Is and What it Can Be. In D. Cole (Ed.), *Conflict Resolution Technology*. Cleveland, OH: Organization Development Institute.

HERCUS, T. & OADES, D. (1982). The Human Resource Audit: An Instrument for Change. *Human Resource Planning, 5*(1), 43-49.

HEYDINGER, R. & ZENTNER, R. (1983). Multiple Scenario Analysis: Introducing Uncertainty into the Planning Process. In J. Morrison, W. Renfro & W. Boucher (Eds.), *Applying Methods and Techniques of Futures Research*. San Francisco: Jossey-Bass.

HINRICHS, J. (1980). *Controlling Absenteeism and Turnover*. Scarsdale, NY: Work in American Institute.

HOFER, C. & SCHENDEL, D. (1978). *Strategy Formulation: Analytical Concepts*. St. Paul, MN: West Publishing.

HOLLOMAN, C. & HENRICK, H. (1972, June). Adequacy of Group Decisions as a Function of the Decision-Making Process. *Academy of Management Journal*, pp. 175-84.

HOLLOWAY, C. (1986). *Strategic Planning*. Chicago: Nelson Hall.

HOLMES, B., MORGAN, G. & BUNDY, C. (1976). *Methods in Adult Education* (3rd ed.). Danville, IL: The Interstate.

HOOVER, K. (1982). *The Professional Teacher's Handbook* (3rd ed.). Boston: Allyn & Bacon.

HOPE, V., HOPE, M. & HOPE, T. (1987). Packages and Seminars. In R. Craig (Ed.), *Training and Development Handbook* (3rd ed.). New York: McGraw-Hill.

HORN, R. & ZUCKERMAN, D. (1980). *The Guide to Simulation/Games for Education and Training* (4th ed.). Beverly Hills, CA: Sage Publishing.

HOSMER, L. (1982). *Strategic Management: Text and Cases on Business Policy*. Englewood Cliffs, NJ: Prentice Hall.

HOULE, C. (1972). *The Design of Education*. San Francisco: Jossey-Bass.

HOULE, C. (1961). *The Inquiring Mind*. Madison, WI: University of Wisconsin Press.

HOUSE, R. & DESSLER, G. (1974). The Path-Goal Theory of Leadership: Some Post Hoc and A Priori Tests. In J. Hunt (Ed.), *Contingency Approaches to Leadership*. Carbondale, IL: Southern Illinois University Press.

How Many Trainers are There? (1983). *Training, 20*(12), 132.

HRD Tomorrow. (1984). *Training and Development Journal, 38*(11), 58, 60, 62, 64-65.

HREBINIAK, L. & SNOW, C. (1982). Top-Management Agreement and Organizational Performance. *Human Relations, 35*(12), 1139-58.

HUFF, A. (1982). Industry Influences on Strategy Reformulation. *Strategic Management Journal, 3*, 119-31.

HUGHES, R., ROSENBACH, W., & CLOVER, W. (1983, June). Team Development in an Intact, Ongoing Work Group. *Group and Organizational Studies*, pp. 161-81.

HULETT, D. & RENJILIAN, J. (1983). Strategic Planning Demystified. In S. Sherwood (Ed.), *Organization Development: Present Practice and Future Needs*. Washington, D.C.: American Society for Training and Development.

Human Resources to Play a Bigger Role in Strategic Planning? (1982). *Training and Development Journal, 36,* (10), 9.

HUNKINS, F. (1972). *Questioning Strategies and Techniques.* Boston: Allyn and Bacon.

HUNKINS, F. (1980). *Curriculum Development: Program Improvement.* Columbus, OH: Charles E. Merrill.

HUSE, E. (1982). *Management* (2nd ed.). St. Paul, MN: West Publishing.

HUSE, E., & CUMMINGS, T. (1985). *Organization Development and Change* (3rd ed.). St. Paul, MN: West Publishing.

HUCZYNSKI, A. (1983). *Encyclopedia of Management Development Methods.* London: Gower.

HUSSEY, D. (1988). *Management Training and Corporate Strategy: How to Improve Competitive Performance.* Oxford: Pergamon Press.

Index to Computer Based Learning. (1985, annual). Milwaukee: University of Wisconsin.

Instructional Design Competencies: The Standards. (1986). Iowa City, IA: International Board of Standards of Training, Performance and Instruction.

INZERILLI, G. & ROSEN, M. (1983). Culture and Organizational Change. *Journal of Business Research, 11*(3), 281–92.

ISAAC, S. & MICHAEL, W. (1971). *Handbook in Research and Evaluation.* San Diego: Krapp.

ISAACSON, L. (1985). *Basics of Career Counseling.* Boston: Allyn & Bacon.

IVES, C. (1976). Secretarial and Clerical Training. In R. Craig (Ed.), *Training and Development Handbook: A Guide to Human Resource Development* (2nd ed.). New York: McGraw-Hill.

JACKSON, S. (1986). Task Analysis. In M. Smith (Ed.), *Introduction to Performance Technology.* Washington, D.C.: The National Society for Performance and Instruction.

JACOBS, R. (1985-1986). Naturalistic Inquiry and Qualitative Methods. *Performance and Instruction, 24*(10), 25.

JACOBS, R. & MCGIFFIN, T. (1987). A Human Performance System Using a Structured On-The-Job Training Approach. *Performance and Instruction, 26*(5), 8–11.

JAIN, S. (1984). Environmental Scanning in U.S. Corporations. *Long Range Planning, 17*(2), 117–28.

JAMES-NEILL, M. (1982). The Learning Journal. In L. Porter & B. Mohr (Eds.), *Reading Book for Human Relations Training.* Arlington, VA: NTL Institute.

JANIS, I. (1971, November). Group Think. *Psychology Today, 5,* 43–46.

JANIS, I. (1973). *Victims of Group Think: A Psychological Study of Foreign Policy Decisions and Fiascos.* Boston: Houghton Mifflin.

JANIS, I. & MANN, L. (1977). *Decision Making.* New York: The Free Press.

JELINEK, M. (1979). *Institutionalizing Innovation: A Study of Organizational Learning Systems.* New York: Praeger.

JENKS, R. (1970). An Action-Research Approach to Organizational Change. *Journal of Applied Behavioral Science, 6*(2), 131–48.

Job-Related Basic Skills: A Guide for Planners of Employee Programs. (1987). *Business Council for Effective Literacy Bulletin, 2,* 1–45.

JOHNSON, G., & ROHAN, T. (1982, April 19). Why Executives Jump Ship. *Industry Week,* pp. 62-70.

JOHNSON, S. (1983). Critical Incident. In F. Ulschak (Ed.), *Human Resource Development: The Theory and Practice of Need Assessment.* Reston, VA: Reston Publishing.

JOHNSTON, J., JR. & ASSOCIATES (1986). *Educating Managers: Executive Effectiveness through Liberal Learning.* San Francisco: Jossey-Bass.

JOINSON, D. (1982). Using Checklists as an Aid to Transfer of Training. [rpt. of a June 1977 *Training* article.] In *Adult Learning in your Classroom,* Minneapolis, MN: Lakewood Publications.

JONES, L. (1980). *Great Expectations: America and the Baby Boom Generation.* New York: Ballantine.

KANTER, R. (1977). *Men and Women of the Corporation.* New York: Basic Books.

KANTER, R. (1983). *The Change Masters.* New York: Simon and Schuster.

KANTER, R. (1983). Change Masters and the Intricate Architecture of Corporate Culture Change. *Management Review, 72*(1), 18-28.

KAPPAUF, C. & TALBOTT, S. (1982). Forecasting, Planning and Strategy: What Needs to be Forecast. In S. Makridakis & S. Wheelwright (Eds.), *Handbook of Forecasting: A Manager's Guide.* New York: John Wiley & Sons.

KATZ, D. & KAHN, R. (1978). *The Social Psychology of Organizations* (2nd ed.). New York: John Wiley.

KAUFFMAN, D. (1976). *Teaching the Future.* Palm Springs, CA: ETC Publications.

KAUFMAN, R. & ENGLISH, F. (1979). *Needs Assessment: Concept and Application.* Englewood Cliffs, NJ: Educational Technology Publications.

KEEGAN, W. (1974, September). Multinational Scanning. *Administrative Science Quarterly,* pp. 441-21.

KEICHEL, W. III (1981, October 5). The Decline of the Experience Curve. *Fortune,* pp. 139-40; 144; 146.

KEICHEL, W. III (1982). Corporate Strategists Under Fire. *Fortune,* 106(13), 34-39.

KEISER, T. & SEELER, J. (1987). Games and Simulations. In R. Craig (Ed.), *Training and Development Handbook* (3rd ed.). New York: McGraw-Hill.

KELLY, H. (1983). Case Method Training: What it Is, How it Works. *Training, 20*(2), 46-49.

KEMP, J. (1971, December). Which Medium? *Audiovisual Instruction,* 32-36.

KEMP, J. (1980). *Planning and Producing Audiovisual Materials* (4th ed.). New York: Harper and Row.

KEMP, J. (1985). *The Instructional Design Process.* New York: Harper and Row.

KERR, S. (1975). On the Folly of Rewarding A, While Hoping for B. *Academy of Management Journal, 18,* 796-83.

KIEFER, C., & STROH, P. (1984). A New Paradigm for Developing Organizations. In J. Adams (Ed.), *Transforming Work.* Alexandria, VA: Miles River Press.

KILCOURSE, T. (1984). Management Team Development: A Problem-Centered Technique. *Journal of European Industrial Training, 8,* 3-12.

KINLAW, D. & CHRISTENSEN, D. (1986). Management Education: The Wheat and the Chaff. *Training, 23*(12), 45-48, 50, 52.

KINN, J. (1976). Scientist and Engineering Continuing Education. In R. Craig (Ed.), *Training and Development Handbook: A Guide to Human Resource Development* (2nd ed.). New York: McGraw-Hill.

KIRKPATRICK, D. (1959). Techniques for Evaluating Training Programs. *Journal of the American Society of Training Directors, 13,* 3-9; 21-26.

KIRKPATRICK, D. (1960). Techniques for Evauating Training Programs. *Journal of the American Society of Training Directors, 14,* 13-18; 28-32.

KIRKPATRICK, D. (1985). *How to Manage Change Effectively: Approaches, Methods and Case Examples.* San Francisco: Jossey-Bass.

KIRKPATRICK, D. (1985). Management Development. In W. Tracey (Ed.), *Human Resources Management and Development Handbook.* New York: Amacom.

KLEIN, H. (1979). Commentary (on Utterback). In D. Schendel and C. Hofer (Eds.), *Strategic Management: A New View of Business Policy and Planning.* Boston: Little Brown and Co.

KLEMP, G., JR. (1979). Identifying, Measuring and Integrating Competence. In P. Pottinger and J. Goldsmith (Eds.), *Defining and Measuring Competence.* San Francisco: Jossey-Bass.

KNOWLES, H. (1987). Enhancing HRD with Contract Learning. *Training and Development Journal, 41*(3), 62-63.

KNOWLES, M. (1986). *Using Learning Contracts: Practical Approaches to Individualizing and Structuring Learning.* San Francisco: Jossey-Bass.

KNOWLES, M. (1986). *Using Learning Contracts: Practical Approaches to Individualizing and Structuring Learning.* San Francisco: Jossey-Bass.

KNOWLES, M. (1980). *The Modern Practice of Adult Education: From Pedagogy to Andragogy* (rev. ed.). Chicago: Association Press.

KNOWLES, M. (1984). *The Adult Learner: A Neglected Species* (3rd ed.). Houston, TX: Gulf Publishing.

KOESTLER, A. (1964). *The Act of Creation.* New York: Macmillan.

KOLB, D. (1984). *Experiential Learning: Experience as the Source of Learning and Development.* Englewood Cliffs, NJ: Prentice Hall.

KOLB, D. & GLIDDEN, P. (1986). Getting to Know Your Conflict Options. *Personnel Administrator, 31*(6), 77-78, 80-86, 88, 90.

KOMACKI, J., HEINZMANN, A., & LAWSON, L. (1980). Effect of Training and Feedback: Component Analysis of a Behavioral Safety Program. *Journal of Applied Psychology, 65,* 261-70.

KONDRASUK, J. (1981). Studies in MBO effectiveness. *Academy of Management Review, 6,* 419-30.

KOONTZ, H. & O'DONNELL, C. (1972). *Principles of Management: An Analysis of Managerial Function* (5th ed.). New York: McGraw-Hill.

KOTTER, J. & SCHLESINGER, L. (1979, March-April). Choosing Strategies for Change. *Harvard Business Review,* pp. 106-14.

KOZOL, J. (1986). *Illiterate America.* New York: Anchor Press.

KRAJCI, T. (1987). Outplacement En Masse: A Marketing Approach. *Personnel Administrator, 32*(5), 90-94.

KRATHWOHL, D., BLOOM, B. & MASIA, B. (1964). *Taxonomy of Educational Objectives, Handbook 2: Affective Domain.* New York: David McKay.

KRECH, D., CRUTCHFIELD, R., & BALLACHEY, E. (1962). *Individual Society.* New York: McGraw-Hill.

KRUGER, M. (1983). How to Make a Management Advisory Committee Work for You. *Training and Development Journal, 37*(6), 86-90.

LACOURSIERE, R. (1980). *The Life Cycle of Groups: Group Development Stage Theory.* New York: Human Sciences Press.

LAIRD, D. (1985). *Approaches to Training and Development* (2nd ed.). Reading, MA: Addison-Wesley.

LAMBERT, W. (1986). Liven-up the Lecture Method, Please! *Performance and Instruction, 25*(4), 2.

LAWLER, E. III (1977). Reward Systems. In J. Hackman & J. Suttle (Eds.), *Improving Life at Work.* Santa Monica, CA: Goodyear.

LAWLER, E. III (1984). The Strategic Design of Reward Systems. In C. Fombrun, N. Tichy, & M. Devanna (Eds.), *Strategic Human Resource Management.* New York: John Wiley & Sons.

LAWLER, E., MOHRMAN, A., MOHRMAN, S., LEDFORD, G., CUMMINGS, T., & ASSOCIATES (1985). *Doing Research that is Useful for Theory and Practice.* San Francisco: Jossey-Bass.

LAWRIE, J. (1987). How to Establish a Mentoring Program. *Training and Development Journal, 41*(3), 25-27.

LEACH, J. & CHAKIRIS, S. (1985). The Dwindling Future of Work in America. *Training and Development Journal, 39*(4), 44-50.

LEBELL, D. & KRASNER, O. (1977, July). Selecting Environmental Forecasting Techniques from Business Planning Requirements. *Academy of Management Review,* pp. 373-83.

LEE, C. (1985a). Human Resource Development: A Useful Bit of Jargon? *Training, 22*(1), 75-76.

LEE, C. (1985b, October). Trainers' Careers. *Training, 22*(10), 75-81.

LEE, C. (1981). Identifying and Developing the Next Generation of Managers. *Training, 18*(10), 36; 38-39.

LEE, C. (1986). Training for Women: Where do We Go from Here? *Training, 23*(12), 26-27, 29-32, 34, 39-40.

LEEMHUIS, J. & ECKBLAD, J. (1985). Planning Doesn't Stop at the Top. *Training and Development Journal, 39*(12), 62-63.

LEFKOE, M. (1985). Shifting Context: A Better Approach to Training? *Training, 22*(2), 43-47.

LEIBOWITZ, Z. & SCHLOSSBERG, N., (1981). Training Managers for their Role in Career Development. *Training and Development Journal, 35*(7), 72-79.

LEONTIADES, M. & TEZEL, A. (1980). Planning Perceptions and Planning Results. *Strategic Management Journal, 1,* 65-76.

LEVIE, W. & DICKIE, K. (1973). The Analysis and Application of Media. In R. Travers (Ed.), *Second Handbook of Research on Teaching.* Chicago: Rand McNally.

LEVINE, E. (1983). *Everything You Always Wanted to Know about Job Analysis.* Tampa, FL: Mariner Publishing.

LEVINE, E., ASH, R., HALL, H., & SISTRUNK, F. (1983). Evaluation of Job Analysis Methods by Experienced Job Analysts. *Academy of Management Journal, 26*(2), 339-447.

LEVINSON, H. (1970, July-August). Management by Whose Objectives? *Harvard Business Review, 48*(4), 125-34.

LEVY, A. & MERRY, V. (1986). *Organizational Transformation: Approaches, Strategies, Theories.* New York: Praeger.

LEWIN, K. (1951). *Field Theory in Social Science.* New York: Harper.

LEWIN, K. (1947, June). Frontiers in Group Dynamics: Concept, Methods and Reality in Social Science. *Human Relations, 1,* 5-41.

LEWIS, A. & MIEL, A. (1972). *Supervision for Improved Instruction.* Belmont, CA: Wadsworth.

LEWIS, P. (1975). *Organizational Communications: The Essence of Effective Management.* Columbus, OH: Grid.

LEWIS, W. (1983). Avoiding Planning Backlash. In K. Albert (Ed.), *The Strategic Management Handbook.* New York: McGraw-Hill.

LIKERT, R. (1967). *The Human Organization.* New York: McGraw-Hill.

LINCOLN, Y. & GUBA, E. (1985). *Naturalistic Inquiry.* Beverly Hills, CA: Sage.

LINKOW, P. (1985). HRD at the Roots of Corporate Strategy. *Training and Development Journal, 39*(5), 85-87.

LINSTONE, H. (1978). The Delphi Technique. In J. Fowler (Ed.), *Handbook of Futures Research.* Westport, CT: Greenwood Press.

LINSTONE, H. & TUROFF, M. (Eds.). (1975). *The Delphi Method: Techniques and Application.* Reading, MA: Addison-Wesley.

LIPPITT, G., LANGSETH, P., & MOSSOP, J. (1985). *Implementing Organizational Change: A Practical Guide to Managing Change Efforts.* San Francisco: Jossey-Bass.

LOCHER, A. & TEEL, K. (1977, May). Performance Appraisal—A Survey of Current Practices. *Personnel Journal, 56*(5), 245-47, 254.

LOCKE, E., FEREN, D., MCCALEB, V., SHAW, K., & DENNY, A. (1980). The Relative Effectiveness of Four Methods of Motivating Employee Performance. In K. Duncan, M. Gruneberg, & D. Wallis (Eds.), *Changes in Working Life.* Rochester, MN: Wiley.

LOCKE, E., SHAW, K., SAARI, L., & LATHAM, G. (1981). Goal Setting and Task Performance 1969-1980. *Psychological Bulletin, 90,* 125-52.

LODGE, G. (1983). Educators Must Advocate Holism to Prepare our Human Resources for the Coming Decentralization. *Personnel Administrator, 28*(12), 48-55.

LONDON, M. (1985). *Developing Managers: A Guide to Motivating and Preparing People for Successful Managerial Careers.* San Franscisco: Jossey-Bass.

LONDON, M. & STUMPF, S. (1982). *Managing Careers.* Reading, MA: Addison-Wesley.

LORANGE, P. & VANCIL, R. (1977). *Strategic Planning Systems.* Englewood Cliffs, NJ: Prentice Hall.

LUNDBERG, C. (1984). Zero-in: A Technique for Formulating Better Mission Statements. *Business Horizons, 27*(5), 30-33.

LUSTERMAN, S. (1977). *Education in Industry.* New York: The Conference Board.

McCall, M., Jr. & Kaplan, R. (1985). *Whatever it Takes: Decision Makers at Work.* Englewood Cliffs, NJ: Prentice Hall.

McCall, M., Jr. & Lombardo, M. (1983, February). What Makes a Top Executive? *Psychology Today,* 26–31.

McCarthy, D. (1985). Sales and Dealer Training. In W. Tracey (Ed.), *Human Resources Management and Development Handbook.* New York: Amacom.

McCord, B. (1976). Job Instruction. In R. Craig (Ed.), *Training and Development Handbook: A Guide to Human Resource Development* (2nd ed.). New York: McGraw-Hill.

McCormick, E. (1979). *Job Analysis.* New York: Amacom.

McDermott, L. (1984). The Many Faces of the OD Professional. *Training and Development Journal, 38*(2), 14–21.

McGehee, W. & Thayer, P. (1961). *Training in Business and Industry.* New York: John Wiley.

McLean, J. (1978). Simulation Modeling in J. Fowles (Ed.), *Handbook of Futures Research.* Westport, CT: Greenwood Press.

McNeil, J. (1976). *Designing Curriculum: Self-Instructional Modules.* Boston: Little Brown.

McQuigg, B. (1985). Tuition-aid Plans. In W. Tracey (Ed.), *Human Resources Management and Development Handbook.* New York: Amacom.

Macmillan, I. (1978). *Strategy Formulation: Political Concepts.* St. Paul, MN: West Publishing.

Madsen, D. & Finger, S., Jr. (1978). Comparison of a Written Feedback Procedure, Group Brainstorming and Individual Brainstorming. *Journal of Applied Psychology,* 63, 120–23.

Mager, R. (1968). *Developing Attitude Toward Learning.* Belmont, CA: Fearon-Pitman.

Mager, R. (1972). *Goal Analysis.* Belmont, CA: Fearon Publishers.

Mager, R. (1973). *Measuring Instructional Intent or Got a Match?* Belmont, CA: Fearon-Pitman.

Mager, R. (1975). *Preparing Instructional Objectives* (2nd ed.). Belmont, CA: Fearon-Pitman.

Mager, R. & Beach, K., Jr. (1967). *Developing Vocational Instruction.* Belmont, CA: Fearon-Pitman.

Mager, R. & Pipe, P. (1970). *Analyzing Performance Problems, or 'You Really Oughta Wanna.'* Belmont, CA: Fearon-Pitman.

Magnus, M. & Dodd, U. (1981, July). Relocation: Changing Attitudes and Company Policies. *Personnel Journal,* pp. 538–45.

Mahler, W. (1976). Executive Development. In R. Craig (Ed.), *Training and Development Handbook: A Guide to Human Resource Development* (2nd ed.). New York: McGraw-Hill.

Mahler, W. (1985). Executive Development. In W. Tracey (Ed.), *Human Resources Management and Development Handbook.* New York: Amacom.

Mahoney, F. (1981a, September-October). Team Development, part I: What is TD? Why Use It? *Personnel,* pp. 13–24.

Mahoney, F. (1981b, November-December). Team Development, part 2: How to Select the Appropriate TD Approach. *Personnel,* pp. 21–38.

MAHONEY, F. (1982a, January-February). Team Development, part 3: Communication Meetings. *Personnel,* pp. 49-58.

MAHONEY, F. (1982b, March-April). Team Development, part 4: Work Meetings. *Personnel,* pp. 45-55.

MAHONEY, F. (1982c, May-June). Team Development, part 5: Procedure Meetings. *Personnel,* pp. 31-41.

MAHONEY, F. (1982d, July-August). Team Development, part 6: Variation of Procedure Meetings. *Personnel,* pp. 64-69.

MAHONEY, F. (1982e, September-October). Team Development, part 7: Its Role in the Workplace. *Personnel,* pp. 52-59.

MAIER, N. (1963). *Problem Solving Discussions and Conferences.* New York: McGraw-Hill.

MAIER, N., SOLEM, A., & MAIER, A. (1975). *The Role-Play Technique.* San Diego, CA: University Associates.

MALASKY, E. (1984). Instructional Strategies: Nonmedia. In L. Nadler (Ed.), *The Handbook of Human Resource Development.* New York: Wiley-Interscience.

MANDEL, T. (1983). Future Scenarios and their Uses in Corporate Strategy. In K. Albert (Ed.), *The Strategic Management Handbook.* New York: McGraw-Hill.

MANSFIELD, R. (1987). Training and the Law. In R. Craig (Ed.), *Training and Development Handbook* (3rd ed.). New York: McGraw-Hill.

MANSFIELD, R. (1986). *Company Strategy and Organizational Design.* New York: St. Martin's Press.

MARCH, J. & OLSEN, J. (1975). The Uncertainty of the Past: Organizational Learning Under Ambiguity. *European Journal of Political Research, 3,* 147-71.

Marketplace Directory. (1986). St. Cloud, MN: Lakewood Publications.

MARKLEY, O. & HARMAN, W. (1982). *Changing Image of Man.* New York: Pergamon Press.

MARKOWITZ, J. (1981, September). Four Methods of Job Analysis. *Training and Development Journal, 35*(9), 112-18.

A Marriage Made in Marketing Heaven. (1987). *Training, 24*(5), 12, 14.

MARROW, A., BOWERS, D., & SEASHORE, S. (1967). *Management By Participation.* New York: Harper & Row.

MARSHALL, J. (1982, September). Organizational Culture: Elements in its Portraiture and Some Implications for Organization Functioning. *Group and Organization Studies,* pp. 367-84.

MARSHALL, R., BRIGGS, V., JR., & KING, A. (1984). *Labor Economics: Wages, Employment, Trade Unionism and Public Policy* (5th ed.). Homewood, IL: Richard D. Irwin.

MARTIN, J., FELDMAN, M., HATCH, M., & SITKIN, S. (1983, September). The Uniqueness Paradox in Organizational Stories. *Administrative Science Quarterly,* pp. 438-53.

MARTINO, J. (1978). Technological Forecasting. In J. Fowles (Ed.), *Handbook of Futures Research.* Westport, CT: Greenwood Press.

MARTINKO, M. & GEPSON, J. (1983). Nominal Grouping and Need Analysis. In F. Ulschak (Ed.), *Human Resource Development: The Theory and Practice of Need Assessment.* Reston, VA: Reston Publishing.

MASON, J. (1986). Developing Strategic Thinking. *Long Range Planning, 19*(3), 72-80.

MASON, R. & MITROFF, E. (1981). *Challenging Strategic Planning Assumptions: Theory, Cases, and Techniques.* New York: Wiley.

MECKEL, N. (1981). The Manager as Career Counselor. *Training and Development Journal, 35*(7), 64-69.

MEIDAN, A. (1981). *The Appraisal of Managerial Performance: AMA Management Briefing.* New York: Amacom.

Mentoring, Aid to Excellence: Proceedings of the First International Conference on Mentoring. (1986). Vacouver, BC: International Association for Mentoring.

Mentoring in the U.S.A. (1986). London: PA Personnel Services.

MICALI, P. (1982). The Power of the Questioning Approach. [rpt. of March 1981 Training article.] In *Adult Learning in your Classroom.* Minneapolis, MN: Lakewood Publications.

MIGLIORE, R. (1983). *An MBO Approach to Long-Range Planning.* Englewood Cliffs, NJ: Prentice Hall.

MILES, R. (1978, September-October). The Origin and Meaning of Miles' Law. *Public Administration Review,* pp. 399-403.

MILES, R. & RANDOLPH, W. (1980). Influence of Organizational Learning Styles on Early Development. In J. Kimberly, R. Miles & Associates (Eds.), *The Organizational Life Cycle.* San Francisco: Jossey-Bass.

MILES, R. & SNOW, C. (1984, Summer). Designing Strategic Human Resources Systems. *Organizational Dynamics,* pp. 36-52.

MILKOVICH, G. ANNONI, A., & MAHONEY, T. (1972). The Use of the Delphi Procedure in Manpower Forecasting. *Management Science, 19*(4), 381-88.

MILKOVICH, G. & GLUECK, W. (1985). *Personnel/Human Resource Management* (4th ed.). Plano, TX: Business Publications.

MILLER, D. & BARNETT, S. (Eds.). (1986). *The How-To Handbook on Doing Research in Human Resource Development.* Alexandria, VA: American Society for Training and Development.

MILLER, D. & FRIESEN, P. (1977, October). Strategy Making in Context: Ten Empirical Archetypes. *Journal of Management Studies, 14*(3), 253-80.

MINTZBERG, H. (1979a). *The Structuring of Organizations.* Englewood Cliffs, NJ: Prentice Hall.

MINTZBERG, H. (1979b). Organizational Power and Goals: A Skeletal Theory. In C. Hofer & D. Schendel (Eds.), *Strategic Management: A New View of Business Policy and Planning.* Boston: Little Brown.

MINTZBERG, H., RAISINGHANI, D., & THEORET, A. (1976, June). The Structure of 'Unstructured' Decision Processes. *Administrative Science Quarterly, 21*(2), 246-75.

MIRABEL, T. (1978). Forecasting Future Training Costs. *Training and Development Journal, 32*(7), 78-87.

MIRABILE, R., CALDWELL, D. & O'REILLY, C. (1986, September). Designing and Linking Human Resource Programs. *Training and Development Journal,* pp. 60, 63.

MIRVIS, P. & BERG, D. (Eds.) (1977). *Failures in Organization Development and Change.* New York: John Wiley.

MISA, K. & STEIN, T. (1983). Strategic HRM and the Bottom Line. *Personnel Administrator, 28*(10), 27-30.

Models for Excellence. (1983). Washington, DC: American Society for Training and Development.

MOLES, J. (1979). Planned Social Change and the Negotiation of Reality: Social Scientists, Policymakers, and Planners. In E. Blakely (Ed.), *Community Development Research: Concepts, Issues and Strategies.* New York: Human Sciences Press.

MOLLOY, W. (1982). Making Roleplays Pay Off in Training. [rpt. from May 1981 *Training.*] In *Adult Learning in your Classroom.* Minneapolis, MN: Lakewood publications.

MOORE, J. (1982). The Role Relocation Plays in Management Planning. *Personnel Administrator, 27*(12), 31-36.

MOORE, M. & DUTTON, P. (1978). Training Needs Analysis: Review and Technique. *Academy of Management Journal, 3*(3), 532-45.

MOORHEAD, G. (1982 December). Group Think: Hypothesis in Need of Testing. *Group and Organization Studies,* pp. 429-43.

MORANO, R. & DEETS, N. (1982, May). Professional Retraining: Meeting the Technological Challenge. (1985). *Training and Development Journal,* pp. 99-101.

MORGAN, B. & SCHIEMANN, W. (1986). Employee Attitudes: Then and Now. *Personnel Journal, 65*(10), 100-106.

MORRIS, L. & FITZGIBBON, D. (1978). *Evaluator's Handbook.* Beverly Hills, CA: Sage.

MORRISEY, G. (1976). *Management by Objectives and Results in the Public Sector.* Reading, MA: Addison-Wesley.

MORSE, E. & MARTIN, K. (1983). Motivating the Organization to Implement Strategy. In K. Albert (Ed.), *The Strategic Management Handbook.* New York: McGraw-Hill.

MURPHY, J. (1980). *Getting the Facts: A Fieldwork Guide for Evaluators and Policy Analysts.* Santa Monica, CA: Goodyear.

A Myth Worth Burying. (1987). *Training and Development Journal, 41*(9), 8, 11.

NADLER, D. (1977). *Feedback and Organization Development: Using Data-Based Methods.* Reading, MA: Addison-Wesley.

NADLER, L. (1980). Defining the Field—Is it HRD or OD, or . . .? *Training and Development Journal, 34*(12), 66-68.

NADLER, L. (1979). *Developing Human Resources* (2nd ed.) Austin, TX: Learning Concepts.

NADLER, L. (1984). Human Resource Development. In L. Nadler (Ed.), *The Handbook of Human Resource Development.* New York: Wiley-Interscience.

NADLER, L. (1982). *Designing Training Programs: The Critical Events Model.* Reading, MA: Addison-Wesley.

NADLER, L. & FETTEROLL, E. (Eds.). (1985). *The Trainer's Resource 1985: A Comprehensive Guide to Packaged Training Programs.* Amherst, MA: Human Resource Development Press.

NADLER, L. & WIGGS, G. (1986). *Managing Human Resource Development: A Practical Guide.* San Francisco: Jossey-Bass.

NAISBITT, J. (1982). *Megatrends: Ten New Directions Transforming Our Lives.* New York: Warner Bros.

Nanus, B. (1982, April). QUEST—Quick Environmental Scanning Technique. *Long Range Planning, 15,* 39-45.

Nash, M. (1983). *Managing Organizational Performance.* San Francisco: Jossey-Bass.

Neilsen, E. (1984). *Becoming an OD Practitioner.* Englewood Cliffs, NJ: Prentice Hall.

Nelson, A. (1982). Learning from Experience is a Good Learning Experience. [rpt. from July 1978 *Training.*] In *Adult Learning in Your Classroom,* Minneapolis, MN: Lakewood Publications.

Newell, T., Redfoot, R., & Sotar, L. (1987). After the Layoffs: Orienting New Employees. *Training and Development Journal, 41*(9), 34-36.

Newman, K. (1980). Guidelines on Developing Program Policy. *Training and Development Journal, 34*(7), 20-24.

Newstrom, J. & Lilyquist, J. (1979, October). Selecting Need Analysis Methods. *Training and Development Journal, 33*(10), 52-56.

Niehaus, R. & Sheridan, J. (1984). Human Resource Forecasting: A Survey of Practice and Potential. *Human Resource Planning, 7,* 85-97.

Nilsson, W. (1987). *Achieving Strategic Goals through Executive Development.* Reading, MA: Addison-Wesley.

Nininger, J. (1982). *Managing Human Resources: A Strategic Perspective.* Ottawa, ONT: The Conference Board of Canada.

Nkomo, S. (1986). The Theory and Practice of Planning: The Gap Still Remains. *Personnel Administrator, 31*(8), 71-73; 75-76; 78-80; 83-84.

O'Connor, R. (1980a). *Preparing Managers for Planning.* Research Report no. 788. New York: The Conference Board.

O'Connor, R. (1980b). *Company Planning Meetings.* Report no. 781. New York: The Conference Board.

O'Connor, R. (1982). *Evaluating the Company Planning System and the Corporate Planner.* Report No. 817. New York: The Conference Board.

Odiorne, G. (1984). *Strategic Management of Human Resources: A Portfolio Approach.* San Francisco: Jossey-Bass.

Odiorne, G. (1981, January). The Change Resisters. *Personnel Administrator,* pp. 57-63.

Odiorne, G. (1971). *Training by Objectives: An Economic Approach to Management Training.* New York: Macmillan.

Odiorne, G. (1972). Evaluating the Personnel Program. In J. Fomularo (Ed.), *Handbook of Modern Personnel Administration.* New York: McGraw-Hill.

Odiorne, G. (1979). *MBO II: A System of Managerial Leadership for the 80's.* Belmont, CA: Fearon-Pitman.

Oldham, G. & Hackman, J. (1981, March). Relationships Between Organizational Structure and Employee Reactions: Comparing Alternative Frameworks. *Administrative Science Quarterly.* pp. 66-83.

Olian, J. & Rynes, S. (1984, Spring). Organizational Staffing: Integrating Practice with Strategy. *Industrial Relations,* pp. 170-83.

Olivas, L. (1980). Auditing your Training and Development Function. *Training and Development Journal, 34*(3), 60-65.

OLMOSK, K. (1972). Strategies for Change. In J. Pfeiffer & J. Jones (Eds.), *The 1972 Annual Handbook for Group Facilitators.* La Jolla, CA: University Associates.

OLSON, P. & FREEMAN, L. (1979). Defining Competence in Teacher Licensing Usage. In P. Pottingher and J. Goldsmith (Eds.), *Defining and Measuring Competence.* San Francisco: Jossey Bass.

OSBORN, A. (1953). *Applied Imagination.* New York: Charles Scribner's Sons.

PACE, R. (1983). *Organizational Communication: Foundations for Human Resource Development.* Englewood Cliffs, NJ: Prentice Hall.

PAGE, W. (1982). Long-term Forecasts and Why You Will Probably Get it Wrong. In S. Makridakis & S. Wheelwright (Eds.) *The Handbook of Forecasting: A Manager's Guide.* New York: John Wiley & Sons.

PAINE, E. & NAUMES, W. (1974). *Strategy and Policy Formation: An Integrative Approach.* Philadelphia, PA: W. B.

PARNES, S. & MEADOW, A. (1963). Development of Individual Creative Talent. In C. Taylor & F. Barrow (Eds.), *Scientific Creativity: Its Recognition and Development.* New York: Wiley.

PASCALE, R. (1984, May). Fitting New Employees into the Company Culture. *Fortune,* pp. 28, 30, 34, 38–40.

PASTIN, M. (1986). The Fallacy of Long-Range Thinking. *Training, 23*(5), 47–50, 52.

PATTAN, J. (1986, March). The Strategy in Strategic Planning. *Training and Development Journal, 40*(3), 30–33.

PATTEN, T., JR. (1979a, January-February). Team Building, part 1. Designing the Intervention. *Personnel,* pp. 11–21.

PATTEN, T., JR. (1979b, March-April). Team Building, part 2. Conducting the Intervention. *Personnel,* pp. 62–68.

PEARCE, J., & ROBINSON, R., JR. (1985). *Strategic Management: Strategy Formulation and Implementation* (2nd ed.). Homewood, IL: Richard D. Irwin.

PEDLER, M. & BOYDELL, T. (1980). Is All Management Development Self-Development? In J. Beck & C. Cox (Eds.), *Advances in Management Education.* Chichester, UK: Wiley-Interscience.

PEPPER, A. (1984). *Managing the Training and Development Function.* Alderhsot, Hants, UK: Gower.

PERCIVAL, F. & ELLINGTON, H. (1984). *A Handbook of Educational Technology.* New York: Nichols Publishing.

PETERS, D. (1985). *Director of Human Resource Development Instrumentation.* San Diego: University Associates.

PETERS, T. & WATERMAN, R., JR. (1982). *In Search of Excellence.* New York: Harper & Row.

PETRIE, H. (1981). *The Dilemma of Inquiry and Learning.* Chicago: University of Chicago Press.

PETTIGREW, A. (1979, December). On Studying Organizational Cultures. *Administrative Science Quarterly, 34*(4), 470–581.

PFEIFFER, J., GOODSTEIN, L., & NOLAN, T. (1986). *Applied Strategic Planning: A How To Do It Guide.* San Diego, CA: University Associates.

PHILLIPS, J. (1983). *Handbook of Training Evaluation and Measurement Methods.* Houston, TX: Gulf Publishing.

PHILLIPS, J. (1984). Evaluation of HRD Programs. In L. Nadler (Ed.), *The Handbook of Human Resource Development.* New York: Wiley-Interscience.

PIGORS, P. (1987). Case Method. In R. Craig (Ed.), *Training and Development Handbook* (3rd ed.). New York: McGraw-Hill.

PINCHOT, G., III. (1985). *Intrapreneuring: Why You Don't Have to Leave the Corporation to Become an Entrepreneur.* New York: Harper & Row.

PINTO, P. & WALKER, J. (1978). *A Study of Professional Training and Development Roles and Competencies.* Baltimore, MD: American Society for Training and Development.

POLACK, F. (1973). *The Image of the Future.* San Francisco: Jossey-Bass.

POPHAM, W. (1968). *Objectives and Instruction.* Chicago: Rand McNally.

POPHAM, W. & BAKER, E. (1970). *Establishing Instructional Goals.* Englewood Cliffs, NJ: Prentice Hall.

PORRAS, J. & BERG, P. (1978). The Impact of Organization Development. *Academy of Management Review, 3*(2), 249-66.

PORRAS, J. & WILKINS, A. (1980). Organization Development in a Large System: An Empirical Assessment. *Journal of Applied Behavioral Science, 16*(4), 506-34.

PORTER, L. (1982a). The Learning Journal: Some Mechanics. In L. Porter & B. Mohr (Eds.). *Reading Book for Human Relations Training.* Arlington, VA: NTL Institute.

PORTER, L. (1982b). Giving and Receiving Feedback: It will Never Be Easy, but it *Can* Be Better. In L. Porter & B. Mohr (Eds.), *Reading Book for Human Relations Training.* Arlington, VA: NTL Institute.

PORTER, M. (1979, March-April). How Competitive Forces Shape Strategy. *Harvard Business Review, 57*(2), 137-45.

PORTER, M. (1980). *Competitive Strategy: Techniques for Analyzing Industries and Competitors.* New York: The Free Press.

POSNER, G. & RUDNITSKY, A. (1982). *Course Design: A Guide to Curriculum Development for Teachers* (2nd ed.). New York: Longman.

POULIOT, L. (1984). Executive Management, and Supervisory Programs. In L. Nadler (Ed.), *The Handbook of Human Resource Development.* New York: Wiley-Interscience.

PRATT, D. (1980). *Curriculum: Design and Development.* New York: Harcourt, Brace, Jovanovich.

PROBST, C. (1985). Job Aids & Non-Aids in Everyday Life. *Performance and Instruction, 24*(8), 24-25.

RAIAG, A. (1985). Power, Politics and the Human Resource Professional. *Human Resource Planning, 8*(4), 201-8.

RALPHS, L. & STEPHEN, E. (1986). HRD in the Fortune 500. *Training and Development Journal, 40*(10), 69-76.

RAMBO, L. (1976). Training for Special Groups: Minorities, Women, and the Disadvantaged. In R. Craig (Ed.), *Training and Development Handbook: A Guide to Human Resource Development* (2nd ed.). New York: McGraw-Hill.

Ramsey, J. (1985). Supervisory Development. In W. Tracey (Ed.), *Human Resources Management and Development Handbook*. New York: Amacom.

Rath, G. & Stoyanoff, K. (1983). The Delphi Technique. In F. Ulschak (Ed.), *Human Resource Development: The Theory and Practice of Need Assessment*. Reston, VA: Reston Publishing.

Raudsepp, E. (1983, April). The Politics of Promotion. *Office Administration and Automation,* pp. 28–31.

Rawlinson, J. (1981). *Creative Thinking and Brainstorming*. New York: John Wiley & Sons.

Rebedeau, F. & Tagliere, D. (1976). Sales Training. In R. Craig (Ed.), *Training and Development Handbook: A Guide to Human Resource Development* (2nd ed.). New York: McGraw-Hill.

Reed, P. (1976, Summer). Human Resource Development: Vital Element in Corporate Renewal. *Directors and Boards,* pp. 20–25.

Remer, P. & O'Neill, C. (1980). Clients as Change Agents: What Color Could my Parachute Be? *Personnel and Guidance Journal, 58,* 425–29.

Renfro, W. & Morrison, J. (1983). The Scanning Process: Methods and Uses. In J. Morrison, W. Renfro, & W. Boucher (Eds.). *Applying Methods and Techniques of Futures Research*. San Francisco: Jossey-Bass.

Ribler, R. (1983). *Training Development Guide*. Reston, VA: Reston Publishing.

Roach, J. & Allen, M. (1983). Strengthening the Strategic Planning Process. In K. Albert (Ed.), *The Strategic Management Handbook*. New York: McGraw-Hill.

The Road Ahead for HRD: Bumpy but Better. (1982). *Training, 19*(10), 68–71, 74–75.

Robbins, S. (1986). *Organizational Behavior: Concepts, Controversies and Applications* (3rd ed.). Englewood Cliffs, NJ: Prentice Hall.

Roberts, R. & Wolf, M. (1983). Human Resources Strategy. In K. Albert (Ed.), *The Strategic Management Handbook*. New York: McGraw-Hill.

Robinson, J. (1982) *Developing Managers Through Behavior Modeling*. Austin, TX: Learning Concepts.

Robinson, J. (1985). Behavior Modeling Training. In W. Tracey (Ed.), *Human Resources Management and Development Handbook*. New York: Amacom.

Robson, B. (1983, October). Moving on! *Black Enterprise,* pp. 99–104.

Roche, G. (1979). Much Ado About Mentors. *Harvard Business Review, 57*(1), 14–31.

Rock, R. Eisthen, M. (1983). Implementing Strategic Change. In K. Albert (Ed.), *The Strategic Management Handbook*. New York: McGraw-Hill.

Roeber, R. (1973). *The Organization in a Changing Environment*. Reading, MA: Addison-Wesley.

Rogers, T. (1981). Strategic Planning: A Major OD Intervention. In K. Schaeffer (Ed.), *Organization Development: Strategies for the Future*. Madison, WI: American Society for Training and Development.

Rokeach, M. (1973). *The Nature of Human Values*. New York: The Free Press.

Romiszowski, A. (1981). *Designing Instructional Systems: Decision Making in Course Planning and Curriculum Design*. New York: Nichols Publishing.

Ronan, W. & Lotharn, G. (1974). The Realiability and Validity of the Critical Incident Technique: A Closer Look. *Studies in Personnel Psychology, 6,* 53-64.

Rosenberg, S. (1983, August). The Power of Team Play. *Management World,* pp. 26-28.

Rosenthal, D. (1983, October). Apply Strategic Planning in Mapping a Career Path. *Marketing News,* p. 10.

Rossett, A. (1982). A Typology for Generating Needs Assessments. *Journal of Instructional Development, 6*(1), 28-33.

Roth, L. (1986). *Management Development Trends: A Corporate Perspective.* [Reprint from *Career Center Bulletin, 5* (4)]. New York: Center for Career Research and Human Resource Management, Columbia University.

Rothman, J. (1974). *Planning and Organizing for Social Change: Action Principles from Social Science Research.* New York: Columbia University Press.

Rothman, J., Erlich, J., & Teresa, J. (1976). *Promoting Innovation and Change in Organizations and Communities: A Planning Manual.* New York: John Wiley.

Rothschild, W. (1976). *Putting it All Together: A Guide to Strategic Thinking.* New York: Amacom.

Rothwell, W. (1982). *Strategic Planning.* Unpublished training package.

Rothwell, W. (1983a). Training Conflict with Reality? Try Critical Research. *Training. 20*(7), 11-12.

Rothwell, W. (1983b). Curriculum Design: An Overview. *Personnel Administrator, 28*(11), 53-54; 56-57.

Rothwell, W. (1983c). *A Process Approach to Curriculum Design in Management Training.* A presentation delivered to the Region V Conference of the American Society for Training and Development in Springfield, Illinois.

Rothwell, W. (1983d). The Life Cycle of HRD Departments. *Training and Development Journal, 37*(11), 74-76.

Rothwell, W. (1984a). Applying Critical Theory and Research to Organization Development. *Organization Development Journal, 2*(3), 25-27.

Rothwell, W. (1984b, May). Thinking Strategically: The Business of Career Decisions. *Training News,* pp. 19-20.

Rothwell, W. (1984c). How to Conduct a Real Performance Audit. *Training. 21*(6), 46-49.

Rothwell, W. (1984d). Strategic Needs Assessment. *Performance and Instruction Journal, 23*(5), 19-20.

Rothwell, W. (1984e). Curriculum Theory Reconsidered: Strategic Planning and Organizational Training. *Journal of Educational Technology Systems, 12*(4), 327-36.

Rothwell, W. (1984f). Strategic Curriculum Design for Management Training. *Journal of Management Development, 3*(3), 39-52.

Rothwell, W. (1985a). Administering the Climate Survey: A Toolkit. *Journal of Technical Writing and Communication, 15*(4), 323-38.

Rothwell, W. (1985b). *Management Training in Support of Organizational Strategic Planning in Twelve Illinois Organizations.* Unpublished doctoral dissertation, Urbana, IL: University of Illinois.

Rothwell, W. (1987). *A Directory of Continuing Education Courses, Resources and Facilities in Illinois Community Colleges and Universities.* Springfield, IL: Office of the Auditor General.

Rothwell, W. & Kazanas, H. (1986-8). Strategic Planning and HRD: Results of a Comprehensive Survey. Unpublished Manuscript. Urbana, IL: University of Illinois.

Rothwell, W. & Kazanas, H. (1987). Participation: Key to Integrating Planning and Training? *Performance and Instruction, 26*(9/10), 27-31.

Rothwell, W. & Kazanas, H. (1988). *Strategic Human Resources Planning and Management.* Englewood Cliffs, NJ: Prentice Hall.

Rowe, A., Mason, R., & Dickel, K. (1986). *Strategic Management: A Methodological Approach.* Reading, MA: Addison-Wesley.

Rowland, K. & Summers, S. (1981, December). Human Resource Planning: A Second Look. *Personnel Administrator,* pp. 73-80.

Rowntree, D. (1982). *Educational Technology in Curriculum Development* (2nd ed.). New York: Harper & Row.

Rumelt, R. (1979). Evaluation of Strategy: Theory and Models. In D. Schendel and C. Hofer (Eds.), *Strategic Management: A New View of Business Policy and Planning.* Boston: Little, Brown and Company.

Rummler, G. (1976). The Performance Audit. In R. Craig (Ed.), *Training and Development Handbook: A Guide to Human Resource Development* (2nd ed.). New York: McGraw-Hill.

Ryans, J. & Shanklin, W. (1985). *Strategic Planning: Concepts and Implementation Text, Readings and Cases.* New York: Random House.

Salinger, R. (1976). Correspondence Study. In R. Craig (Ed.), *Training and Development Handbook: A Guide to Human Resource Development* (2nd ed.). New York: McGraw-Hill.

Saltzman, A., Moly, R., & Hartshorn, G. (1976). Vocational and Technical Education. In R. Craig (Ed.), *Training and Development Handbook: A Guide to Human Resource Development* (2nd ed.). New York: McGraw-Hill.

Saunders, C. (1980). The Process of Strategic Choice. In W. Glueck (Ed.), *Business Policy and a Strategic Management* (3rd ed.). New York: McGraw-Hill.

Saylor, J. & Alexander, W. (1966). *Curriculum Planning for Modern Schools.* New York: Holt, Rinehart & Winston.

Saylor, J. & Alexander, W. (1974). *Planning Curriculum for Schools.* New York: Holt, Rinehart & Winston.

Saylor, J., Alexander, W., & Lewis, A. (1981). *Curriculum Planning for Better Teaching and Learning* (4th ed.). New York: Holt, Rinehart & Winston.

Schein, E. (1969). *Process Consultation.* Reading, MA: Addison-Wesley.

Schein, E. (1978). *Career Dynamics: Matching Individual and Organizational Needs.* Reading, MA: Addison-Wesley.

Schein, E. (1983a, Summer). The Role of the Founder in Creating Organizational Culture. *Organizational Dynamics,* pp. 13-28.

Schein, E. (1984). The Coming Awareness of Organization Culture. *Sloan Management Review, 25*(2), 3-16.

SCHEIN, E. (1985). *Organizational Culture and Leadership: A Dynamic View.* San Francisco: Jossey-Bass.

SCHEIN, V. (1983b). Strategic Management and the Politics of Power. *Personnel Administrator, 28*(10), 55-58.

SCHENDEL, D. & HOFER, C. (1979). Strategy Evaluation. In D. Schendel and C. Hofer (Eds.), *Strategic Management: A New View of Business Policy and Planning.* Boston: Little, Brown and Company.

SCHMIDT, T. (1983). *Planning Your Career Success.* Belmont, CA: Lifetime Learning.

SCHMIDT, W. & POSNER, B. (1982). *Managerial Values and Expectations: The Silent Power in Personal and Organizational Life.* New York: AMA Membership Publications Division.

SCHOENNAUER, A. (1981). *Problem Finding and Problem Solving.* Chicago: Nelson Hall.

SCHÖN, D. (1971). *Beyond the Stable State.* New York: Random House.

SCHÖN, D. (1975). Deutero-Learning in Organizations: Learning for Increased Effectiveness. *Organizational Dynamics, 4*(1), 2-16.

SCHÖN, D. (1987). *Educating the Reflective Practitioner: Toward a New Design for Teaching and Learning in The Professions.* San Francisco: Jossey-Bass.

SCHOULTZ, C. (1986, September). Reading Between the Lines: The High Cost of Ignorance. *Training and Development Journal,* pp. 44-47.

SCHREIBER, C. (1982). Using Demographic and Technological Forecasts for Human Resource Planning. In G. Mensch & R. Niehause (Ed.), *Work, Organizations and Technological Change.* New York: Plenum.

SCHWARTZ, B., SVEDIN, U. & WITTROCK, B. (1982). *Methods in Futures Studies: Problems and Applications.* Boulder, CO: Westview Press.

SCOTT, D. & DEADRICK, D. (1982). The Nominal Group Technique: Applications for Training Needs Assessment. *Training and Development Journal, 36*(6), 26-33.

SCRIVEN, M. (1967). The Methodology of Evaluation. In R. Stake (Ed.), *Perspectives on Curriculum Evaluation.* AERA Monograph. Chicago: Rand McNally.

SEASHORE, C. (1982). Developing and Using a Personal Support System. In L. Porter & Mohr (Eds.), *Reading Book for Human Relations Training.* Arlington, VA: NTL Institute.

SEKARAN, U. (1986). *Dual-Career Families: Contemporary Organizational Issues.* San Francisco, CA: Jossey-Bass.

SELFRIDGE, R. & SOKOLIK, S. (1975, Winter). A Comprehensive View of Organization Development. *MSU Business Topics, 23*(1), 46-61.

SELLERS, J. (1985). Scientist and Engineer Development. In W. Tracey (Ed.), *Human Resources Management and Development Handbook.* New York: Amacom.

SHANKLIN, W. & RYANS, J. JR. (1985). *Thinking Strategically: Planning for Your Company's Future.* New York: Random House.

SHARPLIN, A. (1985). *Strategic Management.* New York: McGraw-Hill.

SHAW, M., CORSINI, R., BLAKE, R., & MOUTON, J. (1980). *Role Playing: A Practical Manual for Group Facilitators.* San Diego, CA: University Associates.

SHEEHY, G. (1974). *Passages: Predictable Crises of Adult Life.* New York: E. P. Dutton.

SHEPARD, H. (1960). An Action Research Model. In *An Action Research Model for Organization Improvement.* Ann Arbor: University of Michigan.

SHERIDAN, J. & MONAGHAN, J. (1982). Environmental Issues Scanning: Starting a Self-Sustaining Research Program. *Human Resource Planning, 5*(2), 57-68.

SIMERLY, R. & ASSOCIATES. (1987). *Strategic Planning and Leadership in Continuing Education.* San Francisco: Jossey-Bass.

SIGBAND, N. (1969, April). Needed: Corporate Policies on Communication. *S.A.M. Advanced Management Journal,* pp. 61-67.

SIMPSON, E. (1969). *Psychomotor Domain: A Tentative Classification.* Urbana, IL: University of Illinois.

SINETAR, M. (1986, May). Relo Shock. *Personnel Journal,* pp. 44-49.

SMIRCICH, L. (1983, September). Concepts of Culture and Organizational Analysis. *Administrative Science Quarterly, 28*(3), 342-58.

SMITH, E. (1982, September). Strategic Business Planning and Human Resources: Part II. *Personnel Journal,* pp. 680-82.

SMITH, M. & MARCINUK, R. (1982). Training Cost Accounting at New England Telephone. In R. Craig (Ed.), *The Nature and Extent of Employee Training and Development.* Washington, DC: American Society for Training and Development.

SMITH, R. (1982). *Learning How to Learn: Applied Learning Theory for Adults.* New York: Cambridge Books.

SMITH, R. (1983). *Helping Adults Learn How to Learn.* San Francisco: Jossey-Bass.

SMITH, R. (1984). OD Can Be a Discipline. *Training and Development Journal, 38*(1), 102-4.

SPAID, O. (1986). *The Consummate Trainer: A Practitioner's Perspective.* Englewood Cliffs, NJ: Reston Book.

SPECTOR, A. (1984). Instructional Strategies: Media. In L. Nadler (Ed.), *The Handbook of Human Resource Development.* New York: Wiley-Interscience.

SPECTOR, A. (1985). *Identification and Analysis of Human Resource Development Policy in Selected U.S. Corporations.* Unpublished doctoral dissertation. Washington, DC: George Washington University.

SPECTOR, P. (1981). *Research Designs.* Beverly Hills, CA: Sage Publications.

SPENCER, L., JR. (1984, July). How to Calculate the Costs and Benefits of an HRD Program. *Training, 21,* 40-51.

SPIEGEL, H. (1979). Theoretical Research and Community Development Practice. In E. Blakely (Ed.), *Community Development Research: Concepts, Issues and Strategies.* New York: Human Sciences Press.

SPRADLEY, J. (1979). *Ethnographic Interview.* New York: Holt, Rinehart and Winston.

SPRUELL, G. (1985). Say So Long to Promotions. *Training and Development Journal, 39*(5), 70-75.

SREDL, H. & ROTHWELL, W. (1987). *The ASTD Reference Guide to Professional Training Roles and Competencies.* 2 vols. Amherst, MA: Human Resource Development Press.

STAKE, R. (1978). Responsive Evaluation. In D. Hamilton et al. (Eds.), *Beyond the Numbers Game.* Berkeley, CA: McCutchan.

STAKE, R. (1981). *Recommendations for Those Considering the Support of Naturalistic Case-Study Research.* ERIC Document ED 202 868. Urbana, IL: University of Illinois.

STANISLAO, J. & STANISLAO, B. (1983, July-August). Dealing with Resistance to Change. *Business Horizons,* pp. 74-78.

STARLING, G. (1984). *The Changing Environment of Business.* (2nd ed.). Boston: Kent.

STAW, B. (1976). Knee-Deep in the Bid Muddy: A Study of Escalating Commitment to a Chosen Course of Action. *Organizational Behavior and Human Performance, 16*(1), 27-44.

STEADHAM, S. (1980, January). Learning to Select a Need Assessment Strategy. *Training and Development Journal, 34*(1), 56-61.

STEINER, G., MINER, J., & GRAY, E. (1982). *Management Policy and Strategy: Text, Readings, and Cases* (2nd ed.). New York: Macmillan.

STEVENSON, H. (1976). Defining Strengths and Weaknesses. *Sloan Management Review, 17*(3), 51-68.

STEWART, L. & GUDYKUNST, W. (1982, September). Differential Factors Influencing the Hierarchical Level and Number of Promotions of Males and Females Within an Organization. *Academy of Management Journal,* pp. 586-97.

STINSON, P. (1983, September). Making the Right Moves. *Black Enterprise,* pp. 55-60.

ST. JOHN, W. (1981, November). In-House Communication Guidelines. *Personnel Journal,* pp. 872-78.

STOKER, R. (1987). Literacy in the Workplace. In R. Craig (Ed.) *Training and Development Handbook* (3rd ed.). New York: McGraw-Hill.

STONE, W. & HEANY, D. (1984). Dealing with a Corporate Identity Crisis. *Long Range Planning, 17*(1), 10-18.

STONICH, P. (Ed.). (1982). *Implementing Strategy: Making Strategy Happen.* Cambridge, MA: Ballinger Publishing.

STOVER, J. & GORDON, T. (1978). Cross-Impact Analysis. In J. Fowles (Ed.), *Handbook of Futures Research.* Westport, CT: Greenwood Press.

Strategy and HR Policy. (1988). *Personnel Administrator, 33*(1), 20, 22.

STRAUSS, G. & SAYLES, L. (1960). *Personnel: The Human Problem of Management.* Englewood Cliffs, NJ: Prentice Hall.

STRAUSS, J. & BURACK, E. (1983). The Human Resource Professional: A Challenge in Change. *Human Resource Planning, 6*(1), 1-9.

STREET, W. (1974). Brainstorming by Individuals, Coacting and Interacting Groups. *Journal of Applied Psychology,* 59, 433-36.

STUBBART, C. (1982). Are Environmental Scanning Units Effective? *Long Range Planning, 15*(3), 139-45.

STUFFLEBEAM, D. (1968, July 30). Toward a Science of Educational Evaluation. *Educational Technology, 8*(14), 5-12.

STUMP, R. (1985). *Your Career in HRD: A Guide to Information and Decision Making.* Alexandria, VA: American Society for Training and Development.

SULLIVAN, E. (Ed.). (1983). *Guide to External Degree Programs in the United States.* New York: Macmillan.

SULLIVAN, R. & MIKLAS, D. (1985, May). On-the-job Training that Works. *Training and Development Journal,* pp. 118-20.

SWANSON, R. & GRADOUS, D. (1986). *Performance at Work: A Systematic Program for Analyzing Work Behavior.* New York: Wiley.

TANNENBAUM, R. & SCHMIDT, W. (1973, May-June). How to Choose a Leadership Pattern. *Harvard Business Review,* pp. 162-80.

TANNER, D. & TANNER, L. (1980). *Curriculum Development: Theory into Practice* (2nd ed.). New York: Macmillan.

TAYLOR, P. & RICHARDS, C. (1985). *An Introduction to Curriculum Studies* (2nd ed.). Windsor, Berhshire, UK: NFER-Nelson Publishing.

TERRY, P. (1977, June). Mechanism for Environmental Scanning. *Long Range Planning, 10,* 2-9.

TESSIN, M. (1978, February). Once Again, Why Training? *Training,* p. 7.

THIAGARAJAN, S. (1986). Alternatives: 25 Ways to Improve Any Lecture. *Performance and Instruction, 24*(1), 22-24.

THOMAS, P. (1980, February). Environmental Scanning—the State of the Art. *Long Range Planning, 13,* 20-25.

TICHY, N. (1983). *Managing Strategic Change.* New York: John Wiley.

TICHY, N., FOMBRUN, C., & DEVANNA, M. (1982, Winter). Strategic Human Resources Management. *Sloan Management Review,* pp. 47-61.

TOFFLER, A. (1980). *The Third Wave.* New York: William Morrow.

TOUGH, A. (1979). *The Adult's Learning Projects* (2nd ed.). Toronto: Ontario Institute for Studies in Eduation.

TRACEY, W. (1981). *Human Resource Development Standards.* New York: Amacom.

TRACEY, W. (1984). *Designing Training and Development Systems* (rev. ed.). New York: Amacom.

Trainer Tally Varies—Depending upon Who is Counted. (1982). *Training, 29*(10), 22-24, 26.

TREGOE, B. & ZIMMERMAN, J. (1984). Needed: A Strategy for Human Resource Development. *Training and Development Journal, 38*(5), 78-80.

TREGOE, B. & ZIMMERMAN, J. (1985). The New Strategic Manager. In J. Ryans, Jr. & W. Shanklin (Ed.), *Strategic Planning: Concepts and Implementation.* New York: Random House.

TUCKMAN, B. & JENSEN, M. (1977, December). Stages in Small Group Development Revisited. *Groups and Organization Studies,* pp. 419-27.

TYLER, R., (1949). *Basic Principles of Curriculum and Instruction.* Chicago: University of Chicago Press.

ULSCHAK, F. (1983). *Human Resource Development: The Theory and Practice of Need Assessment.* Reston, VA: Reston Publishing.

ULSCHAK, F., NATHANSON, L. & GILLAN, P. (1981). *Small Group Problem Solving: An Aid to Organizational Effectiveness.* Reading, MA: Addison-Wesley.

Using Mission Statements to Plan Training. (1982, November). *Training,* pp. 23, 25.

UTTAL, B. (1983, October 17). The Corporate Culture Vultures. *Fortune, 108*(8), 66-72.

UTTERBACK, J. (1979). Environmental Analysis and Forecasting. In D. Schendel & C. Hofer (Eds.), *Strategy Management: A New View of Business Policy and Planning.* Boston: Little, Brown and Company.

VAILL, P. (1982). Strategic Planning. In E. Pavlock (Ed.), *Organization Development: Managing Transitions.* Washington, DC: American Society for Training and Development.

VAILL, P. (1982, Autumn). The Purpose of High Performing Systems. *Organizational Dynamics,* pp. 23-40.

VANCIL, R. & LORANGE, P. (1975, January-February). Strategic Planning in Diversified Companies. *Harvard Business Review, 53*(1), 84-85.

VAN DE VEN, A. & DELBECQ, A. (1972, June). Nominal Versus Interacting Group Processes for Committee Decision-Making Effectiveness. *Academy of Management Journal,* pp. 203-12.

VAN DE VEN, A. & DELBECQ, A. (1974). The Effectiveness of Nominal, Delphi, and Interacting Group Decision Making Processes. *Academy of Management Journal, 17,* 605-21.

VAN DE VEN, A. & MORGAN, M. (1980). A Revised Framework for Organizational Assessment. In E. Lawler, D. Nadler & C. Cammann (Eds.), *Organizational Assessment: Perspectives on the Measurement of Organizational Behavior and the Quality of Work Life.* New York: Wiley-Interscience.

VAN GUNDY, A. (1981). *Techniques of Structured Problem Solving.* New York: Van Nostrand Reinhold.

VAN GUNDY, A. (1984 August). How to Establish a Creative Climate in the Work Group. *Management Review,* pp. 24-28.

VAN GUNDY, A. (1984). *Managing Group Creativity: A Modular Approach to Problem Solving.* New York: Amacom.

VAN GUNDY, A. (1982). *Training Your Creative Mind.* Englewood Cliffs, NJ: Prentice Hall.

VAN MAANEN, J. (1976). Rookie Cops and Rookie Managers. *Wharton Magazine, 1,* 49-55.

VAN MENTS, M. (1983). *The Effective Use of Role-Play.* New York: Nichols.

VANSTON, J. JR. (1985). Technology Forecasting. In W. Tracey (Ed.), *Human Resources Management and Development Handbook.* New York: Amacom.

VARNEY, G. (1977). *Organization Development for Managers.* Reading, MA: Addison-Wesley.

VARNEY, G. (1980, April). Developing OD Competencies. *Training and Development Journal,* pp. 30-33.

VERDUIN, J. (1980). *Curriculum Building for Adult Learning.* Carbondale, IL: Southern Illinois University Press.

VINTON, D. (1987). Delegation for Employee Development. *Training and Development Journal, 41*(1), 65-67.

VOTH, D. (1979). Social Action Research in Community Development. In E. Blakely (Ed.), *Community Development Research: Concepts, Issues and Strategies.* New York: Human Sciences Press.

VROOM, V., GRANT, L., & COTTEN, T. (1969, February). The Consequences of Social Interaction in Group Problem-Solving. *Organizational Behavior and Human Performance,* pp. 77-95.

VROOM, V. & MACCRIMMON, K. (1968). Toward a Stochastic Model of Managerial Careers. *Administrative Science Quarterly, 13,* 26-46.

WAGSCHALL, P. (1983). Judgmental Forecasting Techniques and Institutional Planning: An Example. In J. Morrison, W. Renfro, & W. Boucher (Eds.), *Applying Methods and Techniques of Futures Research.* San Francisco: Jossey-Bass.

WALKER, J. (1973). Individual Career Planning: Managerial Help for Subordinates. *Business Horizons, 16*(1), 65-72.

WALKER, J. (1980). *Human Resource Planning.* New York: McGraw-Hill.

WALL, J. (1974, November-December). What the Competition is Doing: Your Need to Know. *Harvard Business Review, 52*(6), 22-24, 28, 30, 32, 34, 36, 38.

WALSH, W. & ANDERSON, B. (1985). Evaluating Relocation Management Firms. *Personnel Adminstrator, 30*(4), 27-34.

WALTON, R. (1969). *Interpersonal Peacemaking: Confrontations and Third Party Consultation.* Reading, MA: Addison-Wesley.

WANOUS, J. (1980). *Organizational Entry: Recruitment, Selection, and Socialization of Newcomers.* Reading, MA: Addison-Wesley.

Wanted: A Manager to Fit Each Strategy. (1980, February 25). *Business Week,* pp. 166-73.

WARD, L. (1982). Eight Steps to Strategic Planning for Training Managers. *Training, 19*(11), 22-23, 25, 28-29.

WARR, P., BIRD, M. & RACKHAM, N. (1970). *Evaluation of Management Training.* London: Gower.

WATSON, C. (1979). *Management Development Through Training.* Reading, MA: Addison-Wesley.

WEBER, C. (1984). Strategic Thinking: Dealing with Uncertainty. *Long Range Planning, 17*(5), 60-70.

WEBER, R. (1982). The Group: A Cycle from Birth to Death. In L. Porter & B. Mohr (Eds.), *Reading Book for Human Relations Training.* Arlington, VA: NTL Institute.

WEINSTEIN, L. (1982, August). Collecting Training Cost Data. *Training and Development Journal, 36,* 31-34.

WEISBORD, M. (1978). *Organizational Diagnosis: A Workbook of Theory and Practice.* Reading, MA: Addison-Wesley.

WEISS, A. (1987). Select, Don't Settle. *Training, 24*(9), 90.

WEISS, C. (1972). *Evaluation Research: Methods for Assessing Program Effectiveness.* Englewood Cliffs, NJ: Prentice Hall.

WEISS, C. (1983). The Stakeholder Approach to Evaluation: Origins and Promise. In A. Bryk (Ed.), *Stakeholder-Based Evaluation.* San Francisco: Jossey-Bass.

WEISS, H. (1984). Contributions of Social Psychology to Productivity. In A. Brief (Ed.), *Productivity Research in the Behavioral and Social Sciences.* New York: Praeger.

WERTHER, W. & DAVIS, K. (1985). *Personnel Management and Human Resources.* (2nd ed.). New York: McGraw-Hill.

WEST, E. (1986). Want a Winning Budget? Prepare a Winning Strategy. In H. Birnbrauer (Ed.), *The ASTD Handbook for Technical and Skills Training.* Vol. II. Alexandria, VA: American Society for Training and Development.

What's Wrong with Management? (1982). *Dun's Business Month,* 119(4), 48-52.

WHEELER, M. (1988). Whose Objectives are These, Anyway? *Training,* 25(1), 76.

WHEELWRIGHT, S. & BANKS, R. (1979). Involving Operating Managers in Planning Process Evolution. *Sloan Management Review,* 20(4), 43-59.

WHITE, S. & Mitchell, T. (1976). Organization Development: A Review of Research Content and Research Design. *Academy of Management Review,* 1(2), 57-73.

WHITLOCK, G. (1976). The Role of Universities, Colleges, and Other Educational Institutions in Training and Development. In R. Craig (Ed.), *Training and Development Handbook: A Guide to Human Resource Development* (2nd ed.). New York: McGraw-Hill.

WHYTE, W. (Ed.). (1955). *Money and Motivation: An Analysis of Incentives on Industry.* New York: Harper.

WHYTE, W. & HAMILTON, E. (1964). *Action Research for Management.* Homewood, IL: Irwin-Dorsey.

WILES, J. & BONDI, J. (1984). *Curriculum Development: A Guide to Practice* (2nd ed.). Columbus, OH: Charles E. Merrill.

WILKINS, A. (1983). The Culture Audit: A Tool for Understanding Organizations. *Organizational Dynamics,* 12(2), 24-38.

WILKINS, A. & OUCHI, W. (1983, September). Efficient Cultures: Exploring the Relationship Between Culture and Organizational Performance. *Administrative Science Quarterly,* pp. 468-81.

WILLARD, E. (1986). Budgeting in a Training Group. In H. Birnbrauer (Ed.), *The ASTD Handbook for Technical and Skills Training.* Vol. II. Alexandria, VA: American Society for Training and Development.

WILSON, I. (1974, July). Socio-Political Forecasting. *Michigan Business Review,* pp. 16-18.

WILSON, I. (1978). Scenarios. In J. Fowles (Ed.), *Handbook of Futures Research.* Westport, CT: Greenwood Press.

WILSON, I. (1983). The Benefits of Environmental Analysis. In K. Albert (Ed.). *The Strategic Management Handbook.* New York: McGraw-Hill.

Win New Allies with a Training and Education Committee 1982. *Training,* 19(2), 67.

WINER, L. (1983). Applying Strategic Planning in Human Resource Development. *Training and Development Journal,* 37(11), 81-82, 84.

WISE, G. (1976, October). The Accuracy of Technology Forecasts, 1890-1940. *Futures,* pp. 411-419.

WISSEMA, J., BRAND, A., & VAN DER POL, H. (1981). The Incorporation of Management Development in Strategic Management. *Strategic Management Journal,* 2, 361-77.

WITKIN, H. (1949). The Nature and Importance of Individual Differences in Perception. *Journal of Personality,* 18, 145-70.

WLODKOWSKI, R. (1985). *Enhancing Adult Motivation to Learn: A Guide to Improving Instruction and Increasing Learner Achievement.* San Francisco: Jossey-Bass.

WOHLKING, W. & WEINER, H. (1981). Structured and Spontaneous Role-Playing. *Training and Development Journal,* 35(6), 111-12, 114-18, 120-21.

WOLFE, J. (1976, August). The Value of Environmental Cognition: A Simulation-Based Test of Emery and Trist's Causal Textures. *Proceedings of the Academy of Management.*

Women Are Moving into Management—Slowly. (1983, December 21). *Chemical Week*, pp. 72-77.

WOODCOCK, M. (1979). *Team Development Manual.* New York: John Wiley.

WOODMAN, R. & SHERWOOD, J. (1980, April-June). Effects of Team Development Intervention: A Field Experiment. *Journal of Applied Behavioral Science*, pp. 211-17.

Work and Family: A Changing Dynamic. (1986). Washington, D.C.: The Bureau of National Affairs.

WULF, K. & SHAVE, B. (1984). *Curriculum Design: A Handbook for Educators.* Glenview, IL: Scott, Foresman & Co.

ZEMKE, R. (1981). Curriculum Development as Strategic Planning. *Training, 18*(4), 29.

ZEMKE, R. (1982a). Job Competencies: Can They Help You Design Better Training? *Training, 19*(5), 28-31.

ZEMKE, R. (1982b). Can Games and Simulations Improve Your Training Power? *Training, 19*(2), 24-31.

ZEMKE, R. (1982c). Behavior Modeling: The 'Monkey See, Monkey Do' Principle. [rpt. from June 1978 Training.] In *Adult Learning in Your Classroom.* Minneapolis, MN: Lakewood Publications.

ZEMKE, R. (1985a). Stalking the Elusive Corporate Credo. *Training, 22*(6), 44-51.

ZEMKE, R. (1985b). In Search of a Training Philosophy. *Training, 22*(10), 93-94, 96, 98.

ZEMKE, R. (1984). Customer Education: The Silent Revolution. *Training, 22*(1), 27, 30-33, 37-39.

ZEMKE, R. (1986). Development and Delivery: Classroom Training Still Most Common Option. *Training, 23*(10), 58-59.

ZEMKE, R. & KRAMLINGER, T. (1982). *Figuring Things Out: A Trainer's Guide to Needs and Task Analysis.* Reading, MA: Addison-Wesley.

ZENGER, W. & ZENGER, S. (1982). *Curriculum Planning: A Ten-Step Process.* Palo Alto, CA: R & E Research Associates.

ZENTER, R. (1985). Scenarios in Forecasting. In J. Ryans, Jr. & W. Shanklin (Ed.), *Strategic Planning: Concepts and Implementation.* New York: Random House.

ZEY, M. (1984). *The Mentor Connection.* Homewood, IL: Dr. Jones-Irvine.

ZEY, M. (1988). A Mentor for all Reasons. *Personnel Journal, 67*(1), 46-51.

ZWICKY, F. (1969). *Discovery, Invention, Research through the Morphological Approach.* New York: Macmillan.

NAME INDEX

A

Abell, D., 168
Ackerman, R., 201
Ackoff, R., 261, 262
Adair, C., 418
Adams, E., 355
Aguilar, F., 125
Aiken, M., 293
Ajimal, K., 57
Albert, M., 67, 251
Albrecht, K., 355
Alderfer, C., 250
Allen, M., 440
Allevras, J., 212
Alpander, G., 12, 226
Anderson, R., 418
Anshen, M., 266
Anthony, W., 126
Archer, S., 262, 424

Argyris, C., 185, 238, 241, 251, 472
Aronoff, C., 263, 266
Ary, D., 471
Avakian, A., 364

B

Bailey, R., 399
Baird, L., 21
Baker, E., 65
Baker, H., 245
Baker, J., 373
Ball, S., 476
Bandura, A., 316, 416
Barney, D., 370
Bates, C., 115
Bauer, R., 266
Beach, D., 164
Beaudin, B., 430

547

Beck, L., 101
Beckhard, K., 186, 318
Bedeian, A., 237, 240
Beer, M., 60, 168, 355
Bell, C., 250
Bellingham, R., 361
Benne, K., 238
Berger, M., 17, 65
Bernardin, H., 349
Bibeault, D., 212
Biklen, D., 262
Birnbrauer, H., 370
Bittel, L., 370
Blakely, E., 262, 264
Blank, W., 410, 419
Blessing, B., 35
Blomquist, C., 308
Bloom, B., 203, 480
Bobbitt, F., 174
Bolles, R., 355
Bolt, J., 168
Bortz, R., 357
Bouchard, T., Jr., 437
Boulding, E., 251
Bourgeois, L., 129
Bowers, D. and Franklin, J., 246
Bowman, B., 166
Boyatzis, R., 189
Boyd, B., 415
Brakken, D., 204
Brandenburg, D., 468, 469, 474, 475, 476, 482, 484
Brett, J., 124
Bridges, E., 141
Briggs, L., 204
Brightman, H., 293
Brimmer, A., 343
Broadwell, M., 403, 417
Bronikowski, R., 343
Brookfield, S., 181, 191
Brown, L., 359
Bruner, J., 357, 193
Buell, V., 89, 260, 264
Burack, E., 351, 361
Burke, W., 215, 243, 245, 246, 253
Byars, L., 7, 45

Byrne, J., 358

C

Caffarella, R., 364
Calish, I., 201
Calvert, R., 21
Campbell, J., 476
Campbell, D., 141, 472
Cantwell, J., 378
Carnevale, A., 21, 22
Catalanello, R., 476
Cathcart, J., 317
Chakiris, B., 378
Chandler, A., 3, 211
Charles, D., 22
Chin, R., 237
Chinoy, E., 349
Clark, C., 437
Clark, G., 217
Cleland, D., 66
Connell, H., 370
Cook, T., 472
Cooke, P., 416
Coon, A., 437
Cooperrider, D., 241
Corey, S., 241
Corson, J., 266
Craft, J., 13, 50, 171
Crites, C., 369
Cross, L., 215
Cullen, J., 477
Cummings, D., 408
Cummings, L., 211
Cutlip, S., 261
Cyert, R., 167

D

Dalton, D., 211
Dalton, G., 361
Daly, A., 370
Danforth, T., 358
Danis, C., 192

Datta, L., 476
Davies, I., 188
Davis, L., 187, 190
Davis, S., 65, 213
Day, G., 259
Deal, T., 65, 341
Dean, R., 361
Debono, E., 293, 441, 462
Deegan, A., III, 53
Delbecq, A., 55, 102, 316
DeMeuse, K., 246, 476
Deming, B., 477
Dennis, S., 360
Denova, C., 410, 479
Derr, C., 172
Desatnick, R., 154
Dewey, J., 16
Dick, W., 405, 408, 410, 421, 479, 480, 482
Diebold, J., 261
Diffenbach, J., 115
Digman, L., 80, 404, 473
Dillman, C., 408
Doeringer, P., 343
Doll, W., 343, 359
Downs, A., 247
Duhaime, I., 212
Duke, R., 418
Dunn, S., 114
Dyer, L., 54, 97, 245

E

Eastburn, R., 370
Easterby-Smith, M., 57
Eitington, J., 417
Ellington, H., 418
Emery, F., 117
Estrin, D., 309

F

Fahey, L., 115, 167
Faris, J., 473

Feldman, D., 341
Fenn, R., 370
Feuer, D., 80, 216, 273, 404, 473
Fiedler, F., 238, 347
Finnegan, G., 403
Fisher, B., 141
Flanders, D., 343
Fleishman, E., 100, 209
Foltz, R., 21, 50, 153, 343
Ford, L., 415
Fordyce, J., 246
Francis, G., 250
Fratzreb, R., 304
French, W., Jr., 236, 237, 240, 241, 242, 250
Fresina, A., 309
Friedlander, F., 250
Friedman, D., 360
Friedman, P., 323, 443
Fritz, R., 311
Frohman, M., 241

G

Gagné, R., 180, 410, 480, 482, 497
Galbraith, J., 211
Galosy, J., 90, 91, 178, 197, 414
Gardner, J., 306
Gay, G., 173
Geber, B., 88
Gerstein, M., 50
Gibbons, A., 100, 407
Gibson, J., 211, 238, 239
Gilbert, T., 400
Gilbert, W., 81, 187
Gilfillan, S., 114
Gilmore, F., 4
Ginzberg, E., 356
Glueck, W., 114, 135, 321, 341, 428
Godiwalla, Y., 115, 116
Goldner, F., 349
Goldstein, I., 100, 406, 407, 472
Golembiewski, R., 472
Goodacre, D., 472
Goodman, P., 250

Gordon, J., 21, 22, 34, 368
Gray, B., 121, 343
Greene, M., 191
Greenlaw, P., 101
Greiner, L., 60
Grinyer, P., 129
Guest, R., 245
Gupta, A., 167
Gutteridge, T., 357, 369

H

Hagberg, J., 355
Hage, J., 212
Hague, H., 306
Hall, D., 303, 361
Hamblin, A., 204
Hammer, N., 343, 359
Hand, H., 472
Hanson, M., 369, 414
Hare, A., 141
Harless, J., 400, 403, 476
Harley, J., 343
Harrison, R., 341
Hartley, J., 419
Harvey, L., 52, 154, 250
Hay, R., 266
Heinich, R., 419
Heller, K., 212
Helmer, O., 430
Hennings, D., 443
Hensey, M., 442
Heydinger, R., 440
Hofer, C., 3
Holloman, C., 141
Holloway, C., 2, 3, 6
Holmes, B., 411
Hoover, K., 406, 420, 421
Hope, V., 378
Horn, R., 418
Houle, C., 192
Hrebiniak, L., 150
Huczynski, A., 411, 437
Hughes, R., 245
Hulett, D., 153

Hunkins, F., 175
Huse, E., 8, 9, 57, 250

I

Inzerilli, G., 66
Isaac, S., 472
Isaacson, L., 358
Ives, C., 370

J

Jackson, S., 407
Jacobs, R., 403, 473, 483
Jain, S., 115
James-Neill, M., 315
Janis, I., 141, 239, 247, 355
Jenks, R., 241
Johnson, G., 363
Johnson, S., 102
Jones, L., 172

K

Kanter, R., 66, 317, 341, 349
Kappauf, C., 115
Katz, D., 238, 243, 424
Kaufman, R., 98
Keegan, W., 125
Keichel, W., 5, 201, 248
Keiser, T., 418
Kelly, H., 415
Kemp, J., 418, 419, 479
Kerr, S., 215
Kiefer, C., 341
Kilcourse, T., 245
Kinn, J., 370
Kirkpatrick, D., 245, 370, 484
Klemp, G., Jr., 188
Knowles, M., 92, 93, 113, 192, 361, 363, 365, 369, 410, 423, 427, 434
Koestler, A., 293
Kolb, D., 241, 442

Komacki, J., 472
Kondrasuk, J., 203
Kozol, J., 364
Krajci, T., 357
Krathwohl, D., 203
Krech, D., 184
Kruger, M., 221

L

Laird, D., 31, 81, 87, 98, 315, 401, 411, 413, 414, 417, 490
Lambert, W., 411
Lawler, E., III, 215
Lawrie, J., 307
Leach, J., 341, 172
LeBell, D., 115
Lee, C., 22, 23, 24, 343, 359
Leemhuis, J., 120, 246
Leibowitz, Z., 369
Leontiades, M., 7
Levie, W., 418
Levine, E., 349
Levinson, H., 202
Levy, A., 250, 252, 262, 425
Lewin, K., 238, 438
Lewis, A., 173
Lewis, P., 347
Lewis, W., 218, 240
Likert, R., 246
Lincoln, Y., 473, 483
Linkow, P., 59, 154
Linstone, H., 438
Lippitt, G., 241
Locher, A., 100
Lodge, G., 80
London, M., 307
Lorange, P., 219
Lundberg, C., 62
Lusterman, S., 378

M

McCall, M., Jr., 252, 401

McCarthy, D., 370
McCord, B., 417
McCormick, E., 349, 407
McGehee, W., 81
McLean, J., 418
McQuigg, B., 378, 380
MacMillan, I., 167
Madsen, D., 437
Mager, R., 203, 400, 407, 408, 409, 410
Magnus, M., 342
Mahler, W., 370
Mahoney, F., 245, 246
Maier, N., 416
Malasky, E., 411
Mandel, T., 440
Mansfield, R., 122
Markley, O., 251
Markowitz, J., 349
Marrow, A., 187
Marshall, R., 88, 343
Martin, J., 65
Martinko, M., 103
Mason, J., 57
Mason, R., 56, 252, 265, 441, 442
Meckel, N., 369
Meidan, A., 202
Micali, P., 443
Migliore, R., 101
Milkovich, G., 100
Miller, D., 129, 472
Mintzberg, H., 167, 212, 496
Mirabel, T., 477
Mirabile, R., 154
Mirvis, P., 253
Misa, K., 13, 21
Moles, J., 262
Molloy, W., 416
Moore, J., 303
Moore, M., 81, 82, 83, 429
Moorhead, G., 141
Morano, R., 369
Morgan, B., 341, 342
Morrisey, G., 46, 61
Morse, E., 215
Murphy, J., 473

N

Nadler, L., 31, 36, 37, 89, 208, 302, 303, 306, 316, 340, 341, 345, 347, 397, 413, 429, 489
Naisbitt, J., 364, 492
Nanus, B., 115
Neilsen, E., 241
Newell, T., 212
Newman, K., 209
Newstrom, J., 104
Niehaus, R., 16
Nilsson, W., 97, 105
Nininger, J., 19, 48, 210
Nkomo, S., 13, 14, 16, 343

O

O'Connor, R., 11, 207, 347
Odiorne, G., 91, 201, 304
Oldham, G., 211
Olson, P., 188
Osborn, A., 293, 440

P

Pace, R., 264
Page, W., 114
Paine, E., 11, 54, 175
Pascale, R., 309
Pastin, M., 66, 79
Pattan, J., 153
Patten, T., Jr., 245
Pearce, J., 152, 159, 166, 223
Pedler, M., 306
Percival, F., 419
Peters, T., 65
Pettigrew, A., 65
Phillips, J., 467, 471, 472, 473, 486, 487, 488
Pigors, P., 415
Pinchot, G., 114
Pinto, P., 24
Polack, F., 251
Popham, W., 203
Porras, J., 187
Porter, M., 125, 315
Posner, G., 420
Pouliot, L., 370
Pratt, D., 80, 175

R

Raia, A., 167
Rambo, L., 359
Ramsey, J., 370
Rath, G., 102
Raudsepp, E., 343
Rawlinson, J., 437
Rebedeau, F., 370
Remer, P., 355
Renfro, W., 115
Ribler, R., 421
Roach, J., 11
Robbins, S., 65, 66
Roberts, R., 12, 13, 49, 51, 224, 225
Robinson, J., 316, 416
Robson, B., 343
Roche, G., 306
Rock, R., 204
Roeber, R., 115
Rogers, T., 220, 240
Rokeach, M., 464, 465
Romiszowski, A., 214, 419
Rosenthal, D., 355
Roth, L., 208, 404
Rothman, J., 262
Rothschild, W., 46, 496, 497
Rothwell, W., 1, 11, 12, 13, 47, 51, 56, 57, 59, 187, 248, 250, 252, 347, 348, 351, 400, 407, 430
Rowe, A., 80, 123
Rowland, K., 13, 50
Ryans, J., 4, 11, 119

S

Salinger, R., 373

Saltzman, A., 370
Saylor, J., 174, 185, 487
Schein, E., 13, 53, 65, 347, 355, 497
Schendel, D., 495
Schmidt, T., 355
Schmidt, W., 465, 466, 467
Schon, D., 164
Schoultz, C., 364
Schwartz, B., 430
Scriven, M., 479, 482
Sekaran, U., 360
Selfridge, R., 242
Sellers, J., 370
Shanklin, W., 114
Sharplin, A., 6, 8, 106
Shaw, M., 416
Shepard, H., 241
Sheridan, J., 115
Sigband, N., 218
Sinetar, M., 342
Smircich, L., 63
Smith, E., 418
Smith, M., 477
Smith, R., 476
Spaid, O., 411, 437
Spector, A., 419
Spector, P., 208, 472
Spencer, L., Jr., 477
Spiegel, H., 262
Spradley, J., 67
Spruell, G., 341, 358, 172
Sredl, H., 3, 12, 18, 26, 189, 214, 342, 400, 403, 404, 407, 413, 419, 472
Stake, R., 472, 473
Stainslao, J., 201
Starling, G., 114, 267
Staw, B., 347
Steadham, S., 104
Stewart, L., 343
Stinson, P., 343, 359
St. John, W., 218
Stoker, R., 368
Stone, W., 57, 66
Stonich, P., 59, 220
Stover, J., 439
Strauss, J., 16

Street, W., 437
Stubbart, C., 115
Sullivan, E., 373
Sullivan, R., 403
Swanson, R., 399

T

Tannenbaum, R., 238
Tanner, D., 173
Terry, P., 437
Thiagarajan, S., 411
Thomas, P., 115
Tichy, N., 252
Toffler, A., 66, 261
Tough, A., 311
Tracey, W., 98, 209, 407, 411
Tregoe, B., 113
Tyler, R., 80

U

Ulschak, F., 98, 104
Uttal, B., 66
Utterback, J., 5, 114

V

Vaill, P., 341
Vancil, R., 10
Van de Ven, A., 438
Van Gundy, A., 437, 441, 462
Van Ments, M., 416
Varney, G., 24
Vinton, D., 314
Voth, D., 262
Vroom, V., 349

W

Wagschall, P., 430
Walker, J., 304, 342, 348, 349, 351

Wall, J., 125
Walsh, W., 304
Walton, R., 243
Wanous, J., 37, 352
Ward, L., 153, 154
Warr, P., 204
Watson, C., 16
Weber, C., 57
Weinstein, L., 477
Weiss, A., 163
Weiss, C., 473
Werther, W., 101, 306, 342, 343, 349, 379
Wheeler, M., 479
White, S., 215
Whitlock, G., 370
Whyte, W., 241

Wilkins, A., 67
Wilson, I., 115, 267, 440
Wissema, J., 432
Witkin, H., 192
Wohlking, W., 415, 416
Wolfe, J., 129
Woodcock, M., 246
Woodman, R., 245

Z

Zemke, R., 21, 35, 36, 51, 63, 64, 65, 131, 316, 402, 416, 418, 473
Zenter, R., 55
Zey, M., 307
Zwicky, F., 440

SUBJECT INDEX

A

Action research, 184, 240
American Society for Training and Development (ASTD), 1, 24
Analysis in environmental scanning, 118
Arab oil embargo of 1973, 5
Assessing learner needs, 403-404
Association for Educational Communications and Technology (AECT), 24
Artificial experience approach
    drawback, 56
    steps in the use of, 56
Assessment centers, 98, 101

B

Behavior modeling *see* employee development

Budget, annual, 216-218

C

Career planning (CP):
    develop conducive climate, 344
    establish career policy, 345
        sample of, 346
    model of:
        assessing strengths and weaknesses, 356
        clarify values and identities, 355
        establish long-term career strategy, 356
        making decisions, 356
    purpose of, 355
    steps in establishing formal program, 344-354

steps in the use of, 53
Career education *see* employee education
Career path analysis, 349–351
Cause:
    definition, 158
    examples, 158
Change direction, 206
Characteristics of learners, 405–406
Chief Executive, 15
Clarifying the corporation's role in society, 284
Classification schemes, 260
Coercion *see* organization development
Committee, advisory:
    membership, 222
    purpose of, 222
    responsibilities, 222–227
Communicating, strategy, 218
Community polls, 265
Competencies:
    definition of, 188–9
    importance, 25
Competency analysis, 124
Comprehensive HR information system, 304
Comprehensive needs assessment:
    definition, 80
    description, 80
    environmental scanning, 117
    steps in, 87
Confrontation meetings *see* employee development
Conglomerate diversification, 163
Consumer market segments, 264
Context shifting, 188
Continuing education *see* employee education
Coordinative planning, 8
Correspondence study, 373
Criteria for objectives, 203
Critical incident technique, 101
Culture:
    and formal purpose, 65
    major characteristics, 65

Culture audit, 67
Curriculum:
    developmental, nonemployee, 106
    educational, 106
    training, 106
Curriculum definition, 117
Curriculum design:
    competency-based, 189–190
    experience-centered approach, 186
        advantage, 186
        disadvantage, 186
    goal-centered approach, 187
    learner-centered approach, 187
    performance-based, 187, 191
Curriculum development, 175
Curriculum planning:
    alternative approaches to
        course-centered, 180
        future-oriented, 183
    process, 178
    results, 193

D

Data collection:
    issues, 98, 99
    methods, 98–102
Delphi procedure, 98, 102
Disadvantaged workers, 272
Discrepancy:
    definition of, 268

E

Educational approach, 57
Effort, HRD:
    definition, 2
Employee appraisal, 98, 100, 363
Employee committees *see* employee development
Employee development (ED):
    behavior modeling, 316

definition of, 302–303
establish action plans, 305–306
executive in residence, 308
field trips, 314–315
identify educational needs, 303–306
long-term, formalized transfer programs, 307
long-term, formal mentoring programs, 307
long-term, informal mentoring programs, 306
long-term rotation programs, 309–311
methods for employee development, 306–318
planning long-term experiences, 321–322
problems with traditional programs, 319–320
professional conference, 315–316
specialized methods for, 321–323
special job assignments, 311–312
strategic, 320–321
think tank experience, 316–317
Employee education, 37 (*see also* training)
Employee education (EE):
adult, 364
career, 368
continuing, 359
cooperative, 370
definition of, 340–342
external degree programs, 373
external instruction sponsored by:
community colleges, 372
universities, 372
methods of delivering, 370–378
planning educational efforts
individual component, 363
organizational component, 357–362
occupational, 370
organizational strategy for HRD, 380
sources of information, 379
tuition reimbursement programs, 378
Employee performance appraisals
future-oriented, 140
Employee retreat *see* employee development
Environmental scanning:
definition, 113, 114
description, 113
and external trends, 126
for HRD, 117
methods of, 138–142
opportunities, 142
parts, 114
relations with external groups, 126–127
results of, 142
sources of information, 135
steps in, 118–126
threats, 142
uses of information, 138
Environmental scanning and comprehensive needs assessment, 117
Environmental sectors:
distribution, 126
economic trends, 121
geographic issues, 125–126
market issues, 125
political influence on business, 122
trends, 122
social trends, 124
supplier issues, 126
technological issues, 123
trends, 123
Espoused theory, 185
Event, 15
Experiential methods, 56
External degree programs *see* employee education
External environment, 118, 261
External groups *see* external stakeholders
External instruction *see* employee education
Externally directed HR activities, 260

Subject Index   557

External stakeholders *see* nonemployee development
Evaluating:
    educational resources, 489
    employ development, 492
    employee education, 489
    the HRD effort, 494
    training, 478
Evaluation (E):
    analyzing and interpreting data, 473
    concurrent:
        strategic approach, 484
        traditional approach, 483–484
    content of, 468
    data collection techniques, 475
    definition of, 464–465
    design of, 471–472
    formative:
        functions of, 474
        importance of, 465–466
        method of, 469–470, 481
        strategic approach, 480–481
        traditional approach, 479–480
    post-instructional
        purpose of, 469
        sample, 472–473
        state of the art, 473–474
        strategic approach, 488
        traditional approaches, 468–485
    role of evaluator of, 468
    strategic
        definition of, 495–496
    summative
        strategic approach, 482–483
        traditional approach, 482
    testing
        strategic approach, 478–479
        traditional approach, 477–478
    timing, 469

F

Field trips *see* employee development

Forecasting methods, 129
Formal curriculum, 185
Fortune 500, 13, 14, 16, 114
Futuring approach
    definition, 54
    steps in the use of, 54

G

Geographical scope of business operations, 261
Grand strategy, 7, 8
Grand strategy selection matrix, 161
Group cohesiveness, 238
Group discussion, 98, 101
Group dynamics, 327
Group norms, 238
Group's stage of development, 239
Group think, 239
Growth in consumer education, 277

H

Human Resource (HR):
    audit, 304
    enterprise strategy, 15
    functional strategy, 15
    grand strategy, 15
    practices, 13
    supplies, 305
Human Resource Development (HRD):
    activities:
        employee development, 38
        learning needs, 38
        nonemployee development, 38
        organization development, 38
    basic purpose, 117
    categories of activities, 36
    choosing organizational strategy for
        definition, 152
        history, 173
        importance, 153

prescription, 153
product, 173
reasons for, 153
steps in, 155
uses, 165
drastic cutbacks, negative effects, 164
Effort
clarifying purpose, 61
philosophy, 63
maintenance subsystem, 17
policies, 208
practitioners
future trends, 26
key roles, 26
use of public seminars, 26
strategy
steps in choosing, 155-165
traditional, 17
traditional forms, 36
types of, 36
Human Resource Planning (HRP):
key assumptions, 13
levels of, 14-15
methods of, 15
model of, 12
values of, 13

I

Implementing Organizational Strategy (IOS):
communicating about, 218
definition of, 201
examine leadership, 209-210
issues in, 228
review and revise HRP policies, 208-209
review reward systems, 214-216
review structure, 211-214
steps in, 202-229
Impromptu problem-solving *see* employee development
Individual development program, 53
Individual learning contract, 363

Individuals:
classification of, 91
life cycle stages, 92
in organizational settings, 36-37
Industry conference: *see* employee development
In-house:
externally-developed instruction, 371
formal group instruction, 371
informal group instruction, 371
Instructional efforts, 275
Instructional needs:
logical grouping, 90
methods of, 270
types of, 81
Instructional objectives, 274
Integration, vertical, 163
Interpersonal approach, 59-60
Interview, 98-99

J

Job analysis:
future-oriented, 140
Job loading, 314
Job-market:
job category or family, 89
position, 89
task, 89
Job performance
definition of, 399

L

Leadership, 209
Leadership behavior, 238
Learners:
career market, 90
classifying, 89
work group, 94
Learning and rewards, 215
activity-oriented, 215

Subject Index

goal-oriented, 215
learning-oriented, 215

M

Management retreat *see* employee development
Management by objectives (MBO), 140, 202
Managers, 127
Manpower planning, 12
Market:
    segments, 89
    steps in, 53
Market development, 164
Market-driven approach, 50
Methods of collecting data, 265-266
Models for excellence, 25

N

National opinion polls, 265
National Society for Performance and Instruction (NSPI), 25
Needs assessment:
    data collection methods, 97
    future-oriented, 132-134
    history of, 81
    identification of learners, 88
    levels of, 97
    problem-solving, 81
    strategy, 97
Needs of communities, 361
Nominal group technique (NGT), 48, 102
Nonemployee development (ND):
    analyze deficiencies, 269
    analyze present and future criteria, 266-267
    analyze relationships between corporation, public and stakeholders, 263
    choice of delivery methods, 274
    definition of, 259
    delivery methods, 272-273
    design instruction, 271-272
    externally-oriented instruction, 273
    external stakeholders, 262-263
    general public, 261
    instructional and noninstructional needs, 268
    pinpointing discrepancies, 268
    selecting content, 272
    seminars, 272
    steps in, 260
Noninstructional need:
    levels, 4
    objectives, 4

O

Objectives, instructional:
    affective, 203
    by type of change, 207
    cognitive, 202
    course, 204
    levels of, 203-207
    long-term, 204
    medium-term, 204
    psychomotor, 203
Observation, 98-99
Occupational education *see* employee education
Open-house, 266
Operational objectives, 202
Operational planning, 8
Organizational culture, 65, 240
Organization analysis, 81
Organization development (OD):
    action research, 240-241
        model of, 242
        steps in, 241
    change method, 237
    coercion, 237
    external consultant, 236
    external environmental change, 237
    definition of, 236

family group, 237
future environmental demands, 237
group cohesiveness, 238
group norms, 238
interpersonal peacemaking, 243-244
intervention, 241
leadership behavior, 238
long-term change, 237
methods of, 240-241
organizational change, 237
organizational culture, 240
organizational mirror, 246-248
organizational structure, 238
persuasion, 237
problems associated with traditional, 250
process consultation, 244
role analysis technique, (RAT), 242-243
status of work group, 238
strategic, 250
    steps in, 251-253
strategic planning intervention, 248-249
    steps in, 249
survey-guided development, 246
team building, 244-245
work group, 237
work group norms, 238
Organizational learning, 237
Organizational mirror, 246-247
Organizational philosophy and culture, 63
Organizational strategy for SHRD, definition, 2
Organizational strengths and weaknesses, 56
Organizational structure, 238

P

Performance, 188

Performance productivity measures, 98, 100
Persuasion *see* organization development
Planning and organizational culture, 11
Primary groups, 262
Priority matrix, 141
Process consultation, 244
Product development, 164
Product development life cycle, 52
Professional conference *see* employee development
Pulse-taking approach, 56
Purpose:
    advantages, 45
    definition, 6, 45
    importance, 47
Purpose statement, 4, 63

Q

Quality circles *see* employee development

R

Rand Corporation, 102
Rational problem solving, 264
Reward, systems, 214-216
    extrinsic, 215
    intrinsic, 215
Rifle approach, 60

S

Second generation (strategic) planning, 3
Segmentation, 260
Situation analysis, 80
Skill-based pay, 216
Social audit, 266
Social monitoring, 287

Staff meetings: *see* employee development
Stages of socialization, 362
Stakeholder, 6, 131-132
Status of work group, 237
Strategic business planning (SBP):
    culture, 66
    key assumptions, 6
    levels, 7
    steps, 3-5
Strategic business plans (SBU):
    and HRD, 48-49
    and HRP, 13
    and HR plans, 48
    levels, 8
    methods, 9
    types, 7-8
Strategic business unit, 8
Strategic human resource development (SHRD):
    definition, 2
    distinction between traditional and strategic, 16
    key assumptions, 19
    model of, 18
    and strategic business planning, 21
    values, 21
Strategic organization development, 250-253
Strategic orientation, 259
Strategic performance system, 21
Strategic planning, 8, 237
Strategic thinking, 57-58
Strategy
    enterprise, 7, 8
    environmental, 113
    formulation, 57
    functional, 8, 223
    HRD, 225
    organizational, 218
    for HRD, 226
Strategy-making, 237
Strengths and weaknesses, 100-106
Structure, organizational, 211
    changes of, 212
    and strategy, 213
Surveys, 140, 265

T

Task, 89
Task analysis, 100, 140, 198
Task force *see* employee development
Team approach, 9
Team building, 244-245
Think tank experience *see* employee development
Time horizon, 271
Top-down approach, 13, 49-50
Training (T):
    analyze future setting, 432
    analyze setting, 406-442
    carrying out work analysis, 407
    characteristics of future learners, 430-432
    content selection, 419-423
    creating tests, 408-409
    definition of, 397-398
    delivery methods, 411-419
    delivery of, 443
    future oriented, 134-135
    future-oriented work analysis, 432
    and HR Planning, 399
    and individual learning, 37
    and organizational strategy for HRD, 399
    preparing training objectives, 407-408
    problems with traditional mode of, 423-424
    selecting content, 442
    sequencing objectives, 410
        sequence strategic objectives, 433
    strategically-oriented tests, 433
    strategic and:

business planning, 426
HR planning, 425
organizational strategy for HRD, 425
and Strategic Business Planning, 400
strategic instructional objectives, 433
strategic model of, 426–427
strategic training needs, 429–430
traditional model of, 400–403
uses of strategic model of, 427–429
use strategic delivery methods, 434–442
Trend, 5

W

Work analysis, 81, 348–349
Work force analysis, 351–354
Work group, 237
WOTS-UP Analysis:
definition, 155
uses, 159